LATH. A wood or metal lattice on which plaster is laid.

LINTEL. Load-bearing horizontal beam above masonry doorway, arch or window opening.

LOCKSET. Hardware for door latch and lock.

MANSARD ROOF. A four-sided roof with gently sloping upper portions and steeply sloping lower portions.

MASONRY NAIL. Fastener of hardened steel, often ridged, for attaching objects to masonry.

MASTIC. Viscous adhesive.

MITER. An angled cut, usually 45°, at the end of a piece of wood; used for joints.

MOLDING. Strips of wood or other material used for decoration or to protect exposed edges.

MORTISE. A cutout area in a piece of wood, often used to recess hardware.

NEWEL POSTS. Structural vertical members of balustrade.

NIPPLE. A fastener for a light fixture, or a fitting that extends joints between pipes.

NOSING. Rounded front edge of stair tread.

OFFSET HANGER. Device for mounting ceiling boxes.

ORIENTED STRAND BOARD. A type of reconstituted wood panel, or CD plywood, used for sheathing.

PANELS, ACOUSTICAL. Sound-absorbing panels.

PARQUET. Wood tile.

PARTICLE BOARD. A sheet of material made from compressed wood chips.

PILOT HOLE. Hole drilled to receive shank of screw; prevents splitting of wood.

PIPE-JOINT COMPOUND. Threaded-joint sealer.

PLACING. Correct term for what is commonly called "pouring" concrete.

PLASTIC JOINT TAPE. Sealer for threaded pipe joints.

PLASTIC LAMINATE. Durable thin sheet of plastic that may be glued to a surface to protect it.

PLATE, SOLE. Bottom beam to which a wall partition frame is anchored.

PLATE, TOP. Top beam of wall frame.

PLATFORM FRAME. Construction in which each story is built separately atop the one below.

PLYWOOD. A sandwich of thin layers of wood glued together with the grain of alternate layers at right angles.

POINTING. Replacing of old mortar.

PUTTY, WOOD. A compound used to fill and conceal cracks and depressions in wood.

R VALUE. Measurement of a material's ability to slow the passage of heat.

RABBET. Notch in the face of a piece of wood, along its edge or at the end; used for a joint in which the edge or the end of a second piece of wood is set in the notch.

RAFTERS. Diagonal supports for roof.

RAIL. Horizontal member of doorframe or sash frame.

RAKES. Sloping edges of roof framing gable.

RECEPTACLES. Points at which appliances plug into house circuits.

REINFORCING ROD (BAR). Metal rod or bar embedded in concrete to increase the concrete's tensile strength.

RIDGE. Horizontally running peak where roof slopes meet.

RISE. Vertical distance from roof ridge to top of walls.

RISERS. Vertical boards between stair treads, or vertical water pipes.

RUNNERS. Long metal strips in frame of suspended ceiling.

SANITARY T. Fitting used to join drainpipe to stack.

SASH. Movable part of window.

SCAFFOLD. Temporary platform used while working on walls or roofs.

SEAMING TAPE. Material used to join pieces of carpet.

SHAKES. Irregularly shaped, thick wood shingles.

SHEATHING. Layer undersiding on exterior wall.

SHED ROOF. A roof with one slope.

SHIM. A thin strip of material which may be inserted between parts for aligning or spacing.

SHORING. Temporary supports.

SILL, WINDOW. Bottom horizontal piece of frame.

SISTERS. Reinforcement rafters or joists.

SLEEPERS. Floor joists laid on concrete slab.

SLOPE. Inches of vertical rise per foot of horizontal span.

SOFFIT. Covering of underside of roof overhang.

SOFTWOOD. Lumber from coniferous trees, used for general construction.

SPACKLING COMPOUND. Material used to fill holes and depressions.

STACK. Vertical run of drain and vent pipes.

STILE. Vertical member of doorframe or sash frame.

STOOL, WINDOW. Inner sill of window.

STORY POLE. Gauge used to check height of a course of masonry or siding.

STRINGERS. Boards fit against ends of stair treads and risers.

STUB-OUT. A pipe that protrudes through the wall for connection to a plumbing fixture or waste pipe.

STUCCO. Siding material of thick mortar.

STUD. Vertical support made of wood or metal within walls.

STUD, CRIPPLE. Short stud above header in rough frame for an opening.

STUD, JACK. Short stud supporting header over door or window.

STUD, KING. Full-length stud alongside jack stud.

SUBFLOORING. Rough flooring laid over joists to serve as base for finished floor.

T FITTING. Plumbing branch fitting in which branch enters at right angle.

TAP-ON FITTING. Device for joining plumbing branch by drilling holes directly into supply pipe.

TERMINALS. Connections for wires.

THRESHOLD. Strip on floor below door.

THRESHOLD, TRANSITIONAL. Metal plate used as joint between two types of flooring.

THROWING MORTAR. Depositing mortar from trowel.

TILES, ACOUSTICAL. Sound-absorbing tiles.

TOENAILING. Fastening two pieces of lumber with nails at an angle.

TRAP, HOUSE. Bend in main drainpipe isolating drains from sewer gases.

TRAP, P. P-shaped trap used on many plumbing fixtures.

TREADS, STAIRWAY. Horizontal surfaces of stairs.

TRUSS. An assemblage of beams typically arranged in a triangle to form rigid framework.

TRUSSED-RAFTER CONSTRUCTION. Trusses and rafters are joined by metal fasteners and braced upright by horizontal planks; no structural horizontal members are present.

UNDERLAYMENT. Moistureproof and sound-deadening layer between subfloor and finished floor; base for finished flooring.

UNDERWRITERS LABORATORIES, INC. (UND. LAB INC.; UL). U.S. organization that tests, and establishes standards.

UNION. Fitting for joining two pieces of threaded pipe.

VALLEY. Trough formed at joint between sloped roof sections.

VENEER. Very thin sheet of material used as surface layer or sandwiched with other layers.

VENT PIPES. Pipes that allow air into and gases out of drainage system.

VOLUTE. Spiral end of railing.

WAINSCOTING. Wall panels that rise from the floor midway up the wall; upper edge is capped with molding.

WALER. Large horizontal board used in shoring.

WALL, WET. Specially constructed wall designed to conceal pipes.

WALLBOARD. Panels of gypsum plaster sandwiched between sheets of paper, used for walls and ceilings.

WALLS, BEARING. Also called load-bearing. Walls that support second-floor joists or the roof.

WALL, KNEE. Wall meeting low end of sloped ceiling.

WALLS, NONBEARING. Nonsupporting walls.

WINDOW, AWNING. Window hinged at top.

WINDOW, CASEMENT. Window hinged at side.

WINDOW, DOUBLE-HUNG. Window with vertical sliding sashes.

WINDOW, HOPPER. Window hinged at bottom.

WINDOW, PREHUNG. Factory preassembled window.

WINDOW, SLIDING. Window with horizontally sliding sash.

Z BAR. Hardware serving as weather seal on storm door.

TIME
LIFE
BOOKS

COMPLETE HOME IMPROVEMENT AND RENOVATION MANUAL

Time-Life Books

COMPLETE HOME IMPROVEMENT AND RENOVATION MANUAL

*by the Editors of the Time-Life
Home Repair and Improvement Series*

Introduction by Bob Vila

PRENTICE
HALL
PRESS

New York • London • Toronto • Sydney • Tokyo • Singapore

Time-Life Books Inc. is a wholly owned subsidiary of
THE TIME INC. BOOK COMPANY

President and Chief Executive Officer	Kelso F. Sutton
President, Time Inc. Books Director	Christopher T. Linen

TIME-LIFE BOOKS INC.

Managing Editor	Thomas H. Flaherty
Director of Editorial Resources	Elise D. Ritter-Clough
Director of Photography and Research	John Conrad Weiser
Editorial Board	Dale M. Brown, Roberta Conlan, Laura Foreman, Lee Hassig, Jim Hicks, Blaine Marshall, Rita Thievon Mullin, Henry Woodhead
Production Manager	Prudence G. Harris
PUBLISHER	Joseph J. Ward

Time-Life Books Complete Home Improvement and Renovation Manual
was produced by
ST. REMY PRESS

PUBLISHER	Kenneth Winchester
PRESIDENT	Pierre Léveillé
Senior Editor	Dianne Stine Thomas
Senior Art Director	Diane Denoncourt
Designer	Shirley Grynspan
Contributing Editorial Assistants	Jennifer Meltzer, Fran Slingerland
Contributing Designer	Chantal Bilodeau
Index	Shirley J. Manley
Administrator	Natalie Watanabe
Production Manager	Michelle Turbide
Coordinator	Dominique Gagné
Systems Coordinator	Jean-Luc Roy
Proofreader	Judy Yelon

THE CONSULTANTS

Richard Day, a do-it-yourself writer for 25 years, is a founder of the National Association of Home and Workshop Writers and the author of several home repair books. He has built two houses from the ground up, and now lives in southern California.

Mark M. Steele, a professional home inspector in the Washington, D.C., area, is an editor of home improvement articles and books.

Rosalind Stubenberg, consulting editor, is an editor and consultant who served as an editor for *Time-Life Books*.

Maurice Gagnon, special consultant for Canada, is a professional woodworker. He specialized in custom woodwork in Montreal.

Prentice Hall Press
15 Columbus Circle
New York, New York 10023

LC No. 90-52528

ISBN 0-13-921883-1

Manufactured in the United States of America

FOREWORD

While Bob Vila operated his own residential remodeling and design business, his house in Newton Center, Massachusetts, was selected "Better Homes and Gardens" Heritage House of 1977. After hosting the PBS "This Old House" television series for ten years, he is now producing a new television series on home remodeling, "Home Again with Bob Vila." He continues his interest in residential and commercial property development in the Massachusetts area.

For most of us, home renovation is an investment in the future. For some, the goal is to boost the value of a house quickly, in order to sell and make a profit. Adding a second bathroom to a house, for example, is one of the best investments you could make to increase the value of your home. For other homeowners, the focus is on improvements that enhance their family's quality of life, such as a new deck or an added room for a growing family. Then there are some—like me—who get involved in renovation for the sheer love of doing it.

This book is about home renovation for both value and enjoyment. It has been compiled from the best-selling Time-Life Books Home Repair and Improvement series, which has helped hundreds of thousands of men and women become seasoned home-improvement do-it-yourselfers.

The step-by-step information here is timeless; whatever the state of the economy, these improvement ideas will come in handy. When the economy is booming, homeowners fix up their houses to cash in on profits. On the other hand, during a recession, people postpone dreams of buying a bigger or better house—and renovate their present home to better suit their needs.

There was a time when hiring home-renovation professionals was more affordable than it is today. When I got started renovating townhouses in Boston's Back Bay in the early '70s, for example, I could hire college students at $3.50 an hour to do the demolition. Those days are gone; now it makes sense to do your own demolition—and haul it yourself to the dump. More and more homeowners are now becoming do-it-yourselfers. For economic reasons, they have to; they have no choice. Of course, there are times when you will need to hire a professional, and *The Complete Home Improvement and Renovation Manual* will help you there, too, by giving you an overview of what is involved in renovation jobs.

For years, I've been helping people turn average homes into their dream houses. Most people don't realize how easy it is to transform a home and increase its value and comfort with a few simple projects. All it takes is a little imagination, a little hard work, the right tools, and knowing how to use them properly and safely. This book gives you hundreds of ideas plus the step-by-step advice you need to complete them successfully. Won't you join me on a quick tour of the book?

Chapter 1 can help you with a variety of interior improvements for floors, walls, ceilings, stairways and even storage space. If you like the look and feel of wood, for example, here is everything you need to install a new wood floor, from start to finish. Or panel a room with wood, or design a home library with floor-to-ceiling bookshelves. Wish you could make better use of your attic? Turn to step-by-step instructions for opening the floor, then installing a spiral or disappearing stairway. Dreaming of refinishing your basement? The Time-Life Books do-it-yourself instructions will teach you how to install wallboard and partitions like a pro. Or, with the view of saving money, cut energy costs with better insulation.

Now let's move on to Chapter 2, and remodeling your kitchen or bathroom—two top priorities of many homeowners. Learn how to plan the most efficient layout for your kitchen, where to place appliances and how much counterspace you need. In many cases, you'll also read the best materials to use. (Years ago, my wife and I made the mistake of installing real maple butcher block counters right next to the kitchen sink; the water stains were constant!) Find out, too, the best arrangement for bathroom fixtures to maximize your space. Before you begin work in either room, read about your local building, plumbing, electrical and mechanical codes, and when they govern your projects. Then go to work, using tried and true techniques for working with tile, laminating countertops and laying new flooring.

Chapter 3 takes a look at your home's windows and doors—and creative options for them. Add a new prehung door or window to your house—or convert a window to a door. Add a bay window or a picture window. Every step of the way, the instructions are designed for structural safety and professional-looking results. From installing the frame to custom-fitting the trim to choosing and fitting the lock, you build valuable skills.

Chapter 4 helps you tackle improvements to your home's heating and cooling, wiring and plumbing systems. It helps you with planning a variety of improvements—pathways for piping, a new electrical circuit, a new duct run for your heating system. Illustrated instructions guide you all along the way—for improvements as simple as hooking up a toilet or as time-consuming as installing a freestanding fireplace. Perhaps most important, this chapter gives you the basics you need for working confidently and safely with pipes and electrical wiring.

Let's step outside the house for a moment in Chapter 5, and consider shopping for roofing and siding materials. Find out which improvements are safe for the average do-it-yourselfer to do, the steps to follow and how to work safely at heights. Investigate the siding materials that are available, then install new siding. Or improve your property with a new brick garden wall or patio, or ensure your family's privacy by building a tall, attractive fence.

In my opinion, Chapter 6 is mostly about quality of life. It shows how to build the features that many homeowners enjoy most. You will discover that turning an ordinary porch into a year-round sunporch is not really difficult after all. Nor is planning and constructing a basic deck, complete with railing and stairway. But if you are looking for more of a challenge, try out your home-improvement skills every step of the way. Build a new addition onto your house, from foundation to walls to roof.

For handy reference, there are two other important sections of the book. Pages 10-15 help you cope with emergency situations and, beginning on page 454, the "Tools for Home Improvement" section gives valuable information on how to choose tools, and techniques that help you use them like a professional.

I hope that you enjoy doing home renovation as much as I have over the last 17 years. My guess is that, once you start, you will find it rewarding not just in dollars, but in the joy you get any time you complete a task. Not only will you have made your home a more comfortable, more convenient, more enjoyable environment; you will have the satisfaction of knowing that your effort and skill made it happen.

Today, a little do-it-yourself skill and some careful planning can still add plenty to the value of your house—not to mention your daily life. And if you enjoy the process as well, then you have the best of all possible worlds.

TABLE OF CONTENTS

How to Use this Book

Time-Life Books Complete Home Improvement and Renovation Manual is divided into six main chapters and two handy reference sections. The Emergency Guide on pages 10-15 provides information that can be indispensable, even life-saving, in the event of a household emergency. Take time to study this section *before* you need the important advice that it contains.

The home improvement chapters—the heart of the book—are organized and color-coded for easy access, and provide step-by-step instructions for specific renovation projects. Before deciding whether you should attempt a repair,

read all the instructions carefully. Then be guided by your own confidence and experience and the tools available to you. For renovations that may seem too complex or time-consuming for your level of expertise, you may wish you call for professional help. You may still save time and money by shopping for materials yourself, and you will be better equipped to find the right professional for the job and to discuss the repair in an informed manner.

These chapters also offer information on basic how-to techniques, from connecting bathroom and kitchen fixtures to wiring new electrical switches. In some cases, charts aid you in selecting the proper materials for the job. Highlighted throughout the chapters, safety information guides you to the equipment and practices that will help you minimize risk during your renovations.

The final section presents many of the tools that you will need for home renovation, and basic instructions for using them properly, as well as valuable advice on building a tool kit to suit your needs and setting up a home workshop. If you are a novice when it comes to home repair, read this section before undertaking a major job.

Doing your own home renovations is easy and safe if you work logically, follow instructions, and practice safe work habits whenever necessary. Before beginning any electrical repair, for example, turn off power to the circuit, then confirm that the power is off, as instructed. Likewise, many plumbing repairs require closing the main shutoff valve and draining supply lines. Ask local authorities about electrical, plumbing, building or sanitation codes that might apply to your renovation project.

INTRODUCTORY TEXT
Describes key techniques, maintenance tips and other information about the repair, based on the experience and advice of professionals.

CROSS-REFERENCES
Direct you to important information elsewhere in the book, including safety information. Be sure to read referenced pages before beginning the procedure.

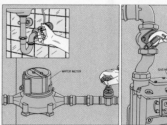

ILLUSTRATIONS
Show the action required for each step of the project.

STEP-BY-STEP PROCEDURES
Follow the numbered repair sequence carefully. Depending on the result of each step, you may be directed to a later step, or to another part of the book, to complete the repair.

LEAD-INS
Bold lead-ins summarize each step or highlight the key action pictured in the illustration.

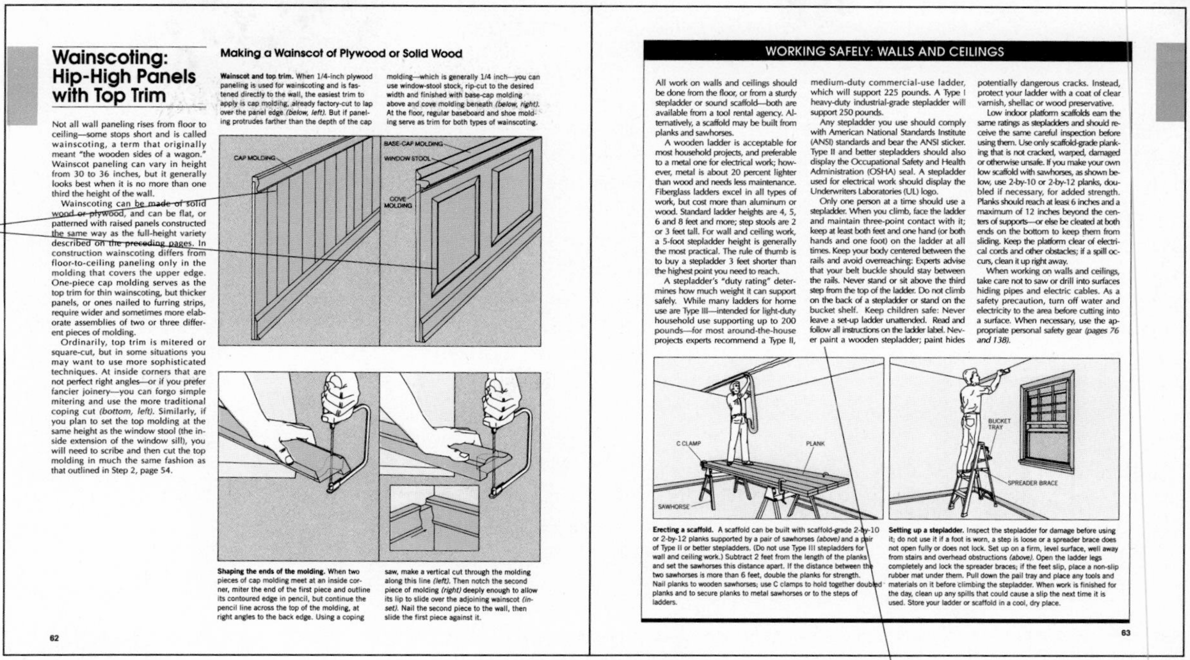

Wainscoting: Hip-High Panels with Top Trim

Not all wall paneling rises from floor to ceiling—some stops short and is called wainscoting, a term that originally meant "the wooden sides of a wagon." Wainscot paneling can vary in height from 30 to 36 inches, but it generally looks best when it is no more than one third the height of the wall.

Wainscoting can be made of solid wood or plywood, and can be flat, or patterned with raised panels constructed the same way as the full-height variety described on the preceding pages. In construction wainscoting differs from floor-to-ceiling paneling only in the molding that covers the upper edge. One-piece cap molding serves as the top trim for thin wainscoting, but thicker panels, or ones nailed to furring strips, require wider and sometimes more elaborate assemblies of two or three different pieces of molding.

Ordinarily, top trim is mitered or square-cut, but in some situations you may want to use more sophisticated techniques. At inside corners that are not perfect right angles—or if you prefer fancier joinery—you can forgo simple mitering and use the more traditional coping cut (bottom, left). Similarly, if you plan to set the top molding at the same height as the window stool (the inside extension of the window sill), you will need to scribe and then cut the top molding in much the same fashion as that outlined in Step 2, page 54.

Making a Wainscot of Plywood or Solid Wood

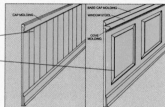

Wainscot and top trim. When 1/4-inch plywood paneling is used for wainscoting, the easiest trim to apply is cap molding, already factory-cut to lap over the panel edge (below, left). But if paneling protrudes farther than the depth of the cap molding—which is generally 1/4 inch—you can use window-stool stock, rip-cut to the desired width and finished with base-cap molding above and cove molding beneath (below, right). At the floor, regular baseboard and shoe molding serve as trim for both types of wainscoting.

CAP MOLDING — BASE-CAP MOLDING — WINDOW STOOL — COVE MOLDING

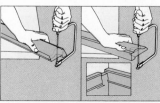

Shaping the ends of the molding. When two pieces of cap molding meet at an inside corner, miter the end of the first piece and outline its contoured edge in pencil, but continue the pencil line across the top of the molding, at right angles to the back edge. Using a coping saw, make a vertical cut through the molding along this line (left). Then notch the second piece of molding (right) deeply enough to allow its lip to slide over the adjoining wainscot (inset). Nail the second piece to the wall, then slide the first piece against it.

62

WORKING SAFELY: WALLS AND CEILINGS

All work on walls and ceilings should be done from the floor, or from a sturdy stepladder or sound scaffold—both are available from a tool rental agency. Alternatively, a scaffold may be built from planks and sawhorses.

A wooden ladder is acceptable for most household projects, and preferable to a metal one for electrical work; however, metal is about 20 percent lighter than wood and needs less maintenance. Fiberglass ladders excel in all types of work, but cost more than aluminum or wood. Standard ladder heights are 4, 5, 6 and 8 feet and more; step stools are 2 or 3 feet tall. For wall and ceiling work, a 5-foot stepladder height is generally the most practical. The rule of thumb is to buy a stepladder 3 feet shorter than the highest point you need to reach.

A stepladder's "duty rating" determines how much weight it can support safely. While many ladders for home use are Type III—intended for light-duty household use supporting up to 200 pounds—for most around-the-house projects experts recommend a Type II, medium-duty commercial-use ladder, which will support 225 pounds. A Type I heavy-duty industrial-grade stepladder will support 250 pounds.

Any stepladder you use should comply with American National Standards Institute (ANSI) standards and bear the ANSI sticker. Type II and better stepladders should also display the Occupational Safety and Health Administration (OSHA) seal. A stepladder used for electrical work should display the Underwriters Laboratories (UL) logo.

Only one person at a time should use a stepladder. When you climb, face the ladder and maintain three-point contact with it; keep at least both feet and one hand (or both hands and one foot) on the ladder at all times. Keep your body centered between the rails and avoid overreaching: Experts advise that your belt buckle should stay between the rails. Never stand or sit above the third step from the top of the ladder. Do not climb on the back of a stepladder or stand on the bucket shelf. Keep children safe: Never leave a set-up ladder unattended. Read and follow all instructions on the ladder label. Never paint a wooden stepladder; paint hides potentially dangerous cracks. Instead, protect your ladder with a coat of clear varnish, shellac or wood preservative.

Low indoor platform scaffolds earn the same ratings as stepladders and should receive the same careful inspection before using them. Use only scaffold-grade planking that is not cracked, warped, damaged or otherwise unsafe. If you make your own low scaffold with sawhorses, as shown below, use 2-by-10 or 2-by-12 planks, doubled if necessary, for added strength. Planks should reach at least 6 inches and a maximum of 12 inches beyond the centers of supports—or else be cleated at both ends on the bottom to keep them from sliding. Keep the platform clear of electrical cords and other obstacles; if a spill occurs, clean it up right away.

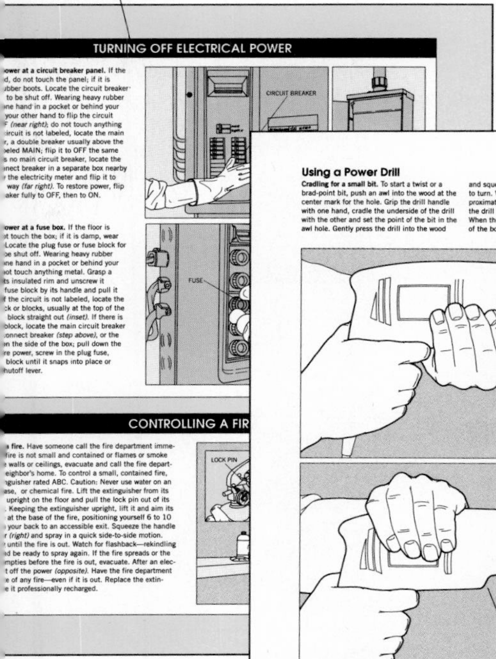

When working on walls and ceilings, take care not to saw or drill into surfaces hiding pipes and electric cables. As a safety precaution, turn off water and electricity to the area before cutting into a surface. When necessary, use the appropriate personal safety gear (pages 76 and 138).

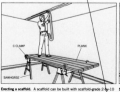 

Erecting a scaffold. A scaffold can be built with scaffold-grade 2-by-10 or 2-by-12 planks supported by a pair of sawhorses (above) and a pair of Type II or better stepladders. (Do not use Type III stepladders for wall and ceiling work.) Subtract 2 feet from the length of the planks and set the sawhorses this distance apart. If the distance between the two sawhorses is more than 6 feet, double the planks for strength. Nail planks to wooden sawhorses, use C clamps to hold together doubled planks and to secure planks to metal sawhorses or to the steps of ladders.

C CLAMP — PLANK — SAWHORSE — BUCKET TRAY — SPREADER BRACE

Setting up a stepladder. Inspect the stepladder for damage before using it; do not use it if a foot is worn, a step is loose or a spreader brace does not open fully or does not lock. Set up on a firm, level surface, well away from stairs and overhead obstructions (above). Open the ladder legs completely and lock the spreader braces; if the feet slip, place a non-slip rubber mat under them. Pull down the pail tray and place any tools and materials on it before climbing the stepladder. When work is finished for the day, clean up any spills that could cause a slip the next time it is used. Store your ladder or scaffold in a cool, dry place.

83

Using a Power Drill

Cradling for a small bit. To start a twist or a brad-point bit, push an awl into the wood at the center mark for the hole. Grip the drill handle with one hand, cradle the underside of the drill with the other and set the point of the bit in the awl hole. Gently press the drill into the wood and squeeze the trigger slowly until the bit starts to turn. When the bit has made a hole that is approximately 1/8 inch deep, increase the speed of the drill to its maximum and bear down firmly. When the bit has drilled almost to the full depth of the board, reduce the pressure but maintain the speed of the drill as the bit bores through the last fraction of an inch. If the hole must be perfectly perpendicular to the surface of the wood, set a combination square against the board and sight the bit against it (inset) as a jig for precision work.

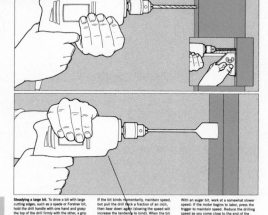

Steadying a large bit. To drive a bit with large cutting edges, such as a spade or Forstner bit, hold the drill handle with one hand and grasp the top of the drill firmly with the other, a grip that resists the twisting tendency of the drill better than the cradling grip illustrated at the top of this page. Press the bit firmly into the awl hole and begin the hole at a fairly high speed.

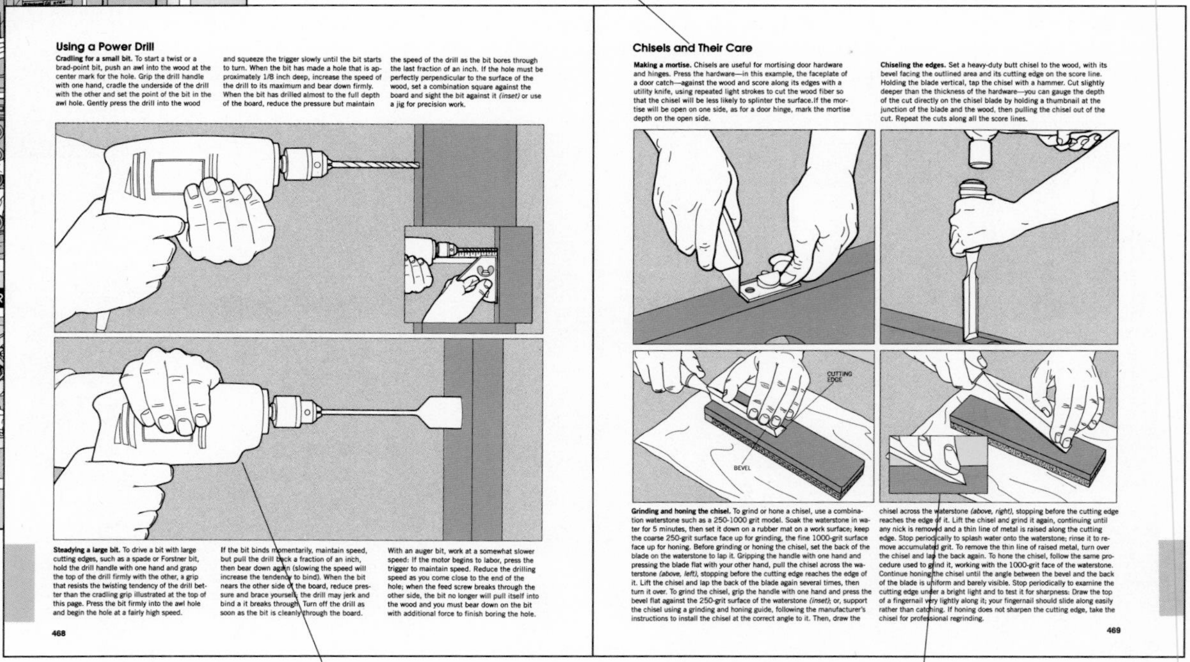

If the bit binds momentarily, maintain speed, but pull the drill back a fraction of an inch, then bear down again (slowing the speed will increase the tendency to bind). When the bit nears the other side of the board, reduce pressure and brace yourself, the drill may jerk and bind as it breaks through. Turn off the drill as soon as the bit is cleanly through the board.

With an auger bit, work at a somewhat slower speed: If the motor begins to labor, press the trigger to maintain speed. Reduce the drilling speed as you come close to the end of the hole; when the feed screw breaks through the other side, the bit will no longer will pull itself into the wood and you must bear down on the bit with additional force to finish boring the hole.

468

Chisels and Their Care

Making a mortise. Chisels are useful for mortising door hardware and hinges. Press the hardware—in this example, the faceplate of a door catch—against the wood and score along its edges with a utility knife, using repeated light strokes to cut the wood fiber so that the chisel will be less likely to splinter the surface. If the mortise will be open on one side, as for a door hinge, mark the mortise depth on the open side.

Chiseling the edges. Set a heavy-duty butt chisel to the wood, with its bevel facing the outlined area and its cutting edge on the score line. Holding the blade vertical, tap the chisel with a hammer. Cut slightly deeper than the thickness of the hardware—you can gauge the depth of the cut directly on the chisel blade by holding a thumbnail at the junction of the blade and the wood, then pulling the chisel out of the cut. Repeat the cuts along all the score lines.

CUTTING EDGE — BEVEL

Grinding and honing the chisel. To grind or hone a chisel, use a combination waterstone such as a 250-1000 grit model. Soak the waterstone in water for 5 minutes, then set it down on a rubber mat on a work surface, keep the coarse 250-grit surface face up for grinding, the fine 1000-grit surface face up for honing. Before grinding or honing the chisel, set the back of the blade on the waterstone to lap it. Gripping the handle with one hand and pressing the blade flat with your other hand, pull the chisel across the waterstone (above, left), stopping before the cutting edge reaches the edge of it. Lift the chisel and lap the back of the blade again several times, then turn it over. To grind the chisel, grip the handle with one hand and press the bevel flat against the 250-grit surface of the waterstone (inset), or support the chisel using a grinding and honing guide, following the manufacturer's instructions to install the chisel at the correct angle to it. Then, draw the chisel across the waterstone (above, right), stopping before the cutting edge reaches the edge of it. Lift the chisel and wind the blade, continuing until any nick is removed and a thin line of metal is raised along the cutting edge. Stop periodically to splash water onto the waterstone; rinse it to remove accumulated grit. To remove the thin line of raised metal, turn over the chisel and lap the back again. To hone the chisel, follow the same procedure used to grind it, working with the 1000-grit face of the waterstone. Continue honing the chisel until the angle between the bevel and the back of the blade is uniform and barely visible. Stop periodically to examine the angle: Draw the top of a fingernail very lightly along it; your fingernail should slide along easily rather than catching. If honing does not sharpen the cutting edge, take the chisel for professional regrinding.

469

Emergency Guide

While catastrophes in the home are rare, being prepared for an emergency situation when it does arise can spare the need for costly, and otherwise unnecessary, home repair or renovation. Halting the discharge of water from a leaking pipe *(page 14)*, for instance, can save damage to walls, floors and ceilings—damage that can cost thousands of dollars to repair. And being armed with the right fire extinguisher and knowing how to use it properly *(opposite)* can aid in smothering a small kitchen fire that may otherwise spread. Familiarizing yourself with the plumbing, electrical and heating systems in your home will help in attacking problems when they occur. In storm-prone ar-

eas, prepare for violent weather that sometimes strikes with little or no notice by keeping on hand plastic sheeting and plywood to seal doors *(page 15)* and windows against flying debris hurled around by high winds. Follow the instructions for shutting off the electricity *(opposite)* and gas supply *(below)* to your house. Read the manuals that come with household appliances as guides to safely operating home machinery.

With the right preparation, home improvement projects can be carried out safely. But if a life-threatening situation should occur, it is important to act quickly and administer the appropriate aid. Read the first aid information provided on these

pages to acquaint yourself with some quick-action steps to take. Enroll in a Red Cross-approved course in cardiopulmonary resuscitation (CPR) so you are better prepared to aid victims who suffer an electric shock or heart failure. Learn how to dress minor cuts and other injuries *(page 13)* that occasionally happen in the course of working with tools.

Install smoke detectors in your home for early detection of smoldering flames. Post the phone numbers of your community's fire department, police department and ambulance service, as well as the numbers of your family doctor and the poison control center if children are present in your home.

SHUTTING OFF THE WATER AND GAS SUPPLY

Shutting off the water supply. If water is leaking from a plumbing fixture, close its shutoff valve *(inset)*. If water is leaking from an undetermined source, turn off the water supply at the main shutoff valve *(below)*, usually located near the water meter or where the main water supply pipe enters the house. If your water supply is provided by a well, look for the main shutoff valve on the main water-supply pipe near the pressure gauge or pump.

Shutting off the gas supply. The main shutoff valve is located on the main gas-supply pipe for the house at the gas meter, usually in the basement. Use an adjustable wrench to shut off the gas supply, turning the valve handle *(below)* until it is perpendicular to the supply pipe. To shut off the gas at the boiler or furnace, grip the valve handle on the supply pipe leading to the unit and turn it until it is perpendicular to the supply pipe *(inset)*.

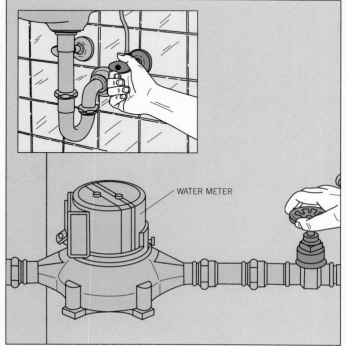

WATER METER

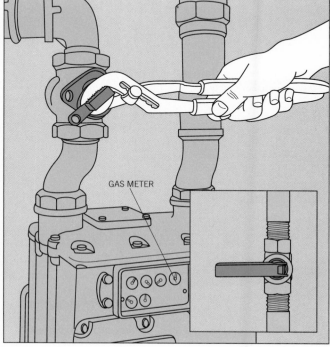

GAS METER

TURNING OFF ELECTRICAL POWER

Shutting off power at a circuit breaker panel. If the floor is flooded, do not touch the panel; if it is damp, wear rubber boots. Locate the circuit breaker for the circuit to be shut off. Wearing heavy rubber gloves, keep one hand in a pocket or behind your back and use your other hand to flip the circuit breaker to OFF *(near right)*; do not touch anything metal. If the circuit is not labeled, locate the main circuit breaker, a double breaker usually above the others and labeled MAIN; flip it to OFF the same way. If there is no main circuit breaker, locate the service disconnect breaker in a separate box nearby or outdoors by the electricity meter and flip it to OFF the same way *(far right)*. Before working in the vicinity of the shut-off circuit, confirm that the power is indeed off *(page 272)*. To restore power, flip the circuit breaker fully to OFF, then to ON.

Shutting off power at a fuse box. If the floor is flooded, do not touch the box; if it is damp, wear rubber boots. Locate the plug fuse or fuse block for the circuit to be shut off. Wearing heavy rubber gloves, keep one hand in a pocket or behind your back and do not touch anything metal. Grasp a plug fuse by its insulated rim and unscrew it *(right)*; grip a fuse block by its handle and pull it straight out. If the circuit is not labeled, locate the main fuse block or blocks, usually at the top of the box; pull each block straight out *(inset)*. If there is no main fuse block, locate the main circuit breaker or service disconnect breaker *(step above)*, or the shutoff lever on the side of the box; pull down the lever. Before working in the vicinity of the shut-off circuit, confirm that the power is indeed off *(page 272)*. To restore power, screw in the plug fuse, push the fuse block until it snaps into place or push up the shutoff lever.

CONTROLLING A FIRE

Extinguishing a fire. Have someone call the fire department immediately: If the fire is not small and contained or flames or smoke come from the walls or ceilings, evacuate and call the fire department from a neighbor's home. To control a small, contained fire, use a fire extinguisher rated ABC. Caution: Never use water on an electrical, grease or chemical fire. Lift the extinguisher from its bracket, set it upright on the floor and pull the lock pin out of its handle *(inset)*. Keeping the extinguisher upright, lift it and aim its nozzle or hose at the base of the fire, positioning yourself 6 to 10 feet away with your back to an accessible exit. Squeeze the handle levers together *(right)* and spray in a quick side-to-side motion. Keep spraying until the fire is out. Watch for flashback—rekindling of the fire—and be ready to spray again. If the fire spreads or the extinguisher empties before the fire is out, evacuate. After an electrical fire, shut off the power *(opposite)*. Have the fire department inspect the site of any fire—even if it is out. Replace the extinguisher or have it professionally recharged.

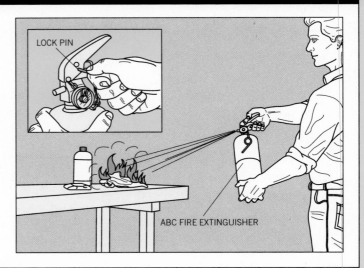

RESCUING A VICTIM OF ELECTRICAL SHOCK

1 **Freeing a victim of electrical shock.** A person who contacts live electrical current is usually thrown back from the source; sometimes, however, muscles contract involuntarily around the source. Do not touch the victim or the source. Immediately shut off power at the main circuit breaker, the service disconnect breaker or the main fuse block *(page 11)*. If power cannot be shut off immediately, unplug the source using a rag or cloth to prevent electrical shock *(inset)*, if possible, or use a wooden broom handle or other implement to knock the victim free *(below)*.

2 **Handling a victim of electrical shock.** Call for medical help immediately. Check the victim's breathing and pulse; if you are qualified, administer artificial respiration if there is no breathing and cardiopulmonary resuscitation (CPR) if there is no pulse. If the victim is breathing and has no back or neck injury, place him in the recovery position *(below)*, tilting the head back with the face to one side and the tongue forward to maintain an open airway. Keep the victim calm until medical help arrives.

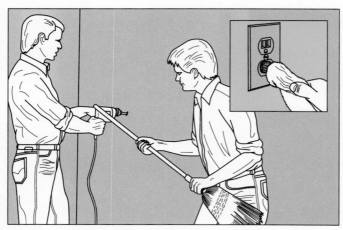

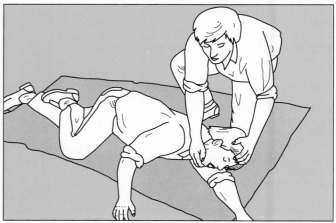

TREATING INJURIES

Treating the victim of a fall. Call an ambulance immediately, then cover the victim to regulate body temperature in case of shock *(below)*. Caution: The victim of a fall should not be moved until qualified medical help arrives, especially if there is pain in the area of the neck or back, or if clear spinal fluid can be seen flowing from the ears or nose. Help the victim to stay calm and keep others from crowding around. When qualified medical help arrives, make sure they are advised of possible spinal cord injury.

Treating a strained back. Lie down on a flat surface and apply an ice pack to the sore area to reduce swelling and soothe pulled muscles *(below)*. After 24 hours, a heating pad may be used to lessen pain and speed healing. If the pain does not decrease after several days, seek medical attention.

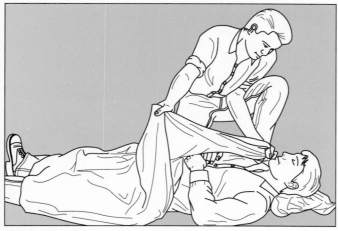

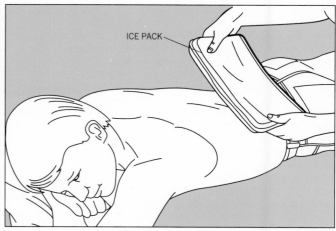

ICE PACK

Pulling out a splinter. Wash the skin around the splinter with soap and water. A metal splinter may require treatment for tetanus; seek medical help. Otherwise, sterilize a needle and tweezers with rubbing alcohol or over a flame. Ease out the splinter from under the skin using the needle *(below)*, then pull it out with the tweezers. Wash the wound again with soap and water. If the splinter cannot be removed or the wound becomes infected, seek medical attention.

Treating a cut. To stop a wound from bleeding, apply direct pressure with a clean cloth or gauze dressing and elevate the injury *(below)*. If the cloth or dressing becomes blood-soaked, add another one over the first; avoid lifting the cloth or dressing to inspect the wound. Continue applying direct pressure and elevating the injury until the bleeding stops. If the wound is minor, wash it with soap and water, then bandage it. Seek medical attention if the wound is deep or gaping or if bleeding persists.

Treating a burn. Gently remove any clothing from the burn; do not remove any clothing adhered to it. If the burn is severe, gently cover it with a gauze dressing and seek medical help immediately. Otherwise, flush the burn in a gentle flow of cool water from a faucet *(below)* or cover it lightly with a clean cloth soaked in water. Flush or soak the burn for at least 5 minutes, then bandage it. Do not apply antiseptic sprays, ointments or chemical neutralizers of any kind.

Removing a particle from the eye. Facing a mirror, use the forefinger and thumb of one hand to hold open the injured eye. Inspect the eye for the particle; if necessary, slowly rotate the eye to help expose it. Caution: Do not remove a particle that is on the cornea, is embedded or adhered, or cannot be seen. Otherwise, gently wipe away the particle using the twisted end of a tissue moistened with water *(above, left)*. Or, holding the eyelids of the injured eye apart with your fingers, position the injured eye under a gentle flow of cold water from a faucet *(above, center)*. If you are outdoors flush the injured eye the same way, using a flow of water from a garden hose *(above, right)*. Caution: Remove any nozzle from the garden hose to prevent any eye injury from a strong jet of water. Do not allow a child to flush an injured eye on his own; hold his head with one hand and use the other hand to flush the injured eye for him.

Quick fix for a pinhole leak. If you suspect a leak in the supply line, first check the water meter. If its needle or dial is moving and no one in the house is using a faucet or appliance, there is a leak somewhere. To locate it, look for stains on ceilings and walls, and listen carefully along supply pipes. As a temporary repair, turn off the water supply at the main shutoff valve, jam a pencil point into the hole and break it off *(below, left)*. A toothpick may also work, but for steel pipes, the graphite in the pencil lead will better seal the leak. To secure the plug, dry the surface of the pipe and wrap two or three layers of plastic electrical tape around the pipe for three inches on each side of the leak, overlapping each turn by half *(below, right)*. For a more permanent solution, you will have to replace the damaged section of pipe *(page 242)*.

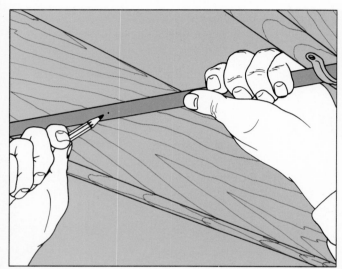

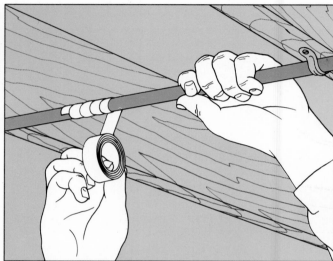

Sealing cracks or punctures. For a larger crack or puncture, close the main shutoff valve and drain the supply line. Wrap the pipe with an old bicycle inner tube and secure it with hose clamps *(right)*. Turn the water back on, slowly at first, to test for leaks. Replace the damaged section as soon as possible *(page 242)*.

To install a commercial pipe-leak clamp, remove the screws that hold the two halves of the clamp together, then fit them over the damaged pipe so that the rubber cushion seals the leak. Insert and tighten the screws *(inset)*.

Small leaks can also be patched using pipe cement or epoxy. The pipe must be drained of water and dried thoroughly for the cement to set properly. Roughen the damaged area with emery cloth, apply a thick coat of cement and allow it to dry overnight. Point a heat lamp or 100-watt bulb at the pipe to speed curing.

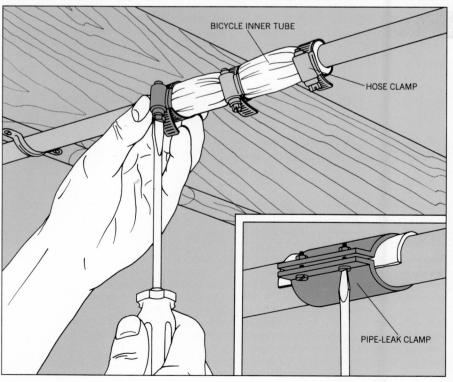

BICYCLE INNER TUBE

HOSE CLAMP

PIPE-LEAK CLAMP

THAWING FROZEN PIPES

Using a hair dryer. When thawing frozen pipes, always open the nearest faucet to allow melting ice to drain, and close the main shutoff valve about 3/4 of the way off. If you still have electricity, one of the safest remedies is to aim a hair dryer 3 to 4 inches from the affected area. Apply heat to the open faucet first, then work back along the pipe, as shown. When water begins to trickle from the tap, open the main shutoff valve: the flow of water will speed thawing.

Using heating tape. Electric heating tape draws only a small amount of current to keep tap water safely above the freezing point. Some models are equipped with a thermostat that turns the tape on and off as needed; these may be permanently plugged in. Starting at a faucet or fixture, wrap the tape tightly around the exposed pipe, taping 6 to 8 turns per foot. Secure the spirals with plastic tape every 6 inches.

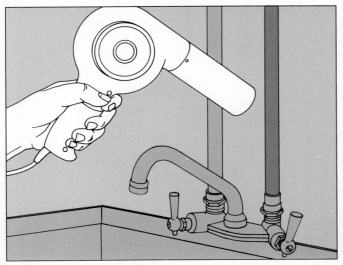

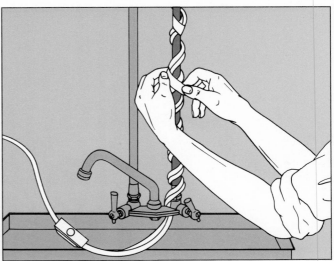

SEALING WINDOWS AND DOORS

Shielding unprotected openings. To prevent storm damage, cover windows and doors with 1/2-inch plywood sheets cut to fit. Nail the plywood to the exterior wood frame *(near right)* using 2-inch common nails spaced about 12 inches apart. Remove nails and plywood with a pry bar or claw hammer after the storm has subsided, and fill nail holes with wood filler. To attach plywood sheets to metal frames, drill pilot holes and use screws: Caulk the holes when the plywood is removed. In hurricane regions, install shutters or window shields that can be closed in the event of a storm.

Use 4- to 6-mil plastic sheeting to seal a broken window. Staple the plastic around the window frame, or tuck the plastic under 1-by-2 wood slats, nailing 1 1/2-inch common nails through the slats and plastic into the window frame *(far right).* Cover the floor and sill under the window with rags or towels if it rains. Remove the slats with a pry bar or claw hammer.

PLYWOOD

PLASTIC SHEETING

WOOD SLAT

1 INTERIOR IMPROVEMENTS

Laying a new wood floor is often easier and less time-consuming than laying many of the so-called quick and easy floor coverings of synthetic sheet or tile. Wood, unlike most resilient materials, does not require a smooth, carefully prepared surface. In most cases, you use the existing floor or a plywood subfloor covered with strips of asphalt-saturated building paper. A new subfloor is probably unnecessary if you have old wood or resilient flooring in reasonably good shape. In this case, drive down raised nails, renail loose boards and replace badly warped ones, and cement down loose tiles or torn sheeting.

If you suspect that the old floor may conceal damage or decay, check underneath it. Remove damaged flooring and subflooring and patch the hole with plywood equal to the thickness of the old finished floor. If the damage is ex-tensive, remove the entire floor, check for and repair any structural damage; then lay a new plywood subfloor. Before trying to floor over concrete, check for excess dampness by laying a 16-inch square of heavy plastic over the slab and sealing the edges with tape. If drops of water have condensed on the plastic after several days, the concrete is a poor choice for a finished wood floor.

If the concrete is suitable, provide a moisture barrier for the new floor by cover-ing the concrete slab with polyethylene film sandwiched between two layers of 1-by-2 sleepers (opposite). Then lay a plywood subfloor on the sleepers.

A ceramic-tile floor makes an unstable base for a new wood floor. Nailing tongue-and-groove flooring on top of ce-ramic tiles will loosen and crack the tiles—even if they are covered with ply-wood. Remove old tiles and install a new subfloor before you lay the strip flooring.

To install a new subfloor or replace a damaged old one, use C-D grade ply-wood at least 5/8 inch thick. Check the joists underneath before laying subfloor-ing, and if they are more than 16 inches apart, or are made of lumber smaller than 2-by-8, reinforce them (page 109), or in-stall new joists in the spaces between the old ones. In rooms such as attics, where small joists may cover long spans, it may be necessary to increase the thickness of the plywood subfloor to 3/4 inch.

Always lay plywood subflooring with the outer grain perpendicular to the joists, and stagger the sheets so that the joints do not align. Where two sheets meet at a joist, trim them so that there is a bearing surface for both, and leave 1/8-inch spaces at the sides and 1/16-inch spaces at the ends to allow room for expansion of the subfloor.

Laying a new subfloor. Apply a 1/4-inch bead of subfloor construction adhesive in a serpen-tine pattern to each joist or sleeper. Spread only enough adhesive to lay one or two sheets at a time. Before the adhesive sets, lay the ply-wood on top of the joists and nail down each sheet with eightpenny ringed or coated nails sold for this purpose. Stagger the nails and space them 6 inches apart, 3/8 inch from the edges at end joints. Space the nails 10 inches apart between the ends of the sheets.

If the two outer joists in the room are hidden beneath walls, install cleats (inset) to provide a bearing surface for the outer subfloor sheets. Nail two 2-by-4s to each hidden joist. Then screw the 2-by-4s into the joists with 3/8-inch lag screws, 6 inches long and spaced 16 inch-es apart.

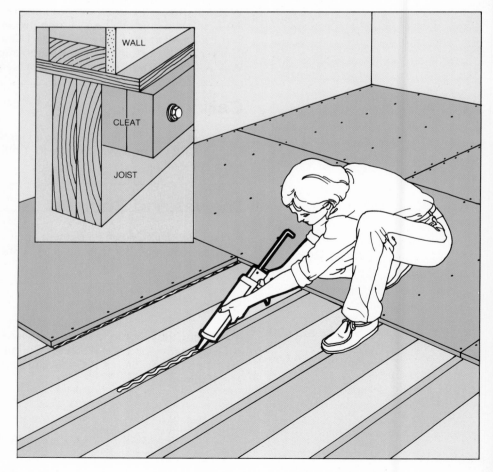

An Antimoisture Sandwich

1 **Laying bottom sleepers.** Sweep the floor clean and apply a coat of masonry primer. When the primer dries, snap chalk lines 16 inches apart at right angles to the long dimension of the room. Cover each line with a 2-inch-wide ribbon of either a synthetic rubber-based adhesive or an asphalt mastic designed for bonding wood to concrete. Embed random lengths of pressure-treated 1-by-2s in the adhesive or the mastic, flat side down, leaving about a 1/2-inch space between ends. Secure the sleepers with 1 1/2-inch concrete nails 24 inches or so apart.

2 **Attaching the top sleepers.** Lay sheets of 4-mil polyethylene film over the sleepers, overlapping joints 6 inches. Nail a second course of 1-by-2s on top of each first course, sandwiching the film between the two layers.

Floating a Floor to Reduce Noise

Uncarpeted wood floors upstairs are noisy. The best way to muffle the sounds of footsteps is to lay carpeting, but for excessively noisy areas, you can adapt the "floating floor" techniques that were developed to soundproof apartment buildings.

To construct a floating floor, staple 1/2-inch insulation board, available from lumberyards in 4-by-8 sheets, to the existing floor or subfloor. Mark the position of the joists on each sheet and do not staple into any joists. Glue 1-by-3 furring strips to the board with subfloor construction adhesive, placing the strips parallel to one another between joists. Then fasten a 1/2-inch plywood subfloor to the furring strips *(right)* and install the finish flooring. You can further muffle airborne noise by laying insulating batts between the open floor joists underneath the subfloor.

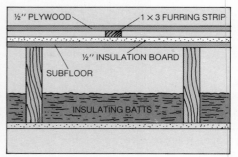

Installing a Wood Floor Board by Board

A floor of oak strip boards—or of the less common hardwoods, such as maple, pecan, hickory and ash, that can be found at specialty lumberyards—is durable and elegant in appearance, yet remarkably simple to install. And with the aid of a power nailer, available at tool-rental agencies, the job goes fast.

Flooring boards that are of conventional hardwood are 3/4 inch thick and 2 to 4 inches wide. The boards are milled with interlocking tongues and grooves on their sides and ends, and can be blind-nailed through their tongues *(page 25)*, a technique that makes the joints between boards uniform and hides the nailheads. Broader hardwood planks, which may be as wide as 8 inches, must be screwed into the subfloor *(page 25)* as well as blind-nailed to keep them from buckling.

Before they are nailed in place, floorboards are extremely susceptible to warping and swelling caused by moisture. Bring your home to its normal humidity before the wood is delivered: In winter, heat the room adequately, and in summer keep the air conditioner running. Insist that hardwood flooring be delivered on a dry day, at least three days before you plan to lay your floor. Untie the bundles and stack the boards in loose piles to let them adjust to the humidity and temperature of the room.

When laying the floor, you will have to nail the first few boards by hand before you will have room to use the power nailer for the rest of the floor. The nailer, which consists of a spring-operated mechanism that drives barbed flooring cleats, is triggered by the blows from a rubber-headed mallet. The cleats feed into the nailer like bullets from the clip in an automatic rifle: Each blow of the mallet drives home a cleat and simultaneously reloads and cocks the machine. To get the knack of working with the nailer before you use it, practice on a scrap of flooring set atop some spare plywood.

How to Buy Hardwood Flooring

Hardwood flooring—no matter what the wood—is graded according to the standards that are set by the National Oak Flooring Manufacturers Association. The boards are rated in order of decreasing quality as "clear," "select," "No. 1 common" or "No. 2 common," depending on color, grain and imperfections such as knots and streaks.

All strip flooring is sold in random lengths. Individual boards range from 9 to 102 inches long, but the boards are always sold according to a "flooring board foot" formula, based on the premilled size of the boards. To determine the amount of flooring you will need, calculate the area of your room in square feet. If you are buying 3/4-by-2 1/4-inch boards, the most common size, increase the area measurement by 38.3 percent to convert to flooring board feet and to account for wastage. For example, a 16-by-20-foot room totals 320 square feet. Multiplying 320 by 1.383 gives 443 flooring board feet. For boards of other dimensions, ask your flooring distributor for the proper conversion factor.

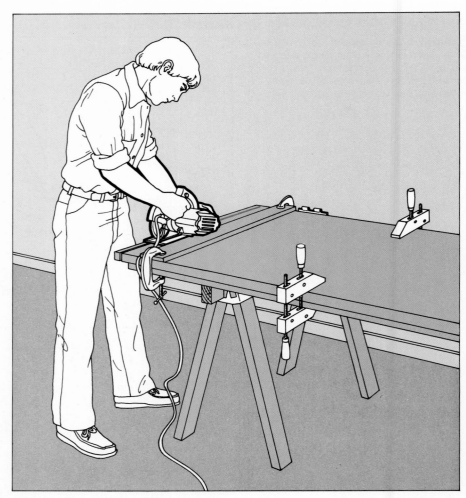

1 **Trimming for a new floor.** Saw a strip off the bottom of each door that opens into a room where you will lay a new wood-strip floor. Use the uncut edge of a piece of plywood as a guide to making a straight cut. To determine the depth of the cut, simulate the new floor with scraps of flooring laid next to the doorstop; include the height of a threshold if you plan to install one. Expose the subfloor and measure up from it to find the new floor height of tiled or carpeted rooms. Finally, mark and cut off the bottoms of the doorstop and doorcasings.

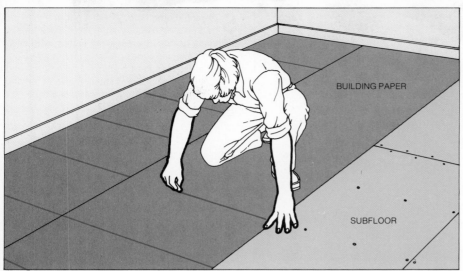

2 **Marking the joists.** Unroll strips of 15-pound asphalt-saturated building paper across the room and mark on each the positions of the joists. When installing a new wood floor on a plywood subfloor, simply use the subfloor nailing pattern as a guide to the joist positions. If these positions are hidden by existing flooring—and if they cannot be determined from below, as would be the case if you were working above an unfinished basement—drill pilot holes to locate the joists.

BUILDING PAPER

SUBFLOOR

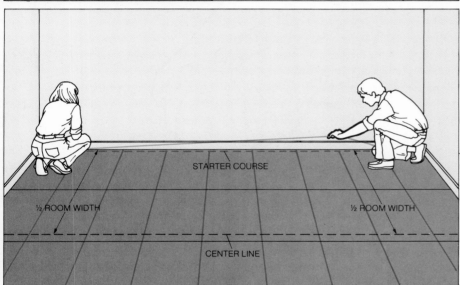

3 **Aligning the starter course.** Find the midpoints of the walls parallel to the joists and snap a chalk line between them to mark the center of the room. Measure equal distances from the center line to within roughly 1/2 inch of the end wall and snap a chalk line between the points. Using this line to mark the starter course along the wall will guarantee that the center boards of the room look straight even if the room is not truly square. The gap between the first course and the baseboard will be hidden by the shoe molding *(page 24)*.

STARTER COURSE

½ ROOM WIDTH   ½ ROOM WIDTH

CENTER LINE

4 **Face-nailing the first course.** With a helper, align a long flooring board, tongue out, along the starting chalk line. Drive eightpenny finishing nails through predrilled holes at each end of the board, as near to the grooved edge as possible. Drive additional nails through predrilled holes at every joist and also at midpoints between joists. The nailheads will be covered later by shoe molding. In the same way, nail down the other boards to complete the first course.

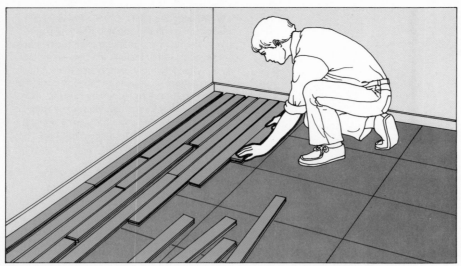

5 **Arranging the field.** Working out from the starter strip, rack seven or eight loose rows of flooring boards in a staggered pattern with end joints in adjoining rows at least 6 inches apart. Find or cut pieces to fit within 1/2 inch of the end wall. Then jam each board snug, groove to tongue, and blind-nail (page 25) the second and third courses along joist lines.

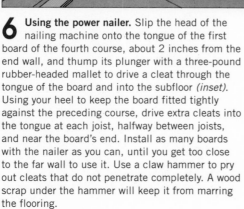

FLOORING CLEAT

HEAT REGISTER OPENING

6 **Using the power nailer.** Slip the head of the nailing machine onto the tongue of the first board of the fourth course, about 2 inches from the end wall, and thump its plunger with a three-pound rubber-headed mallet to drive a cleat through the tongue of the board and into the subfloor (inset). Using your heel to keep the board fitted tightly against the preceding course, drive extra cleats into the tongue at each joist, halfway between joists, and near the board's end. Install as many boards with the nailer as you can, until you get too close to the far wall to use it. Use a claw hammer to pry out cleats that do not penetrate completely. A wood scrap under the hammer will keep it from marring the flooring.

7 **Dressing a board to fit.** To work around openings in the floor, such as heat registers (inset), trial-fit boards over the gaps, decide whether the tongue or the groove will be saved, mark and cut them. Clamp the end of the board firmly to a workbench before sawing.

8 **Framing special borders.** Using a miter box, saw boards at 45° angles to frame a fireplace hearth *(inset)*. Rip off the boards' tongues when necessary to make them fit flush to adjoining boards. Face-nail them into place.

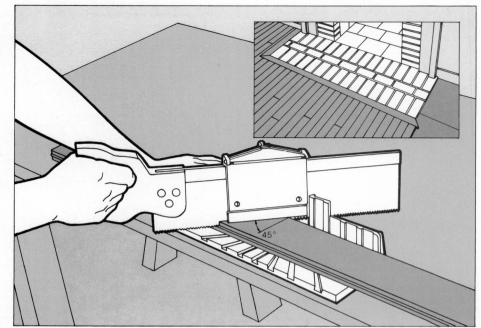

9 **Reversing tongue direction.** To install tongue-and-groove boards in a hall or closet opening onto the groove side of the starting course, join groove to groove with a slip tongue, available in 3-foot lengths from flooring distributors. After placing the slip tongue into the back-to-back grooves, put the nailer's head over the tongue of the loose board and nail it to the floor.

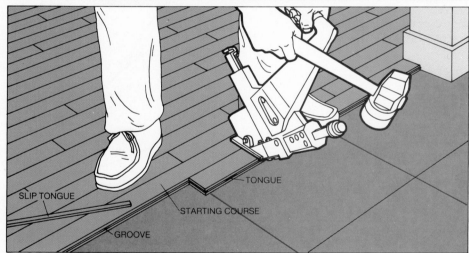

10 **Installing the final boards.** If a gap of more than 1/2 inch remains at the far wall, dress off the tongue sides of several boards *(Step 7)*, wedge them into the gap and face-nail them into place. To hold them tight for nailing, use your foot to angle a pry bar between the wall and the boards. Slip a scrap of wood between the pry bar and the wall to protect the baseboard.

11 **Finishing off a doorway.** Face-nail a clam-shell reducer strip (so called because its rounded top makes it resemble half a clam shell) at a doorway where a new wood floor meets a lower floor. The reducer strip, available at flooring distributors, is milled on one side to fit over the tongue of an adjoining board. The strip can also be butted to the ends of floorboards that run at right angles to a doorway.

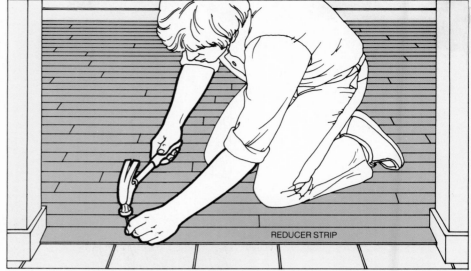

REDUCER STRIP

12 **Laying the expansion strips.** Wedge strips of 3/4-inch corkboard into the space where the floor meets glass sliding doors, ceramic tiles or a laid stone floor. The cork acts as a cushion that compresses or expands to compensate for shrinkage or swelling of the floorboards.

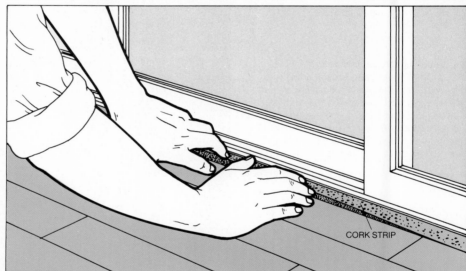

CORK STRIP

13 **Installing shoe molding.** Fasten 3/4-inch shoe molding over the gap between the flooring and the baseboard with fourpenny finishing nails. Drive the nails horizontally through the middle of the molding into the baseboard to allow the new floor to shrink or expand without tearing the shoe molding.

Techniques for Fastening a Plank Floor

Blind-nailing a board. Drive and set eightpenny finishing nails at a 45° angle through the corner of the tongue of the board. Pilot holes are not essential but may be helpful.

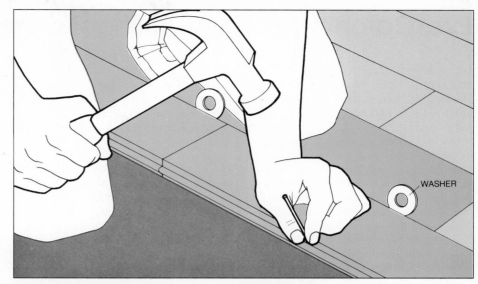

WASHER

Drilling fastening holes for screws. Use a 3/4-inch spade bit to drill partly through the ends of the planks. A piece of masking tape on the bit, 1/4 inch from the squared end of the spade portion, will serve as a sighting guide for the depth of the hole. Stagger additional screw holes at 20-inch intervals along the faces of long boards.

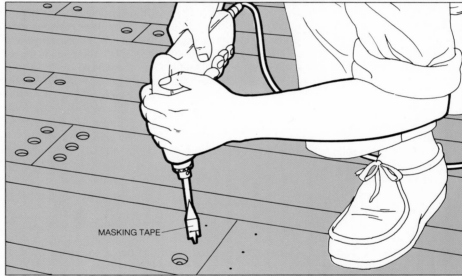

MASKING TAPE

Securing the planks. Drive 1 1/2-inch, No. 6 flat-head wood screws through the planks. Then cover the screwheads with hardwood plugs 1/4 inch deep and 3/4 inch in diameter, bought from a flooring distributor or cut from a length of 3/4-inch hardwood dowel. Use white water-base glue to hold the plugs.

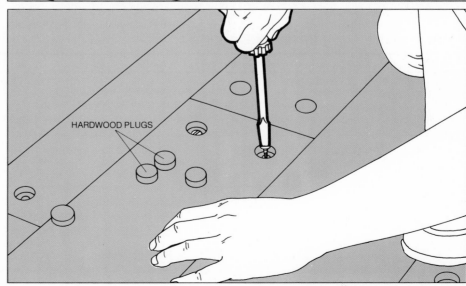

HARDWOOD PLUGS

Eye-Catching Patterns in Sheet and Tile

For centuries, the most common flooring materials in North America were wood planks, rough stones or dirt. Synthetics and modern industry changed all that. In 1863 a Briton named Frederick Walton invented a new kind of flooring—linoleum, made by mixing linseed oil, ground-up cork and natural resins. It was inexpensive, impervious to most spills and colorfully decorated with built-in patterns, and its popularity inspired the development of other man-made resilient flooring materials.

As a result, when installing a new floor today, you can select the material best suited to the demands of a particular room. Durability and economy of upkeep can govern the choice for a workroom while appearance and comfort determine what will go underfoot in a living room or den. Although wood (pages 18-25) is still the most versatile material, synthetic floorings are the most popular for kitchens and playrooms. These floorings are called resilient because they cushion the impact of feet or dropped objects. They come either as tiles that can be installed in a variety of designs (pages 27-28), or in rolled sheets that can be cut to fit irregularly shaped rooms.

Resilient tiles, generally 9 or 12 inches square, lend themselves to imaginative design and are available in a variety of materials (below). Wood tile, often called parquet, is installed in much the same way as resilient tile (page 29) and also can provide variations in pattern. Choose tiles according to the amount of traffic they will bear as

well as the floor design you have in mind.

You can lay a tile floor all in one color, of course, but once you know how to design a floor you can use tiles to hide visual defects—stripes running across the width make a narrow room look broader, for example—or to define areas of the room or to decorate your floor with any design that strikes your fancy.

Begin by measuring your room and calculating the number of 9- or 12-inch tiles you will need; then draw the floor on graph paper (page 27) and work out the design you want by filling squares representing tiles of different colors.

Resilient tile can be laid on almost any surface except strip flooring, which shifts too much to provide a firm base. Cover a strip floor with a 1/2-inch hardboard or plywood underlayment (page 18). You can lay a new resilient tile floor over an old one if you remove wax and other finishes and repair indentations, holes or loose tiles.

If you want to lay tile on concrete, check the slab for moisture (page 18), as the combination of dampness and alkali deposits in the concrete will make the tile buckle. If there is moisture on the floor, do not lay resilient tile on the concrete; install a moisture-resistant underlayment first (page 19). If the concrete passes the moisture test, remove paint and stain, repair any cracks or holes, flatten bumps with a rented electric concrete-grinder, and fill in any depressions with a floor-patching compound, available at hardware stores.

Then, using a roller or brush, coat the slab with a clear waterproofing solution, also available at hardware stores.

After you have made your design and prepared your floor, set up guidelines by the method shown opposite, center. Tiles are laid either on the square, with their edges parallel to the walls, or on the diagonal, with their edges at a 45° angle to the walls; the guidelines you make will ensure that they are correctly aligned in either direction. Then test your plot by making a dry run of tiles (opposite, bottom) so that you can adjust your borders and avoid the tedious business of cutting tiny pieces of tile to fit along a wall. If you are trying a complex design you may want to do a dry run over the entire floor.

Following the dry run, laying the floor is largely a matter of setting tiles in adhesive—your floor dealer can tell you which to use. Most resilient tiles require solvent-based adhesives. Wood tiles, which are laid by a similar process, need a more viscous mastic, either solvent based or latex based. Caution: Solvent-based adhesives are flammable; keep the room well ventilated and extinguish any flame before starting. The adhesives work best when the room is warmer than 70°.

Although ceramic- and quarry-tile floors are best laid in mortar, they can be set in water-resistant organic adhesive. The tiles often have lugs on their edges, creating gaps that are filled with grout (page 32).

Selecting the Right Resilient Flooring

Material	Form	Advantages	Limitations
Vinyl	Tile, sheet	Outstanding durability; fine resistance to stains, dents; deadens sound; easy maintenance; variety of colors and patterns	Relatively expensive; poor resistance to burns
Wood	Tile, block, strips	High wear resistance; rich appearance, prefinished; supplies extra insulation	Expensive; more difficult to install than most tiles; stains easily; requires more maintenance
Rubber	Tile	Very resilient; resists dents; quiet; waterproof	Slippery when wet; poor resistance to grease; requires frequent polishing to maintain gloss
Cork	Tile	Most resilient flooring; deadens sounds	Wears rapidly; poor resistance to heavy loads; stains badly unless coated with vinyl

Creating the Design

Planning on paper. On graph paper, plot a design for a floor laid on the square *(near right)* or on the diagonal *(far right)*, letting each block represent one tile. If you plan to use 9- rather than 12-inch tiles, multiply the dimensions of the room by 1.33 to find how many tiles to plot to a side. For example, if you use 12-inch tiles, the 20-foot-square design *(near right)* requires 20 per side. If 9-inch tiles are used, it requires 26.6 per side, but plot it for 27; always count fractions of tiles as whole tiles.

Order as many 12-inch tiles as there are square feet in the room. The number of 9-inch tiles you need will equal the number of square feet in the room multiplied by 1.78. For two colors of tile, count the squares of one color and subtract from the total to see how many tiles you need in each; add 5 percent for waste and repairs.

Guidelines for the dry run. Divide the room into equal quadrants with two chalked strings stretched between nails set at the midpoints of both pairs of opposing walls. Make sure the strings form 90° angles at their intersection by measuring from the intersection 3 feet on one string and 4 feet on the other. The diagonal between the 3- and 4-foot points should measure exactly 5 feet. Do not snap the chalk lines yet.

If your pattern is to be laid on the diagonal, measure the shorter guideline from the intersection to the wall, then set nails into the wall at points that distance to either side of the guideline nail. Repeat this on the opposite wall and stretch chalked strings diagonally between the nails *(inset)* so that they bisect the angles formed by the original guidelines.

Making a dry run. For a pattern laid on the square, lay dry tiles in one quadrant, starting from the intersection and duplicating the colors plotted on your graph paper. If the dry run ends more than half a tile from the walls, snap both chalk lines and remove them. If the last tiles are less than half a tile's width from the wall, move the rows to make larger gaps so you will not have to cut and lay small pieces. Set the chalk lines in the new place and snap them.

To check a diagonal pattern, lay dry tiles point to point along the perpendicular lines defining one quadrant and lay an extra row along the diagonal guideline *(inset)*. When laying a checkerboard pattern, you will achieve the best effect if the floor ends at each wall in a sawtooth line of half tiles. Add a border of tiles set on the square wide enough to make the diagonally laid field end in a sawtooth; if differences in the widths of borders on two adjacent walls are disturbing, make the borders at least two tiles wide.

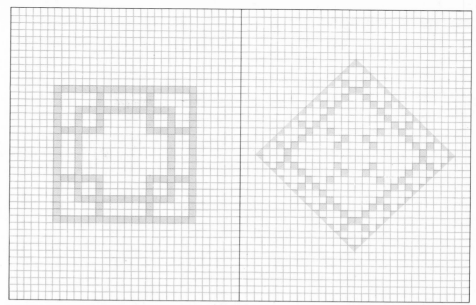

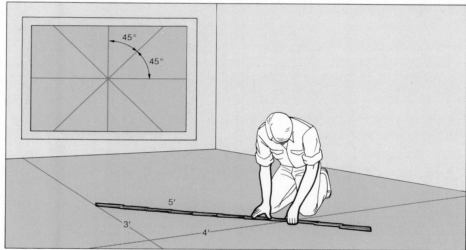

Setting the Tiles

Setting tiles and adhesive. With a notched trowel held at a 45° angle to the floor, spread adhesive along one chalk line—if you are laying tiles in an on-the-square pattern—working from the intersection toward a wall. Leave small parts of the line uncovered for guidance, and make your layer about half the thickness of your tile. Set this row of tiles, butting each tile against one already laid and dropping it into place. Do not slide a tile: that will force adhesive onto its surface. Set another row of tiles along the perpen-

dicular chalk line, then fill the area between the rows in a pyramid pattern so that each new tile butts against two already laid *(inset, top)*. When you finish a section, roll it with a rented 100-pound tile roller or a rolling pin on which you place most of your weight. To lay a diagonal pattern *(inset, bottom)*, set tiles point to point over the perpendicular chalk lines. Lay another row of tiles with their sides along the diagonal chalk line. Then fill in the area between rows, working from the intersection toward the wall.

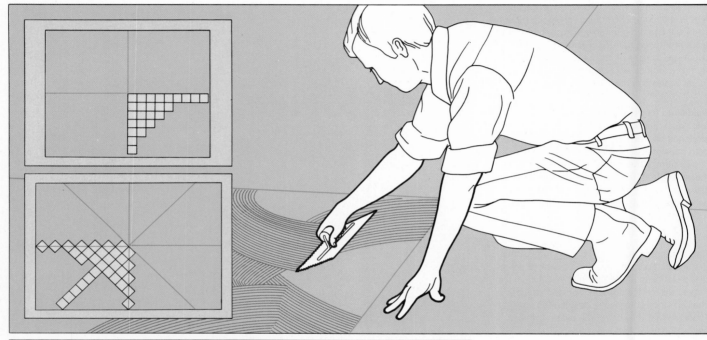

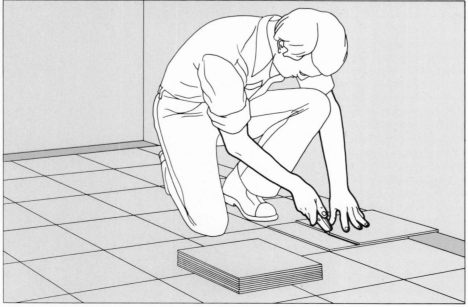

Trimming a border tile. Place two loose tiles squarely on top of the last whole tile in a row and slide the upper one across the untiled gap until it touches a wall; then, using the edge of the top tile as a guide, score the one beneath with a utility knife. Snap the tile along the scored line. The piece that was not covered by the guide tile will fit into the border, its snapped edge against the wall.

If your floor is diagonally laid, score tiles from corner to corner, using a straightedge, and snap them to make triangular half tiles to fill the sawtooth edge of the diagonal pattern. If you also have a square-set border, trim the tiles for it as above.

Two Patterns for Parquetry

Parquet—wood tile—comes in a variety of sizes, shapes and finishes with which you can lay a handsome floor in patterns such as the two traditional ones shown at right, "Haddon Hall" and "Herringbone." Design and installation techniques are much like those for resilient tile floors, but there are a few exceptions. When you plot your design on graph paper (page 27), you may have to use more than one square of the graph to represent each tile, depending on the shape of tile you are using. And if you are using square tiles, indicate on the plot the direction of the grain in each tile. In elongated tiles and strips, the grain runs lengthwise.

While resilient tile floors have a border of trimmed tile on four sides, wood floors should have a border of whole tiles on the sides of the room where there are doorways, because the glue under a full-sized wood tile provides a stronger bond in heavily trafficked areas. Guidelines are set up just as they are for resilient tile (page 27), but when you make a dry run, you may need to adjust the lines to get a full-tile border on a door side.

Wood tiles absorb moisture, so before you lay them let them rest loosely around the room for 72 hours so that they will adjust to the humidity. Also, leave a 1/2-inch space between the border tiles and the walls to allow for the tiles' expansion. You may insert a thin strip of 1/2-inch cork, available at lumberyards, in the space.

Spread the proper mastic for wood tiles 1/8 inch thick and allow to set for two hours, until it is tacky. Then lay the tiles, paying special attention to the grain patterns marked on your plot and to locking tongues and grooves tightly.

Laying the "Herringbone" pattern. Lay the first 6-by-12-inch tile along a diagonal guideline, one corner set in the intersection. Lay the second tile at the end of and perpendicular to the first and the third tile at the end of and perpendicular to the second, as shown. Use the chalk lines and these three tiles as guides for laying the next three and continue until you reach the wall. Repeat in the other sections of the room until you have completed the floor (inset).

Setting wood tiles in place. Making sure that the grain pattern duplicates that on your graph paper, slip a wood tile into position so its tongue and groove fit with those of adjacent tiles. Tap it with a mallet cushioned by a wood block while holding adjacent tiles in place. The tiles should be laid in the pyramidal manner used for resilient tiles (page 28, top). Measure border tiles as you would resilient tiles (page 28, bottom), but mark them with a pencil instead of scoring them, and cut them with a fine-toothed handsaw.

Laying the "Haddon Hall" pattern. Starting at the intersection of your guidelines, lay an 18-inch square of four 6-by-12-inch tiles bordering one 6-by-6-inch tile. The first two 6-by-12-inch tiles should be laid perpendicular to one another along the guidelines. Lay the floor pyramidally from this block until it is complete (inset).

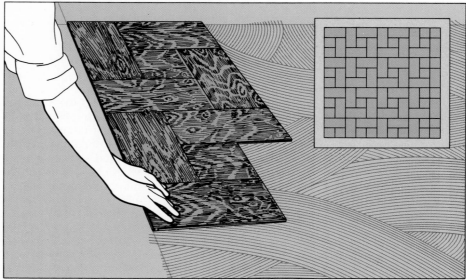

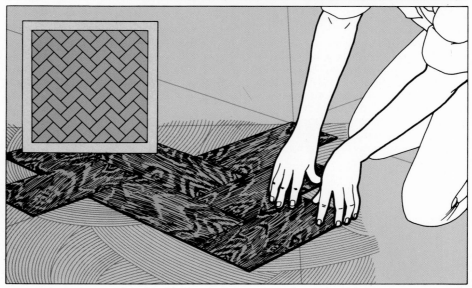

Embedding Stone and Ceramic Tiles in Mortar

For many floors, the merits of hard mineral materials may well outweigh the desirability of resilience provided by wood or vinyl. Vestibules, halls and hearths can benefit from the beauty and durability of tiles of ceramic or stone; ceramic tile for bathrooms is discussed in Chapter 2 *(pages 152-157)*. While hard tiles are best laid in a thin bed of mortar over a concrete subfloor, as described on these pages, today's adhesives make it possible to lay them on underlayment of 5/8-inch exterior-grade plywood, using the methods for laying resilient tiles *(pages 26-28)*.

The hard surfacing materials come in a dazzling variety. Ceramic-tile retailers offer choices that range from unglazed earth-colored pavers 6 inches square and 1/4 inch thick, and 8-inch square quarry tiles 1/2 inch thick, to colorful glazed and patterned creations up to a foot square. Tiles with abrasive grain fired into the glaze reduce slipperiness.

Slate and various kinds of sandstone, limestone and quartzite, all available in tile-shaped rectangles of uniform thickness, also make good-looking, impermeable floors and can be laid like ceramic.

But for millennia the most desirable of all stones has probably been lustrous, gemlike marble. Though marble tiles come in various dimensions, a common and practical size is 1 foot square—1/2 inch thick if American, 1 centimeter (2/5 inch) thick if imported from Europe. Marble honed to a soft gloss is best for floors; highly polished surfaces are slippery and easily scratched. Despite its density, marble absorbs liquid, but transparent silicone sealer will protect it.

Remove the old tile, if any. The original surface—such as the bare concrete subfloor shown below—must be level to within 1/8 inch. By rolling a straight piece of pipe in various directions, find high and low spots. Level high spots with a rub brick or a rented concrete grinder, and fill low spots with mortar.

If your tiles have a directional pattern, such as the grain of marble, arrange a number of them to determine whether to set them with the grain running one way, or in a checkerboard-parquet style or at random. Lay out the tiles, using the method shown on page 28, but in place of chalk lines stretch mason's string tautly between nails driven into the wall plates 3/4 inch from the floor.

The technique given here uses a thinset mortar, which can be made by mixing three cups of portland cement and three cups of fine masonry sand into two cups of latex tile-setting liquid (a bond-strengthening suspension of latex in water, sold by cement dealers). A batch will cover 6 square feet. It is applied with a rectangular "box-notch" trowel. Your dealer can recommend the correct notch size for the tile you select.

For most vestibules and halls, the job is finished with wood baseboards and molding—the ones you removed for the renovation, or new ones. For a formal look, make bases of the same material as the floor. Ceramic tilemakers can supply such trim. For stone floor base and trim, ask your dealer to saw 12-by-12 tiles into 4-by-12 strips. Smooth and bevel or round the rough edges: Wearing eye protection *(page 130)* or other necessary personal safety gear *(page 76)*, use silicon-carbide sanding disks in an electric drill, with grits 80, 150 and 320 in succession. Secure the trim to the wall with water-resistant organic adhesive.

1 Making the mortar bed. Divide the room into equal quadrants: Drive nails into the wall plates at the midpoints of both pairs of opposing walls, 3/4 inch from the floor. Stretch two strings tautly between the nails and check for 90° angles as shown on page 27, center.

Dampen the concrete subfloor and, starting in one of the corners where the reference strings cross, use a box-notch trowel to spread a low mound of mortar. Then hold the trowel nearly vertical, and drag the teeth on the subfloor so you leave a row of mortar ridges. Do not try to substitute a sawtooth-edged mastic trowel for this job; teeth at least 1/4 inch deep and 1/4 inch apart are necessary to get the mortar to the correct level.

2 **Laying the first tile.** Place a tile on the ridged mortar with one corner at the crossed strings, and while twisting it slightly several times press it down firmly; use full body weight on big tiles. Using a rubber or wood mallet, tap the tile edges until it lines up exactly with the strings. Check with a level along both dimensions and diagonally; tap down any high sides. Pick up any excess mortar for reuse.

Check the first tile by lifting it off the mortar to determine whether it has made full contact; if not, make a new bed with more mortar, place a mound of mortar on the tile, then re-lay the tile with more twisting and pressure. Dampen the backs of highly absorbent tiles with a sponge. If you are using quarry tiles that have deeply scored backs, trowel mortar into the scores before setting.

3 **Filling in the field.** Lay tiles, aligned with strings, in all four directions from the first, and allow to set overnight; remove the strings, then fill in the quarters. Unless the tiles have self-spacing lugs cast on their bottom edges, use wood spacers such as rounded toothpicks to hold them 3/32 to 1/2 inch apart. Tiles may not be cut to precise size, so measure frequently from the center lines and adjust spacing to keep joints squared. With a level on a straight 2-by-4, check and adjust the height of the tiles against the central tile as you set them. At obstacles, use the techniques shown in Step 4.

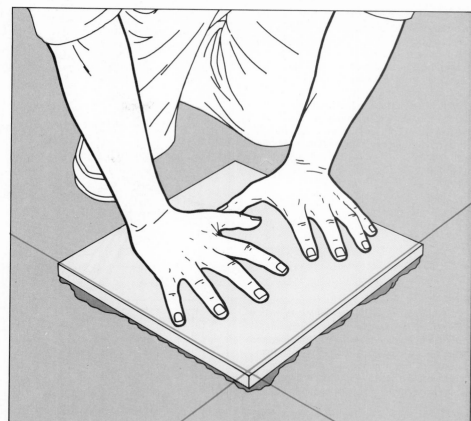

4 **Cutting border tiles.** Mark to measure the tiles that will be used for the floor's border, following the method shown on page 28. If the tiles are stone or thick ceramic, ask your dealer to cut them. If they are small, thin ceramic tiles, cut them yourself: Using a rented tile cutter, push the handle forward to draw the scoring wheel across the tile's surface. Then flip the handle back and gently tap it, so that the flanges on both sides of the wheel will strike the tile and snap it along the scored line.

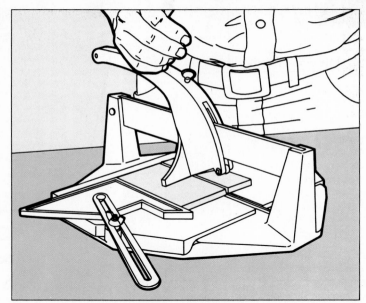

5 **Setting a threshold.** For ceramic or marble tile floors, a marble threshold is generally installed in interior doorways by removing the doorstops with a putty knife and pry bar, then setting the threshold in a bed of raked mortar as you would a tile. Saw off the doorstops to fit and replace them. Marble companies cut thresholds to length and bevel them to accommodate the newly tiled floor to adjacent floors. Bathroom thresholds should rise 1/4 inch above the floor to make a dam against spills. Outside doors may need new weatherproof metal thresholds.

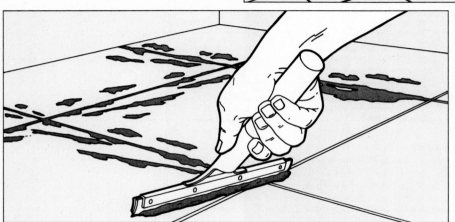

6 **Grouting between tiles.** Using a window-washing squeegee, pack into the spaces between tiles a floor grout of portland cement and latex tile-setting liquid mixed in proportions that make it barely fluid. Squeegee each joint from both directions, crossing the tile edges at a slight angle. Then use a damp cloth to wipe the tiles and recess the grout slightly. As soon as the grout starts to set, clean the film of cement from the tiles with a damp sponge. The gray grout made with portland cement is inconspicuous and does not show dirt; an alternative is white grout mixed with powdered concrete coloring pigments, available from many building-supply dealers.

Estimating and Installing Wall-to-Wall Carpet

Two principal types of carpet are glue-down (also called cushion-back) and stretch-in carpets. A glue-down carpet typically has a cushion layer of foam rubber, jute or action backing and is secured directly to the subfloor with latex adhesive. An increasingly popular version of glue-down carpet is called double-stick carpet—which involves gluing the cushion to the floor, then the carpet to the cushion. Some carpets, called unitary back, have no backing at all, and require higher-grade adhesive that must be allowed to "breathe" in order to set.

A stretch-in carpet has a separate undercushion stapled to the subfloor onto which it is placed. It is stretched and hooked onto tackless strips nailed to the edges of the subfloor or stairs—a procedure that is often best left to professionals.

While both types of carpets are still equally common, the glue-down carpet (pages 35-36) is often favored over the stretch-in carpet by the do-it-yourselfer because few special tools are required to repair or replace it. In addition, glue-down carpet is usually less expensive than carpet installed over separate padding.

Most carpets are tufted: That is, their pile—whether made of wool or any of several synthetics—is machine-stitched into a backing that is made beforehand (below). They may be made with loop pile or cut pile, a distinction that is important to the techniques used when cutting carpet to fit your room (page 34). Sculptured carpets are made with both loop and cut pile.

When newly manufactured carpet is rolled up as it comes off the machine, the pile fibers are pressed down in the same direction, never to return to their original position. This "pile direction" affects appearance and installation technique.

You can tell pile direction by stroking it: Stroking against the pile direction will raise the nap. When you "look into" the pile, with the fibers leaning toward you, a carpet takes on its deepest hue. When you "look over" the pile, the carpet appears flatter and lighter in color. If possible, carpet should be installed with the pile leaning toward the main entrance to the room, presenting its fullest, richest appearance. To help hide the seam where two pieces of carpet are joined, the pile of at least one side should lean over the seam. In a doorway connecting two rooms, the pile from both sides may lean over the seam, but within a room the pile of every section of carpet must lean the same way or the pieces will show up as different hues.

Pile direction is one of several factors that must be taken into account when you are planning the layout of a carpet in a room and calculating how much to buy. Some others to remember are:
• Unless you have some carpet installation experience, you may be wise to begin in a small room requiring carpet with no seams.
• Run the longest seam in the room toward the major light source—usually the largest window. A seam running parallel to light rays is much less apparent than one running across them.
• Keep seams away from high traffic areas, such as between doors of a room. The foot traffic thus directed along the seam length may loosen it.
• A tool called a carpet tractor is useful when making seams. Available from some carpet equipment suppliers, it pulls the two edges together for a tight seam.
• The best way to determine how much carpet you will need is to make a scale drawing of the area to be carpeted on graph paper. Choose a scale that will keep the drawing a convenient size; equating each square of the graph paper to a square foot usually works well.
• Make separate measurements of the entire length of each wall and then the shorter distances between its various features, such as doorjambs. Double-check for error by making sure the sum of the parts is equal to the whole. Compare diagonal measurements and the distances between walls to see if the walls are skewed or bowed. Plot the walls, doors and windows on the graph paper.
• Include the areas where the carpet will extend into doorways or bays as part of the room's overall dimensions; then add 3 inches to the length and the width of the floor for error. You may also have to add 1/2 inch for trimming each factory-cut edge; ask the carpet dealer for the manufacturer's recommendations.

Now, bearing in mind the rules about pile direction and the location of seams, figure out how many running yards of carpet 12 feet wide you need to cover the room, keeping the seams and the amount of wasted carpet to a minimum. To do this, experiment with graph paper cut to represent a length of carpet 12 feet wide.

If the carpet is patterned, you must take into account the repeat—the distance from the point where a pattern begins to where it begins again—in order to be sure of matching the pattern along a seam. If your scheme involves matching the pattern only lengthwise across two original edges of the carpet, simply allow for a full extra repeat on one of the lengths, and you will be able to adjust it to match. Take your scale drawing to your carpet dealer to have your estimates checked. If the carpet will meet an adjoining surface other than carpet, buy the length of binder bar needed; install it as described on page 151.

Before starting, nail uneven boards, remove grills from heating vents and sweep the floor. You may wish to remove shoe moldings, then put them back (page 24) or repaint the baseboards before laying the carpet. The floor must be dry. A remedy for occasional moisture in a concrete floor is a layer of concrete sealer. However, if water rising from the ground leaves the floor permanently damp, it is best to forgo carpeting entirely, as the moisture will rot the cushion-back. Test for water seepage with a sheet of plastic taped to the floor, as described on page 18.

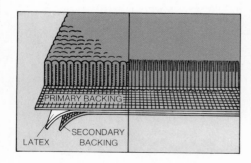

The making of a tufted carpet. The pile yarn of tufted carpet is stitched through a layer of open-weave fabric—the primary backing. A second fabric backing is stuck onto the underside of the first with a coating of latex. When the yarn is left uncut the result is loop-pile tufted carpet (left). But the tops of the loops are often split or cut off, making cut-pile tufted carpet (right).

Rough-Cutting and Seaming

Once you have carefully planned the carpeting of a room, as described on page 33, unroll your carpet. Before cutting it, check for any defects and make sure that it is the size you ordered. Unroll the carpet in an empty room, basement, driveway or yard—over newspaper if necessary—and give it time to flatten.

Cut-pile carpet should be cut from the back *(right)*. Loop-pile should be cut from the front *(below)* to be sure the cut carpet does not remain joined by loops across the cut. When you lay out the pieces in the area to be carpeted, place them so that the pile leans in the same direction. Position the carpet by kicking it, or by flapping smaller pieces as if shaking a tablecloth, until the excess extends up all walls equally. Make relief cuts at corners *(right, inset)*, using a utility knife. Seams across the width of the carpet require special cutting with a row-running cutter.

Two Ways to Cut a Carpet

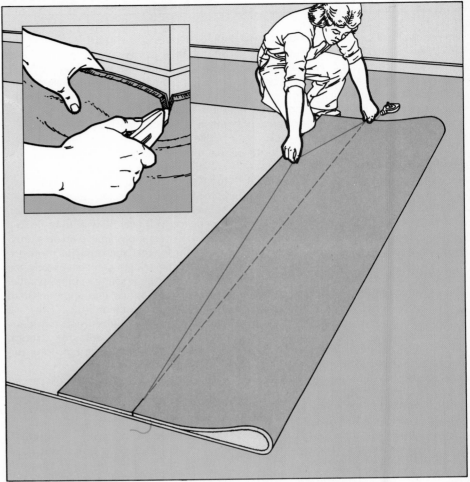

Cutting a cut-pile carpet. Measure along the face of the unrolled carpet, cut notches in the edges, fold the carpet back and snap a chalk line across it with a string held between the notches. Cut along the chalk line with a row-running "cushion back" cutter guided by a good straightedge. Extend the blade of the knife only enough to cut the backing.

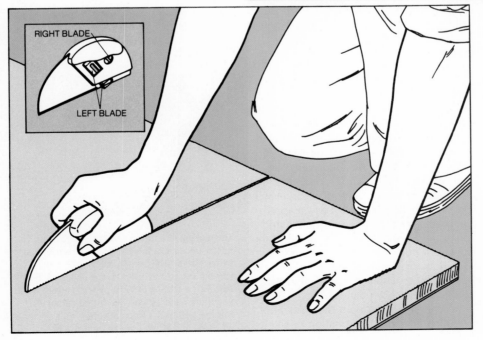

Cutting loop-pile carpet. Measure the carpet and cut it from the face between rows of loops with a row-running "cushion-back" cutter or with a utility knife. If the rows are not straight use a straightedge. If you use the row runner *(inset)*, retract both blades and separate the pile by sliding the runner along the backing. After making a path, extend the blade on the side of the tool next to the section of carpet you will use and make the cut.

Glue-Down: Easy to Install

Glue-down carpet is the easiest type to install. It requires no stretching, no specialized tools and no tackless strips. It is simply cemented down—or, in some cases, stuck to the floor with double-faced tape *(page 36, bottom)*. Also, glue-down carpet is usually less expensive than carpet installed over separate padding.

Although it goes down easily, once cemented glue-down is impossible to remove intact—the cushion-backing rips off the face of the carpet as it is pulled up. The carpet cannot be used again and the backing and adhesive must be scraped off the floor; unless recarpeted, the floor will have to be refinished. And the foam backing of some cheap glue-down carpets may decompose in a few years; heavier backing generally lasts longer. Although weight is not the only determinant of carpet life, 26 ounces per square yard is the recommended minimum for a typical room, and 28 ounces for public areas such as stairs or hallways.

For cementing most glue-down carpets, use a multipurpose latex adhesive, available at hardware stores. Caution: When shopping for glue-down carpet, be sure to ask about backing material. Special adhesive is required for carpets with vinyl backing or those used below ground level. Often the backing material is difficult to identify—even for the carpet dealer. If unsure of the material, contact the manufacturer.

Before laying the carpet, it should be preconditioned to room temperature—at least 65°—for 72 hours. Remove all dust, wax and paint from the floor, patch cracks and secure loose tiles or floorboards. The floor must be dry; a permanently damp floor is best left uncarpeted. While installing the carpet, and for 72 hours thereafter, make sure the room is well ventilated.

Many floors are so large that carpet cannot be laid without a seam. In such cases, begin to cement under the seam area *(Step 1)*. If the room needs only one piece, lay the carpet out, fold it in half with the triangular folds described in Step 4 and proceed with installation according to that and subsequent steps.

1 **Preparing to make a seam.** Before applying adhesive *(below)*, rough-cut *(page 34)* and lay out the carpet. Snap a chalk line on the floor where the seam will run. Align the edge of one piece of carpet with the line and pull the other piece so that its edge overlaps the first by 1/4 inch. Fold both pieces back about 3 feet. With a 3/32-inch V- or U-notched trowel, spread a thin, even layer of adhesive on the exposed floor. Roll one piece of carpet onto the adhesive, lining it up with the chalk mark.

Then pull the carpet back to inspect the backing. If the floor pattern has been imprinted on the backing, the carpet should adhere well. Working from there toward the wall, use your hands to rub out any air bubbles that may be trapped beneath the carpet.

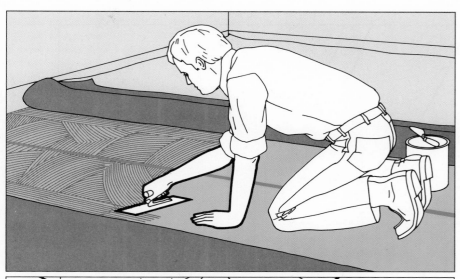

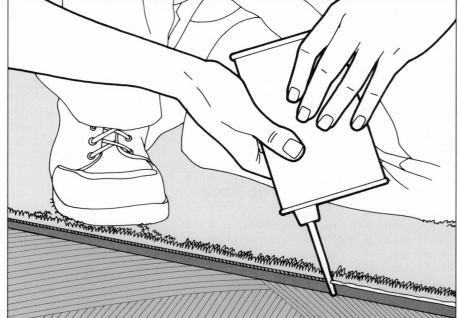

2 **Gluing the seam.** Apply a bead of seam sealer *(above)* to the primary backing—just between the pile and the cushion—at the edge of the cemented-down piece of carpet. Work carefully; seam sealer may ooze to the top, and will attract dirt. If any adhesive gets on the pile of the carpet, wipe it off immediately with a clean white rag moistened with seam solvent, available from a carpet dealer. (Caution: Seam solvent is corrosive, and attacks rubber backing; do not leave it on the face pile, and wash your hands immediately.) To make the job easy and accurate, notch the nozzle of the applicator at the height of the primary backing, and then run the tip along the floor while the adhesive feeds onto the carpet edge.

3 **Making a compression seam.** Unfold the second piece of carpet and position it on the floor. Butt the edge of this piece of carpet against that of the glued-down piece and work any bulges resulting from the overlap away from the seam with your fingers until you reach the unglued area. When gaps occur at the seam, seal them by pulling and pressing the carpet edges together with your fingers until the two pieces meet all along the seam.

4 **Completing the cementing.** Fold one piece of carpet back from the wall until you reach the part that has already been cemented to the floor. To prevent the carpet from grabbing along the wall as you fold it back, first fold each corner of the carpet at a 45° angle toward the center of the seam. Trowel the adhesive onto the exposed floor and unfold the carpet in reverse order, rubbing any wrinkles or ridges out toward the wall with your hands or with the pa-

per core of a carpet roll. Repeat this process on the other side of the room. When the carpet is cemented down, crease it along the walls with a screwdriver.

Trim off excess at a distance above the floor equal to the thickness of the carpet. Then tuck the edge of the carpet against the wall with the screwdriver. Tamp down the flanges of the doorway edgings.

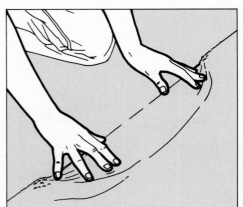

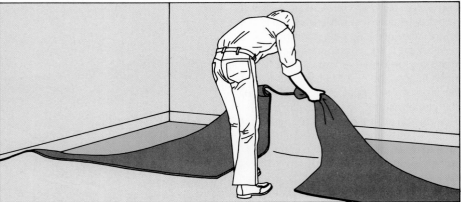

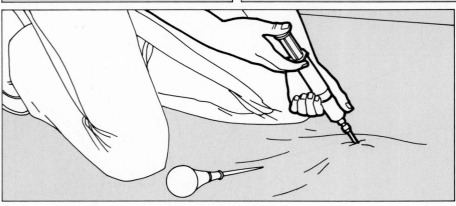

5 **Flattening a bubble.** Where the carpet is not adhering to the floor, poke an awl through the carpet and use a plastic syringe—available from a carpet-supply dealer—to inject a special quick-drying cement called contact adhesive into the hole. Then press down on the carpet with your hands until it holds firmly to the floor.

Easier Yet—Taped Cushion-Back

Short of just letting the carpet lie loose on the floor, no installation could be easier than sticking down cushion-back carpeting with double-faced tape. Unfortunately, the carpet is likely to develop wrinkles between the strips of tape, and is likely to come unstuck altogether if it gets much wear. In addition, the floor surface will be ruined by the tape. It does, however, provide a simple, quick and cheap way to carpet an area where permanence is unimportant and where the floor will always be covered.

In a lightly traveled room, you need to apply tape only around the perimeter, flush with the walls, with a double strip of tape in

front of any doorways. In a busier room, lay tape not only around the perimeter, but also diagonally 1 foot apart across the floor.

Stick down the tape, folding under a corner of each strip to provide a tab for removing the paper covering the face of the tape. Position the rough-cut carpet on the floor and fold back one side in the triangular manner described in Step 4 above. Peel the protective cover from the strips of tape and roll the carpet onto the taped area. Then press the carpet onto the tape with your fingers. Finish the job by trimming the carpet along the walls .

Truing Up Hills and Valleys for Resurfacing Walls

The key to a smooth wall or ceiling is a flat, sound substructure for the surface material. While some walls are sound enough to be resurfaced directly, others need extensive preparation to compensate for surface damage or crooked framing members. You may have to make a grid of thin wood furring strips to serve as a flat base. You may even have to build a false wall in front of the old one.

To assess the condition of an uneven wall or ceiling, you will need a carpenter's level and a long straight-edged board. First hold the level against the wall at several places to check it for plumb, or against the ceiling to check that it is level. Then slide the board across the wall or ceiling as you look for gaps between board and surface. If neither check discloses major flaws, you can probably install the new surface over the old with only minor preparations. If you plan to use adhesive, make sure the old surface is clean and tight; if the new surface will be fastened to the old framing, mark the positions of the wall studs or ceiling joists.

On surfaces where only small areas are damaged or out of true, you can use plywood or wallboard patches to repair the damage, shimming the patches to bring them flush with the surrounding surface. When the surface is badly dam-

aged, however, or very uneven, you will have to build out the entire wall or ceiling with a grid of furring strips, shimming them as necessary to produce an even base. For the shims, use cedar shingles, making the required thickness by sliding two shingles together with their thin ends in opposite directions.

Sometimes, if the existing surface is basically true, you can check by eye alone to see if the shimmed furring strips are true. But you may need to rule off the wall or ceiling with reference lines and strings and take careful measurements to level the grid. On the sound sections of wall or ceiling around your working area, use erasable pencil or chalk.

In laying out a furring grid, you will have to deal with interruptions in the surface. Remove moldings and trim, and adjust the depth of door and window jambs to suit the new wall thickness. You will have to reposition some electrical outlet boxes—or adjust their depth with box extensions, an easier task.

The pattern for the furring grid may require some preliminary thought. Although furring strips usually run horizontally, some materials, plywood paneling for example, require vertical supports as well, and you must plan the layout of the panels in advance, so that the verti-

cal supports will match the panel edges.

Furring out from a masonry wall presents other problems. Many experienced do-it-yourselfers prefer the use of mastic furring anchors: At points aligned with furring strip locations, dab on mastic and press the anchors into it. When the anchors have set, drive the furring strips over them to clinch the nails. However, on any masonry wall below ground level, you must put a moisture barrier of vinyl sheeting—after installing the anchors and before attaching the furring strips. A false wall may also be needed for the outlet boxes or switches for a new electric circuit.

Sometimes built-ins or plumbing fixtures make it impossible to fur out a wall or build a false one. Sometimes, too, a surface will be too badly damaged to serve as the base for a new one—plaster may be too loose or wallboard too crumbly. In such cases, remove the existing wall surface and start from scratch, laying the resurfacing material directly against the framing studs. This is not as drastic as it sounds. Wallboard can generally be pulled off, or plaster broken, wearing safety goggles and using a hammer, after which the lath can be pried out with a utility bar. Before installing the new surfacing material, sink any protruding nails.

Gridiron Pattern of Furring Strips

A framework for plywood paneling. The furring strips on this wall, backed by thin wood shims where needed, make a flat, plumb base for vertical 4-foot-by-8-foot plywood panels. The horizontal strips are 1-by-2s, spaced 16 inches apart from center to center. Vertical furring strips, also 1-by-2s, are placed across the wall at 48-inch intervals, center to center.

Small gaps between vertical and horizontal furring strips prevent moisture damage by letting air circulate behind the paneling. Additional 1-by-2s frame the corners and window to support the panel edges, and a furring strip that spans two studs will support an electrical outlet. The horizontal 1-by-4 furring strips at the top and bottom of the wall serve as the backing for the crown and base moldings that will be nailed to the wall after the paneling is in place.

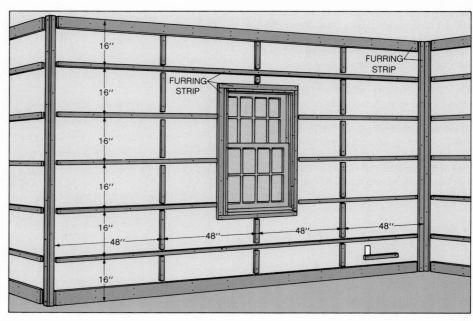

Prying Off Molding and Trim

1 **Removing a length of molding.** To salvage a length of shoe molding, first cut through the paint at the seam between the molding and the baseboard with a utility knife, then drive a thin pry bar into the seam near an end of the molding. Place a wooden block behind the pry bar to protect the baseboard, and slowly pry the molding loose. Work along the seam, using wedges to hold the seam open as you go, until the whole length of molding is loose enough to remove in one piece. Use the same technique to remove baseboards and other moldings.

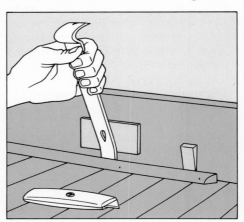

2 **Removing window or door trim.** To avoid splitting window or door casings as you pry them loose, use a nail set to drive the existing nails completely through one section of each mitered corner. Then you will be able to pry off the casing, using the technique described in Step 1, left.

Guidelines and Shims to Position Furring

1 **Setting up reference lines.** With a pencil and straightedge, rule off the wall *(top right)* with a gridwork of lines marking the vertical locations of framing studs in the wall and horizontal positions where furring strips will be installed. Then snap a chalk line against the ceiling, 2 inches out from the wall.

On a ceiling *(bottom right)*, mark two reference lines by first marking the location of concealed joists, then snapping a chalk line along each of the two walls that parallel the joists. Place these chalk lines about 2 inches below ceiling level. Drive nails partway in along each chalk line at the positions for furring strips, and then run taut strings across the joists between opposing nails.

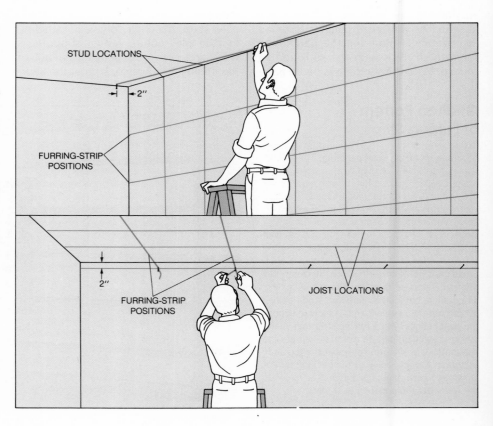

STUD LOCATIONS

2"

FURRING-STRIP POSITIONS

2"

FURRING-STRIP POSITIONS

JOIST LOCATIONS

2 **Positioning the first furring strips.** Suspend a plumb bob from the ceiling chalk line (2 inches from the wall) so that it hangs in front of a wall stud, and measure the distance from the plumb line to the wall at each intersection of stud and furring-strip line. Record each measurement. Repeat at the other studs.

When you have found the point with the smallest measurement—the highest point along the wall—nail a horizontal furring strip with a single nail to the wall at this point. Position the plumb bob in front of this point and note the distance from the plumb line to the face of the furring strip. In positioning the strip, leave room at the corner for a vertical furring strip. When several points along the wall are the same short distance from the plumb line, nail a furring strip to the wall with a single nail at each such point.

Use the same procedure to locate the lowest point on the ceiling, measuring from the intersections of the strings to the ceiling. At the lowest point, slip a furring strip under the strings and then nail it with a single nail to a joist. Measure and make a note of the distance between the string and the furring strip at this point.

3 **Shimming the first furring strip.** Reposition the plumb bob, hanging it from the ceiling chalk line in front of the stud nearest one end of the furring strip. Place wood shims as necessary behind the strip until the distance between its face and the plumb line measures the same as the distance at the first nailing point. Drive a nail through the furring strip and the shims and into that stud. Position the other end of the furring strip in the same way.

On a ceiling, shim out one end of the furring strip until the distance from the string to the face of the furring strip is the same as at the first nailing point. Nail the strip to the joist nearest the end of the strip. Then repeat at the opposite end.

4 **Truing a furring strip.** Press the edge of a long straight board against the first furring strip, spanning two nailed points, and note where the furring strip, when pressed against the wall, bows away from the straight edge. Build these points out with shims at each stud as you nail the furring strip in place.

Repeat Steps 3 and 4 to install a second furring strip at the top or bottom of the wall, adjusting it with shims so it is set the same distance from the plumb line as the first strip. On a ceiling, use the same technique to true and nail the first furring strip, then install and true a second strip at one side, setting it the same distance from the reference strings as the first strip.

5 **Installing the remaining furring.** Hold the edge of the long straight board vertically, spanning the two trued furring strips, and use it as a reference for installing and shimming the rest of the horizontal strips in the grid. Then install vertical strips where they are needed, shimming them to lie flush with the horizontal strips. At corners, install full-length vertical strips; at midwall, cut them to fit between the horizontal strips. Short vertical strips need not be fastened to studs; they can be secured to the old wall with adhesive or nails.

Use the same techniques to install the remaining furring strips on a ceiling. Then add short cross strips where they are needed to support the panel edges.

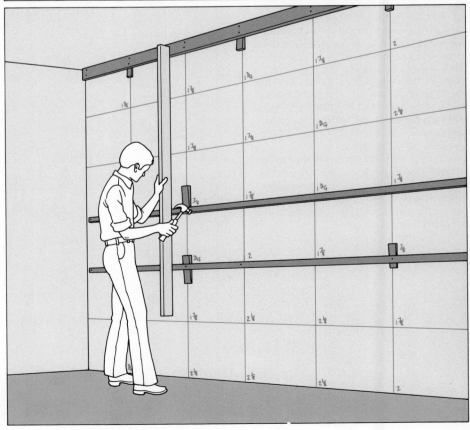

Covering Walls with Wood Veneer Panels

Nothing brings the warmth and elegance of wood to a room as quickly and effectively as veneer paneling for the walls. Available in hundreds of styles, wood-veneer panels are far less costly than are solid-wood boards *(page 48)* and even easier to install than gypsum wallboard *(pages 80-86)*. Vertical joints can be disguised by an incised pattern on the panels, and other edges hidden by special moldings. The panels are attached to a framework of studs or furring strips *(pages 37-40)* just as wallboard is or, even better, to wallboard itself.

Yet, for all its advantages, paneling also has several disadvantages that have limited its use to certain rooms, such as recreation rooms and dens. It is more expensive than wallboard and, because of its construction, it is more flammable and more vulnerable to damage.

Typically, veneer paneling is a backing of plywood or particleboard veneered in one of several ways—with a thin layer of fine wood, with a thin sheet of less desirable wood *(chart, page 42)*, or with a simulated wood grain printed on paper or vinyl. The panels come in sheets 5/32, 3/16 or 1/4 inch thick, and this thinness, along with the materials used, makes them the least fire-resistant of all common wall surfaces. National fire-testing laboratories give most veneer panels the same poor flame-spread rating, Class C or its equivalent, FS-200—ratings you should find stamped on each panel back.

Fire-prevention experts warn against putting large expanses of veneer paneling directly over wall studs or furring strips, particularly in such fire-prone areas as halls, stairways, kitchens and utility rooms. Instead, they recommend that you either apply panels directly to an existing wall of gypsum or plaster, or cover any stud wall or furring framework with 1/2-inch gypsum board. When you apply the panels, avoid placing wallboard joints and panel joints along the same studs. The wallboard underlayer not only multiplies the wall's fire resistance ninefold, to a far safer level, but also triples

its resistance to impact and decreases sound transmission by 43 percent.

All veneer panels come in sheets 4 feet by 8 feet, and some are available as tall as 12 feet—but the latter are expensive, and 8-foot sheets should suffice to cover the loftiest wall. Both the real-wood veneers and the printed-wood panels are made in a variety of colors and grains, and most styles have a vertical-groove pattern that makes them look like boards. The spacing between grooves is designed to seem random, but in fact a groove always falls at or near a 16- or a 24-inch interval, to make it easy to find the studs or furring strips when you are fastening the panels. At the edges, vertical half-grooves disguise joints.

To estimate how many panels you will need to cover an area, measure the total width of the walls in feet, and divide by 4. Some suppliers recommend that you then subtract one half panel for a door and one quarter panel for a window, on the assumption that pieces cut from window and door panels can be used elsewhere; in practice, however, they are not likely to fit anywhere else.

After you buy the panels, store them in the room where they will be used, stacked one atop another with small wood blocks between. Give them 48 hours to adjust to the temperature and humidity of the room; this will reduce the danger of shrinkage or expansion after the panels are installed. Next, if the panels have a real-wood veneer with truly random graining, stand them against the wall and arrange them to suit your taste. A few panels may have a stronger grain than others, a few may be lighter or darker, or the horizontal joints of the core may show in some grooves. Printed panels, which are flawless and nearly identical, can go up in any order.

You can cut plywood veneer panels with a handsaw or power saw. For long straight cuts, most carpenters prefer a portable circular saw *(page 454)* fitted with a special plywood blade that has six teeth per inch. For short straight cuts and

curved cuts, use a saber saw *(page 454)* with a 10-tooth-per-inch blade. The chief advantage of circular and saber saws is that they cut on the upstroke. Saw with the panel face down; this enables you to mark your cutting lines on the back of the panel and confine most of the splinters from the cut to that surface. With most other types of saw, including a table saw but not a radial-arm saw, you will have to control splinters by marking the finished side of the panel and cutting with that side facing up.

How you fasten panels to a wall depends on whether you plan to remove them in the future. The choices are colored nails alone, or nails used with panel adhesive. Applying panel adhesive, which goes on studs or furring strips in a bead from a caulking gun, is faster and easier than hammering in the many nails needed if nails alone are to hold the panels. But glued panels are much harder to salvage. If you elect to use adhesive, buy one 11-ounce tube for every three panels. As for nails, buy special paneling brads, colored to match the panels and sold by panel suppliers. To fasten panels directly to studs or furring strips, use 1-inch nails; when you also nail through wallboard or plaster, be sure to use 1 5/8-inch nails.

Once in place, paneling requires little attention beyond an occasional wiping with a damp cloth and mild detergent. Scratches cannot be removed, but they can be concealed with matching wood stain. If they are no deeper than the panel's finish layer, you may be able to hide them: Rub clear wax into them with a damp cloth. For concealing deep mars, some manufacturers offer putty sticks in colors that match their panels. Over time, some panels fade when exposed to light and air, leaving unfaded areas behind pictures that were hung flat against the wall. To prevent this—or to soften the line between faded and unfaded areas—stick push pins or tacks into the backs of picture frames, creating a 1/2-inch air space between them.

Four Basic Variations in Wall Panels

Choosing a panel. Use the chart below to help you choose paneling that suits your needs. Listed vertically are four panel types; listed horizontally are their characteristics. All of the panels are composite to some extent, composed of wood particles, wood fibers or plywood. Also the four categories are not mutually exclusive. Some manufacturers of plywood veneer panels use particleboard instead of plywood for the core, for example; some enhance the appearance of plywood veneer panels by printing additional wood grain over the grain already present. Whether the grain pattern on a panel is simulated photographically or the real thing may be unimportant to you if it looks genuine. Panels less than 1/4 inch thick need a solid backing.

Panel	Composition	Advantages	Disadvantages
Simulated pattern on particleboard	Compressed and glued wood particles covered with a paper-, vinyl- or wood-printed finish; 3/16 inch thick	Most economical	Weak, rigid and brittle; does not hold nails well; dulls saw blades quickly
Simulated pattern on hardboard	Heated and compressed wood-fiber covered with paper- or wood-printed finish; 5/32 or 3/16 inch thick	Great variety of styles; can simulate brick, stucco or marble as well as wood; stronger than particleboard	Dulls saw blades quickly
Simulated pattern on plywood	Plywood covered with a paper-, vinyl- or wood-printed finish; 5/32 or 3/16 inch thick	Stronger and more flexible than particleboard or hardboard; more economical than plywood veneered with real wood. Can be bent to fit curved walls	Splinters easily; usually thinner and less solid than real wood veneer
Wood veneer on plywood	Real wood veneer over a plywood backing. Veneer can be hardwood or softwood, ranging in quality from inexpensive pine to rosewood. Surface is protected by a clear or slightly tinted plastic coating. Usually 1/4 inch thick	Texture and patina of real wood; best resistance to moisture, sound and impact. Each panel is unique	Two to four times as expensive as printed panels; splinters easily

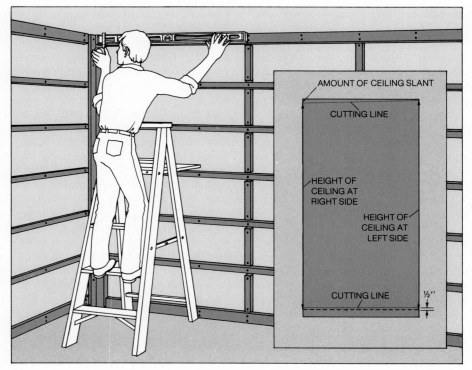

AMOUNT OF CEILING SLANT

CUTTING LINE

HEIGHT OF CEILING AT RIGHT SIDE

HEIGHT OF CEILING AT LEFT SIDE

CUTTING LINE

½"

Fitting and Cutting Panels to Cover a Wall

1 Establishing cutting lines. At either an inside or an outside corner of the room, hold a 4-foot level against the top of the wall to check whether the ceiling slants. If it does, measure the gap between the level and the ceiling at the ceiling's highest point. Measure this distance down one side of the panel and draw a line from that point to the opposite corner of the panel *(inset)*. If you are using a circular saw, saber saw or radial saw *(pages 454)*, mark the cutting line on the back of the panel; for any other type of saw, mark on the front.

Measure the distance from floor to ceiling at the corner of the room and 4 feet away from the corner, along the wall. Subtract 1/2 inch from both measurements and mark these distances down the corresponding sides of the panel, measuring from the top cutting line or from the actual top of the panel, depending on whether the ceiling slopes. Draw a bottom cutting line across the panel between the marks.

2 **Sawing the panels.** If you use a portable circular saw *(page 454)* to trim the panel, measure the distance from the left side of the saw blade to the left side of the base plate and clamp a straight-edged piece of wood to the panel, at this distance from the cutting line. Use the straight edge as a guide while you cut the panel.

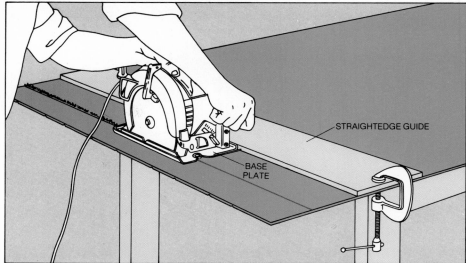

STRAIGHTEDGE GUIDE

BASE PLATE

3 **Applying panel adhesive.** If you are using panel adhesive, apply it in a continuous 1/8-inch-wide serpentine bead to all the studs, furring strips or wall surfaces that will underlie panel edges. On intermediate studs or furring strips, apply the adhesive in 3-inch-long beads 6 inches apart; on a solid wall surface, apply intermediate rows of adhesive in continuous vertical lines about 16 inches apart. You may want to measure and mark these lines with pencil or chalk.

4 **Plumbing the first panel.** Place the panel in position and wedge shims beneath it to lift it 1/4 inch off the floor. Using a 4-foot carpenter's level, plumb the panel's outer edge by having a helper adjust the shims. Do this carefully, because the eventual appearance of all the paneling, especially at the corners of the room, will depend on how vertical the grooves are in the first panel. Tack the panel in place temporarily with four panel nails along the top edge.

WOOD BLOCK

5 **Securing the panel.** Press the panel against the wall to compress the adhesive, then pull out the bottom of the panel and insert two 8-inch wood blocks between the panel and the wall, one at each side. Let the adhesive dry for the time the manufacturer recommends, then remove the blocks and push the panel against the wall again, tapping it with your fist to make a tight seal. Wipe away any adhesive on the finished face of the panel with a rag dipped in paint thinner. Nail the edges of the panel to the wall, spacing the nails 1 foot apart; then nail the panel to the wall along the intermediate studs or furring strips at 2-foot intervals, placing the nails either in the grooves or 1/8 inch from their edges. Set all panel nails with a nail set.

6 **Setting adjoining panels.** Before adding a second panel, run a felt-tip pen, the color of the grooves, along the edge of the panel just installed, staining the furring strip, stud or wall surface. This will keep the joint between panels inconspicuous, even if the panels shrink. Then install subsequent panels the same way as the first, plumbing each one by butting it against the edge of the last panel installed and trimming ends as necessary.

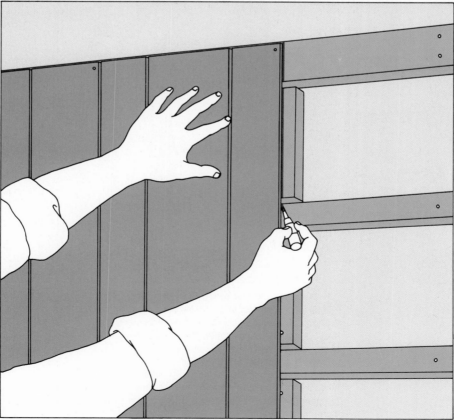

7 **Trimming a panel to fit a corner.** First cut the corner panel to the proper height *(Steps 1 and 2)*, then determine its width by measuring the distance from the corner of the room to the edge of the last panel installed, at both ceiling and floor. Mark these distances on the top and bottom edges of the corner panel, positioning them so that the factory-cut edge of this panel will fall against the panel already in place. Snap a chalk line between the two marks and cut along the line. Install the cut panel as you would a full-width panel, shaving down the cut edge, if necessary, with a block plane so that the edge fits against the corner stud.

Continue to panel around the corner by installing the first panel of the next wall as in Steps 1 through 5, using a level to plumb the panel. If this wall is less than 4 feet wide—the width of one panel—trim the panel to fit, but be sure to use its factory-cut edge to plumb it.

DISTANCE TO CORNER AT CEILING

DISTANCE TO CORNER AT FLOOR

Matching Paneling to Odd-shaped Openings

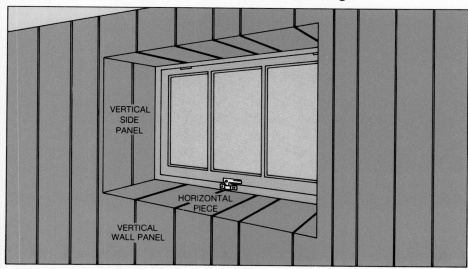

VERTICAL SIDE PANEL

HORIZONTAL PIECE

VERTICAL WALL PANEL

Making grooves turn a corner. When paneling around a corner where one surface is horizontal, as at the bottom or top of a recessed window, align the grooves of the horizontal and vertical panel pieces where the two surfaces meet. For the horizontal panel, use the waste piece cut from the vertical panel, trimming it as needed to fit the space. To line up the grooves, measure the distance from a groove in the vertical panel to the side of the window opening, and match this distance on the horizontal panel, using the corresponding groove as a reference point.

Locating Studs or Joists

For most work on walls and ceilings, it is necessary to determine the positions of concealed studs and joists, and there are several techniques for doing so.

You can tap lightly along a wall or ceiling and listen for a change from a hollow to a solid sound, then move over 16 inches—the most common distance between framing members—and tap again. Alternatively, skim an electric razor along the surface and listen for a change in pitch. A magnetic compass needle may shift when passed over a nail in a stud or joist. Slight ridges or depressions at stud or joist positions can be detected in the oblique glare of an exposed light bulb. Another method—reliable as well as affordable—is the density sensor shown at right.

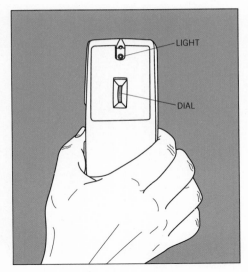

LIGHT

DIAL

Using a density sensor. Roll the dial upward to the "Start" position and place the tool flat on the surface. Press the two buttons on the sides of the tool, turning on the red light, and slowly roll the dial downward until the green light comes on and the red light goes off: Still pressing the two buttons on the sides, slide the tool slowly along the surface. The edge of a stud or joist is indicated when the red light comes on; the other edge is indicated when the green light comes on and the red light goes off.

Making Way for Electric Boxes, Service Panels and Pipes

Marking for an electrical box. To mark the location of an electrical box on a section of paneling for a new wall, first make sure the electricity is off *(page 272)*. Use the front edge of the box, which typically protrudes beyond the studs, for marking the cut. Rub the edge of the box with a piece of chalk *(left)* or lipstick, set the panel in its exact position over the box, and strike the face of the panel with a padded wood block to transfer the chalked outline onto the back of the panel *(right)*. If the outline is not completely clear, use a spare electrical box as a pattern to fill in the missing sections with a pencil. When you are paneling directly over an existing wall, a protruding switch or receptacle will prevent you from using the edges of the electrical box to mark the panel. Instead, you can plot the location of the box by the use of coordinates *(page 82)*.

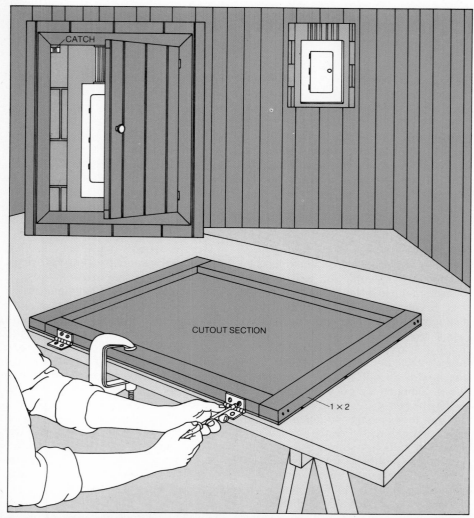

Making a door for a service panel. Using the system of coordinates shown on page 82, transfer the location of the service panel to the back of the wood paneling and cut out the opening. Use the cutout section for a door, framing it with 1-by-2 strips glued to the back. If necessary, trim one long edge so that it will fit easily after hinges are mounted. Screw hinges onto the strips along one edge, set the door into its opening and screw the other wings of the hinges to one of the framing studs surrounding the service panel. Attach a knob to the front of a door, and a catch to the back and to a framing stud. For a more finished look, you can frame the opening with mitered molding, as shown in the inset at left.

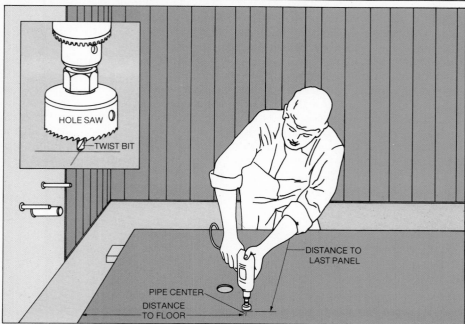

Perfect holes for protruding pipes. Establish the center of the pipe by measuring the distance from the outside of the pipe to the floor and to the last panel installed. Add half the pipe diameter to both measurements, then subtract 1/4 inch from the vertical measurement, in order to allow that much clearance at the floor. Transfer these vertical and horizontal coordinates to the panel back, indenting the point where they meet.

Use a hole saw matching the pipe diameter to drill a hole at this point, drilling only until the twist bit of the saw *(inset)* breaks through the face of the panel. Remove the saw, turn the panel over and finish sawing the hole from the face side.

Solid-Wood Boards: An Elegant Way to Panel

Whether you choose the classic rich hue of mahogany or the casual, rustic look of knotty pine, the room that you panel with solid wood will have a warmth and charm that can be achieved with few other wall coverings.

Many kinds of wood can be used for board paneling. Good hardwoods include birch, cherry, mahogany, maple, oak, pecan, rosewood, teak and walnut; popular softwoods are cedar, cypress, fir, hemlock, pine, redwood and spruce. Prices depend on the availability of the wood, which frequently varies with geographic location. Oak, for example, is more abundant, and therefore less expensive, on the East Coast of the United States. Some woods, such as mahogany or teak, are available only as imports and are always expensive.

The species of wood and the way you position the boards—vertically, horizontally or diagonally—have the greatest effect on the look of board paneling, but other factors are also important. Any board can be milled with a smooth or a rough-sawed surface. The grade of the wood can vary the effect, too—a clear grade provides an even, formal look; a knotty grade is more casual. Most boards are a nominal 1 inch thick (actually 3/4 inch), but the width of boards ranges from 2 to 12 inches and varying widths are frequently intermixed on one wall.

Board edges may be square-cut for a contemporary look or they may be shaped with designs ranging from simple to elaborate, and milled to interlock or overlap. Those with interlocking tongue-and-groove joints are the easiest to work with, especially if the boards are installed in a diagonal pattern.

After you make the esthetic decisions, consider practical matters. Check avail-ability and prices at several lumberyards in your area; ordering wood that is not stocked locally will add considerable shipping costs. Then calculate the square footage of the walls you will cover. Converting this figure into the number of board feet of lumber you need can be tricky, as it depends on the installation pattern, the average width of boards, and in some cases whether they are hardwood or softwood; ask your lumber dealer for help. Count on buying 10 to 20 percent more than the minimum figure to cover inevitable waste.

Another consideration is board length. If you order in bulk, you will receive boards ranging in length from 8 to 14 feet. If you plan a diagonal installation that requires both short and long boards, a bulk order will serve your purpose best. But if you plan a vertical installation, it probably will be more economical to order boards all one length to minimize waste, although the price per board foot will be higher.

Once the planning and purchasing are done, you are ready for the installation. This task calls not so much for woodworking expertise as for patience and care, because wood boards have non-conforming personalities all their own. There is no way to avoid the slight cups, crooks, bows and twists that characterize wood. To keep all the boards exactly vertical, horizontal or diagonal, you must measure, cut and cajole each board into place individually, adjusting as you go.

Add to wood's normal idiosyncrasies the ravages wrought by years of exposure to the elements and you have barn boards, widely used for creating rustic-looking interiors. If you use barn boards, you can skip over decisions about color, grain, edge treatments and length. Barn boards come straight off the side of an old barn—their charm lies in their weathered appearance and in their irregularity, so you take what you can get.

Because barn boards are filled with nails, most mills refuse to machine-shape their edges to form joints. You put them up just as they are, trying out different arrangements to match the edges as well as possible. To make knotholes and gaps less conspicuous, cover the wall with black felt or black roofing paper before installing the boards.

Despite wood's many peculiarities, you can do an entire paneling job using a portable circular saw (*page 454*) with a hollow-ground blade to cut the boards (a table or radial-arm saw is faster), a block plane (*page 219*) to trim and smooth ends, and several measuring tools to keep you on course. You will need scribers, a level, a plumb bob, a steel square and a combination square. Plan to leave the boards in the room that is to be paneled for at least two days before you start installing them. Stack the boards in layers separated by 2-by-4s so they will become acclimated to the temperature and humidity of the room. This will reduce the wood's tendency to warp after the paneling has been installed.

While the boards acclimate, prepare the wall with furring. Horizontal strips, as shown on page 50, are adequate for vertical and diagonal patterns. Apply the furring strips using the techniques on pages 37-40, with one exception: Leave a 3/4-inch space all around the opening for a door or window. After all the boards are installed, when you are ready to put on the trim, add jamb extensions. The width of these extensions should equal the combined thickness of the furring strips and the new wall surface.

Choosing Patterns and Edges

A pattern for every purpose. Solid-wood paneling can be installed in one of several patterns. A vertical application is the most versatile—a traditional and formal look can be achieved with smooth, polished woods and elaborate trim, a contemporary look with rougher woods and a minimum of trim.

Dramatic diagonal and herringbone patterns are best in a modern setting. Boards on adjoining walls can be placed for a zigzag effect or to continue the same sloping line from one wall to the next. These patterns look best on walls with few doors or windows.

A horizontal application is the least common. In a high-ceilinged room it can be exciting, but in a room of average height the pattern seems to lower the ceiling to an uncomfortable level.

Most professionals prefer to install solid boards without using base, ceiling or corner moldings, because these can detract from the bold, simple lines of the pattern. The door and window trim should be of the same wood as the paneling—strips cut with mitered corners to form a simple frame around the opening.

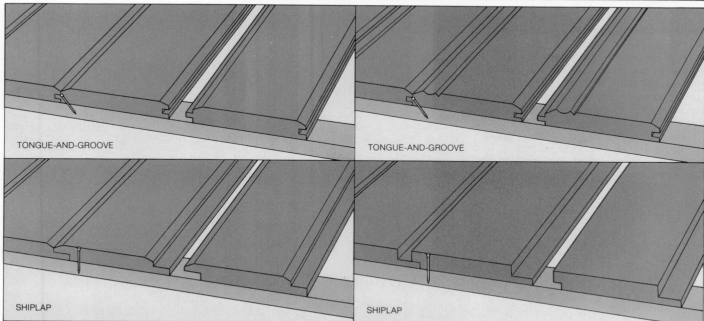

TONGUE-AND-GROOVE

TONGUE-AND-GROOVE

SHIPLAP

SHIPLAP

Milled edges for tight joints. Neat, gap-free joints that allow boards to expand and contract slightly with atmospheric changes are made possible by milled edges. Interlocking tongue-and-groove edges are the most common of these and are easy to install in any pattern. They can be milled so that the top edge of the joint is beveled, which creates a V-shaped seam between boards, or with rounded or even elaborately molded edges for a more decorative effect. Such boards are blind-nailed to furring strips through the base of the tongue; the nailheads are hidden by the next board.

Shiplap joints, where the edges of the boards do not interlock but do overlap each other, are easier to use in vertical or horizontal installation patterns than in diagonal ones. The boards typically come with their top edges beveled to form V-shaped seams, or with straight edges, which produce a slightly gapped joint. Shiplapped boards are generally nailed through the face of each board because nailing through the narrow edge tends to split the wood.

Straight edges for a modern look. Straight-edged boards and battens installed vertically or horizontally produce a casual, contemporary effect. Board-and-batten and reverse board-and-batten patterns are made of wide boards set about 1/2 inch apart with a narrower batten —generally a 1-by-2—nailed either over or under the gap. The contemporary-vertical pattern uses battens set on edge between the wider boards. Board-on-board paneling is similar to board-and-batten, except all the boards are the same width and the gap between boards in the first layer is about half the width of boards. With any of these patterns, when face-nailing is necessary, forestall splitting by placing nails as far as possible from the board edges.

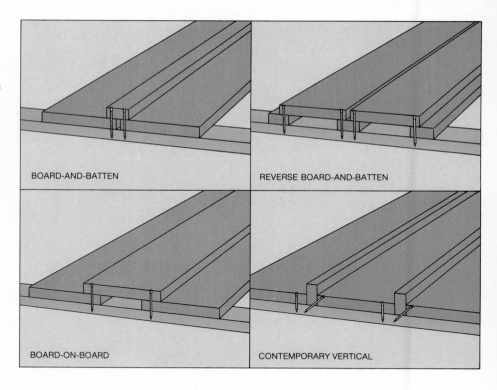

BOARD-AND-BATTEN

REVERSE BOARD-AND-BATTEN

BOARD-ON-BOARD

CONTEMPORARY VERTICAL

Installing the Classic Vertical Paneling

1 **Planning the layout.** To be sure that the last board on a wall will not be a narrow strip, first calculate how many whole boards will fit on the wall by measuring the length of the wall in inches and then dividing it by the width of a board (measured from its grooved edge to the base of the tongue). If the space for the last board is less than half a board width, determine how many inches are needed to widen it to half a board, then cut that amount from the grooved edge of the first board before you begin the installation.

2 **Starting off plumb.** Measure the starting corner from floor to ceiling and cut a board to that length, then set the board flat against the wall with its grooved edge butting the adjoining wall. Check for plumb by holding a carpenter's level against the tongue edge of the board. If the grooved edge does not fit flush with the corner when the board is plumb —and if the space will not be covered by a board on the adjacent wall—scribe the board to match the corner, using the technique on page 54, and trim the edge to the scribed line with a block plane.

If you install the first board at an outside corner, where the adjoining wall will not be paneled, trim 1/2 inch from the grooved edge of the board, then place that cut edge plumb and flush with the corner. Plane as necessary for a precise fit.

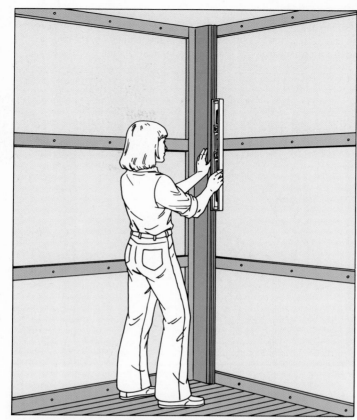

3 **Nailing the first board.** Drive a sixpenny finishing nail at a 45° angle through the base of the tongue and into each horizontal furring strip, sinking the head with a nail set. If the board is wider than 6 inches, also face-nail it to every furring strip, a third of the way across the board from the grooved edge in the corner *(inset)*. Sink the nail heads and cover with wood filler.

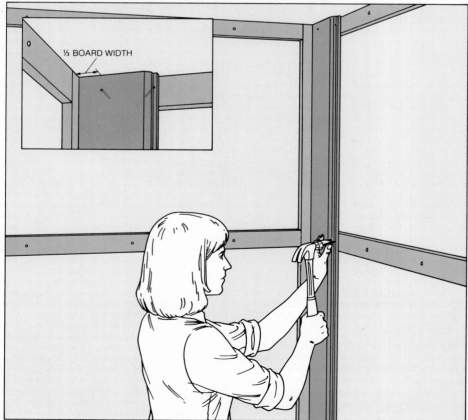

⅓ BOARD WIDTH

4 **Fitting individual boards.** To adjust each board to variations in ceiling height, cut a template—a board 3 inches shorter than the average ceiling height—and use it as a measuring device. Place the template where the next board will go, rest it on the floor, and measure from the top of the template to the ceiling. Then lay the template on the board to be cut, bottom ends flush, and transfer this measurement to it. Cut the board along this line, slide it into place on the wall, grooved edge over the tongue of the previous board, and nail it in place.

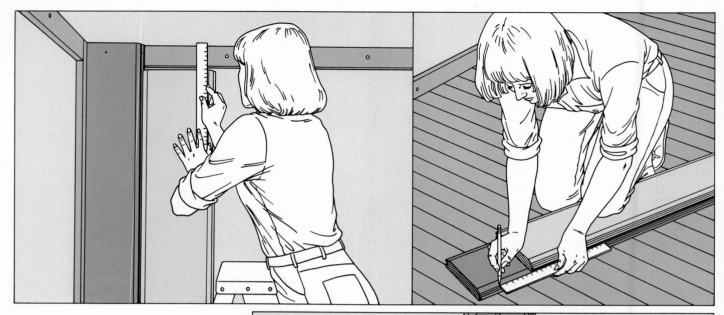

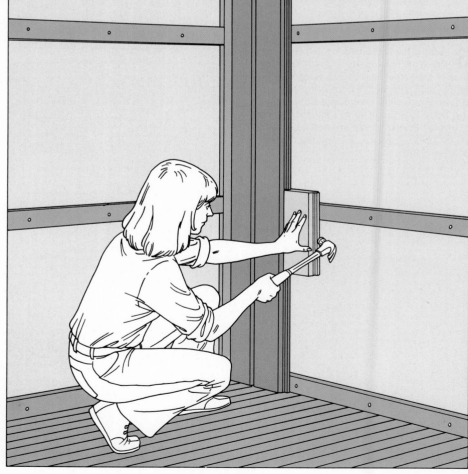

5 **Locking tongue-and-groove joints.** To tighten the joint between two boards that do not fit together snugly, cut a scrap of board about a foot long and use it as a hammering block. Slip its groove over the tongue of the outer board and gently tap the edge of the scrap until the joint is tight. Then move the scrap along the board, closing the entire joint. Check the board for plumb, readjusting the joint at top or bottom if necessary, and nail the board in place.

6 **Cutting to fit around an opening.** When you reach an opening, such as a window framed by furring strips *(page 37)*, lock the groove of a full-length board into position, with its tongue edge overlapping the opening. Reach behind the board and mark the back where it crosses the horizontal furring-strip edges closest to the opening. Mark the same furring strips where the tongue edge of the board crosses them. Then ease the board off the wall.

Measure the distance from the marks on the top and bottom furring strips to the edge of the vertical furring strip and transfer this measurement to the board at the top and bottom marks, drawing two lines that are perpendicular to the tongue edge. Connect the two lines with a third, parallel to the tongue edge. Drill 1/4-inch pilot holes just inside the two corners formed by the three lines, then cut out the notch with a saber saw; the pilot holes will allow the blade to turn easily at the corners.

Measure and cut short boards to fit above and below the opening. Then cut a board to fit the other side of the opening in the same way.

Making Neat, Tight Corners

Mitering for an outside corner. Where paneling continues around a corner, lock the final board on the first wall into place, tongue edge extending beyond the corner, and mark the corner line on the back of the board. Remove the board and clamp it face down on two sawhorses with a straight-edged 1-by-2 strip on top to guide the saw. Set the blade of a circular saw *(page 454)* at a 45° angle pointing toward the waste edge and make a beveled cut along the guideline. Lock and face-nail the board in place with the beveled edge extending beyond the corner *(inset)*.

To bevel the adjoining corner board, draw a guideline on the back of the board, marking the desired width of the board as determined in Step 1; measure this distance from the tongue edge. Then clamp the board face down and cut along the line, with the saw blade angled toward the grooved edge of the board. Before setting the board in place, spread wood glue on both beveled edges; then tape them together until the glue dries. Trim the corner with a block plane.

Snugging boards at an inside corner. After locking the next-to-last board in place, pull its tongue edge slightly away from the wall, slip on the grooved edge of the final board and push both boards against the wall at once. Face-nail the boards as in Step 3, page 51. To ensure a tight fit—especially important in a corner where no adjoining paneling will cover the edge of the final board—cut the final board exactly to size, scribing the cut edge *(below)*, if necessary, to conform to the corner. Then use a block plane to bevel the corner edge about 5° toward the back face of the board *(inset)*.

Contouring a Panel Edge to Fit an Irregular Shape

Scribing a panel. To fit a panel tightly against an irregular edge, such as a masonry fireplace wall, cut the panel off just wide enough to fit between the last-installed panel and the farthest point—such as a deeply scored masonry joint. Then place the newly cut edge of the panel against the greatest projection on the irregular edge—for example, a fireplace mantel. Keep the other panel edge plumb as it overlaps the last panel installed. Place one leg of a pair of scribers against the newly cut edge and rest the other leg against the point on the fireplace edge farthest from it. Tighten the scriber clamp to lock it in this position. Starting at the top corner of the greatest projection and holding the legs of the scribers horizontal, transfer the outline of the irregular edge onto the panel. Cut along the scribed line with a saber saw or coping saw, then fit the contoured panel between the edge and the last panel installed.

To fit a 4-foot-wide panel to an irregular edge back from the direction of panel installation—for example, the other side of a fireplace—first measure over 4 feet from the edge of the last panel installed going beyond the contoured edge. From a plumb line through this point, measure back to the most distant point on the unpaneled edge and use the same procedure to mark and cut a contoured panel for this surface.

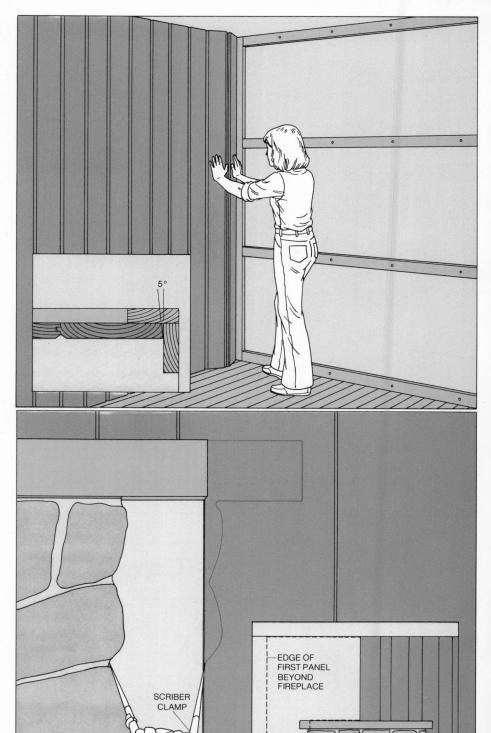

5°

SCRIBER CLAMP

EDGE OF FIRST PANEL BEYOND FIREPLACE

The Cabinetmaker's Art Displayed on a Wall

Few wood wall coverings can match the grace and joinery of Georgian paneling—the raised paneling perfected by 18th Century artisans. Made of wood rectangles whose beveled edges are clinched between vertical stiles and horizontal rails, this traditional wall covering is most often associated with posh clubs and law offices, but it can bring a classical elegance to any room.

With the proper tools, you can make authentic raised paneling of solid wood. Or, to save time and money, you can create a facsimile by adding stiles, rails and other embellishments to flat plywood panels. Softwoods were traditionally used for raised paneling; some, like clear white pine, can be stained and varnished for rich color and grain. Or you can finish the paneling with paint, as was common in colonial times.

There are choices, too, in the treatment of details. With solid-wood paneling, you can leave the edges of stiles and rails square or shape them with a router. With frame-on-plywood paneling, you can add a rectangle of molding several inches within the frame of stiles and rails, or add a raised panel of 1/8-inch hardboard with beveled edges. These bevels are naturally much narrower than those on solid-wood panels,

and the entire assembly must be painted, rather than stained.

With either type of paneling, the planning stage is crucial. Make a scale drawing of the existing wall, showing door and window openings, electric switches and outlets, and any other protruding fixtures. Then superimpose a sketch of the paneling on this drawing. A common pattern *(below)* uses four levels of rails: one near the floor, a second about 32 inches above the floor, a third just above the tops of doors and windows, and a fourth just below the ceiling.

The width of individual panels should not exceed 24 inches, except at doors and windows, where the frame should be wide enough to span the opening. Plan the frame layout so that each hole for an electric switch or outlet will fall on a flat surface, rather than on a joint or a section of molding; you may have to move electrical elements or have a licensed electrician do so. For frame-on-plywood paneling, position stiles to cover the joints between plywood panels.

The width of stiles, rails and moldings depends on the proportions of the wall, but it should fall within a general range—stiles, 4 to 6 inches; rails, 2 1/2 to 3 1/2 inches; base moldings, 3 1/2 to 5 inches; crown moldings, 3 inches;

door and window casings, 3 inches. Refine your sketch to include these dimensions, then transfer your pattern directly to the wall; if the proportions seem correct and the pieces are properly positioned, you are ready to begin building.

For frame-on-plywood paneling, which is assembled directly on the wall, use furniture-grade 1/4-inch plywood, and paint or stain it before installing it. Nail it to furring strips attached to the wall in the pattern used for regular plywood, but add horizontal furring strips at rail heights. Solid-wood paneling is fastened to the wall in completed sections.

To make frame-on-plywood paneling, you need no special tools, but for the special cuts and joints of raised paneling, you will need a doweling jig, router and table saw. For best results, use grooved dowels for secure glue bonding, and use carbide-tipped router bits that have ball-bearing guides, called pilots.

For table-saw work, you will need a dado head—a combination of blades that makes a wider cut than one blade alone—and special wooden guides on the saw table: one bolted to the rip fence, the other parallel to the rip fence on the opposite side of the blade. To speed production, finish each step for all the pieces before proceeding to the next step.

The Structure of a Wall of Raised Panels

Dissecting the parts. Stiles (vertical) and rails (horizontal), made of 3/4-inch boards, secure the panels. The interlocked stiles and rails have glued dowel joints and their edges are dadoed (grooved) to hold the beveled panel edges.

The bottom rail *(inset, bottom)* rests on blocking made of inexpensive 3/4-inch lumber slightly narrower than the base molding that covers it, and the whole structure is nailed to the furring strips behind the edges of every rail, and behind the top and bottom blocking. One third of the way up the wall, chair-rail molding covers a joint between frame sections. Crown molding trims the wall near the ceiling *(inset, top)*, and casings border the doors and windows. At floor level on both sides of the door are rectangular plinth blocks, which separate the curves of door casing from those of base molding.

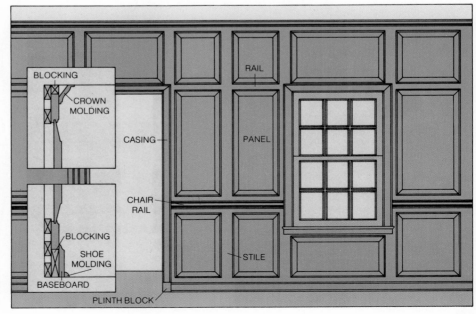

A Facsimile with Plywood

1 Laying out the frame. With a pencil and a long straight-edged board, mark positions for the edges of stiles and rails on the plywood-paneled wall, making sure that all joints between panels will be covered by stiles and that no stile or rail edge will cross an electric outlet or switch. Mark the position of the bottom edge of the bottom rail; it should be 1 inch lower than the height of the planned base molding. Finally, cut all of the stiles, making them 1/2 inch shorter than the overall wall height for ease in installation.

2 Attaching the stiles and rails. Line up a stile with one set of stile-edge marks, checking it with a level for plumb. Nail the stile in place with eightpenny finishing nails long enough to reach through stile and paneling to the horizontal furring strips; use two nails at each strip. Nail the other stiles in place, then measure and cut rails for a snug fit between stiles, using a miter box to ensure perfectly square rail ends. Line up the rails with the pencil marks and tap them into position with a mallet, placing a wood block between mallet and rail. Nail the rails in place.

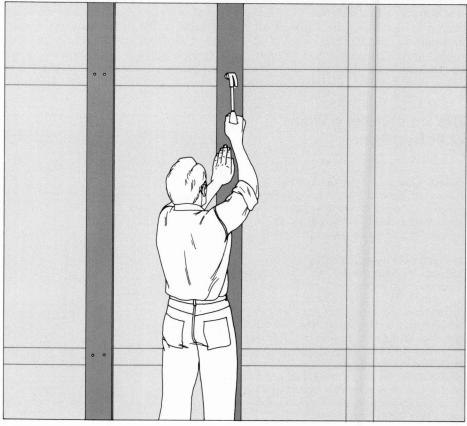

3 **Adding mitered molding.** Finish the edges of stiles and rails with mitered quarter-round *(page 87)* or patterned molding, installed so the mitered cuts slant inward and the overall length of the molding equals the distance along a stile or rail. Nail the molding in place with 1-inch brads, starting with a stile and working clockwise around to the remaining three sides of the rectangle. Repeat for each frame, then fill any cracks at miter joints with wood putty.

4 **Adding embellishments.** For a raised-panel effect in the rectangle *(above, left)*, cut a piece of 1/8-inch hardboard 2 inches shorter and narrower than the inside measure of the rectangle. Bevel its edges with a table saw *(page 454)*, then center it and attach it with glue and 3/4-inch brads. Repeat for the other rectangles.

Alternatively, add a molding rectangle of the same dimensions and location as the raised panel described above, right. Outline its position in pencil, then use the technique described in Step 3 to nail mitered molding along the outline. Repeat for the other rectangles. Countersink all nails and fill holes with wood putty.

Building a Frame for Solid-Wood Panels

1 **Laying out a frame.** Nail horizontal furring strips to the wall along the floor and the ceiling, at each rail level and at the midpoint between any rails more than 2 feet apart *(pages 39-40)*. Nail blocking over the strip at floor level *(page 55)* and mark the exact positions of stile edges on all the strips. Also, mark for the joint between top and bottom sections of the panels. The strips must be wider than the rails or doubled so that each rail edge is backed by furring.

Use the stile-edge marks to calculate the exact stile, rail and panel dimensions. Stiles for the bottom section of panels reach from the top of the blocking to the joint line; stiles for the top section reach from the joint line to 2 inches below the ceiling. Measure the distance between stile edges to determine rail lengths. If you plan to shape the edges of stiles and rails, allow for this decorative edge in calculating the length of the rail, which must meet the stile at the break line *(inset)* where the shaped edge begins.

Cut stiles and rails, lay them face down on the floor in the relative positions they will occupy on the wall, and mark rail and stile with matching numbers at each joint, to speed later assembly.

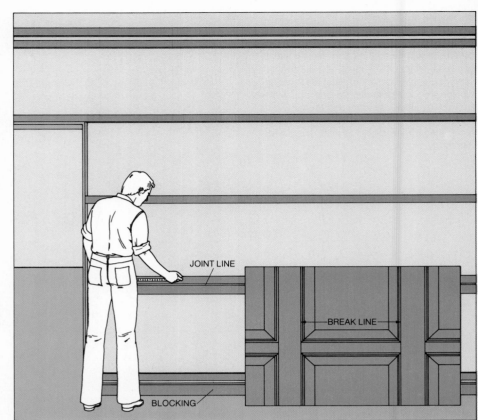

2 **Cutting grooves in rails and stiles.** Assemble a 1/4-inch dado head on the table saw and lock the rip fence 3/8 inch from the near edge of the dado head. Then clamp an auxiliary fence—a 2-by-4 nailed to a piece of plywood—to the saw table on the other side of the blade, separated from the rip fence by the thickness of the lumber used for stiles and rails. Set the dado head to cut 1/4 inch above the table. With the power on, feed rails and stiles—one edge down and the outside face against the rip fence—over the dado head.

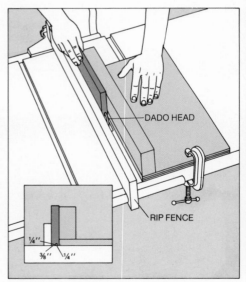

3 **Shaping stile and rail edges.** Clamp a stile, face up, on a worktable and put the desired edge-forming bit in a router. Rest the router base on the stile face with the bit an inch or so in from one end of the stile; turn on the router and push it toward the stile until the pilot comes into contact with the edge of the wood *(inset)*. Slowly move the router to the near end of the stile until the bit clears the corner, then move the router in the opposite direction, shaping the entire edge of the stile.

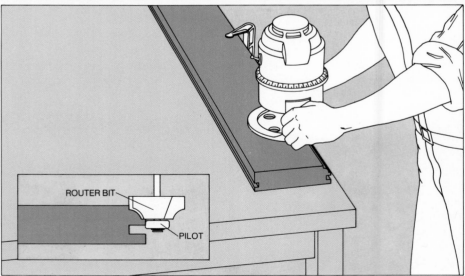

If the clamp blocks the router, switch off the motor, reposition the clamp, and then restart the shaping cut an inch away from the stopping point, bringing the pilot against the still-uncut edge of the stile.

Shape the opposite edge of the stile in the same way, then repeat the shaping process on all the remaining stiles and rails except along those edges that are going to be covered by chair-rail molding, door casing or base molding.

4 Preparing a shaped stile for joints. On the back of a stile that has a shaped edge, mark the points where the rail edges intersect the stile. Then use a combination square *(below, left)* to mark the converging lines of a 45° angle from these points. Use a tenon saw or other fine-tooth saw *(below, right)* to cut along the lines, down to the break line of the shaped edge. Keep the cutting edge of the saw horizontal. Repeat wherever a rail intersects a stile.

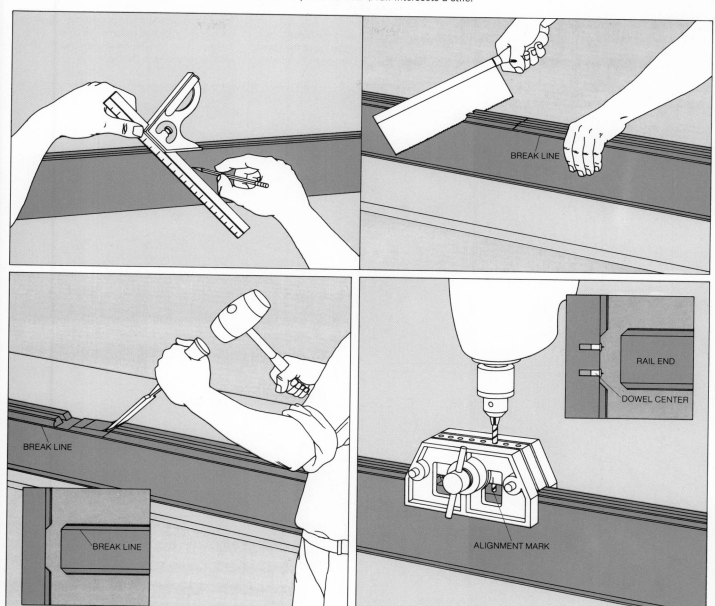

BREAK LINE

BREAK LINE

BREAK LINE

RAIL END

DOWEL CENTER

ALIGNMENT MARK

5 Chiseling out the joint. Using a wood chisel with the beveled edge facing down, remove the wood between saw cuts. Chisel off chips about 3/4 inch long and 1/16 inch thick until you have a flat surface at the level of the break line.

Use a miter box to cut a 45° angle across each corner of the matching rail. Position the rail for the cut by aligning the saw blade over the point where the break line intersects the rail end *(inset)*. Repeat for all other rails.

6 Drilling holes for dowels. Mark guidelines for the doweling jig by drawing lines across both ends of the cutout section of a stile, 1/2 inch in from the bottom of the bevel. Center the jig over each line and drill a 5/16-inch hole, 1 1/8 inches deep. Slide a 5/16-inch metal dowel center into each of the holes *(inset)*; align the matching rail and tap its free end to force the points of the dowel centers into the wood. Then remove the rail, align the jig over the dowel center marks, and drill holes in the rail to match those in the stile.

Cutting and Assembling the Raised Panels

1 Joining boards edge-to-edge. Select several 3/4-inch-thlck boards long enough to make one or two raised panel sections and with a combined width slightly greater than the planned width of one panel. Lay the boards edge-to-edge across pipe clamps positioned near the board ends and at 20-foot intervals. Place additional clamps across the top of the boards parallel to and midway between those on the bottom; then tighten all the clamps, increasing the pressure evenly until the seams between boards are nearly invisible hairlines.

If there are still gaps between the boards, remove the clamps and carefully recut the board edges on a table saw that has been fitted with a sharp carbide-tipped blade. Test the boards again in the clamps.

When no gaps show between board edges, loosen the clamps, spread a film of carpenter's glue on each board edge and reclamp the boards. After the glue is dry, remove the clamps, cut the panels to size, and sand the faces.

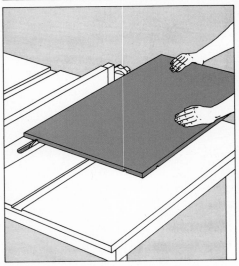

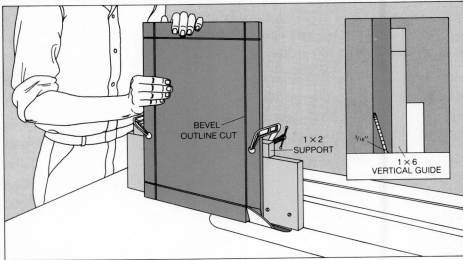

2 Outlining the bevel. Set the cutting height of a table-saw blade at 1/16 inch and position the rip fence 2 inches from the blade (*page 454*). Hold a panel face down, one edge against the rip fence, and make a 1/16-inch-deep cut down the length of the panel face. Make the same cut 2 inches in from the other three edges of the panel. Outline the bevels for all panels in this way, and make similar cuts on several pieces of scrap the same thickness as the panels, to use in setting the saw blade for the bevel cut.

3 Cutting the bevel. To set up the saw, tilt the blade away from the rip fence at a 15° angle, and fasten a 1-by-5 board to the rip fence as a vertical guide, anchoring the guide to the fence with countersunk flat-head stove bolts. Then position the guide so that its face is 3/16 inch away from the saw blade at table level, and adjust the cutting height of the blade so that the highest part of the blade reaches exactly to the bevel outline you have drawn on one of the pieces of scrap lumber *(inset)*.

Slide a panel into the space between the blade and the vertical guide, with the back of the panel against the guide and the end grain down. To steady the panel, rest a length of 1-by-2 on top of the guide and clamp the panel and the 1-by-2 together. Turn on the saw and, keeping your hands well above the table, push the panel over the blade. Repeat this procedure on the opposite end of the panel, and then on the two sides, repositioning and reclamping the 1-by-2 support before each cut.

Assembling the Pieces and Erecting the Wall

1 Joining the parts. Place the panels, rails and stiles of the lower paneling section face down on the floor, with the adjoining edges facing each other and the bottom edge toward the wall. Using a wooden mallet, first tap 2-inch-long dowels into all of the rail holes, then tap panels into the rail grooves; finally, tap stiles onto the dowels protruding from the rails. If the joints fit tightly, as they should, disassemble the parts, spread a thin film of glue inside the dowel holes and on all of the facing edges of the joints—but not in the grooves. Reassemble the parts, using pipe clamps stretched from stile to stile to close the joints. Drive 1/2-inch brads through the backs of rails and stiles into both ends of all dowels. Then remove the clamps and assemble the remaining sections in the same way.

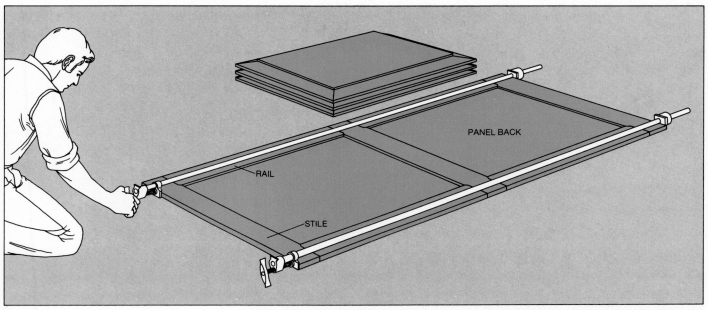

PANEL BACK

RAIL

STILE

2 Raising the paneling. With helpers providing support at each stile, tilt the lower paneling section against the wall, then lift it and set the bottom rail on the blocking. Slide a carpenter's level along the top of the paneling while a helper wedges thin wooden shims between the blocking and the bottom rail to level the section. Fasten the stiles to the wall at each furring strip with pairs of eightpenny finishing nails.

Raise the upper paneling section into position on top of the lower one, aligning the stiles exactly, and nail the upper stiles to the furring strips. Nail blocking between the top rail and the ceiling. When all sections are in place, cover the joint between the upper and lower sections with chair rail, and add ceiling, corner and base moldings *(pages 87-90)*. Frame the door and window openings with casings that match the wood of the stiles and rails. Use a nail set to countersink all nails, and fill the holes with wood putty.

BLOCKING

Wainscoting: Hip-High Panels with Top Trim

Not all wall paneling rises from floor to ceiling—some stops short and is called wainscoting, a term that originally meant "the wooden sides of a wagon." Wainscot paneling can vary in height from 30 to 36 inches, but it generally looks best when it is no more than one third the height of the wall.

Wainscoting can be made of solid wood or plywood, and can be flat, or patterned with raised panels constructed the same way as the full-height variety described on the preceding pages. In construction wainscoting differs from floor-to-ceiling paneling only in the molding that covers the upper edge. One-piece cap molding serves as the top trim for thin wainscoting, but thicker panels, or ones nailed to furring strips, require wider and sometimes more elaborate assemblies of two or three different pieces of molding.

Ordinarily, top trim is mitered or square-cut, but in some situations you may want to use more sophisticated techniques. At inside corners that are not perfect right angles—or if you prefer fancier joinery—you can forgo simple mitering and use the more traditional coping cut (bottom, left). Similarly, if you plan to set the top molding at the same height as the window stool (the inside extension of the window sill), you will need to scribe and then cut the top molding in much the same fashion as that outlined on page 54.

Making a Wainscot of Plywood or Solid Wood

Wainscot and top trim. When 1/4-inch plywood paneling is used for wainscoting and is fastened directly to the wall, the easiest trim to apply is cap molding, already factory-cut to lap over the panel edge (below, left). But if paneling protrudes farther than the depth of the cap molding—which is generally 1/4 inch—you can use window-stool stock, rip-cut to the desired width and finished with base-cap molding above and cove molding beneath (below, right). At the floor, regular baseboard and shoe molding serve as trim for both types of wainscoting.

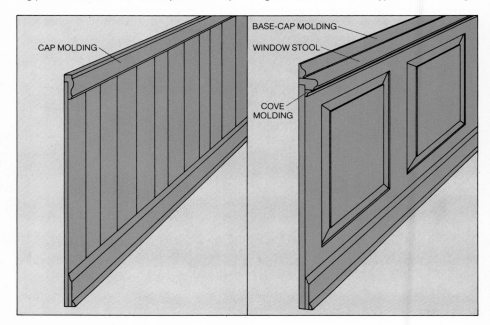

CAP MOLDING

BASE-CAP MOLDING
WINDOW STOOL
COVE MOLDING

A Coped Joint for a Cap Molding

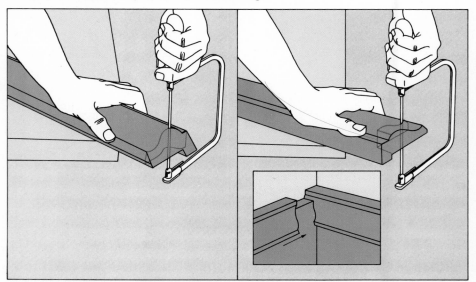

Shaping the ends of the molding. When two pieces of cap molding meet at an inside corner, miter the end of the first piece and outline its contoured edge in pencil, but continue the pencil line across the top of the molding, at right angles to the back edge. Using a coping saw, make a vertical cut through the molding along this line (left). Then notch the second piece of molding (right) deeply enough to allow its lip to slide over the adjoining wainscot (inset). Nail the second piece to the wall, then slide the first piece against it.

All work on walls and ceilings should be done from the floor, or from a sturdy stepladder or sound scaffold—both are available from a tool rental agency. Alternatively, a scaffold may be built from planks and sawhorses.

A wooden ladder is acceptable for most household projects, and preferable to a metal one for electrical work; however, metal is about 20 percent lighter than wood and needs less maintenance. Fiberglass ladders excel in all types of work, but cost more than aluminum or wood. Standard ladder heights are 4, 5, 6 and 8 feet and more; step stools are 2 or 3 feet tall. For wall and ceiling work, a 5-foot stepladder height is generally the most practical. The rule of thumb is to buy a stepladder 3 feet shorter than the highest point you need to reach.

A stepladder's "duty rating" determines how much weight it can support safely. While many ladders for home use are Type III—intended for light-duty household use supporting up to 200 pounds—for most around-the-house projects experts recommend a Type II,

medium-duty commercial-use ladder, which will support 225 pounds. A Type I heavy-duty industrial-grade stepladder will support 250 pounds.

Any stepladder you use should comply with American National Standards Institute (ANSI) standards and bear the ANSI sticker. Type II and better stepladders should also display the Occupational Safety and Health Administration (OSHA) seal. A stepladder used for electrical work should display the Underwriters Laboratories (UL) logo.

Only one person at a time should use a stepladder. When you climb, face the ladder and maintain three-point contact with it; keep at least both feet and one hand (or both hands and one foot) on the ladder at all times. Keep your body centered between the rails and avoid overreaching: Experts advise that your belt buckle should stay between the rails. Never stand or sit above the third step from the top of the ladder. Do not climb on the back of a stepladder or stand on the bucket shelf. Keep children safe: Never leave a set-up ladder unattended. Read and follow all instructions on the ladder label. Never paint a wooden stepladder; paint hides

potentially dangerous cracks. Instead, protect your ladder with a coat of clear varnish, shellac or wood preservative.

Low indoor platform scaffolds earn the same ratings as stepladders and should receive the same careful inspection before using them. Use only scaffold-grade planking that is not cracked, warped, damaged or otherwise unsafe. If you make your own low scaffold with sawhorses, as shown below, use 2-by-10 or 2-by-12 planks, doubled if necessary, for added strength. Planks should reach at least 6 inches and a maximum of 12 inches beyond the centers of supports—or else be cleated at both ends on the bottom to keep them from sliding. Keep the platform clear of electrical cords and other obstacles; if a spill occurs, clean it up right away.

When working on walls and ceilings, take care not to saw or drill into surfaces hiding pipes and electric cables. As a safety precaution, turn off water and electricity to the area before cutting into a surface. When necessary, use the appropriate personal safety gear (pages 76 and 130).

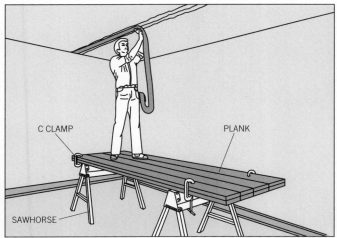

Erecting a scaffold. A scaffold can be built with scaffold-grade 2-by-10 or 2-by-12 planks supported by a pair of sawhorses *(above)* and a pair of Type II or better stepladders. (Do not use Type III stepladders for wall and ceiling work.) Subtract 2 feet from the length of the planks and set the sawhorses this distance apart. If the distance between the two sawhorses is more than 6 feet, double the planks for strength. Nail planks to wooden sawhorses; use C clamps to hold together doubled planks and to secure planks to metal sawhorses or to the steps of ladders.

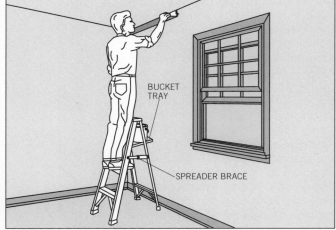

Setting up a stepladder. Inspect the stepladder for damage before using it; do not use it if a foot is worn, a step is loose or a spreader brace does not open fully or does not lock. Set up on a firm, level surface, well away from stairs and overhead obstructions *(above)*. Open the ladder legs completely and lock the spreader braces; if the feet slip, place a non-slip rubber mat under them. Pull down the pail tray and place any tools and materials on it before climbing the stepladder. When work is finished for the day, clean up any spills that could cause a slip the next time it is used. Store your ladder or scaffold in a cool, dry place.

Superinsulation: Thicker Walls to Hold in Heat

Greatly increasing the thickness of house insulation—a technique that is called superinsulating—is one of the best ways to slash heating bills. In some newly built superinsulated houses—with wall insulation values of R-40 and ceiling insulation values of R-60 and higher—the savings can be as much as 50 percent and more compared with the cost of heating a similar house with conventional insulation. Superinsulating an older house can yield comparable savings by stopping drafts and reinforcing inadequate insulation while improving comfort.

Many features found in new superinsulated houses—thermal blocks between structural parts to interrupt the flow of heat, for example, and special roof sheathing—are impractical for existing homes. But other superinsulating techniques are adaptable to existing houses. The primary technique is to bolster existing insulation with thick extra layers. It is simple, for instance, to lay extra fiberglass batting in an attic, adding an R value of about 3.33 per inch of thickness. It is also possible to superinsulate exterior walls.

Before extra insulation can be added, the exterior walls must be thickened to accommodate it. And thickening the walls involves major construction: A wall frame must be built, then covered over with an attractive surfacing material after the new insulation is installed. In almost every case this frame, which can be built of 2-by-4s or 2-by-3s, is best added to the inside of an existing wall. It can rest on the existing floor and can be covered with inexpensive wallboard (pages 80-86). Thickening walls on the outside requires a heavy ledger board bolted to the studs to support the new frame, plus expensive exterior siding. However, if your house is due for new siding anyway, superinsulating from the outside may prove feasible.

The major drawback to superinsulating a wall inside is that living space must be sacrificed. A new wall cavity providing room for 6 inches of new insulation will use up 5 square feet of space for every 10 feet of wall thickened; fully superinsulating a two-story, 20-by-40-foot house means the loss of 120 square feet.

Of course, space can be saved by superinsulating only some of the walls. The south wall—warmed by the sun for most of the day—needs superinsulation only in the harshest climates. Or limit your superinsulation to the north wall, or to the north wall and the west or east wall, whichever faces the direction of prevailing winds in your locale.

The major physical obstacles to superinsulating walls are windows, doors, electrical boxes and heating outlets. For windows and doors, use 2-by-2 furring strips to extend the jambs back into the rooms; the recesses inside the extended jambs can be covered with wallboard. Electrical cables connected to boxes, forced-air ducts and radiator pipes must be brought into the new room perimeter. The vapor barrier of a superinsulated wall also requires special consideration: It must be better than its counterpart in an ordinary wall. Because less air seeps through a superinsulated wall, less moisture is carried out of the wall cavity. Instead, any moisture that gets inside the wall can condense, matting and ruining the new insulation. The best defense is a continuous sheet of 6-mil polyethylene sheeting, spread over the new insulation. The sheeting will bolster the performance of the standard foil vapor barrier that comes with the new insulation.

If there is an existing vapor barrier, it must be perforated so that moisture can pass through it. Otherwise, even a tiny amount of moisture that penetrated the wall would be permanently trapped between two virtually impervious barriers.

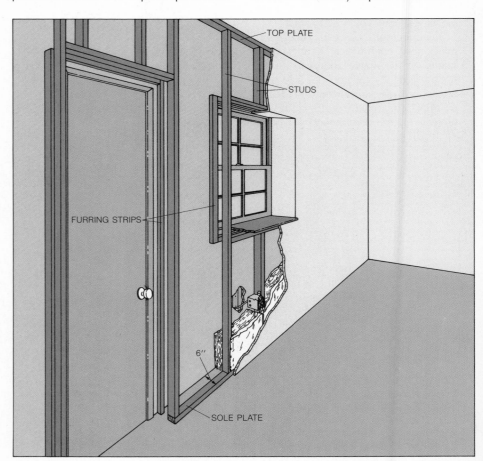

TOP PLATE

STUDS

FURRING STRIPS

6″

SOLE PLATE

A superinsulated wall. An inner frame, consisting of studs, a sole plate and a top plate, thickens an exterior wall from the inside to provide space for 6 extra inches of fiberglass insulation. Window and door recesses in the existing wall are extended inward by the frame and by furring strips, used for securing a new vapor barrier, wallboard and trim. An electrical outlet is relocated onto a stud of the new frame, its front flush with the surface of the new wallboard.

Moving Existing Utilities

Detouring a heating duct. To make room for the sole plate of the new wall frame, move any floor register that is within 6 inches of the existing wall. First lift off the register grille. Working from below, cut away a section of the ceiling under the register if necessary, and pull the elbow free from the end of the duct. Cut the duct short and replace the elbow to reroute the air flow to a new opening cut in the floor. Install the grille over the new opening.

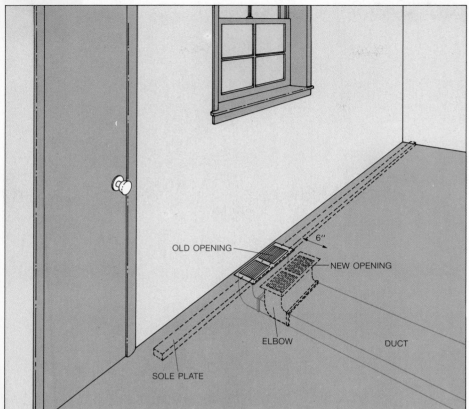

OLD OPENING

6"

NEW OPENING

ELBOW

DUCT

SOLE PLATE

Pulling an electrical box forward. If there is enough slack in cables connected to an electrical box, you can avoid having to rewire the wall by simply moving the box from the existing wall to the new inner wall. Turn off the electricity to the box at the house service panel *(page 11)*. Hammer a hole through the existing wall surface, and pry out any staples holding the cables near the box. Pull the cables and box loose from the existing wall frame without damaging them. After securing the new wall frame, remount the box, positioning it so that its front edge will be flush with the new wallboard. If the box has external mounting straps, this will be simple. If not, the box may need to be replaced with one that does *(Chapter 4, page 241)*.

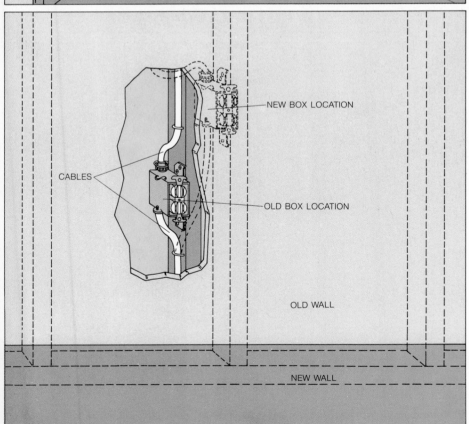

NEW BOX LOCATION

CABLES

OLD BOX LOCATION

OLD WALL

NEW WALL

Framing the Inner Wall

1 **Adding nailing blocks.** If ceiling joists run parallel to the exterior wall and the new wall frame cannot be located directly under a joist, install nailing blocks between joists to secure the top plate of the new frame. First use a pry bar to lever the baseboards and ceiling moldings off the exterior wall and adjacent walls. If the ceiling is covered with wallboard, use a utility knife to cut it away between the exterior wall and the center of the closest joist. If the ceiling is plaster, cut it away with a mason's chisel and a hammer. Cut nailing blocks from lumber the same size as the joists. Nail the blocks at 24-inch intervals between the joists, with the bottom edges flush. If the joists run perpendicular to the exterior wall, nailing blocks are not necessary. The top plate of the new wall can be nailed at the points where it crosses the joists.

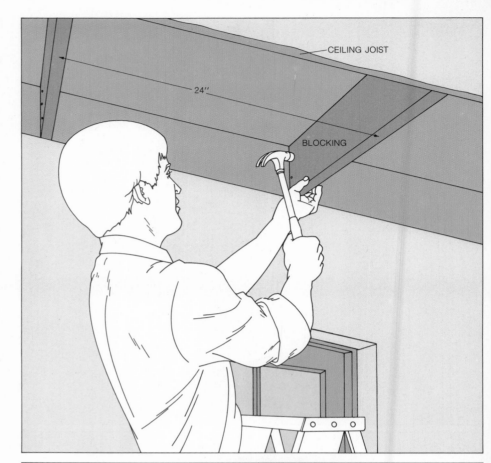

2 **Extending door and window jambs.** Nail 2-by-2 furring strips around the door and window openings to provide a nailing surface for wallboard that will be installed later. To install strips around an untrimmed opening, such as the window shown here, set the furring strips exactly 1/2 inch from the sides and top of the opening to accommodate the wallboard; at the bottom of a window, nail the furring strip flush with the window sill. For openings trimmed with casing, such as the doorway shown here, space the strips 1 inch or more from the outer edge of the trim.

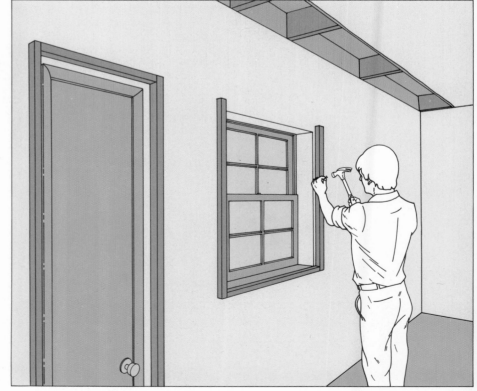

3 **Assembling the wall frame.** Cut two boards to serve as the new top and sole plates, the same length as the existing wall. On the face of one of the boards make marks at 16-inch intervals to indicate stud positions. With a helper, hold the marked board against the wall and mark it for additional studs at each of the vertical furring strips framing the doors and windows. Transfer the marks to the other board. Make two cuts in the sole plate to remove the section cor-responding to the doorway, and nail the remaining pieces to the floor.

Cut full-length studs to the height of the room minus 3 inches to allow for the combined thickness of the top and sole plates. Set the marked top plate on edge, and nail a full-length stud to it at each mark, skipping the marks above a door or window. To frame around a window (inset), cut two boards the width of the opening. Nail the two horizontally between the studs bounding the opening at the same height as the horizontal furring strips on the existing wall. Nail short studs, called cripple studs, above the header and below the sill at the marked 16-inch intervals.

To frame around a door, nail a horizontal header at the height of the furring strip above the door. Nail cripple studs above the header at the 16-inch marks on the top plate.

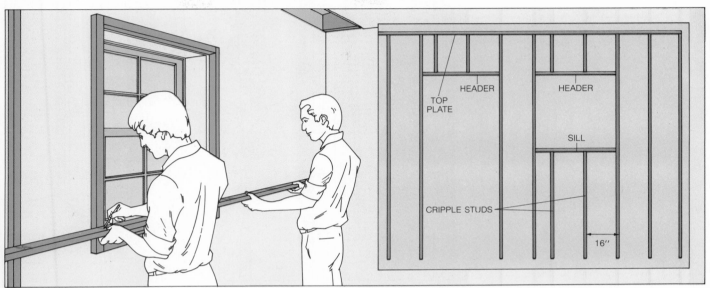

4 **Erecting the wall frame.** With a helper, lift the assembled top plate and studs onto the sole plate. Toenail the bottom ends of the studs to the sole plate. Plumb the frame, and nail the top plate to the ceiling joists or nailing blocks.

Fasten the end studs of the new wall frame to the adjacent walls with toggle bolts if the adjacent walls are hollow where the frame meets them; then nail it in place if the frame falls at stud locations.

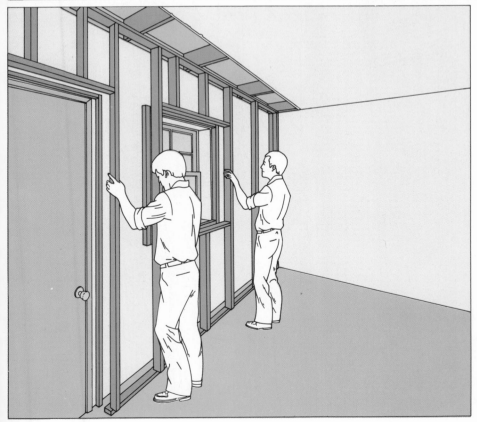

Installing the New Insulation

1 Perforating the old vapor barrier. Using a power drill fitted with a 1/4-inch twist bit, bore holes through the old wall surface to relieve vapor pressure at 1-foot intervals vertically and horizontally. Push the drill bit at least 2 inches into the wall to ensure that it pierces the vapor barrier of the existing insulation.

2 Stapling on new insulation. Wearing gloves, a long-sleeved shirt and a dust mask, fit fiberglass insulation between the studs of the new wall frame, keeping the foil vapor barrier of the material toward you. Staple the flanges of the foil facing to the studs every 6 inches with a staple gun. If necessary, cut the insulation to fit with a long pair of scissors or with a butcher knife; odd-sized pieces and scraps can be butted together to fill all of the spaces around doors and windows. Do not pack any of the insulation tight; compressing the fibers will greatly decrease the effectiveness of the material.

3 **Adding the second vapor barrier.** Fasten a single piece of 6-mil polyethylene over the new insulation, stapling every 6 inches along the studs. At every window and door, slash the plastic from corner to corner in an X pattern *(below,* *left)*; fold the four triangles into the opening, and staple the plastic to the furring *(below, right)*.

Cover the stud wall and the recesses of the window and door openings with wallboard *(pages 80-86)*.

Finishing the Wall

Trimming the window. At the bottom of the window recess, use a piece of stair-tread lumber to create a finish sill. Cut the tread as long as the window recess is wide and 3/8 inch wider than the depth of the recess from the window sash to the new face of the wall. Place the back edge of the tread 1/16 inch from the window sash, and nail through the top of the tread into the framing and furring strip below. Cover the seams between wallboard panels here and elsewhere in the room with joint compound and tape *(pages 80-86)*.

Removing Walls

Taking down a partition, even one structurally essential to the house, is a job well within the capability of most homeowners. Before you start, make sure you understand all of the wall's functions, and know how well they can be served when it is gone. Check to be certain that the space the wall divides will not seem ill-proportioned without it. Note that besides serving as a partition a wall may carry plumbing or gas pipes, electrical cables or heat ducts. Keep in mind that although removing a wall may join two spaces together it does not actually add any more space than the few square feet on which the wall stands.

To size up the job, first look the wall over. An outlet or switch indicates wiring behind the wall. (But no outlet or switch does not necessarily mean there is no wiring.) A bathroom directly above may be hooked to plumbing that goes down through the wall. From the basement you may be able to detect whether heating pipes or conductors rise within the wall.

If all you find is wiring that terminates at outlets in the wall, you can remove it when you break the wall. A hot-air duct connected to a wall register can be cut back to the floor and capped with a grid. Even if you encounter many pipes and cables, you may be able to remove the bulk of the partition and leave part of one end of the wall to carry the various conductors, which can be moved there by a plumber or an electrician.

More critically, you should be aware that the wall may bear weight from above, thus serving as a vital structural element of the house. If it does, you will have to limit the width of the opening to 14 feet, because a bigger span entails too many risks and difficulties. To replace the weight-carrying function of the wall, you will have to install a visible overhead beam, as well as end posts for this beam that may also be visible, so that instead of removing the wall without a trace you build a bridge. These intrusions can be minimized by surfacing the structural members with wallboard to match the walls, or by positioning furniture, such as bookcases, to hide the posts.

A key clue to a bearing wall is joists crossing its top plates perpendicular to them *(diagram, below)*. You may be able to see the direction of the joists from your attic; you may have to cut a peephole in the ceiling next to the wall to be removed. The basement can also yield clues. If you find a girder or a wall running under and parallel to the partition in question, you can be quite sure that the partition carries weight down to this support. If any doubt remains, assume that the wall bears weight.

As the converse of a bearing wall, a nonbearing wall usually runs parallel to the joists and perpendicular to the long walls of the house. Walls enclosing small spaces like closets are probably nonbearing walls—but be sure to check. Because nonbearing walls serve no structural function, they can be removed without leaving a bridge.

Tearing off the surfaces of the wall you are removing is not difficult, but prepare for dirty work, especially if the material is plaster. When the wall is gone, you will confront breaks in the ceiling, walls and floor. Ceilings and walls are easy to patch. The break in the floor of newly joined rooms can be built up with any wood as thick as the flooring, and the whole room carpeted or tiled. If the floors are of valuable hardwood and will remain exposed, you may need professional help to patch and refinish them.

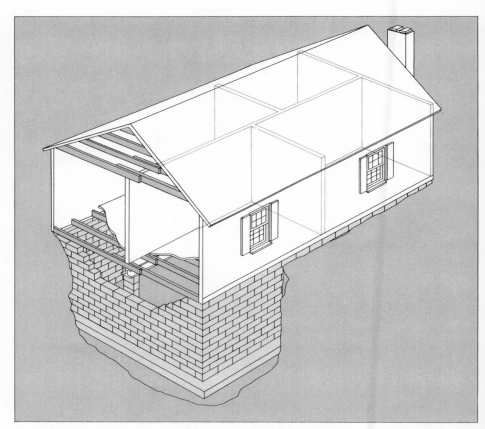

Bearing and nonbearing walls. This simplified diagram of a frame house shows how the cumulative weight of a house is passed down to its underground footings. Apart from the roof, which is supported by the outer walls parallel to the ridgepole, the weight load consists of the house structure itself plus whatever is on the floors, such as furniture, appliances, bathtubs or people. The joists under the floor are beams that transfer this load to the tops of the walls at both ends. The side walls that hold up one end of the joists carry the weight to the foundations, which take the burden to the footings. (End walls usually do not carry much weight.) Since a single wood joist is neither long enough nor strong enough to span the usual distance from one side wall to another, house framers provide two joists and rest their inside ends on an interior bearing wall, such as the one that runs the length of the house shown above. The interior bearing wall carries the weight down to a solid support, sometimes a bearing wall that rests on its own footings, often to a steel girder whose ends rest on the foundation.

Taking Out a Nonbearing Wall

1 **Stripping the wall.** After you have determined that you can remove the partition without encountering any insuperable difficulties *(page 70)*, tear off the trim and turn off all electrical circuits to the outlets, fixtures and switches. Tape down dropcloths, wear a dust mask and goggles, close doors and open windows. The wall surfaces can be cut out with a keyhole saw. A job of this size will go faster, however, using a circular saw set to the thickness of the wall surface. Caution: Use a circular saw only after making sure that there are no pipes or cables behind the wall. Cut chunks of wall from between the studs, using a metal cutting blade if the wall is plaster on metal lath. Saw the studs in two near the middle, and work the halves free from their nailing, as shown. Or, if you can reuse the studs and prefer to remove them whole, drive them from their nails at the bottom with a baby sledge then pull them away from their upper nails.

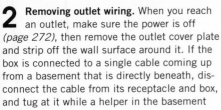

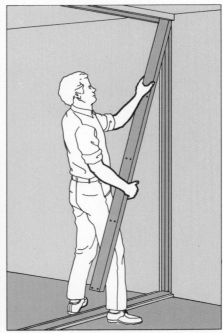

2 **Removing outlet wiring.** When you reach an outlet, make sure the power is off *(page 272)*, then remove the outlet cover plate and strip off the wall surface around it. If the box is connected to a single cable coming up from a basement that is directly beneath, disconnect the cable from its receptacle and box, and tug at it while a helper in the basement watches to identify it by its movement. Trace the cable back to a junction box, disconnect it and pull it free from below. If you cannot trace a cable's origins, or if the outlet is tied into the middle of the run of a cable, or if unrelated cables pass through the wall, you may need to call for professional help to reroute the wiring.

3 **Removing the last stud.** At the end of the partition, the last stud is nailed to a pair of close-set studs in the adjoining wall. In prying it loose, begin at the bottom and use a wide wood scrap held against the wall as a fulcrum for the pry bar so that the bar will not break through the covering of the adjoining wall. When the stud is safely away from the wall, wrench it free. The top plate is usually nailed upward to blocks between adjacent joists. Pry it down, beginning at the nailhead nearest one end, using a wood scrap as a prying surface.

71

4 **Removing the sole plate.** Somewhere near the center of the sole plate, make two saw cuts about 2 inches apart. Chisel out the wood between the cuts down to the subfloor. Insert a crowbar and pry up one end of the plate. With a scrap of 2-by-4 as a fulcrum, pry up the other end.

Repair the gaps made in the adjoining walls and the ceiling. If you are planning to cover the floor with resilient tiles or carpeting, fill in the space where the sole plate rested with a board thick enough to make the surface even.

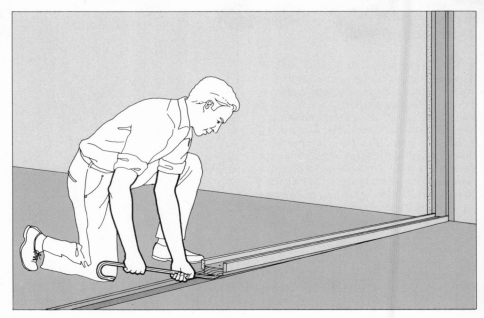

How to Leave a Section in Place

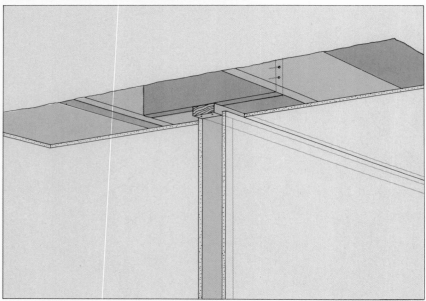

1 **Securing the top plate.** Remove the surface and studs *(page 71, Steps 1-3)*—but not the plates—of the wall back to the stud nearest the end of the part that you wish to preserve. Cut a hole about 1 foot wide in the ceiling, centered on the upper end of the stud and running to the second joist on either side. Saw the upper plate off 1 1/2 inches out from the stud, and pry down the part of it remaining over the opening. Butt-nail a block as wide as the joists between the joists on each side of the plate, resting the edge of the block on the outer end of the plate. Nail through the plate up into the block.

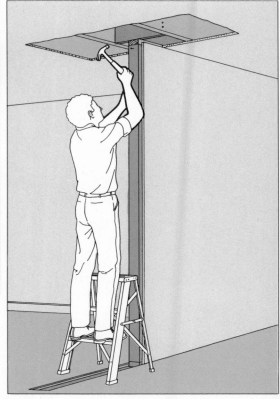

2 **Reinforcing the stud.** Saw the sole plate down to the floor level 1 1/2 inches out from the stud and chisel through the rest of it. Remove it as in Step 4, above. Nail a reinforcing stud, running from plate to plate, against the existing stud. Surface the reinforcing stud with wallboard and finish it with corner beads and tape.

Taking Out a Bearing Wall

The beam that will carry the weight hitherto supported by the wall is the main consideration when you plan to remove a bearing wall. For spans of up to 8 feet, make a doubled wood header, choosing boards as directed in the table below. For greater spans use American standard 8-by-17 steel girders (i.e., 8 inches high and weighing 17 pounds per foot). Commonly called I beams, they are 5 1/4 inches wide and are sold by steel-supply dealers to the length ordered. (Have plenty of help on hand, and wear safety helmets when raising it into place.) Four-by-four posts are used to support the header beam.

Do not remove a bearing wall if the load above it is uncommonly heavy—a concrete-floored bathroom or a bedroom containing a water bed or attic storage, for example. Even for ordinary weights, the posts that carry the load downward from the beam must rest on solid structure. For spans of up to 8 feet—a job most homeowners can confidently tackle—the posts can be positioned above joists in the floor, which carry the weight to the beam or other weight-bearing structure originally provided to support the wall.

In going beyond 8 feet with girders, the problems of post support become more critical, often demanding special blocking beneath the floor to bear the load downward. By concentrating weight once carried by the wall on two posts, you alter the structural design of the house; you may have to consult an engineer, to determine whether all the supporting members below the post will be strong enough. Amateurs should not attempt to bridge openings wider than 14 feet.

Wood headers that run to a side wall can rest on support posts within the wall, leaving an unbroken surface when the job is done. Allow 3 1/2 inches of extra length on the end of a header that goes into a wall. The joists above a bearing wall need the support of temporary walls on both sides while the job is under way. If the temporary walls will block access to your working area, place the new header or girder next to the partition that must come down before you build the temporary walls.

1 **Building a wood header.** Cut a piece of 1/2-inch plywood the same size as the header pieces; sandwich it between them. Secure the sandwich: Drive 16-penny nails through the boards from one side. If the header will be fitted into an adjoining wall, cut a notch out of its upper corner (3 inches deep, 3 1/2 inches long) to fit around the top plate in the adjoining wall.

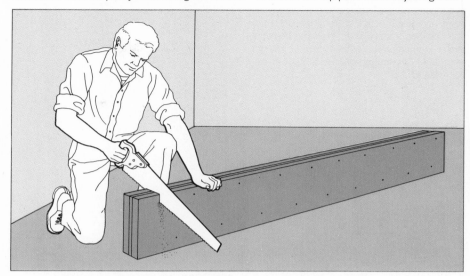

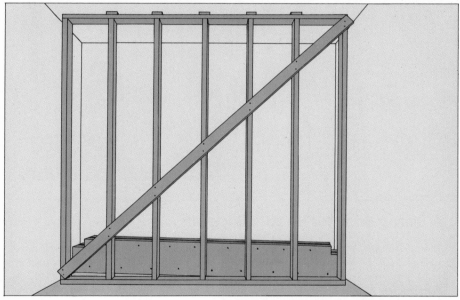

2 **Installing temporary support walls.** Put up stud walls about 30 inches out from the partition on both sides. In toenailing the studs, use double-headed nails to make later removal easy. Brace the wall with a diagonal 1-by-4 nailed to every stud. The temporary wall should run the width of the span, but need not abut a side wall closer than 2 inches. Find the positions of the joists above *(page 46)*, and shim tightly between them and the top plate, using pairs of shingles as wedges. Caution: Make sure that the support walls are vertical and firmly secured by their tight fit.

Remove the existing wall surface and studs in the manner shown on page 71, Steps 1-3.

Header Dimensions

Maximum span	Board size
3'6"	Two 2 x 6
5'	Two 2 x 8
6'6"	Two 2 x 10
8'	Two 2 x 12

3 **Prying out the plates.** The doubled top plates of a bearing wall are interlocked with those in the adjoining wall. To remove them, cut out a 2-inch chunk with a saber saw and begin prying a length of the doubled plate down far enough to use it as a lever. Get a firm hand hold on it and work it free from its nailing in the adjoining wall. Similarly remove the other section. Cut and remove the sole plate *(page 72, Step 4)*.

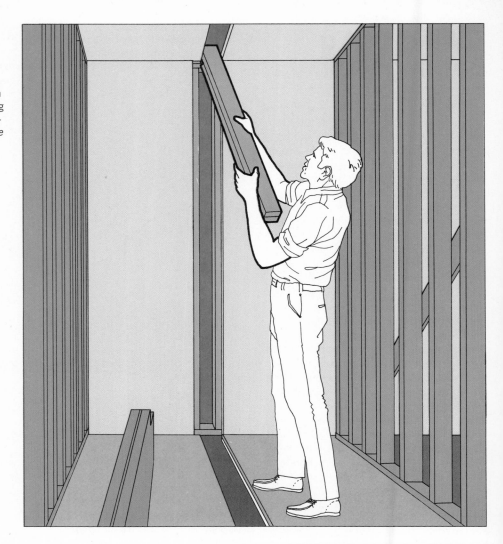

A Strong Base for Header Supports

The great weight that is held up by header supports must be transmitted directly downward through structural components to the foundation of the house. Usually header supports are placed on the sole plate of an adjoining nonbearing wall that runs perpendicular to the wall being removed. The plate transmits the weight to a joist directly beneath it, which in turn carries it to the top of a girder or bearing wall underneath *(top right)*; the girder or bearing wall is supported by the house's foundation. But sometimes carpenters place the sole plate of a wall adjoining a bearing wall not above but between joists *(bottom right)*. In this case the plate and post need special blocking under them to carry the weight directly downward to the girder or bearing wall below. If

you find there is no girder or wall directly below, consult an architect or contractor regarding proper placement of the posts.

To determine whether or not blocking is needed, drive a long nail through the subfloor next to the side-wall plate, find where it protrudes beneath, and then determine whether the plate rests above a joist. If not, cut two pieces of board the width and thickness of the joists and long enough to fit tightly between the joists. Nail the pieces together with six tenpenny nails and butt-nail them to the joists with two 16-penny nails for each board at each end, eight nails in all. This blocking should fit snugly between the bottom of the subfloor and the top of the girder or wall below; any gaps above or below the blocking should be shimmed.

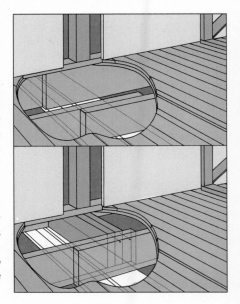

4 **Installing the header.** After the partition has been removed, the breaks in the side walls will reveal pairs of close-set studs placed to provide nailing for wall surfacing *(page 71, Step 3)*. Cut the wall back to the nearest studs on either side of these nailing studs, and pry the nailing studs free. Place the header, notched edge up, on the sole plates of the side walls for each end. Cut a 4-by-4 post precisely as long as the distance from the top of the resting header to the joist above it that runs nearest the wall. Check the posts to be sure they fit snugly, with no gap or surplus.

5 **Raising the header.** With helpers, raise the header to the joists. Check whether it fits flush against the bottoms of all joists; if the center ones are low, put the header down and raise the sagging joists by tightening some of the shims on top of the temporary walls. With the header in position, jam one 4-by-4 under each end. Use a level in order to get the post truly vertical. Toenail the post to the sole plate and the header using three tenpenny nails. Nail a piece of 1-by-4 about 1 foot long to join the side of the header to the top of the 4-by-4 and to provide a nailing surface for the wallboard.

Now you can remove the temporary walls. Patch the wall, then surface the header with wallboard *(pages 80-86)*.

Butting a Header to a Wall

1 **Positioning support studs.** Dismantle the wall surface and studs back to the stud nearest the desired end of the wing wall. Cut the doubled top plate flush with the stud and remove it *(page 74, Step 3)*. Cut the sole plate 3 1/2 inches out from the stud and remove the remainder *(page 72, Step 4)*. Use the procedure described in the box on page 74 to ascertain whether the existing stud stands over a joist, and install blocking if it is needed. Make a header to fit the opening.

2 **Raising the header.** Rest the header end on the protruding sole plate and cut two 4-by-4s exactly long enough to reach from the top of the header to the joist above nearest the stud. Raise the header and force one post between it and the sole plate. Drill through the post and stud and use three 3/8-by-4 1/2-inch lag bolts and washers to secure the post; make sure to countersink their heads. Similarly, secure the second post. Cover the posts and header with wallboard *(pages 80-86)*.

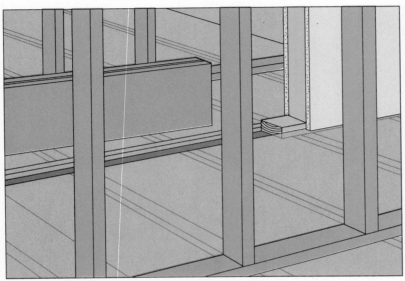

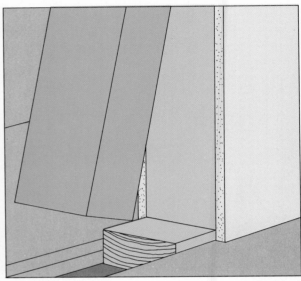

Using Personal Safety Gear

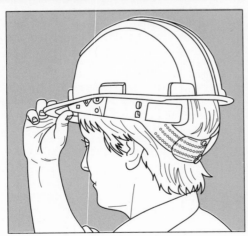

Reusable dust mask. Replaceable cotton fiber or gauze filters permit repeated use protection against nuisance dust and mist. Choose a model of neoprene rubber or soft plastic with an adjustable headstrap.

Disposable dust mask. For single-use protection against nuisance dust and mist. Choose a model with sturdy headstraps, a foam seal inside the top and a metal nose clip on the outside that conforms to the shape of your nose.

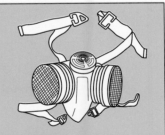

Dual-cartridge respirator. For protection against toxic dust, mist and vapor. Fitted with interchangeable filters or cartridges for protection against specific hazards. Contaminated air purified as inhaled through filters or cartridges, then expelled through exhalation valve.

Using head protection. To prevent impact injury to your head when tearing down old walls or working in tight spaces with little headroom, wear a safety helmet. Choose one with the correct American National Standards Institute (ANSI) or Canadian Standards Association (CSA) rating for the job: a type rated A or B if there is any electrical hazard. Adjust the suspension harness for a snug fit.

Using respiratory protection. For dusty work when a dust mask is not used or for work using chemicals that emit hazardous vapors, ensure that the work area is provided with a constant supply of fresh air; also clean up periodically during the job. Choose the best respiratory-protection device; ensure that it is approved by the National Institute of Occupational Safety and Health (NIOSH) and the Mine Safety and Health Administration (MSHA). A disposable dust mask is adequate for single-use protection only. For repeated use, choose a reusable dust mask or respirator, fitted with the appropriate filter or cartridges. Consult the accompanying instructions for proper use and care of the equipment.

Structural Changes to Create New Spaces

Few houses have a spare room that can be used for a specialized activity or hobby. More often than not, making space for a special purpose—without enlarging the house—means dividing up an existing room. In a couple of weekends, you can frame and cover a partition wall, hang a door and install its latch.

Before you carve up a room, however, determine how the new barrier will affect the present use of the space. If the new wall will block a window, the room will be darker. And if you block a thoroughfare, traffic may not flow smoothly.

Much of the new wall's construction takes place on the floor. Here wall studs are nailed to the top plate and the rough frame for a doorway is built.

The simplest wall, without a door, requires little more than accurate measuring, marking and sawing. Such a wall can extend out from an existing wall, or it can be fastened flat against a masonry wall to provide a nailing surface for wallboard or other finishing material.

A wall containing a rough frame for a door requires more measuring steps. Buy a prehung door before you begin the wall, and follow the manufacturer's instructions concerning the clearances to allow within the rough frame for the door and its jamb (the finished frame). To attach a wall to wood framing, find studs and joists hidden behind the wallboard (page 46).

In a masonry basement, the new wall is attached in a different manner. Use an electric drill with a 1/2-inch masonry boring bit to drill the concrete or block for 5/16-inch lead shield anchors. Then attach the new wall using three 5/16-inch lag bolts in each stud.

After the studs are in place and you have added any necessary plumbing or electrical runs, cover the framing with 1/2-inch gypsum wallboard. Wallboard comes in 8-, 10- and 12-foot lengths and 4-foot widths; it can be installed horizontally or vertically, whichever requires fewer cuts. If you have measured the framing carefully, the parallel edges of a standard sheet will fall at the centers of two studs, where they must be fastened. But you almost always have to trim a sheet at the end of a wall or where you must patch a hole cut for nailing blocks (page 78). To trim wallboard, score the paper covering with a utility knife, snap the core along the score, and cut through the paper on the other side. Holes can be cut with a wallboard or keyhole saw. Cut pieces large enough so that the parallel edges will lie at stud or joist centers for nailing.

To fasten the sheets to wood framing, use wallboard adhesive and wallboard nails. To cover nailheads and seams, use joint compound and two joint knives, 6 and 10 inches wide. You will also need perforated joint tape and, for outside corners, strips of metal corner bead. See pages 80-86 for wallboard techniques.

Each coat of joint compound takes about 24 hours to dry, then the third and final coat must be sanded smooth. Always wear a dust mask and goggles for this dusty job.

Techniques for Erecting a Stud-Wall Partition

1 **Marking the top and sole plates.** Cut a pair of 2-by-4s to the length of the planned wall and place them flat on the floor, side by side, with their ends aligned. These will be the top plate and the sole plate of the partition. Using a steel square, pencil pairs of parallel lines 1 1/2 inches apart (the same width as the shorter arm of a steel square—and the width of a 2-by-4) across both plates simultaneously, to indicate stud positions. Pencil an X in each of these rectangles to mark its center. Mark the first stud position flush with one end of the plates; place a mark for the center of the second stud 16 inches in from the end of the plates, and continue marking at 16-inch intervals. Mark the last stud position flush with the opposite end of the plates, no matter how close it is to the next-to-last stud.

Since the partition will be bearing no weight but its own, your building code may permit the economy of spacing studs at 24-inch intervals, center to center. Either 16- or 24-inch spacing will permit the use of standard 4-by-8-foot sheets of wallboard with a minimum of cutting.

16"

2 **Marking the position of the wall.** For a wall that will run perpendicular to overhead joists, snap a chalk line across the bottoms of exposed joists or across the finished ceiling, to indicate an edge (inner or outer) of the top plate. Then drop a plumb line from several points along the line so that a helper can mark where the plumb bob touches the floor. Then snap a chalk line connecting the floor marks, to establish a matching position for the sole plate.

If the new wall will parallel the joists, try to position it directly under a joist so that the top plate can be nailed to it. If this cannot be done, cut away any ceiling covering between the joists on either side of the plate so that you can toenail blocks at 16-inch intervals between the joists to support the the top plate *(inset, near right)*. Snap a chalk line across these nailing blocks to establish a position for the top plate. If the new wall will meet an existing stud wall at a point between studs, cut two holes in the old wall and toenail 2-by-4 nailing blocks at one third and two thirds of the distance from floor to ceiling *(inset, far right)*. To patch holes you have cut in the wall or ceiling, nail pieces of wallboard to the exposed studs or joists and to the nailing blocks after the new wall has been erected but before it is covered with wallboard.

To find the length of the new studs, measure the distance between the floor and ceiling chalk lines at three or more points along the wall. If these measurements vary by less than 3/4 inch, subtract 3 inches from the shortest measurement (to allow for the combined thickness of the plates); cut all the studs to this length. But if the variation in measurements exceeds 3/4 inch, measure and cut each individual stud after the sole plate has been installed *(Step 3)*. For a basement concrete floor, prevent rot by using a pressure-treated 2-by-4 sole plate, treated to 0.40 Ground-Contact retention rating.

3 **Assembling the top plate and studs.** With the top plate on edge on the floor, hold each stud end against its marked position and drive two 16-penny nails through the top of the plate into the end of the stud.

At the point where the new wall will meet the old, drop a plumb line from the ceiling corner to the floor. If the plumb bob hangs slightly away from the wall, mark its position on the chalk line on the floor to indicate where the end of the sole plate should fall.

Lay the sole plate flat, its end butted against the existing wall or even with the plumb mark if there is one, its edge even with the chalk line. Drive 12-penny nails at 1-foot intervals through the plate and into the floor; for a concrete floor, use either masonry nails or hardened cut nails.

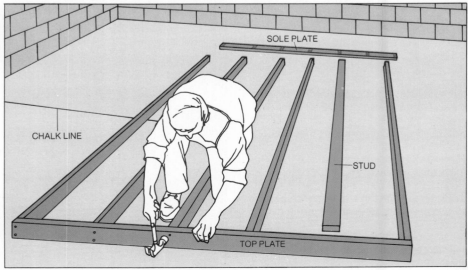

4 **Erecting the wall.** With the aid of a helper, lift the wall frame onto the sole plate, and set the edge of the top plate even with its chalk line. Check to be sure the stud nearest the existing wall is plumb, then fasten the ends of the top plate directly to the joists or to nailing blocks with 16-penny nails, shimming small gaps with thin wedges as necessary. Fasten the end stud to a masonry wall with lead shield anchors and 3/8-inch lag bolts, to a stud or to nailing blocks with 12-penny nails; shim if necessary to plumb. Fasten the sole plate to the concrete floor using a lag bolt at each end and one approximately every 4 feet. Then nail the rest of the top plate.

Center the bottom of each stud over its mark on the sole plate, check to be sure it is plumb, and toenail the stud to the plate with three tenpenny nails—two on one side and the third centered on the other side.

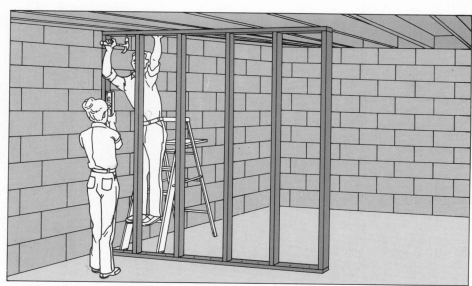

5 **Constructing a corner assembly.** To reinforce the wall at a corner and create nailing surfaces for wallboard, toenail an extra stud to the top and sole plates of the first wall, 1 1/2 inches in from the last stud. Cut three 10-inch nailing blocks from 2-by-4s, sandwich them between these last two studs at the top, middle and bottom of the wall, and fasten each block with four tenpenny nails.

Construct the second wall as you did the first one *(Steps 1-4)*. Nail its end stud to the corner nailing blocks with 16-penny nails *(inset)*.

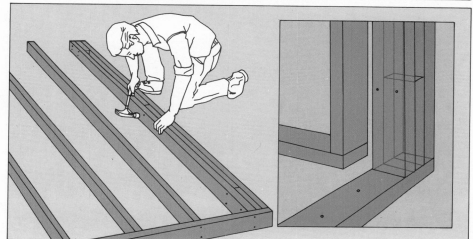

Building a Frame for a Door

1 **Forming the opening sides.** Calculate the size of the rough door opening: the door width plus 2 1/2 inches and door height plus 3 inches. Then mark all stud positions on a top and sole plate as you would for a solid wall *(Step 1, page 77)*. Add marks to position the outer studs and the shorter jack studs that will form the sides of the opening. Cut the two outer studs to the same length as the other studs, and the two jack studs 1 1/2 inches shorter than the planned height of the rough opening, to allow for the sole plate thickness. Lay a jack stud on top of an outer stud, with bottom ends aligned, and fasten the two together by driving a pair of 12-penny nails into each end of the assembly. Stagger more nails at 1-foot intervals in a zigzag pattern to forestall warping. Do the same with the other pair of door-framing studs. Then nail the full-length studs to the top plate *(Step 3, page 78)*.

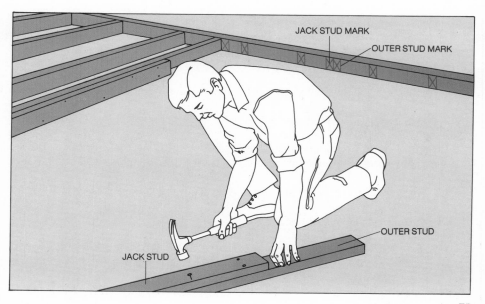

2 **Adding a header and cripple studs.** Cut a 2-by-4 header to fit horizontally between the outer studs of the door opening. (A single header is sufficient for a nonbearing wall only; a bearing wall requires more support.) Then lay the header flat across the tops of the jack studs, and drive two 16-penny nails through each outer stud into an end of the header. Cut 2-by-4 cripple studs to fit between the top plate and header. Check with a square to make sure they will be vertical; then fasten each one at the position marked for it, using pairs of 16-penny nails driven through the top plate and the header *(inset, near right)*.

Turn the marked sole plate face down, and saw three fourths of the way through it at the inside edge of each jack-stud mark. Then install the sole plate and wall as in Step 3, page 78, and Step 4, page 79. In the door opening do not fasten the sole plate to the floor. With the frame upright and all studs nailed in place, use a handsaw to cut away the section of sole plate within the door opening, sawing down to meet the cuts on the underside of the plate *(inset, far right)*.

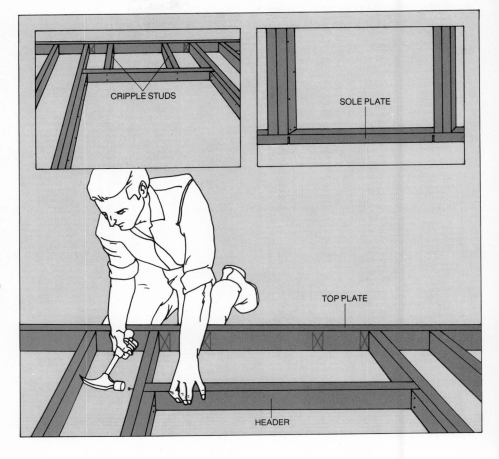

CRIPPLE STUDS

SOLE PLATE

TOP PLATE

HEADER

- Stack and store wallboard flat on the floor; if it leans it may bow or break.

- Cut wallboard short instead of long to fit into a space. The base molding will cover up to 1 1/2 inches of space at the bottom of the board. Trying to force wallboard into too small a space crumbles the edges.

- Be sure you use wallboard with beveled edges for ease in finishing the joints with joint tape and compound.

- Always use special wallboard nails or drywall screws that are treated to prevent corrosion.

- Perforated tape, which has holes for joint compound to penetrate, is easier to embed than plain tape.

- Premixed joint compound is easier to work with than the powdered form that you mix with water. It has uniform consistency and will retain its moisture for a year after being opened and resealed.

- Applying wallboard horizontally gives you the advantage of fewer joints to finish, although the weight of longer lengths makes placing it a two-person job. It is the best method for high-ceilinged rooms and for hallways, where vertical joints are especially noticeable.

- Take safety precautions when you are working with dried joint compound, whether sanding new compound or removing old. Wear a face mask, goggles and hat to keep the dust out of lungs, eyes and hair.

The Professional's Way with Wallboard

Wallboard, also called plasterboard, gypsum board or drywall, is the sensible solution for covering interior walls and ceilings, much less costly and easier to install than wet plaster troweled over wood or metal lath. Wallboard is made of a core of gypsum plaster, pressed into a sandwich, with sheets usually 1/2 inch thick, 4 feet wide and 8 feet long. Heavy white, gray or creamy paper covers the front and heavy kraft paper covers the back. Water-resistant wallboard with a green facing is available for use in the bathroom.

Wallboard is not notably strong—it breaks if you bend it too much and its corners crumble if you tip its 64-pound weight onto one of them. A stout hammer blow will punch right through it cleanly; you can break it neatly and quickly along a scored line, and saw it rapidly with any kind of wood saw. It will hold a hook strong enough to hang light pictures, and it readily accepts wallboard anchors of various types. If you have to cut into wallboard, you can patch it to the original smoothness, and it makes a good match for the existing smooth plaster.

Wallboard is fastened to house framing with corrosion-resistant wallboard nails or drywall screws, sometimes also with an adhesive. Making smooth joints to hide the seams between sheets takes practice. Using wallboard that has a slight bevel along the long edges makes the job easier. Adjacent bevels are filled in with joint compound—a homogenized, water-based plaster-of-paris filler-glue—reinforced by paper joint tape 2 inches wide. Outside corners are strengthened with angled metal strips called corner bead.

The joint compound is spread and feathered out with joint knives made especially for the task. Professionals use four widths—a 6-inch knife for applying the compound and embedding the tape, 10-inch and 12-inch knives for feathering out the next two applications and a 16-inch knife for extra feathering on butt joints that are not tapered. However, two joint knives—6 and 10 inches—will serve if you take care to make the applications as smooth as possible. Textured surface finishes also help to hide joints.

Wallboard is put up on walls after ceilings are covered. These, too, are usually made of wallboard. The standard 8-foot-long sheet of wallboard fits the height of a wall built of commonplace 93-inch studs, but can be shortened for walls less than 8 feet high. For higher walls, you can buy wallboard in lengths to 16 feet, or you can apply 8-foot-high sheets horizontally. On most ceilings, wallboard can be put up as shown on page 83. Installing wallboard on a sloping ceiling such as above a stairway or under a gabled attic roof, however, is best left to a professional; it is extremely difficult to fit joints, and nearly impossible for the do-it-yourselfer to fill them smoothly.

If the wallboard is to be installed vertically, estimate your needs by measuring the perimeter of the room and dividing the number of feet by four. You will need an extra sheet or two to allow for waste. To install wallboard horizontally, treat each wall separately in making measurements.

Cutting the Sheets

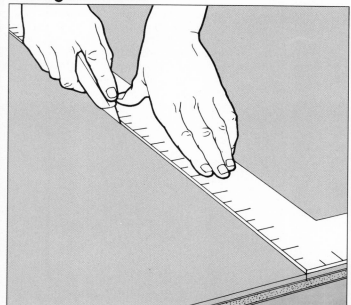

1 **Scoring wallboard.** Measure the size of the panel needed and mark the face accordingly, using a carpenter's square and pressing hard with the pencil to indent the surface. Score the pencil line along the straightedge with a utility knife.

2 **Snapping the core.** Place two 2-by-4 scraps under the wallboard just behind the scored line. With the palm of your hand give the sheet a sharp push, snapping the core in a clean break along the scored line. Finish by bending the panel slightly at the break and slicing through the backing paper with a utility knife.

Fitting the Boards

Measuring for cutouts. Cut holes for fixtures that will protrude through the wallboard before setting the panel in place. Position them by measuring the distance from the ceiling to the top and bottom of the fixture. Record the measurements on the face side of the panel with a pencil. Next measure the width of the cutout—either the distance from the corner or the adjacent fastened panel to both edges of the fixture—and make corresponding marks. Connect the marks with a straightedge to outline the hole.

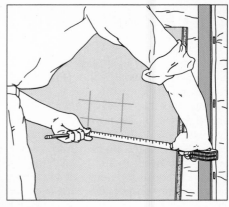

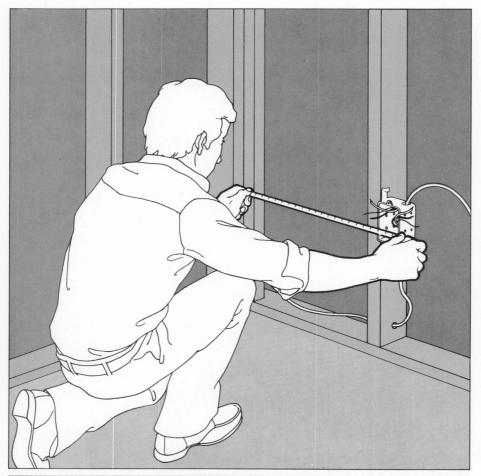

Measuring for openings. To mark a panel for a small opening such as the hole for an electrical outlet, use a professional's trick with a steel tape and pencil. Measure across from the point where the side edge of the panel will rest to the near and far sides of the installed box. Similarly, measure from the point where the top or bottom edge of the panel will fall (whichever is closer) to the top and bottom of the box.

To transfer these measurements to the panel (not yet installed), grasp the measuring tape between thumb and forefinger of one hand so that a length of tape corresponding to the first measurement projects beyond your thumbnail. Rest the side of your forefinger against the appropriate edge of the panel and hold a pencil against the end of the tape with the other hand. Move both hands down the panel simultaneously, keeping them parallel, to mark the first of the four edges of the opening. Repeat with each of the other three measurements. Cut the opening with a keyhole or wallboard saw *(below)*. For a larger opening, such as a window, mark the wallboard in the same way. Cut all four sides with a saw or, if you wish, saw three sides, then score and break the fourth.

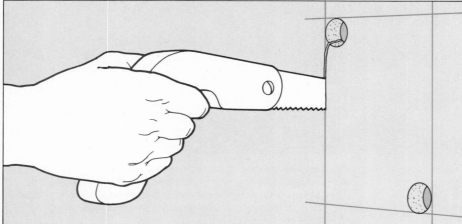

Cutting for fixtures. Drill holes in two diagonally opposite corners of the penciled shape. Force a keyhole saw through the board and cut along the lines Raise the panel into place and nail. A wallboard saw used in place of a keyhole saw will make its own starting holes without drilling.

Fitting around windows and doors. Add fire stops, short horizontal 2-by-4s, between the studs of an exterior wall. For a window, measure down from the ceiling to the top and bottom of the jamb on both sides, and across from the last installed panel to the closest side jamb edge. If the panel will surround the window, also measure to the farthest side jamb edge. Mark these distances on the face of the panel and then connect the marks.

If the panel will enclose three sides of the window, cut along the two parallel lines with a keyhole saw *(page 82)*. Then score the remaining line and snap the score *(page 81, Steps 1 and 2)*. If the panel will surround the window, drill holes at the corners and cut with a keyhole saw.

For a door, mark only the distances from the ceiling to the jamb top and from the last installed panel to the side jamb edge—or edges. Make all cuts with a keyhole saw.

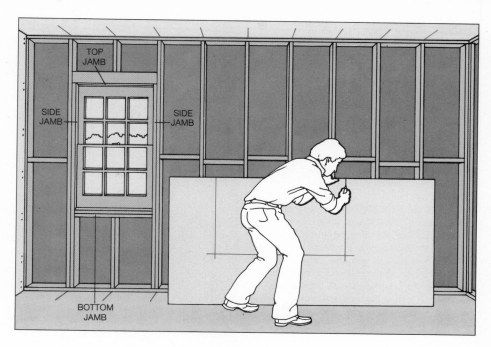

Installing the Sheets

1 Fastening wallboard to ceiling joists. Cover the ceiling with wallboard before starting on walls. Measure and trim the first wallboard panel for a ceiling so that one narrow end fits into a corner and the opposite end falls directly at a joist's midpoint. Use a caulking gun to apply beads of wallboard adhesive, if desired, to the joists within the panel area. Then, with a helper or two, lift the panel into place and drive a wall-board nail or drywall screw into each joist where it crosses the lengthwise center of the panel. Drive a second row of fasteners into the joists, 8 inches in from the wall edge of the panel, then a third row 3/8 inch in from the outer edge. Fasten each supported edge of the panel with a row of fasteners spaced 8 inches apart, placed 3/8 inch in from the edge. Install fasteners through the middle of the panel 8 inches apart on each joist.

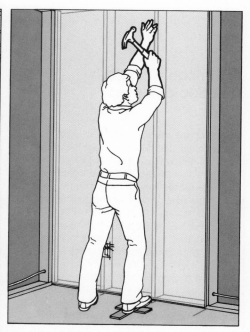

2 Positioning the board. Mark ceiling and floor to indicate stud centers. Lean the first sheet into position in a corner. Shove a piece of wood shingle under the bottom, slide a scrap under the shingle; use these as a foot-operated lever and fulcrum to push and hold the sheet up against the ceiling. Align the edge away from the corner with the center line of the stud. Using the ceiling marks to indicate locations of studs now behind the sheet, drive a wallboard nail into each stud about 1 foot down from the ceiling. These fasteners will hold the board in place, and you can let up on the lever.

3 **Fastening the board.** Drive pairs of wallboard nails or drywall screws into each stud 2 inches apart at intervals of about a foot between pairs. At seams, place fasteners 3/8 inch in from the edges. Fewer fasteners may be installed if adhesive is used. Between the edges, use the marks on the floor and ceiling to help nail or screw into studs you cannot see. If you miss, remove the fastener and try again; joint compound will later fill the hole. Drive each nail flush, then hammer again to set it a fraction of an inch below the surface *(inset, top)*. Be careful not to make this blow so hard that you break the paper covering *(inset, middle)*, or hit it at an angle with the same result *(inset, bottom)*. Drive screws slightly below the wallboard surface. Running the end of a joint knife over the fasteners will indicate by a clicking sound whether any protrude. Drive these in farther. Dimpling the nail and screw heads slightly below the surface allows them to be covered with joint compound and hidden.

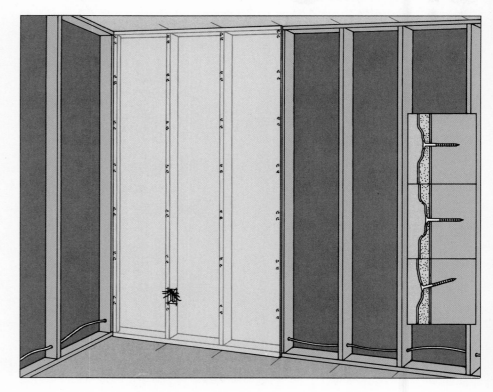

A Horizontal Pattern for Special Cases

Putting up the board. Mark the stud positions on the ceiling and floor. Drive eightpenny nails partway into the studs 4 feet down from the ceiling. With a helper, lift the wallboard so it butts against the ceiling, resting on the nails. Secure the wallboard by nailing it to the intermediate studs about a foot from the ceiling. Then finish nailing *(Step 3, above)* and remove the eightpenny nails. If the wall is more than 8 feet high, put up the second sheet similarly.

Before putting up the bottom sheet, measure from the bottom of the last installed sheet to the floor in at least four places; the ceiling and floor rarely will be parallel. Mark these distances on the new sheet. If the distances are fairly uniform, snap a chalk line between the marks, then score and break the sheet. Otherwise connect the marks with separate straight lines and cut the sheet with a keyhole saw. With a helper, raise the wallboard—using two fulcrums and levers—and nail in place.

Concealing the Joints

1 **Applying joint compound to seams.** Ladle premixed joint compound into a baking pan long enough to accommodate a 10-inch as well as a 6-inch joint knife. Using the 6-inch knife, spread compound like butter to fill the trough formed by the tapered edges of the wallboard, with a layer covering the adjacent surface approximately 1/16 inch deep. (To fill joints at corners, follow the instructions on the next page.) Run the knife down the joint in one motion to smooth out the compound. Wipe the knife frequently against the lip of the pan; otherwise the compound will harden on the knife and score grooves in the wet compound.

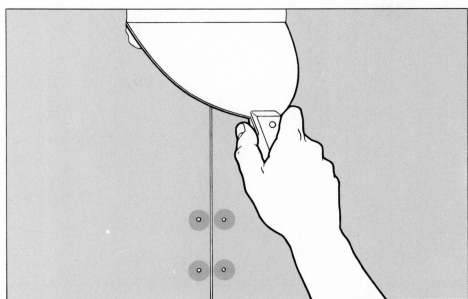

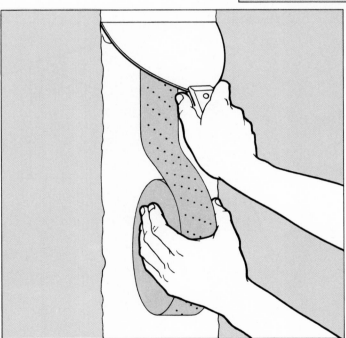

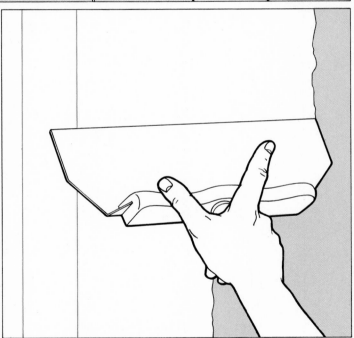

2 **Taping the joint.** With your finger, press one end of the perforated tape into the wet compound at the top of the joint. Unwind the tape with one hand and use the other hand to embed the tape in the joint compound with the knife. Watch for air pockets and wrinkles in the tape; if they appear, lift the tape, pull it tight, and embed it again. If the tape becomes badly wrinkled, peel it up and tear off the damaged section. Start again with fresh tape, positioning the ends of the sections as close together as possible. When you reach the bottom, tear the tape off the roll against the knife.

3 **Feathering the joint.** As the tape is embedded, compound will squeeze out along the sides of the joint. Run the knife down each side, spreading the compound outward. Press hardest on the outside edge of the knife so the compound gradually spreads to a feathered edge. Apply joint compound to the nail dimples on the intermediate studs, feathering the edges. A day later, apply a second coat to the joints with a 10-inch taping knife, feathering about 10 inches on either side of the joint. After another day, apply a third layer of joint compound, thinned with water if necessary to make it spread evenly, and feathered just beyond the 10-inch line.

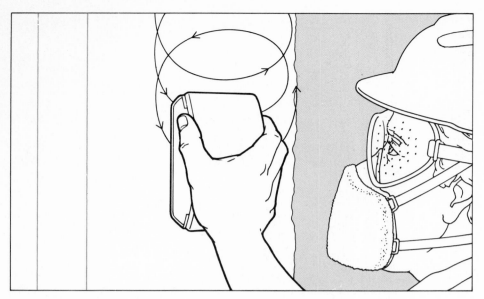

4 **Smoothing the surface.** When the last coat of compound is completely dry, smooth the surface with 100-grit garnet abrasive paper on a sanding block, working in a circular motion from top to bottom. Do not sand onto the paper itself, or the surface will become rough. Similarly, sand over the filled-in nail dimples. Caution: Much dust is generated. Wear protective goggles *(page 130)* and dust mask or respirator and hat *(page 76)*, and keep the working area well ventilated. Brush away the dust and seal the joint with primer.

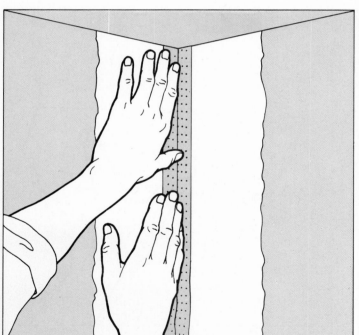

Taping inside corners. Use the 6-inch knife to slather joint compound into the crack in the inside corner of a wall, or between a wall and the ceiling, buttering the compound in crosswise. Run the knife along each side of the joint to smooth the compound. Using one 2- to 3-foot-long strip at a time, bend the paper tape in half where it is creased for this purpose. Press the crease lightly into the corner by running your fingers along the joint. Draw the knife along each side of the joint, embedding the paper and feathering the edges. When applying the second and third coats, do one side at a time. Allow the compound to dry one day between coats.

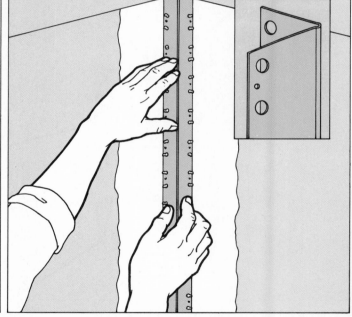

Strengthening outside corners. Butter a 1/8-inch-deep layer of compound over both sides of the corner. Press a reinforcing strip of metal corner bead *(inset)* into the compound so it fits flat on each side—although it may stick in place without fastening, it is best to secure it with nails or screws. Place the fasteners every 6 inches along both flanges, leaving about 8 inches of corner bead free at both ends. Avoid fastening to either the top plate at the ceiling or the sole plate at the floor. Run the knife from ceiling to floor, smoothing out the compound that oozes through the perforations, and feathering. Apply two more coats of compound at one-day intervals. When completed, the rounded tip of the metal bead will still show but will be covered by the wall finish. Dust off and seal the sanded corner with primer.

The Right Way to Nail Molding

Fasten molding in place with the same care used in cutting or in correcting angles. The strips can pull away from the wall if they are incorrectly nailed, and a misplaced hammer blow can easily dent the soft pine generally used for molding.

After making sure that joints are properly fitted, begin nailing a strip of molding at one corner and continue across the room to the opposite end. If the wall is longer than your molding or if the length of a strip of molding proves unwieldy, cut and splice as described on page 88. Remove from the path of the molding any irregularities—such as accretions of paint on old walls or lumps of joint compound at the top or bottom of newly installed wallboard—that might keep the molding from fitting tightly.

Before finishing molding, set the nails about 1/8 inch into the wood and fill the holes with wood putty.

Fastening baseboard. Affix baseboard to the wall by driving two eightpenny finishing nails into the molding at each corner and at each stud. Drive one of the nails through the middle of the molding straight into the stud, and the other nail, at a 45° angle, into the sole plate near the bottom of the molding.

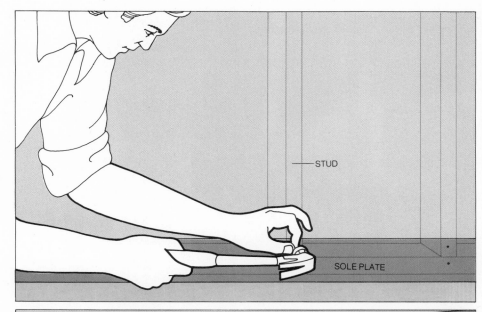

Fastening ceiling molding. Attach ceiling molding by driving nails straight through the middle of the molding at corners and into the studs. Use eightpenny finishing nails—or longer nails if the molding is particularly heavy. Nailing up long strips of molding requires a helper to hold up one end. If you must work singlehanded, cut miter laps at 5-foot intervals, and fasten each strip by nailing it first to the stud nearest the middle of the strip, then nailing back toward one end of the strip and finally nailing forward to the other end.

Finishing mitered corners. Hold the mitered ends of two strips of molding firmly together by driving fourpenny finishing nails through the molding into the wall close to the corner. For baseboard and ceiling moldings, drive two nails at each side of the corner: For the base shoe, drive one nail into the baseboard at each side.

Fastening the base shoe. Nail the base shoe to the floor *(below)* with fourpenny finishing nails at intervals of about 16 inches. Drive the nail at a 45° angle downward into the floor just above the middle of the base shoe; nailing too near the top of the shoe can split the wood.

Fitting the base shoe to doorways. To improve the appearance of the base shoe where it juts into the room past the molding for doors, bookcases and other built-ins, sculpt the obtrusive end into a curve. Holding the base shoe in place, mark a freehand line on the base shoe *(below)*. Begin the line at the point where the base shoe protrudes past the frame, and curve the line away from the frame. Set the base shoe on a solid surface, plane along the line and sand smooth.

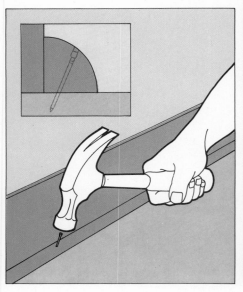

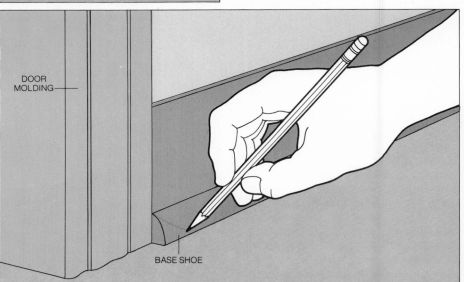

DOOR MOLDING

BASE SHOE

Blending New Trim and Old

When you add a partition to a room, you may be able to buy new moldings that match. If so, set your miter box at a 45° angle and saw enough of the old molding for the run from its original corner to the new wall. Then miter the new molding and join it to the old.

If the molding is antique, and you cannot make a perfect match, the most practical, inexpensive and pleasing solution is not to make a match at all. Reproducing the pattern of antique molding is costly, and new molding that fails to match the old exactly is generally obtrusive. Use instead a plain new molding or clear pine board cut to the same height as the old molding. The new moldings in this application butt against the old walls. With the miter box set at a 90° angle, square-cut the ends of the new molding to fit their run, and nail them to the new wall. Using the same setting, cut the old moldings to lengths equal to the distance from their original corners to the face of the new moldings. Nail them into place.

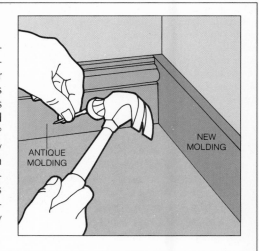

ANTIQUE MOLDING

NEW MOLDING

CEILINGS

Creating any new living space usually involves installing or replacing a ceiling. Simply patching the existing surface is often less satisfactory in the long run than putting in a new one, and sometimes patching is just as much work. For one thing, a new ceiling lets you have the kind of overhead material that both suits your taste and matches the uses you plan for the room. In many cases a new ceiling can make up for architectural deficiencies. Dividing a room, for example, may make the ceiling too high for the room's size; lowering the ceiling restores proper proportions. Recessing light fixtures in it can make a low ceiling seem higher. Soundproofing a ceiling can deaden the upstairs or downstairs din and adapt a room for quiet uses such as a study.

Planning and preparation, essential to any home-improvement project, is especially important in the case of ceilings. Supporting a new ceiling is not complicated. Most ceilings are simply attached directly to the joists supporting the floor of the room above, or to furring strips nailed across the joists at intervals (pages 95-97). Where no ceiling joists exist, as in an attic, you can nail horizontal collar beams across the rafters and attach the ceiling to them. Hanging a suspended ceiling (below) requires little more technical skill than hanging a picture; prefabricated snap-together metal strips strung from the joists provide a framework for drop-in panels. Fluorescent lighting can be incorporated into a suspended ceiling (pages 93-94), giving added function to a room's ceiling.

Suspending a Ceiling

Suspended ceilings are usually made of 2-foot-by-4-foot acoustical panels supported by a metal grid. This framework consists of long main runners connected at 4-foot intervals by 2-foot cross Ts. The runners are usually hung at right angles to the joists and are held up by hanger wires attached to the bottom edges of the joists. The outer edges of the ceiling are supported by edge framing, which is L-shaped in cross section, and which is attached to the walls with the vertical stroke of the L uppermost.

Both the hardware—framing, runners and hanger wires—and the acoustical panels are adaptable to all room sizes and designs. Runners, sold in 8-, 10- or 12-foot lengths, are made of light aluminum sheet metal that can be cut to fit easily enough with tin shears. Tabs at the ends interlink and lock to extend the length. Holes for hanger wires occur every 3 inches, and slots for cross Ts are positioned every 6 inches. Edge framing is flexible enough to accommodate the slight irregularities in wall surfaces. Use a utility knife to trim the panels.

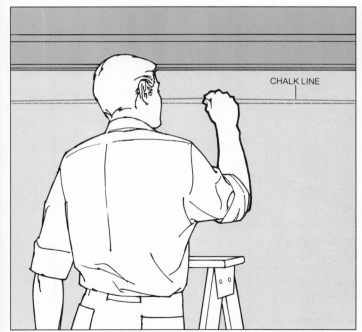

1 **Measuring ceiling height.** Mark the proposed ceiling height—allowing room below the joists to clear ducts, pipes or other obstructions—on the wall at the corners of the room. In each corner, drive a nail part-way into a stud at the level marked. Stretch a chalk line tautly between the nails, and snap the line across each wall.

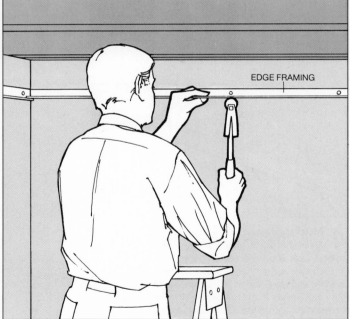

2 **Installing edge framing.** Screw or nail edge framing into studs along each wall at ceiling height. Where the ends of two strips of framing meet at a corner, lap one end over the other.

3 **Positioning runners and cross Ts.** To ensure a symmetrical arrangement of the panels, start by marking the centers of the walls at joist level. Since the short ends of the panels will abut the walls parallel to the joists, these walls must be divided into centered 2-foot intervals. Measure from center to corner, and determine the distance in inches beyond the last even number of feet. If this overage is 6 inches or more *(top right)*, snap a chalk line across the joist bottoms from the center of one wall to the center of the other. If the overage is less than 6 inches, mark the joists along a line a foot to one side or the other of the midpoints *(bottom right)*. In either case, mark across the joists at 2-foot intervals on both sides of the first line.

In centering the long dimension of the panels on the walls perpendicular to joists, measure in the same way from center to corner. The overage is the distance to the corner from the last 4-, 8- or 12-foot mark. If the overage is 6 inches or more *(top right)*, plan to space cross Ts at 4-foot intervals on both sides of the center mark. If the overage is less than 6 inches *(bottom right)*, space cross Ts from points 2 feet on either side of the center. Mark the walls above the edge framing for cross Ts.

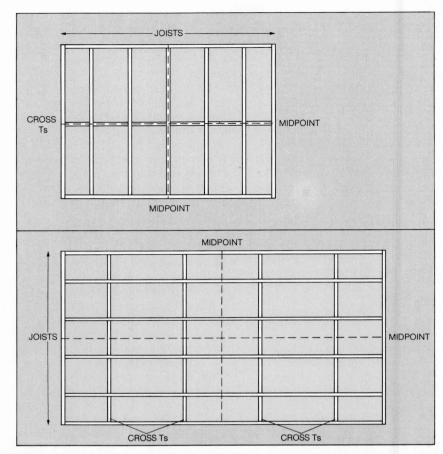

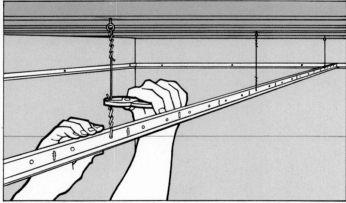

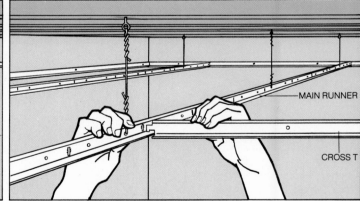

4 **Attaching runners.** Along the lines marked across the joists, attach an eye screw to the bottom edge of every other joist. Insert a hanger wire in each eye, secure the wires by twisting and bend the free ends to a 90° angle. Ensure alignment of the cross-T slots in the runners by stretching a line between center marks on the walls perpendicular to the joists. Hang the runners so that a T slot lies just above the string. Add lengths of runners as needed and cut off the excess. Set each runner in place with its ends resting on the edge framing. Thread hanger wires through the holes in the runners. Level each runner by adjusting the hanger wires, then secure each wire by twisting it around itself.

5 **Connecting the cross Ts.** Connect the runners with cross Ts at the proper intervals by fitting the ends of the cross Ts into the slots in the runners along the two walls perpendicular to the joists; rest the outer ends of the cross Ts on the edge framing.

Install panels in all the full-sized openings in the grid. Lift each panel diagonally up through the framework, turn it to the horizontal and rest its edges on the flanges of the runners and the cross Ts. Check the alignment of full-sized panels and grid, then trim panels to fit the smaller spaces around the border of the grid and install them.

Inserting a Fluorescent Light Fixture

Suspended ceilings offer a variety of opportunities for installing either fluorescent or incandescent light fixtures. The simplest method is to replace one full-sized panel with a troffer type of fixture—one with a shallow rectangular reflector the same size as a panel.

Such a fixture usually comes with a light-diffusing screen of transparent plastic, and a receptacle for housing the connections to a power source. If the original ceiling fixture employed a hanging cord switch, you will have to install a wall switch for the troffer.

1 Connecting cable to cover plate. Knock out one of the punch holes in the cover plate from the light fixture, and insert the threaded end of a cable connector through from the top, or ridged, side. Screw the lock nut tightly to hold the connector to the plate.

Cut 6 inches of sheathing off the end of a length of plastic-sheathed cable, wire size No. 14 for a 15-ampere branch circuit, or No. 12 for a 20-ampere branch circuit. Peel off 3/4 inch of insulation to bare the ends of the black- and white-insulated wires. Slip these wires through the clamp on the cable connector and out the nozzle until 1/4 inch of the cable sheathing comes through. With a screwdriver, tighten the cable clamp to secure the cable.

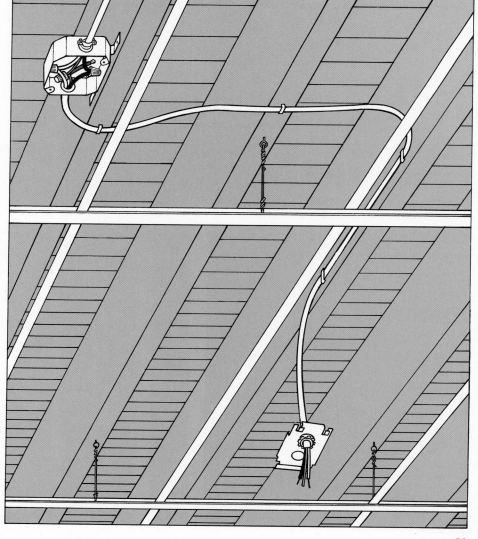

2 Running cable to a junction box. Cut the cable long enough to reach from where you want to place the light fixture to the junction box that holds the original ceiling light. Turn off the current at the service panel. Unscrew the original fixture from the fixture box. Carefully remove the wire caps without touching any bare wire ends. Use a voltage tester to be certain the power is off *(page 272)*. If the tester glows, turn off the proper circuit before working with the wires. Disconnect and straighten the wires. Locate a knockout—a removable part of the junction box that allows cable entry, and fasten the cable into it with another cable connector. Attach the grounding wire to other grounding wires and grounding jumper wires in the fixture box. Connect the wires from the power source and from the fixture with wire caps, white to white and black to black. Screw a cover plate to the box.

3 **Putting up the fixture.** With the power off, leave grid openings surrounding the fixture empty in order to have ample space in which to work. With the help of a partner, angle the fixture into place and set it on the grid.

4 **Connecting cable to fixture wires.** With the power off, wire-cap the white-insulated wires from the light fixture to the white wire of the cable. Wire-cap the black-insulated wires from the fixture to the black wire of the cable. Then push the wiring into the opening on the fixture; attach the cover plate. Staple the cable within 12 inches of the fixture. From below, open the fixture and attach the cable grounding wire to a grounding screw on the fixture.

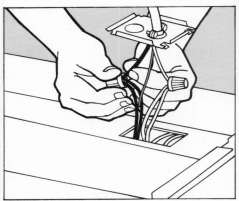

Providing a Wall Switch

1 **Making connections in the junction box.** If the original ceiling light used a pull cord as a switch, install a wall switch for the new fixture. From the wall near an entry door to a new knockout hole in the ceiling junction box, run No. 12 or 14 cable *(page 93, Step 1)* with a cable connector. Staple the cable to the joints at 4-foot-maximum intervals and at bends. Make sure the power is off *(page 272)*. In the ceiling junction box, join the white-insulated wire of the power source cable to the white wire of the cable from the new light fixture. Join the black-insulated wire from the power source cable to the white wire from the switch cable, coding the white wire black to show that it is being used as a hot wire. Join the black-insulated wire from the switch cable to the black wire from the fixture cable. Wire cap the three bare grounding wires from the cables together with a short green-insulated or bare grounding jumper of the same wire gauge and connect the other end of the jumper to the bonding screw at the back of the metal junction box. Fold the wires carefully back into the box and cover the box with a blank cover.

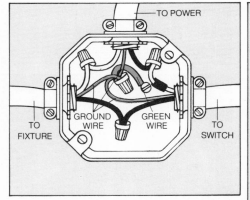

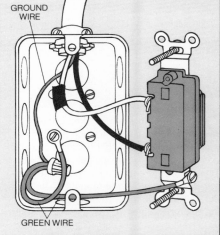

2 **Connecting the switch.** At the wall, run the cable into the box. Connect the bare grounding wire with green-insulated jumping wires leading to grounding terminals in the box and on the switch. If the switch has no grounding terminal, see that its metal yoke contacts the metal box when installed. Connect the black- and white-insulated wires to the terminal screws. Mark the white wire to flag it as hot. Screw the switch to the box, install a switch plate and turn on the power.

Putting Up a Tile Ceiling

1 **Planning the job.** Acoustical tiles, 12 inches by 12 inches, make a suitable ceiling for a new living space in a basement, attic or unfinished room. At ceiling level, make chalk marks at the centers of all four walls. Measure from each mark to an adjacent corner. This distance will be a number of feet plus, usually, a fraction of a foot. If the fraction is less than 3 inches, move the center markers 6 inches right or left. Mark 12-inch intervals from the center markers to the adjoining walls. To determine how many 1-by-3 furring strips you need, count the number of marks on one of the walls parallel to the joists and add two extra. Cut each strip the length of the walls perpendicular to the joists. To estimate the number of tiles required, count the number of 12-inch intervals on two adjoining walls; add one to each of these figures and multiply them.

Any extensive electrical wiring that is to be installed in the room should be completed before you put up the furring.

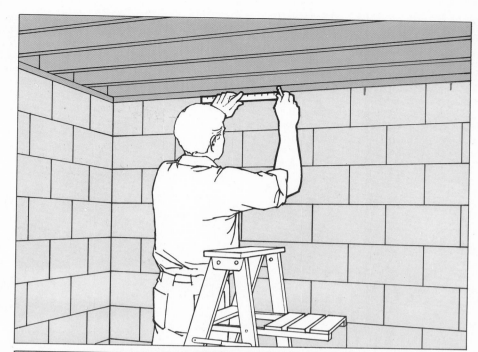

Holding the Edge

Where you find a gap between the end joist and the wall, supply a nailing surface for the ends of the furring strips by adding a false joist. Cut a 2-by-4 or 2-by-6 just enough shorter than a joist so that you can raise it to rest flat on the side sill plate at one end, and then slide it over to rest on the sill at the other end. Cut 1-by-3s to a length equal to the width of a joist. Every 2 or 3 feet nail these segments—called kickers—to the outer edge of the false joist, with their upper ends against the subfloor. Position the joist's inner edge to lie where the furring strips will end. The kickers provide solid nailing for the strips, which in turn hold the joist in place.

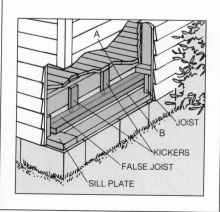

2 **Putting up furring strips.** Tape a carpenter's level to the narrow side of a straight 2-by-4 and check the joists lengthwise and crosswise to see how level a base they will provide. If they vary sharply, start by holding the first strip at right angles to the joists at their lowest level. Center the ends between the nearest pair of chalk marks and attach the strip to the joist with an eightpenny nail. Using a level to guide you, shim the rest of the strip down from the high joists. Level the other strips from the first one, attaching a strip between each remaining pair of chalk marks and against the end walls.

3 Adjusting fixtures. If a furring strip crosses an existing ceiling fixture, disconnect the fixture: Turn off the electric circuit *(page 11)*. Carefully remove the screws or nuts holding the fixture; pull it away from the box. Carefully remove the wire caps without touching any bare wire ends; disconnect the wires. Detach the ceiling box from the joist or loosen it from the hanger and slide it back along the cable out of the way of the strip. Reattach the box; lower it if necessary so the bottom rim will be flush with the ceiling when the tiles are installed. Leave the power off.

4 Putting up the first tile. Snap a chalk line down the center of the next-to-last furring strip on one side of the room and another line intersecting the first at right angles—between the last pair of chalk marks at one end of the room. Set the tile in the corner where the lines intersect with the raised, or tongue, edges toward the corner and the stapling flanges toward the center of the room. Align the finished rims with the chalk marks. Staple both ends of the flanges on the grooved edges to the furring strips.

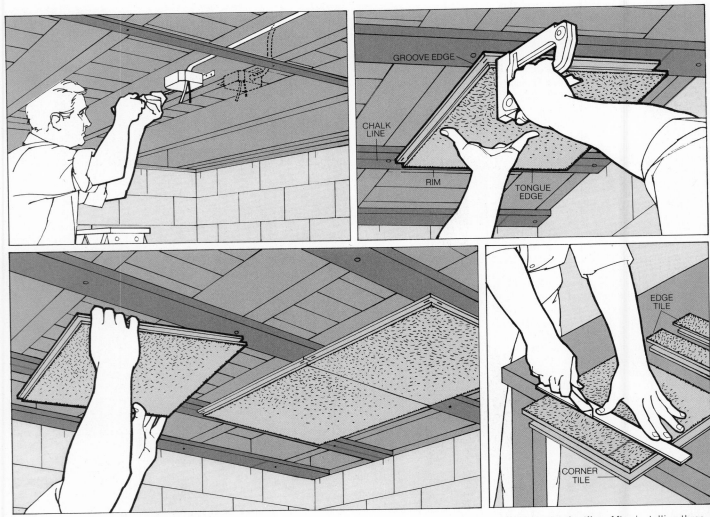

5 Attaching adjacent tiles. With the adjoining raised edges toward the corner, slide the tongue of the next tile into the groove on the stapled edge of the preceding tile. Then align the rims of the new tile with the chalk line or the rims of the preceding one. Staple the flanges on the projecting grooved edges of the new tile to the furring strips.

6 Adding border tiles. After installing three tiles, measure the distance from their outer rims to the walls at both ends of each tile. Deduct 1/4 inch from each measurement and use the results to mark the required sizes for the corner and edge tiles. Be sure to measure from the rims along the grooved edges. Draw lines between the marks and cut the tiles with a utility knife. Slide the pieces into place, starting with the corner tile, and anchor them to the furring strips with 1 1/2-inch common nails.

7 **Marking the site of an outlet box.** Be sure the power is still off. Before you reach the area where you must tile around the outlet box of a ceiling fixture, remove the fixture and relocate the box *(page 96, Step 3)*, if you have not already done so. Reattach the box to a joist so that it will be more or less in the middle of a tile and so that its lower rim will be flush with the surface of the ceiling. Tile as closely as possible to two adjacent sides of the relocated box, then slip the tongue of a fresh tile into the groove of a tile already installed on one side of the box. Slide the loose tile up to the box and mark the tongue of the tile at the point where it touches the midpoint of the rim of the box, but do not mark the face of the tile. Slide the same tile up to the adjoining side of the box and mark the point on the tile's other tongue where it touches the midpoint of the rim.

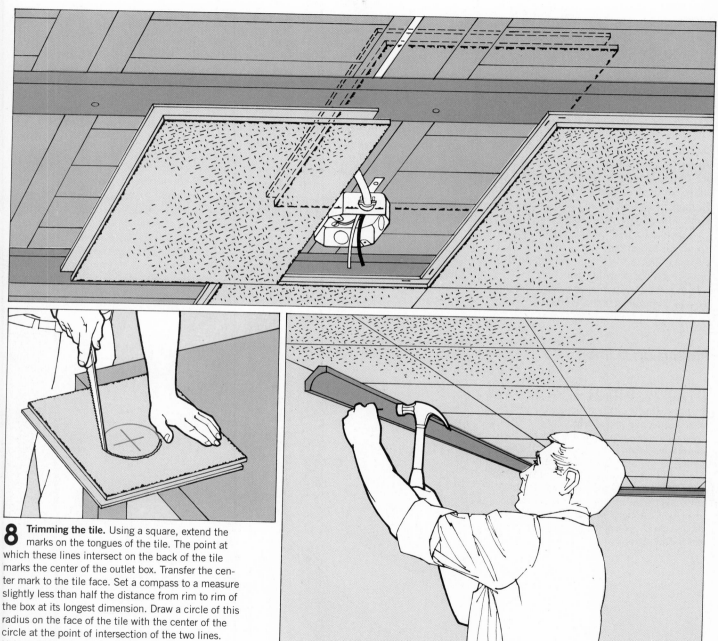

8 **Trimming the tile.** Using a square, extend the marks on the tongues of the tile. The point at which these lines intersect on the back of the tile marks the center of the outlet box. Transfer the center mark to the tile face. Set a compass to a measure slightly less than half the distance from rim to rim of the box at its longest dimension. Draw a circle of this radius on the face of the tile with the center of the circle at the point of intersection of the two lines. Using a keyhole saw held with the blade pointed outward at a slight angle, make a beveled cut around the circle through the face to the back of the tile. The box should be flush with the face of the tile or stick out 1/16 inch. Staple the tile in place around the box as described on page 96 Step 5. Reattach the fixture and turn the circuit back on.

9 **Finishing the ceiling.** After installing the tiles, insulate as necessary and put up wallboard *(pages 80-86)*. (You can also work in the reverse order, putting up wallboard first and then the tiles.) After the wallboard is finished, use the procedure shown on pages 87-88 to miter-joint 1 1/2-inch cove molding to cover the line between walls and ceiling. Attach the molding as described on pages 89-90.

Hanging Shelves and Cabinets

Once you have determined the wall type and selected the appropriate fastener for hanging a shelf or cabinet securely *(inside back cover)*, make sure it will be perfectly level. Supports should usually be spaced from 20 to 32 inches apart, depending on the load. If supports are more than 32 inches apart, most wood shelving will sag under its own weight. Nor should the ends of a shelf extend more than 8 inches beyond the outside supports; the ends might bow and the shelf would lose stability.

If your wall is hollow, it is probably backed by wood or metal studs. Locate the studs according to the instructions on page 46; and, if possible, attach the supports to them. Since most studs are about 16 inches apart, a support attached to every other stud will work for most loads.

In leveling a shelf or cabinet, do not rely on visual judgment; use a level *(Step 4)*. Wall, ceiling and floor lines are seldom straight, even in new homes.

The most common methods for hanging shelves use braces that are attached directly to the wall, or brackets that fit into upright standards installed on the wall. Braces are usually used to put up a single, stationary shelf. Heavy angle irons, like the one shown below, or braces made from molded metal can be used to support heavy weights. But whether braces are decorative or utilitarian, all are attached to walls in much the same way.

Standards are most often used to support several shelves on removable brackets. Most standards are attached as described in the instructions on page 100. Brackets differ, however; the most widely used brackets, with instructions for installing them, are on page 101.

Shelves are also installed in closets and corners, across windows or in hallways, where they can be supported at the sides instead of—or in addition to—the back. For this kind of installation, specialized mountings are required.

Wall storage devices are not, of course, limited to shelves. One way to put vertical space to work is to use perforated hardboard, or pegboard. This composition board comes in thicknesses of 1/8 inch for light loads, and 1/4 inch for heavier jobs. Holes punched at 1-inch intervals over its surface vary from under 1/4 inch in the 1/8-inch-thick board to about 3/16 inch in the 1/4-inch board. Pegboard can be attached to a wall by inserting fasteners through the holes. To maintain space behind the board for insertion of pegboard hooks, frame the back of the pegboard with 1/2-inch molding or insert a cylindrical rubber spacer between the pegboard and the wall. Tool departments and hardware stores carry hooks, clamps and other support devices in sizes appropriate to the thickness of the board (1/8 inch, 1/4 inch).

With imagination, you can use pegboard in many ways and in many rooms, as well as creating your own storage devices from objects you have at home. Big, bulky equipment, for example, can be lifted onto braces installed to be used as hooks. Dowels will support snow tires in a garage, or plants on a porch. Even wood soft-drink cases make splendid compartmental storage for small items.

Putting up a Shelf

1 Leveling the first brace. Decide where you want your shelf, and place the first brace against the wall at that location. Balance a carpenter's level on top of the bracket, then adjust the position of the brace until the air bubbles in the end vials of the level are centered. With an awl, scratch circles through the screw holes. Remove the brace and drill pilot holes. Center the drill bit precisely; even a small error can throw off the alignment. Attach the brace with the appropriate fastener *(chart, inside back cover)*.

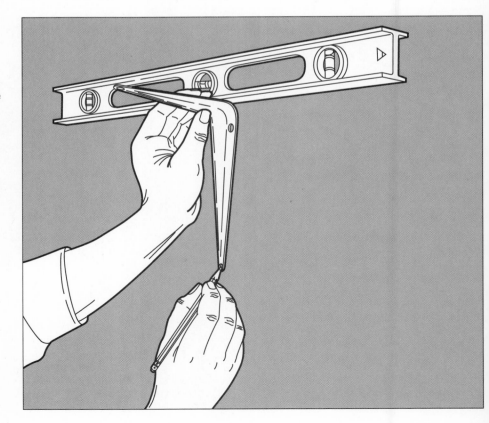

2 **Positioning the other braces.** If the shelf is short enough to require only two braces, decide on the amount of overhang you want at each end. Measure in that amount from each end and mark the shelf lightly on its underside. If the shelf will need more than two braces, mark the positions of the braces at each end in the same manner. Then measure the distance between the position of these braces and divide this measurement by the number of additional braces you intend to use plus one. The resulting figure will provide an equal distance from brace to brace.

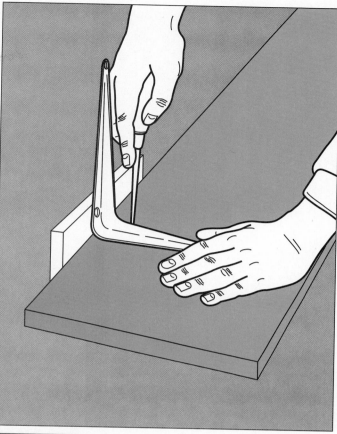

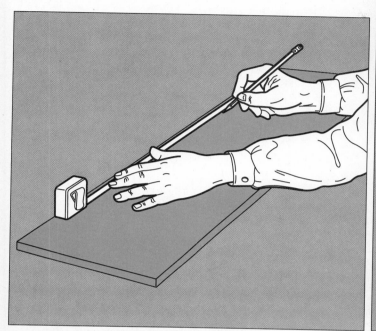

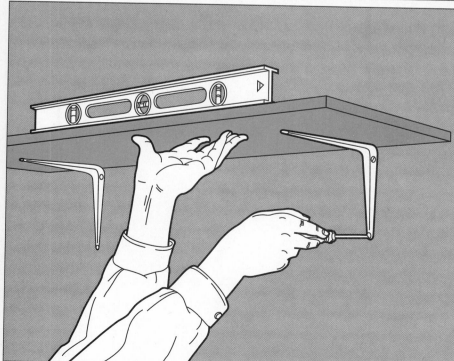

3 **Setting the second brace.** At one of the marked positions on the shelf (except where the brace already attached to the wall is to align), nail a piece of square or rectangular scrap wood to the shelf, as shown, or ask a helper to hold it in place for you. This will square the brace against the back edge of the shelf. Mark the screw holes, drill pilot holes and attach the brace to the shelf with wood screws. Then remove the scrap wood. Attach all other braces, if any, in the same way, centering them carefully on the positions marked on the underside of the shelf.

4 **Leveling the shelf.** Rest the shelf, its braces attached, on the brace already fastened to the wall. Make sure the brace is centered on the mark made for it on the shelf. Put a carpenter's level on the shelf and adjust the shelf position until the middle bubble in the level is centered. With an awl, scratch the wall through the screw holes in the braces. Remove the shelf and drill all pilot or anchor holes in the wall. Replace the shelf and fasten the braces to the wall. Drill pilot holes in the shelf through the holes in the brace that was first fastened to the wall. Drive in wood screws.

Hanging a Shelf on Standards

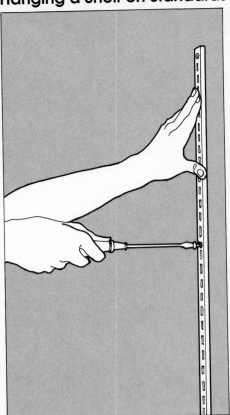

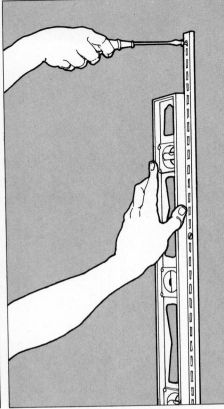

2 **Attaching the standard.** Align the standard vertically with a level. Mark the positions of the other fastener holes and, if necessary, swing the standard aside when you drill the pilot or anchor hole. Make sure that the drill bit is centered precisely. Then attach the remaining fasteners.

3 **Hanging the shelf.** Insert one shelf bracket in the first standard. Fit a bracket into the corresponding holes of a second standard. Place the second standard against the wall, centering it on the mark made for it, and set the shelf, with a level on it, on top of the brackets. Adjust the shelf until the bubble in the level is centered. Mark the top and bottom of the second standard on the wall; remove the shelf and attach the second standard as described in Steps 1 and 2. If the shelf is to be supported by more than two standards, repeat Steps 1 to 3 for each.

1 **Positioning the first standard.** Mark the location of the shelves lightly on the wall. Determine the location of the end standards, then of the middle ones, if any, as described in Step 2, page 99, but mark the positions on the wall, not on the shelves. Place a standard against the wall on the spot marked for an end standard. (Check to make sure the standard is top end up; some standards are made to be oriented in one way only.) Mark one fastener hole—the center one if there are more than two—and drive in an appropriate fastener. Do not tighten, so you can swing aside the standard to insert the remaining fasteners.

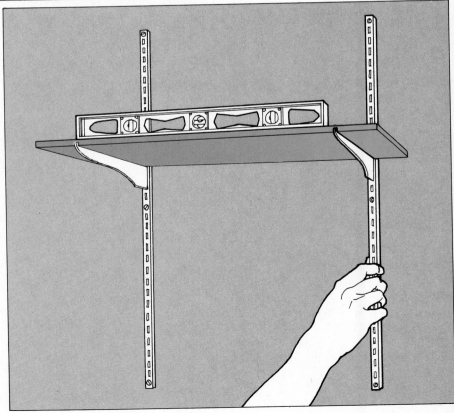

Types of Standards and Brackets

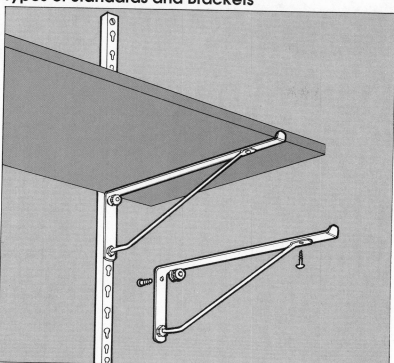

Keyhole. Because of their triangular design, brackets of this type can support very heavy weights. Slip the bolts that come with the brackets into the holes in the standards. Press the bolts down and tighten the bracket nuts.

Tracked. This slotted metal standard is fitted with sliding inserts equipped with a bolt and flat nut. To attach a bracket, press an insert into the track of the standard. The top of the insert must be at shelf level minus the thickness of the bracket. Tighten the bolt with a hex wrench *(inset)* until the nut grips the standard. Slip the spade pin at the end of the bracket sidewise into the standard slot and turn the bracket until it fits into the groove on the face of the insert. (These standards will also hold lamps with spade-pin attachments similar to those on the brackets.)

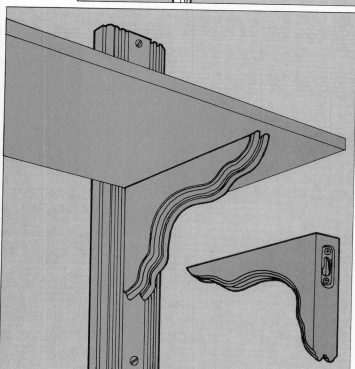

Carved wood. These decorative brackets are hooked over screws driven into their standards. To attach them, partially drive a screw into the standard at the level on the wall where you want to hang the shelf. Then fit the small, metal-lined hole on the bracket's inner surface *(inset)* over the projecting screwhead.

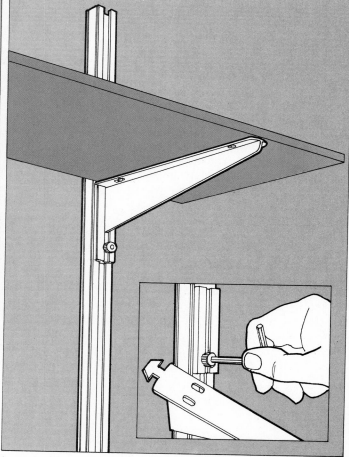

A Showcase for Your Books: The Home Library

Books have a way of accumulating. Whether you buy paperbacks or first editions, the acquisitive instinct never seems to wane; soon you have run out of storage space. Floor-to-ceiling bookshelves covering an entire wall, or more, may supply the answer. Treated architecturally and provided with such amenities as a built-in ladder and a lighted reading ledge, the wall of books becomes a library—a gracious addition to any home.

Although a bookcase that covers an entire wall may look imposing, it is relatively simple to construct. Rather than building one monolithic cabinet, you can assemble the book wall in modules—small, sturdy, self-contained units that are screwed to the wall studs and to each other and rest on a common base.

Modular construction offers some distinct advantages. Since each unit is relatively light, it is easy to move. Thus you have the option of doing most of the work in your shop and assembling the finished unit on site. Perhaps more important, the short shelves of a modular unit, with their built-in vertical supports, are less apt to sag than a bookcase with a continuous span of longer shelves. Paper, remember, is heavy. The paper used in most books weighs about 58 pounds per cubic foot, and a typical 3-foot shelf fully loaded with hard-cover books is supporting more than 100 pounds.

This book weight is an important factor in your decision on where to place a library wall. A fully loaded, 3-foot-wide floor-to-ceiling module in an 8-foot-high room may weigh over 700 pounds, and a row of such modules adds up to considerable weight on the floor. On floors above ground level, an outside or load-bearing wall is the most desirable place for the library, and ideally the shelves should sit on floor joists that run perpendicular to the wall. In most houses the joists run across the shorter dimensions of the house, but if your house is constructed differently and you suspect you may run into structural problems, you should check out your library design with a structural engineer.

The most efficient wall in terms of book storage space obviously is one without doors or windows. But the modules can be adapted to surround a window or to pass over a door—although this is likely to place the top shelf so high that you will need to plan for access to it. The floor-to-ceiling bookshelves shown here, for instance, are designed with a top shelf 12 inches below the ceiling in an 8-foot-high room. This puts the top shelf within arm's reach of the average person. If you are taller or shorter, you may want to change the height of the top shelf. Or you can install a ladder, which puts even high shelves within easy reach.

To design a library wall that is balanced and pleasingly proportioned, plan it on paper first. Start by making a scale drawing of the area the bookcases will cover, indicating the position of any architectural features or electric outlets. Divide this scale drawing into equal-sized sections no more than 38 inches wide, the optimum span for a bookshelf. If you are planning to cover one wall only, calculate the divisions corner to corner, allowing at least 1 inch of clearance for installation. At each of these divisions, mark off the width of the modules' vertical supports.

If you are covering two adjacent walls with shelves, lay out and build the longer wall first, the shorter wall second. Subtract from both walls the depth of the completed bookcase (the total width of the standards, the back and the face frame). Add 1 inch to the length of the longer bookcase or the one that is built first. This provides a surface for joining the two bookcases, leaving an inaccessible dead space in the corner.

At this stage in your planning decide what else, in addition to standard-sized books, you may want the library wall to hold. If you have oversized art books, you will probably need extra-deep shelves. You may want slanted display shelves for magazines, a well-lighted reading ledge for reference books, or cabinets for stereo components. Finally, to complete your scale drawing, calculate in linear feet the amount of shelving you will need for your books, and decide how many shelves you can fit in each module. In general, shelves are spaced 10 to 12 inches apart for hardcover books, 8 to 10 inches apart for paperbacks; an average of seven books will fit into a running foot of space. But these figures can vary widely, and the spacing of your present shelves may be the most accurate guide.

Once you have found a design that suits your needs and looks attractive, preview it in full scale by sketching it lightly on the wall. Since the bookcase modules have backs, the marks will later be concealed. Then, in preparation for building the modules, measure the distance from ceiling to floor at several points along the wall. The vertical standards for the modules will be cut to a length equal to the height of the lowest point on the ceiling line minus the height of the common base and less an additional inch for clearance during installation. If there are any irregularities in the ceiling line, they will be concealed by moldings attached to the finished units. In addition, during installation you will use shims to compensate for any irregularity in the back wall *(Step 1, page 106).*

A library built in modules. The unbroken expanse of bookshelves in this library is actually composed of a series of relatively narrow floor-to-ceiling modules resting on a common base that matches the height of the existing baseboard. The modules are attached side to side with wood screws and are screwed to the wall studs through a horizontal hanging bar inside the back of each unit. Each module has two vertical standards cut from 3/4-inch plywood or, where ceilings are more than 8 feet high, from solid lumber. The inner face of each standard

is rabbeted top and bottom to take the top and bottom of the module, and dadoed slightly below its midpoint to accept a stationary center shelf. A 1/4-inch plywood back reinforces these connections. In a typical module the shelves are 10 inches deep and, except for the stationary center shelf, rest on adjustable shelf pins. The same basic module can be modified to incorporate slanted display shelves and cabinet doors. Similarly, a reading ledge can be fitted into dadoes in the sides of one module, replacing three shelves. The shelf unit that spans the top of the

door is simply a box, attached to the flanking modules with screws. A movable ladder hooks over the stationary shelf to provide access to the upper books.

A face frame of solid lumber hides the module joints and conceals the rough plywood edges. A fascia board spans the tops of the modules and supports a cornice molding; it and the floorline shoe molding serve to conceal any floor or ceiling irregularities and make the library wall look as if it is permanently built in.

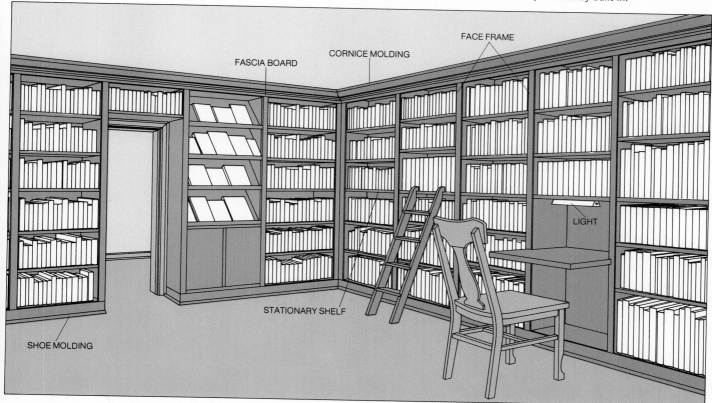

Building a Bookshelf Module

1 Cutting the plywood components. Cut standards to the desired width from large sheets of 3/4-inch plywood; crosscut each standard to the desired length. Cut a top, bottom and stationary shelf for each module, making these pieces the same depth as the standards and as long as the planned inside width of the modules plus 3/4 inch. Cut adjustable shelves 1/8 inch shallower than the standards and less the thickness of the shelf edging you plan to use. Shelves are 1/4 inch shorter than the inside width of the modules, to accommodate shelf pins. Cut a 4-inch-wide hanging bar for each cabinet, the inside width of the modules. Cut back panels from 1/4-inch plywood or hardboard, the full outside dimensions of the modules.

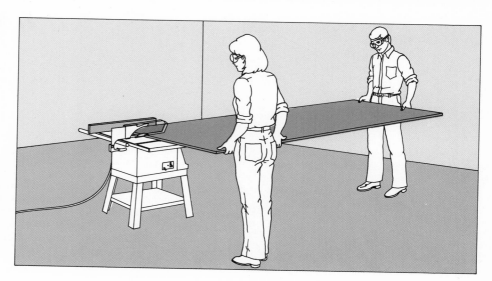

2 **Positioning the shelves.** With a fine-pointed pencil and a combination square, mark a line for a 3/4-inch-wide rabbet at each end of all standards, and a 3/4-inch-wide dado for the center shelf, positioning the dado at the midpoint of the standard minus the height of the base *(Step 2, page 106)*. Measuring carefully, mark the positions of holes for the shelf pins 1 inch from the front and back edges of each standard. Space these marks 2 inches apart, beginning 1 foot in from the ends of the standards and stopping 1 foot short of the marks for the dadoes.

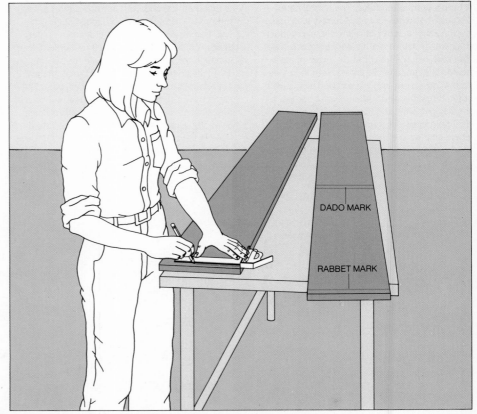

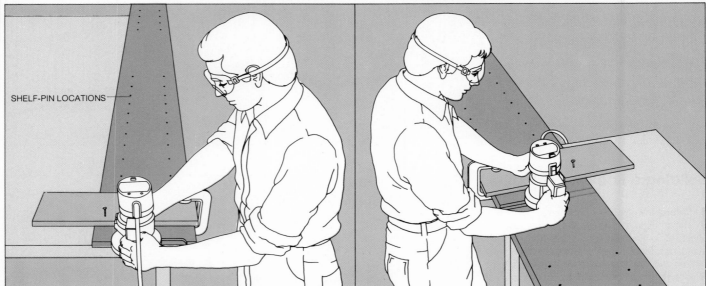

3 **Cutting the shelf supports.** Clamp a length of straight-edged scrap wood to one end of a standard, as a guide for the router base, and cut the first rabbet 3/4 inch deep and 3/4 inch wide *(page 454)*. In order not to splinter the corner of the plywood, begin the rabbet 2 or 3 inches in from one edge. Guide the router to complete the forward cut first, then bring the router back to complete the rabbet. Reposition the guide, and cut an identical rabbet at the op-

posite end of the standard. The top and bottom of the module will fit into the rabbeted ends of the standards.

Use the same length of scrap wood to guide the router between the dado lines marked for the stationary shelf, making this cut, too, 3/8 inch deep. Finally, use an awl to make a slight depression at every shelf-pin mark, and drill a 1/4-inch hole 1/2 inch deep, taping the bit 1/2 inch from its tip to keep from drilling too deep.

4 **Assembling the frame.** Working with a helper, test-fit the joints between the standards and the top, bottom and stationary shelf of each module. If necessary, use a hammer and a block of wood to seat the center shelf snugly. If the fit is not perfect or the modules do not line up precisely, adjust the depth of the rabbets and dadoes until they do. Then assemble the pieces with glue and sixpenny finishing nails. Spread glue on the ends of the horizontal pieces as well as inside the rabbets and dadoes. Drive the nails partway into the center line of the rabbets and dadoes, spacing the nails 4 inches apart and at least 1 inch from the edge of the standard.

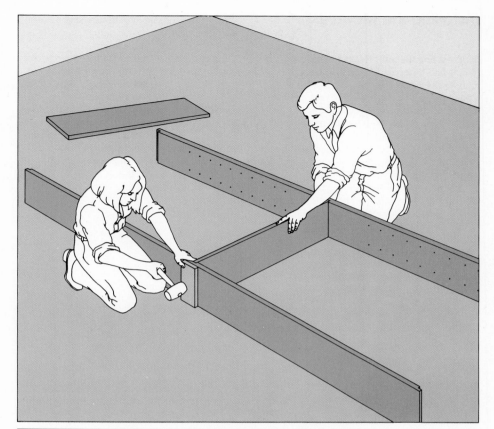

5 **Squaring the frame.** To make sure the frame is squared, measure diagonally between opposite corners while the glue is still moist. If the measurements are not exactly equal, push the corners with the longer measurement toward each other, then measure again. Repeat until the measurements are identical, then set all of the nails. Apply glue to the ends and top edge of the hanging bar. Slide it into the top back of the module. Secure the bar with sixpenny nails, putting two through each standard; nail every 6 inches through the top.

Glue and nail the 1/4-inch-thick back panel into place. Drive 3/4-inch box nails through the panel into the edge of the frame at 3-inch intervals. Drive two rows of nails at 3-inch intervals through the back panel into the hanging bar. Paint or finish the completed module as desired.

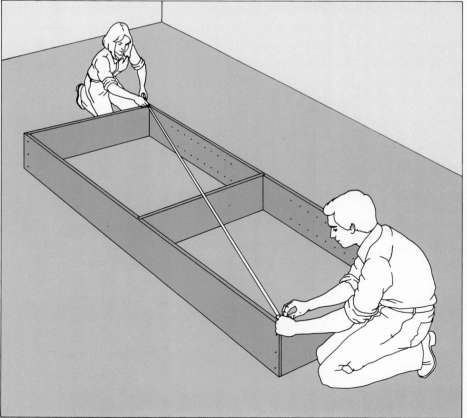

Installing the Modules

1 **Preparing the wall.** Remove the shoe molding and baseboard along the planned location for the bookcases; sweep the edge of a straight 6-foot board across the wall and mark any pronounced bumps in the surface. Determine the height of these bumps by holding a carpenter's level against the board, to make sure it is perfectly vertical, and measuring the depth of the gaps between the edge of the board and the low points on the wall. Note your findings on your scale drawing *(page 102)* or on the wall. In installation, the unit base and the hanging bar in each module must be shimmed until they are flush with the highest point in the wall. Mark every wall stud location at the top and bottom of the wall. Extend the top marks out onto the ceiling, far enough to clear the front edge of the modules when they are set in place.

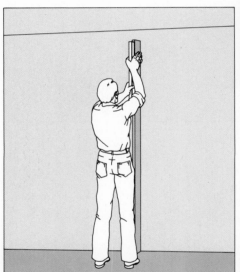

3 **Installing the modules.** With a helper, place the first module at the end of the base. Use the carpenter's level to check vertical alignment and, if necessary, have your helper slide a horizontal shim behind the hanging bar to plumb the module before you screw it in place. Drill two pilot holes through the hanging bar and shim into each stud, one above the other, 2 inches apart, using the stud marks on the ceiling as a guide. Secure with 3-inch flat-head screws.

Butt the second module against the first. Align their front edges, then clamp them together with C clamps, using scraps of wood under the clamp jaws. If necessary, shim the second module before you screw it to the studs. Drill pilot holes for two 1 1/4-inch wood screws 1 inch in from the edge at the top and bottom of the adjoining standards and below the stationary shelf, and screw the modules together.

2 **Making the common base.** Using a continuous strip of plywood or lumber, cut to the height of the room's baseboards, assemble a common base that will support all the modules. Cut the front and back rails to the planned total length of the bookcase less 1 inch; cut the endpieces and the interior braces—known as spreaders—to the width of the standards minus the combined thickness of the front and the back rails. Set the four framing pieces on edge, forming a rectangle, and butt-join each corner with three sixpenny finishing nails driven through the rails. Nail the spreaders inside the frame, at intervals of 2 feet.

Move the base into position and, if necessary, shim it out from the wall at the studs to the distance that you determined in Step 1. Level the base by tapping shims under its corners as necessary, as well as into any gaps beneath the spreaders. Then fasten the base to the wall by driving two eightpenny nails into each stud in the wall behind, through the back rail and the shims. Use sixpenny finishing nails to toenail through the spreaders and the shims into the floor. If the ends of any shims protrude beyond the base, use a chisel to notch them; then break them off flush with the bookcase by pulling up firmly on the protruding ends.

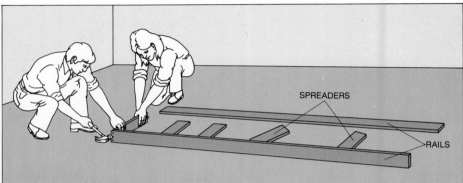

SPREADERS

RAILS

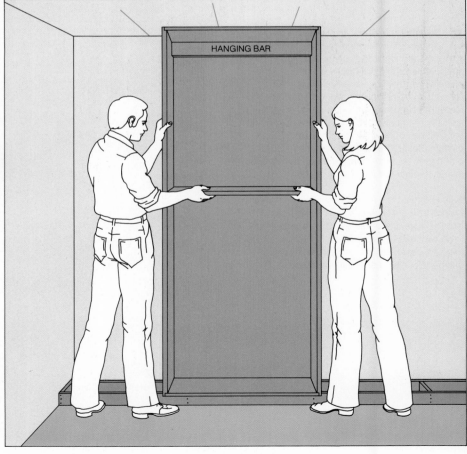

HANGING BAR

4 **Attaching the facings.** Using solid lumber, cut a fascia board to span the top of all the modules, a rail to span the bottom, and vertical stiles—as wide as the combined thickness of two adjoining standards—to cover up the front edges. The bottom rail can be one long board or several boards butted together. First install the fascia board, aligning its top edge with the top edges of the modules. Secure it with sixpenny finishing nails every 10 inches, setting the nails.

Next attach vertical stiles, cut to fit between the bottom edge of the fascia board and the top edge of the module bottoms. At the two ends of the wall, align the outside edges of the stiles with the outside edges of the standards, allowing the inside edges to lap over the shelves. Cut horizontal facings to fit between the vertical stiles at each stationary shelf, and nail these facings to the front edge of each shelf. Finally nail on a bottom rail, flush with the bottoms of the stiles.

Cover the nailheads with wood putty, and paint or stain the facings to match the modules. To cover any gaps between the ceiling and the fascia board, install a cornice molding, mitering joints if the bookcase covers more than one wall. Nail shoe molding at the base of the bottom rail. If one end of the library wall will be exposed, conceal the back edge of the end module with a length of quarter-round molding.

FASCIA BOARD

STILES

5 **Trimming the shelf edges.** Conceal the front edges of plywood shelves either with 1/4-by-3/4-inch pine edging strips *(above, left)* or with veneer tape *(above, right)*.

To attach the edging strips, clamp the shelf in a woodworking vise and cut a section of edging to match. Spread yellow glue on the shelf edge and on one face of the strip. Press the surfaces together and secure them at 8-inch intervals with 1 1/2-

inch finishing nails, setting the nails. Cover the nailheads with wood putty, and finish to match the shelf.

To use veneer tape, cut a strip of tape 1 inch longer than the shelf. One type is simply adhered according to directions, using a hot iron. To apply the other type, spread contact cement on the shelf edge and allow it to soak in. Add a second coat and at the same time spread cement on the back of the

tape. Place three or four small wooden dowels on the shelf edge—to keep the glued sides from sticking—then carefully line up the tape with the shelf edge. Working from the center outward, press the tape onto the edge, removing dowels as you go. Roll the tape smooth with a larger dowel, then rub the dowel over the corners of the shelf to crease the excess tape, and cut off the excess with a razor blade. Sand the tape edges with 120-grit sandpaper, blending them into the edges of the shelf.

Opening the Floor for a New Stairway

If you can reach your basement only through an exterior door, if valuable attic storage space is accessible only by balancing on a chair, if you must tiptoe through an adjoining bedroom to get to an upstairs study—you know you need a stairway. The first step is to create an access hole in the upper floor—a stair opening with new framing to do the work of the structural members you cut out.

Since the addition of new stairs changes the layout of two floors, framing the opening requires forethought. Try to locate the stairs so that existing walls will not have to be removed or shifted to accommodate the new construction; most stairs, for instance, need clearance of at least 3 feet between the top or bottom tread and a facing wall in order to provide turning space for entering or leaving the stairs. Also try to position the new stairs to avoid interference with plumbing lines, electrical wiring and heating ducts. And if you can plan the stairs so the longer sides of the opening run parallel to the joists, as shown, below, you will simplify the framing.

Consult local building codes, which often specify minimum dimensions for clear passageway and headroom—factors that determine the minimum width and length of a stair opening. Some codes stipulate that main stairs provide an opening at least 32 inches wide between the handrails—stairs with two handrails, each occupying 3 1/2 inches, would need an opening at least 39 inches wide. The opening must be even wider if its sides are finished with wood or wallboard.

The length of a stair opening also is governed by practical considerations. A conventional stair opening need only be long enough to provide adequate clearance overhead. A minimum of 76 inches is required by most codes for basement stairs and 80 inches for main stairs. Remember that the code requirement is a minimum. Greater clearance is advantageous—to accommodate tall people and to simplify the job of moving furniture.

How the opening is measured and marked depends on the type of stairway to be installed. For most types, follow the procedure for a cleat basement stairway *(page 116)*; the instructions for a spiral stairway and a disappearing stairway are given on pages 112-115. However, openings for all types of stairs are cut and reinforced in essentially the same way, following the basic techniques illustrated here for a basement stairway.

Cutting a stair opening requires the removal of some finish flooring, subflooring, joists and—for all but unfinished basements, shown here to simplify illustrations—sections of finished ceiling. Careful shoring is particularly important for an opening that runs perpendicular to joists. In this case, as many as six joists may have to be cut for a conventional stair, and posts or walls erected underneath as permanent supports for the uncut portions, called tail joists.

For a spiral stairway the opening must be finished before stair installation; in most other cases, finish work is done after installation. Use scraps of ceiling material to patch gaps around the stair opening. Special moldings called landing nosing, available from stairway manufacturers and at lumber-supply stores, can be installed around the upper edges of the opening if a balustrade will be installed *(page 123)*. Otherwise, hide the exposed edges of plaster, plywood and finish flooring with decorative moldings.

Anatomy of a stair opening. For most openings parallel to joists, cut portions of two joists and fasten the cut ends, or tail joists, with joist hangers to doubled 2-by-10 headers. The header hangers are nailed to "trimmer joists" on the sides of the opening. On the right side of this example the trimmers consist of a new joist fastened to an existing one; on the left, two new trimmer joists have been installed between existing floor joists to narrow the width of the opening to the dimensions required for the stairway.

An opening across joists is made similarly but should run along a bearing wall that supports the trimmer joists. An opening along a foundation wall requires special techniques *(page 111)*.

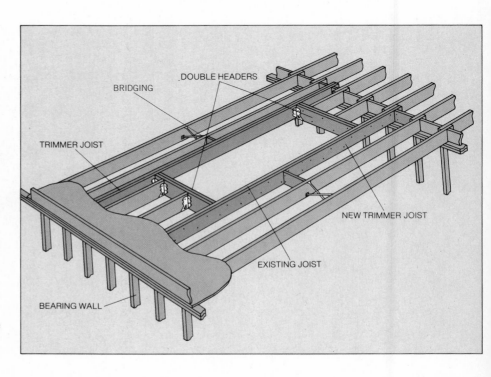

1 **Supporting the floor.** Shoring must be erected, using straight 4-by-4s for bottom plates, top plates and posts. First mark the opening of the subfloor underside, locating it as described on page 117, Step 2, for most stairways and on page 112 for disappearing stairways and spiral stairways. Double joists on each side of the proposed hole *(page 111)* or triple them if they are to bear the weight of a partition wall above. Install the shoring beyond each end of the opening *(below)*, inserting wedge-shaped shim shingles under each joist *(inset)* from both sides of the top plate. Make sure the posts are perfectly plumb—if necessary, tap them into position with a hammer—then hammer the wedges tightly in.

TRIMMER JOIST (2 × 10)

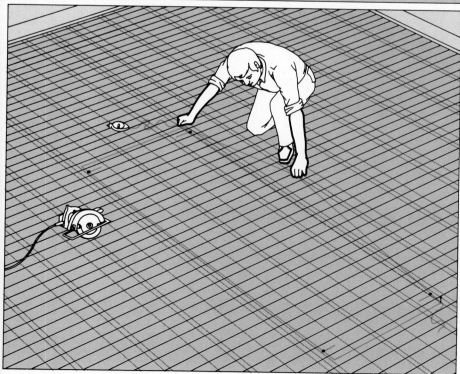

2 **Cutting the opening.** On the upper floor, locate the holes at the corners of the opening of the planned stair, extend the length of the opening 3 inches beyond each end to allow for the thickness of the double headers *(page 110, Step 5)*, and snap four chalk lines to mark out the extended opening. Saw through finish floor and subfloor along the two sides of the opening that are at right angles to the floorboards. Pry up the cut boards using a pry bar. Then, using a circular saw, cut along the two sides parallel to the floorboards.

3 **Removing the subfloor.** To loosen the subfloor from the joists, pound upward with a 2-by-4 along the sides of each joist under the sawed section. Use a pry bar from above to pull the loosened nails.

4 **Cutting the joists.** Hand-saw the joists flush with the opening while a helper supports each joist from underneath to prevent it from pinching the saw as you cut. The cut joists can then be used to make the double headers required to complete the framing *(diagram, page 108)*; cut two lengths to fit between the trimmer joists at each end of the opening and fasten them together with tenpenny nails in a W pattern.

5 **Installing the headers.** Nail 3-inch joist hangers to each end of a double header and butt the header side against the ends of the cut, or tail, joists, bringing its top edge level with the top of the trimmers and tail joists. Then nail the joist hangers to the trimmer joists with framing anchor nails; be sure to use all nail holes in the hangers. Slip 1 1/2-inch joist hangers onto the tail joists from below and nail them to the tail joists and the headers. Then install the other double header in the same way.

Doubling a Joist

Attaching the new joist. Remove the bridging, then use a telescoping house jack to raise the floor 1/4 inch above level. Have a helper hold the new joist tight against both the old one and the subfloor. Then fasten the new and old joists together every 12 to 16 inches, as shown, using 16-penny nails. Clinch the nails—that is, hammer the protruding points flat—and install new bridging. Finally, the shoring can be removed.

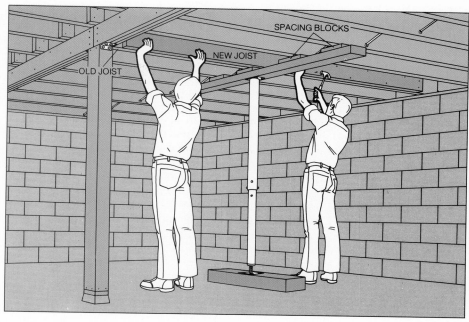

An Opening Next to a Foundation Wall

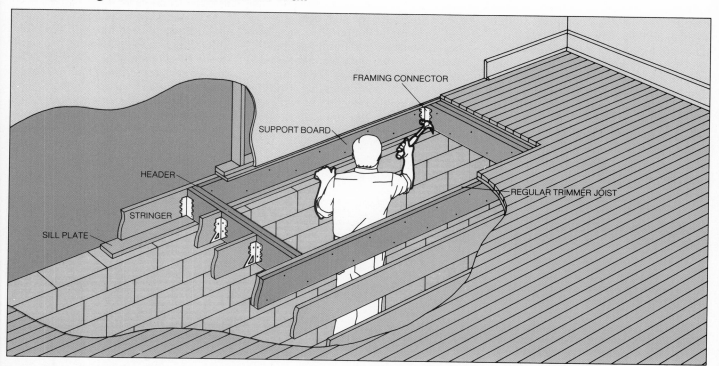

Setting the headers on the wall. If you are installing a basement stair alongside a masonry wall, add a support board to the stringer atop the wall to make one of your trimmer joists. First pound the headers without joist hangers against the regular trimmer, the cut tail joists and the stringer trimmer. Fasten the headers to the regular trimmer and tail joists as in Step 5, opposite. Use metal framing connectors to fasten the headers to the stringer joist and support board. The stairway opening is ready for stairs. The shoring can be removed.

Two Spacesavers—Disappearing and Spiral Stairs

Not every home has enough space for a full flight of stairs to an attic or basement, or an additional flight between main floors. But even the most cramped floor plans can accommodate the two stairways shown below and at right and on pages 114-115. A disappearing stair pulls down from a ceiling to provide access to attic storage space, then folds back into the attic when not in use. A spiral stairway not only adds style and beauty to any room, but also takes 70 percent less space than a regular stairway.

Disappearing stairs, usually made of unfinished softwoods, are sold as preassembled units by major retail chains and home-improvement centers. Most stairs, like the ones shown below and opposite, close manually into a double or triple fold; the folds are hinged to a wood frame and concealed behind a plywood ceiling panel. More complex models slide up and down on a pulley system or have an electric motor for automatic operation. Spiral stairs—of hardwood, aluminum or steel—are available in kits from several manufacturers, listed in classified directories and dealer catalogues under "Stair builders" and "Iron works."

Both disappearing and spiral stairs require stair-well openings (pages 108-111) made to the dimensions specified by the manufacturers. The folding attic stairs come in standard sizes to fit openings 25 to 30 inches wide and 54 to 60 inches long. If you make the opening parallel to the ceiling joists, you need cut only one joist to accommodate the stair; if you must cross the joists, you may have to cut as many as three framing members. In either situation, frame the opening with doubled joists and headers.

Before ordering a disappearing stair, measure the ceiling height and determine the clearance and attic headroom required for the model you have chosen. Clearance, which is measured horizontally on the floor directly beneath the opening, is the amount of space needed to unfold the stairs. Headroom is the free space needed above the ceiling for the supporting hardware and the handrail.

Ordering a spiral stair requires a few more measurements. First, determine the stair diameter and location best suited to your floor plans. Spiral kits come in a range of widths from 3 to 8 feet, but the minimum width is not recommended—carrying even small items is difficult on a stairway less than 4 feet wide. Find the most comfortable direction of entry and exit to and from the stairway on both floors, and decide whether you prefer a right-hand stair (climbed counterclockwise) or a left-hand one.

When ordering a spiral stairway, you must also specify the exact height of the stair from finished floor to finished floor. To get an accurate measurement, drill a 1/8-inch hole through the upper floor and drop a plumb bob to the floor below.

Draw a sketch to accompany your order, indicating the diameter and height of the stairway, the preferred entry and exit direction on each floor and the location of adjoining walls or other obstructions. The manufacturer will help you determine the number and size of treads for either a full spiral (360°) or a three-quarter turn (270°).

To strengthen the floor the stair will rest on, double the joists beneath the center pole (page 111). If the center pole falls between joists, double the joists on either side and insert doubled wood blocking on 3-inch joist hangers between the doubled joists for reinforcement.

Before you begin the installation, mark the location of each tread on the center pole. Counting the landing as one tread, divide the floor-to-floor height in inches by the number of treads in the kit. For example, a kit that includes 12 treads and a landing and is intended for a total height of 104 inches should have its center pole marked for an 8-inch interval between steps. On a well-designed spiral stair, the rise should not be less than 7 inches or more than 9 inches.

Installing a Disappearing Stair

1 **Attaching the stair.** Follow the manufacturer's instructions. After cutting and framing an opening (pages 108-111) to fit the stair, bolt its frame to joists and headers with 3/8-by-4 1/2-inch bolts. To hold it in place while drilling holes and inserting bolts, shim it level on top of two 2-by-4 braces, which are fastened to the double joists by nails driven through the ceiling and removed after the stair is installed.

2 × 4 BRACE

2 **Cutting the side rails to size.** Pull the stair from the stair box, unfold the middle section and, following the angle of the stair, measure the distances from the front and rear edges of this section to the floor. Mark the side rails of the bottom section with these measurements (be sure not to reverse the distances) and draw cutting lines, indicated here by a broken line, between the marks. Saw along the lines on each side rail and smooth the cuts with sandpaper.

A Stairway with a Twist

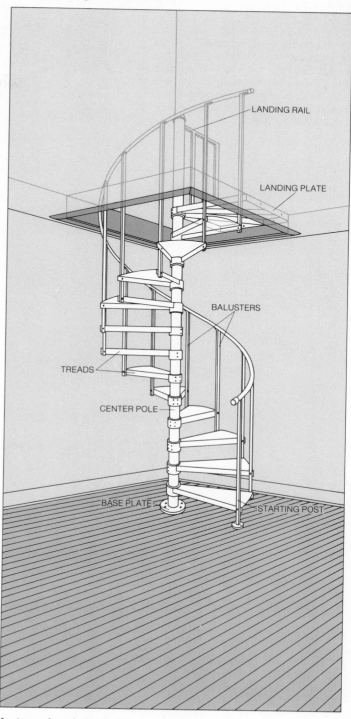

Anatomy of a spiral stair. This typical metal staircase, which comes in a kit, consists of a center pole mounted on a base plate and 12 treads secured to the post and braced at their outer edges by 12 balusters. A landing plate and a landing rail top the stairs; a starting post at the bottom forms the starting point for a curving handrail made either of plastic or metal.

Assembling and Installing a Spiral Stairway

1 **Positioning the center pole.** Follow the manufacturer's instructions. Stretch two strings diagonally from nails driven into opposite corners of the well hole. Drop a plumb line from the intersection of the strings to the floor below and then mark the spot where the plumb bob touches the floor.

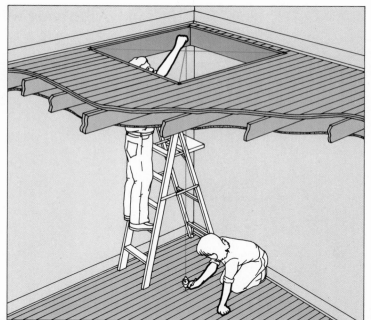

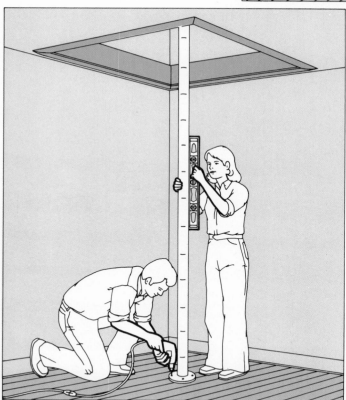

2 **Securing the pole.** Stand the center pole on the floor mark—be sure it is centered and plumb—and using the predrilled holes in the base plate as a guide, drill pilot holes into the subflooring for the lag bolts provided with the kit. On a concrete floor, drill the holes with a masonry boring bit and insert expansion anchors for the lag bolts. Then slide all the treads, face-up, to the bottom of the center pole.

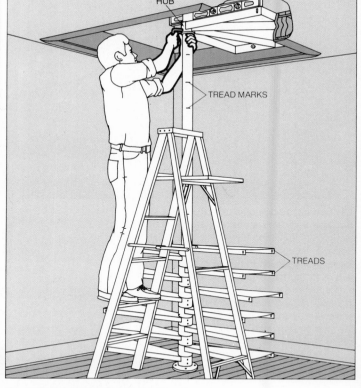

3 **Installing the landing plate.** Align the landing plate with the top tread mark and, while a helper levels the plate, insert the four setscrews into the hub and tighten them loosely against the center pole. Drill pilot holes through the landing-plate flanges into a joist and header of the hole framing and fasten the landing plate to the framing with lag bolts. Make a final leveling adjustment, then tighten the setscrews.

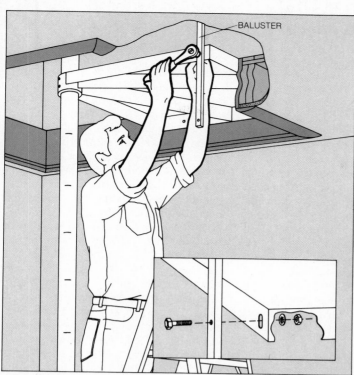

4 **Bolting the top baluster.** Align the upper hole of a baluster with the predrilled hole in the landing-plate flange. Then fasten the baluster to the landing plate with a nut, bolt and washer furnished with the kit *(inset)*.

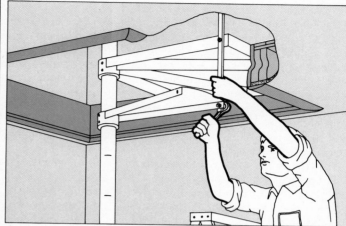

5 **Setting the first tread.** Align the top tread with the top tread mark, and the hole at the back of this tread with the open hole in the installed baluster; then level the tread and bolt it to the baluster, as in Step 4. Tighten the four setscrews in the tread hub. Repeat the procedure down to the floor, fastening each tread to the one below it with the balusters. At the base of the stair, bolt the starting post to the bottom tread and secure the post to the floor with lag bolts, as in Step 2.

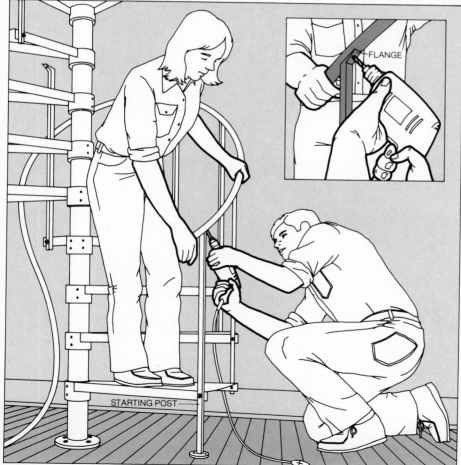

6 **Installing the handrail.** Set the handrail over the starting post and the bottom baluster, leaving a 2-inch overhang beyond the post. Then, using the predrilled flanges on the starting post and baluster as guides *(inset)*, mark and drill pilot holes into the underside of the handrail. Fasten the rail to both the post and baluster with the self-tapping screws that are in the kit. Proceed up the stair, unwinding the rail as you go and marking each hole before drilling; allow a 2-inch overhang beyond the top baluster and saw off the excess rail.

Bolt the landing rail to the landing plate and the center pole, and install the caps that cover the ends of the handrail and the top of the pole.

115

Building Simple Basement Stairways Step by Step

Ancient builders knew the secret of comfortable stairs thousands of years ago, and modern carpenters use the same principles: For comfortable ascent or descent, a precise ratio must be maintained between the distance a person moves forward and the distance he raises or lowers himself. Today builders think in terms of "unit-rise" and "unit-run" to figure the ratio. Unit-rise is the vertical distance between the tops of successive treads; unit-run is the horizontal distance between the back edges of the treads. Adding all the units of rise gives the total rise; the total run is the sum of all the units of run. In any stairs there is one less unit-run than unit-rise because the top tread is actually the upper floor.

For any kind of stairway—the economical basement or patio stairs on page 119 or the finished main stairs shown on pages 120-122—carpenters make sure that the sum of the unit-run and unit-rise falls between 17 and 18 inches. Since stairs should not be as steep as ladders or as shallow as ramps, they keep the unit-rise between 6 and 9 inches. Many building codes go even further. The Federal Housing Authority, for example, requires a unit-run of at least 9 inches and a unit-rise of no more than 8 1/4 inches for most stairs, 9 inches for a basement stair.

Most codes also require nosings—the rounded front edges of stair treads—of 1/2 to 1 1/8 inches on each tread, giving more footroom. Headroom, measured from the finish-ceiling height down to the nose of a tread, is important as well; generally codes require at least 80 inches for most stair wells, or 76 inches for basement stairs.

Two common types of rough stairs are named for the way the treads are attached to support boards. In a cleat stair, the treads rest on small blocks (cleats) fastened to the inside faces of supports called stringers. In a cutout stair, the treads lie on notches cut into supports called carriages. Use 2-by-10s for stringers and 2-by-12s for carriages. Use pressure-treated lumber for all parts of an outdoor stair and for supports of an indoor stair built against an unfinished foundation wall or resting on a concrete floor.

Stringers or carriages are anchored to the stair-well header at the top as well as to the floor at the bottom with framing anchors—steel angle brackets that can be adjusted by bending to hold boards together at any angle. When the lower floor is concrete, a pressure-treated wood kick plate, or small sill, is used instead and the bottoms of the supports are soaked with wood preservative. Stringers or carriages are further anchored by either nailing them to an adjacent wall or resting them on intermediate 2-by-4 posts.

Treads for a stair can be cut from any lumber but you can buy special tread stock, 9 1/2 or 11 1/2 inches wide and rounded on one edge for the nosing. Whatever wood is used, treads should be at least 1 1/16 inches thick for stringers up to 30 inches apart; 1 1/2-inch treads will span up to 36 inches. Add a middle cutout carriage for wider stairs. Risers, the vertically mounted boards that close the spaces between the treads, are usually cut from 1-by-8s or 1-by-10s to be as long as the treads and as wide as the unit-rise.

A carpenter's square, a tool that resembles two rulers joined at a right angle, simplifies laying out stringers or carriages. Placed properly on a board (*Step 3*), the square quickly locates the necessary end cuts and tread positions. But you must be precise—use a sharp pencil.

Handrails, 30 to 34 inches above the tread nosings, are essential along any open portion of a stairway and are advisable along closed portions. For rough stairs, 2-by-3s bolted to the open side of the carriage or stringer serve as posts for 2-by-3 handrails. Screw them to the post and to the inside trimmer joist of the stair opening. Along a wall, use widely available wall rail brackets to support a 2-by-3 or a stock-molded handrail.

Preparing the Supports

1 **Determining the rise and run.** Measure between the upper and lower finish floors, or measure to the subfloor and account for the thickness of unlaid finish floors—8 feet 1 inch total in this example. You can measure by drilling a hole through the stair-well area. Convert the distance to inches (97 in this example), and divide by seven to get the number of risers. Round fractions up for a slightly shallower stair, down for a steeper one. Now divide the number of risers, here 13, into the total rise, 97 inches. The result is 7 6/13, the unit-rise. Since the unit-run—which excludes the nosing width—plus the unit-rise should total 17 to 18 inches, the unit-run can be between 9 7/13 and 10 7/13 inches. Choose a middle distance, here 10 inches; the total run will be 12 times 10 inches—120 inches. (There is always one less unit-run than there are unit-rises.) Mark the lower floor directly beneath the place where the stringers' upper ends will rest. Measure the total run and mark the floor.

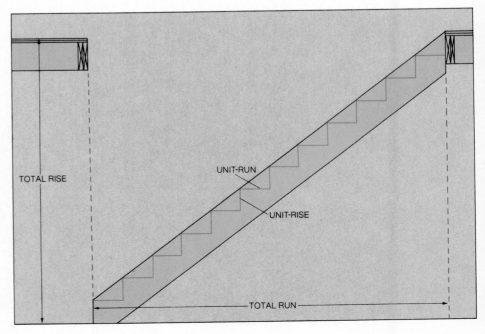

2 **Marking the stair opening.** Draw the first treads and risers on the wall, or, in the case of a stair that is in the middle of a room, on the floor. Measure down from the joists or ceiling to the nose of the treads beginning at the bottom. When you reach a tread mark at which the distance from ceiling to tread nose is less than minimum head room, go to the next lower tread mark and mark the ceiling above with a plumb bob—this point indicates one end of the stair opening.

3 **Marking the floor line.** Place a carpenter's square so that the unit-run measurement, read on one outer scale, intersects the edge of the support board—using a 2-by-10 for a stringer, a 2-by-12 for a carriage. Shift the square until the unit rise, read on the outer scale of the other leg, intersects the same edge of the board. Here the unit rise is 7 6/13, the unit-run is 10 inches. Draw a line around the outer edges of the square. Then extend the unit-run line across the board to mark the floor line.

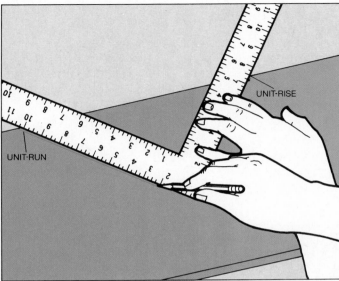

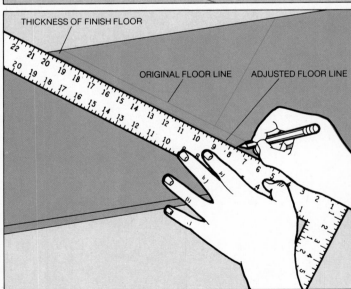

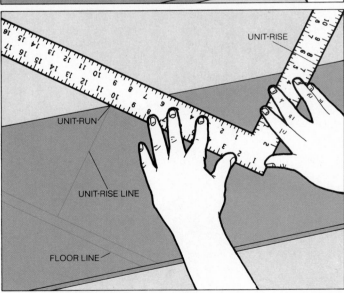

4 **Adjusting for a finish floor.** To allow for the thickness of an unlaid finish floor with a cleat stair, shift the measured floor line toward the end of the board a distance equal to the thickness of the finish floor. Position the cleats to account for the thickness of the treads. To make a similar adjustment in a cutout stair, move the floor line down the thickness of the finish floor, then up the thickness of a tread; the result usually is an adjusted floor line slightly above the original.

5 **Marking the tread lines.** Slide the carpenter's square up the support so that the unit-run measurement, read on one outer scale, is at the end of the first unit-rise line. Make certain the unit-rise measurement, read off the other leg of the square, is also at the edge of the board, then mark around the square. The unit-run line is the tread line. Repeat, moving the carpenter's square up the board to mark unit-run and unit-rise lines for each step.

6 **Marking the header line.** Mark the last unit-run, or tread, and unit-rise lines as on page 117, Step 5. Then extend the unit-rise line down to the lower edge of the board to mark the line where the support will meet the stair-opening header. Check that the units of rise are of equal size, differing by no more than 1/4 inch, then cut the board along the adjusted floor line, first unit-rise line and header line. If the stair is to be set over a kick plate on a concrete floor, cut a 1 1/2-by-3 1/2-inch notch in the bottom front of the board for the kick plate *(opposite, Step 2)*.

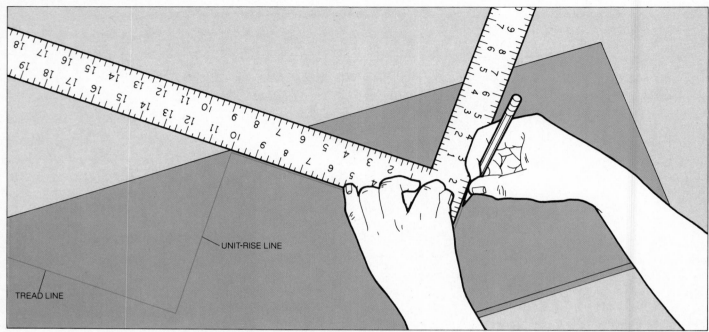

UNIT-RISE LINE

TREAD LINE

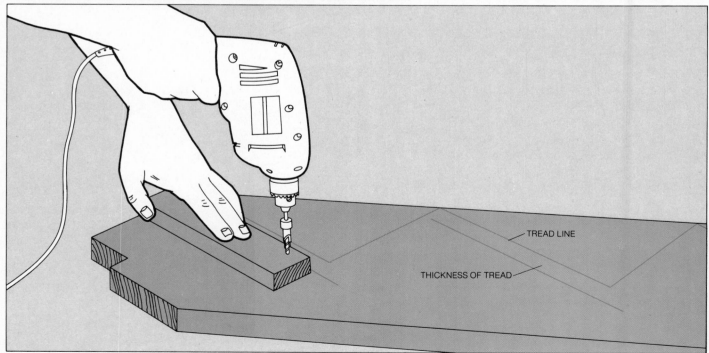

TREAD LINE

THICKNESS OF TREAD

7 **Finishing the support.** For a cleat stair *(above)*, draw a line below each tread line at a distance equal to the thickness of a tread. Place the top of a 1-by-3 cleat, cut to the length of the unit-run, along each new line except in the top one, and use a counterbore bit for drilling pilot holes. Use five screws to secure each cleat. For a cut stair, saw along the tread lines and unit-rise lines; do not cut any deeper into the support board than necessary.

Installing the Supports

1 **Securing a support to the header.** After tacking the top of the support in place against the header and checking to see that the tread lines are level, secure the top of the support with a framing anchor. Bend the end of one leg of the anchor to fit the bottom of the header *(inset)*. Use a center punch to make additional nail holes in a joist hanger if the framing anchor overlaps one at the header. In a cleat stair, fasten the top cleat to the stringer.

2 **Fastening supports to the floor.** For a concrete floor, position a pressure-treated 2-by-4 kick plate under the notches in the support and drill through it to mark the concrete. Then set it aside and use a masonry boring bit to drill holes for three lead anchors. Replace the plate, fasten it with 3/8-by-3-inch lag bolts and washers, and toenail the supports to it. For a wood floor, where a kick plate is not necessary, use a framing anchor to fasten the support to the floor.

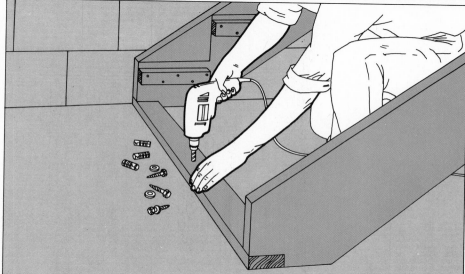

3 **Bracing the supports.** A support running along a wall is fastened to it, using 3/8-by-3-inch lag bolts and lead shields for foundations, tenpenny nails for studs; however, an open stairway requires posts as shown at right. Secure a pressure-treated 2-by-4 plate to the floor beneath the support board with concrete nails or bolts and anchors. Hold a 2-by-4 plumb on the plate, and mark it for an angle cut along the lower edge of the support. Cut the 2-by-4 along this line, then toenail it to the plate and stringer or carriage.

For a cleat stair, cut treads to fit between the stringers, then nail them in place, angling the nails so that they enter the stringer as well as the cleats. For a cutout stair, nail risers to the carriages first. Then butt the treads against the risers and nail them to the carriages.

SUPPORT POST

PLATE

A Craftsman's Pride: The Prefab Stair and Railing

To replace a main stairway or make an attractive passageway to a newly finished basement or attic, the best solution is often a factory-built stairway with a balustrade that you can assemble from stock parts.

The stair builder will make a stairway to your specifications and deliver the finished unit to your home. You must prepare the opening in the upper floor *(pages 108-111)* and, with helpers, secure the stair to the opening and to the adjoining walls. With the stair in place, you can fit the balustrade to it. This is the trickiest, most time-consuming part of the job: The intricate joinery of a balustrade requires not only skill in the use of woodworking tools but also the patience and perfectionism of a fine craftsman.

Ordering the stair correctly is the crucial first step. Some builders have representatives who will help you to choose a stair and write the specifications for it, though it is your responsibility to be sure the installation will comply with local building codes. If you order the stair yourself, you must tell the manufacturer the total rise, total run and width of the stair. Measure the rise and estimate the run as shown on page 116, Step 1; the total run of the stair you receive may be slightly longer or shorter than your estimate, but your calculation will tell you roughly where the bottom of

Installing the Stairway

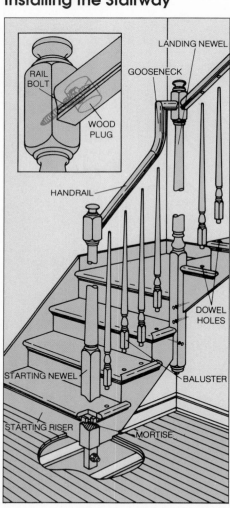

The parts of a balustrade. The structure of a stairway balustrade goes beyond that of hammer-and-saw carpentry to the stronger and more elegant techniques of cabinetwork. In addition to a generous use of finish hardwood, the balustrade uses ingenious joinery—with mortised newels, rail bolts *(inset)* and dowels.

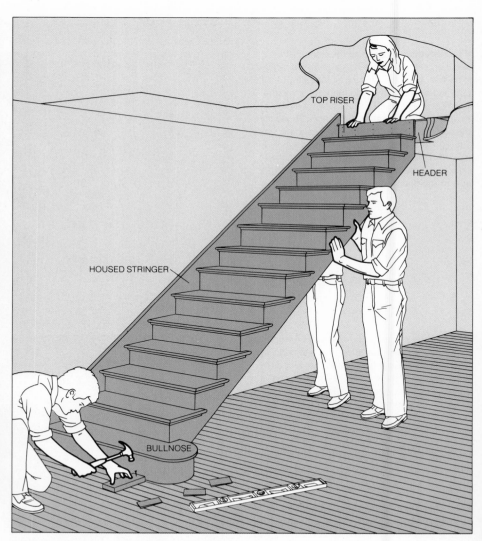

1 **Fitting the stair in the opening.** Follow the manufacturer's instructions. Station a helper on the upper floor and walk the stair into position, with the housed stringer flush to the wall and the top riser against the double header; to hold the stair in position, temporarily nail two 2-by-4 blocks to the flooring in front of the bullnose starting tread. Use shims as necessary beneath the bullnose until the treads are level and the top of the top riser is exactly flush with the surface of the subflooring on the upper floor.

the stair will fall. Minimum stair widths are set by local codes *(page 108)*.

The stair builder must also know whether the stair will be fully or partially open, and whether the open side will be supported by a wall *(opposite)*. A free-standing open side must be strengthened; any open side must have a balustrade. For a stair enclosed by walls, screw handrails to the wall framing. To install a balustrade, simplify the job by using a bullnose starting tread; the starting newel will fit into a hole drilled in the bullnose without the intricate cuts required for a landing newel. From the landing newel, a landing rail must run along all the unwalled sides of the stair opening.

Along with the stairway, the builder will provide a landing tread for the transition between the top of the stair and the finish floor. The parts of a balustrade—the gooseneck, volute, newel posts, balusters and handrail—must be ordered

separately. You will also need finish moldings to conceal joints and shims, rail bolts *(page 120)* to join railing sections to each other and to a landing newel, and hardwood plugs to fill access holes for rail bolts.

The type of gooseneck you order depends on your local building code. A gooseneck leads a stair rail, usually set 30 inches above the tread nosing, up to the height of the landing rail, either 34 or 42 inches above the finish floor. If your code calls for a 34-inch landing rail, use a "one-riser" gooseneck as shown on page 124; the higher rail requires a longer "two-riser" gooseneck.

A spiral volute, supported by a starting newel and several balusters, is a common treatment for the lower end of the handrail; alternatives include a turn in the rail or a straight section called a starting easing. Some builders attach these fittings to the handrail at the mill; goosenecks are fitted on site.

To get a good fit for the balustrade, you should rent, borrow or buy several specialized woodworking tools. The hole for the starting newel calls for a heavy-duty 1/2-inch drill and a bit called a ship auger, 14 inches long and 1 1/2 inches in diameter. A steel square and a pitch block—a wood triangle cut to the dimensions of a tread and riser *(page 124)*—are necessary to calculate the gooseneck dimensions; a precision miter box is essential for making accurate cuts on the rail and gooseneck. A router will make the landing-newel cuts faster and more accurately than a chisel, and a 4-foot level will help you to plumb balusters and newels and adjust handrail heights.

Finally, a caution on woodworking technique: to avoid splitting hardwood parts, always drill a pilot hole before driving a nail or screw. In some cases, as with the riser fastening in Step 2 *(below)*, pilot holes should be drilled before positioning the stair *(Step 1)*.

2 **Fastening the riser to the header.** If the header is plumb and perpendicular to the adjoining wall, fasten the top riser directly to the header with three horizontal rows of 16-penny finishing nails, spaced 10 inches apart horizontally and 2 inches vertically. If the header is out of plumb or square, tap wood shims between riser and header before nailing, using a combination square to be sure the shimming does not force the riser out of plumb with the tread beneath.

3 **Securing the housed stringer.** Locate and mark the positions of the wall studs behind the housed stringer and fasten the underside of the stringer to the center of each stud with two 16-penny common nails.

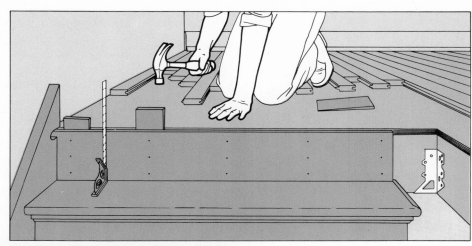

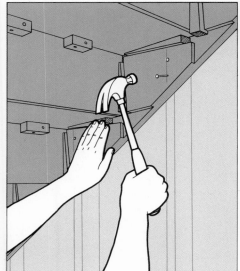

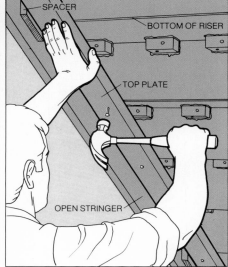

4 **Building a supporting wall.** Under the stair, tack 1/2-inch plywood spacers to the inner face of the open stringer at 3-foot intervals, then nail a 2-by-4 top plate to the risers with eightpenny nails; position the end of the plate on the floor and its outer edge flush to the spacers. Install a sole plate on the finish floor directly underneath, and complete the framing of the wall with studs between the sole plate and top plate. Remove the spacers and install wallboard *(pages 80-86)*, concealing the tops of the wallboard panels behind the stringer.

121

Assembling the Balustrade

1 Marking the bullnose. Cut out the printed paper template supplied by the manufacturer, place it on the bullnose tread with its cutout corner fitted to the corner of the riser and push the tip of an awl through the template and into the tread to mark the centers of the newel post and the bullnose balusters.

2 A hole for the starting newel post. Drill a vertical hole through the bullnose tread and shelves, using a rented heavy-duty 1/2-inch electric drill and a 1 1/2-inch auger. To make sure that the hole is perfectly plumb, have helpers sight the bit against two combination squares *(below)*; drill in short bursts, adjusting the angle of the bit between bursts according to your helpers' instructions. Slide the dowel into the hole until the base of the newel rests on the tread. If the dowel is too long, cut it back; if it is too thick, then sand it down until it fits easily. If the newel is still not perfectly plumb, enlarge one side of the hole with the auger and shim.

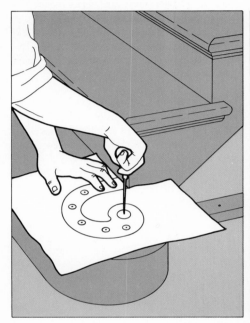

3 Installing the newel. Apply about a pint of woodworker's glue to the drilled hole and the dowel, reset the newel into the bullnose, and get the newel exactly plumb with a 4-foot level while a helper nails braces to newel, stringer and the nosing of the second tread. Allow 24 hours for the glue to set. If you have easy access to the underside of the subfloor, drive a lag bolt with washer up through the subfloor into the end of the dowel.

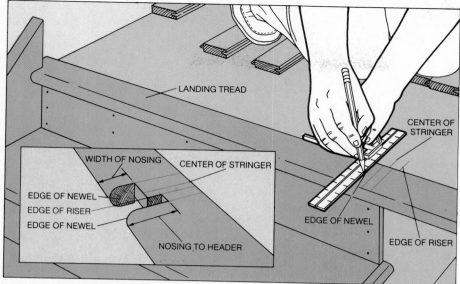

4 **Notching the landing tread.** Using a combination square, mark the landing subfloor in line with the outer edge of the top riser and the center of the open stringer, then slide the end of the landing tread into the matching notch in the housed stringer, set the tread in place on the top riser and transfer the marks to the tread. Across the tread, draw additional lines, centered on the stringer mark, to indicate the edges of the landing newel.

Measure the width of the tread nosing and the distance from the front of the nosing to the header; transfer both of the measurements to the face of the tread *(inset)*. Shade the area that must be notched, cut it out and then fasten the landing tread to the subfloor and headers with eightpenny finishing nails.

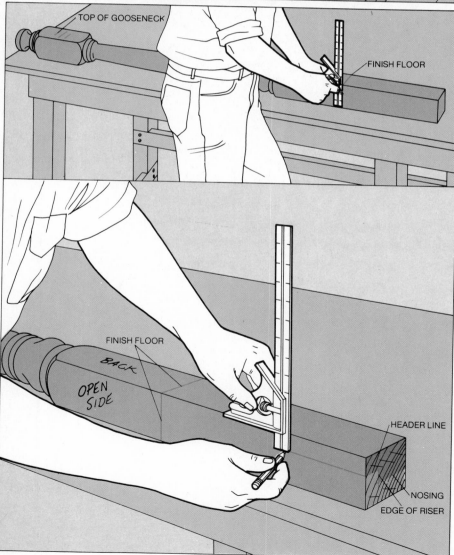

5 **Laying out the landing newel.** Using the dimensions provided by the manufacturer, mark a finish-floor line across the back and sides of the newel *(top)*. To locate this mark, measure down the newel from the point where the top of the gooseneck will meet the front of the newel to the point where the finish floor will meet the newel. On the newel bottom *(lower picture)*, measuring from the front, mark lines for the width of the landing tread nosing *(Step 4)* and also for the distance from nosing to header; then, measuring from the open side of the newel, mark a line for the edge of the riser *(Step 4)*.

Use a combination square to extend the nosing and header lines up the sides of the newel to the finish-floor line and, with a router or a chisel and mallet, cut away the wood in the shaded area from the bottom of the newel to the finish-floor line. Smooth the cuts with a plane.

6 **Fitting the newel to the stringer.** On the stairway, measure the distance from the top of the landing tread to the tread below it and, measuring down the newel from the finish-floor line *(Step 5)*, mark a tread line at this distance on all sides of the newel. Extend the riser line up the front of the newel to the tread line and shade the area that must be removed to allow the newel to fit over the stringer. Cut away the wood in the shaded area, then set the newel in position on the tread below the landing, pushing it tight against the riser; mark the return nosing flush with the front of the newel. Cut the return molding and nosing along the line you have just drawn so that the newel can lie flush against the stringer *(inset)*. Set the post in place to check whether it fits properly; plane the cuts until the post rests snugly against the riser, stringer and cutouts in the landing tread. Then securely fasten the post to the header and stringer with countersunk wood screws or lag bolts.

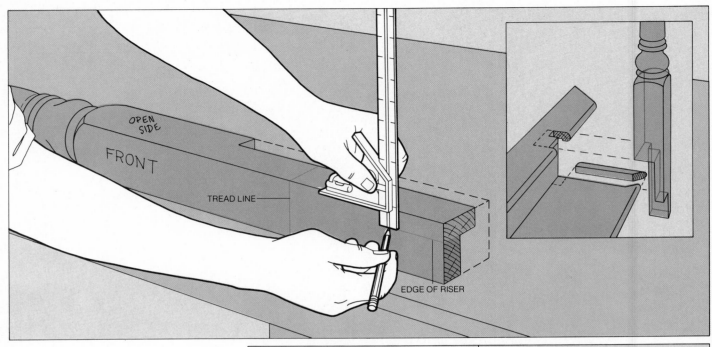

7 **Cutting the bottom of the gooseneck.** Prepare a pitch block—a right-angle triangle of wood with sides that are equal to the unit-rise and unit-run of the stairs—and have your helper hold a carpenter's square upright with the block in its corner, run side down. Set the vertical part of the gooseneck tight against the tongue of the carpenter's square and mark the point where the pitch block touches the gooseneck *(right)*.

Set the rise side of the pitch block on a workbench alongside the carpenter's square, hold the gooseneck against the tongue and, using the block as a straightedge, extend the mark into a line across the railing *(far right)*. Cut the gooseneck along this line in an adjustable miter box.

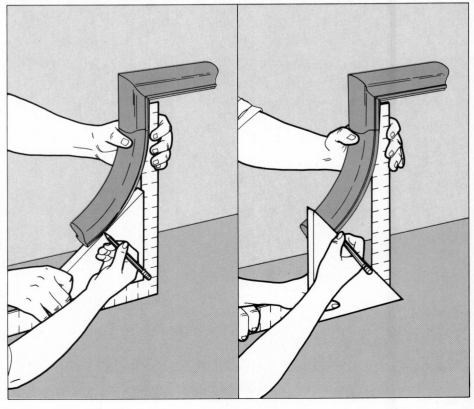

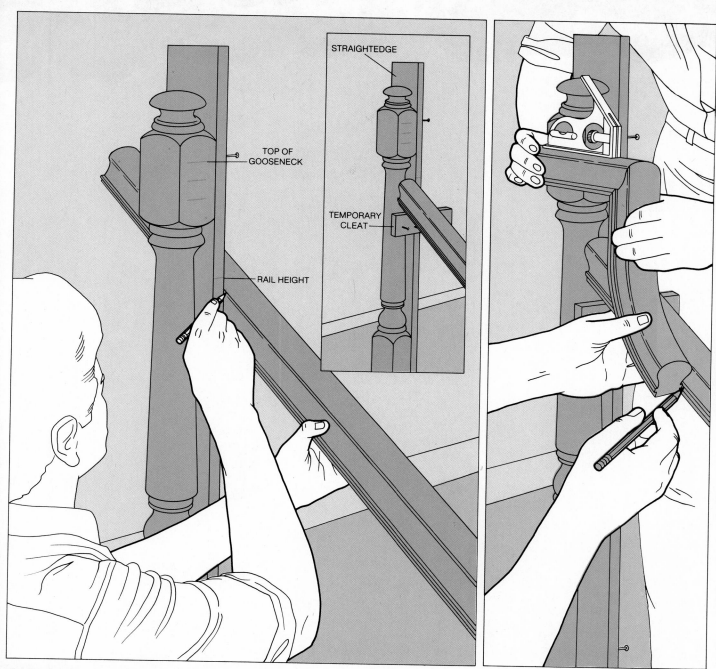

STRAIGHTEDGE

TOP OF
GOOSENECK

TEMPORARY
CLEAT

RAIL HEIGHT

8 **Bracing the rail in place.** Nail a straight piece of 1-inch lumber to the side of the landing newel, with its front edge flush to the front of the newel. Measuring up from the landing-tread nosing, mark the straightedge at the rail height specified by your building code. Set the volute onto the dowel of the starting newel and, holding the upper end of the rail along the landing newel at the marked height and using the straightedge as a guide, draw a vertical line across the rail. Cut the rail along this line and with a combination square, align its top with the mark on the straightedge *(inset)*. Position the rail with a temporary cleat nailed to the straightedge and newel.

9 **Cutting the rail.** Have a helper hold the gooseneck alongside the landing newel at the correct height above the finish floor *(Step 5)*, with about 6 inches of the horizontal gooseneck section in front of the newel. Level the horizontal section with a combination square *(above)* or torpedo level, then mark where the bottom of the gooseneck intersects the rail. Use a miter box to cut the rail at the mark at a 90° angle.

10 **Installing the rail bolt.** Clamp the gooseneck in a vise, with the end of the curved section vertical, and drill a horizontal 1/4-inch hole in this end; locate the hole 15/16 of an inch above the bottom of the gooseneck and drill it 1 7/8 inches deep. Drill a matching 3/8-inch hole in the rail *(inset)*. Mark the center of the railing bottom 1 3/8 inches from the end and drill a hole at this point 1 inch wide and 1 1/2 inches deep.

Screw the lag-threaded end of a rail bolt into the gooseneck; to tighten it, run the nut on the bolt to the end of its thread and turn it with an adjustable wrench. Remove the nut and washer and insert the other end of the bolt into the hole at the end of the rail. Run the washer and nut onto the bolt through the hole in the rail bottom and tighten the nut with a nail set.

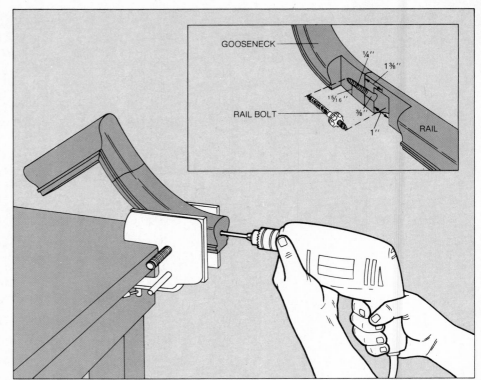

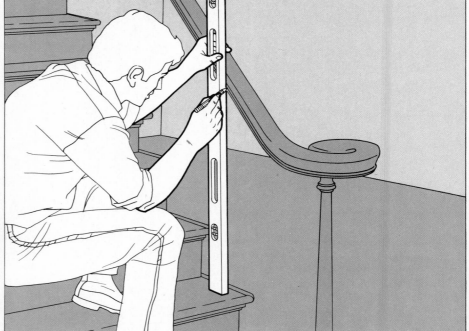

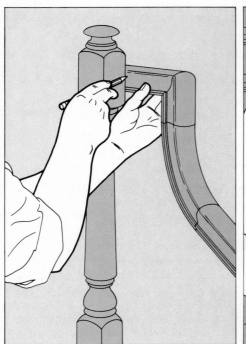

11 **Fitting the gooseneck to the newel.** Set the volute on the starting newel, hold the gooseneck alongside the landing newel at the correct height, and mark the point where the gooseneck meets the newel. Unbolt the gooseneck and cut it at this mark, then refasten the gooseneck and cut its end back in 1/8-inch increments until it fits snugly against the newel. Fasten the gooseneck to the newel with a rail bolt.

12 **Locating the balusters.** On each tread above the starting tread, mark the center line of the stringer and locate points for two baluster holes along this line, with the front of the first baluster directly over the front of the riser below the tread and the second halfway between the back of the first baluster and the front of the riser above the tread. Using a 4-foot level, plumb up from the marks to make correspond-

ing marks on the railing side, then use a combination square to transfer the marks to the underside. Mark the underside of the volute with the paper template supplied by the stairbuilder *(Step 1)*.

Using spade bits matched to the dowels at the bottom and top of the balusters, drill holes 3/4 inch deep into the treads, and 1 inch deep into the volute and railing.

13 **Cutting the balusters to size.** Using a folding rule with a brass extension, measure the distances from the treads to the tops of the holes in the railing and cut the balusters to these lengths. Number the balusters, counting down from the top of the stairway. Loosen the bolt that fastens the gooseneck to the newel and, working down the stairway, try each baluster in place. If the top does not fit the hole in the rail, sand it down; if the baluster forces the rail out of line, shorten it 1/8 inch at a time.

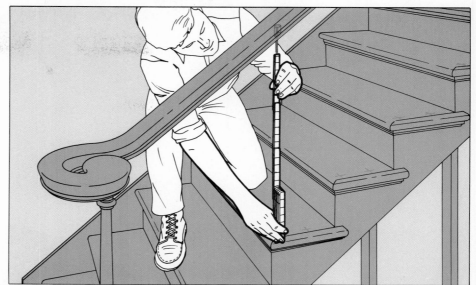

14 **Installing the balustrade.** Starting at the top of the stairway, lightly smear the top and bottom of each baluster with glue, apply a generous quantity to the hole in the tread, and insert balusters in the holes while a helper raises the railing at the volute. Work downward in groups of about six balusters at a time; after inserting each group, set a 2-by-4 block on the railing above it and strike it several times with a mallet. At the bottom of the stairway, coat the dowel on the starting newel with glue, install all of the balusters in the bullnose, and drive the volute down onto the newel and balusters. Wipe up any excess glue immediately with a damp cloth.

Glue the joints on both sides of the gooseneck, tighten the rail bolts and toenail the joints together. Plug the holes beneath the rail bolts with cross-grained wood dowels.

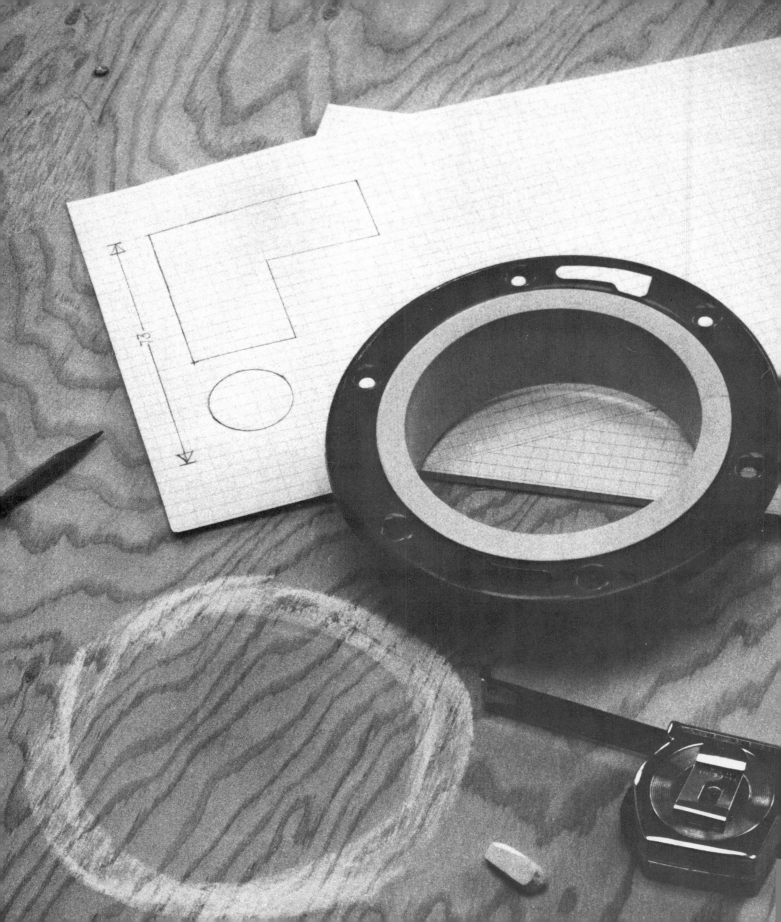

2 RENOVATING KITCHENS AND BATHROOMS

Getting Started Smoothly

Creating a new kitchen or bathroom can be less formidable than it seems at first. The trick is to cut the job down. It may call for no more than the removal and replacement of old fixtures or, at a more ambitious level, the installation of whole new walls *(pages 77-86)*. In any case, the old appliances and fixtures are removed *(opposite page)* and either saved for reuse or discarded.

Before you begin working, you must comply with local government regulations by applying for permits and planning to meet local code requirements. Four different codes affect work on a kitchen or bathroom:

• **The building code** regulates structural changes. Whether building an addition or simply adding a new window or blocking off an old door, in most communities you must take out a building permit to remove a loadbearing wall or to tamper with an exterior wall. Some codes also require permits for less complex work, such as adding or removing a nonbearing partition. To apply for a building permit, you must submit a plan of the work to the local building department. The plan need not be elaborate, but it should be drawn to scale and indicate the location and sizes of existing doors and windows, the proposed locations of new walls, doors or windows, and whether or not any wall you intend to remove is loadbearing.

• **The mechanical code** regulates work on heating and cooling systems, such as extending ductwork and removing radiators. Mechanical codes may also govern the installation of vent fans and range hoods and the installation and relocation of such appliances as gas ranges. For a mechanical permit, you also need a plan indicating the details of furnace, air conditioner and distribution system.

• **The plumbing code** and **electrical code** regulate plumbing and electrical work, and may require plans showing both the existing installation and the proposed changes.

Applying for permits can be time consuming, so investigate your community's regulations well before you begin work. Copies of codes are available through the local building department or at public libraries. Find out what plans are required and how many copies of each you will need to submit (some inspectors require four sets). Also check on how inspections are handled in your area. Generally, two inspections are needed under each permit. The first takes place after all rough-in work has been done—ducts, wiring and pipes in place but not connected to appliances and fixtures, and walls framed but not closed. After each inspector approves the roughed-in work, you are given permission to finish the walls and hook up appliances and fixtures. Then comes a final inspection of the finished work.

In plumbing renovation, make use of as much existing piping as you can. Where extensions are necessary, choose piping materials that are easy to work with; you do not have to match new plumbing materials to old, for example, because adapters make the transition. The easiest piping material is plastic—light in weight, easily cut with a saw and assembled with solvent cement; it now is almost universally used for drains and vents. (In most areas two types of plastic tubing are accepted for hot and cold supply lines.)

While renovation in most rooms of the house can proceed at a leisurely pace, kitchens and bathrooms require relatively swift transitions to minimize the loss of their important functions. Have everything you need on hand before you begin. Do not rely on promised delivery dates of fixtures and supplies which often must be ordered from the manufacturer—a process that can take months.

Stock up on nails, screws, solvent cement, lead-free plumber's solder and paint and tools, including special tools that must be borrowed or rented. And make sure you have replacement parts: The hacksaw blade always seems to break on a weekend after the building-supply stores close.

When you are ready to begin, save time and effort by working in an area that is as uncluttered as possible. Remove furniture, appliances, fixtures and cabinets wherever practical. Working around them, or removing them piecemeal, not only slows things down but exposes them to unnecessary damage. Place doormats at all entrances and hang sheets in open passageways to keep dust and debris out of the rest of the house; if you will be chipping dusty plaster, wet the sheets for additional protection.

Allot enough time to do the job thoroughly and without haste, and allow for delays. If you plan to have a professional handle tricky parts of the job, be sure that your schedules are coordinated. But keep your own schedule flexible; do not place yourself in a position where everything comes to a standstill while you wait for a worker who arrives late or not at all.

The best way to minimize the temporary loss of a kitchen or bathroom during renovation is to work midday or at night, between the peak-use periods of early morning and late afternoon. You may want to set up a temporary kitchen elsewhere in the house, and if you are doing extensive bathroom work in a home with children, it might be wise to establish protocol for use of a neighbor's facilities.

Using Personal Safety Gear

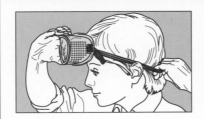

Using eye protection. When chipping tiles, sanding, nailing, sawing, drilling or using chemicals, prevent eye injury by wearing safety goggles. Ensure that any safety goggles you use are approved by the American National Standards Institute (ANSI) or Canadian Standards Association (CSA) and are recommended for the particular hazard. In general, use safety goggles with perforated vent holes for protection from impact injury; with baffled vents for protection from chemical injury; with no vents for extremely dusty work or work using a chemical that emits irritating fumes. Before starting to work, put on the goggles to test their fit; adjust the headstrap if necessary. If the safety goggles are scratched, cracked, pitted or clouded, replace them.

Removing a bathtub. If there is a tile wall around the tub, use a cold chisel and hammer to chip away the tub molding and first course of tile above the tub *(right)* to free the flange. Cut away at least 4 inches of wallboard or plaster above the tub. Remove any fasteners holding the tub flange to the wall studs and remove the tub waste fittings and trap. Then have someone help you pry the tub away from the wall. If it is enclosed by three walls, you may have to cut a hole through an end wall where there are no supply pipes. Lay down some heavy planks and push the tub out through the wall *(below)*.

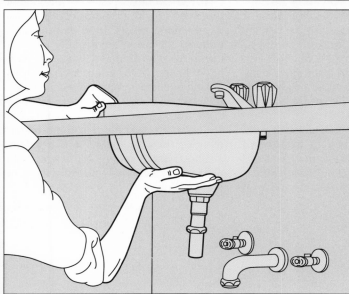

Removing an old sink. Free the sink from its counter by scraping away putty or adhesive, or by unscrewing metal clamps or lug bolts from below. Then lift the sink up and out *(above)*. If it is to be reused, lay it on a pad of newspapers.

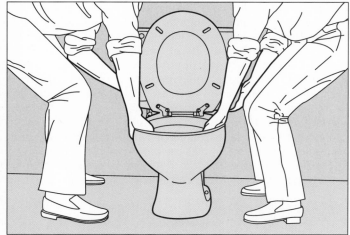

Removing a toilet. If the toilet has a wall-mounted tank, first remove the flush elbow. Otherwise, you and a helper can remove the toilet without taking off its tank. First unbolt the bowl from the floor; if the bolts are impossible to remove, cut through the bolt with a hacksaw. Then, standing over the bowl, twist and rock it to break its seal. With knees bent and back straight, lift the toilet straight up and off the hold-down bolts *(above)*. Let the water from the trap run into a pan. Then gently lay the toilet on its side on a pad of newspapers or an old blanket. Cover the drain hole to prevent loose parts from falling in and to contain sewer gases.

Basing a Kitchen on a Step-Saving Triangle

To prepare two meals—breakfast and dinner—a family cook walks 120 miles a year. As much as a third of this mileage may be waste motion, due to appliances placed not for efficiency but for economy in construction. In an efficient kitchen, three "activity centers" focused at the refrigerator, the sink and the range lie within easy reach of the cook—and according to a study made at Cornell University, better placement of these activity centers can eliminate as much as 40 miles a year from the kitchen marathon.

A kitchen that, whatever its shape and size, is designed for efficient use rather than construction economies, has its major fixtures and appliances in one of the four basic layouts shown on pages 134-135: the U, the L, the corridor and the one-wall. In each layout, the three activity centers make up the three points of a work triangle, and in an efficient kitchen the sides of the triangle add up to no more than 23 feet. Up to a point, the smaller the triangle the greater the efficiency; its minimum size is dictated by the need for working space—each activity center must have a minimum of counter area and storage volume (right and on page 134). Avoid layouts that route household traffic through the work triangle, and allow at least 48 inches between facing base cabinets or appliances—enough space to allow you to stand at an open cabinet, refrigerator or oven while another person edges past.

The sink is the main activity center, accounting for 40 to 46 percent of all kitchen work time. Ideally, it belongs at the center of the work triangle, within 4 to 6 feet of the range and 4 to 7 feet of the refrigerator. Locate the dishwasher within 12 inches of the sink, for convenient loading and the simplest pattern of plumbing connections, but do not set the dishwasher at right angles to the sink—in this arrangement you will have to move away from the sink every time you open the dishwasher door.

A single-bowl sink is adequate for a kitchen with a dishwasher; use a double-bowl model if you plan to wash and rinse dishes by hand. In a double sink, at least one of the bowls should be large enough for a roasting pan—that is, a pan at least 20 inches long.

The range and microwave oven are the cooking and serving center, best located for easy access to the dining area. This is the spot at which most kitchen injuries occur. Avoid an arrangement in which people passing through the kitchen are likely to brush against the range, and never place a range under a window: Grease-laden curtains can blaze up easily, and you must reach across the burners to open and close the window. Wall cabinets over the range should be at least 30 inches above the cook-top surface, and the counter surface next to the range should have heat-resistant areas for hot pots and pans.

In a large kitchen you may want a separate oven and range. An oven is the least used of all major kitchen appliances—it accounts for less than 10 percent of the trips to and from the activity centers and can lie outside the work triangle without a significant loss of efficiency. The bottom of a wall oven should be 3 inches below elbow height, a level that minimizes the chance of burning an arm on an oven rack and is comfortable for turning or basting food.

Locate a refrigerator at the end of a counter, where it will not cut counter space into several small, cramped work areas. Get a refrigerator with hinges away from the counter, so that the open door will not block work space—many models have doors adjustable to open either way. To dissipate the heat of the condenser coils at the back of a refrigerator, allow at least 3 inches between the top of the unit and any overhanging cabinets, and 1 to 2 inches between the side and an adjoining wall or broom closet.

Any of the three activity centers can be located in a kitchen island or peninsula, but islands are seldom practical in average kitchens because they need at least 5 feet of floor space on one of their long sides and at least 3 feet along their short ones. Even though you have adequate space for an island, avoid using it for the range or the main sink: Both centers need more counter space than most island installations permit.

In practice, the counter space for an activity center may vary considerably from the dimensions recommended in the plans opposite and on page 134, top. In a limited space two activity centers can share counter space, but try to keep a shared counter at least as long as the most generous minimum length for the two centers, plus 1 foot. And at some point in the assembly (usually between the refrigerator and sink) try to keep at least 36 inches of counter space for a mixing and food-preparation center.

A large kitchen permits more variations, but has one paradoxical limitation: Try not to exceed the maximum recommended dimensions of the plans. Extra counter space means extra steps between work centers—and extra work for the cook.

The Three Activity Centers

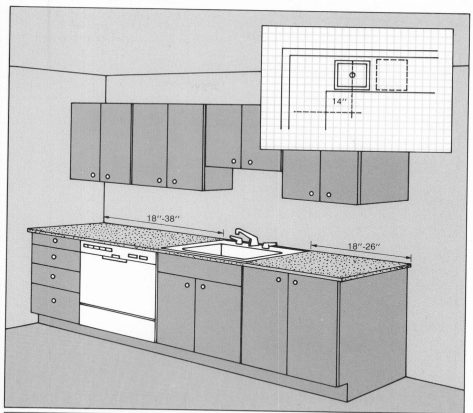

The sink. Provide at least 18 inches of counter space on each side of the sink. If more space is available, add 6 or 8 inches of countertop on one side for preparing food and stacking unwashed dishes, and from 10 to 20 inches on the other for draining and stacking washed dishes. A dishwasher next to a sink will have at least 24 inches of counter space above it. For a sink near a countertop corner *(inset)*, allow at least 14 inches between the sink center line and the corner.

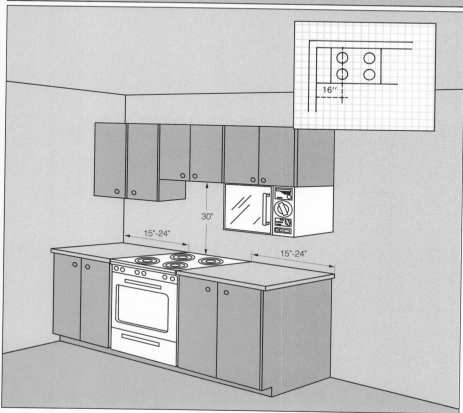

The range and microwave. Allow at least 15 inches of counter space beside the range for resting pots and setting out serving dishes, or up to 24 inches on each side if space allows. For a range next to a wall or another appliance *(inset)*, allow a safety margin of at least 16 inches from the center of the nearest burner. A range with less than 10 inches between burners must have at least 10 inches of counter space on each side, so that pot handles will not jut into the work area.

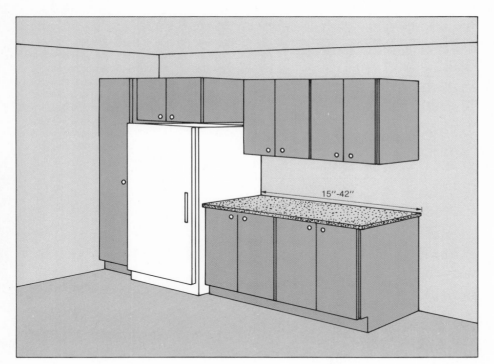

The refrigerator center. Provide at least 15 inches of counter space on the latch side of the refrigerator for setting out supplies. If this counter must also form part of the food-preparation center, provide between 36 and 42 inches of uninterrupted counter space.

The Four Layouts

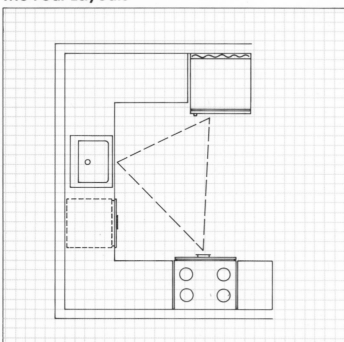

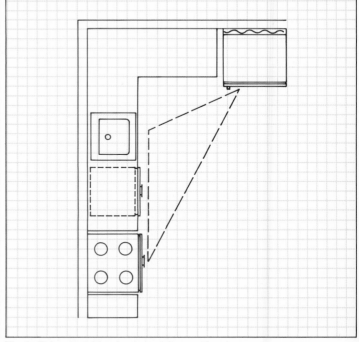

The U. Cabinets and counters set along three walls keep the three activity centers accessible to one another and out of the way of traffic. The back wall should measure between 8 and 13 feet, allowing from 4 to 9 feet of work area between facing counters—a tighter arrangement makes for cramped work areas; a looser one, too many steps between activity centers.

The L. This adaptable plan is best for small square kitchens; in large ones it provides a work triangle isolated from traffic and frees the rest of the room for dining. Its drawbacks are the long distance between two of the work centers and the need for expensive corner cabinets. Arrange the centers with a sink in the middle, creating a refrigerator-to-sink-to-range work flow.

The corridor. In this arrangement, usually found in a kitchen that also serves as a passageway, appliances and cabinets are distributed along two facing walls. Because the work triangle will be broken by traffic, try to locate the range and microwave, and the sink—the most active work centers—along the same wall. The corridor aisle should be at least 4 feet wide to provide adequate clearance between cabinet and appliance doors. If your aisle is narrower, try to stagger the three work centers so that appliance doors do not interfere with one another.

The one-wall. This layout works best in an area less than 12 feet long; if the arrangement is strung out to gain more cabinets and larger counters, the distances between work centers become too large for efficiency. Use scaled-down appliances to provide maximum counter and cabinet space, and save steps by locating the refrigerator at one end, the range and microwave at the other and the sink in between, with most of the counter space between the sink and the range.

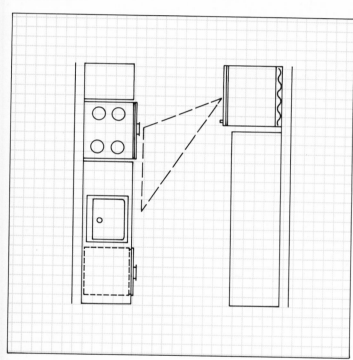

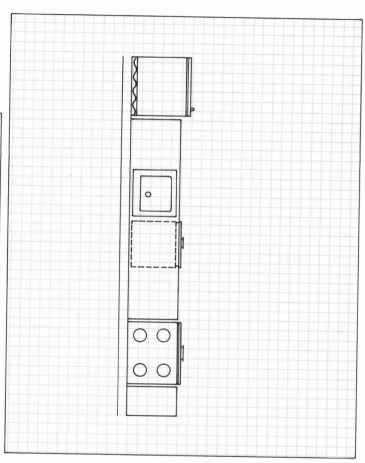

Making a Dangerous Room Safer

According to the National Safety Council, many serious home accidents take place in the kitchen. The placement of appliances and the arrangement of work spaces shown on these pages reduce or eliminate many hazards, but designers and safety experts also recommend safety measures for specific danger points.

• Choose a kitchen range that has controls located at the front or sides, not at the back of the burners.

• Hang an ABC dry chemical fire extinguisher that is especially designed for grease fires. Locate it within easy reach of the range—but be careful: Do not hang it directly above the cook top, where you might have to reach through a fire's flames to get at it.

• Hang kitchen doors so that they swing out of the room rather than into the work triangle.

• Locate hanging or wall-mounted light fixtures at least 6 feet 8 inches above the floor,

unless they hang over an island, a base cabinet or a table.

• Install a feed-through-type receptacle ground-fault interrupter *(page 171)* to protect receptacles at or near a sink. (However, note that a GFI is intended only for ordinary 120-volt circuits.)

• Isolate the storage areas of dangerous tools and chemicals. Store your sharp knives and choppers separately from other utensils, and store cleaning products separately from food.

Bathrooms to Fit the Space

Bathrooms are usually the smallest rooms in a house—and even a large bathroom has a way of seeming inadequate when every member of the family wants it at once. You may be able to use the space more efficiently by adding a second washbowl or partitioning off a toilet; in some situations, you can enlarge a bathroom by removing a wall and picking up a few feet from an adjoining room or closet. But the most satisfactory solution to the problem is another bathroom—a new one, built into whatever space you find available. A full bathroom with standard fixtures can fit into a space 5 by 7 feet, a half bath (toilet and sink) into a space as small as 4 feet square.

In such small rooms, the fixtures must be placed with special care to provide minimum clearances at the front and sides. (Most building codes specify these clearances; if your local code does not, use the diagrams at right as a guide.) At the same time, the layout of the bathroom is influenced by the location of existing plumbing or the routes of new pipes. Juggling positions of your fixtures to meet both requirements calls for ingenuity and patience.

In a room with an existing soil stack or one in which a new stack must be located in a particular area, position the toilet first—it must be near the stack. Try to locate the toilet next to a wall, for convenience in mounting a toilet-paper holder, but remember that some people find the sight of a toilet from an open door objectionable: Always place the toilet away from a door if you can, and if the space is available consider separating the toilet from the other fixtures with a partition.

Because a full bathtub is very heavy, the floor joists under the tub must have extra bracing; the best location for the bracing is under, and parallel to, the flange (*diagram right, bottom*). Position the foot of the tub against a wall that can be opened from the other side for plumbing repairs.

The lavatory is the most frequently used fixture. Place it well away from the tub and toilet, with space around it for the necessary number of towel racks and hooks, toothbrush racks and cabinets or storage shelves. In a windowed bathroom, try to give the lavatory the advantage of natural light for shaving and applying make-up.

When you have chosen the locations of these three fixtures, use the manufacturer's rough-in dimensions to plan the connections of each fixture to its plumbing. Mark the rough-in points on the walls and floors of the room (some fixtures come with rough-in templates that you can tack or tape to walls and floors), then decide upon the routes of the pipes to and from the rough-in points. The details of the routes will depend on the floor plan, the location of existing plumbing and the requirements of your local plumbing code. Three of the most common fixture arrangements, with progressively more complicated plumbing, are shown in the floor plans at right and on page 138. Although these plans are for the smallest practical rooms, the plumbing patterns will also serve large bathrooms and additional fixtures (*page 139*).

In any small bathroom, new or old, you will confront the problem of getting adequate storage and counter space. Some simple solutions:
• Mount shallow shelves along a wall behind the door.
• Set the hinges on the door so that it swings outward.
• Replace a wall-mounted or pedestal lavatory with a vanity that provides both counter space and an enclosed cabinet beneath the washbowl.
• Extend a vanity top over the top of the toilet tank—use a removable extension, so that you can get to the tank for repairs.
• Use the space above the toilet as a storage wall.
• Build shelves or cabinets into the spaces between studs.

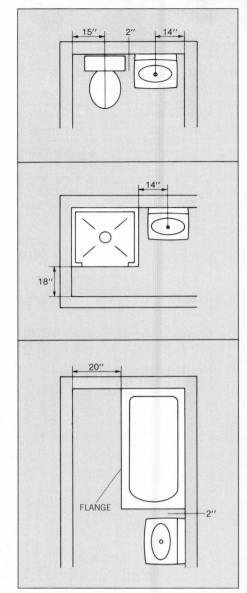

Minimum fixture clearances. For the average adult, the clearances indicated in the floor plans above are the minimums for using standard bathroom fixtures and cleaning around them. Minimum clearances mean minimal comfort: Exceed the figures if you can. A 14-inch clearance between the center line of a lavatory and a wall, for example, allows barely enough room to shave or apply make-up; 18 inches between a shower and a wall allows only enough room to edge out of the shower. When a toilet and a lavatory or tub face each other, 18 inches between them provides no more than knee room in front of the toilet and just enough room to stand in front of the lavatory or to towel off beside the tub. Most bathroom designers—and some municipal codes—specify 24-inch minimum clearances for comfortable use of these fixtures.

Rough-in dimensions. Make large, clear, rough-in marks on walls and floors for pipe-to-fixture connections, with the centers of pipe holes indicated precisely. The dimensions shown here are typical for U.S. and Canadian fixtures (your own may be slightly different). They match the plumbing pattern shown at right, below.

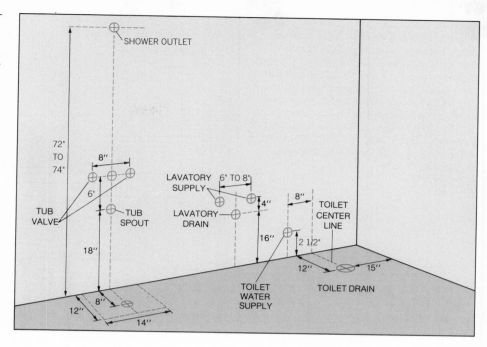

One wall. The simplest bathroom for a limited space has fixtures in a row, with all their plumbing in a single wall. This arrangement calls for the least amount of cutting into the house structure and uses the fewest fittings. While still in the planning stage, be sure to check your local plumbing code.

Three Basic Plumbing Patterns

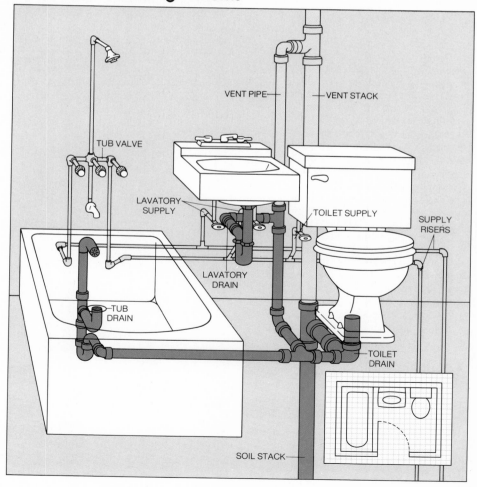

Two walls. A bathroom with plumbing in two adjoining walls provides somewhat more storage and activity space around the lavatory than a one-wall room, and the plumbing is only slightly more complicated. But a two-wall bathroom generally requires more cutting of studs and joists to accommodate the pipes; to minimize cutting or, as here, to clear a door, try to run the supply lines underneath or between joists rather than through the walls. While still in the planning stage, be sure to check your local plumbing code.

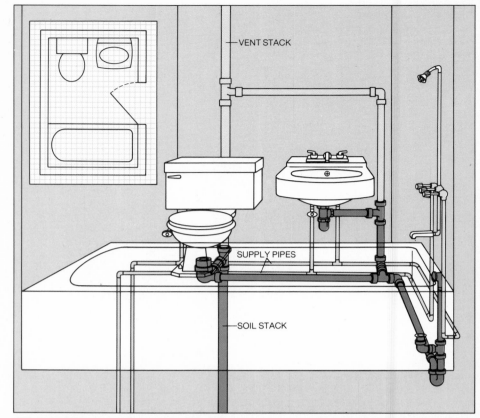

Three walls. Of all the basic bathroom plans, this offers the greatest flexibility and the largest wall and counter spaces—at the cost of added room area and more complex plumbing. The room must be at least 5 1/2 feet by 7 feet 2 inches to accommodate minimum clearances between fixtures; in practice, three-wall bathrooms are usually set up in larger rooms—at least 7 feet 8 inches by 6 feet. Venting is especially difficult. Your local code may require separate vents for each fixture, and even with the single lavatory vent shown here, routing a horizontal connection to the vent stack may be difficult. If the space above the bathroom is unfinished, run the pipe diagonally across it. Otherwise, the vent must be run inside the room, boxed in a wallboard enclosure, or extended up to the attic or roof. While still in the planning stage, be sure to check your local plumbing code.

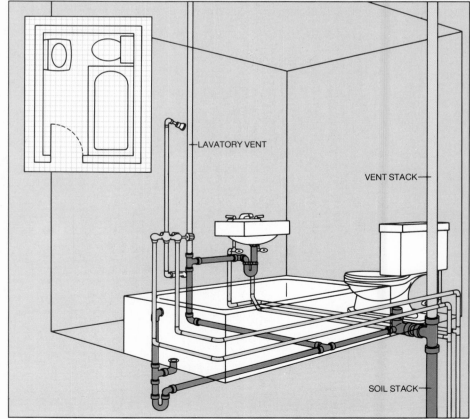

The Luxury That Size Allows

An expanded bathroom. Fixtures can be added to any of the basic bathroom plans with surprisingly little additional plumbing work, provided they conform to the local plumbing code. For example, a 5-by-7-foot one-wall bathroom *(inset)* is expanded with a second toilet and a vanity, installed in what formerly had been an adjoining closet. In the illustration below, the old piping is shown in white, the new piping in color. The new fixtures drain into the stack through a new drain-waste vent system (called a sanitary T) directly beneath the existing one. New drainpipes and supply pipes run horizontally beneath the floor to the new lavatory; the vertical supply risers and the drain behind the lavatory could be concealed by furring out the original wall *(page 256)* or installing a new wet wall as shown on pages 257-259. The lavatory vent could reach the vent stack by a route that runs around the room or up to the attic or roof.

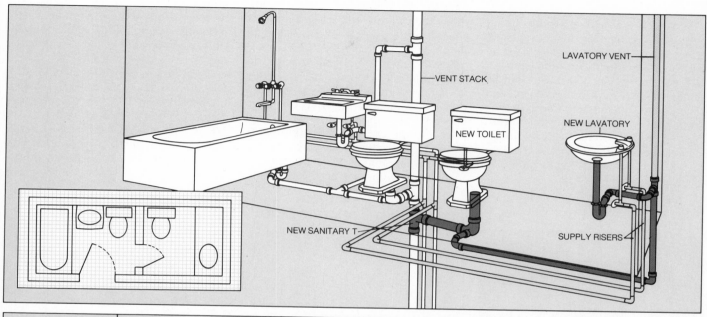

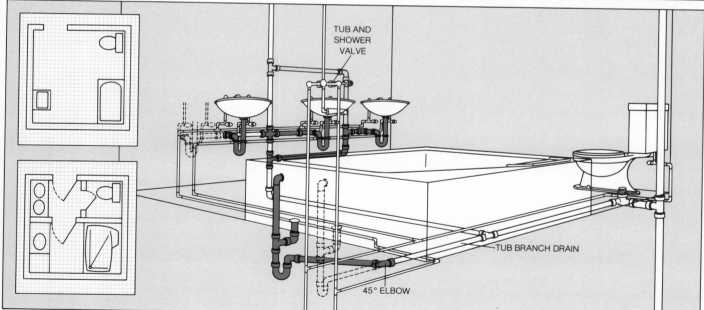

A redesigned bathroom. Many older homes have very large bathrooms equipped with no more than a standard tub, a toilet and a standing lavatory. In a typical 10-by-11-foot room *(top inset)*, the rest of the space is wasted. For maximum versatility, the room can be partitioned into functionally separate sections, separated by new doors *(bottom inset)*. The section nearest the original door becomes a powder room with double vanity sinks and an enclosed toilet. The inner section gets a new oversized tub; a vanity sink and dressing table replace the old standing lavatory. The original plumbing *(white and dotted lines)* follows the plan of a three-wall bathroom, with pipes concealed inside three wet walls. An elbow in the tub branch drain routes the drain to a point beneath the new tub's outlet. The supply lines to the tub and shower valve are in their original positions; the new lavatories tie into the plumbing of the original single lavatory. While still in the planning stage, be sure to consult your local plumbing code.

Layered Flooring: Level, Smooth, Squeak-Free

If a new floor is needed in an extra living space that you set up for a bathroom or other purpose, cemented-down tiles—made of any of a variety of materials *(pages 26-28)*—are the simplest to use.

Since they show every lump, bump and nailhead beneath them, or buckle unless seated properly, the tiles must be laid over a perfectly smooth surface. The concrete slab of a basement or garage will serve if it is first leveled and waterproofed *(below and opposite top)*. Wood subfloors and existing finish flooring need to be covered with an underlayment of smooth 1/4-inch hardboard or 5/7-inch plywood that is nailed in place as a base for the tiles.

In an attic both subflooring and underlayment may have to be added to existing joists, creating a complete floor like the one below, left. Subflooring must be laid before walls are built, underlayment afterward. If the joists are spaced more than 16 inches apart or made of lumber smaller than 2-by-8, you will need to increase or reinforce them *(opposite, center)*. The composite floor—supports plus subfloor plus underlayment—is also preferred on top of concrete, since the tiles are less likely to peel off, and the wood platform adds spring to make the result more comfortable to walk on than tiles that are in direct contact with concrete. To build this platform on a slab, you will have to add sleepers—supports of 2-by-4s that are placed on their sides.

Regardless of the type of floor installed over concrete, the slab should be moistureproofed first. A clear waterproofing solution, available at hardware stores and applied like paint, will do the trick if your basement feels dry, and if you plan to tile or paint directly over it. For a raised floor, seal the slab with asphalt before putting down the sleepers *(opposite, top)*. Neither treatment, of course, will protect your flooring if you are plagued by water in your basement. This problem should be solved before any flooring is laid.

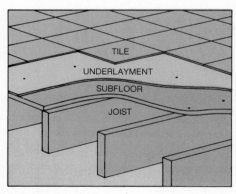

Anatomy of a floor. Whether upstairs or down, floors share a similar structure. At the bottom are the joists, commonly spaced 16 inches apart. Resting on the joists is the subfloor, usually sheets of plywood 15/32 inch thick nailed to the joists.

An additional layer, called the underlayment, is recommended for the tile flooring shown here. Made of 1/4-inch hardboard or 1/4- to 3/8-inch thick APA (American Plywood Association) underlayment plywood, it is nailed to the subfloor—but not the joists—to provide a smooth base. Topmost is the finish flooring of vinyl or wood-block tiles, cemented in place.

Preparing a Concrete Slab

Leveling the slab. If tiles are to be cemented directly to concrete, check for irregularities by rolling a long straight piece of pipe over the surface while, from a low angle, you look for slits of light under the pipe. Flatten bumps of 1/4 inch or more with a rub brick or a rented electric concrete grinder. Fill in low areas with a fast-setting floor-patching compound—ask for flash patch, a filler compound that retains its resilience when set. Apply it with a trowel, then level and feather-edge the patches with a straightedge. When the patching compound cures—usually within 24 hours—waterproof the slab by applying clear waterproofing solution with a brush, roller or squeegee.

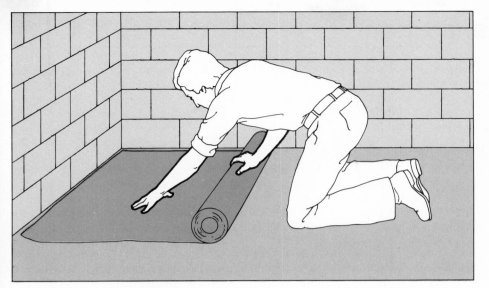

Waterproofing the slab. When a concrete slab is used as the base for sleepers, subfloor, underlayment and finish flooring, it need not be level but it must be dry. To waterproof the surface first apply a thin coating of roofing-type emulsified asphalt, available in 5-gallon cans at building materials/home supply dealers; use a stiff broom to coat the slab. Spread 6-mil polyethylene sheeting over the asphalt and work out any air bubbles with a stiff, dry broom. Press the sheet down evenly and firmly until it lies flat over the asphalt.

Supports for a Subfloor

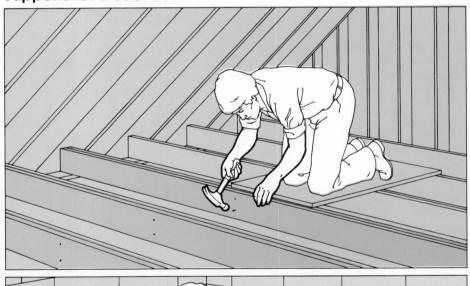

Reinforcing an attic floor. If the joists already in your attic are made of lumber smaller or otherwise different than is required by local building code for supporting a floor, you must strengthen the existing framing. This can often be done by doubling the existing joists. Following your local code, cut new pieces the same size and length; rest them on the 2-by-4 plates that run the length of the attic where joists and rafters meet. Nail them, using 16-penny nails, to the sides of the existing ones in a W pattern 16 inches apart along their lengths; toenail the ends to the plates. If joists are spaced more than 16 inches apart, add extras in between. Cut additional joists the same size and length as existing ones. Insert new joists mid-way between existing ones, resting them on the plates; toenail into place. If new joists do not match dimensions of the existing ones, use wood scraps under both ends of the new joist to make sure joist tops are flush.

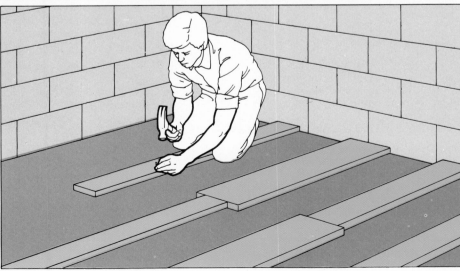

Sleepers for a slab. To provide the base for a floor in a basement or garage lay pressure-treated 2-by-4s or other 2-inch-thick pressure-treated scrap lumber flat across the planned room area at 16-inch intervals, measured from center to center. Install shims to level the sleepers, then use a claw hammer or small sledgehammer to drive 2-inch-long hardened concrete nails through the 2-by-4s and polyethylene sheeting, using only as many nails as needed to keep the sleepers from shifting until the subfloor is in place. If you want to add additional insulation—the air space probably affords enough—use batts of insulation or insulation board between the sleepers, being careful to staple batts with the vapor-barrier side up.

Subfloor and Underlayment

If you are adding a new subfloor for a kitchen or bathroom, remember to install it before walls are put up, since the walls might prevent you from nailing the subfloor edges to the joists (and because you need something to stand on while building walls). Add the underlayment and the finish flooring after walls are in place.

Plywood makes an excellent subfloor material. In APA-rated sheathing, which comes in 15/32-inch thicknesses to span across supports 16 inches apart, it supplies a strong platform and virtually guarantees a squeakproof floor. Furthermore, the standard 4-by-8 sheets are easier to install than the various types of wood boards that are also used for subfloor materials. Grade C-D is commonly used; the C-grade side—a smoother finish—should face upward. For strength, the face grain should run across the supports, as shown, not parallel to them. Also, to obtain maximum strength from a plywood subfloor, make sure that the ends of adjacent sheets are not fastened to the same joist or sleeper. Leave 1/16-inch spaces between the ends and sides of sheets to permit the wood to expand without buckling; double these intervals in a room that is subject to high humidity.

After installation, some leveling of the subfloor may be necessary, but the underlayment will smooth out any minor unevenness and hide joints in the subfloor. The underlayment also prevents damage from nails forced upward by movement of joists as they settle, expand or contract.

In basements, kitchens, bathrooms and other areas that may be wet, the underlayment should be 1/4- to 3/8-inch APA Underlayment, Exposure 1 plywood, which can withstand a certain amount of moisture. If wood blocks, rather than resilient tiles, are to be used, an underlayment-grade plywood need not be installed. In dry locations, APA Underlayment, Interior, may be used. Butt panel ends and edges to a close 1/32-inch fit. Specify a sanded face for use with resilient floor coverings. You can also use 4-by-4 squares of untempered hardboard, very smooth on one side but rough on the other, to hold the finish-flooring adhesive. With plywood, surface texture does not markedly affect the holding power of adhesives. Since hardboard is highly absorbent, do not allow it to become wet. Before installation, unwrap the sheets and stack them loosely against the walls of the new room for 24 hours to adjust to the normal humidity of the room; they will expand or contract slightly, but thereafter hold their shape.

Rows of underlayment are laid perpendicular to those of the subfloor. If you use nails or screws (*box, opposite*) to fasten the underlayment to the subfloor, be sure the fasteners do not penetrate the joists. Otherwise, like the subfloor nails, they may be forced upward by joist movement to mar the finish flooring.

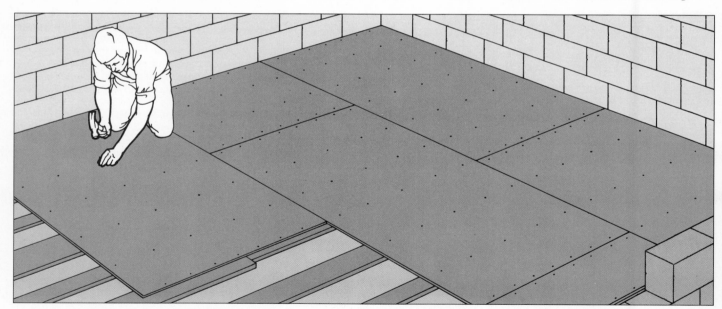

Installing the subfloor. Before starting to cut and lay the subfloor sheets, work out a pattern that avoids alignment of joints while requiring a minimum of plywood. Use full sheets, untrimmed, as much as possible. Lay the first row flush with any existing wall, and cut the last row to fit. Fasten the plywood to joists with eightpenny common nails. At the ends of the sheets, space the nails 6 inches apart and 3/8 inch from the edges. Stagger nails at adjoining ends to keep from splitting the support. Between the ends of the sheets, space the nails 12 inches apart.

Smooth small bumps in the surface of the subfloor with rough sandpaper, and fill holes with flash patch *(page 140)*. Unusually high places may be a result of swelling of joists; if so, pry the plywood up, level the joists with a plane and nail the sheets back.

Installing the underlayment. Hardboard or plywood underlayment *(dark lines in the diagram below)* must be laid so that it always spans the subfloor joints *(light lines)* by at least 2 inches and, like the subfloor, it should be arranged in a staggered pattern with the plywood face grain across supports. If you lay the subfloor before erecting walls and install the underlayment afterward—as you should—this overlapping is almost automatic, since the underlayment sheets will be offset from the subfloor by the thickness of the walls. Install just before laying the finish floor and protect underlayment against damage until the finish floor is installed. Place underlayment sheets—rough surface up, if hardboard—1/8 inch from walls; separate the sheets from each other by 1/32 inch, the thickness of a matchbook cover. To fit the last sheet in each row, follow the procedure used for border tiles, *(page 28)*. Unless underlayment sheets will be cemented down, fasteners should be spaced 6 inches apart, 3/8 inch in from the edges and 8 inches each way elsewhere. Mark off the surface in 4-inch squares as a guide.

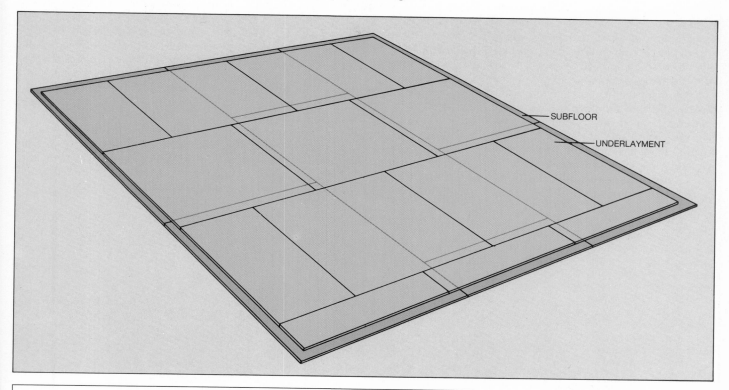

SUBFLOOR

UNDERLAYMENT

Two Fastening Methods

Underlayment can be attached to the subfloor in a variety of ways. They all work, but some work better—or save more time—than others. Although staples and adhesive are used by many professional builders, the two methods described below are recommended for best results for do-it-yourselfers.

• THREEPENNY RING-SHANK NAILS, annular grooved nails, contain deformed rather than smooth shanks that act like barbs when the nails are driven to keep them from loosening. The nails also have thin heads that will sink flush with the surface (ordinary headed nails would create lumps that might show through resilient tile). You can also use special underlayment nails, which have large but very thin heads that can be hammered flush with the surface; in the event of a mis-hit they are easy to pull out. Sand lightly any surface roughness that surrounds the fasteners.

• SCREWS can be sunk flush with the surface of the underlayment and will stay put. However, this method of fastening is extremely time consuming, given the number of screws and screw holes that are needed for just one sheet.

Rolled Flooring: Seamless and Easy on the Feet

Years ago, rolled sheets of flooring were made of only one material—linoleum. Today the material is almost certain to be sheet vinyl—easy to maintain and install.

Sheet vinyl comes in two basic types: inlaid, in which the pattern is pressed through the vinyl; and rotogravure, or "roto" for short, in which the pattern is printed on the surface. Both come in compositions of differing resiliency, some so flexible you can roll them into a ball and others so brittle they split if you try to press them into a corner.

Of the two types roto offers a greater variety of colors and patterns. It is softer and more soundproof; its wear surface is thin and the vinyl sheet has a thick foam-rubber backing called fatback. It is available in 6-,12- and occasionally 9- and 15-foot widths—an advantage, because the variety of widths virtually eliminates the need for seaming, the most difficult part of laying sheet vinyl. But roto's softness makes it easier to puncture, and some furniture—a kitchen table, for instance—can leave a permanent indentation if left too long in one spot. Inlaid sheet vinyl is harder and more durable, but usually comes only in 6-foot rolls.

As the first step in an installation make a plan of the floor, marking the dimensions. Add 6 inches at each wall for overlap and note the width of the pattern repetition, usually printed on the back of the sheet, if you must seam sheets together. The allowance for seaming equals this width; for example, if your pattern repeats every 3 feet, allow 3 feet of extra width when you buy the material.

Remove the shoe molding *(shown on page 38)* and generally the baseboard, too; it is best replaced with cove molding *(page 150)*. Remove all the old wax and sweep the floor clean.

When returning heavy appliances, such as the refrigerator, to the room after the vinyl has been laid, push them back on top of a sheet of hardboard to avoid making deep, permanent ridges in the vinyl.

Leave the fitting of the vinyl to a threshold for the final step of the job. At an existing marble or wood threshold, cut the vinyl as close to the threshold as possible, shaving a little at a time to arrive at a close fit. If there is no threshold, or if you are planning to replace it, use metal edging strips, which is the best transition from new vinyl flooring to the floor covering in an adjoining room. If you use a metal tuck-in strip as a threshold *(page 151)*, leave the vinyl edge in the doorway unglued until the strip is installed.

1 **Rolling out the material.** Let the material adjust to room temperature for an hour or so; then, if you are using more than one sheet of material, start unrolling the larger sheet from the longest and most nearly clear wall of the room. Leave 3 to 6 inches of overlap at each wall.

When you reach a large immovable object, such as a center island or a set of built-in cabinets, reach under the roll and unroll the sheet backward toward the starting wall. Push the unrolled section of the sheet against the object and, about 6 inches above the floor, cut the sheet from its outside edge toward its center with a utility knife. Continue the cut about 6 inches short of the edge of the object, then cut back toward the starting wall for a distance at least 6 inches less than the object's depth.

2 **Fitting around a large object.** Lift the roll over the object and lower it to the floor on the other side. Holding the corner of the flap you have made in the sheet, complete the cutout for the object by cutting, if necessary, to a point about 6 inches from its far edge, then cutting at a right angle toward the outside edge of the sheet.

3 **Fitting around a small object.** Roll the material past a pipe *(near right)* or other small obstruction and slice a slit from the nearest edge of the material to the object. Carefully carve a circle around the object, making several cuts if necessary, then press the sheet together behind the object. If the slit is long, seal the seam *(Step 15).* For a neat job, slide the base ring up the pipe before laying the vinyl, then return it to the finished floor; if the pipe does not have a base ring, use the model shown here, which snaps around the pipe and screws to the floor.

To cut around a toilet flange in a bathroom, feel for the edges of the flange beneath the material and cut around the flange until all of it is exposed *(far right)*. The cut need not be exact: The toilet bowl will overlap the flange, covering any ragged edges.

4 **Reversing the roll.** Unroll the sheet completely, pull it back upon itself and reroll the sheet back from the far edge with the underside of the sheet inside the roll. (The tight original roll in this area compresses the pattern, unless the roll is reversed briefly, the pattern will be smaller in one part of the room than the other.) Unroll the sheet again and press the material into all corners, to the extent that its natural resiliency will allow. Caution: Do not try to force brittle material into a corner; it will split if pressed too tightly.

5 **Laying the second sheet.** Measure the width of uncovered floor from the edge of the first sheet to the wall; to this distance add 6 inches plus the amount of overlap required to match the floor-covering pattern. Mark the total distance on the second sheet and cut off any excess material.

Roll the second sheet out halfway, then pull it over the first sheet until the patterns match. Unroll the rest of the second sheet as you did the first, cutting around objects.

6 **Trimming the edges.** Pull the second sheet off the first and out of the way. At each wall and object, cut the material back to about 3 inches above the floor. Caution: For professional-looking results, take care in making this cut—you are now close to the final trim.

7 **Applying the adhesive.** Pull the first sheet halfway back upon itself. Using a trowel with 1/16-inch grooves, spread adhesive over the floor; do not cover a 6-inch strip along the line at which the first sheet will meet the second, but work the adhesive into corners as closely as possible. Follow the manufacturer's recommendations for the choice of an adhesive and any instructions on its use; the guarantee may depend upon strict adherence to this advice.

At the completion of this step, go on to the next immediately: After about 45 minutes most adhesives become so stiff that the material is hard to adjust.

8 **Setting the vinyl in place.** Lift the edge of the rolled material high above the floor and slowly walk it back into place over the adhesive. Lay it against the wall and press it into place at the corners as closely as its resiliency will allow.

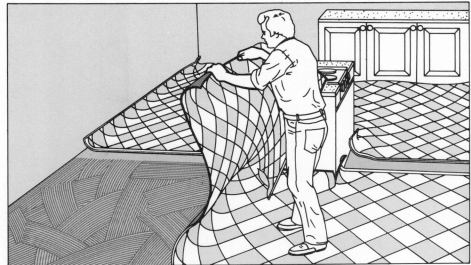

9 **Rolling out the bumps.** Using an ordinary rolling pin or a rented tile roller, and starting from the center, roll the material toward each of its edges. Work slowly, and be sure to flatten any bulges or air bubbles that have risen above the flat surface.

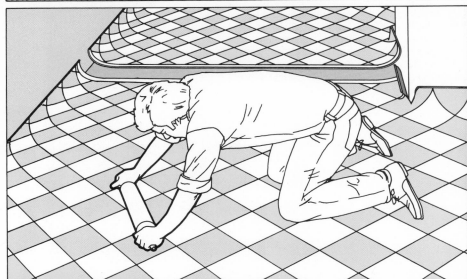

10 **Making the final cuts.** Press a metal yardstick hard along the lines where walls or objects meet the floor, creasing the material sharply at the corners, then slice the material at the wall along the edge of the yardstick with a utility knife. You may not be able to crease inlaid sheet vinyl sharply at a first try; instead, make repeated cuts until the vinyl fits the corner. Caution: Normally, molding will cover cutting errors to about 1/2 inch from the wall, but ceramic cove molding is not removed before laying the vinyl; for this type of molding the cuts must be exact.

11 **Cutting off the trim.** Place a metal yardstick along the overlapping edge of the
second vinyl sheet and cut off the 1/2- to 1-
inch trim at the edge of the sheet. On inlaid
vinyl this trim is likely to be an extra-wide grout
line: Cut along the line to bring its width down
to that of the other grout lines in the pattern.

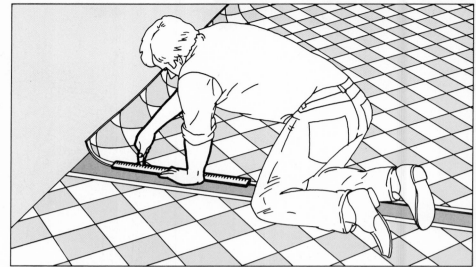

12 **Matching the pattern.** Pull the second
sheet over the first until the patterns of
the two sheets match perfectly. Caution: Note
the pattern carefully to be sure the overlap
continues the pattern in the same manner—a
mismatched pattern will spoil the appearance
of the finished job.

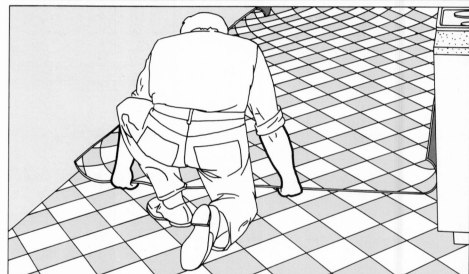

13 **Cutting off the overlap.** Place a metal
yardstick along the edge of the top sheet
and, holding a utility knife straight up and
down and using the yardstick as a guide, cut
through the bottom sheet. Pull the top sheet
back and remove the strip you have cut from
the bottom.

If the material you are using is resilient enough
to permit a cut through two sheets at once,
overlap the second sheet to a segment of pattern repetition and, using a yardstick as a
guide, cut through both sheets at once. This
method assures a perfect match of the pattern.

Lay the second sheet as you did the first, cutting overlaps of 3 to 6 inches around objects,
spreading the adhesive to within 6 inches of
the edge of the first sheet and making a final
trim along each wall and object.

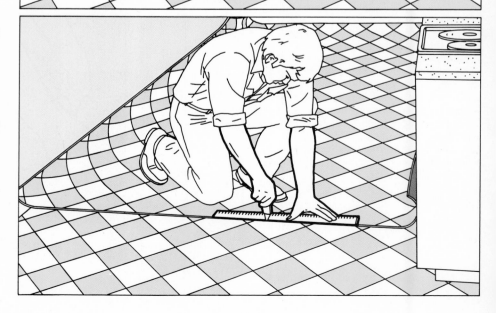

14 **Applying adhesive under the seam.**
Check the manufacturer's directions for sealing the seam between two sheets *(Step 15, below)*. If they do not call for seam sealer below the sheets, simply pull back the butted edges on both sheets and spread adhesive over the bare floor along the entire length of the seam. Then, while the adhesive is still plastic, push the sheets back into place, pressing the edges together until you get a tight fit. Go on immediately to the next step.

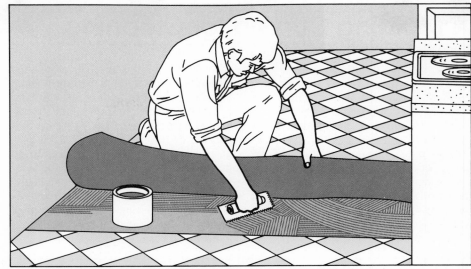

15 **Sealing the seam.** Press the seam together with the thumb and fingers of one hand while applying seam sealer with the other. Most seam sealers are applied with a T-shaped nozzle *(inset)* with the top of the T riding on top of the material and the bottom inside the seam. Caution: Some manufacturers require that sealing be applied beneath the seam—consult the manufacturer's directions for sealing before carrying out Step 14, above. For either method, wipe away all excess sealing immediately and do not step on the seam for at least 24 hours.

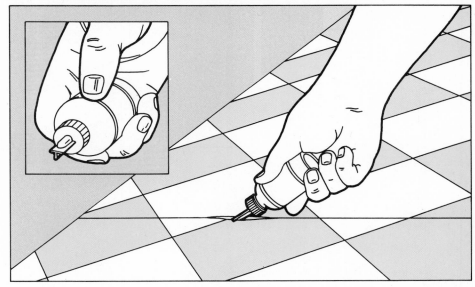

Softer Yet—Carpeting

Although the trend is toward sheet vinyl or tile flooring in bathrooms and kitchens, some people prefer carpeting, particularly in bathrooms—and with good reasons. Carpeting is soft underfoot, and creates a feeling of luxury and warm comfort. But it has its disadvantages as well. It is not as durable as good-quality tile or vinyl, is easily stained and can be ruined by an overflow of water.

If you choose carpeting for your kitchen or bathroom, remember the ever-present moisture in those rooms. Select a carpeting that has the tightest possible weave—the heavier the carpeting gauge, as indicated on the back of the sample, the tighter the weave and the more impervious the material will be to spills.

Carpeting is usually fastened to the floor with double-faced tape rather than adhesive. After clearing the floor, lay the tape along the edges of the room and all permanently installed objects. Cut the carpeting to fit the room as you would sheet vinyl, pull half the carpeting back upon itself and peel the top paper from the tape. Walk the carpet back into place, and press it down; repeat the process for the other half.

A Molding Curved for Cleaning

Vinyl cove base, molded as a single concave strip so that it is easy to clean and moisture resistant, is more practical than wood baseboard for edging rolled flooring. It comes in 2-, 4- and 6-inch widths in rolls and straight sections; also available are premolded corners. It is sold in a variety of colors and can be cleaned and waxed as part of the flooring. Use a 6-inch strip for the best protection against mopping and splashes; a 4-inch strip will just fill the kick space beneath a standard kitchen cabinet.

Installation is simple, but you must take special precautions with the special adhesive, which may be noxious and highly flammable. Turn off all the electrical appliances (including the refrigerator and the freezer) and the pilot lights of a gas range before beginning the job; do not smoke; be sure that all of the windows and doors are wide open; and keep the can of adhesive covered as much as possible, transferring small quantities of the adhesive, as needed, from the can to a piece of scrap plywood.

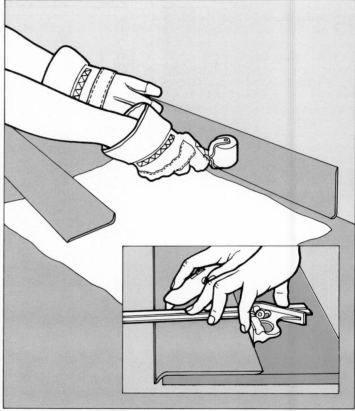

Installing a corner piece. Cover the floor with dropcloths or newspapers, then begin the installation at an inside corner. Using a 3-inch trowel with notches 1/16 inch deep, apply vinyl adhesive evenly to the wide vertical surface of an inside corner piece; the short curved edge that rests on the floor need not be glued. Caution: This adhesive is hazardous; follow the safety instructions in the text above. Fit the piece carefully into the corner. The adhesive will hold it almost immediately and will harden in about 10 minutes. Remove excess adhesive from the wall with a rag soaked in soap and water.

Installing the straight sections. Apply adhesive to the vertical side of a straight 4-foot section of cove base and lay the section along the longest wall adjoining the corner piece. Butt it carefully, then press it against the wall with a steel handroller *(above)* available from your flooring supplier. Add straight sections until you are within 4 feet of the end of the wall. Install the next corner piece and measure a straight length to fill the gap, plus 1/16 inch to ensure a tight fit. To cut this length, true a combination square against the top edge of the cove and make repeated cuts along it with a utility knife *(inset)*.

Thresholds to Mate Materials

The last step in installing a kitchen or bathroom floor is to cover the seams in doorways where the edge of the new flooring material meets adjoining surfaces. In bathrooms, where water spillage is commonplace, raised thresholds act as miniature dams to keep water from seeping under the door and damaging adjacent wood floors or carpeting. A variety of materials are available, including wood, metal, rubber and traditional marble. Marble is difficult to trim and must be bought in the exact length needed to fit between the bathroom doorjambs (below).

In kitchens, three types of metal edging are used to edge vinyl flooring. The binder bar—usually a slightly curved aluminum strip 1 1/2 inches wide—simply covers a seam. A narrower L-shaped edging protects the vinyl edge where it abuts abrasive surfaces such as brick or concrete. The tuck-in, or gripper bar (inset, bottom), used where vinyl meets carpeting, provides a narrow slot into which the carpeting can be tucked and secured.

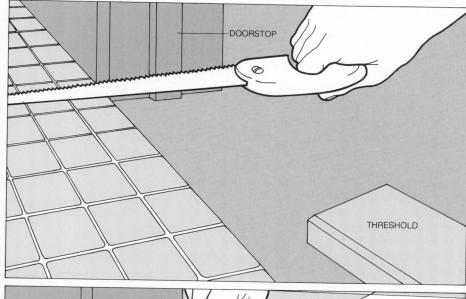

DOORSTOP

THRESHOLD

Setting marble thresholds. Place the threshold, sized to fit between the doorjambs, on the old floor surface and mark its height on the doorstops. Using a keyhole saw, cut the doorstops at the marks, being careful to avoid scratching the jamb. Use a wood chisel, if necessary, to remove the pieces. Spread ceramic-tile adhesive between the doorjambs and along the bottom of the threshold. Then fit the threshold under the trimmed doorstops until it is butted against the floor tiles. Clean off the excess adhesive and let the threshold set at least three hours before grouting.

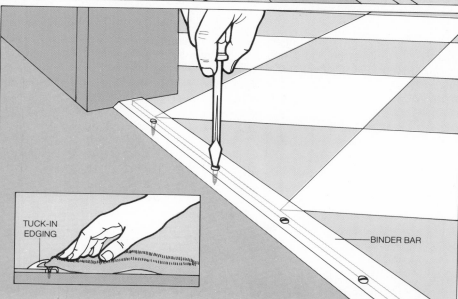

TUCK-IN EDGING

BINDER BAR

Installing metal edging. When adding binder bar, use a hacksaw with a fine-tooth blade to cut the bar to fit the opening. Place it directly over the seam between the two flooring materials and screw it to the subfloor. Do not screw into tiles, which may crack; trim the tiles if necessary, so that the screws go directly into the floor.

L-shaped edging is laid over the vinyl edge and screwed through it into the subfloor. Tuck-in edging (inset) is screwed to subflooring so that carpeting can be tucked snugly into the slotted side while the other side covers the edge of the vinyl floor covering.

Ceramic Tile for Kitchen and Bath: Impervious and Permanent

Ceramic tiles of tough fired clay make a durable, beautiful, impervious surface for kitchen and bathroom walls, floors or countertops. Smooth and shiny glazed tiles are commonly used on walls and countertops; unglazed tiles, less slippery and less easily marred by wear, are better for floors.

Tiles are usually square or hexagonal, range in size from 1 to 12 inches square and come in a wide selection of colors. In addition, a variety of trim tile is available. Most tiles have projections on their edges to space them from their neighbors. Some are designed to fill interior corners where two tile surfaces meet; they are often used instead of baseboard on tiled walls. Other types of trim tiles have rounded edges to give the last row of a surface a finished look or to go around corners and the counter edges.

Laying ceramic tiles involves preparing a smooth surface, planning a pattern and attaching the tiles with adhesive. Tile adhesives include cement-based mortars (most commonly used over a concrete subfloor as shown on page 30), epoxies, latex-mortar and epoxy-mortar combinations and organic adhesives. Most popular with amateur tilesetters are the organics, which are relatively inexpensive, work well for residential tiling, require no mixing and are easier to apply than epoxies.

When buying adhesive, consult a dealer and read the label on the container to make sure the product fits your needs as to bonding ability, setting time and water resistance. Most tile adhesives will bond tile to most other surfaces, but there are exceptions.

Floor adhesives usually harden more quickly than wall adhesives. Thus you can spread adhesive over a large area of wall before setting tile; you must spread floor adhesive a little at a time, but you can walk on a floor 24 hours after tiling it.

Wall adhesives are either Type I, which resists prolonged wetting and should be used around tubs and showers, or Type II, which stands up to intermittent wetting and can be used behind a backsplash. Before tiling any surface that will be wetted frequently, seal it with a thin coat of adhesive *(page 157)*.

After being set in adhesive, the tiles are leveled and the spaces between them are filled with grout—a decorative mortar available in many colors—that seals out dirt and water. Consult a dealer and read the label to make sure you buy a suitable grout. Some tiles, for instance, require a silicone rubber grout *(page 157)*.

Mix mortar-type grout to the consistency recommended by the manufacturer. Mortar-type grouts must dry slowly to "cure," or harden properly. Some floor tiles steal water from grout and impede curing. Before grouting, put a drop of water on the back of a tile; if the tile soaks it up, use more water in the grout.

To make floor grout joints flush with tile surfaces fill the joints with a grout containing a water-retaining aggregate, sprinkle dry grout of the same kind over the grout joints and rub the joints with a piece of burlap, using a circular motion.

After tiling a floor, cover it with polyethylene sheeting. If no condensation appears under the sheeting the next day, remove it, sprinkle water on the floor and replace the sheeting. Let the grout cure for three days. After 10 days seal the grout joints with a sealer sold to protect the grout from dirt or mildew.

For easier installation, small tiles called mosaic tiles are sold attached to sheets of paper or mesh 1-by-1 or 1-by-2 feet in size. Larger wall tiles also can be bought in sheets *(page 156)*. A dealer will tell you how much tile you need if you bring him a sketch showing the shape and dimensions of the area to be covered. Be sure to get enough—and a little extra. Colors and patterns come on and go off the market fairly frequently and even the same color may vary from batch to batch.

Only simple tools are required—a level and chalk line for laying out tilework, a square for keeping it straight and a notched trowel for spreading adhesive. Buy a trowel with notches the size and spacing specified on the label of the adhesive container. For cutting the large unglazed tiles called quarry tiles, rent a heavy-duty tile cutter such as the type used by professionals. For glazed tiles you can use a glass cutter for scoring straight cuts, and for cutting curves and angles get a pair of nippers, a cutting tool similar to pliers that nibbles away tiles a bit at a time. A carbide-tipped hole saw can save you time and work in making large numbers of round holes, as for fitting tile around pipe. Protect your eyes with safety goggles *(page 130)* when using nippers or a hole saw.

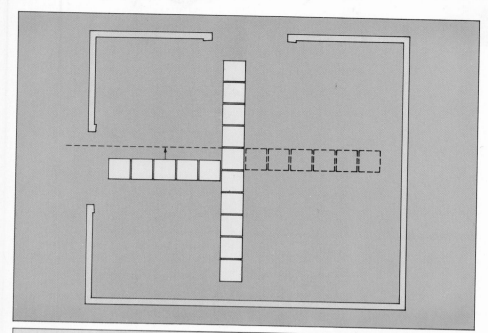

Fitting the Pattern to the Kitchen or Bathroom

Planning a pattern for a floor. Lay a row of dry tile—or squares of tiles—from the middle of a doorway to the opposite wall, guided by a string nailed from the doorway to the wall. If a gap of less than half a tile width remains at the end of the run, remove the first tile and center the remaining tiles. The resulting spaces left for the two border tiles will equal more than half the width of a tile, avoiding awkward cuts on tiny pieces.

If the room has a second doorway, run a second row of tiles inward from this doorway until it nearly reaches the first row of tiles. Slide the first row over until its edge meets the last tile of the second row. Snap intersecting chalk lines as a guide for laying the tiles.

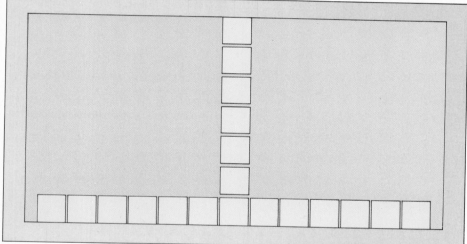

Planning a countertop pattern. Lay a row of dry tiles across the front edge of the counter. Lay a second row perpendicular to the first from the front edge to the backsplash. Adjust the positions of the two rows as at left above so that border tiles are even. If only a small amount of space remains at either of the borders, arrange the tiles slightly farther apart and plan to fill the spaces between them with grout after the tiles have been cemented in place.

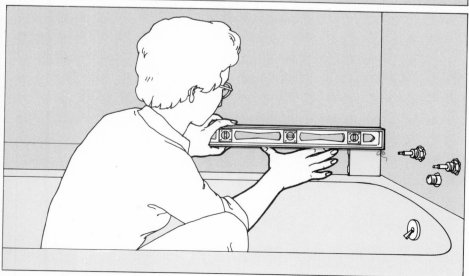

Positioning tiles on a wall. Since horizontal features—tub rim, floor edges, floor cove moldings or countertop—are almost never truly level, use a level to find the lowest point at which the feature meets the wall. Measure one tile width above this point, plus 1/4 inch for clearance under the tiles, and snap a chalk line the length of the wall. Find the highest point of the horizontal feature and measure its distance from the chalk line. If this distance is within 1/8 inch of a tile height, align the tops of the first row of tiles with the chalk line and vary the size of its joint line beneath the tiles. If the distance from the high point to the chalk line is not within 1/8 inch of the tile height, trim tiles to fit between the line and the horizontal feature.

Determine the width of border tiles by measuring the length of the wall and calculating how many whole tiles will fill that space while leaving room for borders more than half a tile wide.

The Tricks of Cutting

1 **Cutting border tiles.** Lay a dry tile over the last fixed tile next to the border. Place another dry tile on top of it and move the second tile to the wall leaving a grout-line space equal to that between other tiles. Mark the first tile where the top tile overlaps it. This portion should fit the border space. Cut at the mark with a tile cutter or score the tile with a glass cutter using a straightedge as a guide. Place the tile over a pencil, lining up the pencil with the scored line on the tile. Press gently on both sides of the tile until it breaks. If the tile is scored too close to the edge to break easily, use tile nippers.

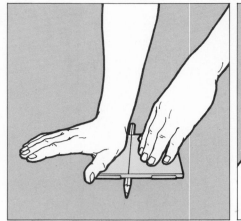

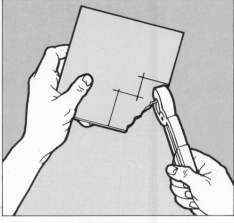

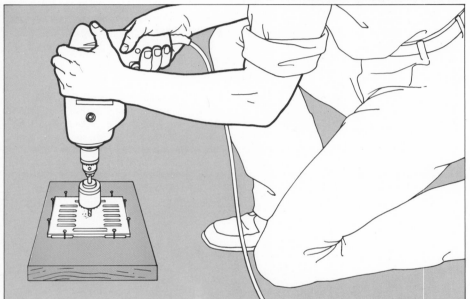

Making irregular cuts. When cutting tile to fit around a doorjamb or other irregular area, first mark the line of the cut. Holding the tile glazed side up, use nippers to nibble away the unwanted part of the tile. Practice using nippers on waste tile before making an unfamiliar cut. Take tiny bites less than 1/8 inch at a time to avoid breaking the tile. Smooth the rough-cut edges with an abrasive stone or a file.

Cutting holes. To cut a hole with a special carbide-tipped hole saw, fasten the tile glazed side down to a plank by driving nails partway in on each side *(left)*. Cut slowly, using firm but not heavy pressure. To fit the tile around a pipe you cannot remove, cut it in two through the middle of the hole. To cut a hole with nippers, outline the hole on the face of the tile, cut the tile through the center of the outline and use the nippers to nibble out the marked area. When the pieces are installed, only a hairline will show between them.

Setting Separate Tiles

1 **Preparing the surface.** Spread adhesive—using the kind of adhesive appropriate to your particular surface *(page 152)*—as thinly as possible with the unnotched side of the trowel. Avoid covering reference lines. Let this skim coat dry.

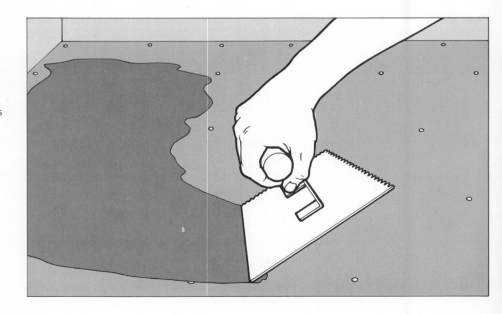

2 **Applying adhesive.** Spread adhesive over an area of about 10 square feet with the notched edge of the trowel, holding the edge against the surface at a 45° angle. Use only about a cup of adhesive at a time so that adhesive flows freely from the notches. Avoid covering reference lines.

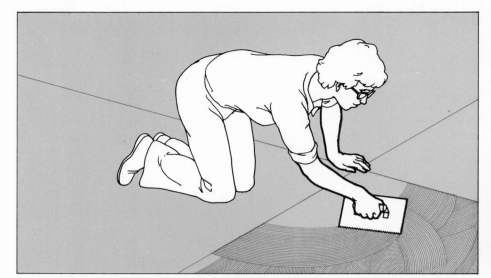

3 **Setting tiles.** Start setting tiles at reference lines *(right)* near the middle of the room and work toward walls. Press each tile in place with your fingertips, twisting it slightly to set it into the adhesive; do not slide tiles into place or adhesive will fill the grout joint and make grouting impossible. When setting thick tiles with indentations on the backs, apply adhesive also to the back of each tile. Butt the spacing lugs on the edges of the tiles tightly together for a proper fit. Check alignment frequently with a straightedge.

Cut each border tile individually as you reach the end of a course, since border spaces may vary slightly. Remove adhesive from the faces of the tiles with the solvent recommended by the adhesive manufacturer.

4 **Beating in the tile.** Pad a scrap of 2-by-4 the length of three tiles with several layers of cloth. Put this beater, padded side down, on the set tiles and tap it gently with a hammer several times along its length. Beating the tiles sets them more firmly into the adhesive and helps to ensure a level floor. Let the adhesive harden for 24 hours before grouting. If you must walk on newly laid tile, cover it first with plywood.

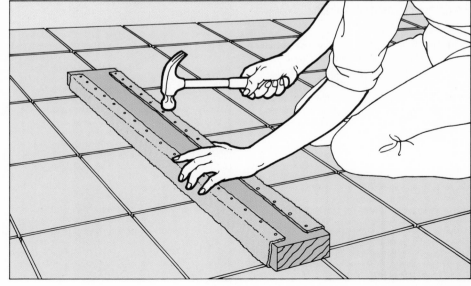

Setting Sheets of Tile

Backed tile. Some tile comes in sheets several tiles square, the tiles attached to one another with flexible grout. Set sheets of backed tile, using the techniques shown for individual tiles *(pages 154-155, Steps 1-4)*. If one or more tiles in a sheet must be cut to fit around pipes or fixtures, cut the affected tiles out of the sheet with a razor blade and trim away the cut grouting. Set the remaining tiles in the sheet, then cut the detached tiles to fit around the obstacle *(page 154)*. Set the cut tiles and, after 24 hours, regrout around them with silicone rubber grouting *(page 157)*.

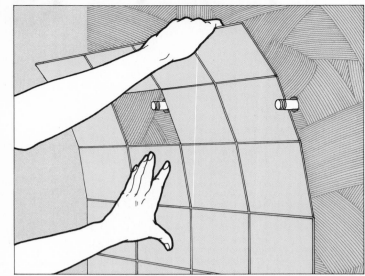

Mosaic tile sheets. Most mosaic tile comes in sheets held together not by grout but by paper on the face of the tiles or by mesh on the back. Roll up the sheet with the back of the tile on the outside. After troweling on adhesive, place the free edge of the sheet where it is to be set and gradually unroll the sheet, pressing the tiles gently into the adhesive. Do not slide sheets into place. Space sheets the same distance apart as the tiles in the sheets. The mesh on mesh-mounted tiles remains in place under the tiles; the paper on paper-faced tiles is removed after the tiles are set by dampening it and peeling it off.

When mosaic tiles must be cut to fit a space, cut the affected tiles out of the sheet, then trim them as necessary and set the cut tiles individually.

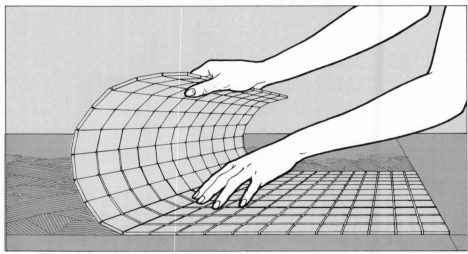

Finishing Techniques

Grouting. Mix grout to the consistency specified on the label. Trowel it into the joints and spread it with a window-washing squeegee or stiff cardboard. After about 15 minutes, wipe up excess grout with a damp sponge, rinsing the sponge frequently. When all grout has been removed, let the tiles dry; polish with a soft cloth.

Applying silicone grouting. Use a caulking gun with the tip cut at a 45° angle to grout between sheets of backed tile with mildew-resistant silicone rubber seal. Fill joints to the same depth as the grouting between tiles. Also grout around any tiles you have set individually. When the silicone rubber is tacky, clean the tiles around the joints, using alcohol on a soft cloth.

Sealing grout. A good way to keep grout joints from becoming discolored by dirt or mildew is to seal them with a penetrating-type liquid water-repellent sealer after the grout has cured for 28 days. On walls, apply the sealer to the grout joints with a small brush such as a watercolor brush. On floors, spread the sealer over the joints and wipe up any excess with a soft cloth.

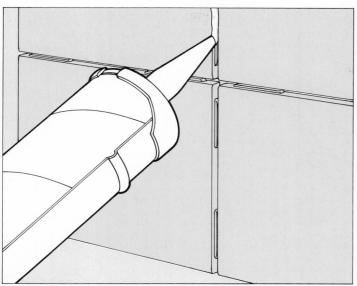

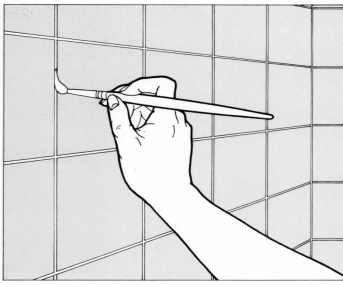

Sealing Tile Flooring

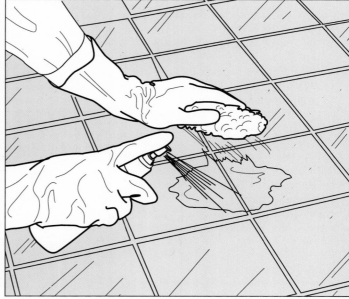

Sealing the flooring. Apply a commercial tile sealer periodically to the flooring to help protect it and ease regular maintenance. Consult a tile dealer for the tile sealer recommended for your type of flooring; if it is of glazed tiles, a tile sealer is not necessary. Clean the tile flooring using a nonacid commercial floor cleaner, then follow the manufacturer's instructions to prepare and apply the tile sealer. Wearing rubber gloves, work from one end of the flooring to the other end of it on a small section at a time, wiping the tile sealer onto the surface with a clean, soft cloth

(above, left) or mop; do not pour the tile sealer directly onto the flooring. Apply only a thin, uniform coat of the tile sealer and wipe off any excess; allow the flooring to dry overnight. If the flooring is of glazed or other tiles that do not require a sealer, apply a commercial grout sealer of liquid silicone to the grout. Following the manufacturer's instructions, spray the grout sealer onto the surface or apply it with a soft cloth, immediately wiping up any excess *(above, right)*; allow the flooring to dry overnight.

Accessories for Bathroom Walls

The essential bathroom accessories— soap dishes, towel bars and toilet-tissue holders—and many less essential ones are available in three types. Flush-set accessories mount on the wall much like tile or paneling; they are installed at the time the wall covering is applied. Recessed accessories, applied at the same stage of wall finishing, are, as the name suggests, fitted into holes in the wall. The third type, surface-mounted accessories, can be installed at any time over the wall covering; some are merely glued on, but the ones held by screws and mounting clips are generally sturdier. The method of fastening the accessory to the clip depends on whether the accessory is ceramic or metal *(right)*.

Vertical or L-shaped grab bars, resembling towel racks but more sturdily mounted, are a useful addition to any bathroom. Like other surface-mounted accessories, they are fixed on top of the wall covering. But plastic anchors should not be used to hold the mounting screws for a grab bar. Some people use hollow-wall fasteners, but it is better to screw a grab bar directly into wood blocking placed behind the wall at the time of framing the room with studs and other supports.

If a wall is being tiled, flush-set accessories are generally installed. Leave an opening for them at the time of tiling, cutting tiles as needed to trim the edges of the space. When setting or replacing a flush-set accessory, use plaster of paris rather than tile adhesive to bond it to the wall. The plaster grips every little crevice around the opening and expands slightly as it sets, strengthening the bond.

Recessed accessories can be installed in any wall that can be cut, and are suitable for tiled walls if a space for them is planned and the underlying material is cut before tiling. The small opening in the wall must be cut to the same dimensions as the accessory's recessed part, the edges at least 1 1/2 inches from a stud.

Surface-Mounted Pieces

Drilling tile. Locate accessories so that their screw holes are as near to the centers of tiles as possible. Use rubber cement to stick a piece of thin paperboard, such as a file card, where the accessory is to be fastened. Hold the mounting clip for the accessory against the card and mark the screw holes. Drill with a masonry bit and a variable-speed drill at low speed; apply light pressure to avoid breaking the tile. After the holes are drilled, peel the paperboard from the wall.

Installing ceramic accessories. Screw the metal mounting clip into plastic wall anchors, setting it with its thickest end up. Slide the accessory down over the wedge-shaped clip until it fits snugly against the wall. Grout the joint between the accessory and the wall.

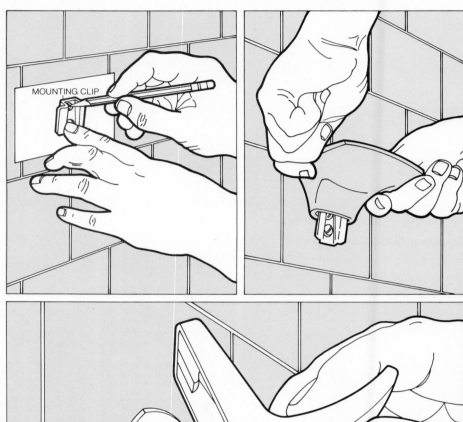

Installing metal accessories. Attach the clip to the wall as shown above, with its angled parts at top and bottom. Place the setscrew in the bottom of the accessory. Slip the top of the accessory over the top angle of the mounting clip and drop the bottom of the accessory over the bottom of the clip. Tighten the setscrew against the bottom of the clip with a small screwdriver.

Flush-Set Accessories

Mixing the plaster of paris. Add water slowly to a pound of plaster of paris in a mixing bowl, stirring constantly. Mix just until the material holds its shape and peaks in the bowl like stiffly beaten egg whites. Avoid excessive stirring; too much air in the mixture will speed setting time. Trowel about a 1/4-inch layer onto the back of the accessory, slightly thinner toward the edges.

Setting the accessory. Press the accessory firmly against the wall while wiggling it to force the plaster of paris into irregularities around and behind the adjacent tiles. Wipe off plaster that oozes out the sides of the front flange. Hold the accessory in place until the plaster stiffens, usually a minute or two. The next day, grout around the flange.

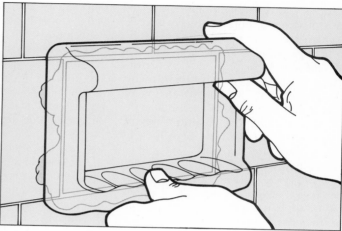

Recessed Accessories

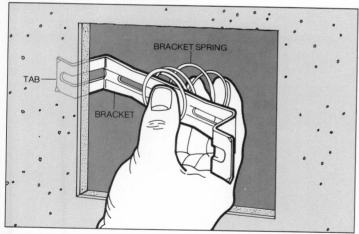

Positioning the hanger bracket. To install a recessed accessory that was planned before the wall was surfaced, screw it directly into wood blocking between studs. For installation after the wall is surfaced, cut and finish the opening, then use a winged bracket to secure the accessory behind the wall *(above)*. Slip the first coil of the bracket spring over the center of the bracket with the remainder of the spring pointing away from the spread tabs. Angle the bracket into the recess, spring first, and position its tabs against the back of the wall surface. The spring, pushing against the far side of the wall section, will hold the bracket in place.

Mounting the accessory. Place a bead of colorless caulking compound around the back of the front flange on the accessory. Insert the accessory into its opening. Put one of the mounting screws through the accessory and engage it in the slot in the mounting bracket. Tighten the screw a turn or two. Do the same with the other screw and then tighten both of the screws to hold the accessory in place.

Plastic Laminates: Easy to Mount and Maintain

Plastic laminate—the tough, impermeable, stain-resistant material that now is almost universal for kitchen countertops—also makes attractive covering for kitchen and bathroom walls, tables, vanities and cabinet doors. Applying laminate sheets is almost as easy as painting and generally far more satisfactory for surfaces subject to heavy wear.

Many laminates used on surfaces other than walls come in sheets 4 by 8 feet in size and 1/16 inch thick; walls require only 1/32-inch material. The sheets expand and contract with changes in temperature and should be allowed to adapt to the room where they will be used—stack them loosely against a wall for 48 hours.

Laminates can be applied over plywood, particle board, hardboard or old laminate. However, it is all but impossible to apply laminate over ceramic tile or linoleum; such surfaces must first be covered with underlayment to which the laminate is then cemented. Two types of contact adhesive are widely used. One, based on water, is nonflammable and nontoxic but lower in bonding strength than the second type, which contains a petroleum-based sol-

vent, highly flammable and toxic. If you must use this type indoors, keep it away from heat, sparks and open flames. Do not smoke while working, extinguish pilot lights and gas burners, open the circuit breakers controlling all nearby stoves, heaters and electric motors—including fans and refrigerators—and provide cross ventilation in the work area.

Because of the hazards of petroleum-based adhesive—as well as the difficulty of handling large sheets of laminate in small rooms—work outdoors as much as possible. Moderate temperatures are necessary; contact adhesives dry slowly at temperatures much below 70° and at higher temperatures dry too fast and lose bonding strength.

Applying laminate to countertops or similar surfaces is easiest when the countertop is being built *(page 163)* or has been removed to a roomy work area. But if removing an already installed countertop is impractical, apply laminate with the countertop in place *(page 162)*.

In either case, remove any metal edging from the countertop and the backsplash. You can later cover these edges with laminate for a finished appearance or install new metal edging *(page 162)*.

The latter process is easier for novices and hides minor misalignments of the top surface laminate. Also remove any metal cove molding that may be attached to the ends or back of the countertop.

Before applying laminate to a top surface, remove the sink or other fixtures recessed into cutouts in the surface. All cutouts in new laminate are made after the laminate has been bonded.

Any surface to be laminated should be clean, dry and even, with protrusions sanded down and holes filled with wood putty. If you apply new laminate directly over the old, flatten bubbles by breaking them with a hammer and sanding them down, or by countersinking a flat-head wood screw through the bubble into the base. Cement loose edges and sand the whole surface thoroughly before applying adhesive; sand, sawdust or laminate chips left on the countertop can make permanent lumps in the finished surface.

Cover the front of a cabinet door in the same way as a countertop but be sure to cover the back of the door with a thinner backing laminate. It will keep the door from shrinking or swelling unevenly with changes in humidity, thus loosening the bond of the adhesive on the front.

Covering a Countertop

1 Cutting laminate. Mark the pieces to be cut out of each laminate sheet 1/4 inch larger in all dimensions than the surfaces to be covered, to provide a margin for error. When laminating a countertop that has been removed from its counter, plan to remove the right-angled backsplash and cover the whole top surface *(Step 4)*. For a countertop being laminated in place with the backsplash attached, cover the top surface up to the bottom edge of the backsplash. Place the marked sheet face up on a firm support or the floor, and score the sheet with a blade called a laminate scriber. Then bend the edge of the sheet *(right)* until it snaps like glass along the scored line. You can also cut the sheet with a saber saw using a fine-tooth blade, but test the blade on a scrap of laminate first to make sure it will not cause excessive chipping.

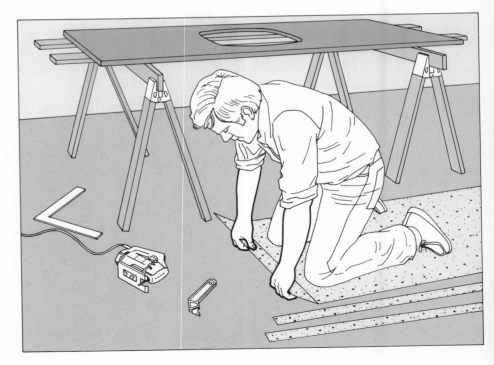

2 **Putting on edge strips.** Attach edge strips first at the short sides of the countertop. If you are laminating a U-shaped countertop, begin at the bottom of the U. If you plan to use metal edging, see instructions on page 162. Apply adhesive to both laminate and edge with a brush or a narrow paint roller, using only a little at a time. When the adhesive has dried, hold an edge strip between thumbs and forefingers *(right)*; position it as accurately as possible and set it in place. Once in contact, it cannot be shifted. Tap all over the surface with a hammer and wood block.

To bend laminate around a gentle curve, soak it in hot water until it becomes flexible, wipe it dry and attach it before it cools.

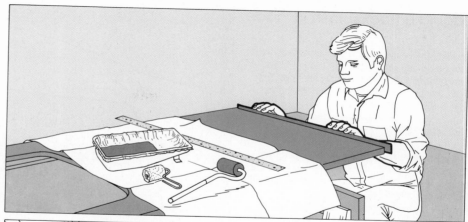

3 **Trimming projections.** Wearing a face shield or goggles *(page 130)* and mask *(page 76)*, trim off laminate projecting at the top, bottom and sides of the edges with a plane, a router fitted with a carbide trimming bit *(right)* or a special laminate trimmer rented from your supplier. Many installers trim the short edges before laminating the long edges so that the long strip laps over the ends of the short ones.

4 **Bonding a top surface.** Apply adhesive to the top surface and the laminate back, using a little extra adhesive around the edges of both. When the adhesive is dry, lay pieces of lumber 3/4 inch thick at 1-foot intervals across the top surface. Lay the laminate face up on the wood supports and aligned with the top surface. Slide out one end support and press that end of the laminate sheet down. Remove remaining supports one at a time, pressing down laminate as you work toward the other end. Tap all over the surface with a wood block and a hammer. Trim off the projecting edges as in Step 3, but coat the edging below with petroleum jelly to prevent scorching by the router or laminate trimmer. Bevel the sharp edges of laminate along the top and at corners, using a file or a router with a bevel cutter.

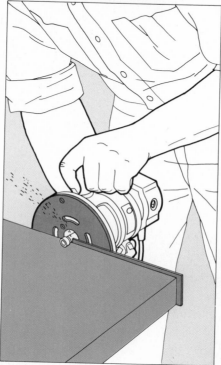

5 **Making cutouts.** Cut out holes for sinks, plumbing and electrical outlets after attaching laminate. If you are relaminating an old surface that already has cutouts, use a panel bit to cut the laminate with a router, following the rim of the original hole. The bit bores its own starter hole in unsupported laminate. If your router *(page 454)* rotates clockwise, as most do, move it clockwise around the curves. If you have made an entirely new countertop, mark each hole as shown on page 164. Drill a 1/4-inch starter hole—and a pilot hole at each corner for cuts with corners—and cut out the opening with a saber saw fitted with a metal-cutting blade. Smooth the edges of the cutout with a router, a laminate cutter or a file.

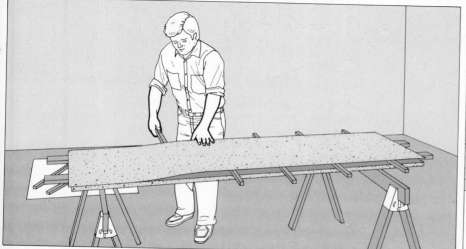

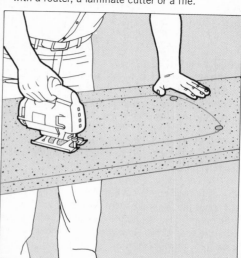

Edging a Backsplash in Place

Covering the backsplash. When laminating the backsplash of a countertop that has not been detached from the counter, apply laminate first to the front of the backsplash and trim the top edge flush with a sanding block. Apply a strip cut as accurately as possible to the top edge of the backsplash *(right)*.

If you are covering a countertop detached from the counter, cover the backsplash as you did the other surfaces—bonding first the sides, then the front and finally the top. Reattach the backsplash after lamination as on page 166, Step 8, putting a small bead of silicone seal along the bottom edge of the backsplash to seal the joint.

With the countertop in place, caulk between the top edge of the backsplash and the wall as needed. If there is no backsplash, seal the wall edges of the countertops *(lower right)*.

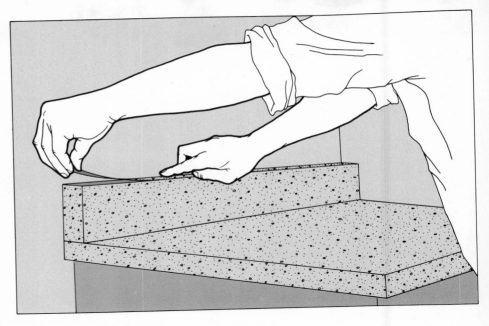

Finishing Edges with Metal

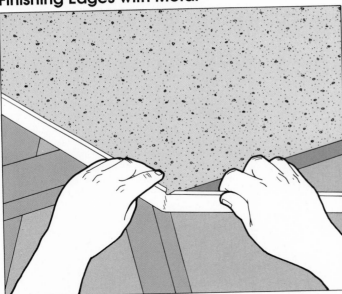

Adding a snap-on edge. If you laminate only the top surface of a countertop, finish the edges with C-shaped metal molding. To allow for error, cut a strip a little longer than the edge it will cover. Slip one end of the strip over the edge where it meets a wall. If the countertop is slightly too thick, trim off the bottom of the countertop around the edge with a router. Secure the molding end with a brad through its bottom lip. Snap the molding onto the countertop edge.

At each outside corner cut a wedge of approximately 10° out of the top and bottom lips of the molding and bend the molding around the corner. At inside corners, miter the ends of two strips. Secure the molding with brads through its lower lip.

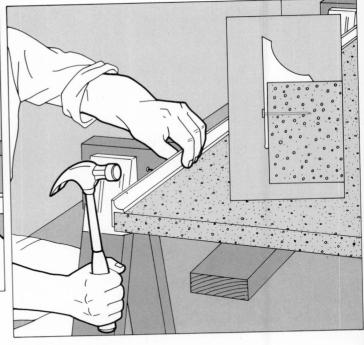

Adding metal cove molding. If, instead of having a backsplash, a countertop adjoins a wall or walls covered with laminate, ceramic tile or other water-proof material, seal the joint between countertop and wall. If the countertop is detached from its counter, before installing it fasten metal cove molding to the wall edges of the countertop by nailing through the flange at the back of the molding *(inset)*. Run a bead of silicone seal along the back of the molding, then install the countertop. If the countertop has not been detached, simply caulk along the joint.

A Custom-Made Counter for a Ready-Made Base

The standard countertop is essentially a long board 1 1/2 inches thick and about 25 inches deep. A vertical backsplash 4 inches high usually runs along the rear edge; the entire assembly rises about 36 inches above the floor. Many countertops have self-rimmed sinks and the units of a cooking range set into them. A flangelike, stainless-steel sink frame may be used to support some sink models and also such inserts as cutting boards.

A countertop may consist of a solid length of hardwood or of a textured synthetic material. It may also consist of a less expensive material, such as particle board or exterior-grade plywood, covered with a decorative surface such as

tile or high-pressure laminated plastic. For installation of plastic laminates and tiles, see pages 154-157 and 160-162.

As an alternative to such an assembly, you can buy a countertop complete with a backsplash and factory-installed laminate. Factory-made tops are easy to install—you need only saw them to length, cut out the openings and screw them to a counter—but they have their drawbacks: L-shaped countertops must be miter cut at a very specific angle; it is often best to take your dimensions to a dealer, and have it cut when ordering the material.

Mitered joints are longer and weaker than butt joints and a long mitered seam in surface laminate provides a channel

through which water can seep, warping or rotting the core below. And the backsplash of a ready-made top cannot be easily fitted to bowed or bumpy walls. When you construct a top from scratch, you can use butt joints, fit the backsplash precisely to the wall and minimize water seepage by locating a 2- or 3-inch laminate seam at the sink cutout, far from the butt joint.

To determine the top's depth, measure the distance from the cabinet front to the wall and add 1 inch for overhang. The length depends on the layout of the cabinets; set a top over the long leg of an L-shaped layout, and add 1 inch of overhang for ends that do not abut a wall.

1 **Assembling the core.** With a circular or saber saw *(page 454)* cut a core 3/4 inch thick to the right length and depth. To join two pieces at right angles with a butt joint, apply white construction glue to the edges, then reinforce the joint with corrugated steel nails driven across the seam at 1 1/2-inch intervals. Turn the board upside down and hammer a second series of corrugated nails across the back of the seam.

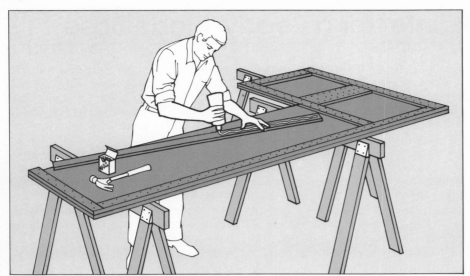

2 Installing the battens. To increase the thickness of the core to 1 1/2 inches, you must add strips called battens, 2 inches wide and 3/4 inch thick. Cut the battens from stock to match the sides of the core, butting at the corners; the locations of the butt joints are unimportant, but the strips must cover the perimeter of the core.

Turn the core upside down, apply a ribbon of white construction glue to the wide surface of a batten strip and press the glued batten to the core, with the outside edges of the mated pieces exactly flush. When the glue has set slightly, hammer a zigzag pattern of 1 1/8-inch nails, set about 1 1/2 inches apart, through the batten and into the core. Repeat the procedure for all the battens. If the countertop contains a butt joint, cut a batten 6 inches wide to the length of the exposed seam and install it along the joint.

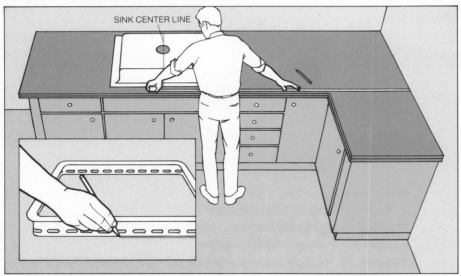

SINK CENTER LINE

3 Positioning a sink. Mark the center of the front edge of the sink cabinet and measure from this mark to the nearest side wall. Set the core on the base cabinets and draw a line across the top of the core from front to rear at the midpoint of the sink cabinet. Mark the center of the sink assembly on the edges of the sink rim, front and rear. Turn the sink upside down, line up the marks with the line on the core and move the sink along this line until the rim is at least 2 inches from the front of the core and 1 inch from the rear. Then trace around the sink's rim.

For a sink supported by a stainless-steel frame *(inset)*, center the rim upright on the pencil line and trace the outline. Cutting-board and hot-plate inserts can be positioned almost anywhere on the countertop, as long as they are at least 2 inches from the front and 1 inch from the rear.

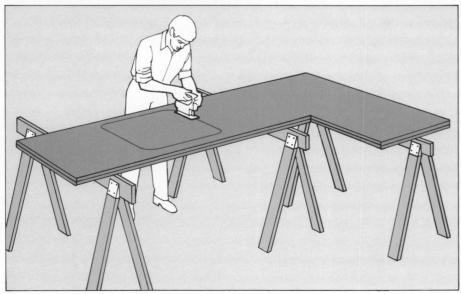

4 Making the sink cutout. Set the sink aside and return the core to the sawhorses. Mark points 1/4 inch inside the outline of the sink rim on all four sides and, using a straightedge and soft pencil, connect the marks to outline a sink cutout 1/4 inch inside the original. Drill a pilot hole 1 inch inside the outline and, beginning at this hole, cut along the outline with a saber saw to form the sink opening. For a sink-frame cutout, simply drill a pilot hole and then cut along the original outline.

To make the splashboard, measure the lengths of the countertop edges that will rest against a wall; where two such edges meet at right angles, subtract 3/4 inch from one of the measurements. With a saber or circular saw *(page 454)* cut strips of core stock 4 inches wide to your measurements. At this point apply tiling or a surface laminate to the core, battens and splashboard by the methods shown on pages 154-157 and 160-162.

5 **Installing the backsplash molding.** Cut metal L molding the length of the backsplash; trim the corner of the wide side of the L at a 45° angle. With the backsplash bottom up, set the molding in place with the wide side of the L flat against the bottom of the splash, and fasten it with lath nails at 1-inch intervals. File the rough ends of the molding smooth.

6 **Measuring a bowed wall.** Set the countertop in place on the cabinets, with its rear edges against the walls. If there are gaps along the line where the countertop meets a wall—an indication that the wall may be bowed—measure the space between the countertop and walls at 12-inch intervals and mark the intervals and measurements on the countertop.

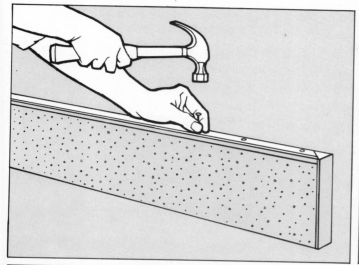

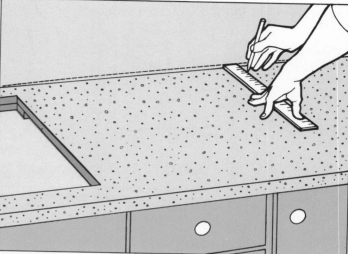

7 **Drilling and caulking for the splashboard.** Return the countertop to the sawhorses and, using a 3/16-inch bit, drill a series of holes starting 1 inch in from the end of the countertop. Locate the holes 3/8 inch from the back edge of the countertop; space them 8 inches apart. Run a bead of caulking around the countertop along the line formed by the holes.

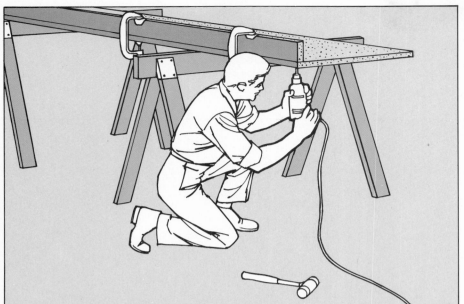

8 **Installing the backsplash.** Secure the backsplash in position with a pair of C clamps and hammer a 2 1/2-inch No. 10 drive-screw into the first predrilled hole and through the backsplash molding. Use a power screwdriver to finish driving the screw. Repeat the procedure at every hole, repositioning the C clamps as necessary. At each gap measurement, tap the backsplash with a mallet until it overlaps the counter edge by a distance equal to the gap, then drive in a screw.

Reading the measurements is easiest if you work from below *(left)*; but if that position is awkward, turn the countertop over and screw from above. Caution: Avoid reshaping the backsplash by more than 1/4 inch—a sharp curve can cause a screw to break through the backsplash. To join backsplash strips at right angles, drive 1 1/4-inch nails spaced 3/4 inch apart through the back of one strip into the end of the other.

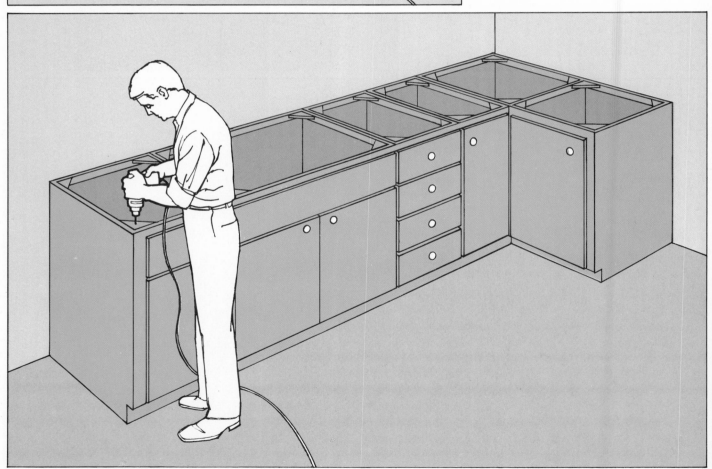

9 **Completing the installation.** Drill 3/16 inch holes through the centers of the braces at the outer corners of the end cabinets. Set the countertop in position and, working from below, drive No. 10 screws up through these holes into the battens above. The thickness of the braces will determine the length of the screws, but be careful not to use a screw so long that it extends through the core of the countertop and punctures the surface. Caution: Do not use an adhesive, rather than screws, to anchor the top—prying off a glued countertop for repair or alteration is not only much more difficult than simply withdrawing the screws but also is likely to damage the cabinets and the countertop.

Fitting Cabinets to the Walls and Floors

The decor of a kitchen is set largely by the style and finish of its cabinets. Its efficiency depends largely on their size and placement. But just as important as the cabinets themselves is the care with which they are installed. Poorly installed cabinets will sag from the start; their doors will swing open on their own or refuse to open at all. Bad installation will ruin good cabinets by wearing out their hinges and weakening their structure.

The installation job begins well before you set to work on the cabinets themselves. Unless you are putting new cabinets against an unused wall, you first must remove the old ones. Do not simply pry them off the wall with a crowbar—old cabinets are worth saving for a workshop or utility room. Take them down by first removing the screws that fasten cabinets to one another, then the screws that hold the cabinets to the walls. If the slots in the screwheads are too worn to accept a screwdriver, use a power drill to drive a bit down through the head. The head will drop off, and you can pull the cabinets from the wall, then remove the screw shank with pliers.

Then, mark the measurements for the new cabinets on the walls. Use a level to find the highest spot on the floor along these walls, and make all vertical measurements from this point. The standard height to the top of a wall cabinet is 84 inches, or 3 or 4 inches lower if the reach is too high for you. Using the level, mark a straight line along the walls at the height you choose. Next, measure the height of your cabinets and mark parallel lines along the walls for the bottoms of the cabinets. Finally, mark lines for the tops of the base cabinets, making adjustments if necessary for a raised or lowered countertop.

The width of a set of cabinets, of course, will depend upon your particular installation, but remember that ready-made cabinets will rarely fit the exact width of a wall. To fill the gaps, filler strips are available in 3- or 6-inch width, in the same material as the cabinets themselves. Trim the strips if necessary, and place them between cabinets of the same height—never at the end of a set.

Walls and floors are not flat—though cabinets are made as if they were—and you will have to shim outward or upward to make them level. If there are conspicuous gaps between the bottom of the cabinets and the wall, hide them with a wood shoe molding stained or painted to match the cabinets and nailed to the studs. To cover gaps between a kick space and the floor, use a vinyl cove molding *(page 150)*—a wood molding is likely to warp from spills and cleaning.

Readying the Walls

Flattening a wall. Using a carpenter's square or level, check the flatness of the walls within the lines you have marked for wall and floor cabinets. Cover the floor with a dropcloth. Wearing goggles, a dust mask and a hat, sand down the high spots and bulges with a sanding block and garnet paper. For very high spots use a wood chisel and a power sander, checking constantly for flatness as you work.

Use an electronic density sensor *(page 46)* to locate all the stud-center positions, and mark them, directly above the line for the top of floor cabinets and above and below the lines for wall cabinets.

Special Wallboard for a Damp Room

Wallboard for such high-moisture areas as bathrooms and kitchens goes into place as easily as in any other room of the house—but it is no ordinary wallboard. The type used in other rooms absorbs moisture through its paper cover, and in a damp room its core becomes soft and spongy. The wallboard designed for bathrooms and kitchens has a tough, almost waterproof cover, and its core is saturated with asphalt that resists absorption and softening.

Water-resistant wallboard is scored, snapped and cut in exactly the same way as the standard type. Before putting it up, rough out all the plumbing in the room, and cut holes in the wallboard to accommodate the protruding pipes. Then nail the new wallboard into place.

A sheet of water-resistant wallboard that is 4 by 8 feet weighs about 10 pounds more than a sheet of standard wallboard, and calls for a different nailing arrangement: You must space nails at 6-inch intervals, rather than 1 foot apart as for standard wallboard, and be sure that the greater weight is adequately supported. Water-resistant wallboard is best supported on studs 16 inches on center. If the studs on your wall are farther apart, or if you plan to cover the wall with tiles more than 5/16 inch thick, add a horizontal 2-by-4 support between the centers of each pair of studs, and then nail the wallboard to the supports as well as to the studs themselves.

The Right Way to Hang Cabinets

1 **Placing the first cabinet.** Remove the cabinet doors. Beginning at an inside corner, have a helper raise the first cabinet to the horizontal line marked for the tops of the cabinets. Check that the cabinet is level, then drill 1/8-inch pilot holes through the holding strips on the back of the cabinet and into the studs. Fasten the cabinet to the wall with 1 1/2-inch, No. 10 screws, allowing some play for shimming *(Step 2)*. Check the fastened cabinet for horizontal level, and move the fastening screws if necessary.

2 **Shimming for plumb.** Check the cabinet edges for plumb and drive shims between the cabinet and wall wherever necessary, using narrow strips of smooth wood. If the cabinet is far out of plumb, loosen screws slightly to make room for the shims. When the cabinet is plumb, tighten the fastening screws; make a final check for both plumb and horizontal level. If you have forced the cabinet out of plumb, loosen the screws and reshim; if the cabinet is not level, remove it and reposition the screws.

3 **Fastening cabinets together.** Install subsequent cabinets along the wall, shimming them out to the same distance from the wall as the first one. As you hang each cabinet, secure it to the preceding one with a C clamp; protect the cabinet with pads of heavy cloth or strips of soft wood between the metal clamps and cabinets. For a cabinet up to 24 inches high, drill two 1/8-inch pilot holes, one third and two thirds of the distance from top to bottom, through the side of the front frame and into the preceding cabinet; drive 2 1/2-inch, No. 6 screws into the holes and pull the cabinets snugly together. For higher cabinets use three screws, positioned at the top, bottom and middle of the frames.

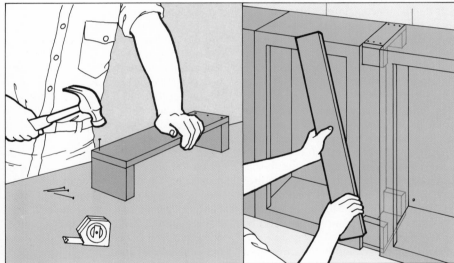

4 **Inserting a filler strip.** Set a filler strip between two installed cabinets and measure the distance from the back of the strip to the wall. Cut two pieces of 1/2-inch plywood to the width of the strip and the length of the distance you have measured; when fitted together at a right angle, the strip and the length of plywood should exactly match the depth of your cabinets. Carefully nail 1-by-3 (or, for a 6-inch strip, 1-by-6) blocks of wood to the ends of the plywood with twopenny finishing nails to make a long, U-shaped assembly *(left)*.

Fasten the plywood-and-block assembly between the cabinets with screws driven through the insides of the cabinets into the blocks. Nail the filler strip to the front wood blocks with twopenny finishing nails, countersink the nails and cover the nailheads with putty.

Installing Floor Cabinets

Leveling with shims. Floor cabinets must be shimmed at both the wall and the floor to make them level and plumb. Slide the first cabinet into place at an inside corner, shimming it at the floor until it is level and meets the height of the line on the wall. Drive these shims in with a block of scrap wood to avoid dents and scratches in the floor or cabinet. Screw the cabinet to the wall *(page 168, Step 1)*, checking to be sure that pulling the cabinet toward the wall does not tilt the top. Shim along the wall to make the cabinet plumb, then tighten the screws, checking again for level and plumb. Install additional cabinets and filler strips by the methods that are shown in Steps 3 and 4 above.

Wiring Designed to Meet Special Requirements

The variety of large and small appliances in a kitchen, and the combination of electricity and wet surfaces in a bathroom or kitchen, are two circumstances that can lead to electrical problems—the problem of overloaded circuits in the kitchen, of electric shock in either room. Both problems can be solved by improving existing wiring to modern standards. This may involve having new branch electrical circuits added and installing ground-fault circuit interrupter (GFCI) outlets.

The National Electrical Code (NEC) calls for no point along the wall-floor line in all rooms being more than six feet from an electrical outlet, eliminating the need for extension cords. In the kitchen area the NEC also requires at least two separate 20-ampere appliance circuits just for powering the refrigerator and small kitchen appliances in kitchen, pantry, breakfast room, dining room or similar spot. Countertop receptacles must be served by two or more different circuits. Each counter space wider than 12 inches needs an outlet of its own, with no point along the countertop being more than 24 inches horizontally from an outlet in that space.

Use the chart of average appliance power ratings below to see whether your kitchen needs more than two appliance circuits. Each appliance circuit may handle up to 2,400 watts of load. In addition, large appliances such as electric ranges, dishwashers and garbage disposers must have properly sized dedicated branch circuits all their own. In the bathroom, at least one outlet must be located next to the washbasin.

Power for a light-duty single use, such as a kitchen range fan or a light fixture over a work area, can usually be tapped from an existing ceiling fixture box or receptacle box, provided its circuit has spare electrical capacity. Running new branch circuits from the service panel is more complicated, and unless you know how to do it, this is best left to a professional electrician. An electrician can install a three-wire 240-volt cable coming from the main service panel and providing two new 120-volt branch circuits. In these, one side of each duplex receptacle can be served by one of the circuits while the other side is served by the other, giving two branch circuits available at each outlet. This is called a split circuit. Overcurrent protection for a split circuit uses a linked double breaker in the service panel.

An excellent way to get additional receptacles without having to cut into a wall for each one is to use a multi-outlet assembly—surface-mounted metal or plastic channels containing a number of prewired receptacles. The assemblies come in 3- to 6-foot lengths, with receptacles spaced 6, 12 or 18 inches apart; a long outlet assembly can be powered by a split circuit.

Ensuring kitchen and bathroom safety, the NEC requires GFCI protection in all new bathrooms and in kitchen outlets within six feet of the sink and certain other locations around the house. Adding ground-fault protection to an existing circuit makes good sense in any bathroom or kitchen. The device monitors the current-carrying conductors for what is called a "ground fault," a current leak caused by faulty electrical insulation in a plugged-in tool or appliance. While too small to trip a circuit breaker, such a current leak can be fatal to anyone who is standing on a wet floor or touching a grounded metal plumbing fixture. But a GFCI, within 1/40 of a second of detecting such a ground fault, safely cuts off all power to the outlet.

GFCIs are one of three types: a circuit breaker professionally installed in the main electrical service panel, a receptacle that can be installed by a homeowner in a new outlet box or as a replacement for an existing outlet, and a simple plug-in GFCI outlet or extension cord. If your bathroom or kitchen has several receptacles that need ground-fault protection, installing a "feed-through" GFCI outlet at the first outlet on the circuit will enable it to provide ground-fault protection to all the receptacles beyond it in the same circuit. Most GFCI outlets are of the feed-through type, having both LINE and LOAD connections; nonfeed-through GFCI outlets have only line connections.

Estimating circuit loads. Even a modest kitchen should have at least two separate 20-ampere circuits for small appliances, and you may need additional circuits if you are likely to run several high-power-using appliances at the same time. Use the chart at the right to estimate the maximum load on your kitchen circuits. The chart gives average power ratings for a wide range of appliances. Combine ratings to determine a total simultaneous load; to convert watts to amperes, divide by the voltage (120). For example, if a coffeemaker and a toaster are in use at the same time, the total load on the circuit would be 1,700 watts, or 14.2 amperes. This is somewhat below the maximum safe load for a 20-ampere circuit, but if a microwave oven is to be used at the same time, it should be plugged into a receptacle fed by another circuit, possibly one served by a split 240-volt cable.

Appliance Power Ratings

Appliance	Watts
Blender	300
Broiler	1,140
Coffee maker	600
Deep fryer	1,350
Food mixer	150
Frying pan	1,200
Refrigerator	850
Rotisserie	1,400
Sandwich grill	1,200
Toaster	1,100
Microwave oven	800

Installing a Ground-Fault Circuit Interrupter (GFCI) Outlet

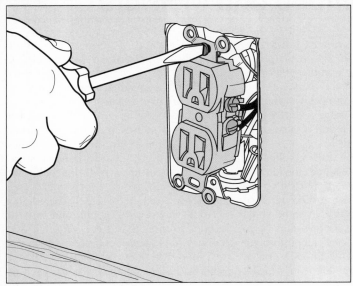

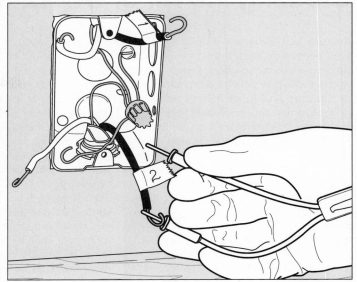

1 **Removing the old outlet.** Shut off the electricity to the outlet *(page 11)* and check that its power is off *(page 272)*; if it is controlled by a double breaker, have an electrician install a GFCI. Otherwise, remove the cover plate and unscrew the mounting strap *(above)*, then pull out the outlet. Caution: Before touching any wire, confirm again that its power is off, then disconnect each wire. Note: A feed-through-type GFCI outlet protects all outlets after it is installed on the circuit. To check if the outlet is the first on the circuit, wrap electrical tape around each wire end and restore the electricity, then plug a working lamp into each other outlet on the circuit. If no other outlet works, the outlet is the first on the circuit.

2 **Identifying the hot black wire.** Shut off the electricity and check that it is off. If one cable enters the electrical box, install the GFCI outlet *(Step 3)*. Otherwise, use a voltage tester *(page 269)* to identify the black wire that is hot—the one that carries current to the electrical box: Label each black wire using masking tape and isolate it from contact with anything, then restore the electricity. Caution: Wearing rubber gloves and standing on a dry spot, hold the tester probes by the insulated handles with only one hand. Touch one probe to the metal outlet box and the other probe in turn to each black wire *(above)*; the tester will glow when its probe touches the hot black wire. Note the hot black wire, then shut off the electricity again.

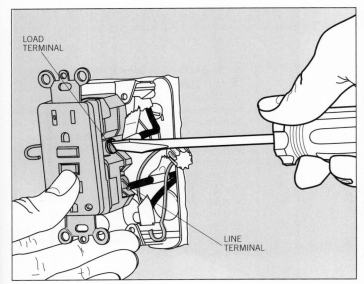

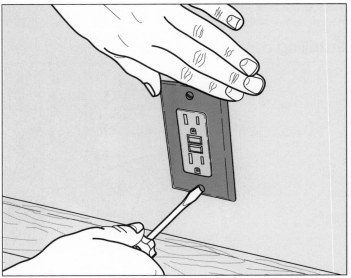

3 **Installing the GFCI outlet.** Buy a receptacle-type GFCI outlet, such as the one shown, at a building-supply center; install it following the manufacturer's instructions. Wrap the hot black wire clockwise around the brass terminal screw marked LINE, then tighten the connection. In the same way, connect the black wire that is not hot to the brass terminal screw marked LOAD *(above, left)*. Use the same procedure to install the white wire of each cable to the corresponding silver terminal

screw. Also connect any grounding wire disconnected from the old outlet to the grounding terminal screw; if there is no grounding wire, install a grounding jumper wire *(page 271)*. Then set the outlet gently into the electrical box, carefully folding the wires. Ensuring that the outlet is straight, screw the mounting strap to the electrical box and the cover plate onto the outlet *(above, right)*. Restore the electricity and test the outlet following the manufacturer's instructions.

Clearing the Air of Odors, Smoke and Moisture

Kitchens and bathrooms require fan-powered ventilation ducted to the outside of the house to remove odors, greasy smoke and water vapor, which can condense into moisture that mists mirrors and windows and damages walls and floors. In a bathroom, a simple wall or ceiling exhaust fan will eliminate condensation. For a kitchen, the ducted blower fan in a canopy hood above the range is generally most effective, although a simple through-the-wall fan may be easier to install. Ductless blower fans also are made for range hoods but this type only filters grease and smoke, churning heat and moisture back into the kitchen.

Metal shells for range hoods are made in a variety of sizes to be mounted under cabinets or on walls or suspended from ceilings. The shells have knockout sections to which ducts and wiring are connected. Most range hoods come with a squirrel-cage-type blower fan and a light prewired to switches on the front of the hood. The wiring terminates in a junction box in the hood; it must be connected to a wall receptacle or junction box.

Wall and ceiling blowers for bathrooms are installed in much the same way as range hoods, though you may need to add a wall switch for the fan. The duct connecting an exhaust fan to the outdoors should be as straight as possible. Its length and the number of elbows in it will affect your choice of blower fans since long runs resist the push of the fan and elbows add still more resistance—a 90° elbow creates as much resistance as 10 feet of duct.

An exit in an outside wall is preferable, with horizontal duct runs from the kitchen pitched slightly downward to keep grease from flowing back to the fan; but roof venting may be necessary. In some cases you may have to vent a downstairs bathroom or a kitchen "island" range through the roof, running duct up through one or more floors and concealing it in a closet or a wallboard enclosure. In cold climates, insulate any duct that passes through the attic to limit condensation. In an older house, you may be able to run duct into an unused flue.

Fans are rated in cubic feet of air moved per minute (CFM). A fan venting directly through an outside wall should have a CFM rating equal to the number of cubic feet in the room divided by 4 for a kitchen or by 7.5 for a bathroom. For a range hood set against an inside wall, use a fan rated at 40 times the number of feet of duct you will use. For fans set over ranges in island or peninsula counters, multiply duct length by 50. Add 50 to 100 CFM for duct runs longer than 10 feet. Variable-speed fans are usually more satisfactory than single-speed ones.

For most kitchen installations, round steel duct 7 inches in diameter is easiest to install, though you may need rectangular duct if you plan to conceal it between studs inside a wall. For bathroom installation, 3-inch or 4-inch duct is generally specified; in this size, flexible plastic duct is easier to handle and to bend around corners than steel. Wrap all duct connections with duct tape.

Where the duct run ends on the outside wall of the house or on the roof, install a wall or roof cap. A wall cap usually comes with an automatic hinged damper to close the duct passageway to back drafts and a screen to keep out birds and insects.

Clean the grease filter of a kitchen vent hood once a week with hot, soapy water. Every six months shut off the power and remove and clean the blower; at the same time, clean the hood interior and as much of the duct as you can reach conveniently. Removing a large build-up of grease deep in the ductwork may be a job for a professional.

Installing a Hood for a Kitchen

1 **Making the duct opening.** Remove a knockout in the range hood for attaching the duct and the wiring. Hold the hood in place while a helper reaches underneath to mark the outline of the duct opening on the kitchen wall or cabinet bottom *(left)*. Turn off at the main service panel all electrical circuits going to or through the kitchen. With a keyhole saw, cut around the outline, staying 1/4 inch outside the mark. If the fan is to exhaust directly out of the wall behind the range, cut a hole for the duct in the outside wall. If the opening must go through a stud, remove a segment of stud, and install the necessary 2-by-4 support segments to frame around the opening.

2 **Making the duct connection.** Attach a hood collar, which is provided by the manufacturer, to the round or rectangular duct opening in the hood. Use sheet-metal screws driven through preformed holes in the collar and the hood. Depending on the direction in which the duct will run, attach a length of duct or an elbow to the collar.

3 **Mounting the hood.** Drill 1/8-inch holes through the cabinet bottom at the locations of the mounting slots, spacing out a recessed cabinet bottom with wood strips *(below)* as necessary. If there is no cabinet from which to hang the hood, support it with right-angle brackets. A hood over a range in an island or a peninsula away from a wall can be attached to ceiling joists or to a soffit built down from the ceiling.

Three Routes for Ducting

TRANSITION FITTING

Using a soffit. If the vent opening is in the cabinet bottom, and if—as is likely—there is open or enclosed space between the tops of the cabinets and the ceiling, run duct up to the soffit and attach an elbow. To connect round duct to a rectangular vent collar, use the transition fitting shown at left. Cut a hole slightly more than 7 inches in diameter through the outside wall. From outside, insert 7-inch round steel duct and connect it to the elbow. You can hide the duct, if necessary, by framing the space above the cabinets and covering it with wallboard *(pages 80-86)*.

If there is no space above the cabinets, you can run ducts in the same way through holes cut in the sides of adjoining cabinets.

Dodging a brick wall. In a single-story brick house you can avoid the chore of cutting through masonry by running duct up into attic space and down through an eave—circling around the top course of the brick wall. Just within the wall install a transition fitting to adapt round to rectangular duct.

Going through the roof. If the most convenient route for the duct is through the roof, run duct straight up, through a hole in the ceiling between two joists, through a corresponding hole in the attic floor and out through a hole in the roof between two rafters. You may have to angle the duct slightly to avoid joists and rafters.

TRANSITION FITTING

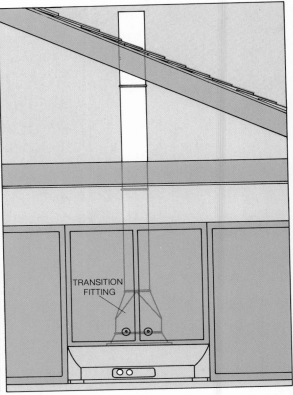

TRANSITION FITTING

Covering the Outside End

Attaching a wall cap. Cut off ducting that protrudes beyond the house siding. Fit a flanged wall cap over the end of the duct; be sure that the cap fits tightly around the duct and that the hinged damper swings freely. Caulk under the flange to make a weathertight seal.

Installing a roof cap. Trim away protruding duct 1/2 inch above the roof surface, cutting at the same angle as the roof pitch. Pull out the trimmed section of ducting. The top edge of the flashing attached to the roof cap should be slipped under the shingles around the hole in the roof.

Cut away shingles that keep the roof cap from fitting over the hole. Working from below, reinstall the duct section. Coat the underside of the roof-cap flashing with roofing cement and press it into place. Apply roofing cement to the underside of shingles that overlap the flashing.

Hooking Up the Fan

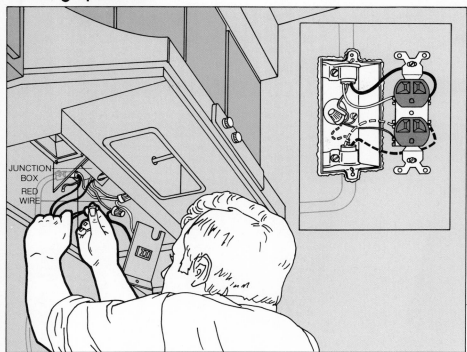

Wiring a range hood. Turn off current to the room and test to make sure that the power is off *(page 269)*. Run a properly sized two-wire-with-ground-type cable to a nearby wall receptacle or junction box *(pages 269-274)*. Attach the black and white wires of the cable *(inset, dash lines)* to the unused terminals on the receptacle. Connect the grounding wire from the cable to the grounding wire of the receptacle and use a jumper wire to connect the pair to the grounding screw in the metal outlet box. At the hood, attach the other end of the cable to the wires at a junction box according to the manufacturer's instructions, making sure that the hood is grounded, and screw the cover of the box in place.

In the typical model shown here, connections are made between the white hood, cable and motor-receptacle wires, between the black hood and cable wires, and between the black motor-receptacle wire and the red hood wire. Screw the grounding wire of the cable to the hood. Finally, follow the instructions for your model to mount the blower unit and install the light bulb, light lens and grease filter.

Installing a Fan in a Bathroom Ceiling

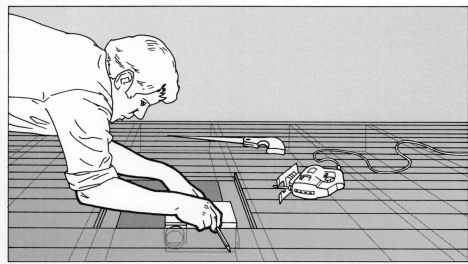

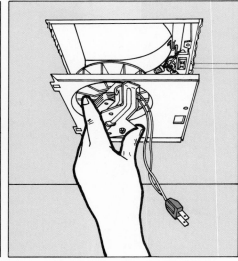

Making the holes. Locate a ceiling joist *(page 46)*, then select a location for the fan between joists. For a location below an attic, drill a locator hole through the ceiling and on through the attic floor above. Remove enough attic flooring to accommodate the fan housing. Detach the housing and set it alongside the joist and over the locator hole. Cut a hole in the ceiling to fit the housing. Screw the housing to the joist, its lip flush with the ceiling. For a location below another room, remove enough ceiling material to enable you to mount the

housing from below. If you plan to vent the fan through an outside wall, cut a duct hole in the wall. If you must vent the fan through the roof, cut a hole in the roof as shown above. From a downstairs bathroom, cut a hole for the duct at a convenient place in the floor of the room above and corresponding holes in the ceiling of that room and the attic floor above.

Wiring and mounting a bathroom fan. Run cable through a connector installed in the outlet box in the fan housing; attach the cable wires to the color-coded box wires. Mount the motor-fan assembly in the housing. Turn off current to the bathroom at the main service panel and test to be sure it is off *(page 269)*. To switch the fan with the bathroom light, run the cable to the light fixture box and splice the black and white cable wires with those of the fixture. To switch the fan independently, wire it to a separate wall switch, tapping an unswitched hot wire as a power source *(pages 269-274)*.

3 DOORS AND WINDOWS

The Trick of Converting a Window to a Door

Adding a new exterior door or window to your house is easier than it sounds. Even making a hole in the wall can be fairly simple if the exterior is wood, aluminum or stucco. Cutting through masonry is heavier work *(pages 192-195)*. But both the door and the window units come ready-assembled in a wide variety of styles and sizes.

The quickest way to add a new door to a frame house—one whose basic structure is made of wood studs, not of solid masonry—is to take out an existing window, lengthen the opening and put a door unit in its place. To take advantage of this simple method, you must be able to find for your door opening a window of suitable size; most ready-made doors are 6 feet 8 inches high and 32 or 36 inches wide. In-side the window casing, measure the height from the underside of the top jamb to the floor and the width between the side jambs. You also need a window with no obstructions hidden in the wall beneath it; check rooms above and below for piping or cables. You may have to cut a hole and inspect the area.

Where you do not have a window of the appropriate size in the appropriate place—or if you wish to put in a window, not a door—you can do that, too, by making a new opening in the wall and framing it as shown on pages 192-195.

For a flush fit outside and inside with wood, aluminum or stucco, choose a door frame 4 5/8 inches thick if your interior walls are wallboard, 5 3/8 inches thick if they are plaster. For brick veneer or solid masonry, either thickness will serve because the door will be recessed flush with the interior wall.

Like prehung interior doors, the exterior models can be hinged on the right or left side. Unlike them, however, exterior doors do not have a split jamb with finished casing on both sides but come with a solid jamb that is trimmed only on the outside. You must assemble the interior trim after you install the unit *(page 182)*. On most doors, the exterior casing or brick mold is 2 inches wide and extends about 1 1/2 inches beyond the jamb. When you are replacing a window with a door, you may need to order wider casing to make it match the size of the existing exterior trim.

Getting at the window. Before you can take the basic frame, or jamb, of a window out of a wall, you have to remove the trim and sashes piece by piece. The first pieces to remove are the strips of interior casing around the window and the stop molding along the sides—and, sometimes, the top—of the jamb. Then comes the apron under the interior sill, or stool, and the sill piece itself. Next is the hardware that holds the glazed sashes.

On the standard double-hung window, shown separated from the trim in the drawing at left, this hardware consists of metal channels and springs. You need to take off the exterior casing to remove them completely. Other types of windows have sash cords or hinges. You can lift out the sashes from the inside and remove the exterior casing afterward; a little experimenting will show what you need to undo.

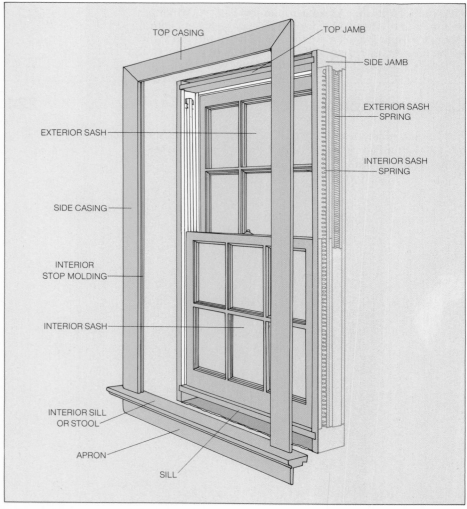

TOP CASING

TOP JAMB

SIDE JAMB

EXTERIOR SASH
SPRING

EXTERIOR SASH

INTERIOR SASH
SPRING

SIDE CASING

INTERIOR
STOP MOLDING

INTERIOR SASH

INTERIOR SILL
OR STOOL

APRON

SILL

Removing the Window

1 **Removing the trim.** Using a utility bar and hammer, pry off the casing from the front of the jamb at the top and sides of the window. Remove the strips of stop molding at the sides of the window and then the apron under the interior sill, or stool. Strike the underside of the stool with a small sledge to knock it up off the frame. Then pull out any nails protruding from the jamb.

SIDE CASING

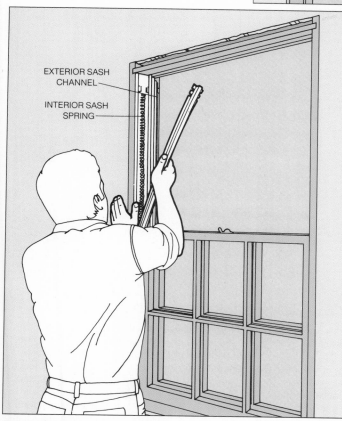

EXTERIOR SASH CHANNEL

INTERIOR SASH SPRING

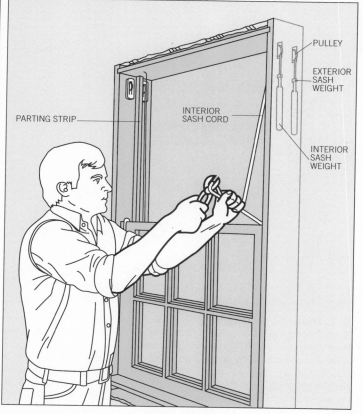

PARTING STRIP

INTERIOR SASH CORD

PULLEY

EXTERIOR SASH WEIGHT

INTERIOR SASH WEIGHT

2 **Taking out the sashes.** Push both sashes down and twist the tops of the metal strips covering the springs for the interior sash *(above, left)*. Pull off the interior strips, release the springs and lift the interior sash out of the window. Working outside the house, use the utility bar and hammer to pry off the top and side exterior casing and the exterior stops. Then twist the tops of the metal strips covering the springs for the exterior sash, pull off the strips and release the springs so you can take out the exterior sash. Remove the remaining metal strips from the sides and top of the jamb. For a double-hung window with cords *(above, right)*, cut the front sash cords and lift the interior sash out of the frame. The sash weights will pull the cords behind the side jambs; weights and cords can be removed when you take off the jambs *(overleaf)*. Pry off the parting strip that separates the sash channels, cut the remaining sash cords and lift out the exterior sash.

3 **Pulling out the jambs.** Remove the exterior casing and stops. With a handsaw, cut the top jamb and the sill in half. Then, with the aid of a utility bar, pry the top jamb and sill out of the opening. Pull the side jambs off the jack studs and remove all the nails that are still protruding from the rough frame.

Preparing the New Opening

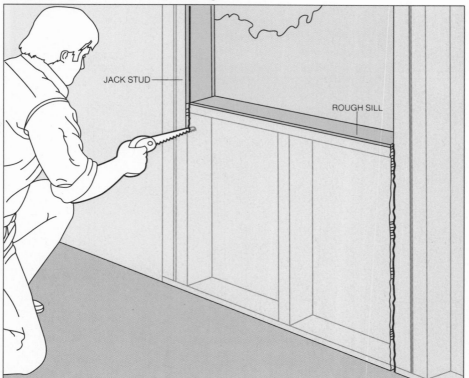

1 **Extending the interior opening.** Remove full sections of baseboard and molding from the working area. Before sawing, turn off power at the service panel to the room's lights and outlets. With a keyhole saw, cut down the wall along one side edge of the window opening past the bottom of the rough sill—about 2 inches. Then, using the inner edge of the jack stud inside the wall as a guide for the saw blade, continue to cut down to the level of the sole plate.

Repeat the procedure on the other side of the window. Using the utility bar if necessary, pry off the wall-finishing material between the cuts. Now the inside of the wall will be exposed so you can see the existing framing.

2 **Taking out the rough sill.** Pull out any insulation material inside the wall. Then examine the sill of the rough opening to determine how it is attached to the jack studs. If the rough sill is toenailed between the studs (*above*), saw it in two near the middle and twist the ends off the studs. If the ends of the sill extend under the jack studs at the sides of the opening and separate jack studs support the bottom of the sill, saw out the sill flush with the inner edges of the studs and then remove it. Twist the cripple stud under the sill off the sole plate at the bottom of the wall.

3 Cutting away the siding. Inside the house, measure from the bottom of the window opening to the sole plate, then add 1 1/2 inches to allow for the depth of the plate. Outside, use a plumb line to snap lines down the siding to this distance from the bottom corners of the opening in the siding. Use a yardstick to draw a horizontal line between the ends of the vertical ones.

For wood, aluminum or stucco siding set the blade of a circular saw *(page 454)*—a carborundum blade for stucco—to the maximum depth of the siding. Plug the saw into a GFCI-protected outlet *(page 171)*, remove any nails in the cutting line and cut along the lines, but avoid sawing into the sheathing; the border of sheathing left around the window opening will be continued for the door opening. Pry off siding between the cuts.

For brick siding, score the bricks along the drawn lines and remove the bricks inside the lines *(pages 192-193)*.

4 Extending the exterior opening. Unplug the circular saw and set its blade to the depth of the sheathing. Then, using the inner edges of the jack studs to guide the blade, saw down the sheathing from the bottom corners of the window opening to the top edge of the remaining siding. Saw horizontally between the bottom ends of the cuts—along the top of the remaining siding. The sheathing will fall out of the opening. Using a handsaw, cut through the ends of the sole plate flush with the jack studs at either side of the opening. Pry the plate off the subflooring.

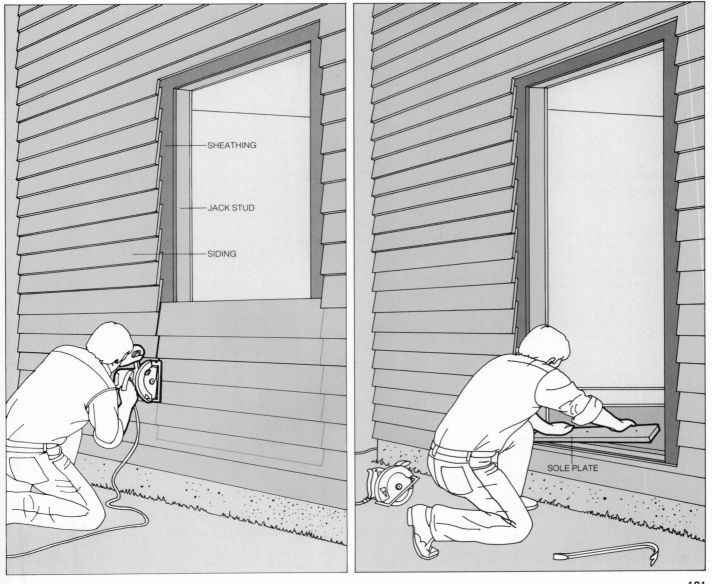

SHEATHING

JACK STUD

SIDING

SOLE PLATE

5 **Putting up flashing.** If there is no flashing above the opening, use metal shears to cut a strip of 6-inch aluminum flashing material long enough to cover the top casing of the door. Shape the flashing *(inset)* by tacking it to a 2-by-4, letting one long edge project 1/2 inch. Use gloved fingers or a block of wood to bend the projection down at a 90° angle against the side of the 2-by-4. Then untack the flashing, turn it over so you can make another bend in the opposite direction and retack it, this time letting the bent edge project 1 1/2 inches or the depth of the top casing. Untack the flashing, and hold the bent section toward you. Then slip the 4-inch flat section up between the siding and sheathing at the top of the opening. You may have to remove nails from the siding above the opening.

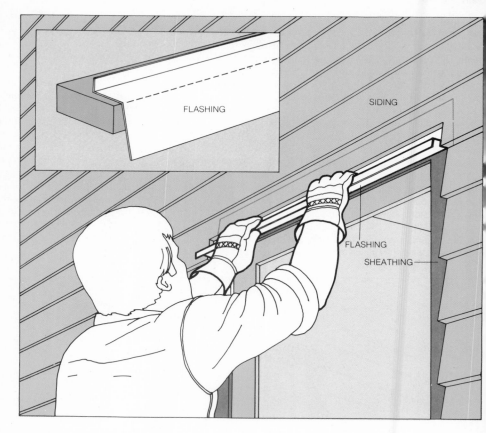

Fitting and Finishing an Exterior Door

1 **Setting the frame in the doorway.** If the door is hung from the frame, remove the pins from the hinges and take off the door. Then center the jamb in the opening and push it back so the outside trim lies flat against the sheathing and butts against the siding at the top and sides. Use a carpenter's level to determine which bottom corner of the sill is higher, then drive an eightpenny casing nail into the side jamb 5 or 6 inches above the high corner. With your hand, push a wood wedge or shim under the opposite corner to level the sill. Nail that side jamb.

Push the frame backward and forward in the opening until it is plumb; if necessary, insert shims at the back of the top casing. Drive nails partway into the side jambs about a foot below the top corners, then hang the door on its hinges and follow the directions on page 214, Step 3, to shim the door from the inside. Pack strips of fiberglass insulating material around the top and side jambs of the door.

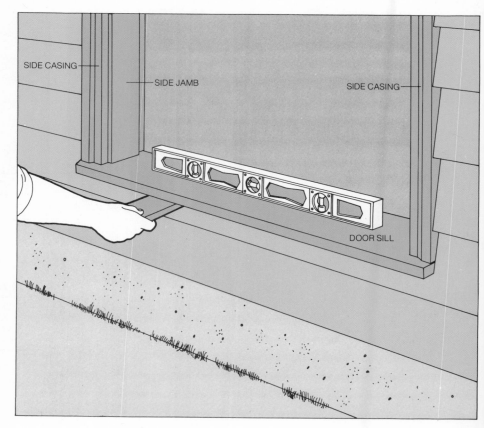

2 **Finishing the exterior.** Nail the top and side casings to the header and jack studs between them, spacing the nails at 12-inch intervals. Drive in the nails in the side jambs and nail the exterior sill to the subflooring in two or three places. Countersink the nails and fill the holes with wood putty. Smooth the flashing across the top and down over the front of the top casing. Finally, caulk around the sides and bottom of the door.

3 **Starting the interior trim.** Inside the house, measure the inside width of the top jamb and add 1/4 inch. Mark this distance on the side of the interior casing that will face the door, then make a 45° outward miter cut from each mark. Center the narrow side of the casing on the inner edge of the top jamb, 1/8 inch above the edge, with the ends extending 1/8 inch beyond the inner edges of the side jambs. Secure the casing first to the jamb, then to the header above the jamb with eight-penny casing nails. You may need to drill pilot holes in the casing to keep from splitting it.

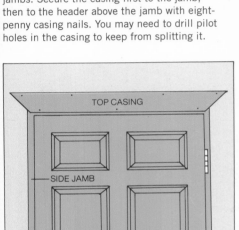

4 **Finishing the interior.** Square off one end of a casing strip, then butt that end against the floor and hold the strip over one side jamb to mark both the point where the strip meets the inner corner of the top casing and also the approximate direction for your miter cut. Miter the casing and attach it—starting at the top—1/8 inch from the inner edge of the side jamb. Repeat the marking, cutting and nailing procedure to trim the other side jamb. Trim to length and replace the molding and base shoe on either side of the opening. Set all the nails and fill the holes with wood putty. Finally, install the lockset, following the manufacturer's directions.

Installing a Simple Frame in a Wooden Structure

To add a door or window to a house of wood-frame construction, you must first cut an opening in a wall and fit the opening with a wooden frame, called a rough frame. The following pages deal with a wide opening and rough frame for a door or window in an exterior loadbearing (also called bearing) wall—a wall that supports the floor above it or the roof. This job requires temporary shoring and a heavy permanent framework around the opening, as well as precise cuts in the sheathing and siding. But the techniques apply to an opening in any wall. The only variations are simplifications—no special support or heavy framework is needed in a nonbearing wall, and less precision in cutting is required in an interior wall.

To determine whether a wall is a bearing wall, study the floor plan of your house. Nonbearing partitions are generally short and parallel to joists and rafters. Bearing walls are usually longer and perpendicular to joists; they usually bear directly on one another and bear on girders or solid walls in the basement or crawl space.

All nonbearing walls are built in much the same way, with one-story vertical studs between horizontal bottom and top plates. But bearing walls can be either platform framed or balloon framed—terms that refer to alternate ways of build-

ing a house. In platform framing *(below, left)*, the most common type, the stories of the house are assembled like a stack of separate boxes: The first-story walls are put up; the second story rests on the first, and so on for succeeding stories. In balloon framing, the house is built like an open box with shelves inside. Long studs, running all the way from the sill of the foundation to the rafters, are assembled first; then the first- and second-floor joists are fitted between them.

Balloon framing *(pages 189-191)* requires additional shoring while you make the opening and different framing. If you can see studs rising alongside the joists in

The Basic Houses: Platform and Balloon

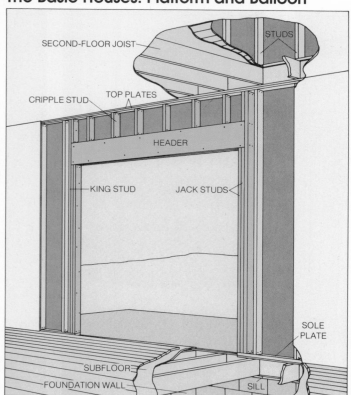 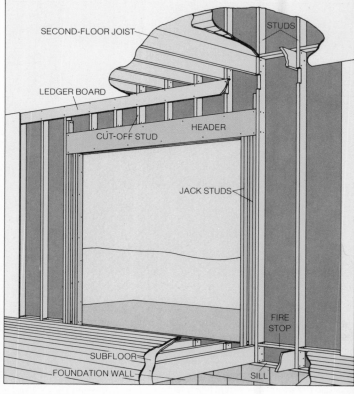

Platform framing. A header—a stiff sandwich made from two large boards and a plywood spacer—bridges the top of this door opening. At the sides, extra full-length studs called king studs are toenailed to the sole and top plates and nailed to the ends of the header. Cripple studs inserted beneath the top plate transmit the weight of the roof and second floor down to the header; short jack studs carry the load from the ends of the header to the sole plate.

Balloon framing. Because the studs in a balloon frame wall are so long, you cannot insert new king studs; the nearest existing stud beyond each side of the opening is used as a king stud. The extra-long header is supported by jack studs in the ordinary way. Additional jack studs are installed at the actual edges of the opening. All the jack studs run past the floor joists to the sill plate. The studs within the opening are cut to fit the top of the header.

the basement or crawl space, your house is the balloon type; if no studs can be seen, the house is the platform type.

You can simplify the framing job by adapting the opening to the special features of your own house. For example, you can save labor by locating the opening at an existing stud. Trace the routes of the cables, pipes and ducts inside the wall you are opening; you may be able to avoid them rather than going to the trouble of moving them. If the top of the rough frame—the header—for the opening would be within 2 inches of the top plate, you can eliminate intermediate cripple studs by making a wider header and setting it against the top plate.

The peculiarities of your house may create special difficulties. Depending on when your wall was built, it may have studs wider than the modern standard. If this is the case, remove the old studs carefully and reuse them or cut new 2-by-6s down to fit. In a brick-veneer house, remove the layer of veneer *(pages 192-195)* before beginning work on the wood frame. And if you are cutting an opening in a second-story wall, rent scaffolding to get at the exterior, and erect temporary shoring *(page 186)* on the first floor as well as the second.

Other difficulties may arise from structural hazards created by an opening—but these problems are usually surmountable without unusual effort. If a particularly heavy load bears directly above an opening, it is advisable to get an architect or structural engineer to determine the header size you need. You should also consult an expert if an opening in an exterior wall is within 4 feet of the corner of the house, or if you find steel columns, wooden posts or diagonal bracing inside a wall. Such cases may require extra support that an engineer can design and that you can install in the course of the job.

The job of installing a new frame starts with the purchase of the new door or window. Locate the nearest studs beyond the sides of the opening and snap vertical chalk lines from floor to ceiling along the facing edges of these studs. At the service panel, make sure you turn off all electrical power in the vicinity *(page 11)*, then cut through the wall along the chalk lines with a circular saw *(page 454)* and remove the wall covering.

The Basic Headers: Wood-Core and Steel-Core

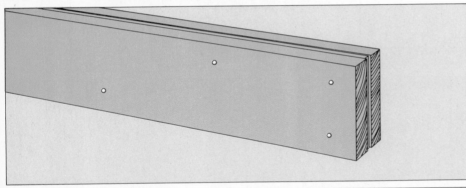

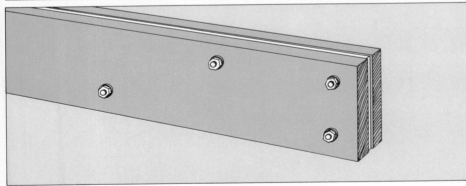

A wood header. The most common header, cheaper than a solid-wood beam and at least as strong, is a sandwich made of two structural-grade boards 2 inches thick and a piece of 1/2-inch plywood. For a bearing wall, determine the width of the board *(chart, below)* and cut a piece of 1/2-inch plywood. Cut all three matching pieces to length and fasten them together from both sides with staggered 16-penny nails every 10 inches. For a nonbearing wall, build the sandwich from 2-by-4s if the opening is less than 6 feet wide, 2-by-6s if it is wider.

A steel-reinforced header. For extremely long spans or where a wooden header of the required width will not fit between the top of the opening and the top plate of the wall, reduce the width of the header by bolting two boards to a steel plate. Check your local building code to determine the thickness of the plate, the width of the boards and the spacing of the bolt holes. Have a steel supplier cut the plate to length and make the holes. Use the plate as a template to drill matching holes in both boards and then bolt the sandwich together with machine bolts.

Matching a Header to Load and Span

Load above opening	Span in feet				
	4	6	8	10	12
Roof only	Two 2x4	Two 2x6	Two 2x8	Two 2x10	Two 2x12
One story	Two 2x6	Two 2x8	Two 2x10	Two 2x12	—
Two stories	Two 2x10	Two 2x10	Two 2x12	—	—

Choosing the right header. To find the dimensions of the boards for a header, match the span of the opening (shown along the top of the chart) with the load above the opening (shown in the left-hand column); for a span between those listed, use the column for the next larger span. If the space for your span and load is blank, use a steel-reinforced header *(above)* in a size specified by your local building code.

Framing for a Door in a Platform Wall

1 **Supporting the load.** Erect and shim a temporary partition parallel to the planned opening and about 4 feet from the wall. To assemble this partition, first nail a double 2-by-4 sole plate, 4 feet longer than the width of the new door or window, to the floor; set a 2 by-4 top plate beside the sole plate and mark both plates for 2-by-4 studs at 16-inch intervals. Cut studs 6 1/4 inches shorter than the distance between floor and ceiling, nail them to the top plate and nail a second 2-by-4 to the plate. With a helper, set the assembly on the sole plate and plumb the end studs in both directions, and then toenail the studs to the bottom plate.

Drive shim shingles between the double top plate and the ceiling at the ceiling joist locations, shimming until the partition fits tightly and immovably. Attach a 1-by-4 brace diagonally across the partition, from the floor at one end to the ceiling at the other end, nailing the brace to each stud. If your house has a basement or crawl space beneath the partition, support the floor joists (page 109), in this case with a horizontal 4-by-6 beam that is supported by 4-by-4 posts.

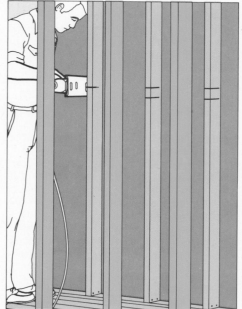

2 **Removing the studs.** With a saber saw, make two cuts about an inch apart through the middle of each stud within the planned opening. Knock out the 1-inch pieces and complete the cuts with a wood chisel if necessary. Pry the studs away from the sheathing with a utility bar. Cut off the nails that protrude from the top and bottom plates with carpenter's nippers.

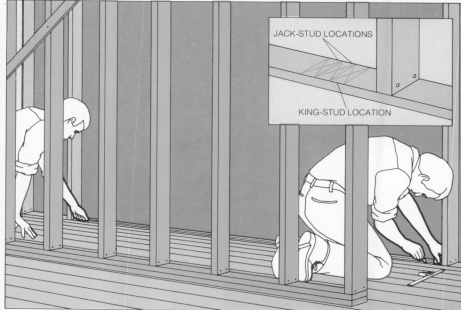

3 **Laying out the framework.** Measure between the outer edges of the side jambs of the finished door or window, add 1 inch (or the shimming space specified by the manufacturer) and draw lines this far apart on the sole plate, centered on the desired location of the finished unit. For an opening more than 6 feet wide, draw lines 1 1/2 and 3 inches beyond each original line, to mark for double jack studs, and a fourth line another 1 1/2 inches away, for the king stud (inset). For an opening less than 6 feet wide—which needs only single jack studs—draw lines 1 1/2 and 3 inches beyond each original line. Drop a plumb bob from the top plate to the king-stud lines and draw matching lines across the top plate. Toenail 2-by-4 king studs between the plates.

4 **Putting in the jack studs.** For a door, measure from the bottom of the threshold to the top of the side jamb, add 1/2 inch (or the dimension specified for shimming space by the manufacturer) and mark each king stud at this total height above the subfloor. For a window, measure from the finish floor to the bottom of the head jamb in an existing window in the room, add the distance between the bottom of the head jamb and the top of the side jamb of the new unit and mark each king stud the total distance up from the finish door. Cut 2-by-4 jack studs to the length between the mark on each king stud and the sole plate. For each side of an opening wider than 6 feet, use a pair of 2-by-4s nailed together with tenpenny nails every 12 inches; for a smaller opening, single jack studs suffice. Nail the jack studs to the plate and the king stud.

5 **Installing the header.** Make a header of the size required by the opening *(page 185)*, and, with a helper, fit it snugly between the king studs and on the jack studs. Nail through the king studs into the ends of the header; toenail up through the jack studs into the bottom of the header.

6 **Putting in cripple studs.** If there is a gap between the header and the top plate of the wall, cut 2-by-4 cripple studs to fit. Nail a cripple stud to each king stud, set additional cripples in place of the studs you removed and then toenail all the cripples to the top plate and the header.

Completing the Rough Frame for a Window

Adding a sill. To install the rough sill and cripple studs that support the finished window sill, first measure the height of your window unit from the top of the side jamb to the point where the bottom of the finished sill will meet the siding. Add 2 inches if the window is less than 40 inches wide, 3 1/2 inches if it is wider, and mark the jack studs at this total distance down from the header. Cut cripple studs to fit between the sole plate and the marks. Nail a cripple stud to each jack stud, then set a 2-by-4 rough sill on the cripples and toenail it to the jack studs. Place a cripple stud at each mark left by the old studs, nailing down through the sill into the top end and toenailing the bottom. If the opening is wider than 40 inches, nail a second horizontal 2-by-4 over the first.

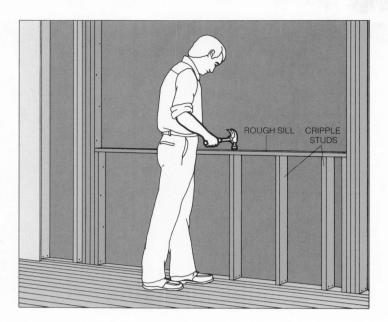

Cutting through the Wall

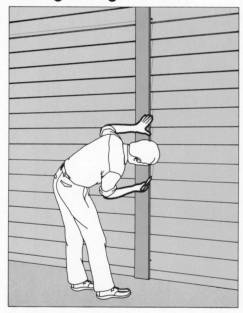

1 Cutting the opening. For a door, drill pilot holes through the sheathing from inside at the corners of the rough frame. Outside, mark the siding 1 1/2 inches below the bottom holes and draw lines connecting the marks and holes, using a straightedge. Cut through the sheathing and siding with a circular saw; wear goggles and a dust mask. Cut through stucco with a masonry blade; otherwise use an old wood-cutting blade. Cut through the sole plate along the jack studs and remove the plate.

Make a window opening the same way, but drill the lower pilot holes 3/4 inch above the rough sill and do not remove the sole plate.

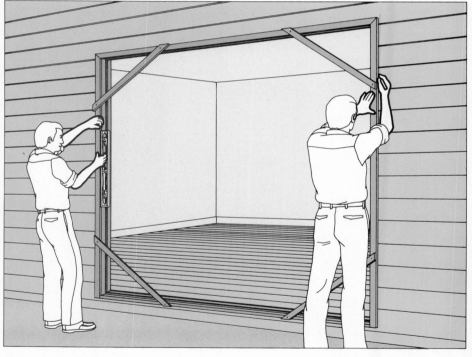

2 Trimming the siding. Cut back the siding around the opening so that the brickmold, or exterior casing, of the finished unit will rest against the sheathing of the wall with its edges 1/8 inch from the siding. For a large unit like the sliding door shown above, which requires precise fitting, enlist the aid of a helper to set the new unit in the opening, with its brickmold tight against the siding. Level the threshold or sill with shims, if necessary, and shim the side jambs until they are perfectly plumb. Trace the outline of the brickmold onto the siding. Set a circular saw to the thickness of the siding, cut along the outside of the lines taking care not to cut through the sheathing—and pry away the cut siding. For a small unit, it may be easier to mark the siding from measurements. Measure the width and height of the unit. Mark these dimensions on the siding at the sides, top and bottom of the opening, extend the marks with a level and a long straightedge, and then cut back the siding.

Additional Support for a Balloon Wall

In balloon framing—standard until about 1930, and still used today in some frame houses that are veneered with stucco or brick—the exterior walls and interior bearing walls have long studs (visible from the basement or crawl space) that run from the sill plate of the foundation to the top plate of the second floor. The first-floor joists rest on the sill, while the second-story joists rest on a horizontal ledger board set into notches in the studs; both sets of joists are also nailed to the sides of the studs.

Making an opening in a balloon type wall differs from making one in the platform type *(preceding pages)* in two respects. In addition to a temporary shoring partition *(page 186, Step 1)* to support the second-floor joists, you must also temporarily shore the studs themselves and the roof by bolting a horizontal board, called a waler, to each stud.

Another difference arises from the sheer length of balloon-frame studs. Because you cannot slip new king studs into the wall at the sides of the opening, you must use two existing studs, one on each side of the opening, as king studs, then bridge the gap between the two with an extra-long header. Extra sets of jack studs are inserted at the actual sides of the opening to complete the framing.

Walers and Wide Headers to Carry the Load

1 Supporting the studs. Have a helper hold a waler—a 2-by-8 about 2 feet longer than the width of the planned opening—against the studs and the ceiling, and nail it to the studs at each end. Then, about 2 inches above the bottom of the waler, fasten it to each stud with a 3/8-inch lag bolt. Nail a short 2-by-12 plank flat on the floor beneath each end of the waler and cut a 4-by-4 post to fit between the waler and each plank. Plumb the posts, shim them tight against the waler and toenail them in place. Support the joists above the opening *(page 186, Step 1)* and the joists beneath the floor *(page 109)*.

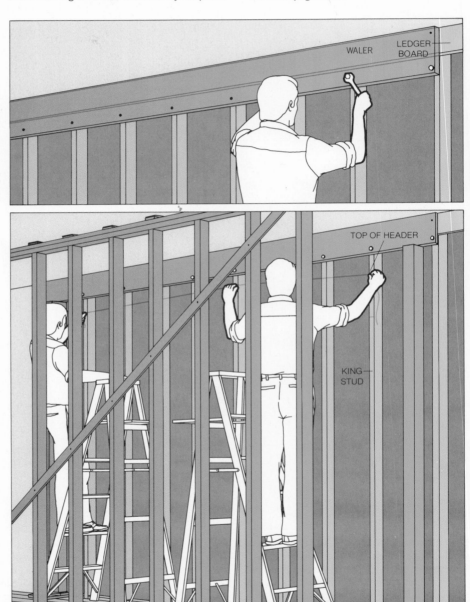

2 Cutting the studs. Mark the heights of the header top and header bottom on the existing studs that will serve as the king studs *(page 187, Step 4)* and, with a helper, snap a chalk line between the marks for the header top. Using a pencil and square, extend the line across the sides of the intervening studs and cut each stud along the line with a saber saw *(page 454)*. Pry out the fire stop between the king stud and the nearest stud or floor joist. For a door, cut each stud within the opening about 6 inches above the floor; for a window, cut each stud about 3 feet below the cuts for the top of the header. Pry out the cut pieces.

JACK
STUDS

KING
STUD

JOIST

3 **Nailing the jack studs.** Measure down from the header-bottom marks on the two existing studs that you are using as king studs to the joist or sill plate below it, cut 2-by-4 jack studs to these lengths and nail the jack studs to the king studs. For an opening more than 6 feet wide, nail a second jack stud to each of the first ones; if the first stud bears on a joist, run the second down past it to the sill plate *(inset).* Make and install the header *(page 187, Step 5)* and toenail the cut-off studs above the header to the top of the header. Nail a 2-by-4 about 1 foot long vertically to the side of each king stud, directly above the header.

4 **Adding jack studs.** Mark the bottom and side of the header for the width of the rough opening and the positions of the extra jack studs at the sides of the actual opening *(page 186, Step 3)*, then drop a plumb line from the header at each mark and have a helper draw corresponding lines on the floor. Knock out the fire stops in the marked stud space. If the extra jack studs are obstructed by the old stud, cut the stud and pry out the pieces. Make doubled jack studs the same length as those of Step 3, toenail them at the marks and nail a fire stop between the two sets of jack studs. Remove the waler and the temporary shoring partition.

Trimming the Studs

Adding the sill for a door. Drill pilot holes at the corners of the opening, with the bottom holes at the level of the subfloor, and cut the opening and trim the siding *(page 188, Steps 1 and 2)*; then knock out the fire stops within the opening and cut the ends of the studs within the opening flush with the top of the joists. Extend the subfloor to the outside of the wall with a sill—a board as thick as the subfloor (usually 3/4 inch), as wide as the studs and as long as the width of the rough opening. Nail this extension to the joists and to the jack studs at each end.

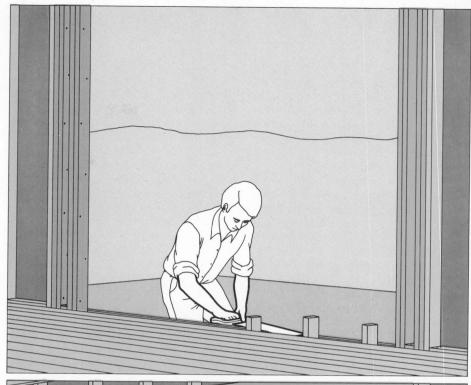

Adding a window sill. Cut off the existing studs at the bottom of the opening so that you can use them as cripple studs. Start by marking the jack studs at the height for the bottom of the rough sill *(page 188)*, use the marks as guides to snap a chalk line on the intervening studs, then cut the studs at the lines with a saber saw *(page 454)*. Nail an extra cripple stud to each jack stud between the sill plate and the mark for the rough sill, and nail the rough sill to the cripple studs. If the opening is wider than 40 inches, nail a second horizontal 2-by-4 over the first.

After cutting the opening and trimming the siding *(page 188, Steps 1 and 2)*, replace the fire stops you removed.

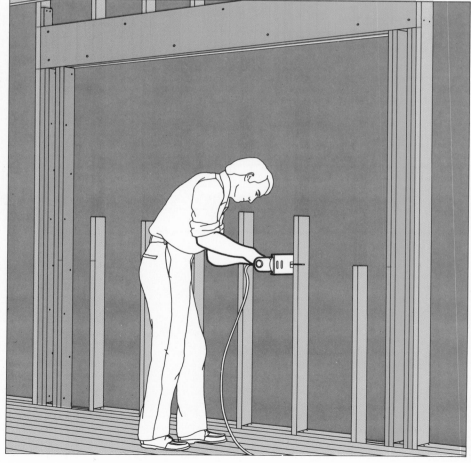

How to Break an Opening through a Masonry Wall

Fashioning a wide door or window opening in brick veneer or solid masonry differs from providing an opening in wood siding. Part of the difference arises from the advisability of making the opening along mortar lines, since mortar is easier to cut than brick or block. This requires adjustments in the opening size.

Ideally, a rough opening would be 3/8 inch wider than the width of the new window unit or new door unit, measured to the outside of the exterior casings, which are called brickmolds; and 1/4 inch taller than the height, measured from the bottom of the threshold or sill to the top of the head brickmold. But if the mortar joints do not fall at the ideal positions, make the opening larger, using the next available joint. The gap between masonry and the top of the brickmold will be filled with caulking and wooden trim strips. Any gap at the sides is filled with brick.

To start the opening, score only the horizontal mortar joints at the sides of the market opening. When all of the whole bricks within the opening are removed, a series of notches—what professional masons call a saw-tooth pattern—will remain. To fill the gaps in the saw-tooth pattern, you will have to cut some of the old bricks into odd-sized sections called bats. To make a bat, score a brick with a cold chisel. Then place the brick on a bed of sand and hammer the chisel sharply along the line; the brick should break cleanly. Before rebricking around the opening, take a sample of the existing mortar to a masonry supplier. He should be able to recommend a mix that will more or less match the color and texture of the old mortar.

Another difference in working with masonry is introduced by its weight—a brick weighs about 4 pounds; an 8-inch concrete block, 30 pounds. Instead of wooden headers, you must use one or more L-shaped steel angles, called lintels, over the opening to support the masonry above—one for an opening in brick veneer, two or three for solid masonry—and the dimensions of each lintel depend upon the span it must cover.

Use the chart below to determine the size and number of lintels you need, and have them cut to order, 16 inches wider than the opening, by a steel-supply house. For an opening through solid masonry, you also must reinforce the brick or blocks with temporary crossbeams until the lintels are in position.

Consult local building codes and obtain a construction permit before you begin the job. On the job, wear safety goggles whenever you must score, split or cut bricks and wear a dust mask when you work on masonry with power tools.

Choosing a Lintel

Opening width (feet)	Lintel size (inches)	
	Exterior	Interior
up to 4	3 1/2 x 3 1/2 x 5/16	3 1/2 x 3 1/2 x 5/16
5	3 1/2 x 3/1/2 x 5/16	5 x 3/1/2 x 5/16
6	4 x 3 1/2 x 5/16	5 x 3 1/2 x 3/8
7	4 x 3 1/2 x 5/16	6 x 4 x 3/8
8	5 x 3 1/2 x 5/16	7 x 4 x 3/8
9	5 x 3 1/2 x 3/8	8 x 4 x 7/16
10	6 x 3 1/2 x 3/8	8 x 4 x 1/2

Choosing the right lintel. Use this table to order L-shaped steel lintels 16 inches longer than the width of the opening. In the second and third columns the first figure indicates the height of a lintel's vertical flange; the second, the depth of its horizontal flange; and the third, the thickness of the steel.

Some brick houses have only a veneer of masonry over a frame structure; they need only exterior lintels. Solid-masonry walls require lintels inside and out. For an 8-inch wall of solid masonry, consisting of one course of blocks and one course of bricks or of two brick courses, use one exterior and one interior lintel. A wall of 8-inch concrete blocks calls for two interior lintels. A 12-inch wall, consisting of three courses of brick, calls for one exterior and two interior lintels.

An Opening in Brick Veneer

1 **Scoring the opening.** Wearing goggles and a respirator, use a circular saw fitted with a masonry cutting blade to score the horizontal mortar joints in a saw-tooth pattern: Score joints to the first vertical joint outside each side of the market opening. Score the bottom of the opening along a horizontal mortar joint. Score the top of the door opening along a horizontal joint and score a corresponding line on the joint 4 inches above the line for the top of the lintel. Caution: Work slowly to avoid overheating the saw or breaking the blade. Do not use a power saw under damp or wet conditions. Plug into a GFCI-protected outlet.

2 **Starting the lintel channel**. At an upper
corner row of the scored opening, chip
through horizontal and vertical mortar joints
with a 4-pound sledge hammer and a cold
chisel. Remove three bricks from each of the
two top courses of the lintel channel. Try not
to break the bricks you remove: You will need
some undamaged bricks to fill the space
above the lintel.

3 **Attaching veneer supports.** Screw a 1 1/2-
by-1 1/2-inch angle iron into each stud
behind the sheathing you have exposed. Use
2-inch wood screws and place the upper flange
of the angle iron snugly against the brick
above it.

ANGLE IRON

STUD

SHOULDER

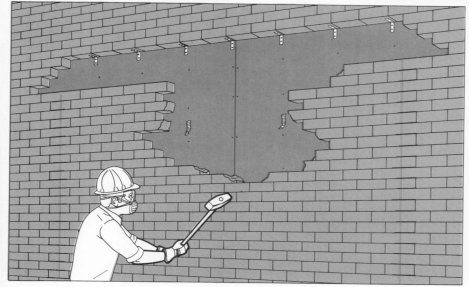

4 **Completing the channel.** Remove the
bottom course of bricks from the lintel
channel, then chisel out an additional 8 inches
of brick at each end of the course to make
supporting surfaces, called shoulders, for
the lintel.

5 **Completing the opening.** Using a 10-pound
sledge hammer, smash against the center of
the opening to remove most of the bricks within.
As you near the edges of the opening, chisel out
the remaining bricks one by one in the saw-tooth
pattern scored in Step 1 *(opposite)*. Break several
bricks in half to make bats and fill the saw-tooth
pattern at one side of the opening with the bats,
laying the bricks in mortar and setting the jagged
edges against the sheathing. Add 3/8 inch to the
width of your door or window unit—measured to
the outside of the side brickmolds—and brick in
the other side with bats and mortar to create an
opening of this width.

6 **Setting the lintel.** Apply a 1/2-inch bed of mortar to the top of each shoulder; then, working with a helper, lift the lintel into the lintel channel, with the horizontal flange on the shoulders and the vertical flange against the sheathing. Place a carpenter's level on the horizontal flange and tap the high end of the lintel into the mortar with a hammer until the lintel is level.

FLASHING

7 **Installing the flashing.** With a heavy-duty staple gun, fasten a length of 18-mil plastic flashing to the studs located between the lintel and the angle irons. Lap the flashing completely over the lintel, then cut it with a pair of scissors, leaving 1/2 inch of the horizontal flange exposed.

8 **Filling in the channel.** Lay a course of bricks directly on the flashing, substituting a piece of 3/8-inch fiberboard 4 inches long for mortar in every third vertical joint between the bricks *(inset)*. When the mortar has set, pull out the pieces of fiberboard, leaving weep holes for escaping moisture. Brick in the remaining two courses, varying the thickness of the mortar beds and joints to match those at the sides of the opening. Install a rough frame *(pages 184-191)*.

FIBERBOARD

ROWLOCK COURSE

9 **Making the sill.** Finish the bottom of the opening to match the other doors and windows in your house. If the other openings have a row of bricks on edge across the bottom, lay a matching row—called a rowlock course—across the new opening, with the back of the mortar bed about 1/2 inch thicker than the front, so that the bricks will slope to shed water; adjust the thickness of the bed to bring the top of the bricks to the level of the bottom of the finish unit. Use

3/8-inch mortar joints between bricks, but adjust the joints so that you finish the course with a whole brick. Caution: The mortar must fill the joints completely to keep moisture out.

If ordinary courses—whole bricks laid lengthwise, with their narrow edges showing—form the sills for the other openings, build the new sill in the same way, adjusting the thickness of the mortar joints between courses to bring the bricks flush

with the finish unit. If the other openings have precast concrete or cut stone sills, order a matching precast sill 8 inches wider than the new opening. Remove bricks at the bottom of the opening to make notches about 6 inches wide on each side, lay a bed of mortar thick enough to bring the sill flush with the finish unit and then set the sill in place, with its outside edge extending 1/2 inch beyond the face of the wall. Use bats to fill the notches at the ends of the sill.

Prehung Units that Make a Tough Job Easy

A prehung door unit is the woodworking equivalent of a ready-to-wear suit. The most difficult part of the work is done in a factory—the jambs are fastened together, the door is hinged and mounted, then the lock holes are cut. You do the final fitting: setting the unit snugly into a new rough opening or an old opening formerly occupied by a door that you have discarded, fastening the unit to the rough frame and—for an exterior door—adding the casing inside the house *(pages 201-203)*.

The only special technique involved is a trick used to shim the jambs of a prehung door. The brickmold prevents you from driving horizontal shim shingles past each other from opposite sides of the door. You must cut off the sharp ends of the shims, then set the butt end of one shim against the brickmold and insert the blunted end of the other alongside it to add just the thickness of the pair.

Prehung door units range from a lightweight interior door to an ornate double front door with sidelights and an overhead transom. Exterior-door units are available with a solid-core wooden door or with a steel-shell door that has an in-

sulating plastic core. Both types of door have wooden jambs. Prehung door units generally come with weather stripping that is already installed, and an adjustable threshold; they are available with double-glazed shatterproof windows built into the door or built into the jamb as a sidelight or transom.

Double-door units *(page 199)*, either exterior doors or interior French doors, are hinged in the same fashion as ordinary doors but they have special hardware and trim. The inactive door—the one that generally remains closed—is held at the top and bottom by flush bolts. To keep the active door—the one that is regularly opened and closed—from swinging past the inactive one, a strip of molding called an astragal is fastened to the edge of the inactive door.

The construction of solid-core interior door units differs from that of their exterior counterparts—there is no brickmold, so you must add casing on both sides of the jamb; the doorstop is a separate piece rather than part of the jamb; and the threshold is often omitted. But the installation techniques are virtually the same. Solid core doors should be used wherev-

er noise, security or the possible spread of fire are important considerations—in a doorway leading to the garage, for example, or for a bedroom door.

In other situations you can save both money and labor by installing a hollow-core wooden door with a split jamb *(page 200)*. In these units, the casing on both sides is installed at the factory, and the two preassembled jamb sections are slipped into the rough opening from opposite sides to sandwich the wall.

In most localities you will have to order the unit from a lumberyard and wait a week or so for delivery. You must specify the width of the jamb (generally 4 inches for walls covered with wallboard and 5 3/8 inches for plaster walls) and the width of the finished door (24 inches for closets, 30 or 32 inches for other interior doors, 36 or 42 inches for exterior doors and 60, 64 or 72 inches for double doors). You must also specify whether the door will open from the right or left and whether it will swing in or out; for a double door, specify which door will be active. And you should provide manufacturer's templates or exact specifications for the lockset *(page 204)*.

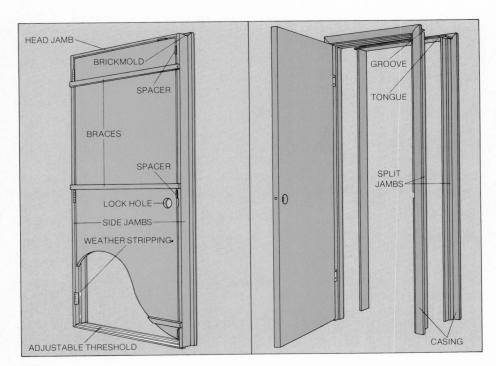

HEAD JAMB
BRICKMOLD
SPACER
BRACES
SPACER
LOCK HOLE
SIDE JAMBS
WEATHER STRIPPING
ADJUSTABLE THRESHOLD

GROOVE
TONGUE
SPLIT JAMBS
CASING

Two basic prehung doors. The exterior door at far left comes with weather stripping and an adjustable threshold to seal the bottom of the door. Before shipping the door, the distributor bores holes for the locks and installs the exterior casing, called brickmold; you must add separate interior casing *(pages 201-203)* after the door is installed. The horizontal braces keep the lock-side jamb from bowing out of line during installation; the cardboard spacers maintain the correct gap between door and jamb.

The interior split-jamb door unit at near left has two jamb sections that fit together with a tongue-and-groove joint. When the section containing the door has been plumbed, shimmed and fastened to the rough frame, the other section is installed from the opposite side of the wall. The casing on both sections is factory-installed; you simply nail it to the rough frame.

Installing an Exterior Door

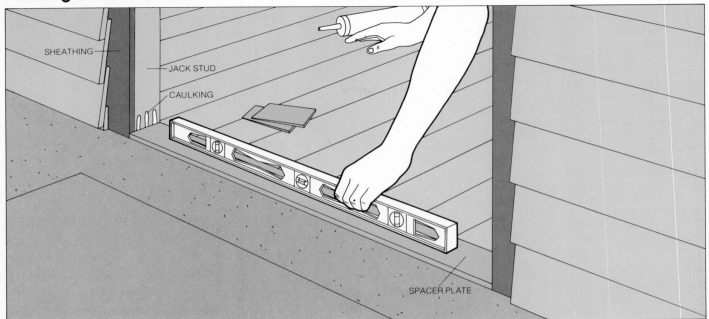

SHEATHING

JACK STUD

CAULKING

SPACER PLATE

1 Preparing the opening. Apply three beads of caulking to the subfloor where the threshold of the new doorframe will rest and continue the beads 6 inches up onto the jack studs at the sides of the opening. If your door unit is not designed to rest on the subfloor, either install the spacer provided by the manufacturer or cut a wooden spacer plate from lumber or exterior-type plywood as thick as the finish floor—usually 3/4 inch; make the plate as wide as the door jambs and long enough to fill the space between the jack studs. Press the spacer into the caulking, with its outside edge flush with the edge of the sheathing, and check it with a carpenter's level. If the spacer is not perfectly horizontal, insert shims below it every 8 inches to level it. Fasten the spacer with galvanized eightpenny common nails in a staggered pattern.

Apply three more beads of caulking on top of the spacer and a long, zigzag bead of caulking to the face of the sheathing around the sides and top of the rough opening. Install a drip cap at the top of the opening (*page 222, Step 3*).

If your door unit is designed to sit on the subfloor, level the threshold with shims when you set the door in the opening (*Step 2*).

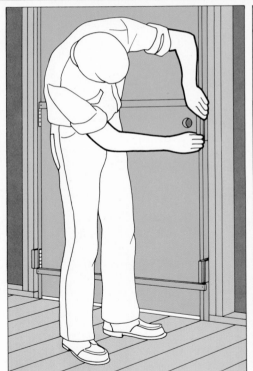

2 Setting the door in place. Set the bottom of the unit on the spacer plate and have a helper outside the house tilt the door upright and hold the brickmold tight against the sheathing. From inside the house, center the unit in the opening and, at the heights of the hinges, insert pairs of shims between the side jambs and the jack studs. Do not nail the jambs to the studs yet—the shims will hold the unit temporarily.

DRIP CAP

BRICKMOLD

3 Plumbing the hinge jamb. Outside the house, hold a level against the face of the hinge-side brickmold; if the brickmold is not perfectly vertical, pull the jamb out at the top or bottom to plumb it. To hold the brickmold plumb, drive 16-penny casing nails through the hinge-side jamb and shims at the top and the bottom of the door and into the stud—but do not drive the nails all the way home.

197

4 Squaring the door. Working inside the house, check the gap between the head jamb and the door. If the gap is wider on the lock side, loosen all of the shims slightly and tighten the pairs of shims at the bottom hinge and the top of the lock-side jamb until the gap is even; if the gap is narrower at the lock side, tighten the shims behind the top hinge and the bottom of the lock-side jamb. Outside the house, make sure the brickmold is still plumb and, at each hinge, drive two 16-penny galvanized casing nails through the jamb and shims into the jack stud.

Inside the house, remove the braces and spacers installed by the manufacturer and open the door. Remove the two outside screws that fasten the top hinge to the jamb (*inset*) and replace them with the longer ones provided by the manufacturer; the longer screws go through the shims into the jack stud for added support.

5 Adjusting the lock-side jamb. Inside the house, check to see whether the top or bottom of the door protrudes beyond the edge of the lock-side jamb; at the same time, have a helper outside check to be sure that the brickmold is tight against the sheathing. If the bottom of the door protrudes inside the house, loosen the shims of the lock-side jamb, hold a block of wood against this jamb near the top and tap the block with a hammer to push the jamb and brickmold outward until the door meets the jamb at both top and bottom. If the top of the door protrudes, push the jamb outward at the bottom.

Have your helper outside the house check to be sure that the door is tight against the stop at both top and bottom; then tighten the pairs of shims at the top and bottom of the lock-side jamb and drive two 16-penny nails partway into the jack stud at each set of shims.

6 Shimming the rest of the door. Tighten or loosen the center pair of shims behind the lock-side jamb until the gap between door and jamb is the same from top to bottom; then drive two 16-penny casing nails through the jamb and shims into the jack stud. If the door is higher than 6 feet 8 inches or if the gap between jamb and door varies on either the lock or hinge side, insert additional pairs of shims midway between the hinges on each side, adjust them until the gap is even and drive two 16-penny casing nails through the jamb and shims.

Insert two pairs of shims between the head jamb and the header, adjust them until the gap between the door and head jamb is even and fasten each pair with 16-penny casing nails. Score the shims across the grain with a utility knife and break off the protruding edges. Trim the edges back flush to the jamb with a wood chisel if necessary. Install more 16-penny casing nails so there is a nail every 16 inches along the jambs. Set all of the nails.

7 Adjusting the sill. Inside the house, close the door and follow the manufacturer's instructions to raise the threshold until a piece of paper slipped beneath the door just catches on the weather stripping. In the widely used model shown here, wedges between the sill and threshold are pushed to the right with the screwdriver, forcing the threshold up; other models have adjusting screws. Do not raise the threshold too high; it can damage the vinyl weather stripping.

Inside the house, fill the space between the jack studs and the side jambs with strips of insulation; outside, caulk the joint between the brickmold and the siding. Install wallboard inside, then install casing to cover the joint between the wallboard and the jambs *(pages 201-203)*.

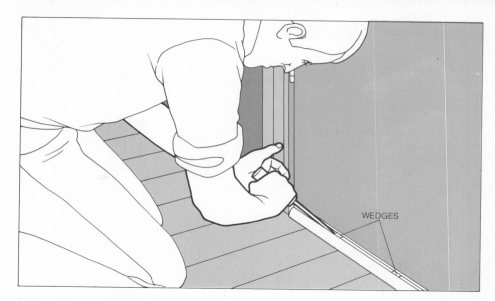

WEDGES

Aligning a Set of Double Doors

Squaring the doors. Center, shim and plumb the doors *(page 197, Steps 1-3)*, treating the jamb for the inactive door as you would the hinge-side jamb of a single door. Loosen the pairs of shims behind the top and bottom hinges of both doors and check the gap between each door and the head jamb where the doors meet *(inset)*. Tighten the shims behind the top hinge of the higher door until the gap is the same for both doors; then tighten all of the shims, recheck the gap and nail through the jamb of the inactive door with 16-penny galvanized casing nails. Replace the top-hinge screws of the inactive door with the longer screws provided by the manufacturer *(opposite, Step 4)*.

Adjust the active door jamb as you would the lock-side jamb of a single door, forcing it out at the top or the bottom until the two doors line up perfectly *(opposite, Step 5)*. Adjust the gap between the side jambs and the doors as you would for a single door *(opposite, Step 6)*.

Insert three sets of shims between the header and the head jamb and adjust them until the gap between the head jamb and the door is even, then drive two 16-penny casing nails up through each set of shims into the header. Replace the screws on the top hinge of the active door with the longer ones provided by the manufacturer.

A Split Jamb for Interior Walls

1 **Installing the door.** Slide the jamb section containing the door into the rough opening and insert pairs of shims behind the side jambs at the heights of the hinges; rest the door on two additional shims. Adjust the shims behind the hinge-side jamb until the jamb is plumb. If the gap between the lock-side corner of the head jamb and the door is more than 1/8 inch, remove the door and jamb from the opening and cut back the bottom of the jamb slightly; otherwise have a helper nail the hinge-side casing to the wall.

2 **Adjusting the casing.** Using a scrap of wood 1/8 inch thick as a gauge, adjust the top casing until there is a 1/8-inch gap between the head jamb and the door, then nail the casing to the header. Adjust the gap between the door and the lock-side jamb similarly and nail the lock-side casing. From the other side of the door, insert pairs of shims above the head jamb, behind the middle of the hinge-side jamb and behind the lock-side jamb. Drive two 16-penny casing nails through each pair and cut the shims off.

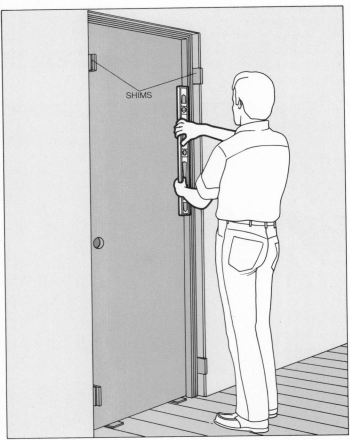

3 **Installing the other half of the jamb.** Fit the tongue of the back jamb into the groove of the door jamb *(inset)* and push the back jamb inward until its casing rests against the wallboard. Fasten the casing with eightpenny casing nails, then drive 16-penny casing nails through the jambs into the rough framing.

Working on the Trim

Molded interior casing does useful work. It strengthens the framework of jams, hides the gaps between the jambs and the wall and conceals the shims that level the door or window. Although these pages show the casing of a door, the instructions apply to both doors and windows.

The casing is one of the most carefully fitted elements of the trim; its position depends on the type of unit it surrounds. On doors and casement windows, the casing is conventionally set back 1/8 inch from the inside edge of the jamb. On double-hung windows, the casing is generally set flush with the inside edge of the jamb, form-ing three-part joint with the interior stop.

Where pieces of casing meet, the joints are generally mitered. The top piece has two 45° miter cuts, fitting similar cuts at the tops of the side pieces to form right angles. Some windows are cased like picture frames, with four casing strips mitered to 45° angles at the ends.

Cutting New Casing

1 **Measuring the head casing.** For doors and casement windows, use a combination square to mark at several points the conventional setback of the casing, 1/8 inch outside the inner edge of the jambs; the marks for the top and side pieces of casing should intersect at a precise corner point. On most double-hung windows, you need not make these marks, because the casing is positioned flush with the inside of the jambs.

Measure the distance between the side jambs at the top; for doors and casement windows, add 1/4 inch to allow for the setbacks at the sides. Mark this distance on the edge of a piece of casing that is long enough to leave room for the miter cuts, which will fan outward from the marks.

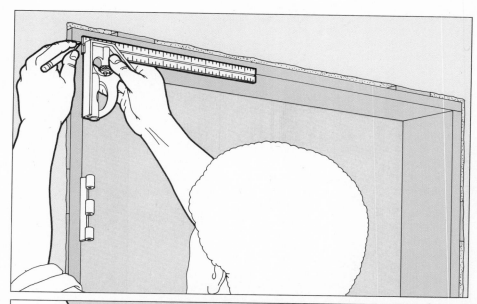

2 **Cutting the miters.** In a miter box bolted to a workbench, place the casing flat side down, set the saw for a 45° cut outward from the mark and, using long, even strokes, saw the strip just outside one of the marks you have made. Reverse the 45° angle and cut the second miter just outside the mark at the other end.

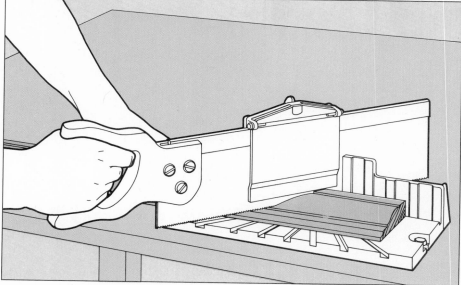

3 **Coping the backs of the miters.** To make the joints fit smoothly, cope a crescent-shaped piece from the back of each mitered end of the top casing strip. Leave an uncoped 1/2-inch margin at the top and bottom edges of the strip.

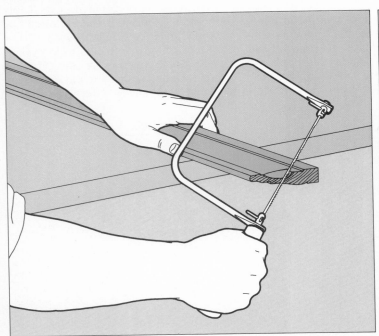

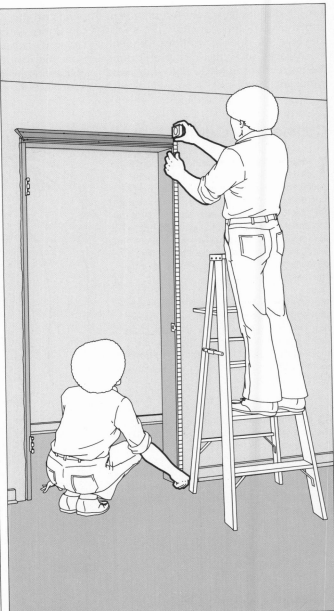

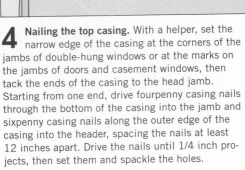

4 **Nailing the top casing.** With a helper, set the narrow edge of the casing at the corners of the jambs of double-hung windows or at the marks on the jambs of doors and casement windows, then tack the ends of the casing to the head jamb. Starting from one end, drive fourpenny casing nails through the bottom of the casing into the jamb and sixpenny casing nails along the outer edge of the casing into the header, spacing the nails at least 12 inches apart. Drive the nails until 1/4 inch projects, then set them and spackle the holes.

5 **Measuring the side pieces.** For a door, measure the distance from the bottom of a miter in the top casing to the floor; for a window, measure to the stool. Add 1/16 inch to this and mark the total length on the narrow edge of a casing strip that is long enough to allow for an outward miter at one end. Square off the strip at one mark and make a 45° outward cut from the other *(page 201, Step 2)*. Stand the side casing in place to check the fit of the miter; plane the side miter with a block plane if necessary. Similarly mark, cut and fit the other side casing.

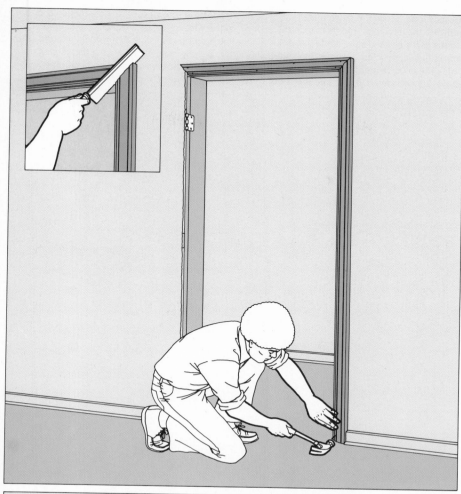

Nailing Casing and Stops

Both casing and stops should be nailed with special care. Drive each nail until the nailhead alone projects above the wood surface, then complete the job with a nail set. Be sure never to drive the nail in at a sharp slant—by doing so you can pull the jamb out of alignment. On a double-hung window with sash pulleys and weight pockets, be careful not to drive the nails into the pocket. And when nailing door casing, do not drive a nail at the location of a strike plate *(page 218)*.

6 **Attaching the side pieces.** With the mitered joint aligned, tack the side casing in position—1/8 inch from the inner edge of the side jamb on a door or a casement window, flush with the jamb edge on a double-hung window. Starting at the top, nail the casing to the jamb and the studs, using fourpenny casing nails at the jamb, sixpenny at the studs. If there is an uneven gap in a miter joint after the casing is nailed in place, you can improve the fit by cutting through the joint with a dovetail saw *(inset)*; the casing pieces are so flexible that lock-nailing *(Step 7, below)* will close the kerf left by the saw.

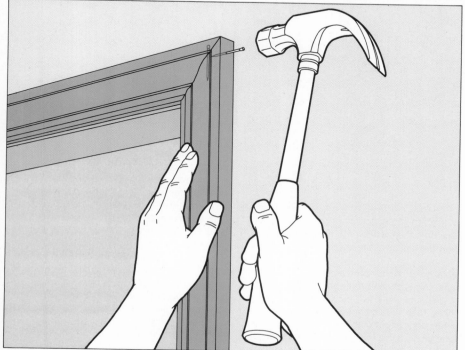

7 **Lock-nailing the joints.** An inch from the outside corner of the casing, drive one fourpenny casing nail vertically down through the top edge of the top casing into the side casing, and another horizontally through the edge of the side casing and into the top casing. The joint should now be even and tight.

Fitting a Lockset

You need only one tool to put in an ordinary lockset—a screwdriver. The lockset manufacturer provides the hardware and, if you buy the lockset before you order a prehung door and give the template and specifications that come with the lockset to the door supplier, he will bore the necessary holes in the door and jamb.

Door locks with latches come in four main types. A passage latch for an interior door has knobs and bolt, but no locking mechanism; a privacy lock *(right)*, for bedrooms and bathrooms, can be locked from the inside with a push button.

An entrance lock *(below, left)* can be locked from both sides—with a key from outside, a push button inside. The type with a dead-locking plunger, which locks the bolt when the door is shut, is more difficult to pick. For extra security add a dead-bolt lock *(below, right)*, which has a heavy bolt that slides into the jamb.

A privacy lock. Screw the strike plate to the jamb; slip the latch bolt into its hole in the door, with the bolt's beveled side facing the strike plate as the door is closed; screw the latch-bolt plate to the door. Depress the latch bolt 1/8 inch and slip the outside-knob unit into the door,

sliding the screw posts, spindle tongue and (on privacy locksets) the locking bar through the latch-bolt holes. Slide the inside-knob unit onto the spindle tongue and locking bar, align its holes with the screw posts and fasten the knob units together with machine screws.

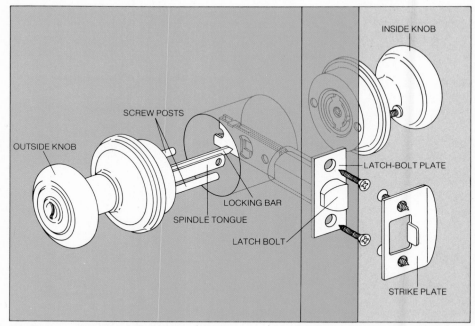

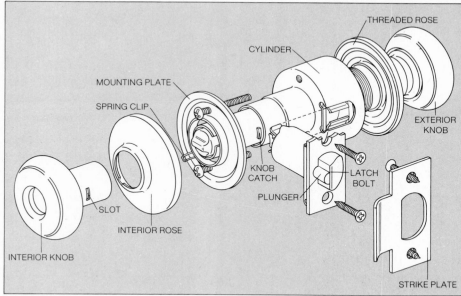

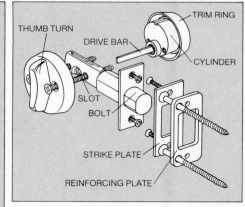

An entrance lock. Install strike plate and latch bolt as you would on a privacy lock *(above)*. Remove the interior-knob assembly according to the manufacturer's instructions: For this widely used model, depress the knob catch with the tip of a screwdriver, then slide the interior knob, interior rose and mounting plate off the spindle. Adjust the lock for the thickness of the door by turning the threaded exterior rose. Depress the latch bolt slightly and slip the spindle into

place from the outside until the cylinder engages the prongs of the latch bolt.

Replace the interior-knob assembly; in this model this is done in three steps: First fasten the mounting plate to the cylinder with machine screws; then slide the interior rose over the spindle and snap it onto the spring clip in the plate; finally, slide the knob onto the spindle until its slot fits over the knob catch.

A dead-bolt lock. Fasten the steel reinforcing plate through the jamb into the stud with 3-inch screws, then fasten the brass strike plate over the steel one. Turn the tip of a screwdriver in the slot of the bolt assembly to extend the bolt, slip the assembly into the door with the drive-bar slot down and screw the bolt plate to the door. Adjust the lock for the thickness of the door: On this model, you can select a trim ring of the correct thickness; on others, you may have to cut off the tip of the drive bar. Slide the cylinder into the door from outside, slipping the drive bar through the bolt-assembly slot and aligning the cylinder and assembly holes. Slide the thumb turn into position over the drive bar and screw it to the cylinder.

The Space Savers: Sliding Doors for Tight Places

Sliding glass doors, running on rollers along a bottom track, combine the transparency of a huge window with the convenience of a door; as an opening between house and yard, they unite two spaces visually and physically. The pocket door *(page 208)*, a variation of the sliding door, glides into a metal frame that is built into the wall and then covered with wallboard. Both are practical solutions to the problem of a space that has no room for a conventional hinged door to swing.

Sliding doors are sold in kits containing finished door panels, a frame and all the needed hardware. Door frames, of wood or aluminum, come in widths from 5 to 20 feet and in heights from 6 1/2 to 8 feet. Wooden doors are more expensive than the metal models, but are more

efficient insulators. If you live in a climate of extreme temperatures but prefer a metal door, you can get a type in which the hollow parts of the metal framing are filled with insulation. The widely used type of wooden sliding door shown on these pages has two door panels, one stationary and one movable, but three- and four-panel units are also available.

Whatever kit you buy, check its contents carefully. Many building codes require the almost-shatterproof tempered glass. In addition, check to be sure that the flexible weather stripping, which seals the unit along the line where the panels meet, fits tightly.

Start the installation with a rough opening *(pages 184-195)* 3/8 inch higher at the top and wider at each side than the

doorframe; for a sliding door take special pains to make the opening plumb and square because the clearances are critical. Run three parallel beads of caulking along the subfloor and set the frame into the opening from the outside. Press the frame down to distribute the caulking.

Both wooden and metal sliding doors are screwed into the rough framing at the jamb, but the details of the trim differ slightly for the two materials: Kits for wooden doors come with special wooden casings that are nailed to the outside of the house to help secure the frame; metal frames are trimmed outside the house with ordinary wooden brickmold. Inside the house, both wooden and metal frames are finished with conventional interior wooden trim.

1 **Securing the threshold.** After assembling the frame and caulking the subfloor along the sill, have a helper hold the frame against the sides of the opening as you nail—or screw—the interior edge of the threshold to the sill every 12 inches.

2 **Fastening the frame.** While the helper checks with a level, plumb the frame *(right)* by hammering shims—five pairs between each side jamb and jack stud and three pairs between the head jamb and the header. Secure the frame temporarily with nails, a foot apart, driven halfway through the brickmold into the rough frame.

Screw the jambs to the jack studs and the header through the predrilled holes. Then drive the nails the rest of the way in and install metal flashing as a drip cap *(page 222, Step 3)* over the head brickmold.

3 **Supporting the threshold.** Cut a piece of scrap wood to the width and thickness of the threshold overhang, align it under the threshold and against the exterior sheathing and nail it to the sheathing *(above)*.

4 **Installing the stationary panel.** Lift the panel into the outside channel of the frame and slide it into the side jamb. If the panel does not slide all the way into the jamb, force it in by pushing down on a length of 2-by-4 angled between the panel and the opposite side jamb. Screw the bottom and top angle brackets that are provided by the manufacturer to the threshold and the head jamb.

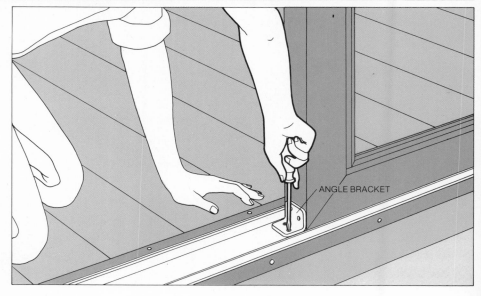

ANGLE BRACKET

5 **Fastening the parting strip.** Screw the parting strip, which separates the stationary and movable panels, into the stationary panel. In the typical model shown here, the strip is located in a rabbet along the center of the jamb.

6 **Installing the movable panel.** Most movable wooden panels are put in by setting the rollers into the inside channel of the frame and tilting the door into the channel at the top of the frame *(below)*. Then set the head stop into the shallow rabbet along the underside of the head jamb and screw the stop to the jamb. Fit the stop snugly against the weather stripping. In some models the head stop is an integral part of the frame. With this type, angle the top of the movable panel into place behind the stop, swing the bottom inward and ease the panel down until the rollers rest in the channel.

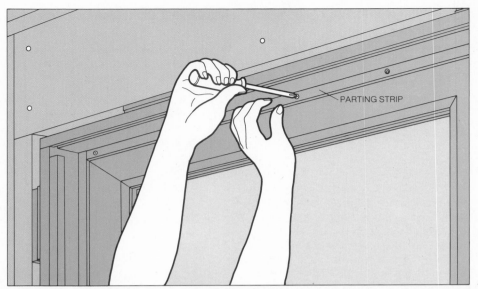

PARTING STRIP

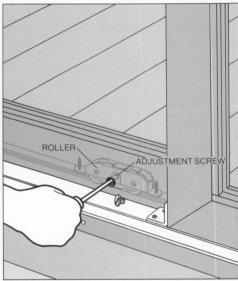

ROLLER

ADJUSTMENT SCREW

7 **Plumbing the movable panel.** Close the movable panel. If it is not plumb against the side jamb, pry off the plastic guard caps in the bottom rail and turn the height-adjustment screws *(above)*, which raise or lower the door over the rollers, until the door meets the side jamb squarely.

207

A Door that Slides into the Wall

A traditional type of sliding door, the pocket door, can be put to good use in a modern house where rooms are compact and wall space is precious. A passageway between a kitchen and dining room, for example, often has little room on either side for a conventional door to swing open—but a pocket door seems to disappear as it opens. It takes up no usable wall space, for it slides inside the wall, filling a channel, or pocket, formed by a prefabricated finish frame.

The frame generally includes a steel split jamb and split stud through which the door slides, wooden nailing strips, an overhead track and such hardware as brackets, gliders, machine screws and special nails. Most frames accommodate doors up to 6 feet 8 inches high and from 3/4 to 1 3/4 inches thick. Some models, like the one shown on these pages, have tracks that telescope to accept doors from 2 to 3 feet wide; other models have fixed tracks, which can be cut down for a door less than 3 feet wide. The door itself, preferably a hollow-core interior door, must be bought separately, along with the door hardware—a pull and, if you like, a lock. To complete the frame, you will need standard stop, jamb and casing stock; to enclose the pocket, use wallboard or other covering to match the rest of the wall.

2 **Hanging the overhead track.** Drive nails partway into the centers of the jack studs 1 1/2 inches higher than the door and with a helper hang the track on the nails. Have a helper raise the lower end until the track is horizontal, then nail both ends of the track to the jack studs.

Snap chalk lines on the floor between the bottom edges of the jack studs so that you can locate the bottom positions of the split jamb and split stud later (*page 209, Step 4*).

Installing a Pocket Door

1 **Cutting the nailing strips.** If your unit has a telescoping overhead track, one method of installation is to first unscrew the wooden nailing strips from the sides of the track. Using a backsaw and miter box, cut the strips 1 1/4 inches longer than the width of the door; the cuts must be perfectly square. Replace the nailing strips and loosen the two screws that secure the center bracket of the track. Telescope the track to the width of the opening and tighten the center-bracket screws. If your model has a fixed overhead track, cut the nailing strips with a handsaw to the length specified by the manufacturer, then cut through the track with a hacksaw and affix the end brackets provided by the manufacturer.

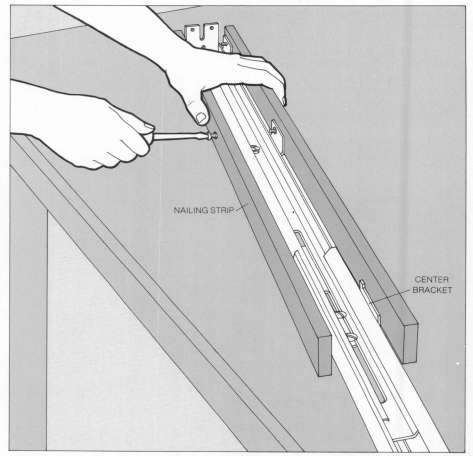

NAILING STRIP

CENTER BRACKET

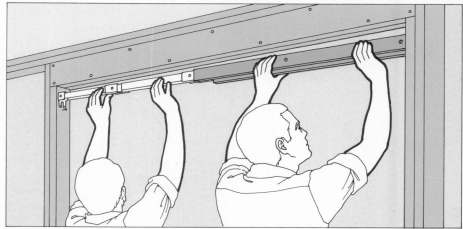

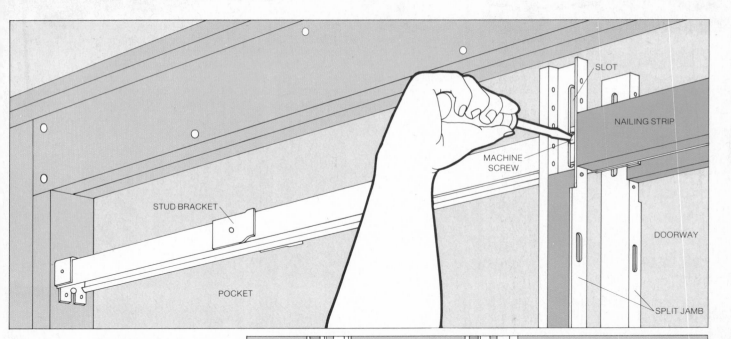

3 **Fastening jamb and stud to the track.**
Rest the split jamb on the floor and fit its top over center bracket of the track and against the ends of the nailing strips. Drive the machine screws provided by the manufacturer through the slots of the jamb top into the holes in the bracket. On a telescoping track, also tighten the two screws at the bottom of the bracket.

Mount the split stud In the same way: Fasten it in the fixed stud bracket located over the center of the pocket and nail it to the floor.

4 **Fastening jamb and stud to the floor.** Set the nailing plate at the bottom of the split jamb between the chalk lines marked in Step 2, plumb the jamb with a carpenter's level and nail the plate to the floor. Repeat the procedure with the split stud. At the top of the jamb nail through the jamb flanges into the edges of the nailing strips for each track *(inset)*.

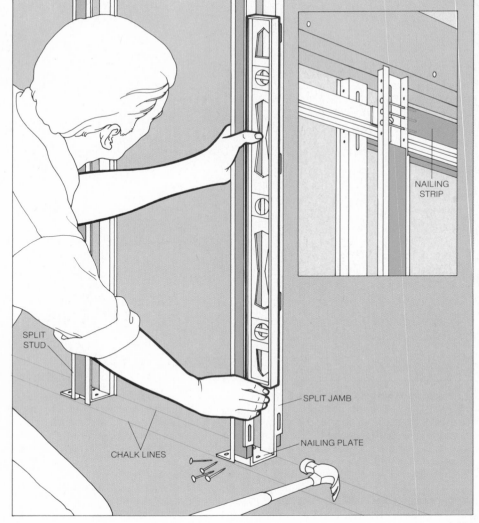

5 **Hanging the door.** Draw a center line along the top edge of the door and, following the manufacturer's spacing instructions, drive the four screws provided by the manufacturer until the screw heads are within 1/4 inch of the surface *(inset)*. Loosen the adjusting screw on one of the gliders, extend the slotted bracket and fit the glider wheel into the part of the track that runs into the door pocket; then, holding the door partway inside the pocket with a helper, push the slots of the glider bracket under one pair of screws and tighten the screws. Slide the door farther into the pocket and install the second glider in the same way, setting its wheel in the part of the track that runs across the doorway. On the telescoping track shown here, the two gliders should face in opposite directions. Align the door edge with the closing jamb, adjusting the door height above the floor by moving the glider brackets along their slots. Then tighten the adjusting screws.

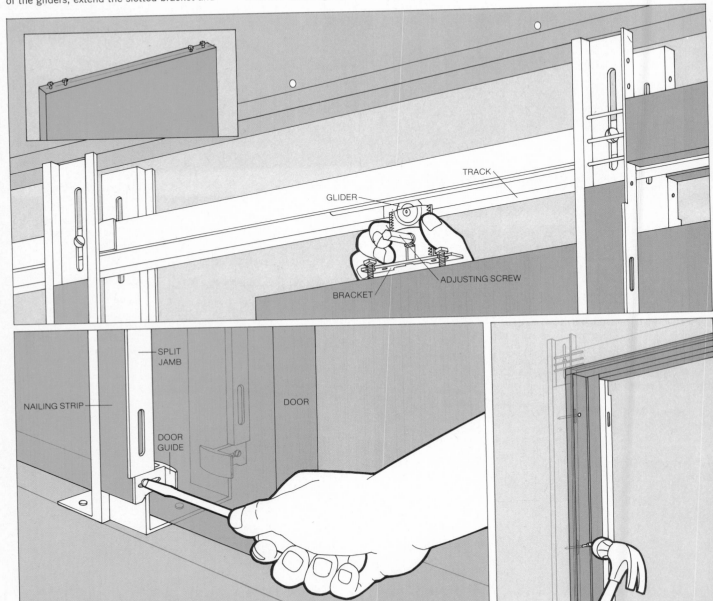

TRACK

GLIDER

ADJUSTING SCREW

BRACKET

SPLIT JAMB

NAILING STRIP

DOOR

DOOR GUIDE

6 **Hardware to hold the door in line.** Set the slotted section of each door guide against the edge of the wooden nailing strip at the bottom of the split jamb, and drive the screw provided by the manufacturer through the slot and partially into the strip. Locate each guide 1/8 inch from the door and tighten the screw.

Using the screw provided by the manufacturer, fasten the rubber bumper to the pocket jack stud, 41 inches above the floor. Slide the door against the bumper. The outer edge of the door should extend 3/8 inch into the doorway; if it does not, either shim the bumper with a metal washer or trim it with a utility knife.

Install wallboard above the opening and over the pocket, using the rough frame, the track nailing strips and the wooden strips on the split jamb and split stud as nailing surfaces.

7 **Installing stop, jamb and casing.** Nail standard doorstop stock to the bottom of the track nailing strips, covering the edges of the wallboard above and extending to within 1/8 inch of the door. Nail stop stock to the split jamb on both sides of the pocket opening; nail through the slots of the split jamb into the jamb nailing strips. At the other side of the rough frame, fasten jamb stock to the jack stud. Install casing and lockset *(pages 201-204)*.

The Fine Art of Fitting and Hanging a Door

A prehung door complete with its jambs *(pages 196-200)* provides an easy way to fill a door opening—but not necessarily the best or only way. Sometimes you must hang a door in existing jambs because the door—and only the door— needs replacing. At other times you must build new jambs, because the space available for an opening does not match any prehung door or because the door you have chosen does not come prehung. Both jobs call for special preparations and some specialized carpentry techniques.

Of the two jobs, the first is by far the easier. You must be sure, of course, that the new door will fit the old opening in height, width and thickness. You should be able to find one of matching thickness, but you may have to settle for one that is slightly oversize in height and width, and then trim it to fit. You can take as much as an inch off the height of a panel or hollow-core door, and as much as 2 inches off the width; trim the width equally from both sides, but trim the height from the bottom alone. If you must cut off more

than an inch from the bottom, order a plain, solid-core door— called a flush door—which can be cut back any reasonable amount on any side.

To build a finish frame for a new opening *(pages 211-214)*, order jamb stock an inch thick for an exterior door, 3/4 inch for an interior door. The width depends on how your walls are made. Use stock 4 5/8 inches wide for standard 2-by-4 stud walls covered with wallboard and 5 3/8 inches wide for walls that are covered with plaster. For walls of different thicknesses, have the lumberyard mill pieces of jamb stock to the width you need or trim the stock yourself with a plane.

Two grades of jamb stock are generally available. The more costly "clear" stock, made from selected lumber, can be finished with stain or varnish, which will reveal the grain of the wood; finger-joint stock, consisting of a number of short pieces of wood glued together, must be covered with paint.

Assembling the jambs involves joint techniques like those required for win-

dows. Grooves called dadoes seat the head jamb between the side jambs, and the hinges fit into recessed insets, called mortises, in the side jambs and the door. Professionals often use a router for these cuts, but a backsaw and a sharp chisel are just as effective. For accuracy in measurement, use a combination square and a marking gauge *(Steps 2-5)* .

Order such accessories as hinges, locks and thresholds when you buy the door and the jamb stock. A solid-core door or any door taller than 6 feet 8 inches requires three hinges. But if all the other doors in your home use three hinges, the new one should as well. Buy rectangular hinges, which are easier to install than the round-cornered ones used on most prehung doors. For both exterior and interior doors, buy locks that adjust to fit the door thickness. If you plan to install a dead-bolt lock in addition to the knob lock, be sure that the backset—the distance between the center of each lock and the edge of the door—is the same for both so that the locks line up vertically on the face of the door.

Making the Side Jambs

1 **Locating dadoes in the jambs.** On two pieces of jamb stock, mark the height of the door plus clearance for a rug or threshold, add a second mark above the first at a distance equal to the thickness of the stock, and extend both marks across the width of the stock with a combination square. Cut the jambs off 1 inch above the dadoes.

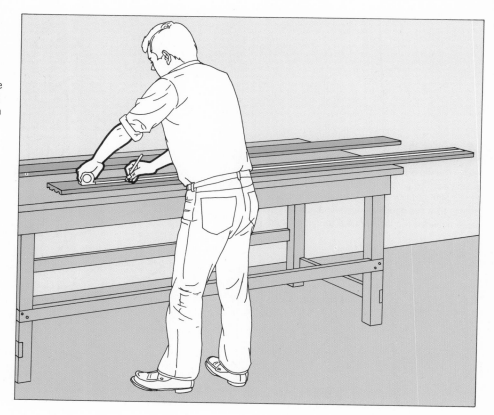

2 **Cutting the dadoes.** Clamp each of the pieces to the top of a workbench and, with a marking gauge set to half the thickness of the stock, mark the gain—that is, the depth of the dado—on both edges of the jamb stock. Cut out the dado grooves with a saw and a chisel, as shown on pages 233-234, Steps 2 through 4.

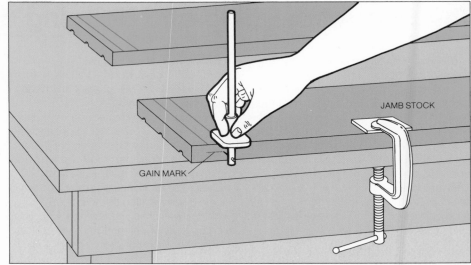

JAMB STOCK

GAIN MARK

3 **Locating the hinges.** On one of the side jambs make one mark 7 inches below the bottom of the dado and another 11 inches above the bottom of the jamb; extend both marks across the width of the jamb and set a hinge, pin side out, against each marked line. Score along the top and bottom of each hinge with a utility knife. If the door requires a third hinge, center it between the marks for the top and bottom hinges and score its location in the same way.

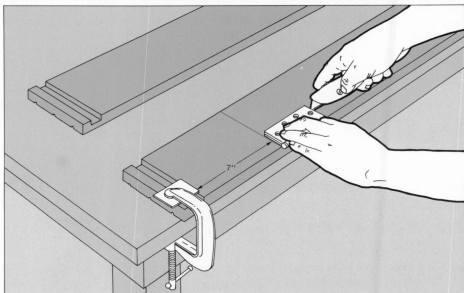

7"

4 **Marking the depth of the mortises.** Set the marking gauge to the thickness of a hinge leaf. (You need not measure the thickness; simply set the needle of the gauge at one side of the leaf and the plate of the gauge at the other.) Run the gauge along the edge of the jamb between the lines scored for each hinge.

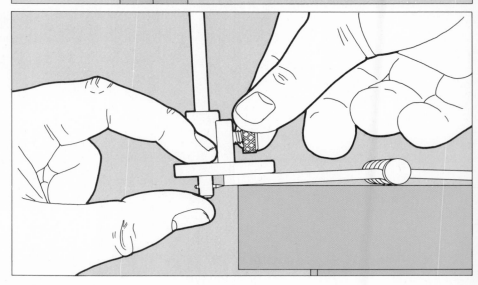

5 **Completing the mortise marks.** Set the marking gauge to the thickness of the door less 3/16 inch and and connect the scored hinge lines on the face of the jamb. Using a utility knife and a straightedge, deeply score all the hinge lines on the face and edge of the jamb.

6 **Chiseling out the mortises.** Use a mallet to drive a 1 1/4-inch wood chisel, held vertically with beveled edge inward, along the scored mortise marks on the face of the jamb *(below, left)*. Then make a series of cuts inside the mortise areas, at a right angle to the edge of the jamb *(below, center)*, tilting the chisel slightly. Next, chisel from the opposite direction to cut out the chiseled wedges. Finally, place the flat edge of the chisel against each gain mark and clean out the whole mortise *(below, right)*.

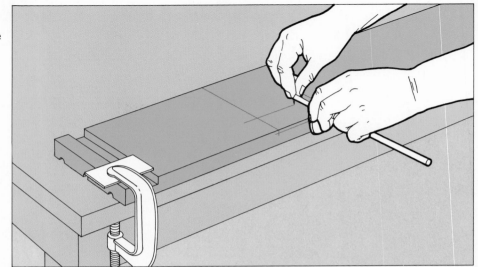

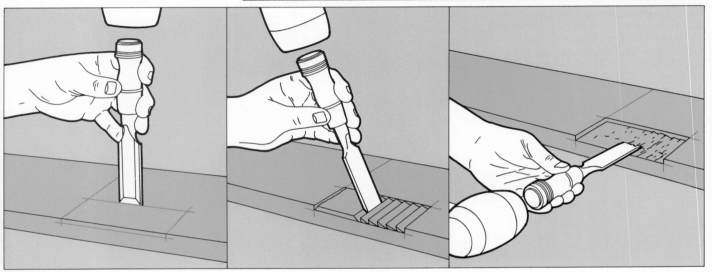

Assembling the Finish Frame

1 **Assembling the frame.** Place a side jamb in a vise, sandwiched between strips of cardboard to protect it from damage, and, on the outside of the jamb, use a square to draw a line corresponding to the center of the dado. Insert a head jamb, cut to the width of the door plus the total depth of the dadoes, into the dado. Countersink and drive two 1 1/2-inch screws along the line into the head jamb. Fasten the other side jamb to the head jamb in the same way. Using the technique on page 216, Step 5, plane a slight bevel on the outer half of the jamb edge so that the casing will fit snugly against the wall.

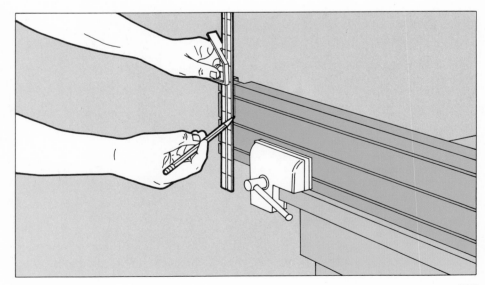

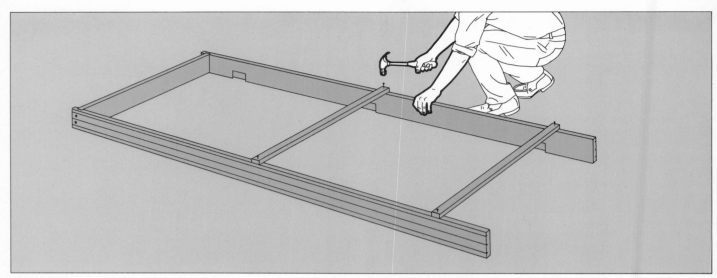

2 **Bracing the frame.** Cut two 1-by-2 spreaders to a length equal to the outer width of the assembled frame. Tack the spreaders to the edges of the side jambs so that they span the finish frame opening at locations just below the center and bottom hinge mortises.

3 **Fitting the frame in place.** Center the frame in the rough opening, push shims between the side jambs and the jack studs, and use a level and a 6-foot length of 3/4-inch plywood to be sure that the side jambs are plumb and straight, adjusting the shims to eliminate warps or bows. Fasten the side jambs to the jack studs *(pages 197-198, Steps 1-6)*.

Fitting the Door to the Frame

1 **Marking the height.** Measure the distance from the floor to the bottom of the head jamb and subtract 1/2 inch plus clearance for a rug or threshold; measure and mark this distance down from the top of the door. Extend the mark across the width of the bottom of the door, using a combination square or a marking gauge. If the door has a plywood-veneer face, score the line deeply with a utility knife and then score a matching line on the other side of the door.

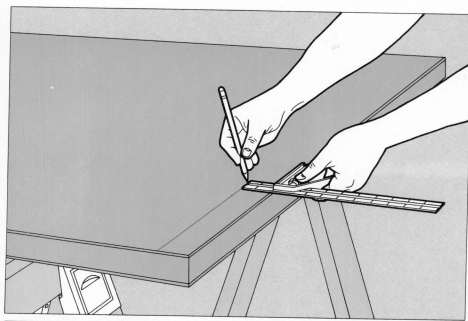

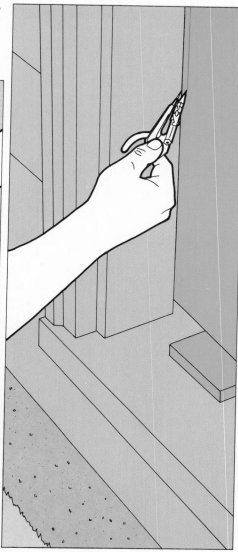

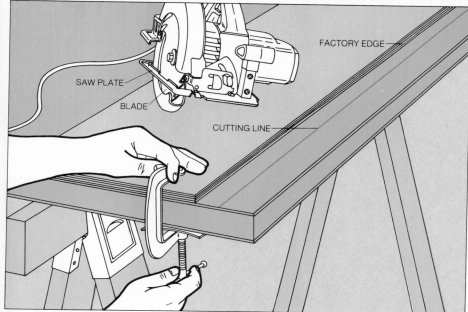

2 **Cutting the door down.** Above the cutting line *(Step 1),* draw a mark across the door at the distance between the blade of a circular saw and the edge of the saw plate; clamp the straight, factory-cut edge of a piece of plywood on this line. Saw along the plywood guide, with the blade set 1/8 inch deeper than the door thickness.

3 **Sizing for width.** Set the hinge-side edge of the door against the side jamb and wedge the top against the head jamb. With a helper holding the door from the other side, scribe the lock-side face of the door by running a compass set to 1/8 inch along the jamb. Plane the door down to the line.

If the clearance at the head jamb is not even, set the points of the compass at the widest point of the gap, scribe the top of the door and plane the top down to the scribed line.

Tack stops to the head and side jambs, positioning them so as to allow for the thickness of the door plus a clearance of 1/16 inch.

4 **Marking the bevel.** Set the spur of a marking gauge to exactly 1/8 inch. On the face of the door that will meet the doorstop, run the marking gauge along the lock-side edge. Using a ruler, draw lines across the top and bottom edges of the door to the adjacent corners.

5 **Planing the bevel.** Set the door on a door jack, adjust a jack plane *(page 220)* for a slanting cut on the edge of the door and plane down to the line made by the marking gauge; then straighten the plane iron and trim away the hump along the middle of the edge.

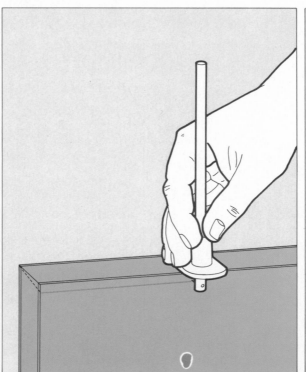

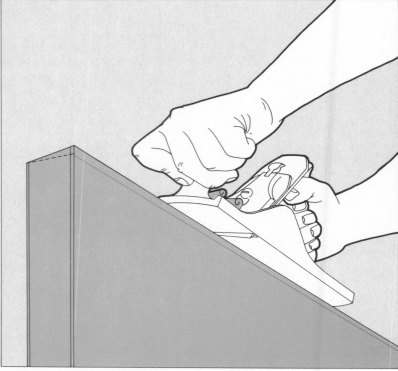

A Door Jack for Easier Work

A simple device called a door jack, which can be assembled from a few scraps of wood and cardboard, offers a handy way to hold a door in place while planing it to size or cutting hinge mortises. It is fashioned from small scraps of lumber; three 1-by-2s and two 2-by-6s. The 2-by-6s, separated by a gap 3/8 inch wider than the thickness of the door, are nailed on edge to a 1-by-2. Cardboard strips lining this gap protect the door finish during the work; a pair of 1-by-2s, nailed across the bottom of the assembly and tacked to the floor, stabilize the jack and raise it above the floor. When the door is set into the jack, its weight forces the middle of the flexible 1-by-2 down toward the floor, and the 2-by-6s squeeze together to seize the sides of the door and hold the top steady.

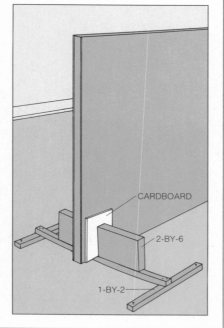

CARDBOARD

2-BY-6

1-BY-2

Putting on the Hinges

1 Determing the hinge locations. With the door in the finish frame, have a helper hold two fourpenny nails as spacers between the top of the door and the head jamb while you drive shims beneath the door to wedge it tight against the nails. Drive a shim between the door and the lock-side jamb about 3 feet from the floor, to push the door against the hinge-side jamb; then nick the edge of the door with a utility knife at the top and bottom of each hinge mortise in the jamb.

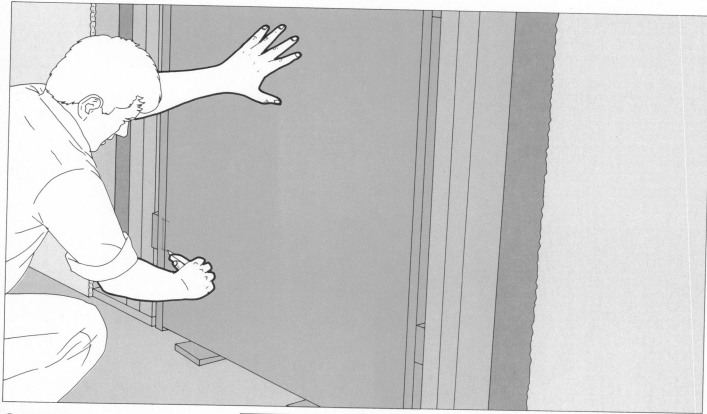

2 Mortising the hinge. Take the door out of the frame and extend the marks across the hinge-side edge. Run a marking gauge, set to 3/16 inch less than the thickness of the door, between each pair of hinge marks to outline the mortise to be cut; hold the gauge so that the 3/16-inch strip to be left uncut is on the side abutting the doorstop. Chisel out the hinge mortises in the door (page 213, Step 6). Separate the hinge eaves and screw them to the door and the jamb, making sure they are right side up.

Set the door upright beside the hinge-side jamb and slip a pair of shims between the floor and the lock-side corner of the door. Slip the top hinge together and insert the hinge pin; then slip the leaves of the lower hinges together. If the hinge leaves do not mesh, loosen the screws slightly and tap the leaves into alignment.

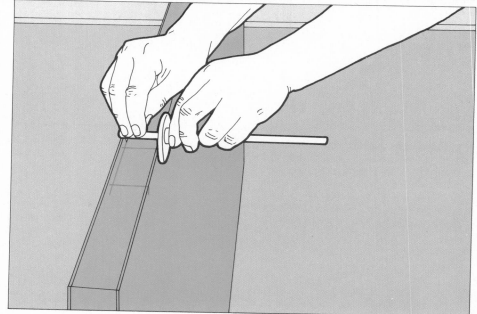

Cutting Holes for a Lockset

1 **Aligning the holes.** Mark the lock-side edge of the door 36 inches above the floor and extend the mark across the edge and 3 inches across the side of the door that faces away from the stop. Fold the manufacturer's template supplied with your lockset over the edge and face of the door, centered on the marked lnes. With a pencil, mark the center of the doorknob hole on the face of the door and the center of the latch-bolt hole on the edge.

Shut the door and drill the knob hole with a hole saw; when the saws pilot bit just breaks through the door, stop drilling and complete the hole from the other side. Drive shims beneath the door to hold it open and drill the latch-bolt hole through the edge of the door and until it meets the knob hole.

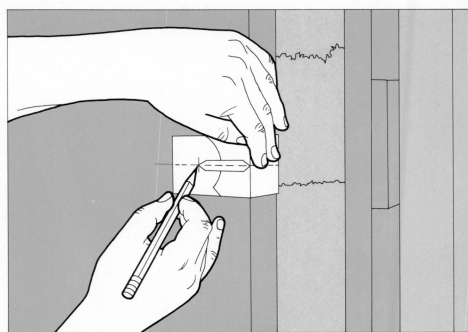

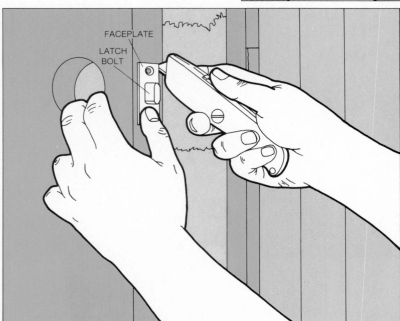

2 **Mortising for the latch bolt.** Insert the barrel of the latch bolt in its hole, with the beveled edge of the bolt facing the doorstop, and outline the faceplate on the edge of the door with a utility knife. Chisel out a mortise as deep as the faceplate is thick *(page 213, Step 6)* and screw the latch-bolt plate to the door.

3 **Locating the strike plate.** Measure from the face of the door nearest the stop to the flat side of the latch bolt *(inset)* with a combination square; measure the same distance on the jamb from the doorstop and mark a vertical line across the face of the jamb about 3 feet from the floor. Shut the door and transfer the 36-inch mark made in Step 1 to the jamb. Hold the strike plate against the jamb, centered on the 36-inch line, with the front edge of the plate's hole against the vertical line; mark the inside of the hole and the outside of the plate. Drill through the marked hole for the latch bolt, mortise for the strike plate and screw the plate to the jamb.

How to Use a Plane

A plane is a versatile tool for many door installation procedures and repairs. Use a 14-inch jack plane, which is held in both hands, for planing the long edge of a door. You can also use it for beveling the edges of swinging doors and for trimming shutters. To plane a door on its hinges or to work on end grains, use a block plane, which is generally about 6 inches long and light enough to be held in one hand while the other hand steadies the work.

When planing, work with the grain and remove the wood in several thin shavings. Apply pressure to the toe, or front, of the plane at the beginning of each stroke, then gradually shift the pressure to the heel, or back, as you finish the cut. For smooth cutting lubricate the bottom of the plane, called the sole, with wax.

To protect the plane iron, always place the plane on its side when the iron is exposed; after the job is completed, retract the iron completely. When the cutting edge becomes dull or nicked, take the iron to a professional sharpener.

Anatomy of a jack plane. The iron and cap iron are fastened together with a cap screw to form a double iron, which rests on a slanting piece called the frog. The lever cap and its cam fasten the double iron in place; adjust locking pressure by turning the lever-cap screw. On the sole, the mouth opening through which the iron projects is adjusted by loosening two frog-bed screws and turning a frog adjusting screw; move the frog forward for fine work, back for coarse planing. The cap iron, which acts as a chip breaker, may also be adjusted. Set it about 1/16 inch behind the cutting edge of the iron for all-purpose planing; move it closer for fine jobs. The adjusting nut controls the depth of the cut the iron makes, and the adjusting lever aligns the iron's cutting edge. A knob and a handle mounted on the sole provide holds for two hands.

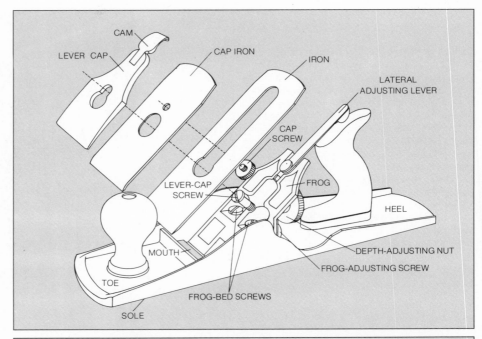

Anatomy of a block plane. The single iron of a block plane lies at a lower angle than the iron of a jack plane, and the bevel of the iron faces up rather than down. The lever cap screw and the locking lever tighten the lever cap directly against the iron; a second lever, secured by a finger rest on the toe of the plane, adjusts the mouth opening. An adjusting nut controls the depth of the cut, and a third lever aligns the cutting edge laterally. On this small plane the vertical flanges, called wings, provide a handhold for one-handed operation.

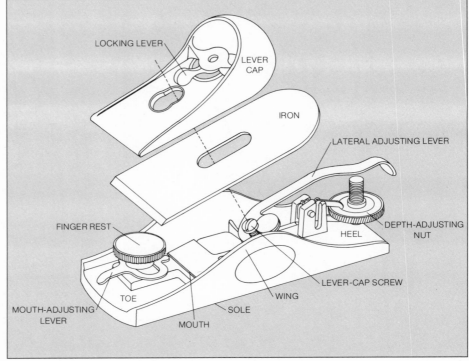

Adjusting the plane iron. Hold the plane—in this example, a jack plane—upside down over a light-colored background and sight along the sole. Turn the adjusting nut until the edge of the iron is visible at the mouth opening, then use the nut to bring the iron to the desired depth of cut; the final turn of the nut should always move the iron outward. If the iron projects unevenly across the width of the mouth, move the adjusting lever to correct ts alignment (inset).

Using a jack plane. Secure the board to be planed in a vise so that you can cut with the grain, and set a jack plane squarely on the edge (below). Grip the handle of the plane with one hand and hold the thumb of the other against the knob, curling the remaining fingers of this hand under the sole and against the face of the board as a guide for a straight cut—provided the wood is smooth; otherwise grip the knob. After a few strokes of the plane, lay a long, straight piece of scrap lumber on the planed surface and mark any high points for further planing. As a final check for squareness, slide a combination square along the full length of the angle formed by the face and edge of the board, and mark and plane any remaining high points.

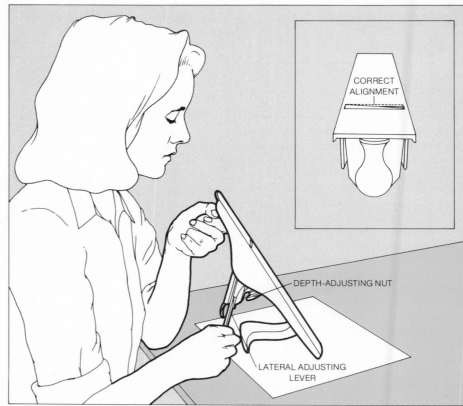

CORRECT ALIGNMENT

DEPTH-ADJUSTING NUT

LATERAL ADJUSTING LEVER

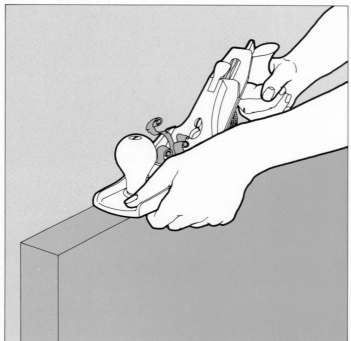

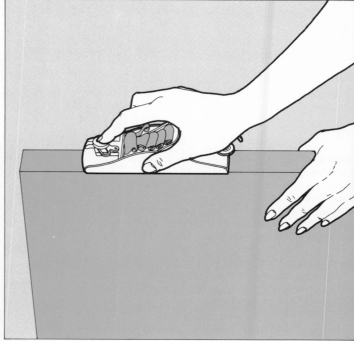

Using a block plane. Mark the parts of the edge to be trimmed and adjust a block plane for a fine cut. With the board steadied with one hand, hold the plane by its wlngs in your other hand, set your index finger on the finger rest and plane the marked areas.

A Factory-Made Window Unit, with All Its Parts

In some ways, adding a new window to a room is like hanging a painting or print: It can offer a pleasing view, decorate an empty wall or brighten a drab area. Of course, a window can do more, too: It can let fresh air into the house.

Once you have cut and framed a rough opening *(pages 184-195)*, installing such a window takes only a few hours—thanks to prefabricated, or prehung, units. A prehung window comes complete with the sashes, jambs and sill, and with the hardware needed to open and lock the sashes. Prehungs come in a variety of sizes and shapes, and in all of the four basic window styles: double-hung, casement, awning and sliding. Many have such features as a removable sash for easy cleaning, a snap-in storm window for winter and a screen for summer, or double or triple glazing; some have plastic-coated weatherproof sashes and exterior trim.

In addition to these built-in conveniences, you have a choice of materials—wood, steel or aluminum. Each has advantages and disadvantages. A wooden window is traditional and elegant but it needs more upkeep than a steel or aluminum unit. Metal windows are almost maintenance-free, but they are poor insulators unless the manufacturer separates their interior and exterior parts with specially fitted insulating material.

If you simply want to replace a window, not add one, you have still another choice: a metal replacement window, consisting of a metal window frame and sashes designed to fit within the jambs and sill of a wooden window that has been stripped of its sashes, stops and balances. Metal replacement windows generally come in kit form; follow the manufacturer's instructions.

Before deciding on any window unit, refer to manufacturers' catalogues at a building-supply store. Note the rough opening sizes required for the prehung windows you are considering, and check them against your available space. (If your space permits, always get a window large enough to double as an emergency exit.) Check for the availability of double or triple glazing and find out whether jamb extensions, helpful for fitting a shallow jamb to a deep wall *(page 223, Step 4)*, are included. When ordering casement or awning units, specify the direction in which the sashes must swing.

One final caution: Some prehung windows are assembled for use in new construction but others are designed for new or reframed openings in existing walls. The installation techniques shown on the following pages apply to the second category alone; do not use them with a unit meant for new construction.

Fitting and Flashing

1 **Squaring the corners.** Set the window unit on a flat surface with the exterior casing—the brickmold—down, and hold a steel square at the corners of the side jambs, head jamb and sill. If these corners are not right angles, clamp the unit to a workbench and push gently against the jamb corners to square it. Turn the unit over, and nail a temporary 1-by-2 brace diagonally between the head brickmold and a side brickmold, allowing 1/2 inch at the top for the drip cap *(page 222, Step 3)*; nail another brace between the sill and the other side brickmold.

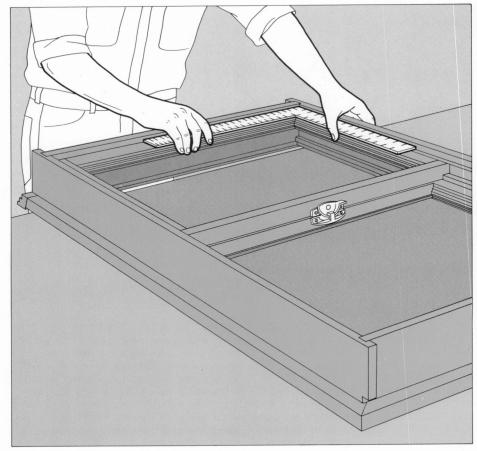

2 **Adjusting for wall thickness.** Tilt the window into the rough opening and push it back until the brickmold lies flat against the sheathing or, in a masonry wall, against the rough frame. If the jambs jut into the room, adjust with filler strips. Push the window out from inside the house until the jambs align with the interior wall. Measure the gap between the back of the brickmold and the sheathing or rough frame. Remove the window from the opening and cut wood filler strips to the lengths of the side and head jambs, making each strip as thick as the gap and as wide as the back of the brickmold. Set the strips against the back of the brickmold and nail them to the jambs with fourpenny nails.

If the jambs are not wide enough to reach the interior wall, you will need jamb extensions rather than filler strips; see page 223, Step 4.

Fastening the Unit into the Wall

1 **Leveling.** Outside the house, center the unit between the jack studs and, with a helper, lift it until the head brickmold fits beneath the drip cap, and the tops of the side jambs butt against the header. Use a carpenter's level to find which top corner of the window is lower than the other. Anchor this corner with an eightpenny finishing nail driven through the brickmold into the header. Lower the other corner to level the head brickmold and nail that corner to the header.

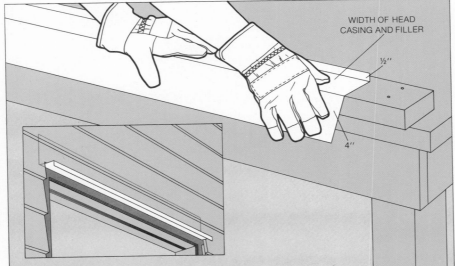

3 **Providing a drip cap.** For a wall with siding, cut a strip of aluminum flashing as long as the exterior head casing and 4 1/2 inches wider than the combined thickness of the brickmold and any filler strips. With an awl, scribe a line on the flashing 1/2 inch from a long edge, then bend the section over a 2-by-4 to a 90° angle at the score line. Turn the flashing over, scribe a second line 4 inches from the other long edge and make a bend in the opposite direction. Insert the 4-inch section between the siding and the sheathing at the top of the window opening (*inset*). Remove any siding nails in the way. You need not make a drip cap for a masonry wall. Because the window is recessed in the masonry and flat against the rough frame, rain flowing down the wall will not run onto it.

2 **Shimming the window.** Inside the house, check to be sure that the head jamb is level; then, while a helper outside the house holds the window flush against the sheathing, insert shims between the finish sill and the rough sill. Drive eightpenny casing nails down through the finish sill and the shims below it into the rough sill. Finally, insert at least two pairs of shims between the side jambs and jack studs on each side of the window frame, and fill the gaps between the jambs and studs with insulation. Caution: Do not insert shims thicker than the space between the jambs and jack studs—larger shims can bow the jambs.

If a metal window unit fits the rough frame exactly, it does not have to be shimmed. In this case, simply fasten the window directly to the rough frame, using 1-inch flat-head wood screws driven through the predrilled holes in the jambs and the finish sill *(inset)*.

ROUGH SILL

FINISH SILL

3 **Securing the brickmold.** Outside the house, fasten the casing to the rough frame with eight-penny nails at 12-inch intervals. Countersink the nails and fill all the holes with wood putty.

Wearing gloves, push the drip cap tightly over the edge of the head brickmold. Run silicone rubber or butyl rubber sealant along the joints where the drip cap and side brickmold meet the siding.

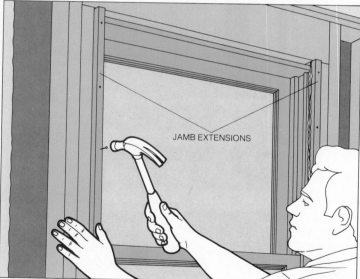

JAMB EXTENSIONS

4 **Adjusting the depth of the jambs.** If the jambs of the installed window do not reach the face of the wall inside the house, glue and nail strips of wood called jamb extensions to the inner edges of the jambs. Your prehung window may come with jamb extensions; if so, fasten them to the jambs, and plane their outer edges flush to the face of the wall with a block plane. If you do not have jamb extensions, you can make your own: Cut 3/4-inch wood strips to the lengths of the jambs and to the required thickness, fasten them sawed side out and smooth the rough edges with sandpaper.

A Choice of Shapes

Prehung windows are made not only in the conventional rectangular form but in unusual shapes that can fit into the most limited and unlikely spaces, such as cramped stair wells and shallow attics. These windows generally have fixed rather than movable sashes and cannot be used for ventilation, but they do bring light to dark spaces and their configurations give them unexpected charm or traditional elegance. Some are circles, half circles or quarter circles. Others, like the fanlight of a period door, are shaped like part of an ellipse. Still others—diamonds, octagons and the like—have straight jambs, but no right angles.

Because of their shapes, these windows call for special steps in installation: For example, the opening for a curved window is cut before the rough framing is assembled, the reverse of the conventional sequence. The methods vary from one window shape to another. The opening for a circular window can be plotted with a string compass (below, Step 1), but the straight sides of half or quarter circles must be leveled or plumbed, and the shape of an oval window is best traced on a wall from the window frame itself. Circular windows are braced differently from oval ones; windows with straight jambs are braced by a third system.

There is one feature, though, that most odd-shaped windows have in common: Virtually all of them need jamb extensions (page 226, Step 6) to fit them to a wall. In many models the shapes of these extensions make them impractical for an amateur to fashion; order them as accessories when you get the window unit.

Putting in a Round Window

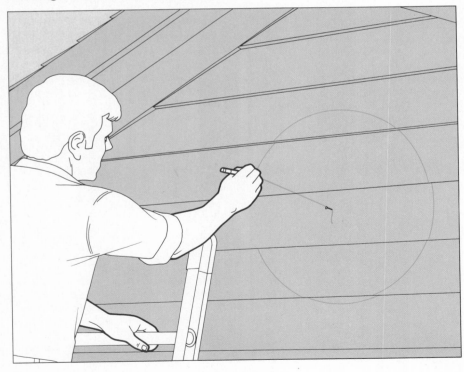

1 **Making the opening.** From inside the house, drill through sheathing and siding to mark the window center. Outside, center a string compass—a length of string with a nail at one end and a pencil at the other—at the hole and draw a circle to the diameter of the outer edges of the brickmold. Drill a starter hole on the circle and, using a saber saw with a 4-inch blade, cut the circle out of the siding and sheathing. If the sheathing is plywood, save the cutout disk for later use (page 225, Step 3). Install a rough frame of jack studs, a header and a rough sill (pages 184-191) projecting 1 inch into the cutout opening.

2 **Installing the braces.** Measure the diameter of the window at the outer edges of the jamb and multiply the measurement by 0.4. Then mark and cut four 2-by-4 braces to this length, beveling their ends in from the marks at a 45° angle.

Toenail the braces to the jack studs, header and rough sill to form an equal-sided octagon.

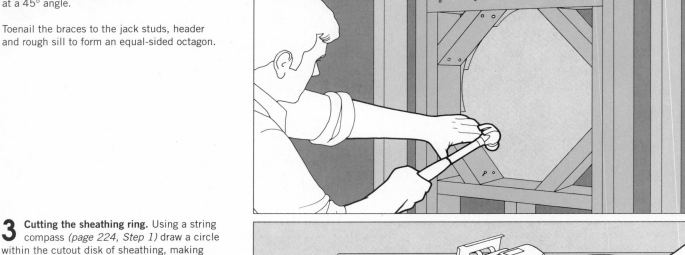

3 **Cutting the sheathing ring.** Using a string compass *(page 224, Step 1)* draw a circle within the cutout disk of sheathing, making the diameter equal to the outer diameter of the window jamb; clamp the disk over the edge of a workbench, turning it as necessary, to cut out a ring. Outside the house, fit the ring into the opening and fasten it to the rough frame and braces with fourpenny nails. Caulk the gap between the ring and the sheathing around it.

If the house has board rather than plywood sheathing, cut the ring from exterior plywood of the same thickness as the sheathing.

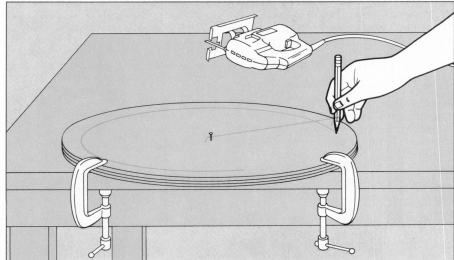

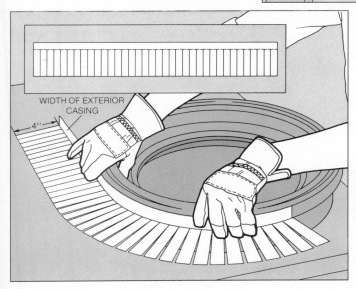

WIDTH OF EXTERIOR CASING

4"

4 **Flashing the window.** Wearing gloves cut a strip of flashing 4 inches wider than the outer edge of the casing and as long as half the circumference of the casing; cut tabs 4 inches long at 1-inch intervals *(inset)*. Bend the tabbed part of the strip to a right angle *(page 222, Step 3)* and shape the untabbed section to a semicircle around the casing. Outside the house, insert the tabbed section of the strip between the siding and the sheathing at the top of the opening.

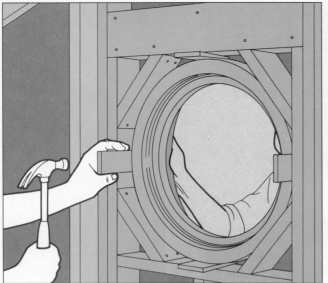

JAMB EXTENSIONS

5 **Shimming and fastening the window.** Have a helper outside the house hold the window in the opening, with the back of the casing set firmly against the sheathing. Inside the house, drive eight shims between the jamb and the framing parts around it, in the following sequence: one at the rough sill, one at the header, one at each jack stud and four at the braces.

Outside the house, fasten the casing to the sheathing and frame with eightpenny nails at 8-inch intervals. Inside the house, score the protruding ends of the shims and break them off; outside, caulk above the flashing and at the joint between the casing and the siding.

6 **Finishing off the window.** Glue jamb extensions, purchased with the window, to the edges of the jamb, and anchor each with two countersunk flat-head screws. Put up the finish-wall material. Using a block plane *(pages 219-220)*, trim the jamb extensions flush with the face of the wall. Nail the interior casing, supplied by the manufacturer, to the jamb extensions.

A Rough Frame for a Diamond-Shape

Anatomy of a special frame. The window shown at right is fastened to diagonal 2-by-4 braces rather than to the frame itself. The rough frame *(pages 184-191)* is 1 inch taller and wider than the window; the braces, marked like those in Step 3, run to the exact midpoint of each side of the rough frame. Each of the four window jambs is shimmed at two points, and outside the house the window unit is nailed to the diagonal braces through the brickmold on each side.

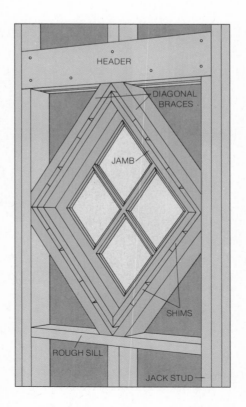

HEADER

DIAGONAL BRACES

JAMB

SHIMS

ROUGH SILL

JACK STUD

Graceful Bays and Bows

A wide bay window or a bow window serves two purposes: It floods a room with light, and it adds space for a seat or a window garden. Both types are available prefabricated. Bay windows, the more common kind, range from 5 to 9 feet wide in 1-foot increments; most have a fixed center window parallel to the wall and two side windows set at an angle. In a bow window the angle between sections is gentler and the unit as a whole takes the shape of a graceful curve; these relatively expensive windows come in 5- to 11-foot widths.

The kits for both bay and bow windows generally include the windows; a head, or ceiling, board; a window seat; and, in many models, an insulating panel below the seat. Some units come with ornamental support brackets called knee braces, which fit beneath the window; for others you may have to make wooden braces yourself according to the manufacturer's instructions, or have an iron shop fabricate metal ones for you.

Bay and bow windows are installed in much the same way. Prepare the rough opening as you would for an ordinary prehung unit *(pages 184-195)*, but consider the manufacturer's instructions before trimming back the siding from the sheathing *(page 188, Step 2)*: Unlike standard windows, some bay and bow units are designed to rest against the face of the siding rather than on the sheathing.

For a window under a roof overhang, cut the opening so the top of the window unit will rest against the soffit when the unit is installed. If the window will have no overhang directly above it, you will need to put on a roof.

Many units are available with roof kits *(pages 229-230, Steps 1-4)*, consisting of a wooden drip cap, precut end and intermediate rafters, thicker hip rafters, and plywood sheathing cut to fit over the rafters. Most roof kits do not include shingles or flashing, but once installed they can be flashed and shingled like any other roof. Some units can be purchased with prefabricated metal roofs. A few manufacturers do not provide a roof: You will have to build your own.

Bay and bow windows are bulky and heavy; do not attempt to install one without helpers to lift the unit into the opening and to steady it on sawhorses while you nail it to the rough frame.

Attaching a Bay Window

1 **Setting the window in the opening.** With at least one helper for every 3 feet of window span, lift the unit into place. First rest the bottom of the insulating panel on the sill, then tilt the window up and into the opening until the brickmold butts against the exposed sheathing. Center the unit between the jack studs and brace it every 3 feet with sawhorses.

2 **Leveling the seat board.** Inside the house use a level to find the higher end of the seat and nail that end into the rough sill, 2 inches from the end jamb. Shim between the insulating panel and the rough sill until the other end is level and nail it in place the same way. Because of their weight, windows 8 feet wide or wider should be shimmed with thin pieces of slate roofing shingle rather than with wood.

3 **Plumbing the jambs.** Hold a carpenter's level first against the edge and then against the side of each end jamb, have helpers move the window slightly from outside the house until the jamb is plumb, then install shims 1 foot apart between the jamb and the jack stud. Wooden shims serve for this purpose. Drive nails through the jamb and shims into the stud, taking special care to avoid driving a nail through the balancing mechanism of a double-hung window.

END JAMB

4 **Anchoring the headboard.** Hammer a wooden shim in snugly every 8 inches between the headboard and the header, then nail through the headboard and shims into the header.

Fill all gaps between the window unit and the rough frame with insulation.

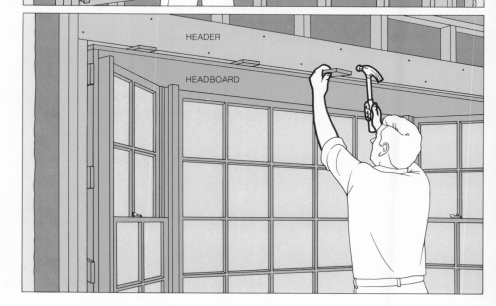

HEADER

HEADBOARD

5 **Fastening the knee brackets.** Outside the house, set a knee bracket—one from the kit or one you make—under each mullion (a vertical strip between two window units), with the long leg of the bracket against the siding; drill pilot holes through the bracket into the cripple stud within the wall. If there is no cripple stud directly in line with the mullion, toe-nail one between the sole plate and rough sill. Fasten the bracket to the stud with 3/8-inch lag bolts, then fasten the short leg to the insulating panel of the unit with a wood screw.

Caulk the joints between the window and the siding of the house. Nail 1-inch quarter-round molding under the window along the joint between the insulating panel and the siding.

Adding a Precut Roof

1 **Marking the siding.** Nail the wooden drip cap supplied by the manufacturer to the trim at the top of the window, then place the three pieces of roof sheathing from the kit against the drip cap and the siding, with the edges of the triangular end pieces overlapping the center piece. Mark the outline of the roof on the siding and remove the roof sheathing; saw the siding along the marks *(page 188, Step 2)* and pry it off.

2 **Strapping the window to the house.** About 10 inches above the top of the window, fasten a length of perforated metal strap to the wall stud behind each corner of the window, using a lag bolt and washer. Pull the strap down to the window corner and fasten it to the top of the mullion post there with a lag bolt.

3 **Installing the rafters.** Attach a hip rafter—thicker than the other rafter pieces in the kit—above each mullion, placing it between the drip cap and the point where the horizontal and vertical cuts in the house siding meet *(below, left)*. Toenail the rafter to the sheathing and the headboard. Attach one of the other rafters flat against the house wall at each end, nailing it to the drip cap, the hip rafter and the sheathing *(below, right)*. Nail the remaining rafters to the headboard and to the sheathing, spacing them at equal intervals between the hip rafters.

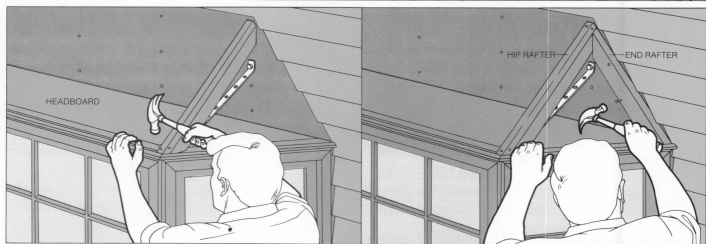

HEADBOARD

HIP RAFTER — END RAFTER

4 **Sheathing the roof.** Place each piece of triangular sheathing completely over the end rafter and halfway over the hip rafter, and nail it to the rafters at 6-inch intervals. Set batts of insulation on the headboard and against the triangular pieces. Place the center piece over the hip rafters and the drip cap; nail it to the rafters.

If your roof kit contains fascia boards to cover the ends of the rafters, place each one tight against the underside of the sheathing and then nail the board to the rafters.

5 **Weatherproofing the roof**. Nail a preformed metal drip edge tight against the edge of each piece of roof sheathing with roofing nails, but do not install the other metal flashing as yet. Nail 15-pound asphalt-impregnated roofing felt over each piece of sheathing and trim away excess felt with a utility knife. Working from the drip edge up, nail shingles to each face of the roof—but do not apply shingles to the hip ridge.

6 **Flashing the sides.** Pry the pieces of siding just above the roof slightly away from the sheathing. Working from the bottom of the roof, slip pieces of flashing bent at a right angle beneath each course of shingles and between the sheathing and the siding of the house. Lap each successive piece over the one below it and nail the upper end of the roof; the next piece of flashing will cover the nail. Renail the siding.

DRIP EDGE

7 **Flashing the top.** Bend flashing 8 inches longer than the length of the middle piece of roof sheathing lengthwise into a right angle and notch the corners to fit under the siding at each end. Slide one edge under the siding, spread roofing cement on the shingles at the roof top and press the lower edge of the flashing into the cement. Bend the notched projections over the hips and seal all edges with roofing cement.

Capturing a View with a Picture Window

Most people consider any large window a picture window, but that term properly applies only if the opening serves as a picture on the wall—a frame for an attractive scene outdoors. You can buy ready-to-install picture windows, but if you build your own window you can make it frame a view just as a picture frame does a painting.

While some striking picture windows are small, most are large and, like a landscape painting, wider than they are tall. The size leads to considerable heat loss in winter (and heat gain in summer), making double-pane insulating glass advisable. You may want to arrange the dimensions of your window to match standard glass sizes. And because such a large, heavy sheet of glass is required, it is best installed by a professional glazier.

The window frame, which resembles that of a standard window except that it does not have a movable sash, fits into a standard rough frame. It requires rabbet and dado joints, but because there are only a few they are most conveniently made by hand with a chisel rather than with a router. Since the wood surfaces will show, the parts should be made of the knotless, kiln-dried pine (called clear pine, but often referred to as shop lumber), which has its thicknesses designated in a special way, as so many quarters of an inch. Thus a shop-lumber 2-by-6 would be designated 8/4-by-6. Make the jambs of 5/4 or 6/4 stock, as wide as the thickness of the wall; use 8/4-by-8 stock for the sill.

The glazier will provide exterior stops; determine their thickness from that professional and make your interior stops the same size—at least 1/2 inch thick for single-pane glass, 3/4 inch for insulating glass. Buy brickmold, or exterior casing, that is wide enough to span the gap between the finish frame and the studs and header of the rough opening; order enough interior casing for all four sides of the frame.

On a frame for insulating glass, the inside dimensions must be 1/2 inch greater in height and width than the glass itself, so that the glass can float on rubber cushions in the glazing compound. For single-pane installation, make sure that you allow 1/4 inch for clearance. And for a good paint seal, both the brickmold and exterior stops should be set 1/8 inch back from, not flush with, the jamb edges.

The parts of a picture window. In this frame, the head jamb is seated in grooves, called dadoes, at the tops of the side jambs. At their bottoms, notches, called rabbets, hold a single sill, its exterior portion sloping downward to shed water. Strips of brickmold, mitered at the corners, are fastened to the outer edges of the head and side jambs and rest on the horns of the sill. The glass is set against interior stops, then sealed on the outside and secured with exterior stops. After the glass is installed, mitered interior casing covers the frame on all four sides.

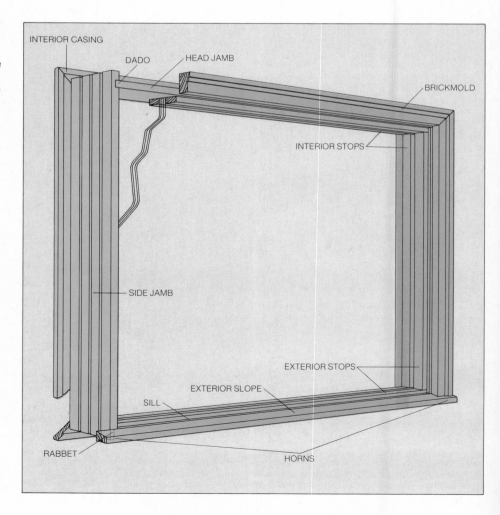

Assembling a Finish Frame

1 Marking dadoes and rabbets. Using a square and a utility knife, mark the thickness of the sill stock across the ends of both side jambs. From this rabbet line, measure up and mark the inside height of the frame for the bottom of the dadoes; then, at a distance equal to the thickness of the head jamb, mark a second line above for the top of the dadoes. Set a marking gauge at 1/2 inch and follow the procedures on page 212, Step 2, to mark the gain, or depth, of the rabbets and dadoes.

Cut the side jambs off 1 inch above the dado marks. Then go on to cut the head jamb to the inside width of the frame plus 1 inch for the combined depth of the dadoes.

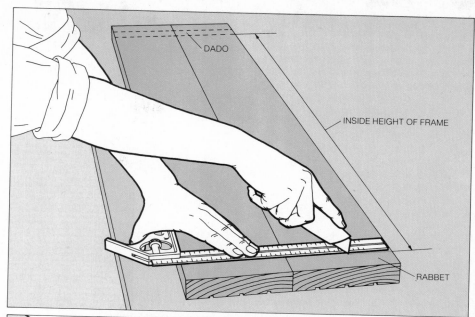

2 Cutting the joints. Saw along the waste side of the rabbet line, cutting across the board evenly down to the gain mark. Do the same for the dadoes, but make two or three additional cuts within the area to be chiseled.

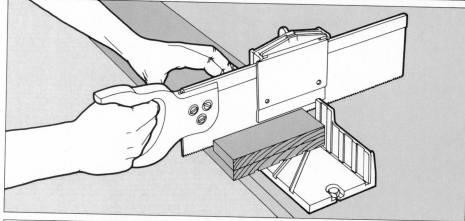

3 Chiseling out the rabbet. Drive a 1 1/2-inch wood chisel, beveled edge up, into the end of the jamb stock at the gain mark, all the way to the saw cut, and split out the waste wood. To finish the rabbet, hold the chisel with its beveled side up in one hand and guide the blade with the other hand to smooth the rough surface *(inset)*.

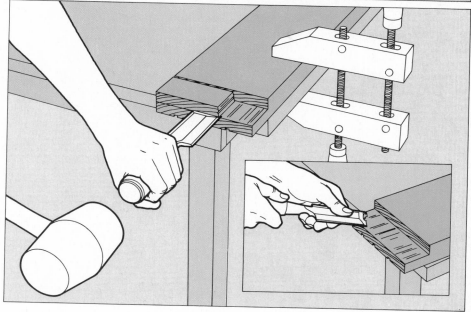

4 **Chiseling out the dado.** Working from each side of the jamb toward the middle, drive a 1-inch chisel, beveled side down, into the edge of the jamb just above the gain mark for the dado. Smooth the groove, using the chisel bevel side up, as on page 233, Step 3.

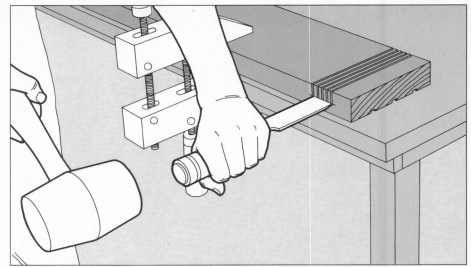

5 **Grooving the sill stock.** Saw along the underside of the sill stock to make three parallel grooves, 1/4 inch deep and as wide as the saw blade; run the grooves 1/2, 3 1/2 and 6 1/2 inches in from the exterior edge of the stock. Move and replace the clamps as necessary. Then trim the grooved sill to a length 1/4 inch more than the inside width of the window frame plus twice the width of the brickmold.

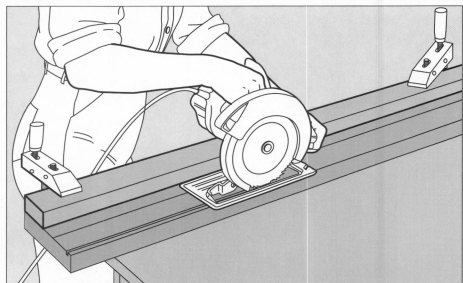

6 **Making the horns.** Across each end of the sill, draw a line at a distance from the sill end equal to 3/8 inch less than the width of the brickmold. Measure from the interior edge of the sill along this line a distance equal to the width of the jamb stock, and draw a perpendicular line from this point to the end of the sill. Cut along these lines to form the sill horns.

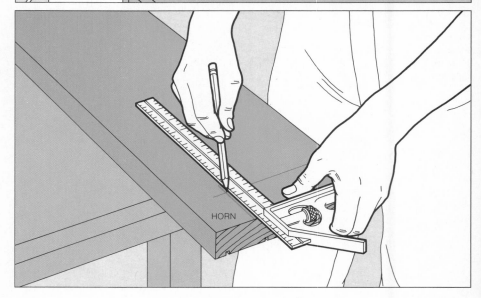

HORN

7 Setting the slope of the sill. Hold a sliding T bevel set at a 15° angle on the end of each horn and draw a line from the inside corner of the horn down to its exterior edge. Connect both ends of these lines with horizontal lines *(inset)* and plane the sill to these marks *(page 216, Step 5).*

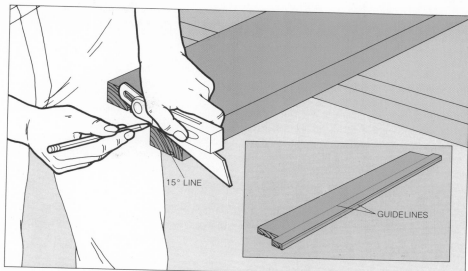

15° LINE

GUIDELINES

8 Assembling the pieces. Insert the head jamb you cut in Step 1 into the dadoes on the side jambs, then insert the sill, exterior edge up, into the rabbets and nail the parts together. Use eightpenny galvanized nails, driving them through the side jambs. Turn the frame over and, with the exterior part of the sill projecting beyond the bench, square and brace the corners of the frame as described on page 221, Step 1.

Attach the brickmold following the procedure for interior casings *(pages 201-203, Steps 1-7)* with one exception: The bottom edges of the side pieces must be mitered, front to back, at a 15° angle to match the sill slope. Apply two coats of wood preservative to the frame, soaking it, and nail it into the rough frame as described on pages 222-223.

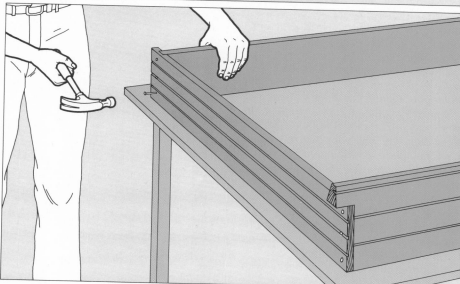

9 Installing the interior stops. Using a combination square, mark the locations of the stops on the face of one of the side jambs. First draw a line 1/8 inch from the outside edge of the jamb for the setback of the exterior stops, then draw a line for the width of the stop. Add 1/4 inch for glazing compound and an additional allowance for glass thickness, measure this total distance from the exterior-stop line and draw a line for the glass channel. Draw a line the width of the interior stop in from the glass channel and extend this line onto all four sides of the frame.

Nail the top and bottom interior stops along the line. Fit the interior side stops between the top and bottom stops: If the interior stops are rectangular, use butt joints; if they have a molded surface, use a coping saw *(page 202)* to cope the joint, so that one stop follows the profile of the adjoining stop. (The exterior stops will be installed by the glazier.)

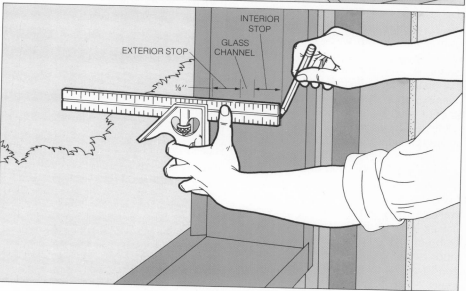

INTERIOR STOP

EXTERIOR STOP

GLASS CHANNEL

1/8"

Bringing the Outdoors in with a Window Wall

Normally, a window fits into an opening in a wall, but in some homes the wall itself, from floor to ceiling, is a window that completely opens a room to the outdoors. Window walls are most often seen in low houses of contemporary design, but within certain limitations they can be built into or added to a home of any style. The major limitation is imposed by requirements of structural stability. Glass walls have comparatively poor resistance to the lateral pressure of high winds and few are strong enough to support the weight of a story above them. If you plan a window wall that is more than 9 feet wide, is less than 4 feet from a corner of the house or must support higher floors as well as a roof, consult an architect or an engineer.

In addition to structural problems, large glass areas bring weatherproofing difficulties. A wall of single-pane glass offers little protection against extremes of heat and cold outdoors, although you can fit storm windows to a completed wall or—at great cost—build the wall with double glazing in the first place. Providing ventilation requires extra construction. The panes of a typical window wall are stationary. You can, however, install windows with movable sashes by adjusting the stud spacing and blocking height to create rough openings that will accommodate prehung casement, sliding or awning windows.

Window-wall construction begins with a braced rough opening like the one on page 184; a header resting on 2-by-4 jack studs and flanked by two 2-by-4 king studs, with the old wall studs and sole plate removed. The header, set tight against the old wall top plate, is higher than that of an ordinary window or door opening, and because it is supported by studs at intervals of 3 feet or less, a sandwich of 2-by-6s and 1/2-inch plywood scraps is adequate (page 185).

Inside this opening is the frame of the window wall itself; a grid of 2-by-6s with rabbeted and dadoed joints. Since these boards will be visible in the completed wall, you may prefer to select the wood, paying extra for lumber with fewer knots than ordinary construction grade. For the studs at the middle of the wall, which consist of a 4-by-6 or paired 2-by-6s, try to get 2-by-6 boards with perfectly square

edges rather than the ordinary rounded edges, to conceal the line where two boards meet.

Use a router and jigs to cut the numerous rabbets and dadoes in the frame pieces. For the rabbets that hold the glass at the outer edges of the frame, adjust the width and depth of the cuts to the type of glass you use. Most single panes require rabbets 1/2 inch deep and 1 1/2 inches wide; double glazing requires rabbets 1/2 inch deep and 1 1/2 inches wide. If you must cut rabbets deeper than 1/2 inch, use

lumber thicker than single 2-by-6s for the middle horizontal blocking, which must be rabbeted on both sides (below, inset); 3-by-6s or paired 2-by-6s will serve.

To minimize the time that the interior of your house must be exposed to the elements, cut all the rabbets and dadoes before you cut through the sheathing and siding of the old wall. Installing the glass is best done by a professional—these large panes and their precise fitting with caulking and wooden stops call for special skills and tools.

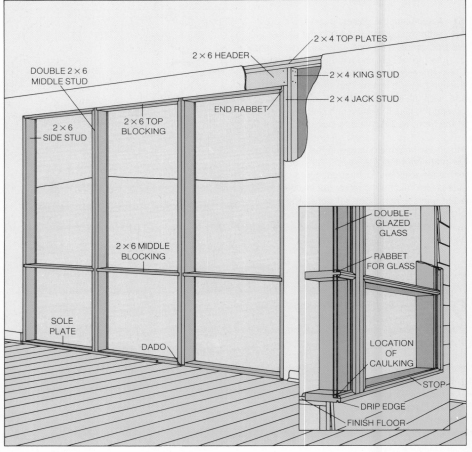

A wall of glass. This typical window wall consists of large panes of glass set in an interlocking grid of 2-by-6s. Above the grid, a doubled 2-by-6 header, supported by 2-by-4 jack studs, fit against the top plate of the main wall. At the bottom of the grid, a 2-by-6 sole plate rests on the subfloor. Between the header and the sole plate, 2-by-6 studs—single at the outer ends of the grid, doubled in the middle (or single 4-by-6s)—and two rows of 2-by-6 horizontal blocking

are joined with dado and rabbet joints to form rectangular openings for panes of glass. All the 2-by-6s of the grid project slightly beyond the siding of the house and are rabbeted at their outer edges to accept the glass—in this example, double panes for insulation (inset). The glass is sealed with caulking secured by stops nailed to the 2-by-6s. Along the bottom face of the sole plate, a shallow groove forms a drip edge to keep water flowing back to the siding.

Routing the Boards

1 **Cutting a drip edge.** Cut a 2-by-6 for the sole plate to fit between the jack studs and, with a router and a 1/4-inch bit, cut a 1/4-inch-deep groove 1/4 inch from one edge along the underside of the sole plate. Guide the router with a straight board temporarily nailed to the 2-by-6, moving and replacing the clamp(s) when necessary.

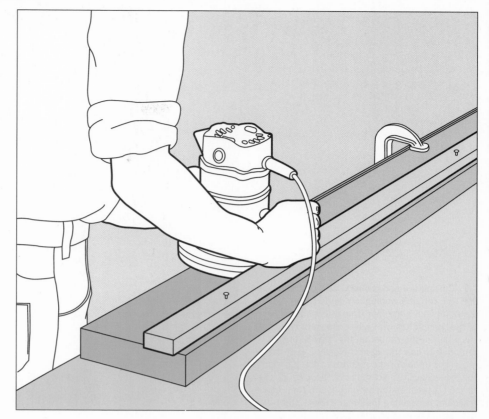

2 **Rabbeting for the glass.** Cutting a rabbet wide enough for most panes of glass 1 to 1 1/2 inches—requires two passes of a router with a 3/4-inch bit set to cut 1/2 inch deep, and two positions of a guide like the one used in Step 1. For a rabbet 1 1/2 inches wide, position the guide so that the first router pass cuts a 3/4-inch notch along the edge of the 2-by-6, then move the guide to widen the rabbet by another 3/4 inch.

Cut rabbets along one edge of the sole plate and of all the 2-by-6s that make up the wall frame; for the blocking within the frame, rabbet both the top and bottom of the outer edge.

Cut the rabbeted 2-by-6s to length for the studs and blocking, allowing 1/2 inch for joints at dadoes and end rabbets *(Step 5)*. Mark the sole plate and the studs for dadoes and end rabbets: End rabbets are 1 1/2 inches wide; dadoes are 3 1/2 inches wide in the sole plate, 1 1/2 inches wide in each of the side studs (3 inches wide if doubled 2-by-6s are used).

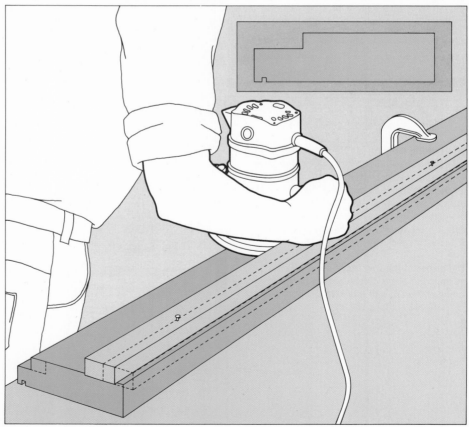

3 **A jig for dadoes and end rabbets.** With a combination square, draw two lines straight across two 2-by-4s, separating the lines by the diameter of the router plate plus 3/4 inch; then set the 2-by-4s 5 1/2 inches apart (the width of a 2-by-6); screw and glue two 1-by-2s to them just outside the lines. Using a 3/4-inch bit set to a depth of 1/2 inch, make two passes with the router to cut a notch 1 1/2 inches wide into the edge of each 2-by-4.

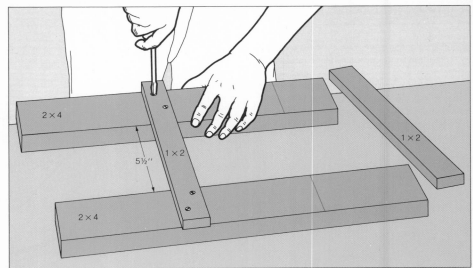

4 **Cutting the end rabbets.** Clamp the jig to the top of a workbench, slide the end of a stud or sole plate into it, aligning one edge of the jig notches with a line drawn to mark the width of the rabbet on the 2-by-6, and temporarily nail the jig to the 2-by-6. Set the router bit in one of the notches of the jig, start the router, push it along one of the 1-by-2s until the bit reaches the second notch; then make a second pass along the other 1-by-2. Cut rabbets at the tops of all the studs and at both ends of the 2-by-6 sole plate.

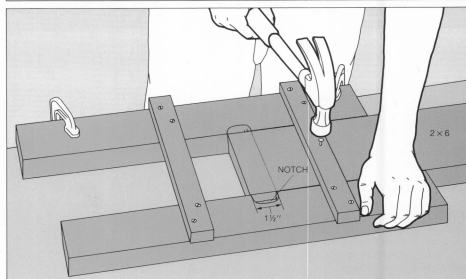

5 **Cutting the dadoes.** Cut the dadoes in the studs as you did the end rabbets in Step 4, aligning the notches of the jig with marks for the edges of each dado. For the dadoes of the sole plate, which are 3 inches wide, move the plate 1 1/2 inches after making the first cuts. Chisel out any remaining wood from the 3 1/2-inch dado.

The pieces of the wall frame are now ready to be nailed in place. Cut away the sheathing and siding of the old wall *(page 188, Steps 1-2).*

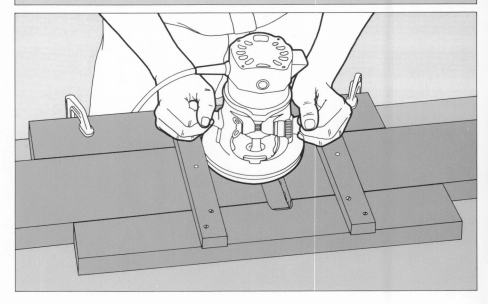

6 **Nailing the studs in place.** Set the sole plate on the subfloor, butted against the finish floor *(page 236, inset)*, and nail it to the subfloor; then set a stud into one of the end rabbets of the plate and nail it to the jack stud. Repeat the procedure for the stud at the other end of the wall. Nail the intermediate studs together in pairs, set them into the sole-plate dadoes and adjust them for plumb; then toenail them to the header and the sole plate.

7 **Putting in the blocking.** Slip the top and middle blocking pieces into the rabbets and dadoes of the studs. Nail through the studs into the ends of the blocks wherever possible so that the nails are invisible; toenail only where necessary, using eightpenny galvanized finishing nails; set the nails.

4 RENOVATING MECHANICAL SYSTEMS

Plumbing

Electricity

Heating, Cooling and Ventilation

Materials and Fittings for Plumbing Tasks

The word plumbing comes from the Latin for lead, and there are still a fair number of lead pipes and fittings around. But today a variety of materials is used in house plumbing—copper, cast iron, steel, brass and plastic. Several are likely to be combined in a house, for each brings a balance of benefits in economy, durability and convenience that makes it the choice for a particular job. And the combination cannot be willy-nilly, for some materials cannot join others without special precautions.

Copper, most popular for water supply lines but also used for drain and vent lines, is convenient to work with and very durable but costly. It is available as rigid pipe in 10- and 20-foot lengths or as flexible tubing in 15-, 30-, 60- or 100-foot coils. Rigid pipe looks neater, but flexible tubing is easier to install, particularly when adding to existing plumbing. Rigid pipe must be soldered with sweat fittings, while flexible tubing can also be joined mechanically with flare or compression fittings, which are costly. Flare fittings are not permitted by most plumbing codes. Flexible tubing comes in two weights: Type K, the heaviest, mainly for underground lines outdoors, and medi-um-weight Type L. Rigid pipe comes in Types K and L, and in lightweight Type M, generally adequate for homes.

Plastic pipe is popular for drains and supply lines because it is light (1/20 the weight of the same size steel pipe), inexpensive, noncorroding and easy to join. Several different plastics are made into pipe, but only CPVC and polybutylene can be used for hot-water supply lines. Other plastics, such as PVC and ABS, can be used for drain and vent lines. Like copper tubing, plastic water supply tube is available in rigid or flexible form. The rigid tube is joined to its fittings with solvent cement. Flexible pipe—either polybutylene, suitable for hot and cold lines, or polyethylene, suitable for cold water—is joined with mechanical fittings and metal clamps.

Galvanized steel is the strongest material available for water supply lines and is preferred for piping exposed to physical damage. It is heavy, and must be joined with threaded fittings. Most plumbing-supply stores will cut the exact lengths you need and thread them.

Cast-iron pipe, the heaviest and most durable of all piping materials, is used only for drains and vents. Today it is joined with metal-clamped rubber gaskets called hubless fittings—old pipes have lead-caulked joints.

The practical considerations of convenience, cost and durability, however, are not the only factors determining the choice of material. Check with your local building department before buying any materials.

All piping is sized nominally by inside diameter. When replacing a section, measure with a ruler its inner diameter and get new pipe the same size. If you are adding a fixture supply line, use the pipe sizes specified by the manufacturer of the fixture.

In addition to pipe, you also need the fittings to join it. A fitting is necessary whenever piping branches off, changes diameter, joins another type, or in the case of rigid pipe, whenever direction changes. The most common fittings are pictured opposite. The shapes are common to all piping—the only difference is the way they are made and joined.

A special precaution must be taken when joining copper water supply tube to steel: Use a bimetallic union to prevent an electrochemical reaction that occurs between dissimilar metals, eroding the joint.

The Difference Between Pipes and Tubes

The material generally called pipe is technically either pipe or tube.

Pipes are sized nominally by inside diameter. Threaded metal, PVC and polyethylene water supply pipes and most drain-and-vent pipes follow pipe sizing.

Tubes are sized according to copper water tube sizes, which are smaller than pipes of the same size. The outside diameters of tubes are made to exact dimensions needed for joining them to their fittings. CPVC and polybutylene, as well as copper, use tube sizing.

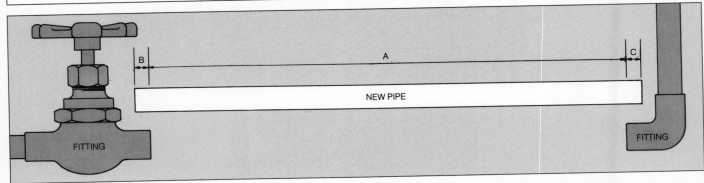

How much pipe do you need? To find out how long a piece of pipe you need between two fittings, measure the distance between the faces of the two (A). Then measure the distance that the new pipe will extend into each fitting (B and C); add both to the first. If only one fitting is in place, mark where the second fitting will go; have someone hold it there while you measure. Keep in mind that no cross connections should exist between the water supply system and any source of contaminated water, according to the U.S. Public Health Service and all plumbing codes.

Four Categories of Connectors

Branches and turns. An elbow takes rigid piping around a curve: Various angles are available up to 90°. A T provides a connection for a new branch at its base. A Y is a variation of the T usually found in drainage and vent lines to allow pipes from individual fixtures to be joined to one main stack. The branch of a Y can also be plugged for use as a cleanout.

Fittings for in-line joints. When two pipes must be connected together in a straight run, a coupling, or sleeve, splices them. A nipple threaded on both ends extends a coupling for steel pipes. Ready-made threaded nipples come in graduated sizes up to 12 inches long. A reducer attaches a length of small-diameter pipe to a larger one. Ts, elbows and Ys are available with a size reduction.

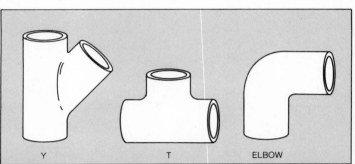

Y   T   ELBOW

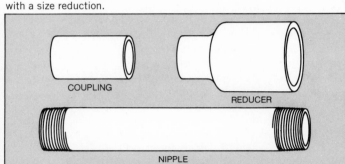

COUPLING   REDUCER   NIPPLE

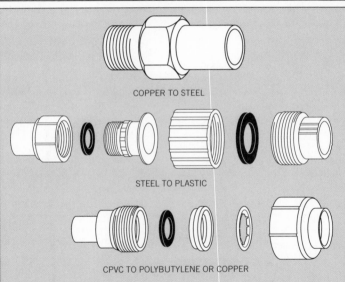

COPPER TO STEEL

STEEL TO PLASTIC

CPVC TO POLYBUTYLENE OR COPPER

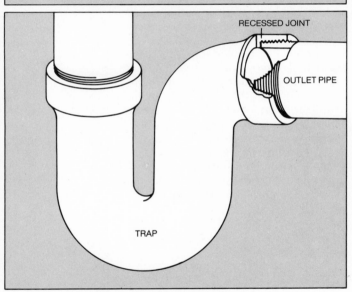

RECESSED JOINT

OUTLET PIPE

TRAP

Transition fittings. To connect one type of pipe material to another, a special fitting is needed to fasten both materials firmly and prevent the electrolytic action that can cause corrosion at joints between dissimilar metals. The copper-steel fitting has one threaded end, to fit steel piping, and one smooth end to solder to copper pipe. The plastic-steel fitting has one threaded end and one CPVC plastic end with an elastomeric washer between metal and plastic to accommodate movements as the dissimilar metals heat and cool. The plastic-copper fitting solvent welds to a CPVC fitting and seals over copper tubing with an O-ring and a gripper ring. No sweat soldering is needed. Transition fittings are also available to join copper, steel and plastic drain pipe to cast-iron pipe.

Drainage fittings. The trap, the one fitting used only in the drainage system, keeps a barrier of water in its U-turn to seal out odors and vermin from sewers. All drainage fittings, whether threaded or not, have recessed joint surfaces so that when a pipe is inserted the inner surface of both pipe and fitting will be flush, eliminating any possibility of waste material snagging in the joint and causing a blockage. Since drain lines depend on gravity to pull waste through the system, the outlets of drainage fittings angle slightly downward.

Copper Piping

The techniques for joining copper piping and fittings are the same whether you are adding new runs or repairing damage in old ones. The first essential step is to cut the pipe perfectly straight, then clean its end of kinks or burrs and clean the mating surfaces of both pipe and fitting. Flexible and rigid copper piping can be cut with a special tool called a tube cutter, or with a fine-tooth hacksaw and miter box. For making smooth bends in flexible copper tube, you may need a tubing bender.

A well-made sweat-soldered joint is the best for either rigid pipe or flexible tube, stronger and more leak resistant than a mechanical connection. When soldering, use noncorrosive flux and lead-free plumber's solder containing tin and antimony, not solder with an acid or rosin core. For use in water-supply piping, avoid solders containing lead.

Caution: Before working on plumbing with a torch, drain all water from the pipes to avoid steam buildup, which will keep the solder from melting. Place sheet metal between the pipe and any surfaces that might ignite.

Because of potential fire hazard, avoid soldering in cramped spaces; instead of sweated joints, use flexible tube and mechanical compression or push-on fittings. Some of these go only with flexible tube; they are more expensive than sweat fittings, but they require little skill to make and are generally preferred for small jobs.

Getting the Right Length and the Right Shape

Using a cutter. Slide the tube cutter onto the pipe and turn the knob until the cutting wheel bites into the wall. Do not tighten the knob all the way or it may bend the wall and the joint will leak. Turn the cutter once around, retighten the knob a little, and continue turning and tightening until the tubing is severed. Use the triangular blade attached to the cutter to ream out the burr inside and, with a file, remove the ridge that the cutter has left on the outer surface. If you cut with a hacksaw, remove the inner burr with a round file.

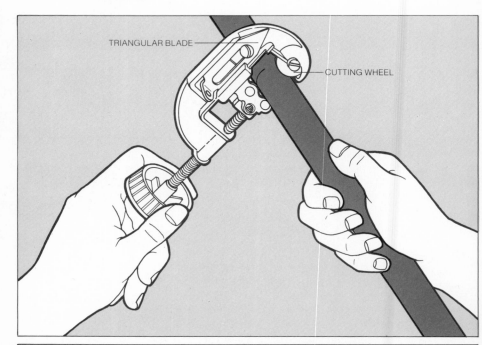

TRIANGULAR BLADE

CUTTING WHEEL

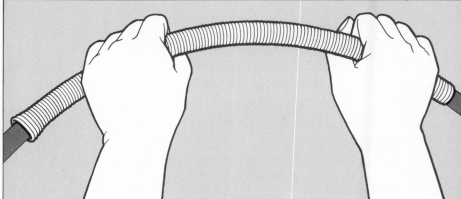

Using a tubing bender. Unlike rigid copper pipe, flexible tube can be bent for easy turns. To prevent kinks in the walls, slip a coiled-spring bender over the section, using a clockwise twisting motion. Bend the tube with your hands or form it over your knee. Overbend the tube a bit, then ease it back to the exact angle you want.

Tap-On Fittings: The Simplest Way to Tap a Line

1 Tapping the existing line. Remove the valve from the tap-on fitting and clamp the yoke around a 1/2-inch supply line, which can be either copper, brass or galvanized steel pipe. Drain the water from the line and drill a hole through the wall of the pipe at the center hole of the yoke, preferably with a cordless drill. (A plug-in drill should be used only in a GFCI-protected outlet. Caution: To avoid electric shock, do not touch the pipe at all.)

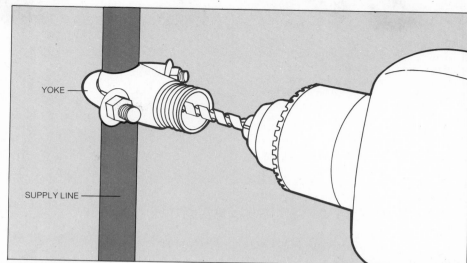

2 Installing the valve. Thread the valve or other fitting back into the center hole of the yoke. Make sure that the yoke is clamped securely to the pipe. The tap-on fitting shown accepts 1/2-inch tube—large enough for most fixtures—or a faucet. Flow is significantly reduced, however. A similar but smaller fitting accepts 1/4-inch tube, used primarily to supply small, low-flow appliances such as humidifiers and ice makers.

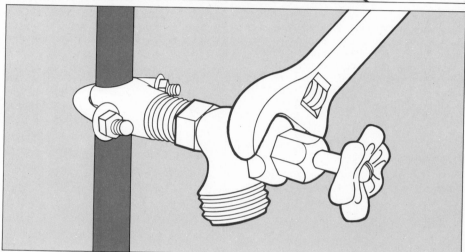

Compression Fittings for Flexible Tubes

Assembling a compression fitting. Cut the supply-line tube square; remove burrs, inside and out. Slip first the flange nut, then the compression ring onto the tube and insert the tube into the fitting—a shutoff valve for a fixture in the drawing—as far as it will go. Slide the compression ring into the joint, making sure that it is squarely aligned, then slide the flange nut over the fitting's threads and screw it down until it is hand-tight. With a wrench, tighten the nut another quarter turn but no more: Overtightening may damage the compression ring and cause a leak.

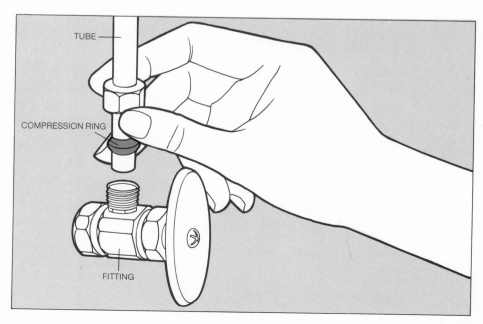

Making a Flare Joint

1 **Flaring the tube.** Since flare joints tend to develop leaks, especially in hot water lines where they expand and contract, they are outlawed by some local codes. If your local code does permit these joints, position them only where they are accessible, and not behind walls, floors or ceilings. Slip a flare nut over the end of square-cut deburred flexible tube and insert the tube into the hole sized for it in a flaring die. Bring the end of the tube flush with the face of the die and tighten the wing nuts. Position the flaring tool over the end of the tube. Clean the point of the tool, then turn the handle clockwise until the point enters the tube. Make sure that the point is centered, then continue tightening until the tube end is flared to a 45° angle. Retrace the tool by turning the handle counterclockwise.

2 **Assembling the joint.** Set the flared end of the tube onto the domed end of the flare fitting. Then slide the flare nut up and thread it to the fitting until it is hand-tight. Finish tightening the nut with a pair of open-end wrenches, one wrench on the flare nut and one on the fitting.

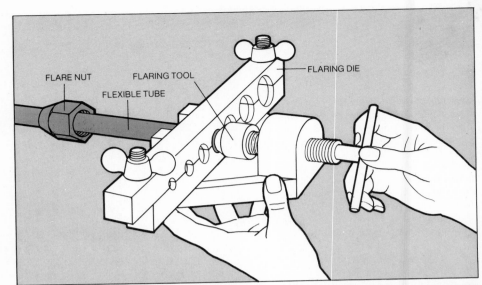

FLARE NUT FLARING TOOL FLARING DIE
FLEXIBLE TUBE

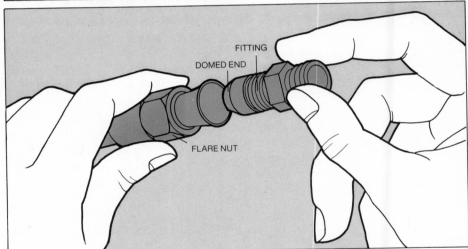

FITTING
DOMED END
FLARE NUT

How to Use a Propane Torch

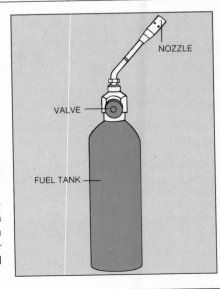

NOZZLE
VALVE
FUEL TANK

The small propane torches generally used to sweat-solder copper joints are made in two parts, a combination valve and nozzle assembly, and a replaceable metal tank of fuel. To assemble the torch, simply screw the nozzle assembly to the threaded fitting at the top of the tank.

While working, wear eye protection (*page 130*). Unless the torch is a trigger-lighting model, light it by striking a match and holding it near the nozzle, turning the valve slightly counterclockwise until a hissing sound is produced—this indicates that gas is flowing. When the torch lights, gradually close the valve until the flame becomes the desired size to heat the area you will work on. Take care not to open the valve all the way: The flame will not get much larger and the gas pressure may blow it out.

It is necessary to hold the torch essentially upright while you work. If the tank is tilted very much, the liquid propane inside may flow into the valve, blocking it so that the flame goes out.

The propane torch is easy and safe to use as long as it is handled properly. Caution is necessary, however, because the joints to be sweated with the flame are generally located near flammable parts of a house structure.

Before starting to work, cover the area behind piping and metal sheeting. And make a habit of shutting off the torch whenever you set it aside, even if only for a moment or two—the flame is silent, nearly invisible and easy to forget about.

Sweat-Soldering a Copper Joint

1 Cleaning the copper. To clean the joint so that melted solder will flow evenly and adhere securely, scour the inner surfaces of fitting sockets with a wire brush. With a piece of emery cloth—not a file or steel wool—clean the end of the pipe that will slide into the fitting socket, rubbing until the surface is burnished bright. Once surfaces are cleaned, do not touch them, since even a fingerprint will weaken the joint. Caution: Wear eye protection *(page 130)* when sweat-soldering; solder sometimes explodes when it contacts moisture.

2 Assembling and heating the joint. Brush a light coating of flux over the surfaces you have cleaned, assemble the joint. Place a piece of sheet metal in back of the joint to protect the surface behind from flame. Wearing safety goggles, light the propane torch and play the flame over the fitting and nearby pipe, heating them as evenly as possible. Touch a piece of lead-free plumber's solder to the fitting and then to the pipe; when the solder melts on contact with both parts, the joint is ready to be soldered. Do not heat further or the flux will burn off and the solder will not flow properly.

3 Soldering the joint. Touch the solder tip to the point where the pipe enters the fitting, but do not let the torch flame touch the solder. The solder should melt only on contact with the hot metal; if it does not, take the solder away and continue heating the joint. When the joint is properly heated, molten solder is drawn into the fitting by capillary action to seal the connection. Continue feeding solder to the joint until a bead of metal appears around the rim and begins to drip. Wipe off excess molten solder with a dry cloth and allow the joint to cool without moving it.

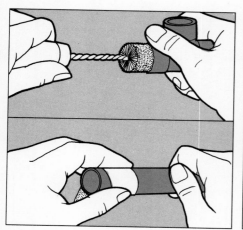

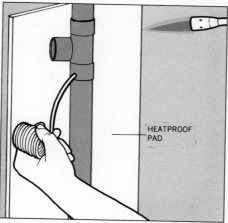

HEATPROOF PAD

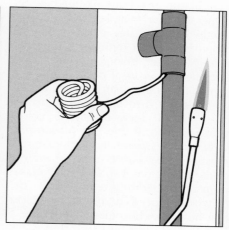

Stopping Leaks in Copper Pipe

Fixing a leaking joint. Leaks in sweat-soldered joints are almost always caused by a poor soldering job. Wearing safety goggles and work gloves, drain all of the water from the line, protect adjacent surfaces with sheet metal and heat the joint until it can be pulled apart. Clean the mating surfaces of both pipe and fitting, then apply flux as described for a new joint. Heat pipe and fitting separately, and cover the fluxed surfaces with solder. When both surfaces have been "tinned," scour them smooth with emery cloth, assemble the joint, and heat and solder it as described for a new joint.

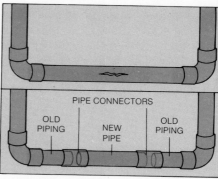

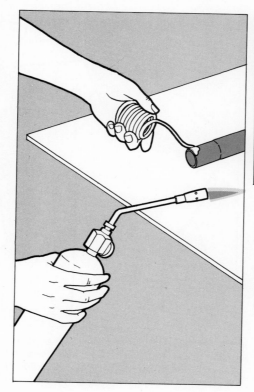

PIPE CONNECTORS

OLD PIPING   NEW PIPE   OLD PIPING

Replacing damaged piping. If a section of copper piping is punctured or burst, it can be patched temporarily but must eventually be replaced. Drain all the water from the line and cut out the damaged section *(top)*. Remove only enough pipe to leave undamaged couplings at each end—sweated or push-on joints are needed for rigid pipe, sweated, push-on or mechanical ones for flexible tube.

Plastic Piping

One of the main reasons that plastic pipe has become so popular is the ease with which it can be assembled. Rigid pipe and fittings are simply solvent welded together, and the resulting joint is stronger than the pipe itself. Flexible plastic tubing cannot be cemented, but can be joined with insert fittings or push-on or mechanical fittings like those used with copper tube. Transition fittings *(page 243)* make it easy to start a run of plastic pipe from existing pipe of another common material.

In the United States, plastic piping is recognized by all regional plumbing codes. However, before buying plastic pipe, check your local code: A few local plumbing codes ban it, while a few others permit it to be used only outdoors, only for drains or only for cold-water supplies. If you use plastic for hot-water lines, reset the temperature-pressure relief valve on your water heater for no more than 180°F, the maximum safe operating temperature for any type of pipe. Rigid plastic pipe carrying hot water becomes slightly flexible and it should be supported with clamps placed at the most every 3 feet and set loose enough to let the pipe move slightly.

Assemble rigid solvent-welded joints only when the air temperature is above 40°F; cold slows the action of the solvent cement, interfering with bonding. Caution: Cement vapors can be hazardous. Work in a well-ventilated area.

Cemented Fittings for Rigid Pipe

1 Cutting the tube. Flexible plastic tube is soft enough to be cut with a sharp knife or even a large pair of shears, but cutting rigid tube demands precision. A tube cutter that is used for flexible copper tube is convenient, but it needs a larger cutting wheel meant for plastic. An equally accurate cut can be made with a miter box and backsaw or a hacksaw with a blade having 24 teeth per inch.

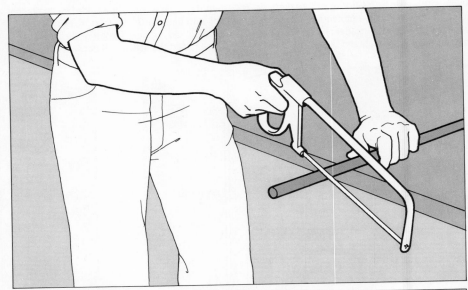

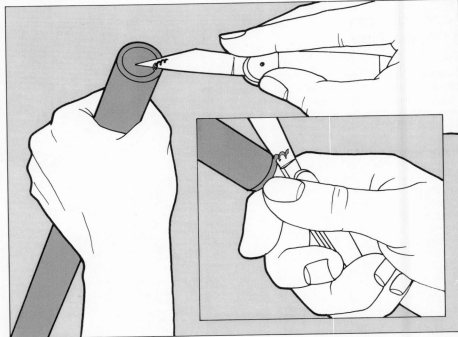

2 Preparing the pipe end. Pare away any burrs from the inside of the pipe end. Then bevel the outside of the end so it will not force the solvent cement from the inside of the fitting *(inset)*. Do not use sandpaper or emery cloth.

3 **Checking the fit.** Clean the pipe end and fitting with a dry rag to remove any grease or moisture, then slip the pipe into the fitting: You should be able to push it in about halfway. If the fit is too tight, the solvent cement may be forced from the joint; too loose and the pipe and fitting may not bond together. In either case the joint will leak: Discard the fitting and try another (with some brands, size may vary slightly). When the fit is correct, adjust pipe and fitting in the position in which they will be set. Mark them so they can be quickly repositioned after solvent cement has been applied.

4 **Priming and gluing the joint.** Although cement alone generally makes a satisfactory joint, most plumbing codes call for you to clean and prepare the mating surfaces of the tube and fitting by brushing on a cleaner/primer; wait about 15 seconds to allow the surfaces to soften. When the primer has dried, use a wide brush to apply a thick coat of cement to the primed surface of the pipe and a thinner coat to the inner surface of the fitting. Do not apply so much cement that it blocks the pipe opening. Immediately slip the pipe into the fitting, twist a quarter turn to evenly spread the solvent cement, and immediately align the pipe and fitting to the marks made in Step 3. Delay may cause the joint to fuse in the wrong position. An even bead of solvent cement should appear around the joint. If the bead is incomplete *(below)*, pull the pipe out immediately and apply more solvent cement. When the joint is properly set, hold it in place for 10 seconds, then wait three minutes before starting the next joint. When the job is done, wait at least one hour—or, better still, overnight—before letting water into the new run of piping.

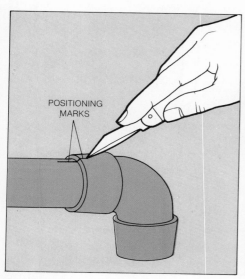

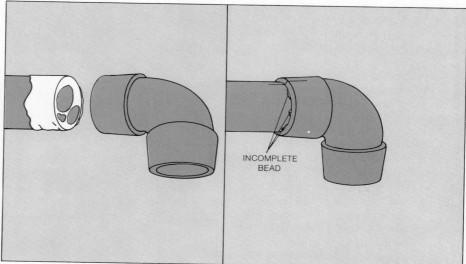

A Clamped Fitting for Flexible Tubing

Attaching an insert fitting. Flexible plastic tubing—polyethylene for cold water—is joined by a ridged insert fitting and two small worm-drive clamps. Slip a clamp loosely to about 1/2 inch from the end of each pipe. Force the pipe ends over the fitting until the ridges are covered. Tighten the clamps with a screwdriver.

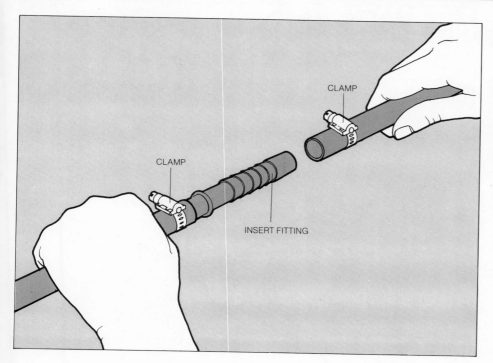

Steel and Brass Piping

Galvanized steel pipe and fittings, as well as the less common brass pipe found in some older homes, must be joined with threaded joints. If you plan only a small extension or replacement job, take careful measurements *(page 242)* and have the plumbing-supply store cut and thread the pipe for you. For a more extensive job, use copper or plastic for it, making connections to the threaded piping with adapters.

Tapered threaded joints make assembly easy, but complicate the job of removing a damaged pipe or inserting a new fitting in existing pipe to make a new branch. The problem is that once a pipe or fitting is in the line it cannot be unscrewed as one piece, since loosening it at one end will tighten it at the other. The solution is to cut out the old pipe and install a new one using a connecting fitting called a union *(opposite, top)*. A simpler device called a slip fitting—a sleeve sealed at both ends by rubber gasket-fitted compression nuts *(opposite, bottom)*—can be used to fix a leaking pipe, and tap-on fittings like the one on page 245 are also available for steel pipe.

Assembling Threaded Pipe

Applying joint sealers. Before assembling a threaded pipe joint, the malepipe threads should be covered with one of the materials below to lubricate, seal, rustproof and, if necessary, allow easy disassembly. Pipe-joint compound *(left)*, the most common material, is spread evenly over the pipe end; use just enough to fill the threads. If you wish to make doubly sure that the joint will not leak, wind wicking into the pipe threads *(center)* before applying joint compound. Use both joint compound and wicking before reassembling an old joint. Plastic joint tape *(right)* is even easier to apply. Wind one and one half turns of tape clockwise over the threads tightly enough for them to show through.

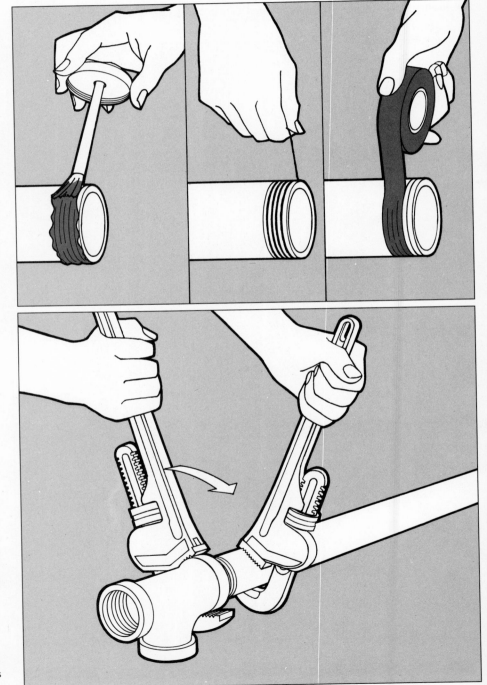

Joining the pipe and fitting. Thread pipe and fitting together by hand to ensure that they are not cross-threaded, then use two pipe wrenches to finish tightening the joint. Turn the fitting with one wrench and hold the pipe with the other so that the rest of the pipe branch will not be twisted or strained. The jaws of the wrenches should face the direction in which the force is applied *(arrow)*. Keep tightening until just three pipe threads are visible outside the fitting. Further tightening may strip threads and cause a leak or crack the fitting.

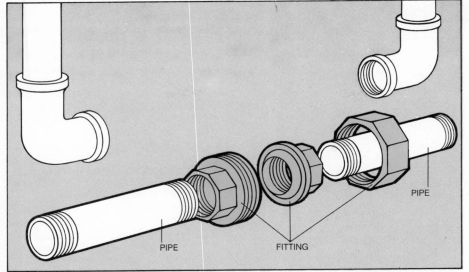

PIPE

PIPE   FITTING   PIPE

Replacing Damaged Pipe with New Pipe and a Union

1 **Preparing the parts.** Hacksaw through the damaged section and unscrew each piece of pipe from its fitting by reversing the procedure shown opposite, bottom. Buy two pieces of pipe and a union whose combined length when assembled will be the same as the old pipe. Prepare the threads of one new piece, slip one union nut onto it and tighten. Slip the ring nut over the end of the second pipe, then thread the other union nut onto it and tighten it.

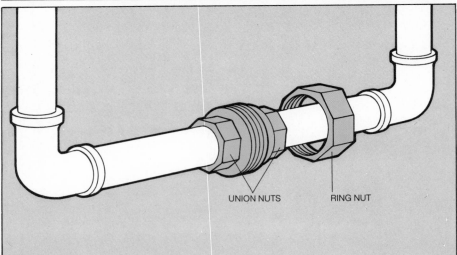

UNION NUTS   RING NUT

2 **Connecting the union.** Prepare the threads at the end of each pipe section opposite the union nut and screw it into one of the existing fittings. When both sections are tightened, the faces of the union nuts should touch. Slide the ring nut to the center of the union and screw it on the exposed threads of the union nuts. Tighten it in place with one wrench while bracing the exposed union nut with another wrench.

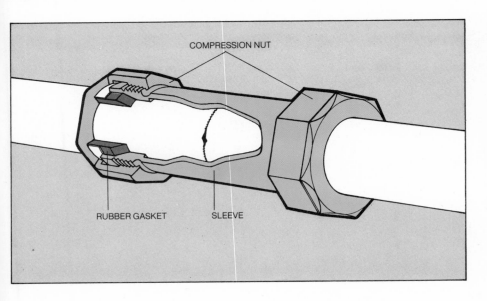

COMPRESSION NUT

RUBBER GASKET   SLEEVE

A Sleeve to Stop a Leak

Installing a slip fitting. Cut through the damaged pipe at the leak with a hacksaw, pull one cut section aside and slide the fitting onto it. Realign the two sections and slide the fitting over the damaged area. Tighten the nut at each end of the fitting. Since this fitting is not as strong as a union, it should be used only on exposed pipe where you can tell if the leak starts up again.

Cast-Iron Piping: Old and New

Because of its low cost and high durability, cast iron has long been the most popular material for drain, waste and vent pipe, but until recently it was also the most difficult to install because of its weight and the difficulty of joining it. The conventional type, still in wide use, is connected at bell-shaped hub joints, which must be sealed with a rope-like material called oakum and molten lead. A newer type, called hubless pipe, is joined with sleeves and clamps (opposite). It can be spliced into an existing system of hub-type pipe to replace a

damaged section—or to add a new one.

Two grades of cast-iron pipe are available, service weight and the thicker-walled heavy weight. Use service weight if your plumbing code permits, because it is easier to work with. Both weights can be cut either with a saw and chisel (below, right) or with a special cutting tool (below, left). Proper support is more important with cast-iron pipe than any other type, both because of its weight and because the hubless joints are slightly flexible. Use pipe straps or the special clamps shown opposite, bottom.

Joining Hubless Pipe

1 **Cutting the pipe.** The easiest way to cut cast-iron pipe is with the cutting tool shown below, left, usually available at rental stores. If you are working inside a wall, there may not be enough space to cut the pipe any other way. Put on safety goggles and wrap the chain section of the tool around the pipe, hook it onto the tool body, tighten the knob and work the handle back and forth until the pipe snaps. Cast-iron pipe can also be cut with hacksaw and chisel (below, right); wear safety goggles. Mark the circumference of the pipe where you wish to sever it, then support the pipe on a 2-by-4 so that the section to be cut off is raised. With a coarse-tooth hacksaw, cut a 1/16-inch-deep groove around the pipe at the mark, then tap around the groove with a small sledgehammer and chisel until the pieces separate.

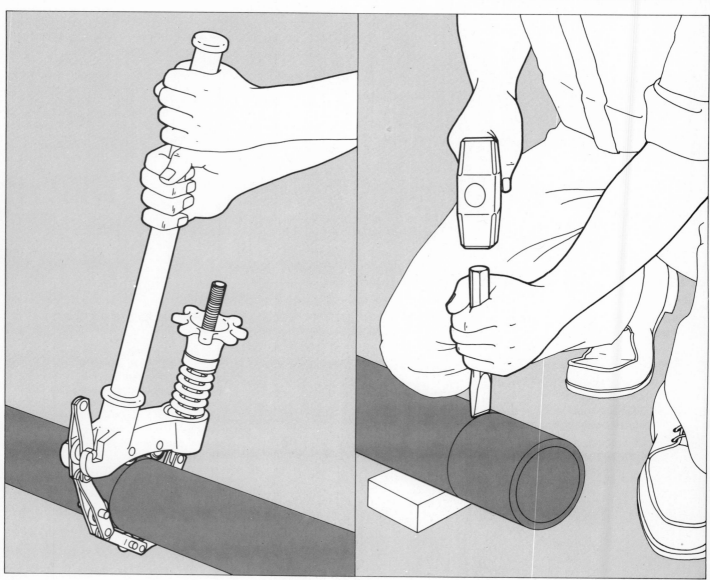

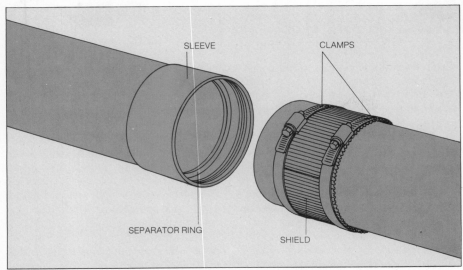

2 **Preparing the joint.** Slip the rubber sleeve onto the end of one pipe, making sure that the pipe end butts firmly against the separator ring at the center of the sleeve. Slide the stainless-steel shield over the end of the second pipe, and position it so that the clamps will be accessible for tightening when the joint is assembled.

SLEEVE

CLAMPS

SEPARATOR RING

SHIELD

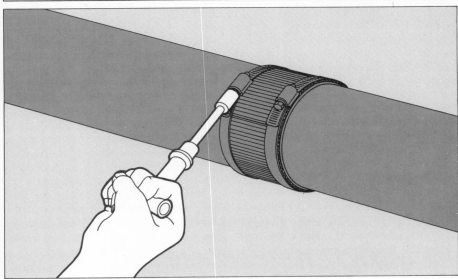

3 **Assembling the joint.** Push the end of the second pipe into the sleeve until it butts against the sleeve separator ring. Slide the shield over the sleeve so that it covers the sleeve completely, then tighten the clamps on the shield. To tighten the clamps, you will need either the special torque wrench shown (the type that auto mechanics use for light-duty turning such as installing spark plugs), or a no-hub joint torque-limiting wrench. Tighten to 60 pound-inches (530 Newton-meters, the metric unit for torque).

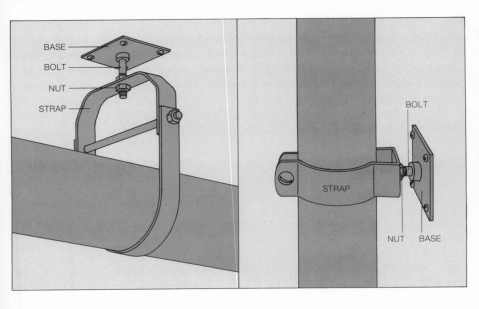

4 **Supporting the pipe.** A horizontal run of hubless cast-iron pipe should be supported at every joint with a special clamp *(far left)*. A long run of pipe between joints should be supported every 4 feet. Screw the base of the support clamp to the ceiling, attach the clamp to the pipe with the bolt provided and adjust the tension of the strap with the nut. A similar clamp *(left)* is used to support a vertical run of cast-iron pipe. It is attached the same way and should be spaced at 3-foot intervals. A third kind of clamp is the stack clamp: Two shaped pieces of strap steel that are held together at the ends with bolts are attached at floor level on vertical runs.

BASE

BOLT

NUT

STRAP

BOLT

STRAP

NUT   BASE

Finding the Best Pathways for the Piping

Remodeling a kitchen or bathroom, or installing a new one, is a major job that requires major planning. Before you turn the first screw or hammer the first nail, you must make basic decisions about the sizes and styles of fixtures and appliances, clearances, floor and wall coverings, lighting, heating and ventilation. Most important of all, you must decide upon the routes of new plumbing lines (opposite). The location of existing plumbing and the distance it can be moved—or whether it can be moved at all—will often dictate the layout of a remodeled kitchen or bathroom, and may limit your choice of locations for a new one.

In most homes, plumbing fixtures are clustered around a vertical core of supply pipes and drain pipes. A bathroom is often located above or behind the kitchen, or over a basement utility room. Each plumbing fixture in these rooms must be supplied with hot and cold water from parallel lines that run through the core. Wastes are carried away from the fixtures by branch drains that run to the soil stack—a large, vertical drain dropping down to the main house drain. Each fixture has a drain trap that prevents sewer gases and vermin from entering the house. And each has a vent pipe that exhausts waste gases through a chimney-like stack and admits air to the drains, preventing water from being siphoned out of the traps.

Roughing-in, the job of installing plumbing where none exists, involves running new piping through the walls, floors and ceilings. Because drain pipes and vent pipes—collectively called the drain-waste-vent, or DWV, system—are the most complicated part of a plumbing network, they are always planned and installed before the supply lines. Drains work by gravity: They are large (1 1/2 to 4 inches in diameter), and must be pitched 1/4 inch per foot on horizontal runs and kept as straight as possible. The maximum length of a fixture's drain piping to the closest vent is rigidly governed by plumbing codes. If length exceeds a specified "critical distance" from an existing vent (chart, right), you must install a new branch vent—and in some circumstances you may have to add an entire vent and drain stack, as in Room 2 in the drawing.

Extending supply pipes usually poses fewer problems. They are relatively small (1/2 or 3/4 inch in diameter) and can be elbowed into sharp turns. But added fixtures can reduce water flow through the supply lines in a system that already has low pressure or constricted pipes. If you have these problems, ask a plumber about remedies before planning plumbing additions.

Concealing new pipes, especially the large drain pipes, can be tricky. If the new kitchen or bathroom is over a crawl space or an unfinished basement, horizontal pipes can easily be run between or beneath the floor joists. For a new installation above a finished ceiling, you must cut away part of the ceiling to install the pipes and you may have to drill or notch joists to accommodate them. There are strict limits on where and how deeply you can cut a joist (page 260); in some cases, you may have to run the pipes below the ceiling, and then conceal them.

Vertical pipes are usually concealed inside a framed structure called a wet wall, substantially thicker than an ordinary partition and created by furring out an existing wall (page 256) or building an entirely new one (pages 257-259). Alternatively, pipes can be run alongside an existing wall and concealed—in cabinets, bookcases, closets or specially made paneling.

Electrical lines for a new bathroom or kitchen pose fewer problems than new plumbing lines. Electrical cable is flexible and can easily be snaked through walls and ceilings; if the existing branch circuit has enough spare capacity (page 280), the new lines can be powered from an existing outlet box or directly from the service panel; call an electrician to do this. Heating ducts are bulkier, but usually not difficult to run: The fans for bathroom ceilings or kitchen range hoods (pages 172-175) are usually vented through lengths of duct run to the outside through the roof or sides of the house.

Since plumbing pipes, electrical lines and vent ducts may have to run over long distances, route them in the same direction if you can to minimize the cutting and patching of walls and ceilings. This part of the planning job is tricky. For example, if you plan to expand a room by removing a wall (pages 70-76), be sure

that you will not endanger the house structure or disrupt vital services.

First determine whether the wall is load bearing (page 70)—almost all outside walls are. Then find out what services the wall contains. Electrical switches or outlets indicate wiring that must be removed or relocated. Heating registers are signs of ducts, which can be rerouted but generally not removed. In some cases, a duct can be cut back and capped with a floor register. Ducts that cannot be cut back or rerouted must be left in place and concealed with drywall or paneling to match the remodeled room.

The presence of plumbing fixtures along a wall, or along a corresponding wall in the room directly opposite or above, indicates pipes within the wall that must be moved. If the plumbing ends at the existing fixtures (you may have to cut a small hole in the wall to check its route), it can be removed and capped (page 260). Supply pipes and small branch drains passing through the wall to fixtures above can usually be rerouted. But large drains and soil stacks usually must be left in place and concealed.

Once you know where you can best place the new services, make a floor plan of the room, indicating the locations and dimensions for walls, doors, windows, and plumbing and electrical outlets. Follow the plan as closely as you can in every step of the remodeling process, from running plumbing and electrical lines to arranging fixtures and appliances—and even to ordering and cutting new wall and floor coverings. Be sure to get a building permit before you begin any work.

Maximum Distance From Fixture Trap to Vent Stack*	
Pipe Size	**Distance**
1 1/2"	5'
2"	8'
3"	10'
*Check local code	

254

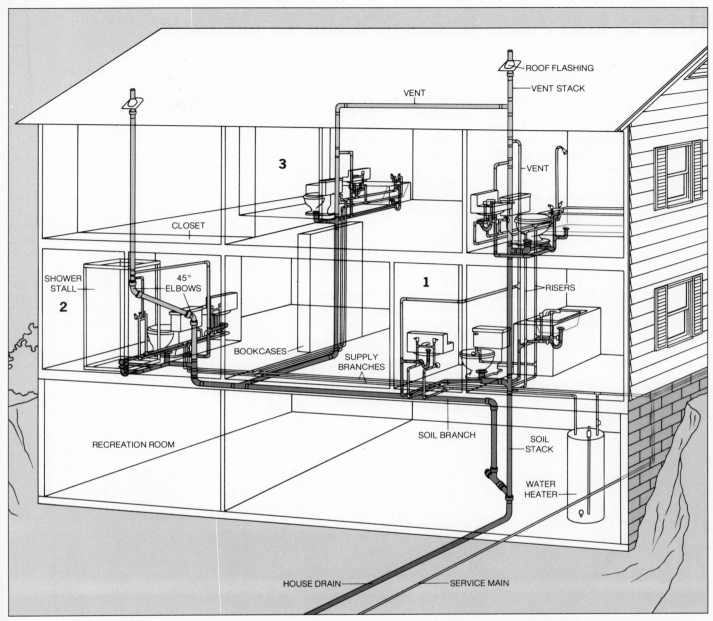

Paths for new pipes. In the two-story house shown above, the existing plumbing core consists of two systems of pipes running from the basement to a first-floor kitchen and a second-floor bathroom. Supply pipes *(colored blue)* carry cold water from the service main and hot water from the water heater. Drains *(colored green)* and vents *(colored yellow)* run to a soil stack that vents gases through the roof and carries wastes down to the main drain.

Three new installations—a powder room next to the kitchen and full baths on the first and second floors—illustrate ways in which new plumbing can be added to an existing system.

1 Powder room. All the newly installed fixtures are close enough to the existing plumbing core to be tied directly into it. A new drain runs across the open ceiling underneath the powder room to the existing stack, and a new branch vent is connected to the existing vent. The supply lines are short extensions of nearby hot and cold vertical lines, called risers.

2 First-floor bathroom. Supply branches and a soil branch (the large horizontal drain) run across the basement ceiling to and from the new bathroom. The pipes that cross the finished ceiling in the recreation room can be concealed by a soffit or a drop ceiling. The vent, too far from the existing vent for a practical branch-vent connection, is a new vent, offset with 45° elbows to carry it into the closet of a second-floor bedroom and onto a new roof outlet.

3 Second-floor bath. An even larger run of the supply piping and drainpiping runs to the second floor across the length and width of a basement and up along a first-floor wall, where it is concealed by floor-to-ceiling bookcases. The vent, however, is close enough to the existing stack to be connected to it by a branch-vent pipe running up through the wall and across the attic. Cleanout openings must be provided at the higher, accessible ends of all horizontally sloped drains. These are closed off by cleanout plugs.

255

How to Run Pipes through Walls and Floors

Renovating a kitchen or bathroom may involve the construction of walls—not just partitions, which are erected like those for any other part of a house, but the kind called wet walls. A wet wall provides space for the plumbing pipes—particularly big drain-waste-vent pipes—and is thicker than an ordinary partition.

The easiest way to provide a new wet wall, if your plan and available space permit, is to add one to an existing wall. Just run the plumbing pipes along the surface of the old wall and attach them to the studs behind. Then nail furring strips, or blocks as shown, to the wall and cover the pipes with a new wall surface *(below)*.

When such a shortcut is not possible you then must erect a new wet wall. It is generally 6 inches thick, instead of the normal 4, and 2-by-6s are used for the horizontal sole and top plates. They may also be used for the vertical studs, but a

simpler construction uses 2-by-4s set sideways and staggered so that there is space to thread pipes between studs, eliminating the need to drill holes.

The way the wet wall is installed will depend on the direction of the joists in the floor and ceiling of the room. If the new wall will run at right angles to the joists, nail the top and bottom plates of the frame to the edge of each ceiling and floor joist that they traverse. However, if the new wall will run parallel to the joists, position the frame under the most convenient ceiling joist, and nail the top plate to the joist through the ceiling. If you must locate the wall between joists, remove sections of the ceiling and install nailing blocks *(opposite, top right)*.

Since a new wet wall is nonbearing, it supports little weight and the placement of studs is not crucial. Ordinarily they are set at 24-inch intervals, but if the position of

one interferes with the placement of a fixture, reposition it as necessary. Be sure to check your local code.

Although supply pipes can be run through ordinary 4-inch walls by cutting holes or notches in their framing, it is not advisable to install the large drain-waste-vent plumbing this way—the large cuts that are necessary will weaken the wall. For the same reason, avoid as far as possible running drains through joists, since they are always part of the basic house structure, and the large notches will weaken them, too. If you must saw or notch studs, joists or top plates, be sure to reinforce them as shown on page 260.

With your walls in place and the roughing-in dimensions marked, you can install the supporting members for your new fixtures. Finally, run the new pipes to the desired locations and install the fixtures themselves *(pages 261-268)*.

An Easy Way to Make a Wet Wall

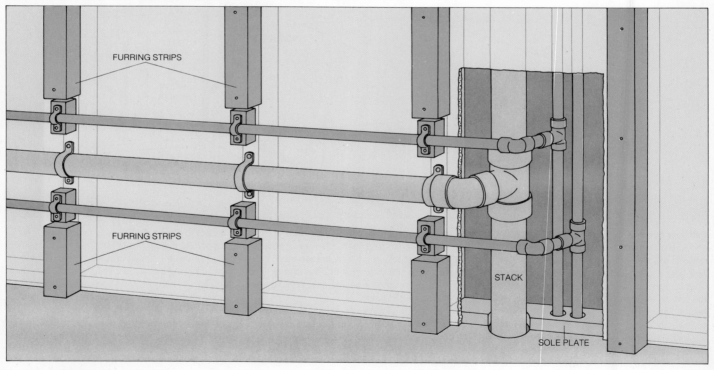

FURRING STRIPS

FURRING STRIPS

STACK

SOLE PLATE

Furring out the wall. Cut out a section from the existing wall, up to 4 feet high, between the two studs where you plan to install the new stack. Cut a hole in the floor and the sole plate for the new stack and drill holes in the sole plate for the risers. Run the pipes through the holes and clamp the pipes to the studs. Cut strips or blocks of wood thick enough to project just beyond the pipes and nail these strips to the studs along the entire length of the wall. Make rough-in holes in new wallboard panels *(pages 136-137)*, then nail the panels to the furring strips or blocks.

A New Wall Designed for Piping

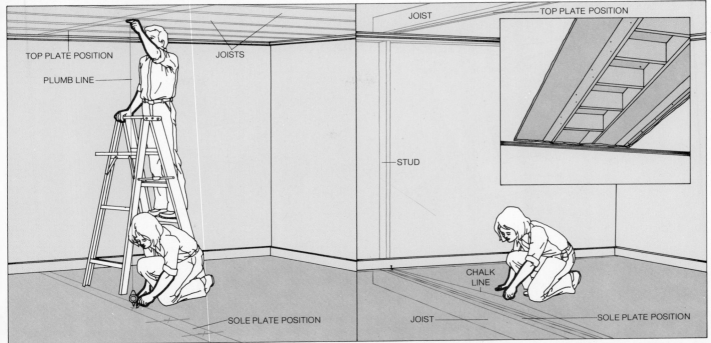

TOP PLATE POSITION

PLUMB LINE

JOISTS

SOLE PLATE POSITION

JOIST

TOP PLATE POSITION

STUD

CHALK LINE

JOIST

SOLE PLATE POSITION

1 **Locating the sole plate and top plate.**
For new walls that run at right angles to the room joists, simply mark the position of the top plate on the ceiling and use a plumb line to find the corresponding spot on the floor for the sole plate *(above, left)*. If the new wall runs parallel to the room joists, find the ceiling joist nearest the intended spot for the frame and position the sole plate and top plate so that the edge of the new wall frame overlaps the joist. Mark both positions with a chalk line *(above, right)*.

If you must locate the wall between joists, cut away the ceiling to expose the two closest joists, then install a series of nailing blocks, of the same size lumber as the joists, at 24-inch intervals between the joists *(inset)*. After installing the blocks, patch the strip with wallboard.

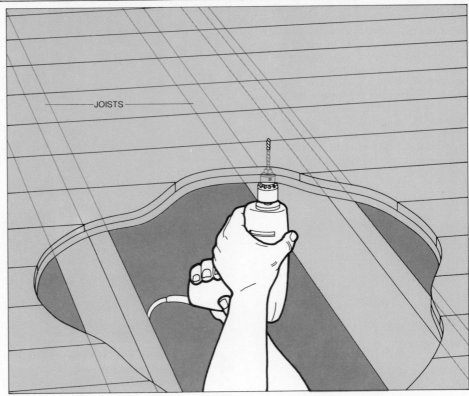

JOISTS

2 **Cutting a hole for a new stack.** If the floor joists run parallel to the new wet wall, drill a small locating hole from the room below for the stack. Make sure that the stack hole will clear the joist. On the floor of the room above, center a piece of the pipe on the hole, draw its outline and saw out the outlined area. When the floor joists run at right angles to the new wall, drill the locating hole from above. If you hit a joist, relocate the stack a few inches to either side of the hole. Drill two smaller holes for the supply pipes. Using an extension bit, drill through a finished ceiling.

257

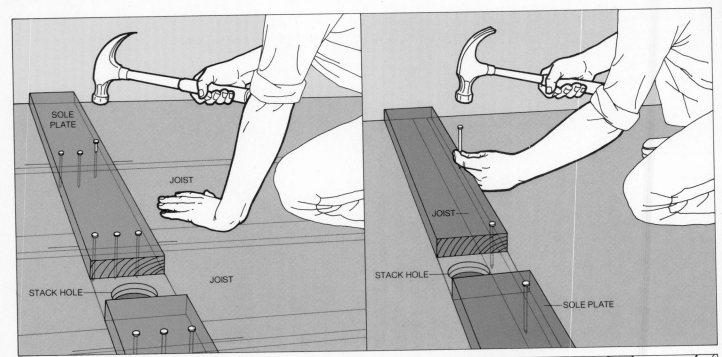

3 **Installing the sole plate.** Remove the floor and ceiling molding from the two walls the new wet wall will touch. Cut two 2-by-6s the length of the distance between the two walls. Use a 2-by-6 as the sole plate and lay it in place on the floor. Mark the position of the hole for the vent stack and cut the sole plate across its width about an inch to each side of the hole. Reposition the two parts of the sole plate and nail them to the floor joists with 16-penny nails; drive three nails at each joist *(above, left)*. If the sole plate runs parallel to floor joists, nail the sole plate at 1-foot intervals, 3/4 inch from the edge of the sole plate *(above, right)*.

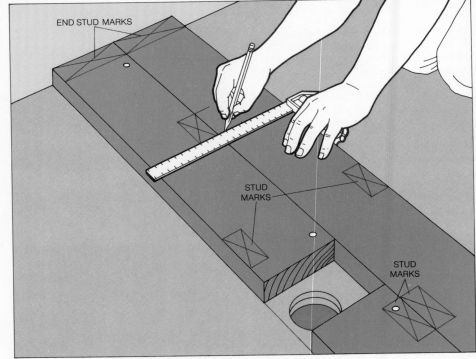

4 **Marking the top plate and sole plate.** Mark positions for end studs at the ends of the sole plate. Then along one edge of the sole plate, mark positions at 24-inch intervals for one row of intervening studs. Along the other edge of the sole plate, mark positions for a second row of studs, each set midway between a pair in the first row. Place the top plate beside the sole plate, and with a square, transfer the stud marks from the sole plate to the top plate.

5 **Assembling the frame.** To determine the length of the studs, drop a plumb line from the ceiling to the floor at three points, and measure the height of the plumb line at each point; the three measurements should be within a fraction of an inch of one another. Take the minimum measurement (to make sure the frame will fit under the ceiling), subtract 3 inches for the combined thicknesses of the top and sole plates and cut to this length two 2-by-6 end studs and the necessary number of 2-by-4 studs. Nail the end studs in place through the top plates. Lay intermediate studs on the floor, butt their ends to the top plate and nail them in place.

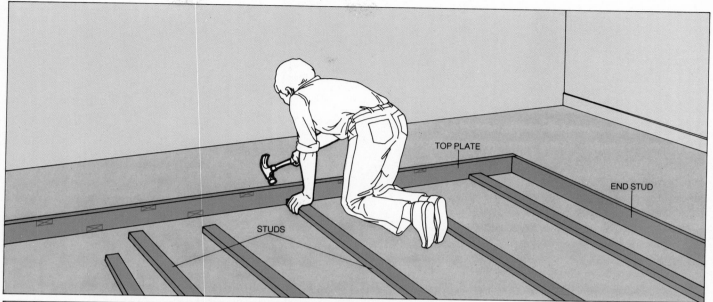

6 **Installing the wet-wall frame.** With a helper, lift the frame and place it on the sole plate so that the end studs rest on the sole-plate marks. Nail the top plate to a ceiling joist or joists, the same way you attached the sole plate to the floor (opposite, top). Plumb the wall and nail the end studs to studs in the abutting walls.

If the frame runs at right angles to the joists, do not nail the end studs to the walls unless you are certain that a stud stands directly behind each end stud. Toenail the end studs to the sole plate. Position each 2-by-4 stud at its mark on the sole plate. Use a level to check that the stud is vertical, shim it if necessary to make a snug fit, then toenail it in place.

Safe Passages for Pipes

In a wet wall. Run new pipe between the back and front studs of a wet wall, clamping the pipe to either row of studs. Use clamps designed for the type of pipe you are using and secure the pipe to each stud along its path.

In studs. Run pipe through notches up to 2 1/2 inches square or through holes within 1 1/2 inches of stud edges. Reinforce a notch with a 1/8-inch steel plate mortised into the stud; in a bearing wall, add a stud at right angles to it.

In top plates. Cut a hole for a stack through the center of the top plates. To reinforce the hole, cut two 2-by-4 supports and notch them at their centers to fit around the pipe. Nail the supports to the top of the plates.

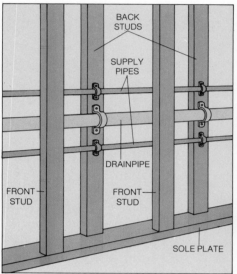

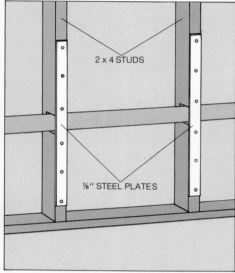

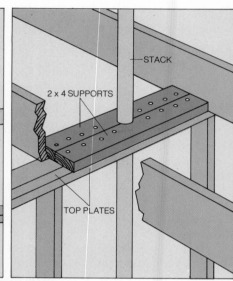

In joists. Notches and holes make passages for pipe in joists as well as studs, but must be more strongly reinforced. Cut a joist notch to no more than one quarter of the joist's height, and locate it in one of the outer quarters of the joist's length, not in the center two quarters; reinforce the notch with a 2-by-4 nailed to both sides of the joist directly under the notch. The maximum safe diameter of a joist hole is one quarter of the joist's height, at a location at least 2 inches from the top and bottom edges. Caution: Limit runs of drain and waste pipe through holes to short distances—on a long run, the pitch of the pipe will locate one or more holes too close to the edges of the joists.

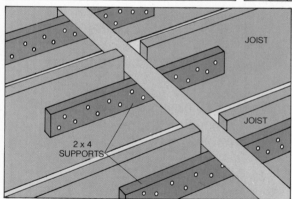

Capping Pipes

All pipes should be sealed when a fixture is removed. Supply lines with shutoff valves require only tape over the valve outlet hole to keep debris out. But drains and supply lines without shutoff valves should be tightly capped. If the pipe is threaded, put pipe dope on the male threads and screw on a matching threaded cap. Elbows and couplings, which have female threads, require plugs. For plastic tubes, solvent weld a matching plastic cap; for copper tubes, solder on a copper cap.

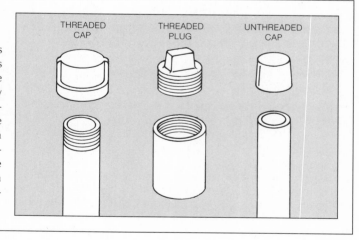

The Final Step: Connecting the Fixtures

Once the framing and rough-in plumbing are in place, installing kitchen and bathroom fixtures is mostly a matter of positioning and connecting supply pipes and drain pipes. With most bathtubs, toilets and sinks, installing new fixtures simply reverses the procedures used to remove the old ones *(pages 130-131)*. You will need the same tools plus a tube cutter or hacksaw to cut pipe.

Most pipe connections require little more than the tightening of slip nuts. But take care not to damage any of the parts by overtightening nuts—always hand-tighten them first, then make an extra quarter turn with a wrench. Use plumber's putty where you want watertight seals and apply pipe-joint compound or joint tape to threaded connections, plastic as well as metal. Check your work by turning on the

water and searching for leaks with your fingers as well as your eyes.

While most fixtures are installed after floors and walls are finished, bathtubs should go in before, since tubs usually rest on the subfloor and are secured to the wall by vertical flange supports nailed to the studs. If you are using a steel or fiberglass tub, which makes more noise than a cast-iron tub when struck by water, you can reduce the racket by laying fiberglass insulation on the subfloor.

Setting a tub snugly into a three-wall enclosure requires some careful movements by at least two people—four if a heavy cast-iron tub is to be installed. It takes less effort to place a tub with a finished end against two walls; the job is easier yet if only the tub's long side adjoins a wall, but you may have to build a

rim-high wood cover at the head end to protect—and conceal—the supply pipes and drain pipes, which are usually connected as soon as the tub is firmly positioned. The faucet spout, handles and shower arm, not connected to the tub, are added after the walls around the tub are finished. Somewhat different techniques are used when a prefabricated tub enclosure is installed *(pages 263-264)*.

Compared to a bathtub installation, putting in a new toilet *(pages 267-268)* is a simple, one-person job. Most parts are supplied by the manufacturer but you must provide a toilet or flange sized to your drain-waste-vent system's waste pipe; a wax gasket to seal the connection between bowl and flange; a set of closet bolts, nuts and washers; and a flexible supply pipe to connect the shutoff valve.

Installing a Bathtub

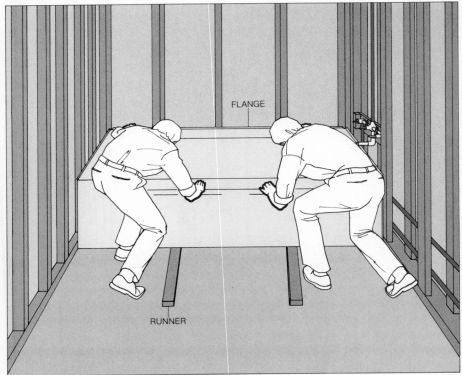

RUNNER

FLANGE

SHIM

2 x 4 SUPPORTS

1 Positioning the tub. To lift and shove a lightweight fiberglass or stamped-steel bathtub into a framed enclosure, you will need at least one helper. For a heavier cast-iron tub, lay a pair of 2-by-4 runners on the subfloor leading into the framed enclosure and enlist three helpers to set the tub on the 2-by-4s.

Two people can then push the tub into the enclosure *(above)*. Ease out the 2-by-4s, letting the bathtub settle onto the subfloor and its flanges onto the horizontal supports. The waterproof wallboard will rest on the flange of the tub; the tile or other finish wall covering will rest on the rim of the bathtub.

2 Leveling the tub. Place a carpenter's level on the tub's rear flange and shove wood shims between the flange and the horizontal supports *(above)* until it is straight. Move the level to the end flanges and shim underneath them. When all the flanges are level, make sure that the tub does not rock. If it does, add more shims for support.

Nail or screw the flanges of steel or fiberglass tubs to the studs. If there are no holes, drive large-headed roofing nails into the studs just above the flanges, so that their heads pin the flange and hold it securely. Cast-iron tubs need not be nailed to the stud wall; their weight keeps them in place.

3 **Attaching the drain pipes.** Unscrew and remove the chrome overflow plate, the lift linkage, the strainer cap and the crosspiece. Connect the waste and overflow pipes with a slip nut and washer, and set them on the waste T. Place the large beveled washer between the back of the tub and the overflow pipe. Place the large flat washer between the drain pipe and the bottom of the tub. Position the assembly and tighten the slip nuts that lock it into place. Roll some plumber's putty into a strand about 7 inches long and 1/4 inch thick. Press the putty around the underside of the crosspiece before screwing it by hand into the tub's drain hole (below) and tightening it with pliers handles and pry bar (inset). Then screw down the strainer cap. Protect the tub surface with dropcloths or paper while you finish the tub walls.

4 **Adjusting the lift linkage.** Loosen the lock nut (below) to turn the threaded rod that shortens or lengthens the linkage used to open and close the drain. Adjust the linkage to the position specified by the manufacturer and tighten the lock nut. Slip the linkage into the overflow hole and reattach the overflow plate.

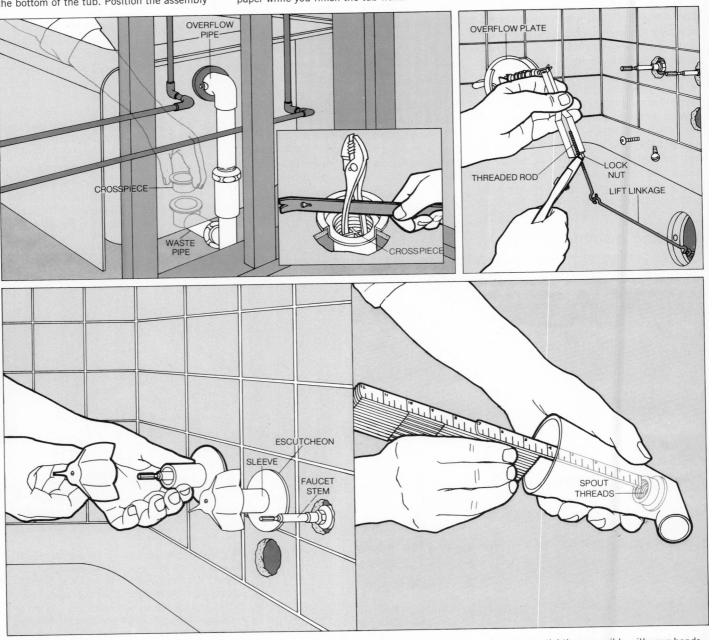

5 **Connecting hardware.** To install most faucet or diverter-valve handles, slide escutcheons and sleeves onto the protruding stems (above) before screwing on the handles. For other types of handles, follow the manufacturer's instructions. Before mounting the spout, measure from the face of the elbow behind the wall to the face of the wall; add the distance from the threads in the spout to the end of the spout, plus 3/4 inch (above, right). Remove the rough-in nipple and replace it with a nipple of the measurement you have made. Use only brass or galvanized steel for the new nipple. Apply a coat of joint compound to the threads of the nipple and screw on the spout as tightly as possible with your hands, ending up in the proper position for use.

To install a shower arm, remove the nipple from the supply pipe. Apply joint compound to the threads of the arm, place the escutcheon over the arm and screw the arm to the pipe by hand.

A Prefab Tub-and-Wall Unit

Prefabricated fiberglass tub enclosures, lightweight and easy to install, usually consist of a tub and three surrounding walls in a one-piece unit or in four-piece packages. Because the one-piece units are too large to fit through a standard doorway they usually must be positioned before the bathroom is framed in. Four-piece enclosures, more practical in remodeled bathrooms, can be brought inside unassembled and then snapped or clipped together at the installation site. Prefabricated shower stalls, which are similarly installed, require the preparation of a special floor drain.

Because the parts of a prefabricated enclosure must fit precisely, the framework should be perfectly square and plumb. Some manufacturers require additional horizontal or vertical framing for greater rigidity. If the enclosure is not already backed with factory-sprayed insulation to deaden splashing noise, regular household insulation can be stapled to the framing and laid on the subfloor.

Fiberglass can be cut and drilled with woodworking tools, but it cracks easily under stress and should be handled with care. Always drill clearance holes before nailing into the material.

1 **Framing the enclosure.** Follow the manufacturer's framing specifications, which may call for additional supports like the horizontal 2-by-4 backing for a grab bar. With one-piece units, which must be slid into the framework, you may get maneuvering room by not nailing the two outer studs on the foot end until after installation—provided that you have access from the other side. Staple soundproofing insulation to the studs *(above)* and lay additional insulation on the subfloor, in thicknesses specified by the manufacturer.

2 **Measuring for openings.** If possible, mark the locations of faucet stems, diverter valve stem, spout nipple and shower elbow directly on the appropriate panel by dry-fitting it against the rough-in plumbing. Where this is impractical, as in the case of a fully assembled enclosure, use a stud to mark the distance from floor to each opening on a single vertical line. Measure the horizontal distances from this line and transfer the markings to the face of the enclosure *(above)*. Drill holes with a spade bit from the face side.

3 Positioning the enclosure. If the enclosure is a one-piece or fully assembled unit, slide it through the wall from the foot end, if possible, and position the openings at the opposite end before nailing the missing studs. Otherwise the enclosure must be positioned from the face of the framework *(left)*, making it necessary to temporarily unscrew protruding plumbing. Tilt the unit so the bottom of the front flange rests across the opening of the framework, then lower the other end and work it flush against the rear studs.

If the enclosure comes in four pieces, position the tub first. Then lay a bead of sealant in the sealant channels, if there are any, and attach the walls to the tub and to one another *(inset)*. Some installations may require clips to be attached from the rear. Use shims to plumb and level the enclosure before connecting the plumbing *(page 262)*.

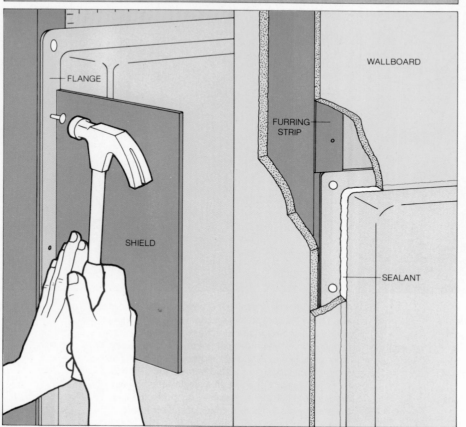

4 Nailing and finishing. Fiberglass cracks easily, so predrill clearance holes if necessary before securing the enclosure to the studs with roofing nails. Use a shield of cardboard or thin plywood when hammering to protect adjacent fiberglass surfaces *(opposite)*. To close off the space—about 2 feet—above the enclosure, nail 1/2-inch furring strips to the exposed portions of studs. Apply a 3/8-inch bead of sealant—equal to the thickness of wallboard—inside the top flange, as shown in the cutaway at left. Measure and cut a piece of wallboard and set the lower edge into the sealant. Then nail the wallboard to the studs through the furring strips. Cover the vertical flanges on either side by lapping them with wallboard panels or, when adjacent walls join the enclosure at right angles, as shown here, by cementing a thin strip of wallboard. Finally, apply sealant to the openings and attach the plumbing hardware.

Three Fixtures for a Kitchen

The kitchen's three basic plumbing fixtures—sink, garbage disposal and dishwasher—are almost a single unit for installation purposes, since the disposal is an extension of the sink drain and all three share a single waste pipe. With proper preparation, the three installations are mostly a matter of tightening nuts and screws.

The easiest way to mount a sink is to attach as many fittings—faucets, strainer, spray hose, tailpiece, flexible supply tubes—as possible before setting the sink into the countertop. This minimizes the difficulty of working in a cramped space.

A disposal requires a 120-volt dedicated appliance circuit with a convenient wall switch. Before working on any wiring, turn off electricity at the service panel (*page 11*). Once the wiring is installed and tested, it takes only a few minutes to fasten the disposal to the sink, and to connect the wires (*Step 4*).

Dishwashers (*page 266*) have three connections: a hot-water supply line, tapped from the sink line and equipped with its own shut-off valve; a waste line tapped to a countertop air-gap device, then to the drain or disposal; and an electrical connection to a 120-volt dedicated appliance circuit, installed by an electrician. All three connections are made through an access panel at the lower front after the dishwasher is positioned. Many local codes require air gaps for dishwasher waste lines to prevent siphonage of waste water back into the cleaning chamber. If you need an air gap device, be sure your sink countertop has a precut hole at the rear. Otherwise you may have to drill a hole through a steel sink or a countertop.

Combining a Sink and Disposal

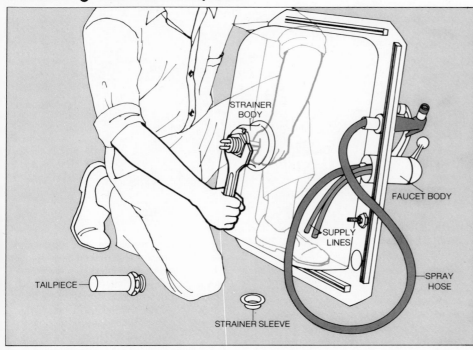

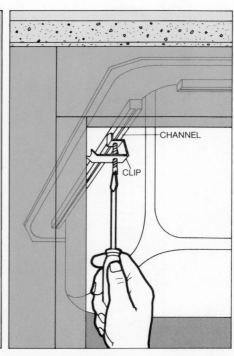

1 Attaching the fittings. Prop the sink on its side for ready access to top and bottom. If the faucet body comes with a rubber gasket, slip it over the stems; otherwise apply a 1/8-inch bead of plumber's putty around the body base before sliding the stems through the holes provided. You may have to partly straighten attached copper supply lines by bending them carefully. If a spray hose is provided, follow the manufacturer's instructions when attaching it to the faucet body and the designated sink opening. For a sink without a garbage disposal (a disposal installation is shown in Step 4, opposite), apply a 1/8-inch bead of plumber's putty to the underside of the strainer body lip before setting it into the drain hole. Slip the rubber and metal washers and a lock nut onto the threaded bottom of the strainer body. Hand-tighten the lock nut. Insert the handles of a pair of pliers into the hole from the top surface to keep the strainer body from turning before tightening (*above*). Then assemble the strainer sleeve, lock nut, washer and tailpiece and attach the tailpiece to the strainer body.

2 Attaching the sink. Apply a 1/4-inch bead of plumber's putty around the top edge of the countertop opening. Lower the sink into the opening. From underneath, slide at least eight evenly spaced clips into channels that rim the sink underside and position them to grip the underside of the countertop. Tighten the clips with a screwdriver (*above*) but do not overtighten or you may crimp the sink rim. Afterward, check the top for a good seal between the sink rim and the countertop; if there are any high spots, tighten the clips to pull them down.

3 **Connecting the pipes.** Attach fixture shut-off valves to the water-supply stub-outs *(opposite)*. If the faucet body has supply pipes attached, fasten them to the valves in the same way you would a toilet supply *(page 268)*. If the pipes are not long enough—or if there are none—use compression couplings to attach flexible fixture supply tubes *(below)*.

Uncap the drain pipe and add a trap adapter and a 1 1/2-inch P trap with slip nuts, installed loosely at first. For a disposal, follow the instructions in Step 4 below; otherwise, slide a slip nut and washer onto the tailpiece. Adjust the trap so that it fits properly, making a trial assembly, then tighten the slip nuts on the trap and trap adapter.

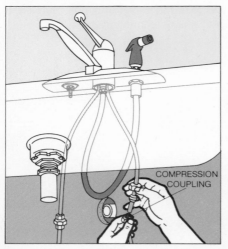

COMPRESSION COUPLING

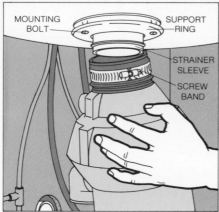

MOUNTING BOLT

SUPPORT RING

STRAINER SLEEVE

SCREW BAND

4 **Attaching a disposal.** With the sink dismounted, insert the disposal strainer in place of the strainer body *(Step 1)*. Slide on the rubber and metal gaskets and loosely thread the mounting bolts before snapping on the support ring. Tighten the bolts, but do not buckle the support ring. After the sink is mounted *(Step 2)*, place the clamp around the disposal collar and lift the disposal *(above)* so it locks into the strainer sleeve. Install a 1 1/2-inch P trap to join the disposal waste pipe to the drain. Tighten the clamp before connecting the electricity.

Running Lines for a Dishwasher

1 **Connecting the unit.** Prepare the dishwasher space: Have an electrician run in a dedicated 120-volt special appliance circuit. Drill or cut a 6-inch hole in the lower rear of any cabinet wall separating the dishwasher space from the sink space. Run a length of flexible copper tubing and the dishwasher drain hose through the hole, along with the electrical cable if necessary. Remove the access panel and kick plate from the lower front of the dishwasher before pushing the dishwasher into its opening. If the leveling legs are not accessible through the access panel, you may have to pull out and push back the dishwasher several times to level it flush with the countertop. The connections can then be made with the dishwasher in or out of its space.

Use a compression fitting to connect the copper tubing to the inlet pipe. Use a hose clamp to connect the drain hose to the outlet pipe. Push the dishwasher into its space and screw it to the countertop through precut holes in front. Turn off power to the circuit *(page 11)*, then connect the wiring and replace the access panel and kick plate. Attach the other end of the tubing to the sink hot-water pipe with a separate shutoff valve, and the drain hose to the sink tailpiece or air gap *(bottom, center)*.

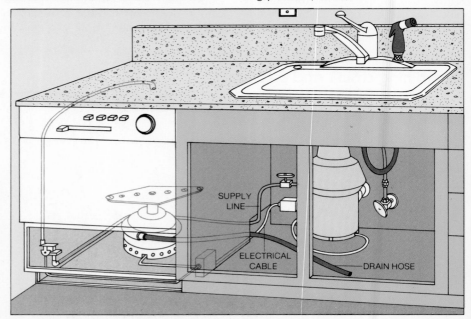

SUPPLY LINE

ELECTRICAL CABLE

DRAIN HOSE

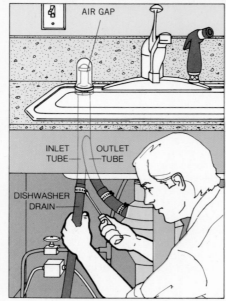

AIR GAP

INLET TUBE

OUTLET TUBE

DISHWASHER DRAIN

2 **Connecting the air gap.** If an air gap is required, raise the stem from below through a hole in the sink or countertop, screw on the plastic top and press in the chrome outer cap. Fasten the dishwasher drain hose to the inlet tube of the air gap with a hose clamp *(left)*. Connect the outlet tube to the disposal, using a section of hose and clamps, or to the tailpiece of the sink, using a Y connector. On some disposals, you may have to punch in a knockout plug at the top, then retrieve the plug with a pair of long-nose pliers.

Hooking Up a Toilet

1 Attaching a shutoff valve. If no shutoff valve exists at the desired location, cut the supply pipe 2 inches from the wall. Slide an escutcheon over the pipe and press it against the wall opening. Slip the coupling nut and compression ring over the pipe. Slide on the valve *(right)*, its outlet hole pointing up, and tighten the nut.

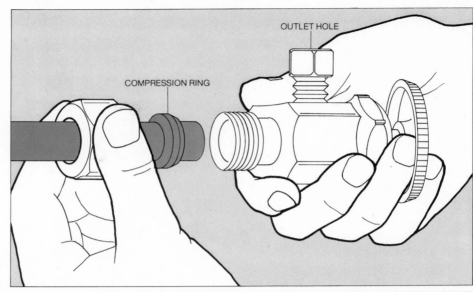

2 Seating the flange. Use a plastic flange with a plastic waste pipe. Solvent cement inside the flange stem and outside the waste pipe. Then immediately push the flange onto the pipe and align it properly, with the toilet bowl flange bolt slots equidistant from the wall behind the toilet. Drill holes into the subfloor through the screw holes and secure the flange to the floor with 1 1/2-inch No. 10 flat-head wood screws.

3 Attaching the wax gasket. Turn the toilet bowl upside down on padding. Slip the doughnut-shaped wax gasket over the ridge around the waste hole, with its flat side toward the bowl. Press it firmly against the bowl bottom and ridge with your fingers *(right)*.

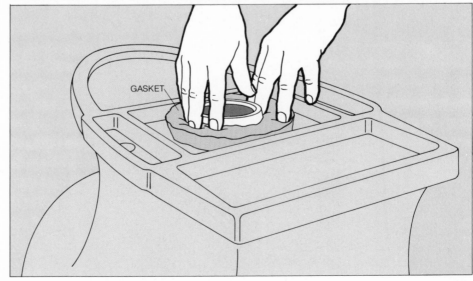

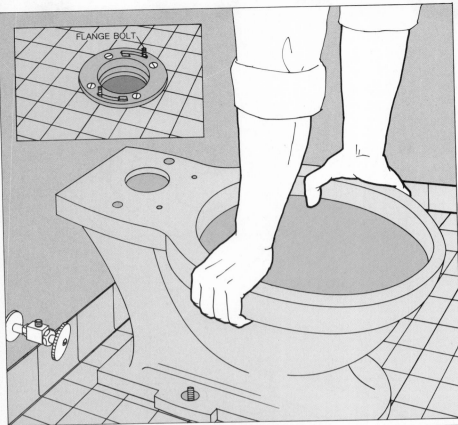

FLANGE BOLT

4 **Setting the bowl.** Insert and position the two flange bolts *(inset)*. Lift the bowl and lower it slowly onto the flange so that the bolts protrude through the bowl's rim holes. Press down firmly on the bowl *(left)* while twisting it slightly in both directions to seal the gasket. Place a level across the width and then the depth of the upper rim. Shim if necessary with copper or brass washers beneath the lower rim, but do not raise the bowl or the gasket seal will be broken. Place washers on the flange bolts before tightening the nuts just enough to keep the bowl from moving. Then place porcelain caps filled with plumber's putty over the bolt ends to conceal them.

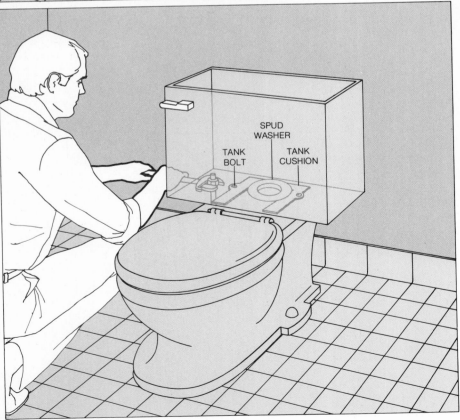

SPUD WASHER

TANK BOLT

TANK CUSHION

5 **Connecting the tank and supply line.** Follow the toilet manufacturer's instructions. If the tank is a separate unit, make certain that the spud washer and tank cushion, if provided, are in place before seating the tank so that the two tank bolts pass through holes in the bowl's rim. Attach the tank with washers and nuts from below. Then attach the seat and cover assembly.

Select the correct diameter flexible supply pipe recommended by the toilet manufacturer. Hold the head of the supply pipe against the tank's threaded inlet stem while bending the pipe slowly to form a gentle curve past the shutoff valve. Mark the pipe where it passes the bottom threads of the shutoff valve and cut the pipe with a tube cutter. Slip a coupling nut up the pipe and hand-fasten it to the inlet stem. Slip on the valve coupling nut and compression ring before inserting the pipe into the valve and tightening both nuts *(left)*. Turn on the valve, and flush the toilet several times to check for leaks.

A Guide for the Home Electrician

The electricity that powers your lights, toasts your bread and operates your power tools is nothing more than a flow of very tiny electrons through what are called conductors. Like drops of water, electrons flow from a higher pressure (higher voltage) source toward a lower pressure (lower voltage) destination. To flow, electrons need a complete circuit from an energized source to ground—a circuit offered by your home's wiring.

This wiring is mostly invisible—safely concealed behind walls and cover plates. More than any other system in your house, your electrical system is standardized, strictly regulated by codes and standards to protect against fire and shock. The types and sizes of electrical equipment, and the methods by which they are installed, are established in the United States by the National Electrical Code and in Canada by the Canadian Electric Code.

Local codes, which have the force of law, generally follow the national codes. If you install new wiring by extending an existing circuit or adding a new one, for example, you may need a permit—and your work may have to be approved by an electrical inspector. Check with your municipality's building department about local regulations concerning the specific job you plan to do.

The watchdogs of electrical equipment are Underwriters Laboratories, Inc. and, in Canada, the Canadian Standards Association; both are independent nonprofit organizations. The tests these groups perform are for the sole purpose of making sure that electrical devices are free of design defects that can cause fire or shock. When you buy supplies, look for the UL or CSA label to be certain you get equipment that has been listed.

Boxes, wires, switches and so on come in standard sizes and shapes so that one manufacturer's products are interchangeable with another's; by matching the data printed on a device, you can be sure of buying a replacement that will fit. Wiring methods are also standardized. Whether your home is in Atlanta or Toronto, the wires will be joined to each other and to terminals in much the same way.

To work on your home wiring, an acquaintance with some electrical terms and concepts is helpful *(pages 270-271)*. If properly installed and maintained, your electrical system will rarely pose a hazard. Working with electrical fixtures and wiring is equally safe, as long as you remember two basic rules: Always turn off the power before working on your wiring *(page 11)*, then confirm that it is off by using a voltage tester *(page 272)*. Never touch any screw terminals, bare wire ends, sockets or metal boxes until you have confirmed that the power to them is indeed off.

Ensuring Safe Work

While electrical wiring is easy and safe if you work logically and follow safety precautions, accidents can happen if work is rushed, improper tools are used or shortcuts are taken. Refer to the guidelines below to undertake an electrical installation properly and safely:

• Never work on your electrical system in damp or wet conditions, and never use any electrical appliance, power tool or extension cord under those conditions.

• Always turn off electricity to the circuit controlling an electrical outlet, light switch or light fixture before working on it *(page 11)*. Also leave a note on the service panel so no one will restore power to the circuit while you are working on it.

• Always use a voltage tester *(page 272)* for a one-handed test to confirm that the power to an electrical outlet, light switch or light fixture is off before touching and disconnecting any wires of it.

• If you cannot locate and turn off electricity to the circuit controlling an electrical outlet, light switch or light fixture on which you will be working, have an electrician inspect the service panel and, if necessary, do the work.

• Never work on the service panel wiring. Entrance wires may remain live even when power is turned off at the main circuit breaker, main fuse block or service disconnect breaker. For this reason, you should not install a new branch circuit yourself; have an electrician do it.

• Avoid touching bare wire ends with your fingers or metal tools even though the power is off and tested for being off. When you might come into contact with bare wire ends or terminals, use backup protection: Wear rubber gloves and use tools with insulating rubber handles; but remember, these do not supply basic protection.

• Remove your watch and any metal jewelry to do an electrical job. Light the work area well. Keep children and pets away from the area while you work.

• Avoid being grounded while you work. Do not touch a metal faucet, water pipe or appliance, or any other ground, when working with electricity. Be sure to use only a wood or fiberglass ladder when doing electrical work; avoid metal ladders for this purpose.

• If your home electrical system has aluminum (silver-colored) wiring, install only electrical outlets and light switches that have a CO/ALR stamp. If in doubt about the type of wiring used in your electrical system, consult an electrician. Likewise, use only electrical devices that bear a recognized seal of approval; look for the UL or CSA stamp.

• Use only electrical methods that conform to the national and local electrical codes: If in doubt, check with your local authorities before starting a job. Apply for an electrical permit for your project, and after working on the electrical system, be sure to have the work checked by an electrical inspector.

Electricity in the Home

If you have a basic understanding of your home's wiring, work methodically and take reasonable precautions, you can tackle any electrical project in this book with confidence.

Electrical current flows in a continuous path, or circuit, from a power source through various switches, fixtures and appliances, and then back to the source. In a household electrical system, the source is the main service panel and the path is your home's wiring. Electricity always takes the path of least resistance. Copper and aluminum are good conductors of electricity and are therefore used to carry current; plastic, rubber, glass and porcelain are nonconductive and are used as insulators for electrical equipment.

The power company delivers electricity to your home usually via large overhead or underground wires—usually three—that arrive at the service entrance. From there, electricity passes through a meter into the main service panel, where it is divided into branch circuits for distribution throughout the house. Two of the three service wires are hot and carry 120 volts each to the neutral wire and 240 volts between hot wires, thus providing power to operate both 120-volt and 240-volt appliances.

To prevent damage to the wiring and guard against fire and shock, each circuit is protected by a fuse or circuit breaker. If there is an overload or short in the circuit, this device will instantly stop the flow of current. The main circuit that brings electric current into the house is also equipped with a fuse or circuit breaker that will turn off all house current at the panel.

Normally, cables that carry 120-volt current contain a black-insulated wire (hereafter referred to as black wire), a white-insulated wire (hereafter referred to as white wire) and a bare copper wire. From the service panel, the hot wire delivers 120 volts of current "under pressure" to light a bulb or to run an appliance. The neutral wire carries the electrons at close to zero volts back to the service panel. The bare grounding wire (or green-insulated wire, hereafter referred to as green wire) in each circuit safeguards the system by providing a second path for wayward electricity to return to the service panel. A main service-grounding wire runs from the service panel to a metal water pipe and a metal grounding rod buried in the earth.

DOORBELL
Power is supplied via a transformer, which steps down 120-volt household current to 6-24 volts.

WATER PIPE
Code now requires that the grounding connection to the water pipe be supplemented by a second grounding connection, commonly a metal rod driven at least 8 feet into the earth.

GLOSSARY

Amperes: The amount of current passing a given point at a given time. Each electrical device has an ampere rating and each circuit is rated for the total number of amperes it can safely deliver.

Circuit: A continuous path for electrical current. In a household electrical system, a branch circuit begins at the service panel, runs to various switches, outlets and fixtures and returns to the service panel.

Circuit overload: Occurs when the combination of lights, tools and appliances is drawing more amperes than the circuit is designed to handle. Normally, the fuse will blow or the circuit breaker will trip, interrupting the flow of electricity to the circuit.

Current: The movement of electrons, measured in amperes.

Grounding wire: The bare copper or green-insulated wire in a cable. Drains off current that escapes its normal path to the service panel, causing a fuse to blow or a circuit breaker to trip.

Hot wire: A wire that carries current forward from the source. Often identified by black (or red) insulation.

Neutral wire: A grounded wire that carries current back to the source. Identified by white insulation.

Short circuit: When an exposed hot wire touches a neutral wire or a grounded metal box, the circuit will heat up suddenly. The fuse or breaker will shut off the power immediately.

Volts: The strength, or pressure, of an electrical current, measured in volts. Household circuits are usually 120 volts, 240 volts or low-voltage.

Watts: The rate at which electrical devices consume energy. Usually listed on a sticker or plate on the lamp or appliance.

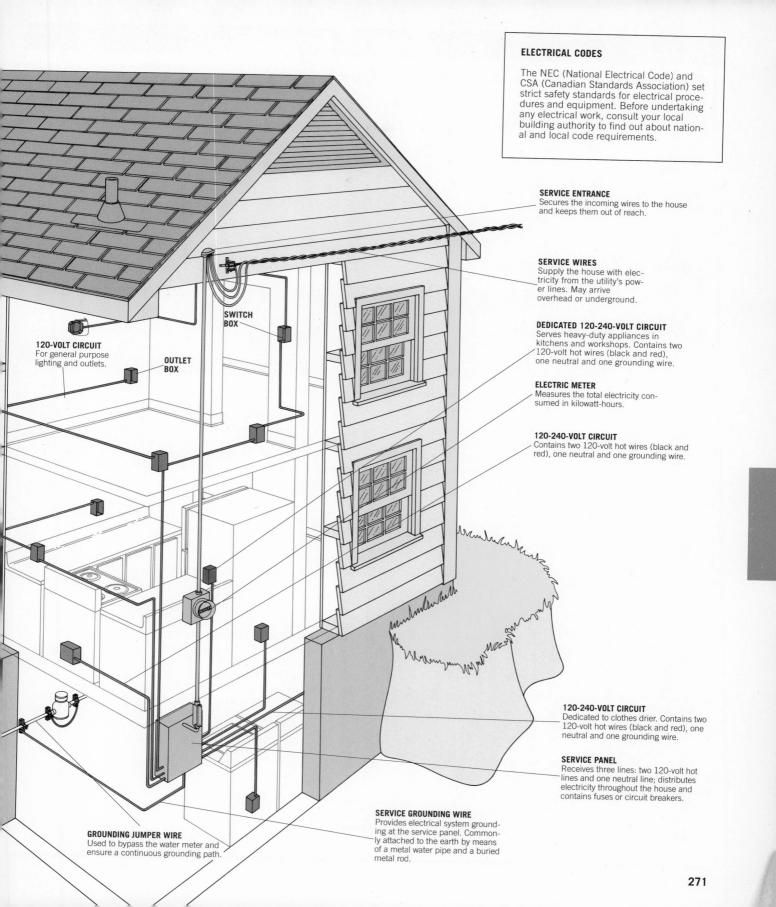

SERVICE ENTRANCE
Secures the incoming wires to the house and keeps them out of reach.

SERVICE WIRES
Supply the house with electricity from the utility's power lines. May arrive overhead or underground.

DEDICATED 120-240-VOLT CIRCUIT
Serves heavy-duty appliances in kitchens and workshops. Contains two 120-volt hot wires (black and red), one neutral and one grounding wire.

ELECTRIC METER
Measures the total electricity consumed in kilowatt-hours.

120-240-VOLT CIRCUIT
Contains two 120-volt hot wires (black and red), one neutral and one grounding wire.

120-VOLT CIRCUIT
For general purpose lighting and outlets.

SWITCH BOX

OUTLET BOX

120-240-VOLT CIRCUIT
Dedicated to clothes drier. Contains two 120-volt hot wires (black and red), one neutral and one grounding wire.

SERVICE PANEL
Receives three lines: two 120-volt hot lines and one neutral line; distributes electricity throughout the house and contains fuses or circuit breakers.

GROUNDING JUMPER WIRE
Used to bypass the water meter and ensure a continuous grounding path.

SERVICE GROUNDING WIRE
Provides electrical system grounding at the service panel. Commonly attached to the earth by means of a metal water pipe and a buried metal rod.

Confirming that the Power is off: Using a Voltage Tester

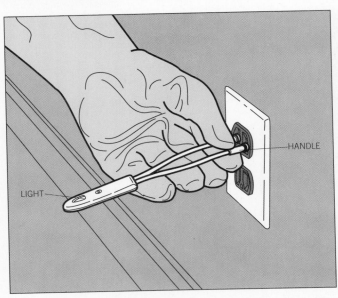

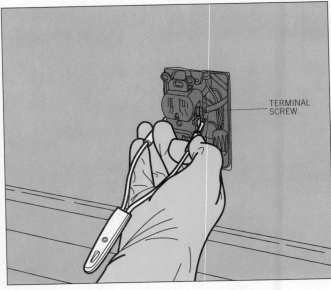

Testing an outlet for voltage. To confirm that the power to an electrical outlet is off, use a voltage tester; test for voltage at each outlet receptacle before you remove the cover plate, then at the outlet terminals after you remove the cover plate. Caution: Wearing rubber gloves and standing on a dry spot, hold the tester probes by the insulated handles with only one hand. To test for voltage at an outlet receptacle, insert the tester probes into the slots of the receptacle *(above, left)*. To test for voltage at the outlet terminals, start by test-ing for voltage between each pair of brass and silver terminal screws, touching one tester probe to each terminal screw of each pair *(above, right)*. Then, touch one probe to the outlet grounding screw—or, if there is none, to any part of a metal electrical box or to the metal grounding bar found in some plastic electrical boxes—and touch the other probe in turn to each brass and silver terminal screw. If the tester glows in any test, shut off electricity to the correct circuit and repeat the test.

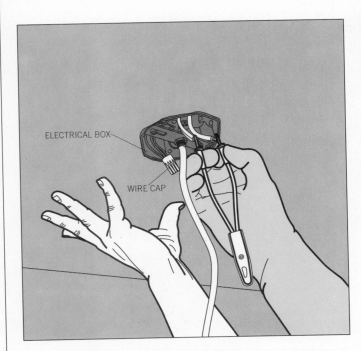

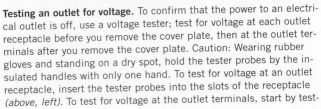

Testing a light fixture for voltage. To confirm that the power to a light fixture is off, use a voltage tester. Caution: Wearing a rubber glove and standing on a dry spot or nonmetallic ladder, hold the tester probes by the insulated handles with only one hand. First, test for voltage between each pair of wire cap connections: Remove the wire caps and touch one probe to each wire end of each pair *(above)*. Then, test for voltage between each wire cap connection and the metal electrical box: Remove the wire cap, then touch one probe to the wire end and the other probe to the electrical box. If the tester glows in any test, shut off electricity to the correct circuit and repeat the test.

Inspecting Electrical Circuits

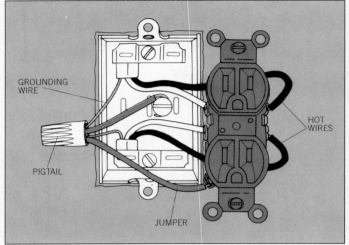

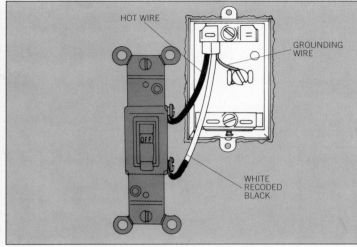

Switch and outlet box makeup. A great deal can be learned about electrical outlet box makeup by inspecting an outlet box and a switch box. First turn off the power at the service panel *(page 11)*, then use a voltage tester to confirm that the power is off *(opposite)*. Unscrew and remove the cover plate—an outlet has one; a switch has two. Unscrew the mounting strap and pull the device carefully from its electrical box without touching any uninsulated wires or terminals. Caution: Before touching any wire, test again to confirm that the power is off. Note the number of cables entering the box. Two or more cables *(above, left)* means that the switch or outlet is located in the middle of the circuit; one cable *(above, right)* indicates that the device is end-of-run, the last device on its circuit. Next, examine the color coding of the wires in the box. Locate the black hot wire, the white neutral wire and the bare grounding wire leading from each cable. When, as in some switch runs, the white wire is used as a hot wire, it may have been recoded black *(above, right)* using a felt-tip marker or black plastic electrical tape. Sometimes a short piece of insulated wire, called a jumper, is used to link two or more wires to a screw terminal; it is attached to the other wires in a pigtail splice connection *(above, left)*.

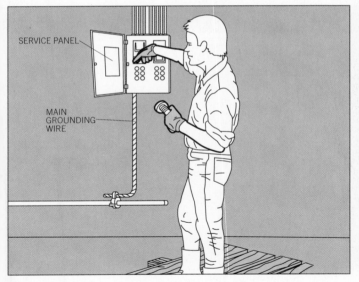

Safety at the service panel. When working at the service panel, even to change a fuse or reset a circuit breaker *(page 11)*, be sure to take basic safety precautions. Dry any wet spots on the floor. To protect your body from making a circuit to the ground, stand on dry boards or wear dry rubber boots and heavy rubber gloves. Work with one hand only; when possible, keep the other hand in your pocket or behind your back to avoid touching metal. Have a nonconductive flashlight at a convenient spot near the service panel so that you do not have to change a fuse in the dark. Do not touch a service panel that is sparking, blackened or rusted; call an electrician. Do not remove the panel cover to expose the service cables; even if you have turned off the main breaker or pulled the main fuse block parts of the box remain charged with current.

Safety outdoors. Electrical code now requires that new outdoor outlets be protected by a GFCI *(page 171)*. This safety device is especially important in damp locations, where electrical shocks can be especially dangerous. As an added safety precaution when using power tools, stand on a dry wooden plank or rubber mat and use a wooden ladder and heavy rubber gloves. Be careful not to touch overhead power lines when working on your roof or siding. Call the power company to locate any underground power lines before digging in the yard.

Grounding for Safety

Grounding at the service panel. Grounding is a safety precaution built into every home electrical system installed since 1967. At the service panel, the main grounding wire is routed to a metal water pipe and grounding rod that is buried in the earth, keeping the home electrical system at ground potential.

In the house wiring, a bare copper or green insulated grounding wire provides an alternate path for leaking current, protecting the circuit from damage and the user from shock. In the example at right, the hot wire supplying current to a lighting fixture has become disconnected from its socket terminal. Since the circuit cannot be completed via the neutral wire, the metal box would become electrified and dangerous. But the grounding wire picks up this leaking current and returns it to the service panel, where the excessive current flow will trip the breaker or blow the fuse.

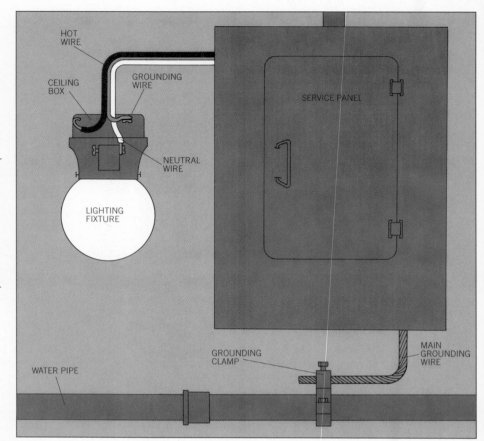

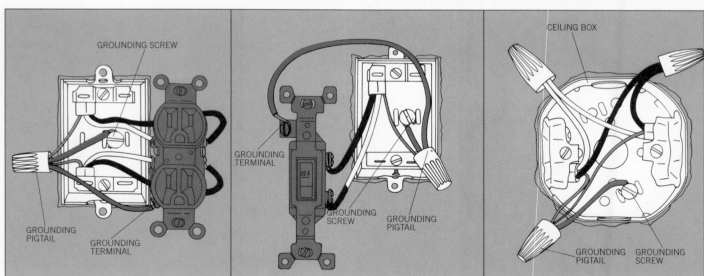

Grounding in outlet, switch and ceiling boxes. The bare copper grounding wire in the cable provides equipment-grounding protection for grounded tools, fixtures and appliances at an electrical box. It is attached to the grounding screw at the back of a metal box and to the grounding terminal on a switch or outlet, and grounds the box, the mounting strap, the device or fixture and all three-prong appliances that are plugged into a grounded outlet. When there is more than one cable in the electrical box, grounding is accomplished using jumper wires in a pigtail connection. In Canada, more than one grounding wire may be attached to the grounding screw at the back of the box.

Wires, Cables and Conduit

Electricity is conducted along house circuits by wires grouped together in the form of cable or, in some cases, contained in conduit. Cable consists of a preassembled combination of wires within a protective outer sheath made of metal or plastic. Conduit is simply piping of steel or plastic through which several wires are threaded after the pipe has been installed.

The hot and neutral wires that conduct electricity in both cable and conduit are individually insulated. The grounding wire is not insulated in plastic-sheathed cable. Metal-sheathed cable uses the armor, and sometimes a metal strip, as the grounding conductor. Metal—but not plastic—conduit needs no grounding wire, since the pipe is its own grounding conductor.

With few exceptions, the wire used for home circuits is Type THHN, which comes in Type NMC cable and has heat-resistant thermoplastic-jacket insulation capable of withstanding a wide range of temperatures up to 194°F (90°C) in dry and damp locations. Type TW, an older variant, is sometimes used outdoors or in a wet location such as a basement.

The type and size of conductor wires provided in metal-jacketed cable and of those intended for installation in conduit are marked on the insulation *(right)*; in plastic-sheathed cable, wire type and size is indicated on the plastic sheathing *(bottom right)*. The wires themselves are copper or aluminum. Wire insulation is color-coded to help avoid error in connecting them to terminals and in splicing them. The hot, or live, wire is covered in black insulation; the neutral wire is always covered in white or gray. The grounding wire is left bare, wrapped in paper, or, in some fixtures, switches and receptacles, insulated in green. If there are other hot wires—in cables for three- or four-way switches or for 240-volt circuits—they are coded red or blue.

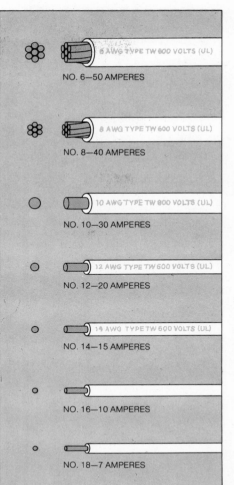

NO. 6—50 AMPERES

NO. 8—40 AMPERES

NO. 10—30 AMPERES

NO. 12—20 AMPERES

NO. 14—15 AMPERES

NO. 16—10 AMPERES

NO. 18—7 AMPERES

Wires for the house. The wires used in house circuits are shown at left. On larger sizes, wire diameter is indicated by a gauge number printed on the insulation and based on the American Wire Gauge system (AWG)—the smaller the number, the greater the diameter. Wire type is also marked. The smaller sizes—No. 18 and No. 16—are too small for printed identification.

Wire sizes No. 14 and No. 12 are used in standard 120-volt circuits for lighting and receptacles for televisions, clocks and other small appliances. Size No. 10 is used in 120-volt circuits carrying electricity to such major appliances as electric clothes driers. Wire sizes No. 8 and No. 6 are the most widely used in 240-volt circuits for electric ranges and central air conditioners. Wire sizes No. 18 and No. 16 are reserved for low-voltage systems like bells and intercoms; in stranded form, they are also used for lamp cord.

The maximum current that a wire of a given diameter can safely carry is stated in amperes and known as the wire's ampacity. The smaller the wire, the greater its resistance to the flow of current and the greater the friction that generates heat, which could destroy insulation and even kindle a fire; thus large currents require large wires. The ampacities given at left are for copper wires, the commonest kind in house circuits. Aluminum wire, which does not conduct electricity as efficiently as copper, has an ampacity approximately equal to that of copper wire two wire gauges smaller; for example, aluminum wire No. 12 has about the same ampacity as copper wire No. 14.

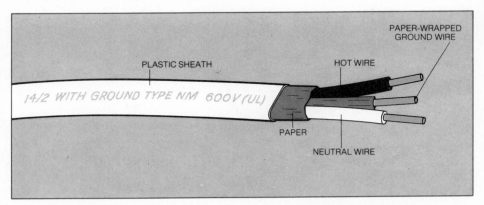

Plastic-sheathed cable. Nonmetallic cable is the commonest form of wiring in houses that were built after 1960. It not only is the least expensive, but it also is the easiest to install because of its flexibility. The insulated hot and neutral wires and the uninsulated grounding wire are enclosed in a protective sheath, generally of plastic. Not all cable has a grounding wire, and for safety's sake cable without one should not be used. Two kinds of nonmetallic cable are usually needed in house wiring: Type NMC is used for indoor wiring and damp indoor locations and for outdoor wiring that is above ground; Type UF is used for buried outdoor branch circuits, which must be fuse- or breaker-protected. Markings on the sheathing show, from left to right: wire size, number of conductors, whether the cable has a grounding wire, and the cable type. Shown here is Type NMC 14-gauge, two-conductor cable with grounding wire.

275

Stripping Wiring

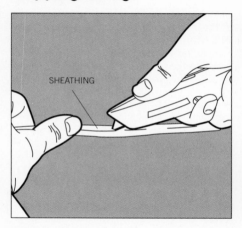

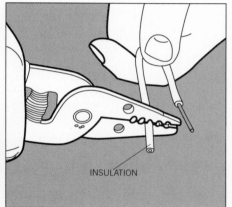

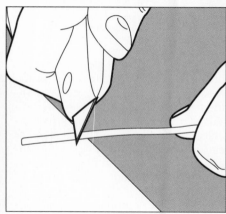

Stripping a cable. To strip a cable, first remove the sheathing from the end of it. Push the blade of a utility knife into the sheathing 8 inches from the end of the cable, then draw the blade back to the end of the cable to cut the sheathing *(above)*: Take care not to cut any wire inside. Peel back the sheathing and use diagonal-cutting pliers to snip it off, then strip each wire *(step right)*.

Stripping a wire. To strip a wire, use wire strippers or a utility knife to remove 3/4 inch of insulation from the end of it. To use wire strippers to strip a wire, open the jaws and insert the wire end into the appropriate-sized slot, then close the jaws over the wire *(above, left)*. Exerting gentle pressure, twist the wire strippers back and forth to sever the insulation and pull it off the wire end. To use a utility knife to strip a wire, hold the wire end on a steady surface and make an angled incision away from you in one side of the insulation *(above, right)*: Take care not to cut the wire inside. Then turn the wire over and make a second incision the same way, gently paring the insulation off the wire end. If you nick the wire inside, snip the wire and start again.

Making a Terminal Connection

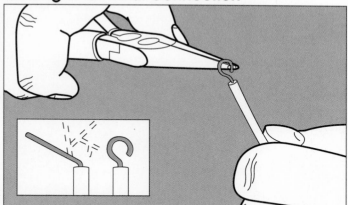

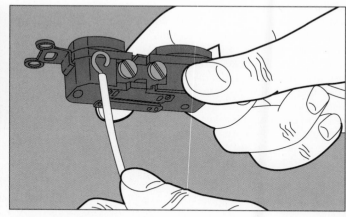

Preparing the wire. To make a terminal connection, first strip the wire *(top, right)*, if necessary; then, for a stranded wire, twist the bare strands tightly together clockwise. Holding the wire, grip the bare end with long-nose pliers and bend it at a 45° angle to the length of the wire. Then, using the pliers to grip the bare end just where it meets the insulation, make a slight upward bend in the end; continue, moving the pliers along the bare end to make one bend after another *(inset)*, until you form an open hook *(above)*.

Making the connection. To connect the wire to a terminal, use a screwdriver to loosen but not remove the terminal screw. Fit the hooked wire end under the head and around the shaft of the screw, orienting it to close in the same clockwise direction as the screw turns to tighten *(above)*; ensure that the hook loops at least three quarters of the way around the screw. Then tighten the screw until it grips the wire end and flattens it slightly. If any bare wire protrudes from under the head of the screw, loosen it and remove the wire, then start again.

Making Wire Cap Connections

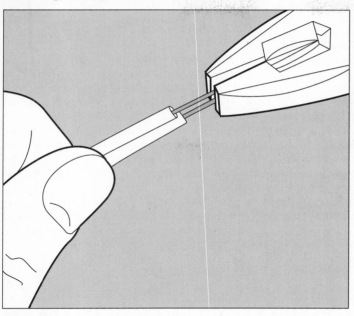
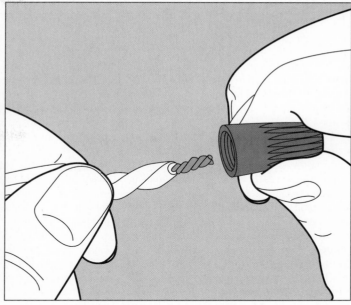

Connecting solid wires. To make a wire cap connection when both wires are solid wires, strip the wires 1 1/2 inches *(opposite)*, if necessary. To join the wires, hold them side by side and use pliers *(above, left)* to twist the wire ends tightly together clockwise; then cut the twist to a length of 5/8 inch by squarely snipping off the tip of it with wire cutters. Slip a wire cap of the appropriate size over the connection *(above, right)* and screw the cap clockwise until it is tight and no bare wire remains exposed. Test the connection with a slight tug; if it is loose, unscrew and remove the wire cap, then untwist the wires and start again.

Two Kinds of Terminals

Screw terminal. Strip only enough insulation to allow the bared end of the wire to be wrapped three quarters of the way around the terminal screw. With long-nose pliers, twist the bare end into a loop, loosen the terminal screw, and hook the loop clockwise around the screw so that when the screw is tightened it will help close the loop.

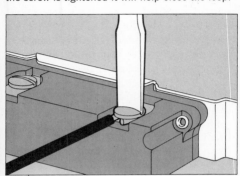
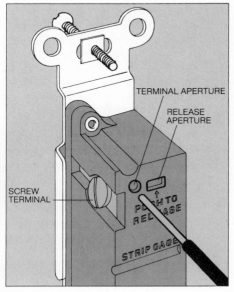

TERMINAL APERTURE

RELEASE APERTURE

SCREW TERMINAL

PUSH TO RELEASE

STRIP GAGE

Push-in terminal. Some switches and receptacles are designed so that you can loop the wire around a screw terminal or insert it through an aperture that automatically grips for a solid connection. To attach a wire to such a push-in terminal, strip the insulation as indicated by the strip gauge marked on the device—usually about 1/2 inch. Insert the bare wire into the terminal aperture *(left)*, and push it in up to the insulation; a spring lock will grip the wire in place. To remove a wire from such a device, insert the blade of a small screwdriver or the end of a stiff piece of wire into the release aperture next to the push-in aperture, press the spring lock and pull the wire free.

Planning a Circuit Extension Step by Step

No matter how simple or how ambitious a job you plan—installing a single receptacle or putting in an extensive circuit with several outlets—the number of steps and the order in which they should be done is the same in every type of home. The job goes much faster if you follow this logical sequence for putting in new boxes, running cable and connecting the cable to an existing circuit.

• First, calculate whether the existing branch circuit has enough spare capacity to permit extension *(page 280)* and whether it is grounded. Only a grounded circuit with spare capacity may be extended. (Most grounded circuits will have three-slot outlets.)

• Choose a location for the new outlet box and break through the ceiling or wall to make an opening in it *(pages 281-289)*. Find the nearest joists or studs and, if the box is to be in a ceiling, determine the direction in which the joists run.

• Select an existing box on the circuit—one that contains an unswitched hot wire, and is positioned as near the new box location as possible to provide power for the new circuit. The best starting point is a box that enables you to run cable to the new box on a direct route between the floor or ceiling joists, but alternative routes may be needed *(pages 290-297)*, depending on such factors as the direction of ceiling joists.

• Shut off the power at the service panel *(page 11)*, and use a voltage tester to make sure that the power is indeed off *(page 272)*. Remove the cover plate of the existing box. Check the wiring inside to see if you can connect the new cable wires to the existing wires or terminals. The insets on the opposite page show the wiring in typical home boxes that can be used to start new circuits. The wires represented as dash lines show how cable for the new circuit would be connected. You cannot bring power from a box that contains an end-of-the-

run switch or light fixture *(opposite)*. Otherwise the added wiring will also be controlled by the wall switch.

• Count the connections in the box to see if there is room for more cable wires and clamps *(page 281)*. If the box is too small you must add a box extension, or gang it to another box, install a deeper box or start the circuit from another place. Check the fuse or circuit breaker at the service panel to be sure that the existing circuit has enough capacity to run all the lights or appliances you may use in the new branch.

• Make a map of the room showing the existing box, the new box, the location of the studs and joists, and the route along which you plan to run cable. At the same time, make a list of the materials you will need. Start with a new box or boxes of the right size and shape, and the hardware for installing them.

• Estimate the amount of cable you will need to reach the new box. Provide an extra 8 inches of cable for connections at each box and an extra 20 per cent to allow for the fact that the cable will rarely run perfectly straight. For most purposes, choose type NMC cable that is the correct gauge for the circuit *(page 275)* and contains the right number of conductors. For example, for a 15-ampere circuit use cable with No. 14 copper wires and for a 20-ampere circuit use cable with No. 12 copper wires. For adding an outlet or fixture that is switched from one location, use two-conductor cable with grounding wire. Three-conductor-with-ground cable is needed for most runs involving multiple switch locations. Finally, list the type and number of cable clamps that will be needed to attach the cable to both old and new boxes *(pages 298-299)*.

• Run the new cable from the existing box to the opening for the new one. This is usually the most strenuous part of the job. It may involve cutting access holes in walls or ceilings, drilling a path for the

cable through beams along the cable's route and snaking the cable through the walls or ceilings *(pages 290-297)*.

• Clamp the cable to both the existing box and the new box. Normally, the existing box is permanently installed in a wall or ceiling; therefore, the cable must be attached with an internal clamp. The new box, which has not yet been installed, will accept an internal or an external cable clamp.

• Install the new box. The procedure you use will depend on the composition of the wall or ceiling and on whether the box can be mounted directly to a stud or joist *(pages 281-289)*. It also depends on whether a remodeling or "old-work" box *(page 281)* is used that mounts to an opening in the wall or ceiling material.

• Connect the wires of the cable to the correct wires or terminals in the existing box *(opposite)*, and then also to the switches, receptacles or light fixtures in the new boxes.

• Test the branch circuit extension. First, with the power still off, and all switches off, clip a continuity tester *(page 306)* to the black wire in the box at the end of the run, and touch the probe to the white wire, the bare wire and to the box. The tester bulb should not glow in any of these tests. If it does, there is a short circuit in the new extension: Check at each new box for improper connections, frayed insulation or a bare wire touching another wire, and make any connections necessary. Then go on to a second set of tests. Have a helper turn on power to the circuit at the service panel and use a voltage tester carefully *(page 272)* to check for power in each device on the new circuit. After these tests, turn off the power immediately and test to be sure it is off. Mount the device and fixtures to their outlet boxes and install all covers.

• Patch up all the holes you have made in the walls or ceilings *(pages 307)*. Then turn on the power again. Your new branch is ready for use.

Wiring an Old Outlet Box with New Cable

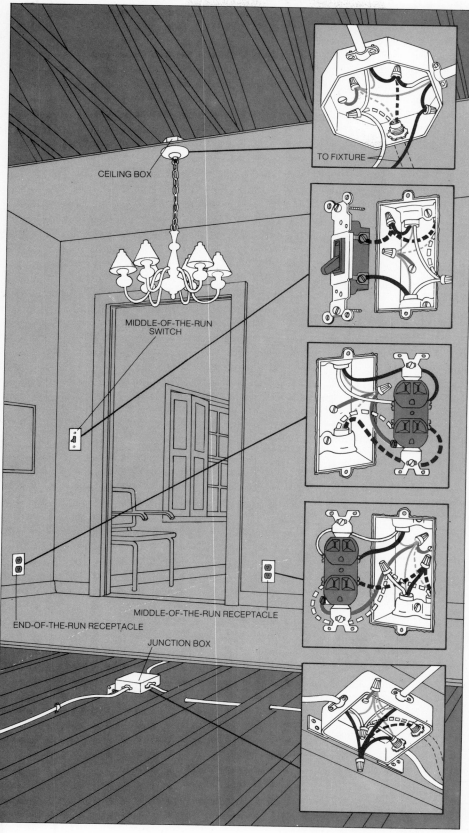

CEILING BOX

TO FIXTURE

MIDDLE-OF-THE-RUN SWITCH

MIDDLE-OF-THE-RUN RECEPTACLE

END-OF-THE-RUN RECEPTACLE

JUNCTION BOX

Middle-of-the-run ceiling box. Make sure that the ceiling box is middle-of-the-run. If it is, the black and white fixture wires will be connected to two separate cables. Otherwise, current will flow in the new branch only when the switch controlling the ceiling box is on. If the box is middle-of-the-run, turn on the power temporarily and use a voltage tester *(page 171, Step 2)* to locate the feed cable coming from the service panel. Turn off the power *(page 11)*, then attach the wires of the new cable *(dash lines)* to the incoming black, white and bare wires.

Middle-of-the-run switch. Determine that the switch is a middle-of-the-run power source—it will be connected to two separate cables. If it is, turn on the circuit's power temporarily and use a voltage tester *(page 171, Step 2)* to identify the black wire that carries current from the service panel. Turn off the power *(page 11)*, then disconnect the black wire from the new cable and to a black jumper *(dash lines)*. Attach the jumper to the switch terminal. Join the new white and bare wires *(dash lines)* to the white and bare wires in the box.

End-of-the-run receptacle. This is the last receptacle connected to a branch circuit, and the easiest location from which to extend wiring—as long as the receptacle is not controlled by a switch. Turn off the power *(page 11)*, then attach the black and white wires of the new cable *(dash lines)* to the unused dark- and light-colored terminals, respectively, on the receptacle *(page 300)*. Join the bare wire to the existing bare wire and the jumper with a wire cap.

Middle-of-the-run receptacle. This receptacle has incoming and outgoing cables. To accommodate the additional wires and clamps, you probably will have to gang the existing box *(page 282)*. Turn off the power *(page 11)*, then remove a black wire from a receptacle terminal and join it with both the black wire of the new cable and a black jumper wire *(dash lines)*. Attach the jumper to the terminal. Use the same procedure for a white receptacle wire and the white cable wire. Attach the new bare wire *(dash lines)* to the other bare wires and the green jumper wire.

Junction box. Since the wires of more than one circuit may pass through a junction box, first locate the wires of the circuit you plan to tap for a power source. Have a helper shut off the circuits at the service panel one by one until you carefully locate, with a voltage tester, the wire controlled by the fuse or breaker in the circuit you wish to tap *(page 171, Step 2)*. Then shut off the circuit *(page 11)* and attach the black, white and bare wires in that circuit to wires of the same colors in the new cable *(dash lines)*, using wire caps of the proper size.

279

Calculating Electrical Load

Determining a circuit overload. If you suspect that a circuit is overloaded, it is a simple matter to calculate the existing load, then compare this to the capacity of the circuit. The maximum load is indicated by the ampere rating of the fuse or circuit breaker. For example, a general lighting circuit would have a maximum load of 15 amperes.

To calculate the existing load on a circuit, list all the fixtures and appliances on the circuit and the watts rating for each device. This information is usually found on a sticker near the socket of a lamp or lighting fixture, or on a small plate on the back or bottom of an appliance *(right)*. Typical watts ratings are listed in the chart below. Add the watts ratings for all appliances and fixtures on the circuit, then divide by 120 volts to convert to amperes. If the total is higher than the capacity of the circuit, the circuit is overloaded. Move a heavy-drawing appliance to another circuit or have an electrician run a new branch circuit from the service panel. When planning a circuit extension or adding a new appliance to the circuit, follow the same procedure to determine the existing and maximum loads of the circuit.

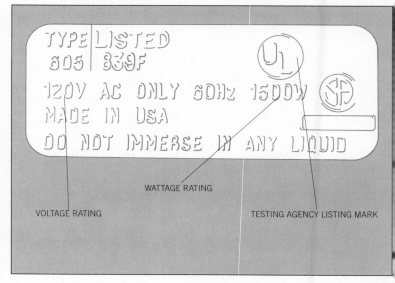

VOLTAGE RATING

WATTAGE RATING

TESTING AGENCY LISTING MARK

Typical Appliance Loads

Appliance	Approximate Watts Rating	Appliance	Approximate Watts Rating	Appliance	Approximate Watts Rating
Household appliances and equipment		**Bedroom and bathroom appliances**		**Kitchen appliances**	
Ceiling fan	50	Electric blanket	150-500	Blender	200-400
Clock	5	Hair dryer	400-1500	Can opener	150
Computer	150-600	Heating pad	60	Coffee grinder	150
Dehumidifier	575	Shaver	15	Coffeemaker	600-750
Humidifier (cold mist)	50-150	**240-volt appliances**		Food processor	500-1500
Iron	1200	Air conditioner	5000	Frying pan	1000-1200
Lamp or fixture	25-150	Clothes dryer	5000	Kettle	1200-1400
Portable heater	1500	Range (per burner)	5000	Mixer	100-225
Projector	350-500	(oven)	4500	Toaster	800-1200
Radio	10-100	Water heater	2500-5000	Toaster-oven	1500
Sewing machine	100	**Large 120-volt appliances**		Trash compactor	500-1000
Stereo system	200-500	Dishwasher	1200-1500	**Power tools**	
Television	150-450	Freezer	300-600	Drill	360
Typewriter	45	Garbage disposer	300-900	Sander	540
Vacuum cleaner	300-600	Microwave oven	800	Saw	600-1500
Videocassette recorder	50	Refrigerator	150-300	Soldering iron	150

Setting Outlet Boxes into Walls and Ceilings

The central element in any permanent electrical installation is an outlet box—a metal or plastic enclosure embedded in a wall or ceiling. A receptacle, switch or light fixture is mounted inside a box, cables enter and leave through holes in the back and sides, and all wiring connections are entirely contained within the box.

Boxes vary in shape according to their position and function: Rectangular wall or device boxes are used with receptacles, switches and wall lights; octagonal or circular ceiling or fixture boxes are used with ceiling lights; and square junction boxes, the largest of all, house connections between two or more cables that branch out to different parts of a circuit.

The existing boxes in your home, installed when the house was built, are probably attached directly to studs or to joists. Plastic boxes, widely used in houses built since about 1970, may be installed in this way, too. When you install new boxes, however, you probably will not have direct access to studs or joists—they are covered over by walls and ceilings. Therefore you must use a box secured in other ways; these are called "old work," remodeling or cut-in boxes. The method you choose depends upon the type of construction in your house.

In a house built after 1950, walls and ceilings are most commonly constructed with plasterboard. Other wall and ceiling materials include wood panels, plywood sheets or sheets of compressed wood fibers called hardboard. Like plasterboard, all these wooden walls are fastened directly to the studs or joists.

A common surface in homes constructed before 1950 and in many of the newer apartments is plaster. It is applied either to wood lath (strips of wood about 1 1/2 inches wide, nailed across the studs and joists about 1/2 inch apart) or to metal lath (a strong mesh that is made of expanded-metal strips) or to rock lath (smooth, hard cement boards nailed to framing). Instructions for installing wall boxes in all these surfaces begin on page 282; instructions for installing ceiling boxes appear on pages 287-289.

Before you install a new box, locate an existing box from which you can run new cable (*page 278*). Make sure that the existing box can safely accommodate additional wires (*chart, below*). If the box has reached its capacity and you cannot find a second box from which to run new cable, you can enlarge a wall box (*page 282, bottom*), add a box extension or replace a box with a deeper one.

How Big a Box to Use

Use the chart at right to determine how many wires you can safely put in an outlet box. Measure the depth of the box, determine the size of the wires already installed or to be added (*page 275*); check the chart for the maximum number of conductors permitted.

The capacity of a box depends not only on the number of wires inside it but also on the number of devices that take up space. Count as one conductor each wire, except grounding wires, that enters the box; do not count jumper wires. Add one connection if the box contains any grounding wires inside it, another if the box contains any internal cable clamps or light-fixture studs, and still another if it contains any switches or receptacles. Then check the total against the number of connections listed in the chart.

A standard 2 1/2-inch-deep wall box might contain a cable with two No. 14 current-carrying wires and a grounding wire inside, plus an internal clamp and receptacle. The box has five conductors; its maximum capacity, according to the chart, is six. The National Electrical Code ruling is clear: Before new wiring is installed, the box should be replaced with one that is deeper, a box extension added or ganged with a second box of the same depth (*page 282, bottom*).

In an older home, the same 2 1/2-inch box might contain a metal-armored cable attached by an external clamp (not counted as a conductor). Here the conductor count would be only four—two conductors, plus a grounding wire and a receptacle. A second cable containing two No. 14 current-carrying wires and a grounding wire can be safely added by using an external clamp.

Matching Connections to Box Size

	Box Depth	Maximum number of conductors No. 14 wire	Maximum number of conductors No. 12 wire
3" x 2" Wall boxes	2 1/2"	6	5
	2 3/4"	7	6
	3 1/2"	9	8
4" Ceiling boxes	1 1/4"	6	5
	1 1/2"	7	6
	2 1/8"	10	9
4" Junction boxes	1 1/4"	9	8
	1 1/2"	10	9

The Three Types of Wall Boxes

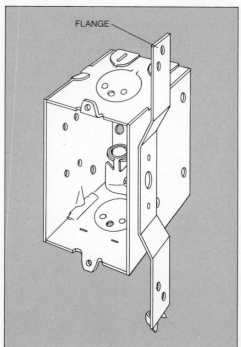

FLANGE

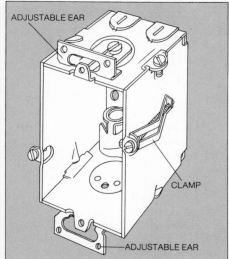

ADJUSTABLE EAR

CLAMP

ADJUSTABLE EAR

A box with side clamps and ears. In plywood paneling or hardboard walls, this box is secured in an opening by clamps that expand behind the wall when the screws at the sides of the box are tightened. The adjustable ears projecting from the top and bottom of the box prevent it from falling backward into the wall space *(page 283)*.

A box with ears and optional brackets. In a wood-paneled or plaster wall with a wood-lath backing, which holds screws well, this wall box can be secured by its adjustable ears alone. For plasterboard and for plaster over metal or rock lath, neither of which holds screws well, use the brackets shown here and follow the mounting method described on page 284. The brackets are purchased separately.

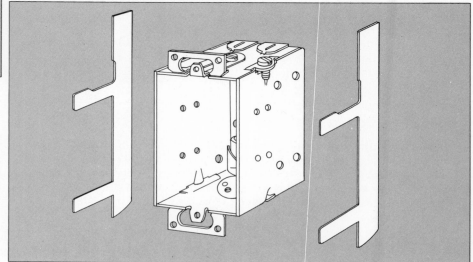

A box with a flange. Nailed to a stud by its flange—or mounting bracket—this type is the easiest wall box to install and is probably the one already inside the walls of your house. Although you cannot add one where the walls are finished, it is a first choice for a basement or attic with exposed studs. If you plan a finished surface over the stud, allow for its thickness; position the flange to bring the front of the box flush with, or 1/16 inch beyond, the surface to be added.

Enlarging a Wall Box

Ganging boxes. Two or more wall boxes of the same depth can be ganged to multiply their size so they can hold extra wires and more than one switch or receptacle. Loosen the screw in the flange at the bottom of one box and pull off the left side. Remove the right side of the other box by loosening the screw at its top. Then hold the open sides together, positioning the notch on one box between the screw head and flange of the other, and tighten the two screws.

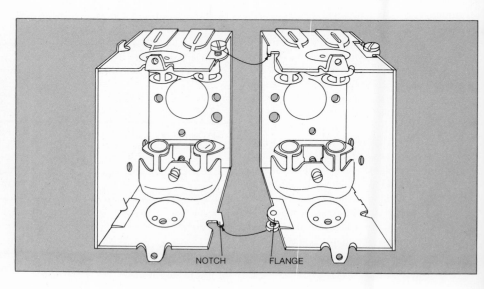

NOTCH   FLANGE

Boxes in Wood Walls

1 **Locating the box.** Mark the wall approximately where you want the box. Then, use a density sensor *(page 46)* to confirm that the location is free of studs or, alternatively, drill a 1/8-inch hole through the wall at this point. If the bit hits a stud, fill the hole with spackling compound and drill a second hole about 6 inches to the left or right. Bend an 8-inch-long piece of coat-hanger wire to a 90° angle at the middle, insert the wire into the wall and turn it through a complete circle. If it does not turn freely within the wall space, indicating the absence of pipes or framing, cover the second hole and repeat the procedure a few inches away until you locate a clear wall space.

2 **Using a template.** Place a box with side clamps face down on a sheet of thick paper. Trace the outline of the box on the paper with a pencil; do not include the detachable ears at the top and bottom of the box. Cut out the paper within the outline as a template and center the template on the hole you have drilled in the wall, with the side of the paper on which you traced the outline against the wall. The template now indicates the exact positions of each of the side clamps. Mark the outline of the template on the wall with a sharp-pointed tool such as an awl.

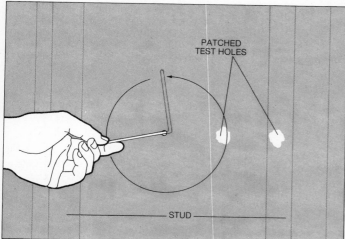

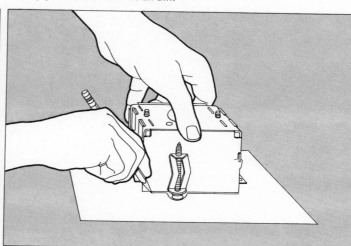

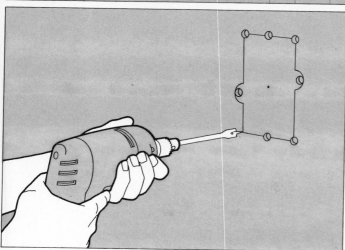

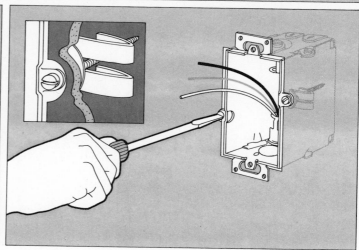

3 **Cutting a hole.** Bore a starter hole for a keyhole saw at each of the four corners on the outline, positioning the point of the bit just outside the outline. Then bore two holes for the side clamps on the box, and two more at the top and bottom of the outline to provide clearance for the long screws that will fasten a switch or receptacle to the box. Cut around the outline with a keyhole saw. Use shallow strokes so you do not jab the blade of the saw into the other side of the wall.

4 Push the box into the wall until the ears hold the front edge flush to the surface of the wall; if necessary, loosen the ear screws and adjust the positions of the ears. Remove the box and attach the unpowered cable through a knockout hole *(pages 298-299)*. Then, holding the box in place, tighten the screws on the sides. Behind the wall, the side clamps will bulge outward, drawing the box into the wall and forcing the ears firmly against the outside surface.

Boxes in Plasterboard

1 **Cutting an outline.** Follow Steps 1 and 2 on page 283, using a standard wall box as a guide for the template. Cut along, and just outside, the template outline with a utility knife. Place the point of the blade at one of the top corners of the outline. If you are right-handed, grip your right wrist with your left hand, bracing your left elbow against the wall, then cut downward. Guide the knife with your right hand while your left hand pushes and steadies the right. Go around the outline twice to cut completely through the paper on the room side of the plasterboard; you need not cut through the board.

2 **Breaking through the plasterboard.** Cut a piece of scrap wood about 3 inches long, 2 inches wide and 1 inch thick. Place one end at the center of the outline you have cut on the wall and strike the other end with a hammer. Try to hit hard enough to break through the paper on the back of the plasterboard. If all of the outlined section does not break away, hammer the piece of wood along the edges of the outline until you have made a rectangular opening of the right size. Then cut away the uneven fragments of plasterboard and paper with the utility knife.

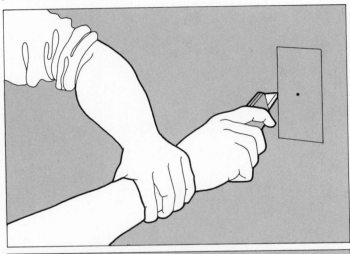

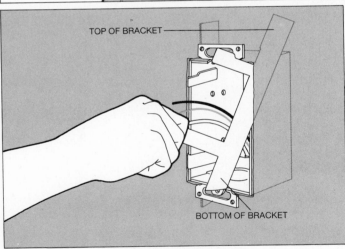

TOP OF BRACKET

BOTTOM OF BRACKET

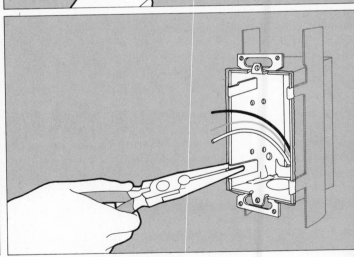

3 **Installing the box.** Attach cable to the box *(pages 298-299)*. Adjust the box ears to bring the front of the box flush with the wall or 1/16 inch beyond, then push the box into the wall and hold it in place with one hand. With your other hand, insert a bracket between one side of the box and the edge of the opening—slide the top of the bracket in first, then the bottom. Caution: Hold the bracket tightly; if it drops behind the wall, it is irretrievable. Pull the bracket toward you by its arms as far as you can, then bend the arms into the box. Install a bracket on the other side of the box in the same way.

4 **Tightening the brackets.** Grip the bend in one of the bracket arms with long-nose pliers and squeeze it tightly against the inside of the box. Repeat this procedure with the other three bracket arms. The arms should be as tight as possible, not only to secure the box firmly, but also to keep the arms out of the way of the wires.

Boxes in Walls of Plaster on Wood Lath

1 **Exposing a lath.** Find a clear wall space for a box by drilling a hole and following the procedure on page 283, Step 1. Using a cold chisel and ball-peen hammer, remove plaster around the drilled test hole, working upward and downward until you have exposed the entire width of a single lath—normally about 1 1/2 inches is enough. Do not loosen any plaster beyond the opening.

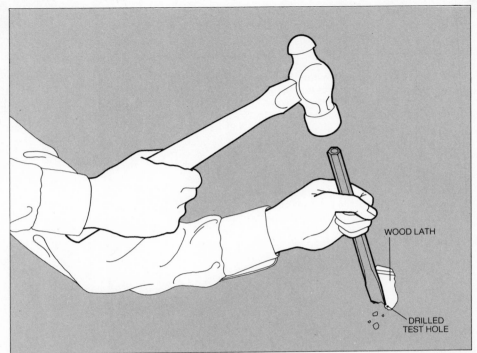

WOOD LATH

DRILLED TEST HOLE

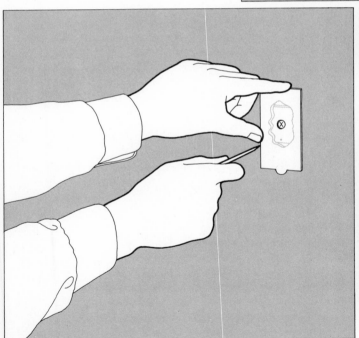

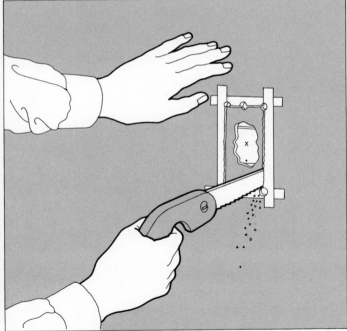

2 **Drawing the outline.** Mark a penciled dot exactly halfway between the top and bottom of the lath. Cut a template for the box (*page 283, Step 2*), using a standard wall box rather than a box with side clamps. Cut a small hole at the exact center of the template and hold the template against the wall with the hole directly over the mark on the lath. Trace the template outline.

3 **Cutting through the wall.** Apply strips of masking tape around the outline to keep plaster from breaking. Score the outline several times with a utility knife. Bore 3/8-inch holes at the outline corners and in the curves at the top and bottom; then cut along the scored lines with a keyhole saw. Work smoothly and evenly; irregular strokes of the saw can jar the laths and crack plaster out beyond the opening.

4 Installing the box. With the power turned off *(page 11)*, remove the masking tape, insert the box in the wall opening and trace the outlines of the ears. Then remove the box and score these outlines with a utility knife. Using a cold chisel and ball-peen hammer, cut away the plaster within the outlines to expose the laths beneath. Chisel in from the outlines toward the wall opening to minimize damage to the wall.

Hold the box in the wall opening and mark the positions of the screw holes in the ears on the exposed lath; drill pilot holes at these points for the mounting screws. Position the movable ears to bring the front of the box flush to the wall surface or 1/16 inch beyond. Then attach cable to the box *(pages 298-299)* and screw the box to the lath.

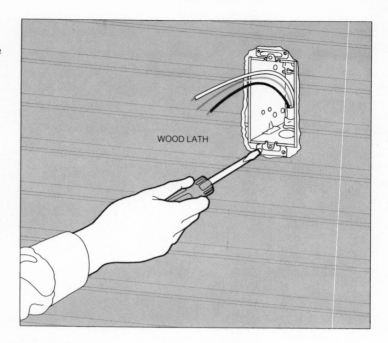

WOOD LATH

Boxes in Walls of Plaster on Metal Lath

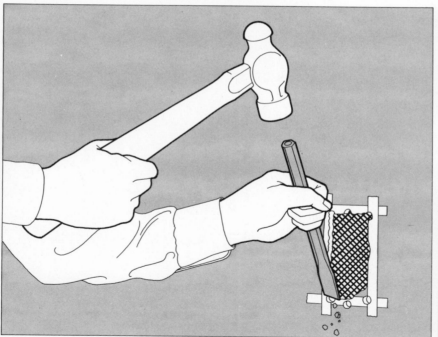

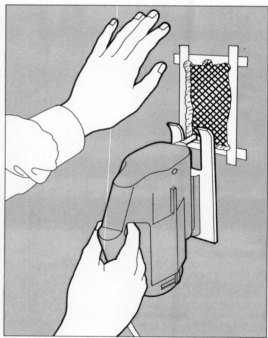

1 Chiseling out the plaster. Locate a clear space for the box and trace the outline of the box on the wall *(page 283, Steps 1 and 2)*, using a template for a standard wall box rather than a box with side clamps. Tape and score the outline *(page 285, Step 3)*. Wearing safety goggles, drill holes at the four corners of the outline and in the curves at the top and bottom, using a 3/8-inch twist bit. With a cold chisel and a ball-peen hammer, remove all of the plaster within the outline so that the metal lath beneath is completely exposed.

2 Cutting out the lath. Fit a fine-tooth blade for cutting metal to a saber saw *(page 454)*, insert the end of the blade in one of the holes that you drilled at the edges of the outline and cut out the exposed metal lath. Caution: This part of the job must be performed very slowly and with special care to prevent the vibration of the saw from damaging the plaster around the opening. Install a standard box, using brackets and following the procedure described for installing wall boxes in plasterboard *(page 284, Steps 3 and 4)*.

Installing Boxes in Ceilings

A ceiling box can be mounted in one of three ways; directly to a joist, suspended between two joists by a device called a bar hanger or hung from the bottoms of joists by a special type of bar hanger called an offset hanger. Your choice among these boxes will depend partly on the material of which the ceiling is made and partly on the access you have to the space above the ceiling.

The ceiling material you are most likely to encounter will be plasterboard or, in older houses, plaster over wood lath. Both are easy to work with when you have access to the ceiling from an attic above. If the attic has floorboards, remove part of a board to get at the joists. If the joists are exposed, the installation job is even simpler but calls for one special precaution. Though the joists will support your weight, the ceiling below them will collapse if you step on it. Create a patch of sturdy flooring by laying three or four planks across the joists at your work area.

If the ceiling lies directly under the roof or under another room, you must install the box from below. Remodeling or "old work" boxes are especially useful for this. Before handling any wires or cables, turn off the power at the main service panel *(page 11)*.

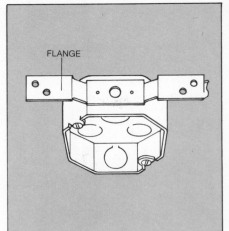

FLANGE

Three Types of Ceiling Boxes

A box with a flange. Screws or nails inserted in the permanently attached flange, or mounting bracket, fasten this box directly to a joist. The installation is simple but the box suffers from one limitation: It can be installed only at the side of a joist, not in the comparatively large spaces between joists.

A box with a bar hanger. This box is screwed to the bar hanger with a threaded stud, the sliding arms of the hanger are extended to meet the joists on either side, and the entire assembly is fastened to the sides of the joists by the flanges at the ends of the arms. Because the construction of this box permits it to be positioned at almost any point between two joists, the bar hanger type has become the most popular.

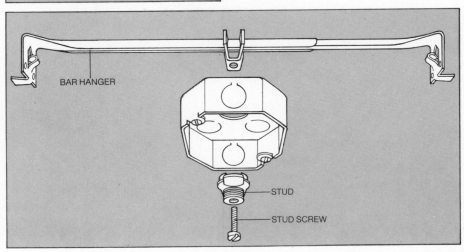

BAR HANGER

STUD

STUD SCREW

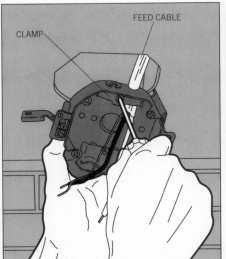

CLAMP

FEED CABLE

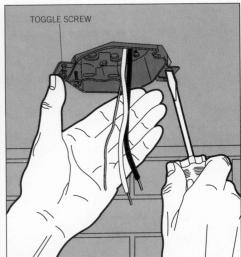

TOGGLE SCREW

An "old work" box. To install this box, hold the electrical box against the ceiling and use a pencil to mark its outline. Wearing safety goggles, use an electric drill to bore a starter hole for a saber saw blade inside the marked outline; then insert the blade of the saber saw into the starter hole and cut along the outline *(above, left)* to make a hole in the ceiling. Have a helper in the attic pass the end of the unpowered cable through the hole. Pull the stripped end of the cable through the knockout behind the clamp, then tighten the clamp *(above, center)*. Fit the electrical box into the hole in the ceiling and tighten the toggle screws *(above, right)* to hold it in place.

Ceiling Boxes Positioned from an Attic

1 **Locating the box.** Choose a place for the new ceiling box and mark the spot on the surface of the ceiling with a pencil or awl. Drill a 1/8-inch hole through the mark. The bit should penetrate the ceiling almost immediately. If it meets prolonged resistance, you are drilling into a joist; cover the hole with spackling compound and drill a second hole at least 2 inches away. When you have found a clear space, bore a 3/4-inch hole, then fit an 18-inch-long extension and a 3/8-inch bit to the drill and bore a hole through the attic floorboard directly above. Go to the attic for the next step. (If your attic does not have floorboards, proceed to Step 3).

2 **Removing a floorboard.** In the attic, find the board with the drilled hole in it. The joists beneath this board can be located by the rows of nails that fasten the board to the centers of the joists. The edges of the joists lie about 1 inch from the rows of nails. Mark the joist edges that are nearest to the hole, using a steel square and an awl to score lines across the floorboard. Bore a 3/8-inch starter hole at one end of each of the lines you have marked; then cut through the board along the lines with a saber saw or keyhole saw. Retrieve the loose section of board you have sawed free, so that you can replace it in the opening when the job is completed.

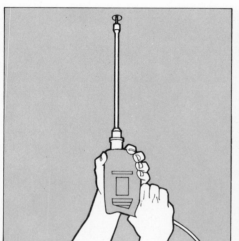

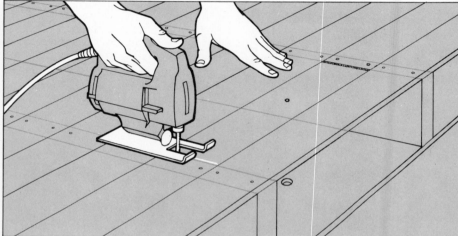

3 **Boring guide holes from above.** If your locator hole is more than 4 inches from the nearest joist, you can mount the box at this point with a bar hanger. To fix the location, center the open end of the box over the hole and trace its outline. If the hole is less than 4 inches from a joist, you must use a flanged box attached directly to the joist. Hold the flange against the nearest joist and trace the outline of the box at this location. For either box, complete this step of the job by boring 3/8-inch holes at the eight corners of the outline, positioning the bit just outside each corner. Then go to the floor below for the next step.

4 **Cutting the box hole from below.** Wearing protective goggles and using a keyhole saw, cut out the outline marked by the drilled holes. A lath-and-plaster ceiling calls for special precautions: Score the plaster with straight lines between the holes; apply masking tape around the outline *(page 285, Step 3)*; and brace a piece of wood against the ceiling just outside the lines of the outline as you make your cuts. A plasterboard ceiling is easier to work with; simply brace the ceiling with your hand as you saw. In either material, begin the cuts by ramming the point of the keyhole saw into one of the holes and work from hole to hole around the entire outline.

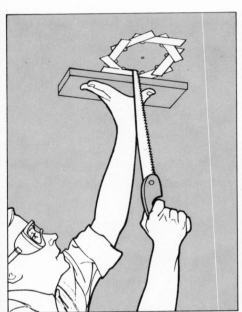
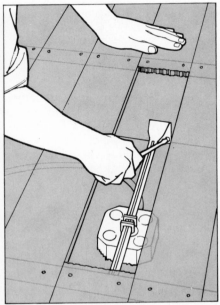

5 **Installing the box.** With power to the cable off, install the cable into the box. If you are working with a bar hanger, fasten the box to the hanger with a threaded metal stud and cut the small tabs from the flanges at the ends of the hanger with metal snips. Holding the box in the ceiling hole with its front flush to the lower surface of the ceiling, extend the arms of the hanger to the joists on either side. Mark the positions of the hanger screw holes on the joists, bore pilot holes for the screws and screw the hanger to the joists *(left)*.

To install a flanged box, hold the box with its front flush to the lower surface of the ceiling and the flange against the side of the joist. Mark the positions of the flange screw holes on the joist, drill pilot holes for the flange screws and screw the flange to the joist.

6 **Replacing the board.** When the cable and the new box have been installed, cut two wooden cleats, each 2 inches wide, 3 inches high and slightly longer than the width of the board you have removed. Nail the two cleats to the exposed sides of the joists, tight against the bottoms of the floorboards. Then insert the loose board in the opening and nail it to the tops of the cleats.

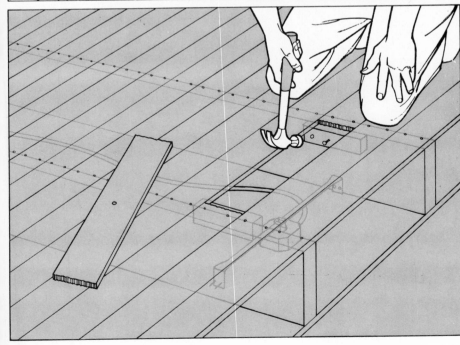

Running Cable from Old Outlet Boxes to New

Having made an opening for a new outlet—but before installing the box—you must run cable to the opening from an existing box. First turn off power to the circuit at the service panel *(page 11)* and test to make sure it is off *(page 272)*. Then find a nearby box—on the turned-off circuit—that can supply power to the new cable. Test to be sure power to that box is indeed turned off; then enlarge the box if necessary *(pages 281-282)*. Then select a route for the cable that calls for the least labor and causes the least damage to your walls and ceilings.

The best route on both counts runs to the maximum extent possible through an unfinished basement or attic, where wall studs and ceiling or floor joists are either exposed or easily uncovered. You can drill 3/4-inch holes through the studs or joists *(page 292)*, then thread cable through the holes; electrical codes re-

quire only that the holes be drilled at least 1 1/4 inches from the edge of a stud or joist, and that you staple the cable to a support *(opposite, bottom)* within 1 foot of a box. Running cable along the side of a stud or joist is even easier: The only code requirement is that you staple the cable at 4-foot-maximum intervals *(opposite, bottom)*. Cables fished through inaccessible locations need not be secured, but the accessible portions must be secured.

Where a finished room lies above a basement or below an attic, these methods suffice for floor or ceiling outlets. A wall outlet needs another step: Boring a hole through the plates, or beams, at the top and bottom of the wall. Through this access hole you can feed the cable inside the wall to the outlet hole.

Running cable in a finished room that has no access to a basement or attic calls

for a radically different procedure. To begin with, you must make holes in a wall or ceiling to get at hidden studs, joists and plates *(pages 293-297)*. Through these access holes you can bore holes through studs and plates, and then, with a fish tape, pull the cable behind a wall from stud to stud, or behind a ceiling between two joists. Other access holes enable you to run cable over a doorway, through a wall, or along a ceiling from an adjoining room *(pages 296-297)*.

Often, you will have to combine several methods of running cable. In the examples shown here, cable for a new wall outlet is connected to an existing wall outlet by running it up through the walls at either end and along basement joists in between. The following pages show techniques for running cable across joists, through an attic and inside a wall inaccessible from basement or attic.

A Cable Route along Basement Joists

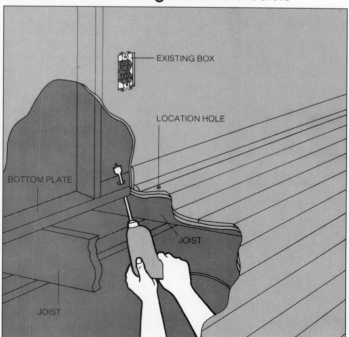

EXISTING BOX

LOCATION HOLE

BOTTOM PLATE

JOIST

JOIST

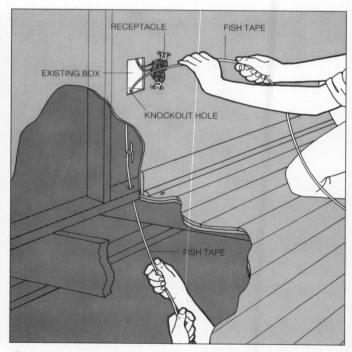

RECEPTACLE

FISH TAPE

EXISTING BOX

KNOCKOUT HOLE

FISH TAPE

1 **Getting from wall to basement.** Wearing safety goggles, bore a 1/16-inch location hole through the floor directly below the existing box you plan to tap. Poke a thin wire through so you can find the hole in the basement. Then, in line with the location hole, drill up through the bottom—or sole—plate with a 3/4-inch spade bit. Directly across the room from the old box, cut an opening for the new one and, using the same method, drill a hole through the plate below it.

2 **Fishing tape through the wall.** With the power off *(page 11)*, detach the receptacle from the existing box and pull it out of the way—you need not disconnect the wires. With a hammer and nail set, remove a knockout from a hole in the bottom of the box *(pages 298-299)*. Push the end of a fish tape through this hole and down behind the wall, and have a helper push a second tape up through the hole in the bottom plate. Maneuver both of the tapes behind the wall until their ends hook together.

3 **Attaching cable to a tape.** From the basement, pull down the end of the upper tape through the hole in the bottom plate; unhook the two tapes. Strip 3 inches of sheathing from the end of a cable and strip all the insulation from the exposed wires. Run the ends of the bare wires through the hook of the upper tape and loop the wires back over themselves. Tape the hook of the fish tape and the looped wires firmly so the cable will not snap or pull loose from the fish tape.

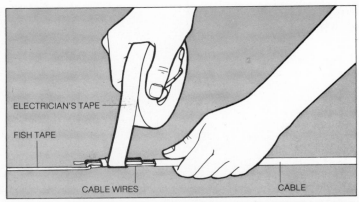

ELECTRICIAN'S TAPE

FISH TAPE

CABLE WIRES   CABLE

4 **Running the cable to the existing box.** From the room, pull the fish tape back through the knockout hole in the existing box until the end of the cable emerges; to make this step of the job easier, have your helper feed the cable up through the bottom plate from the basement. Detach the cable from the fish tape. Cut the cable off cleanly, strip 8 inches of sheathing from the end of it and fasten the sheathed end of the cable to the box with an internal clamp *(pages 298-299)*.

5 **Completing the job.** Run the cable across the basement ceiling, fastening it to the nearest joist with cable staples at 4-foot intervals. (Be careful not to damage the cable sheathing as you nail the staples.) When you reach the hole you have drilled in the opposite bottom plate, fish the cable up to the new box opening by the method shown in Step 2. Attach the cable to the new box and mount the box in the wall *(pages 281-286)*.

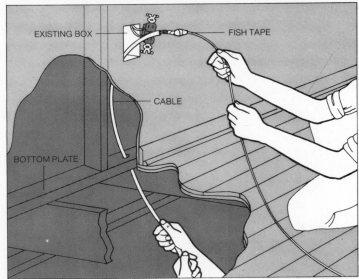

EXISTING BOX   FISH TAPE

CABLE

BOTTOM PLATE

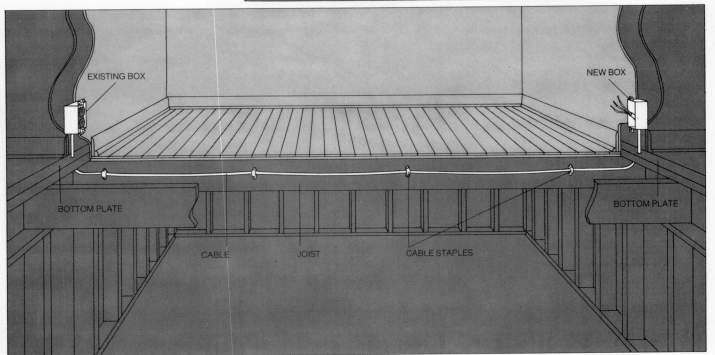

EXISTING BOX

NEW BOX

BOTTOM PLATE   BOTTOM PLATE

CABLE   JOIST   CABLE STAPLES

Alternate Routes in Basements and Attics

Running cable across basement joists. If your route for new cable runs at right angles to the basement joists, run the cable through 3/4-inch holes bored through the middle of each joist. Attach the cable to the existing box *(pages 290-291, Steps 1-4)* and snake the cable through the joists to a point directly below the new box, then fish the cable up to the opening and attach it to the box.

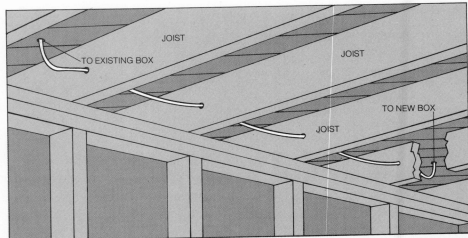

Fishing cable to an attic. Cable can be run along or across exposed attic joists by the same procedures that are used in a basement—except for a slight variation in fishing the cable.

Turn off the power to the circuit on which you are working and test to make sure it is off *(page 272)*. Remove a knockout from a hole in the top of the existing box. Drill a hole through the top plates of the wall at a point directly above the box and have a helper drop a light chain down through the plate, far enough to reach below the box. Push a fish tape through the knockout hole, catch the chain and pull it into the box. Hook the fish tape to the end of the chain and tape the hook and chain together. Pull the chain up until the fish tape reaches the attic, then detach the chain, attach the cable to the tape hook as shown in Step 3 on page 291 and then proceed with Steps 4 and 5 on that page.

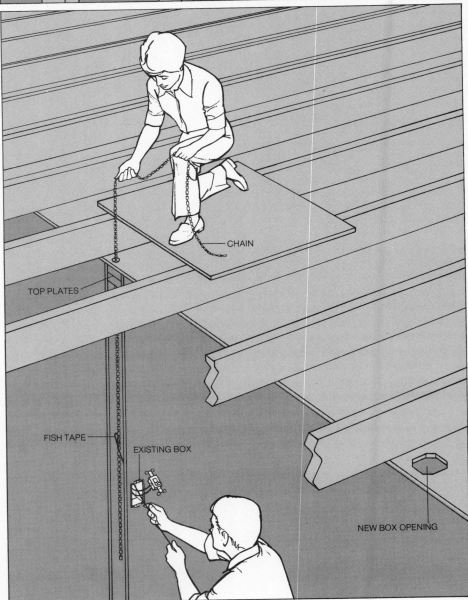

A Route behind a Wall

1 **Exposing the studs.** Make an opening for the new box. Use a density sensor to locate the studs *(page 46)*, and measure the length of the wire from the hole to the stud and mark the wall at that distance.

Turn off the power and test to make sure it is indeed off *(page 272)*. If the wall is plasterboard, use a utility knife to cut a rectangle 3 inches high and wide enough to extend 2 inches beyond the edges of the stud. Knock out the plasterboard rectangle to expose the stud. Locate the next stud and cut a hole over it by the same method. The remaining studs will be the same distance apart as the first two, so that you can simply measure to find them. Use a 3/4-inch spade bit to drill a hole through the center of each stud. In a plaster wall, cut the rectangular hole with a chisel and then saw through the underlying lath *(page 285)*.

2 **Fishing the cable.** Remove a knockout tab in the bottom of the existing box and push a fish tape through the hole and down into the wall. Hook this tape with a second tape pushed through the hole in the nearest stud. With the second tape, pull the first through the stud. Now release the second tape, attach cable to the free end of the first tape, and pull tape and cable back through the stud and into the existing box. Using the same two-tape method, fish the cable through the adjoining studs and into the opening you have cut for the new box. Clamp the cable on both boxes *(pages 298-299)*, install the new box *(pages 281-286)* and patch up the wall *(page 307)*.

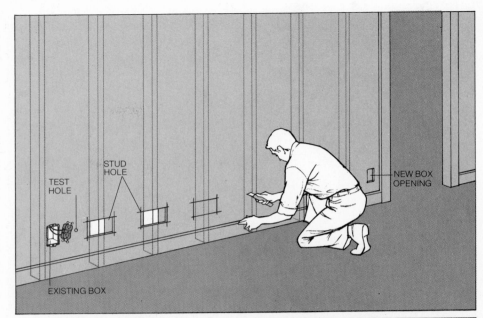

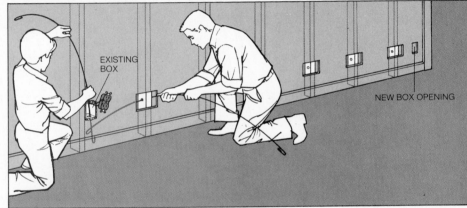

Concealing Cable behind a Baseboard

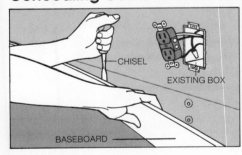

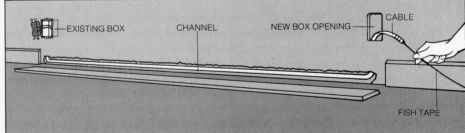

1 **Removing the baseboard.** With power to the circuit turned off, make an opening for the new box *(pages 281-286)*. Directly below the existing box, insert the blade of a wood chisel between the wall and the top of the baseboard, and tap the chisel gently with a mallet until the baseboard begins to separate from the wall. Move the chisel a few inches along the baseboard and repeat the process until you have loosened an entire section. Use the chisel as a lever with one hand and pull the section from the wall with the other hand.

2 **Cutting a channel.** For a plaster wall, chisel a 1-inch hole through the plaster and lath below the existing box in the section behind the baseboard. Make an opening for the new box *(page 283)* and break an identical hole below it. With a hammer and cold chisel, cut a channel between the two holes. Fish cable from the existing box to the first hole, run it along the channel and fish it to the new box

opening. Clamp the cable to both boxes and install the new box. In plasterboard, cut a strip from the section behind the baseboard. Drill holes through the exposed studs, fish the cable into the existing box, run it through the studs and then fish it to the new box opening. Install 1/16-inch-thick metal plates over the cable at stud locations and be careful when installing the baseboard to avoid nailing into the cable.

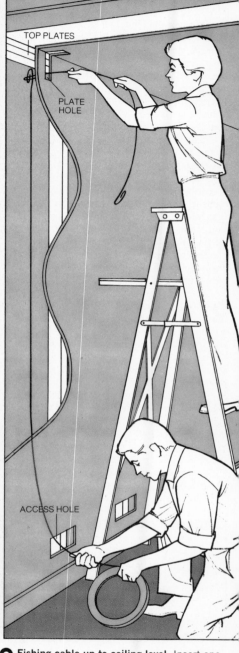

Taking Cable from Wall Box to Ceiling Box

1 **Making access holes.** With power to the circuit turned off, cut an opening for the new ceiling box between two joists (*pages 287-289*). Follow along these joists—not across—to the wall and mark the point midway between them at the top of the wall. If the existing wall box from which you plan to run new cable does not lie directly below this point, you will have to make access holes in the wall to bring cable horizontally to position (*page 293, Steps 1 and 2, top*). From the mark made at the corner of the wall and ceiling directly above the box or hole, outline a 2-inch-long rectangle on the ceiling and a 4-inch-long rectangle on the wall. Cut the plasterboard or score the plaster along the rectangles with a utility knife, and cut through ceiling and wall along the outlines. In plasterboard, break into the ceiling rectangle with a cold chisel and a ball-peen hammer, and cut away the broken fragments with the utility knife. Chisel out the wall rectangle. In plaster, chisel out both rectangles down to the lath, then cut away exposed wood lath with a keyhole saw, or metal lath with a saber saw.

2 **Fishing cable up to ceiling level.** Insert one end of a fish tape through the wall access hole beneath the ceiling, rectangle or, if the existing box lies directly below the ceiling opening, through a knockout hole in the box. Have a helper push the fish tape upward to the top plates. Drill through any fire blocking as shown on page 293, Steps 1 and 2, top. With a second fish tape, hook the top of the vertical tape and pull it out. Disconnect the two tapes, attach the cable to the top end of the vertical tape (*page 291, Step 3*), and have your helper draw the cable down behind the wall and out through the wall access hole (or knockout hole).

PLATE HOLE

CEILING BOX OPENING

JOIST

3 **Fishing cable above the ceiling.** Have your helper insert one end of a fish tape into the ceiling box opening and push the tape between the joists past the rectangular ceiling hole at the top plates. Insert a second fish tape through this ceiling plate hole and hook it over the first tape; then hold it down firmly as your helper slowly pulls the other tape until the two tape ends hook together. Reversing direction, pull your tape completely out of the ceiling plate hole. Disconnect the two tapes, attach the end of the cable to the upper tape and feed the cable into the ceiling plate hole as your helper slowly draws the cable toward and out of the ceiling box opening.

4 **Fastening the cable to the top plates.** If the wall is less than 1/2 inch thick, you must cut a channel for the cable in the top plates. Invert the handle of a keyhole saw and make two parallel vertical cuts, 1/2 inch deep and 3/4 inch apart, across the exposed top plates. Chisel out the wood between cuts. Staple the cable in the groove just below the top edge of the plates.

If the wall is more than 1/2 inch thick, you need not chisel a groove; simply staple the cable to the top plates. In either case, complete the job by patching the two access holes with plaster-board or plaster *(page 307)*.

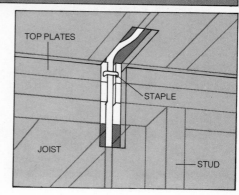

TOP PLATES

STAPLE

JOIST

STUD

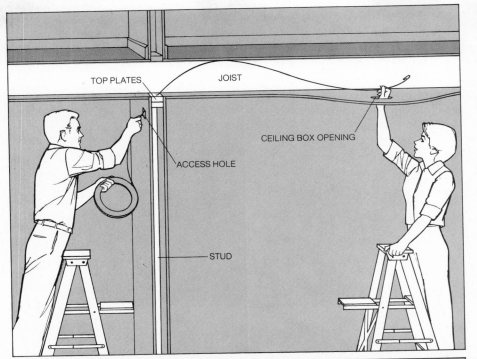

TOP PLATES   JOIST

CEILING BOX OPENING

ACCESS HOLE

STUD

Work from an Adjoining Room

1 **Fishing cable from an adjoining room.** In some cases, this method may be simpler than the one on pages 293-294. Begin in the same way: Cut a ceiling box opening and mark the midpoint between joists at the top of a wall *(page 294, Step 1)*. Then locate the equivalent point on the other side of that wall by measuring off the distance from a corner or a doorway. In the adjoining room, use a density sensor *(page 46)* to locate the top plates and make an access hole 2 inches high and 1 inch wide *(page 294, Step 1)* just below the plates. Using a drill with an extension and a 3/4-inch spade bit, and starting about 1/2 inch inside the plate edge, bore a hole through the plates as close to the vertical as possible. Push a fish tape through this hole into the ceiling space to the ceiling box opening. Have a helper pull the tape through the opening and attach cable to it *(page 291, Step 3)*. Then, reversing direction, pull the cable through the plates and into the adjoining room.

2 **Fishing cable to the wall box.** Have your helper push a fish tape to the top of the wall through the wall opening in the room being wired. Insert a second tape through the access hole in the adjoining room, hook the first one and pull it into the adjoining room. Attach the cable to the first tape *(page 291, Step 3)*, and have your helper pull it through the wall box opening. Then patch up the access hole *(page 307)*.

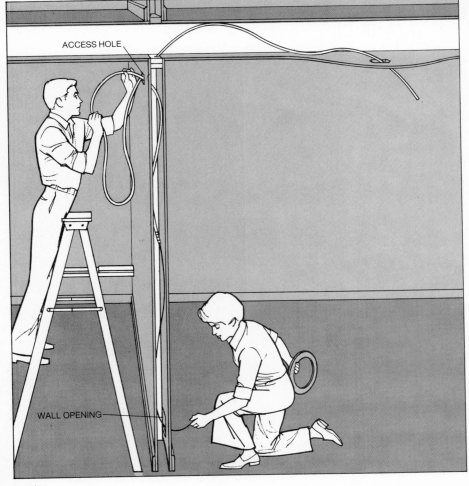

ACCESS HOLE

WALL OPENING

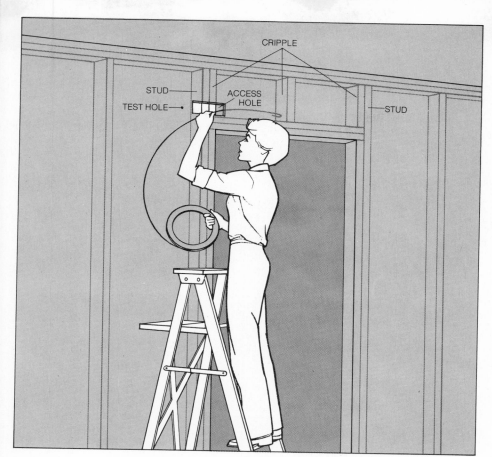

The Best Way to Get Around a Doorway

Fishing cable through the cripples. Use a density sensor (*page 46*) or test hole to locate the exact position of the stud next to the door and cut an access hole (*page 293, Step 1*) wide enough to expose both the stud and the first cripple—a short vertical support—over the doorway. Use the fish tape to locate the next cripple, cut an access hole to expose it and repeat the process until you have cut an access hole at the stud on the other side of the doorway. Drill holes through the studs and cripples (*page 293, Step 1*) and fish the cable through the holes and over the doorway. Patch up the holes (*page 307*).

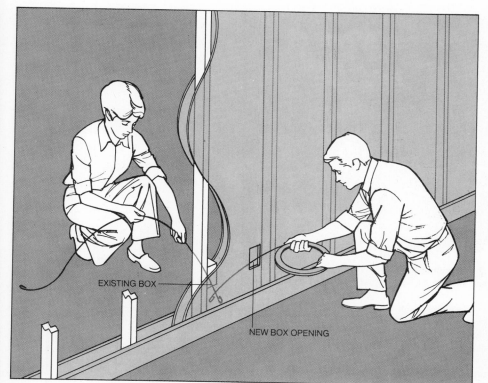

Two Boxes Back to Back

Installing outlet boxes back to back. Measure the distance from a reference point such as a doorway to the existing outlet box, and mark the equivalent point on the other side of the wall. Turn off power to the circuit at the service panel (*page 11*) and test to make sure it is off (*page 272*). Remove the cover plate from the existing box and poke a coat-hanger wire into the space between the sides of the box and the edges of the opening to find the stud to which the box is attached. Go to the adjoining room and mark a second point about 8 inches from the first, measuring away from the stud supporting the existing box. Cut an opening for the new outlet box at the second point (*pages 281-286*).

Have a helper push a fish tape into the wall through a knockout hole in the existing box, and then hook this tape with a second tape inserted through the new opening. Pull the first tape through the new opening, attach 3 feet of cable to it, and have your helper pull the cable back through the wall space and into the existing box. Attach the cable to both the existing and new box, and install the new box (*pages 281-286*).

Connecting Cable to Boxes

Cable enters a box through one of its knockout holes. Choose the hole, preferably an end hole, that provides the most direct path for the cable. Remove the knockout from this hole and fasten the cable to the box. There are two types of knockout holes, and cable is connected to each in a different way.

One type of knockout is U shaped, has a slot in the middle and is almost exclusively found in wall boxes. Cable entering this hole is fastened with an internal clamp (below), usually supplied with the box, that accepts armored or plastic-sheathed cable, but not conduit.

Round knockout holes are provided in ceiling, junction and wall boxes, and they can accept conduit as well as cable. The cable is fastened at the hole by a two-part connector (opposite), which consists of a clamp that holds the cable and a threaded tube that fits into the knockout hole. These connectors are purchased separately.

Usually, you will connect cable to a new box as shown in Steps 1, 2 and 3 below. If you are adding cable to a previously installed wall box, however, start opening the U-shaped knockout from within the box with a nail set and hammer, then insert the looped end of a coat-hanger wire between the wall and the box and pull the knockout back against the box. Fish the cable into the box through the knockout hole and then connect the cable with an internal clamp.

To connect cable with a two-part connector to a previously installed ceiling or junction box, you may remove a section of the ceiling or wall to get at the outside of the box (pages 281-289) or fish the new cable with its two-part connector (minus the locknut) already installed. In this case larger holes will be needed in the framing. Then follow the procedures shown on these pages for new work.

Attaching an Internal Clamp

1 **Removing the U-shaped knockout.** Turn off power to the circuit at the service panel (page 11). Insert the tip of a screwdriver into the slot of the knockout. Pry the knockout away from the box; work it back and forth until it breaks free.

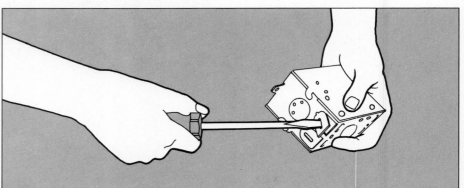

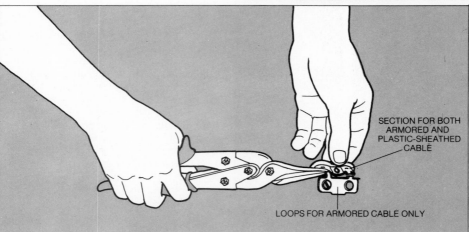

SECTION FOR BOTH ARMORED AND PLASTIC-SHEATHED CABLE

LOOPS FOR ARMORED CABLE ONLY

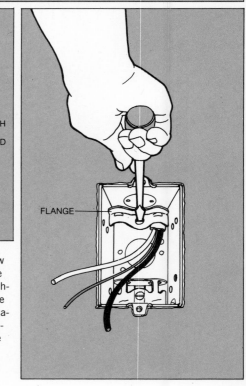

FLANGE

2 **Adapting clamp.** Although some internal clamps are designed exclusively for plastic-sheathed cable, the most common type (above) has extra metal loops to accommodate armored cable. To prepare the latter type of clamp for plastic-sheathed cable, cut off the metal strips holding the loops with metal snips.

3 **Clamping the cable.** With the power off, screw the top part of the clamp loosely to the inside of the box at the end with the knockout. Cut 8 inches of sheathing from the end of the cable, strip the ends of the wires (pages 276-277), and pull the cable into the box through the knockout hole and under the clamp. While holding the cable so that the clamp rests on the uncut end of the sheathing, screw the clamp tightly down against the cable. Then attach the box (pages 281-289).

Attaching a Two-Part Clamp

1 **Removing the round knockout.** Wearing safety goggles, prop the box on a firm surface and open the knockout hole with a nail set and a hammer. Then grip the knockout with a pair of pliers and work it free.

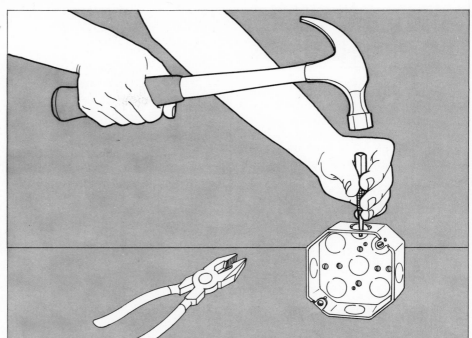

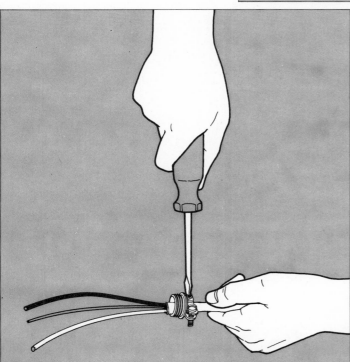

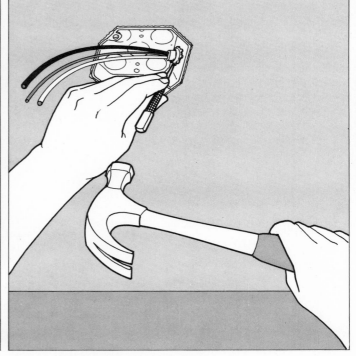

2 **Fastening the connector to the cable.** Cut the sheathing from the end of the unpowered cable and strip the end of the wires *(pages 276-277)*. Slip a connector for plastic-sheathed cable onto the sheathing, with the threaded end facing the stripped wires and with 1/4 inch of sheathed cable reaching beyond the connector. Then tighten the clamp screws onto the cable.

3 **Fastening the connector to the box.** Insert the stripped wires and the threaded end of the connector into the box through the knockout hole. Slip the connector locknut over the wires and screw the locknut onto the connector. Then attach the box to the wall or ceiling *(page 281-289)*. To tighten the connector locknut, position a nail set against one of the points that protrudes from the locknut and hammer the nail set to turn the locknut. Repeat until tight.

Replacing 120-Volt Receptacles

To connect a new receptacle, turn off the power *(page 11)* and follow the wiring patterns on these two pages. If the replacement is identical with the old one, you will probably hook the same wires to the same terminals—but be sure the old one was wired correctly. For 120-volt circuits, always use a three-prong grounded receptacle even if the old receptacle was two-prong, unless the receptacle cannot be grounded. Use green hex-head slotted bonding screws *(not shown)*, available from an electrical supply dealer.

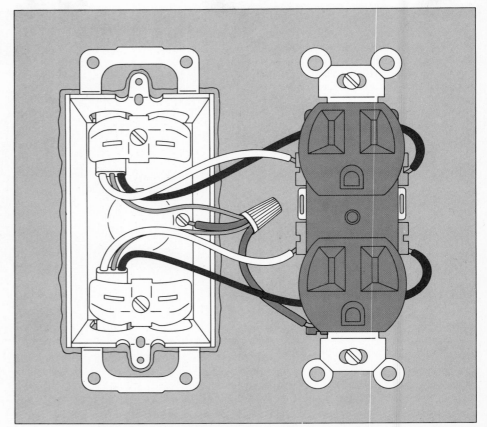

Middle-of-the-run with plastic-sheathed cable. In middle-of-the-run wiring two cables enter the box, each containing a black, a white and a bare copper wire. Connect each of the black cable wires to a brass terminal of the new receptacle; connect each white cable wire to a silver receptacle terminal. Attach one 4-inch green or bare copper jumper wire to the back of the box and another to the green receptacle terminal. Connect both jumpers to the bare cable wires with a wire cap.

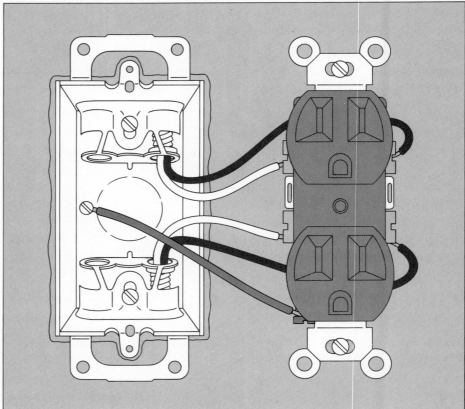

Middle-of-the-run Type AC armored cable. Connect each black cable wire to a brass receptacle terminal and each white cable wire to a silver terminal. Attach a 5-inch green or bare copper jumper wire to the back of the box with a bonding screw and connect this jumper to the green terminal.

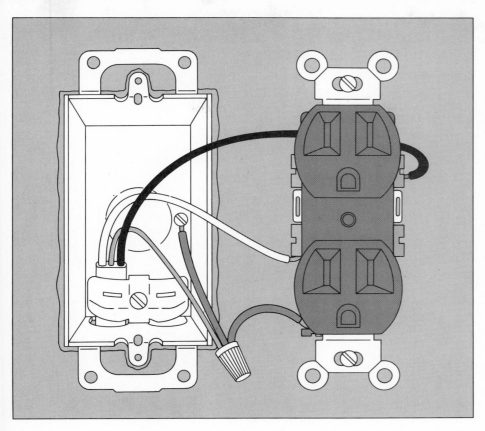

End-of-the-run wiring. In end-of-the-run wiring a single cable enters the box. If the cable is plastic-sheathed, it contains a black, a white and a bare copper wire. Connect the black cable wire to a brass terminal on the new receptacle and the white cable wire to a silver terminal. Attach one 4-inch green or bare copper jumper wire to the back of the box with a hex-head green bonding screw and another jumper to the green receptacle terminal. Then join both jumpers to the bare cable wire with a wire cap.

Armored cable has no bare wire inside the box, since its bonding strip, if present, is cut off and bent back over the outside of the cable. To ground the installation, use a 5-inch green jumper wire and attach it to the back of the box with a hex-head green bonding screw. Then connect the jumper wire to the green screw on the receptacle.

From Switch to Switch-Receptacle Combination

Installing the switch-receptacle. This installation, which combines a single-pole switch with a receptacle that is always hot, is possible only if the switch to be replaced is middle-of-the-run *(opposite)*, because a white neutral wire and unswitched black hot wire must be available for the receptacle. Connect the incoming black cable wire to one of the pair of brass terminals linked by a metal tab. Connect the outgoing black wire to the brass terminal on the opposite side of the switch-receptacle. Attach a 4-inch white jumper wire to the silver terminal and connect it to the two white cable wires with a wire cap. Attach one 4-inch green or bare copper jumper wire to the back of the box with a hex-head green bonding screw and another jumper wire to the green terminal of the switch-receptacle. Connect these jumpers to the bare cable wires with a wire cap.

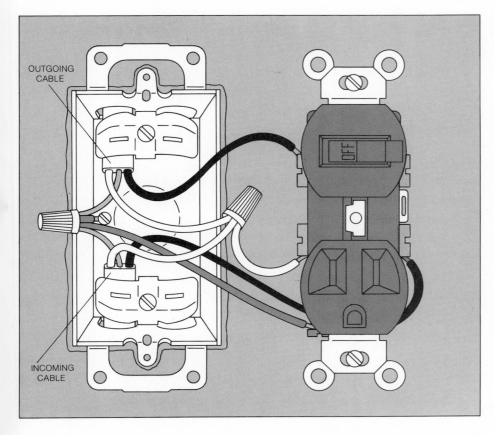

OUTGOING CABLE

INCOMING CABLE

Installing Switch-Controlled Light Fixtures

Once you know how to install boxes and run cables *(pages 281-297)*, extending new circuits for lights and switches becomes easier. As long as there is enough unused capacity in the branch circuit to supply the new loads, you can install special-purpose lights in a living room, a new fixture in a bedroom, or additional three-slot outlets for small kitchen appliances. Using two three-way switches, you can control lights from different locations in a stairwell, garage or two-entrance room. In every case you must run cable from an existing power source *(page 279)* to

newly installed switch and fixture outlet boxes. The route of the cable depends on the location of the circuit you will tap for power and the layout of your home. The route determines the order in which power moves to each device in the circuit. That order, in turn, determines how many wires the cables contain and the way those wires must be joined.

The drawings on these pages show how these relationships work in practice. When a power source is available in an unfinished attic *(opposite, top)*, the easiest cable route for a ceiling light in a

room beneath runs through the attic to the new light and then down through the wall to a single-pole switch. If the attic is inaccessible but power is available at a baseboard receptacle *(below)*, the cable will run through the wall to the switch, then up and along the ceiling to the light. If there is a power source available in an adjacent hallway *(opposite, bottom)*, the cable might run across and up to a switch, then to a ceiling light and—if you install a three-conductor cable between the switch and the light—power can be continued on to supply a wall receptacle.

A new middle-of-the-run switch. The cable for this new circuit starts at a power source, then runs to the switch and on to the light. In this arrangement, the switch wiring *(inset, bottom left)* is called middle-of-the-run and the light-fixture wiring *(inset, right)* end-of-the-run. Throughout, two-conductor cable with grounding wire is used.

At the switch, the hot black wire of the incoming cable is connected to one terminal and the black outgoing wire is connected to the other terminal. The white neutral wires, which must provide an unbroken path for current from the light back to the service panel are joined with a wire cap. The grounding wires, which must also be uninterrupted, are joined to each other and to the metal box. At the light fixture, the hot wire from the switch is connected to the fixture's black wire, the neutral wire to the fixture's white wire, and the bare grounding wire is spliced with a wire cap to the fixture's grounding wire and a green or bare copper jumper wire. The jumper is attached to a hex-head green bonding screw in the back of the metal box.

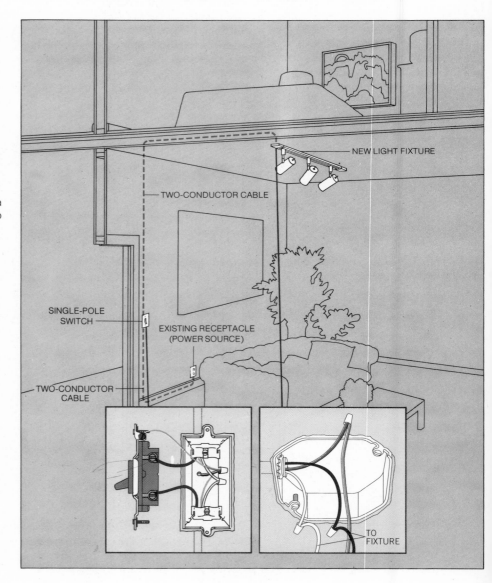

NEW LIGHT FIXTURE

TWO-CONDUCTOR CABLE

SINGLE-POLE SWITCH

EXISTING RECEPTACLE (POWER SOURCE)

TWO-CONDUCTOR CABLE

TO FIXTURE

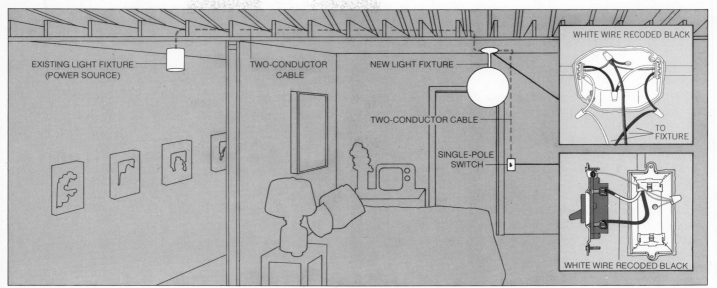

EXISTING LIGHT FIXTURE
(POWER SOURCE)

TWO-CONDUCTOR CABLE

NEW LIGHT FIXTURE

TWO-CONDUCTOR CABLE

SINGLE-POLE SWITCH

WHITE WIRE RECODED BLACK

TO FIXTURE

WHITE WIRE RECODED BLACK

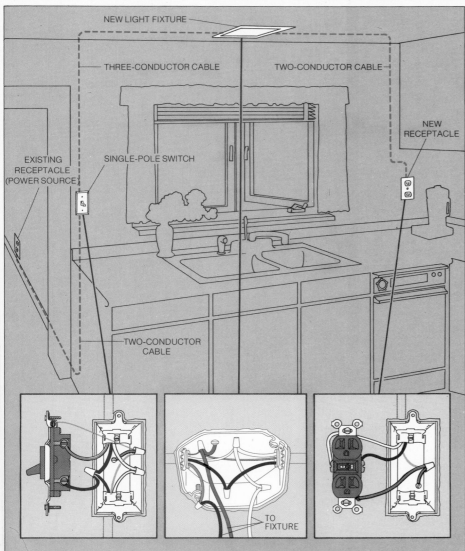

NEW LIGHT FIXTURE

THREE-CONDUCTOR CABLE

TWO-CONDUCTOR CABLE

NEW RECEPTACLE

EXISTING RECEPTACLE (POWER SOURCE)

SINGLE-POLE SWITCH

TWO-CONDUCTOR CABLE

TO FIXTURE

A switch loop. With cable running first to the light fixture, then to the switch, the fixture wiring (inset, top) is called middle-of-the-run and the switch wiring is end-of-the-run, or a switch loop (inset, bottom). Two-conductor cable with ground is used throughout.

At the new fixture, the incoming white neutral wire is joined to the white fixture wire. The hot wire must carry power to the switch, and then back to the fixture. Therefore, the black wire of the incoming cable is joined to the white outgoing wire, to supply power to the switch, and the black outgoing wire, bringing power from the switch, is connected to the black fixture wire. At the switch, the white wire is fastened to one terminal and the black wire to the other; these wires form the loop that carries power to the switch and back to the light. Be sure to indicate the function of the white wire by coding it black at both the switch and ceiling box.

A combination circuit. This circuit runs from an existing hallway receptacle to a switch-controlled light and an unswitched new receptacle. To provide a switched hot wire for the light and an unswitched one for the receptacle, a three-conductor cable runs from the switch to the light.

At the switch, the neutral and grounding wires of the incoming cable are connected as in middle-of-the-run wiring (page 302). The black wire of the incoming cable is connected with a jumper to the switch and the black wire of the three-conductor cable; this wire runs directly to the receptacle. The red wire of the three-conductor cable carries power from the switch to the black fixture wire: the white wire of the three-conductor cable is joined to the white fixture wire and the white wire running to the receptacle. The receptacle wiring is end-of-the-run (page 301).

303

Wiring New Three-Way Switches

A pair of three-way switches, controlling a light from two locations, is more than a mere frill. Stairway lights should always have switches both upstairs and down. Lights in long hallways are best controlled from either end, and you will never have to enter a dark garage or leave a garage light burning if there are switches in both the house and garage.

How three-way switches are installed depends on the relationships of the existing circuit to be tapped for the power source, the switches themselves and the light they control. Three common arrangements are shown here—in a stairway, a dining room and a garage. The variation you choose will depend on the construction of your house and on a power source for the new wiring.

Turn off the power at the service panel *(page 11)*. If a power source is available in an attic, it is easier to run cable to the light fixture and then on to the switches *(below)*. If you take power from a basement, you may decide to run cable first to the switches and then to the fixture *(opposite, top)*. When tapping power from a baseboard outlet, the wiring arrangement at the bottom of the opposite page is often the most convenient.

Three-conductor cable—black and red hot wires plus a white neutral wire—is required for part of a three-way switching circuit, which part depending on the circuit arrangement used. In many wiring variations, white wires serve as hot wires in a three-way switch loop; be sure to recode these wires black, so that they cannot be mistaken for neutral wires. The terminals in three-way switches vary in patterns. Make the tests shown on page 306 to label the terminals. When running three-conductor cable, you often need more wires in an outlet box than the National Electrical Code permits; if necessary, install a larger box or gang two boxes together.

From light to switch to switch. For the stairway light below, controlled by a pair of three-way switches, a two-conductor cable runs from the power source to the light fixture. Another two-conductor cable runs from the light fixture to the upstairs switch, and a three-conductor cable runs from the upstairs switch to the downstairs switch. The only neutral white wire in the circuit is the one in the cable from the power source; all the other white wires are part of a large switch loop and are therefore hot wires that should be coded black.

At the light fixture, connect the white wire of the incoming cable to the fixture, the incoming black wire to the white wire to the switch. At the upstairs switch, connect the incoming white wire to the black wire of the three-conductor cable, the incoming black wire to the common terminal of the switch, and the outgoing red and white wires to the traveler terminals *(page 306)*. At the downstairs switch, connect the black wire to the common terminal, and the red and white wires to the traveler terminals. Connect all grounding wires to each other, to the metal outlet boxes and to the grounding terminals on the switches.

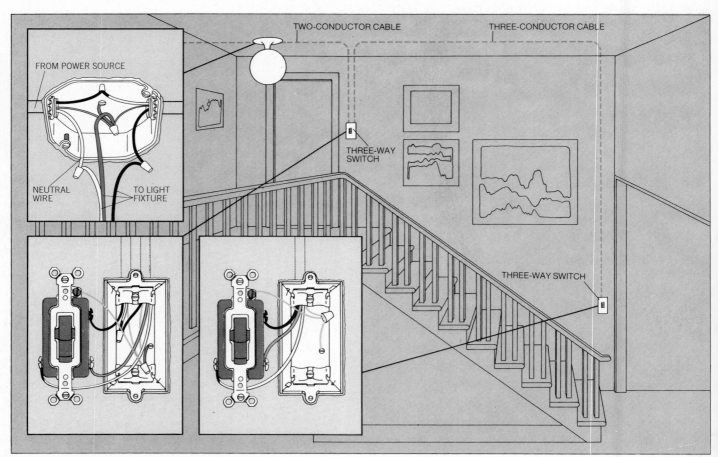

FROM POWER SOURCE

NEUTRAL WIRE

TO LIGHT FIXTURE

TWO-CONDUCTOR CABLE

THREE-CONDUCTOR CABLE

THREE-WAY SWITCH

THREE-WAY SWITCH

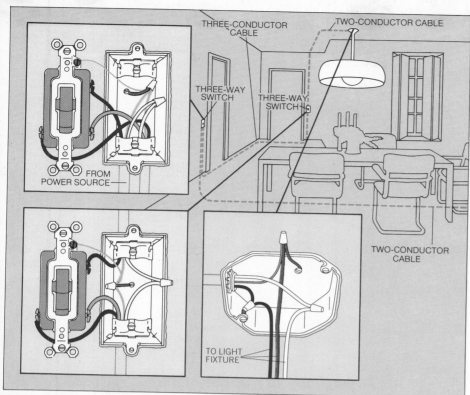

THREE-CONDUCTOR CABLE

TWO-CONDUCTOR CABLE

THREE-WAY SWITCH

THREE-WAY SWITCH

FROM POWER SOURCE

TWO-CONDUCTOR CABLE

TO LIGHT FIXTURE

From switch to switch to light. From a power source in the basement under this dining room, a two-conductor cable runs to the first three-way switch *(left)*, a three-conductor cable runs from the first to the second switch, and a two-conductor cable from the second switch to the overhead light fixture. In this wiring arrangement, the white wire in all three cables is neutral and needs no recoding.

At the first switch, join the two white wires with a wire cap; connect the incoming black wire to the common terminal of the switch *(page 306)*, and the outgoing black and red wires to the traveler terminals. At the second switch, connect the incoming red and black wires to the traveler terminals, join the white wires and fasten the outgoing black wire to the common terminal. Connect the black and white wires to the light fixture. Join all grounding wires to each other and to the boxes. The fixture grounding wire (bare or green-insulated) is simply spliced with the cable grounding wires and grounding jumper in a wire cap.

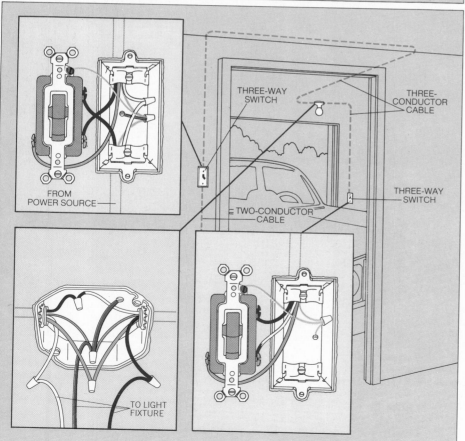

THREE-WAY SWITCH

THREE-CONDUCTOR CABLE

FROM POWER SOURCE

TWO-CONDUCTOR CABLE

THREE-WAY SWITCH

TO LIGHT FIXTURE

From switch to light to switch. In a circuit extended from a house to a garage, a two-conductor cable runs from the power source to the house switch, a three-conductor cable from the house switch to the light fixture, and a three-conductor cable from the fixture to the garage switch. The white wire running from the power source to the light fixture is neutral; beyond the fixture, the white wire is used as a hot wire in a switch loop and should be coded black.

At the house switch, connect the incoming black wire to the common terminal *(page 306)*, join the two neutral wires with a wire cap and fasten the black and red wires of the outgoing cable to the traveler terminals. At the fixture, connect the incoming white wire to the fixture, join the two red wires, join the incoming black wire to the outgoing white wire and connect the outgoing black wire to the fixture. At the garage switch, fasten the black wire to the common terminal, the red and white wires to the traveler terminals. Join grounding wires to each other and to the boxes. The fixture grounding wire (bare or green-insulated) is simply spliced with the cable grounding wires and grounding jumper in a wire cap.

Replacing a Three-Way or Four-Way Switch

If you are replacing a three-way switch because it is defective, you must first determine which of the components is the faulty one. Check three-way switches with a continuity tester as shown in the drawings at bottom.

However, when a four-way switch is used in conjunction with a pair of three-way switches (*shown opposite*), you will have to remove all of the cover plates to determine which of the devices are three-way switches and which is the four-way. A three-way switch has three terminals: a dark-colored one, the common terminal, and two lighter-colored terminals for traveler wires. (On back-wired three-way switches the common terminal is marked COM, or COMMON.) A four-way switch has four brass terminals for traveler wires connecting it to three-way switches. If both three-way switches check out satisfactorily, then you will know that the four-way switch is defective and should be replaced.

Before you put a new switch in, pay close attention to the way the wires are connected to the old switch. Like single-pole switches, the three- and four-way switches interrupt only the hot wire. You may find black, red and white wires connected to either type of switch, but all of them are hot wires regardless of color. White wires that are connected to either switch should be coded black as shown in the drawing at top. Other wires passing through the box go to other devices and should not be disconnected when replacing the switch.

Quiet-action and mercury types are available as replacements for both three- and four-way switches, and there are also three-way switches equipped with lighted handles, dimmer controls and pilot lights that glow when the power is on.

Replacing a three-way switch. Shut off the power to the circuit and without disconnecting the wires remove the switch from its box. Double-check that power is off by touching one probe of a voltage tester to each of the three switch terminals in turn, while the other probe is touching the grounded metal box. Before disconnecting the wires, use a piece of masking tape to designate the wire that is attached to the common terminal—it is usually black or copper-colored, but is always darker than the traveler terminals. Disconnect all three wires. Then connect the wires to the new switch, attaching the marked wire to the dark-colored common terminal. Either traveler wire can be connected to either traveler terminal.

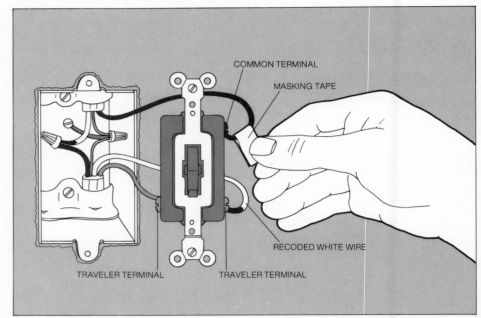

COMMON TERMINAL

MASKING TAPE

RECODED WHITE WIRE

TRAVELER TERMINAL   TRAVELER TERMINAL

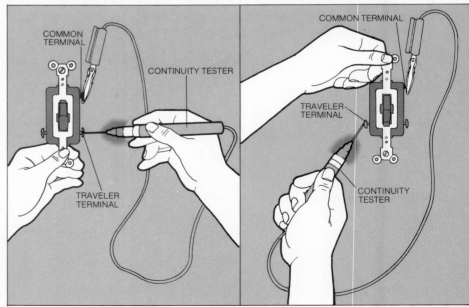

COMMON TERMINAL

CONTINUITY TESTER

TRAVELER TERMINAL

COMMON TERMINAL

TRAVELER TERMINAL

CONTINUITY TESTER

Testing three-way switches. To find which of a pair of three-way switches is faulty, shut off the power (*page 11*), disconnect one switch (*drawing, top*), and attach the clip of a continuity tester (*page 44*) to the common terminal. Place the tester probe on one traveler terminal (*above, left*) and move the switch toggle up and down. The tester should light when the toggle is in only one position, either up or down. Leaving the toggle in the position that showed continuity, touch the probe to the other traveler terminal (*above*). The tester should not light in this position, but should light when the toggle is flipped to the opposite position. If the switch passes both these tests it is good; reconnect it, then remove and check the other switch in the same manner.

The Final Touch: Patching Holes

Installing new wiring usually leaves holes in walls and ceilings. They may be as small as a 1/8-inch test hole or as big as the gap left by a box opening cut in the wrong place. In all but exceptional cases, a simple repair restores the surface to its original condition.

The method depends upon the size of the hole and the composition of the surface. Using spackling compound to fill test holes in plaster or plasterboard; in wood, use plastic wood that matches the wall. For slightly bigger openings such as the open seams around a newly installed box, use plastic wood or patching plaster but stuff the openings with steel wool to support the patches *(right, top)*.

Holes up to 3 or 4 inches, such as the access holes used for running cable or for an opening made by mistake, are patched with new sections of plasterboard, plaster or wood. If the hole lies directly over a stud or joist, you can use these structural beams as a support for the patch *(right, bottom)*. To fill an opening between two studs or joists, you will have to make a backing section of plasterboard, wood or—for a plaster wall—metal screening.

Even large holes in plasterboard are easy to repair. Expand the hole by removing an entire section around it as far as the nearest studs or joists, then replace the section with new plasterboard. Big holes in plaster or wood paneling, however, may require repair by a professional—plaster patches tend to crack and crumble, and wood ones must be applied skillfully in order to avoid gaps. Before working on the patching, be sure to turn off power to the circuit *(page 11)*.

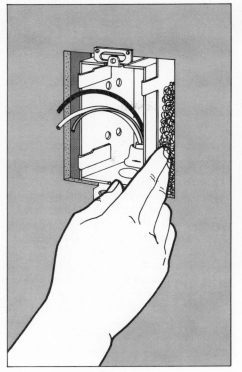

Filling the Gaps around an Outlet Box

Making a steel-wool backing. Turn off power to the circuit at the service panel *(page 11)*. Pack handfuls of steel wool into the gaps at the edges of the box. In a wood surface, fill the gaps flush to the surface with matching plastic wood and sand the patch smooth. In plaster or plasterboard, mix a batch of thick patching plaster and moisten the outer edges of the gaps. Beginning at these edges and working toward the box, apply plaster to a point just below the surface with a putty knife. Let the plaster dry, then fill the gaps with plasterboard joint cement, and smooth the cement about 2 inches outside the gaps with a broad-bladed tool called a taping knife. Allow several days for the patch to dry, then sand.

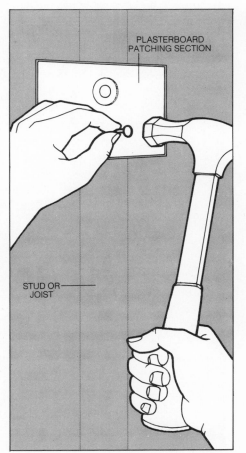

PLASTERBOARD PATCHING SECTION

STUD OR JOIST

Repairing Holes at Studs and Joists

Making a plasterboard patch. In a plasterboard wall or ceiling, measure the exact dimensions of the hole and cut a new section of plasterboard 1/8 inch smaller. Insert the patch with the lighter side facing outward and attach it to the stud or joist with two plasterboard nails. Drive each nail flush with the surface, then gently hammer the nail once more to drive the head a fraction of an inch below the surface so that the crowned face of the hammer makes a small depression, or dimple, in the plasterboard. Fill the cracks around the edges of the patch and cover the dimpled nails with plasterboard joint cement.

In a plaster-and-lath surface, apply enough layers of patching plaster to fill the hole almost completely, let the plaster dry, then fill the hole flush to the surrounding surface with joint cement. When the surface is dry, sand it smooth.

In a wood surface, cut a matching piece of wood to fit the hole and nail it to the stud or joist with finishing nails. Countersink the nails. Fill the countersunk holes and the cracks around the patch with plastic wood, and sand smooth.

Cooling a House without Using Refrigeration

On a sweltering summer day, a house may seem uncomfortably warm even though the air conditioner works constantly—and expensively—to cool it. In the same weather a house without an air conditioner will have a lower electric bill but may be unbearable to live in. For both houses, the best solution to the problems of cooling and its costs may well be a system of attic fans and vents.

In the air-conditioned house, a roof fan could suck hot air out of the attic, or a fan in an attic gable could draw cooler outside air across the attic from a vent in the opposite gable. In a house without air conditioning, a fan mounted in an attic floor (pages 312-313) will pull cool outdoor air into the entire house to cool both the living quarters and the attic.

Attic ventilation in an air-conditioned house can be almost as important as the air conditioner itself. Air trapped in an unvented attic may get as hot as 150°. This heat seeps to the living quarters below, making the air conditioner work harder, but to less effect. An attic temperature of 135° may force the air conditioner below to run continuously to keep the living quarters at 78°. Aided by a roof fan that cuts the attic temperature to 95°, the same

air conditioner may run only intermittently—and the bill for its power may drop by as much as 30 percent.

The roof fan below is housed in an assembly mounted over a hole in the roof. The assembly includes more than a motor and blades: It has flashing to prevent water from leaking through the hole, a bubble-like cover that protects the fan motor from rain and snow, and a screen to keep out birds and large insects. A thermostat turns the fan on and off at preset temperatures that can be adjusted to meet your needs.

When installing a roof fan, be sure to follow the basic rules for safety in high places (pages 340-345); also follow all manufacturer's instructions for the unit. The installation itself is both safe and easy in an asphalt shingle roof, but may split or break wood or slate shingles and is impractical in a metal roof. As an alternative you can install a gable fan, relatively slow in cooling an attic but safer to install in any house. If the attic gable has no vent, the fan is mounted over a special vent with louvers that open by air pressure, then close when the fan turns off (page 311). If you already have gable vents you can install the fan over one of these vents (page 311).

The capacity of the roof or gable fan you install, measured in cubic feet per minute (cfm) at "static air pressure," depends on the size of your attic and the color of your roof (a dark roof absorbs more heat than a light one, and calls for a more powerful fan). To determine the minimum cfm, multiply your attic floor area by 0.7, then add 15 per cent for a dark roof. For example, an attic measuring 2,000 square feet requires either a 1,400 cfm fan under a light roof, or a 1,610 cfm fan under a dark roof. (If your fan is rated at "free air delivery" rather than static air pressure, discount its cfm rating by 25 per cent to arrive at the right figure.)

Whatever the size of the fan you use, your attic must be equipped with vents—ideally, soffit vents at regular intervals under the eaves for a roof fan, both gable and soffit vents for a gable fan. For every 150 square feet of attic-floor area, install at least 1 square foot of "net vent area" that is, of a vent that offers no more resistance to the flow of air than 1/2-inch screening. Vents with metal louvers call for 1 1/2 times the net vent area, with wood louvers, twice as much.

Fitting a Fan into a Roof

1 **Positioning the fan.** Prepare to work safely (page 340). Assemble the fan and carry it up to that part of the house roof that faces away from the street, and near one of the gables. Using a piece of wood as a guide, set the assembly at a point where the top of the fan cover is level with the roof ridge. Measure the distance from the ridge to the center of the fan.

In the attic, locate the two central rafters of the back roof—midway between gables—and, measuring down from the roof peak, locate the point halfway between them that corresponds to the desired fan position. Drive a long nail up through the roof at this point.

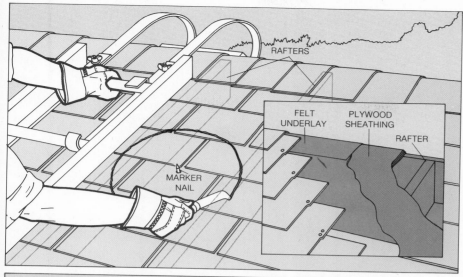

2 **Removing shingles and underlay.** On the outside of the roof locate the marker nail and, using it as a center, mark a circle on the asphalt shingles about 4 inches wider than the hole specified for the fan in the manufacturer's instructions. With a linoleum knife, cut along the outline of the circle until you reach the board or plywood sheathing underneath. Remove the nails holding the shingles and underlay in place, and discard the free shingles and underlay.

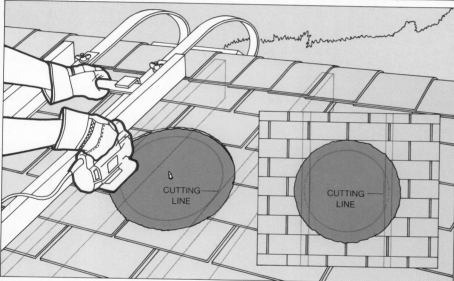

3 **Cutting through the sheathing.** Using a piece of string tied to the marker nail at one end and a pencil at the other, draw the outline of the hole for the fan on the wood sheathing, then cut the hole out with a saber or a keyhole saw. Caution: The hole specified by the manufacturer may be just wider than the distance between the two adjoining rafters; if so, do not cut through the rafters but saw along their inner edges *(inset)*.

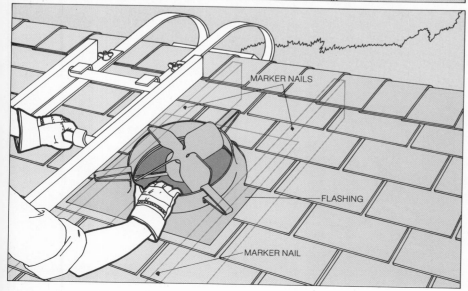

4 **Installing the fan housing.** From the outside, hammer four nails partway into the roof to indicate the centers of the adjoining rafters just above the area to be covered by the fan flashing, and about 6 inches below. Apply roofing cement liberally to the sheathing you have exposed and to the underside of the fan flashing. Remove the fan cover so that you can see through the hole in the fan housing, and slip the flashing up under the shingles until the housing hole lies directly over the roof hole; if necessary, use a pry bar to remove any shingle nails that bar the way. Using the marker nails as guides, drive galvanized steel nails through the flashing and into the rafters below at 3-inch intervals. Remove the marker nails and seal the holes left by them with roofing cement.

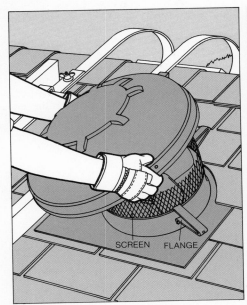

5 **Installing the screen and cover.** Slide the cylindrical screen into the fan opening and secure it to the hooks on the sides of the opening. Set the cover over the opening and bolt it to the flanges at the rim of the housing.

6 **Installing soffit vents.** Calculate the vent area that you will need for your attic *(page 308)* and the number of soffit vents—most vents are 8 by 16 inches or smaller—required to make up this area. Install the vents at regular intervals under the eaves on both sides of the house. To install a vent, hold it against the underside of the eave midway between the outside wall and the edge of the eave, and midway between two of the lookout beams that support the soffit (you can locate a lookout by the exposed nails that hold the soffit to it). Outline the screened area of the vent on the soffit and cut out the outlined area with a saber or keyhole saw. Insert the vent into the opening from below and screw it to the soffit through its flange holes.

7 **Wiring the fan.** In the attic, fasten the fan thermostat to a rafter, with its control dial readily accessible and the temperature-sensing element on its back exposed to the air. To power the fan you must use a 120-volt junction box in the attic or a receptacle on an inside wall in a room below. For the latter location, drill a 3/4-inch hole through the top plates directly above the receptacle. Turn off the power *(page 11)* to the receptacle; remove it from the outlet box. Fish cable from the thermostat to the receptacle through the hole in the top plates; clamp one end of the cable to the thermostat, the other end to the receptacle outlet box. Using wire caps, connect the black cable wire to the black thermostat wire, the white cable wire to the white thermostat wire; connect the bare wire to the grounding screw. To connect the other end of the cable to an end-of-the-run receptacle, attach the black and white cable wires to the proper free terminals; join the bare wire to the existing bare wire with a wire cap, run a jumper wire from this wire cap to the receptacle grounding screw and another jumper wire to the hex-head bonding screw on the back of a metal outlet box. To connect the cable to a middle-of-the-run receptacle *(inset)*, remove a black wire from its terminal and join it to both the new black wire *(dash lines)* and a black jumper wire *(dash lines)* with a wire cap; attach the jumper wire to the terminal. Connect the new white wire *(dash lines)* in the same way. Attach the new grounding wire *(dash lines)* as shown.

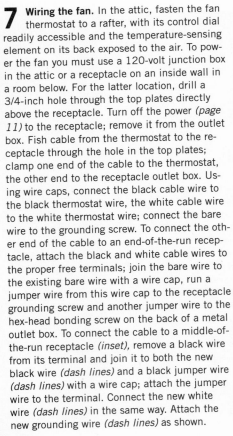

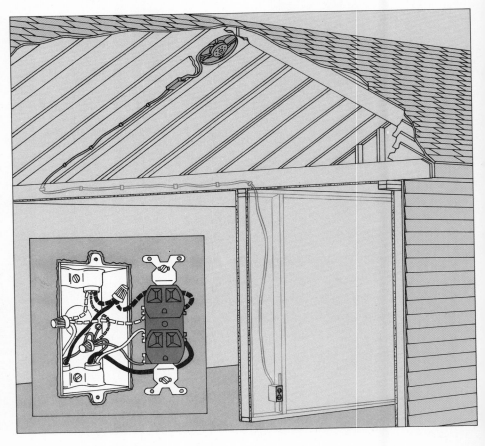

Opening a Gable End for an Attic

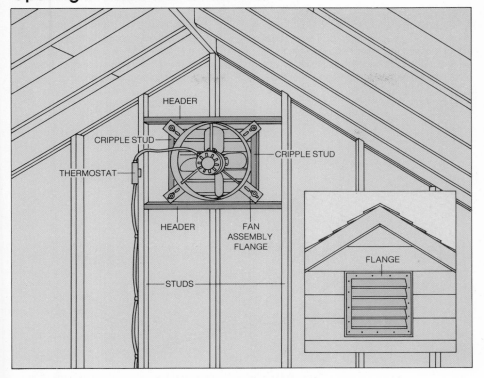

HEADER

CRIPPLE STUD

THERMOSTAT

CRIPPLE STUD

HEADER

FAN ASSEMBLY FLANGE

STUDS

FLANGE

Mounting Fans on Existing Gable Vents

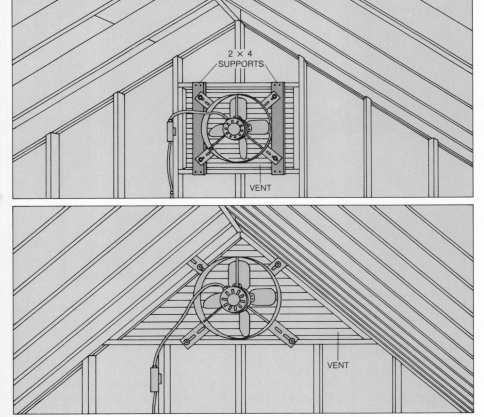

2 × 4 SUPPORTS

VENT

VENT

Cutting a hole for the vent. Inside the attic, outline the hole for the fan vent as high as possible at the center of the gable. In a house with clapboard siding, cut out the outlined area, including the central stud, then cut an additional 1 1/2 inches from the stud above and below the opening. Cut two 2-by-4 headers to fit horizontally between the flanking studs and nail them to the cut stud above and below the opening and to the flanking studs. Cut two cripple studs to fit between the headers and nail the cripples to the headers along the edges of the opening.

Hold the fan assembly in the framed opening with the oil holes of the motor pointing upward; nail the four assembly flanges to the cripple studs. Screw the thermostat to a stud; wire it to a receptacle *(opposite, Step 7)*. Outside the attic, insert the fan vent in the opening and nail it to the siding through the flange *(inset)*; caulk the edge of the vent flange with silicone rubber sealant. Install a standard vent, framed and caulked in the same way in the opposite gable. In a brick wall, drill holes from inside the attic at the corners of the vent area. Outside the attic, connect the holes with a brick chisel and hammer; remove the bricks within the outline. Secure the vents with plug anchors and screws.

Over a rectangular vent. Set the fan at the center of the vent and mark the width of the fan cylinder on the headers above and below. Cut two 2-by-4 supports to fit the vertical distance between the marks, and nail them in place with their inside edges flush to the marks. Screw the ventilator fan to these supports and the thermostat to a convenient stud; connect the thermostat to a receptacle *(opposite, Step 7)*. If the gable vent at the other end of the attic is too small to serve the fan *(page 308)*, add soffit vents *(opposite, Step 6)*.

Over a triangular vent. If the fan flanges extend to the wood vent frame, screw the assembly directly to the frame. Otherwise, install vertical 2-by-4 supports as you would for a square vent, and attach the assembly to these supports.

A King-Sized Fan to Cool a House

A home without air conditioning can be made more comfortable by a single powerful fan, mounted on the floor joists of an attic and controlled by a switch downstairs. The fan pulls cool, fresh air into the house through open windows and drives hot attic air out of the house through gable and soffit vents. Less expensive than central air conditioning, the fan is also much cheaper to run.

The fan should be centrally located, or near a stairwell if there is one. A louvered shutter in the ceiling below automatically closes when the fan is off, sealing off hot summer air. The fan assembly itself houses blades from 24 to 42 inches long and rests on a gasket to reduce vibration.

The size of the assembly determines the construction of the wood frame that supports it. When the spacing of the joists matches the size of the fan blades, the frame consists of a square formed by two joists and two headers. When the assembly is wider than the space between two joists, the frame is more complex *(right and on the following pages).*

For effective cooling, a fan should make one complete change of air per minute in a house in the South, or one change every two minutes in the North, West and Canada. To determine how much air must be moved in your house, multiply total floor area by ceiling height and subtract 10 percent for closets and other unused space. This figure gives you the net air volume of the house and is the minimum air-moving capacity, measured in cubic feet per minute (cfm), required of a fan in the South; a fan elsewhere needs half that capacity. For example, a house with a net air volume of 12,000 cubic feet requires a 12,000 cfm fan in the South, a 6,000 cfm fan elsewhere.

The fan you buy should have two safety devices: an automatic shutoff for an overheated fan, and a safety control that shuts the fan down and closes the shutter's louvers to seal off the attic during a fire.

Ask the dealer for the correct attic vent area for your fan and calculate the net area for metal or wood-louvered vents *(page 308).* Methods for installing vents are shown on pages 310 and 311.

Installing a Fan in the Attic Floor

1 Positioning the fan. Place the shutter upside down on a sheet of cardboard, trace the outline of the area that will fit into the ceiling and, using a utility knife, cut this piece out as a template. Drive a nail through the ceiling at the location you have chosen for the fan. In the attic, set the template over the nail with one edge flush to the inside edge of a joist. Mark the corners of the template on the surface below, and drill small holes at these points.

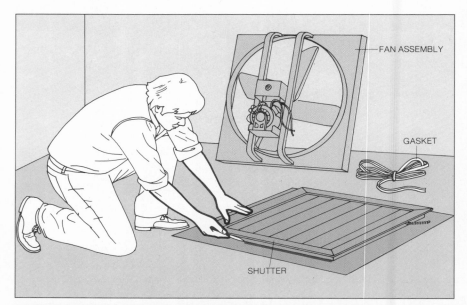

FAN ASSEMBLY

GASKET

SHUTTER

JOIST

CEILING OPENING

2 Cutting the opening. If your roof has trussed-rafter construction, do not cut through it; call for professional advice. Otherwise, in the room below, join the four holes with straight lines to form a square outline and, wearing goggles and gloves, cut along the lines with a keyhole or saber saw. If you meet a joist, do not cut through or under; skip the joist area and resume cutting along the outline beyond the joist. Score the uncut segments of the outline with a utility knife, break up the ceiling board under the joist with a hammer and tear it away with your hands. Working in the attic, cut out the exposed joist 1 1/2 inches outside the edges of the opening. Cut through most of the joist with a circular or saber saw, then, for the last cuts, use a keyhole saw—with the handle reversed, to avoid damaging the ceiling below.

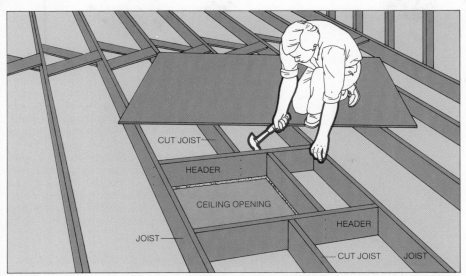

3 **Framing the opening.** Measure the distance between the uncut joists flanking the opening and cut two headers to this length, using wood the same size as the joists. Set the headers at the edges of the opening, and nail them to the sides of the uncut joists and the ends of the cut ones. To complete the frame, cut a third length of wood to fit between the headers, set it flush to the unframed edge of the opening and nail it to the headers.

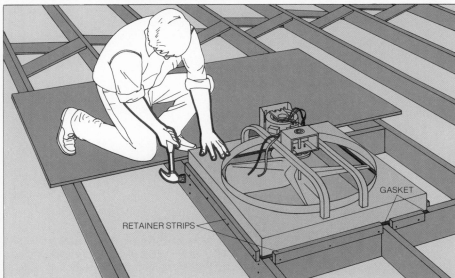

4 **Installing the fan assembly.** Follow the manufacturer's instructions that come with the fan. Set the felt or rubber gasket on the wood frame (in some models this gasket is attached to the fan assembly at the factory) and then lower the fan onto the cushioned frame. Nail 1-by-2 retainer strips to the sides of the joists and headers around the fan assembly, with about an inch of each strip projecting above the frame.

5 **Completing the job.** In the room below, adjust the spring at the side of the shutter to close the louvers gently when you hold them open and release them. Working from a stepladder, lift the vent into the ceiling opening and mark the positions of the screw holes in the shutter flange. Drill pilot holes at these points and screw the shutter through the ceiling to the frame above.

Have an electrician complete the job: in the attic, connecting the black and white fan motor wires to a cable in an outlet box fastened to a nearby joist or header, then running this cable from the box to the basement service panel for a new 20-amp, 120-volt circuit connection. Finally, ask the electrician to install an on-off or a timer switch on a convenient wall in the living quarters.

A Clothes Drier Exhaust Duct

A clothes drier dumps 8 or 9 pounds of vaporized water into a laundry room with every average load—enough moisture to cause damage in most homes. To discharge this exhaust outdoors, you hook up a special clothes-drier vent before you set the drier into its permanent position. Such vents come in kits that consist of a flexible plastic duct, clamps and a hood vent pipe. Make sure you get one the right size to fit your drier's exhaust outlets, and get a vent pipe to suit the installation you plan.

Driers can be vented through a window *(right)*, with a 3-inch-long pipe or through a wall *(opposite)*, with a 12-inch-long pipe. The method you choose will depend on the design and construction of your house as well as where you put the clothes drier. The window vent is easiest to install. Simply replace one pane of glass with a vent plate bored to hole the pipe. Prebored vent plates are available in transparent plastic or in aluminum. However, you can make your own out of a scrap of 1/4-inch exterior plywood and then paint it the same color as the window frame.

If you do not have a convenient window, or if your windows are close to plants that the exhaust would affect, you need a wall vent. This requires making a large hole through the foundation if it is made of concrete block, or through the siding and header joist if the foundation is cast-in-place concrete. Either job is fairly simple with an electric drill.

For efficient venting, the duct should always be as short and straight as possible. Although a plastic duct can bend to snake around pipes or joists, and extra units may be added for stretches of more than the kit's usual 20 feet, loops and long distances slow down the air flow and may cause the duct to clog with lint.

PLASTIC VENT PLATE

VENT PIPE

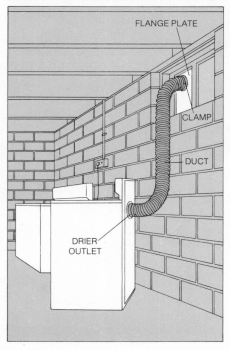

FLANGE PLATE

CLAMP

DUCT

DRIER OUTLET

Installing a Vent in a Window

1 Attaching the vent plate. Chisel out the putty around one pane of glass, pry out the glazing points and remove the pane. Wearing goggles, use a hacksaw to cut the vent plate to fit the window opening. Then, working from outside the house, set the plate into the opening. Anchor the plate with glazing points and seal the edges with glazing compound. Fasten the window closed so that it cannot be opened accidentally. To make a plywood vent plate, use the pipe as a template for drawing a circle of the required size on the wood. Cut out the circle with a keyhole saw, then trim the plywood to fit the window opening. Follow the procedures above for removing the glass and installing the wooden plate.

2 Insert the vent pipe. Slide off the flange plate from the back of a 3-inch-long vent pipe. Working from outside the house, push the pipe through the hole in the vent plate until the back of the hood is flush with the plate.

3 Attaching the duct. From inside the house, slip the flange plate over the back of the pipe and press it firmly against the vent plate. Place a clamp on one end of the duct, then fit the duct over the pipe and anchor it by tightening the clamp. Move the drier to its permanent place and extend the duct to the exhaust outlet on the drier. Use scissors and wire cutters to cut off excess duct. Slide a clamp around the loose end of the duct, then slip the duct over the drier exhaust outlet and tighten the clamp.

To prevent the duct from stretching or sagging, anchor it with strings tied to nails in the wall or ceiling joists, or with perforated metal straps that are held in shape by nuts and bolts and nailed in place.

Installing a Vent in Masonry

1 **Making the opening.** Locate the exhaust opening close to the drier but away from pipes and shrubs, and outline it with masking tape, indoors and out, in a circle the same diameter as the vent pipe. Wearing goggles, use a 1/2-inch masonry boring bit in an electric drill to bore several holes in the circle from outside, penetrating to the hollow core. Knock out the material between the holes with a cold chisel and hammer. Chip away the edges of the opening until it is large enough for the pipe. Then bore and chisel out the opening on the inside of the block.

2 **Sealing the vent pipe.** Spread a 1-inch band of mortar around the exterior opening in the concrete block. Slide the interior flange plate off a 12-inch-long vent pipe and spread mortar around the pipe behind the hood. Push the pipe into the opening, pressing the hood in firmly to squeeze out the excess mortar; wipe it off. Working inside the house, clean away any mortar inside the pipe. Spread mortar around the interior opening in the block, then slip the flange onto the pipe and press it on firmly. Wipe up the excess. Attach the duct to the pipe and drier (*opposite, bottom*).

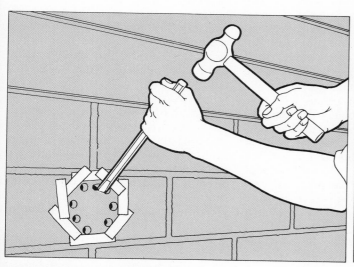

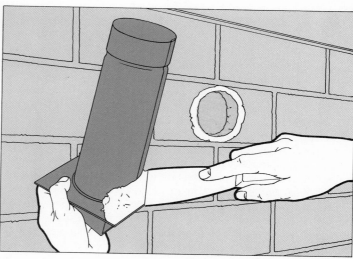

Installing a Vent in Siding

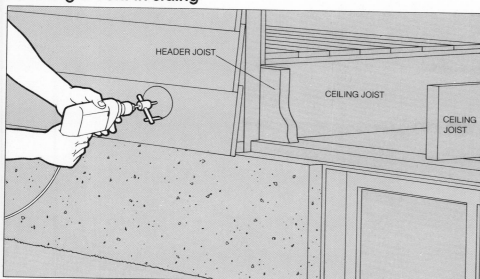

HEADER JOIST

CEILING JOIST

CEILING JOIST

1 **Cutting the opening.** Use the pipe as a template to draw a circle on the siding over the header joist but between the ceiling joists. Then cut the opening through the siding, through the sheathing and through the header joist. As you cut through each layer, remove the material so you can get at the next layer easily. The hole can be cut by drilling a starter hole and using a keyhole saw for wood, or a saber saw with a metal-cutting blade for aluminum or vinyl siding. A circle cutter in a 3/8- or 1/2-inch electric drill is faster, but practice using it before you try it on the wall.

2 **Sealing the pipe.** To weatherproof the opening, seal it all around inside and outside with butyl rubber caulk or silicone rubber applied the same way as mortar in a concrete-block installation (*top, right*).

Extending the Flow of a Forced-Air System

If your house has forced warm-air heating, minor surgery on the existing ductwork can bring heat to a new living space or make an old one warmer. In some cases you need only rebalance the system or add a register—a new opening into the room. In others, you may have to extend existing ducts or run new ones. Most of the work is elementary carpentry, and the metal of ducts and connections is cut and shaped like very stiff cardboard (opposite).

Both registers and ducts must be installed according to a plan. A furnace and its ducts resemble a tree trunk and its branches. Some provide the supply, carrying warm air to the rest of the house. Others are returns, taking cool air back to the furnace to be heated. Before you modify an existing branch or add a new branch to the system, find out where all the ducts run and what they do.

Start at the furnace. While it is running, touch the ducts connected directly to it; supply ducts will feel warm, returns cold. Other exposed ducts in basement or attic are identified the same way.

Now go to the registers. Identify the ones that blow warm air in and the ones that suck cool air out. Remove the registers and examine the spaces behind them. Each register connects either directly to a duct or to a fitting called a boot that makes the duct connection; usually, you can see whether the duct runs down to the register, up to it, or horizontally. For a final check on the routes of supply ducts, cool your house to 50° on a cold day, then set the thermometer at 70°. After about 10 minutes feel the ceilings, walls and floors, tracing the warm surfaces that reveal hidden ducts.

With the map of your system completed, you can choose the points at which to tap it with new registers or extend it with new ducts. Adding new registers to existing supply or return ducts (pages 318-319) can make a room more comfortable in any weather. A return register added to a room that does not already have one can improve air circulation in a heating system. (Returns are not installed in bathrooms and kitchens to avoid spreading moisture through the house.)

In a house with a combined heating-cooling system, a high or low supply register added to complement an existing one enables you to match the circulation to the season. Close the low register in summer and cool air flows down into the room; close the high register in winter and warm air rises from the low one.

Adding new ducts (pages 320-325)—usually to heat a finished attic, a basement room or an addition—is simple if you run the new ducts in accessible locations. As you map your existing system, locate boxed in places—a closet, for example, or a suspended ceiling—and use these spaces for duct runs to save the work of building enclosures.

Such alterations to an existing system have their limitations, particularly in extensions to new living spaces. If your house now seems chilly in winter and your furnace runs almost constantly, it may not be able to heat additional space efficiently. But most heating plants have a little reserve capacity that is rarely called upon—in the average forced warm-air system, the reserve is enough to heat two medium-sized bedrooms, or a basement recreation room plus a small attic bedroom, or a garage converted to living space—and all you need do to take advantage of this untapped heat is provide ducts and registers.

If you are uncertain that sufficient reserve is available, it is best to consult a heating contractor. For a modest fee, the contractor will analyze your system to make sure that your furnace and blower can handle an added load—and advise you on the best route for new ducts.

Working with Sheet Metal

Cutting a round duct with a hacksaw. An open round duct, or pipe (page 322), can be easily be shortened with a pair of tin snips, but the closed pipe shown at right must be sawed. Set the pipe, seam upward, in a snug cradle of 2-by-4s nailed on edge to a piece of plywood. Using a fine-tooth (32-teeth-per-inch) blade, saw through the seam, rotate the pipe slightly and saw again from the top down. To keep the saw from binding, continue to rotate the pipe each time the saw cut penetrates about 1 inch.

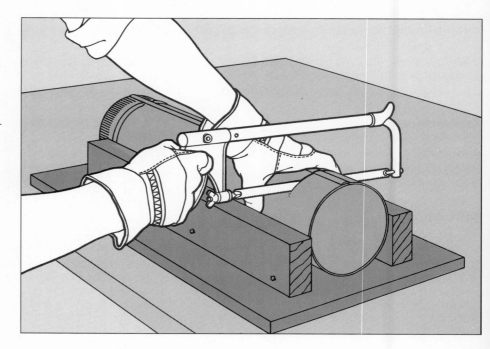

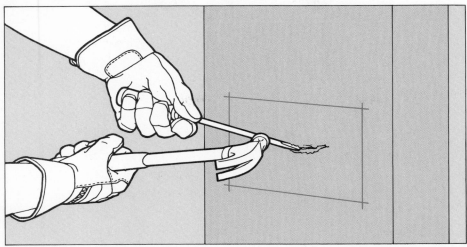

Starting a hole. Press the edge of an old, large screwdriver blade against the duct near the center of the hole you wish to make. Hit the screwdriver shank with a hammer to make a hole large enough to admit the tips of a pair of tin snips.

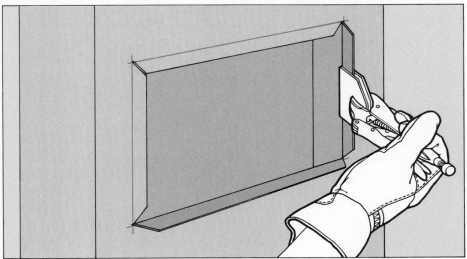

Making a flange. In ductwork, flanges are often necessary in the side or at the end of rectangular duct. (In round duct, collars serve in place of flanges.) To make a flanged opening in the side of a rectangular duct, first outline the hole dimensions on the duct. Then mark a second hole 1 inch inside the first and cut it out, using the techniques above. If the hole is rectangular, snip diagonal cuts in the corners, stopping at the outline. If the hole is circular, make evenly spaced cuts about 1 inch apart to the outline. Fold each of the tabs formed by cutting so they are perpendicular to the duct surface.

You can bend sheet metal with your hands if you wear gloves or, if you must make several flanges, use broad-billed pliers, some of which are calibrated to set the depth of the flange *(left)*. To flange the end of a rectangular duct, snip 1 inch along the duct at the corners.

A Range of Registers

A register for every purpose. The three registers at right typify the models generally used to expand a heating-cooling system. All have vanes or fins to direct the flow of air into a room, and controls to reduce the flow or cut it off entirely.

To deliver air from overhead ducts, round registers, with wide diffusion vanes create air turbulence, so that warm air does not build up at the ceiling and leave a pool of heavier cold air near the floor. A baseboard register is most often used on an outside wall, where it warms the cold air that flows down the windows and the wall. A rectangular register can be fitted into walls, floors or ceilings. The type illustrated is best for tapping into an existing duct that lies so close to the surface that a direct connection can be made *(pages 318-319)*, as is generally the case with ducts inside walls. Ducts in the ceilings and floors may be several inches from the surface, requiring an extension box *(page 319)*.

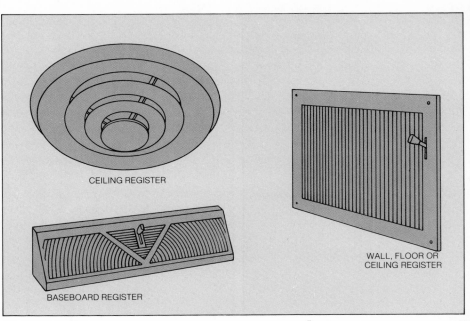

CEILING REGISTER

BASEBOARD REGISTER

WALL, FLOOR OR
CEILING REGISTER

A Direct Connection for a Rectangular Register

1 Cutting the templates. Measure the length and width of the register front, outline these dimensions on a piece of stiff cardboard, and cut out the outlined rectangle. To allow for a collar that lies within the rear edge, or shoulder, of the register, add 1/2 inch to the collar dimensions and transfer these dimensions to the cardboard. Cut out this inner rectangle and save both pieces: The hollow rectangle will serve as a template to mark the surface of the wall that covers the duct; the solid one will be used as a template to mark the metal of a duct.

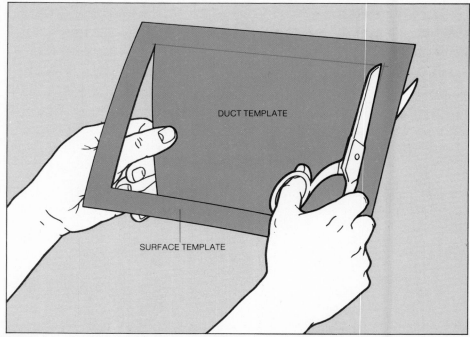

DUCT TEMPLATE

SURFACE TEMPLATE

2 Completing the template. On the metal-marking template, mark lines 1 5/8 inches in from each edge and snip out the corners. The long strips at the edges of the template are guides for flanges to support the register.

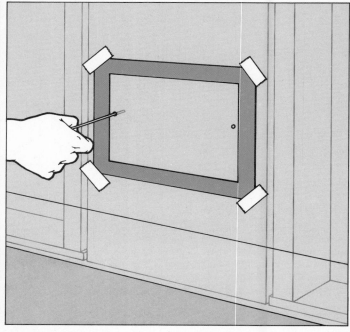

3 Cutting a hole. After you have located the duct you want to tap, set the wall template over the surface concealing it, and tape on the template. Drill 1/8-inch holes just inside the corners and probe behind the surface with a stiff wire to verify the position of the duct; if necessary, move the template to fit completely over the duct. Mark the inner outline of the template on the surface and cut out that portion with a utility knife. If necessary, patch holes later with wallboard compound.

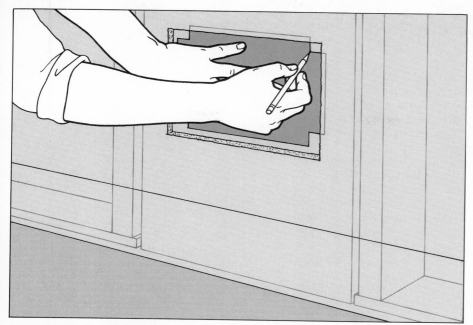

4 **Marking the duct.** Set the duct template against the duct, directly behind the opening in the wall. Mark the cutout corners of the template, then fold the template's flaps back to make a rectangle. Set the rectangle back into position against the duct, with its corners touching the points you have marked; outline the rectangle on the duct, and draw diagonal lines outward from its corners to the corners of the opening. Using these lines as guides, cut a hole and turn the flanges *(page 317)* to lie flat against the outside of the wall. Drill holes in the flanges and attach the register with sheet-metal screws.

An Extension Box for a Recessed Duct

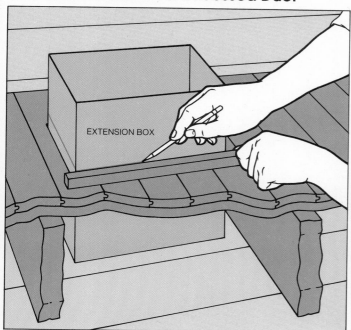

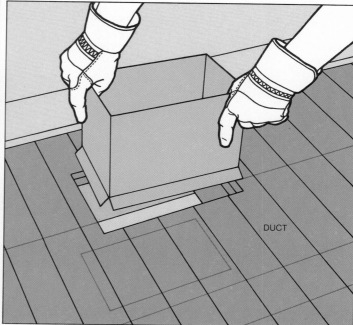

1 **Cutting the box to fit.** To connect a rectangular register to a duct running deep in the joist space of a floor or ceiling, prepare templates for the front and rear of the register and make floor and duct openings by the methods shown above, Steps 1-4. Your supplier will be able to match an open-ended extension box to the collar at the rear of the register. Stand the box on the duct and mark lines 1 inch above floor level on all four sides; a scrap of lumber 1 inch thick makes a handy guide for these marks. Trim off the metal above the marks, and form a 1-inch flange on each side as shown on page 317.

2 **Installing the register.** Invert the box, slide it down into the floor opening until it touches the duct, then flatten the flanges against the duct by pushing the box down. With a long-necked awl, punch small holes through two of the flanges and the duct. Fasten the box to the duct, using sheet-metal screws and a long-necked screwdriver. Finally, set the register in place and fasten it to the floor with wood screws.

Installing Ducts and Fittings

Adding one or two duct runs to an existing system is a matter of simple carpentry and sheet-metal work. All of the parts of a duct run are standardized and easy to hook up *(pages 320-323)*. And the carpentry part of the job is simplified when you use round ducts, run outside a wall and then concealed by a wallboard-sheathed enclosure *(pages 324-325)*, rather than attempt to fit shallow rectangular ducts between the wall studs.

Round duct, called pipe, should be at least 6 inches in diameter. Unless your system uses smaller pipes. (Narrower pipe tends to whistle when air passes through it, and it cannot handle the large volumes of air needed for air conditioning.) A combination of rigid round ducts and flexible ones, made of plastic or spring wire, will carry runs to any point in a house. For short,

sharp turns, install fittings called elbows, either rigidly set at 45° or 90° or adjustable for creating almost any angle you choose.

Your choice of a starting point for a run will depend on the pattern of your existing system *(below)*. In a radial system, runs of round duct start at the furnace warm-air plenum and radiate outward toward the rooms of the house; new runs must also take the plenum as their starting point. In an extended-plenum system, one or more large rectangular ducts run from the plenum, and ducts for individual rooms start at these main ducts; to start a run, choose a point on the extended plenum convenient to the room you plan to serve. Installation of collar fittings to start runs is illustrated opposite. The outlets, called boots, consist of short final sections, usually angled to accept a wall, floor or ceiling register.

How ducts run. No heating system necessarily resembles the one in the drawing below—but the drawing does show how new duct runs can be added to a variety of systems. In both the radial *(left)* and the extended-plenum *(right)* systems, the new runs begin with a fitting called a collar. A run may go directly to a single room *(left)* or be branched at a T or Y to serve more than one room *(right)*; in either case, each run is fitted with a damper to control warm-air flow. The elbow in the run at right is an adjustable type that can be set at any angle; rigid elbows are preset at the factory. Also available are long sections of flexible duct, like the length in the run at left, which combine easy turns with a substantial run. At the ends of the runs, "boots" preset for a variety of angles protrude into the walls or the floors in order to receive register grilles.

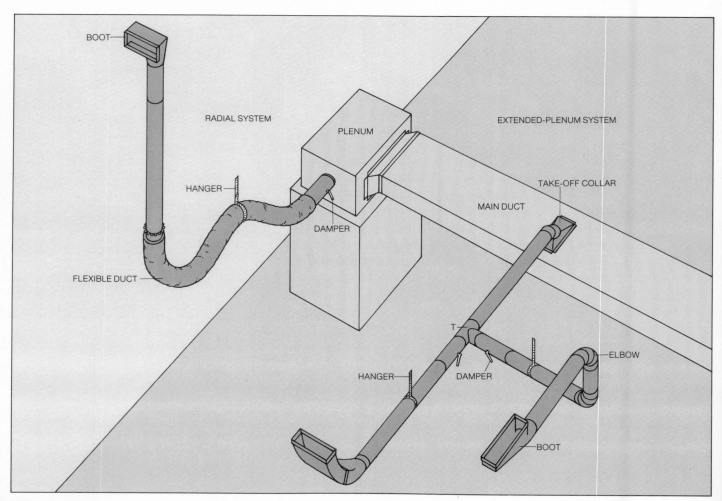

Starting a Run

A straight collar. When installing this fitting as a direct connection to a furnace plenum, wear gloves and a long-sleeved shirt. Cut a hole exactly the size of the collar *(page 317, top)* in the plenum, at least 1 inch below the top of the plenum. Slide the collar into the hole, tabbed end first, until the projecting bead around the middle of the collar meets the side of the plenum, then reach inside the collar and fold the tabs to lie flat against the inside of the plenum. The crimped outer end of the collar will connect to the plain end of the first duct section in the run.

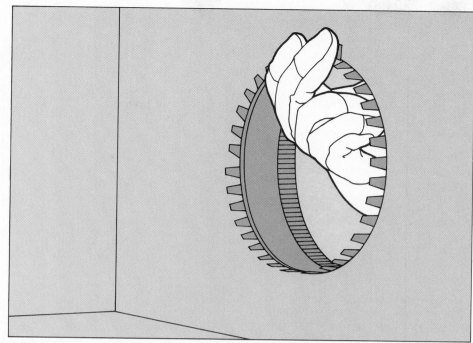

A take-off collar. A take-off is generally needed for the top or side of an extended plenum; from this point, its adjustable elbow can start a run of round duct in almost any direction, even in cramped quarters. Install a take-off—wearing gloves and a long-sleeved shirt—by cutting a rectangular hole in the plenum just big enough to admit the take-off tabs. Slide the take-off in-to the hole, tabbed end first, until the take-off flange rests upon the outside of the plenum; at this point the top of the elbow must clear the joists or ceiling above by at least 1 inch. Reach through the take-off and fold the tabs to lie flat against the inside of the plenum. Finally, on the outside of the plenum, drill or punch holes through two opposite sides of the flange and the plenum beneath it, and secure the take-off to the plenum with sheet-metal screws.

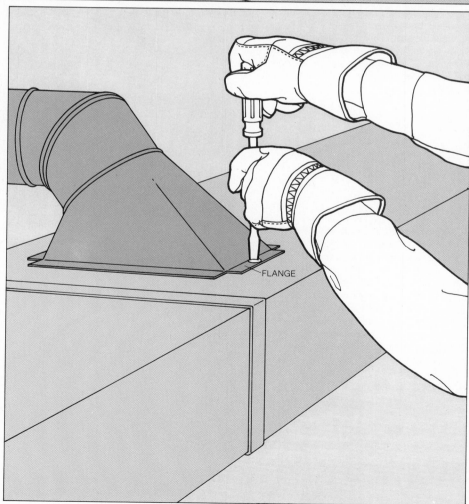

FLANGE

Assembling Duct Sections

A snap-lock assembly. Round duct is generally shipped open in nests of three to 10 sections. Before closing the seams, measure the entire duct run and shorten one section, if necessary, by snipping a length off the plain—not the crimped—end. If the snips pinch the ends flat, pry them open again with a screwdriver.

The type illustrated is assembled by snapping a tongue into a slot (another type is described below). Wearing gloves, start at either end of the duct section and press the duct into a cylinder, then thread the tongue into the slot until the seam clicks shut (inset). Repeat the process at 1- or 2-foot intervals. Caution: Do not hammer a completed snap-lock seam for a tighter seal— you may break the seal.

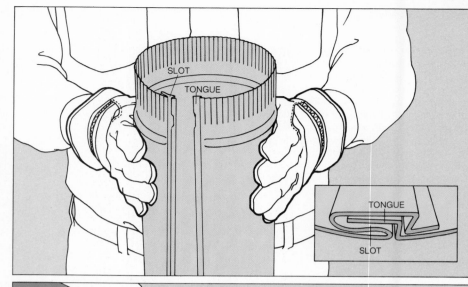

A hammer-lock assembly. In some duct designs, the seam consists of two U-shaped edges *(inset)*. Shape the entire section with your hands and hook the edges lightly together. Then hang the duct over the edge of a suspended 2-by-4 and, starting at either end, hammer the seam shut. Caution: Hammer blows can easily dislodge unsealed parts of the seam. Check constantly as you hammer along the section; an error may force you to reopen an entire seam.

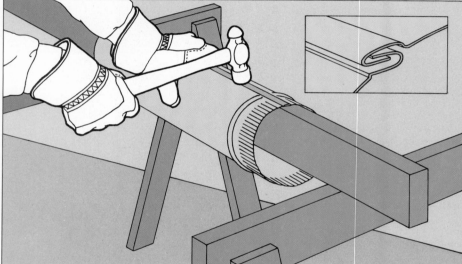

Joining a crimped to a plain end. Slide the crimped end of a duct section, set to face away from the furnace, into the plain end of the next section until the bead of the crimped section touches the edge of the plain one, then align the seams of the two sections. Just outside the bead, drill or punch small holes in opposite sides of the connected ducts, and secure the connection with sheet-metal screws. Seal the connection at the bead with duct tape.

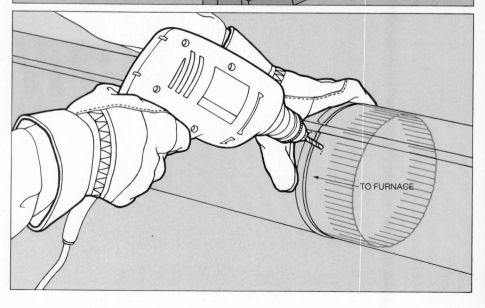

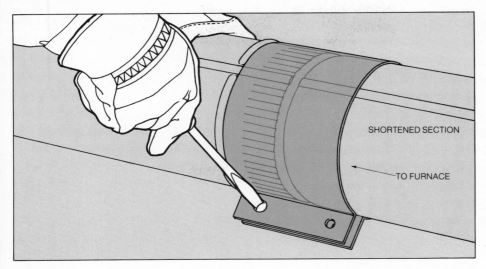

A drawband for a shortened section. To fill a gap shorter than a complete duct section, cut a section about 2 inches longer than the gap. (If the seam is already closed, cut the section at the plain end with a hacksaw, as shown on page 316.) Connect the crimped edge of the short section in the usual way *(opposite, bottom)*. The plain end should meet or nearly meet, but not overlap, the crimped end of the adjoining duct or fitting. Connect the two ends with a drawband—a flexible collar of galvanized steel, tightened by nuts and bolts. Slide the drawband along the plain duct end, bring the two duct ends together and slide the drawband back until it touches the bead of the crimped end. Tighten the drawband and seal the connection with duct tape.

SHORTENED SECTION

TO FURNACE

Dampers and Hangers

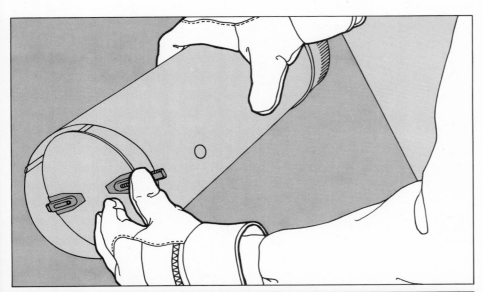

Installing a damper. Each duct run should have a damper, preferably near the furnace, to shut off heat from a room, if necessary, and to balance the entire heating system. Some dealers offer 2-foot duct sections with factory-installed dampers; alternatively, you can buy the damper separately and install it.

In the common model at left, the damper is held in place by spring-loaded shafts. Drill or punch holes for these shafts in opposite sides of the duct, at least 6 inches in from the plain end. Retract the shafts in their slots, set the damper in place, and release the shafts, threading them through the holes you have made. Finish by fastening the damper handle, following the manufacturer's instructions. Before balancing, the damper should be open (parallel with the pipe).

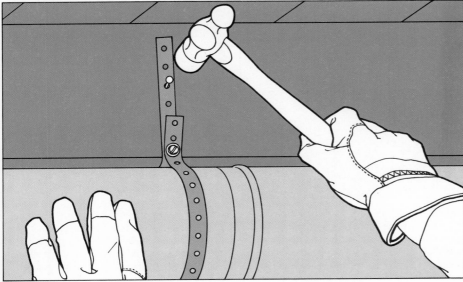

Installing a hanger. Every horizontal part of a duct run must be supported from above at intervals of no more than 10 feet; if the duct sections are relatively short—6 feet or less—shorten the intervals accordingly. The flexible hanger shown at left fits ducts of any thickness and fastens to either joists or ceilings. Secure it around the duct with a nut and bolt, then nail its other end to the supporting surface. Keep a clearance of at least 1 inch between the duct and the joist or ceiling above it.

Adding a New Duct Run

The pictures on these pages illustrate in detail the installation of a common type of new supply duct, in which air is tapped from a furnace plenum in a basement and released high on the wall of an upstairs room. (In schematic form, this duct run appears at the left of the picture on page 320.) Such a run is especially useful in a house with newly installed air conditioning, as a complement to a heating run with an outlet low in the room *(page 316)*. The same installation principles, however, apply to any run of new duct—for example, a heating run that ends at a floor register. In every case, you must make holes in walls, ceilings or floors to provide access to a plenum or an existing duct. After installing the new duct and connecting it to the heat source, attach a boot and a register.

You may be able to hide new duct by running it inside a closet or above a suspended ceiling. More often, you will have to conceal it in a duct enclosure. A two-sided enclosure *(right)* could conceal a vertical duct in the corner of a room or a horizontal duct running along a ceiling-and-wall corner. A frame with three sides could enclose a duct that runs at some distance from a corner.

Anatomy of an enclosed duct. Air passes through a rigid 6-inch round duct in one corner of a room and enters the room through a boot and a register. The duct is boxed in by two adjoining walls and by a wallboard-covered frame of 2-by-2s fastened to the adjacent walls. The boot flanges project 1/2 inch beyond the frame to allow for the thickness of the wallboard. The frame must be at least 8 inches wider than the boot and 3 inches deeper than its depth when measured with its flanges folded back.

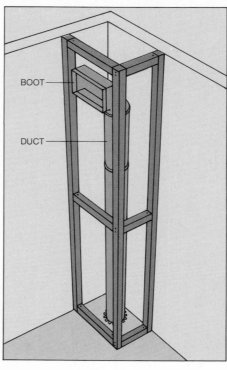

BOOT

DUCT

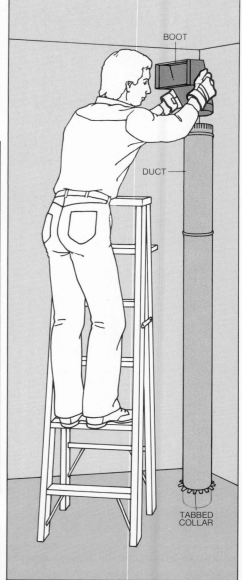

BOOT

DUCT

TABBED COLLAR

Installing the Duct

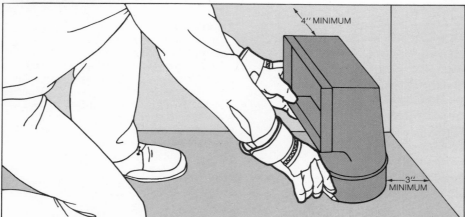

4" MINIMUM

3" MINIMUM

1 Positioning. Set the boot on the floor in the corner selected for the duct, facing the room's axis; the side of the boot face should be 4 inches back from the room's long wall and 3 inches from the short one. Trace around the base of the boot on the floor. At the center of this circular outline, drive a nail through the floor. In the room below, check that there are no ducts, pipes, joists or other obstructions within a circle 7 inches wide around the nail. If necessary, relocate the circle upstairs until a clear passage for the duct is assured.

2 Fastening the duct in place. Using the nail in the boot circle as a center, mark on the floor a circle 1/2 inch wider than the boot circle and cut out the larger circle with a keyhole or saber saw. Open the seam of a starter collar *(page 321, top)*, fold the tabs outward to a right angle, and strap the collar around the duct, crimped edge down. Let about 8 inches of the plain end of the duct protrude from the collar. Slide collar and duct into the hole and nail every third tab to the floor. About 5 or 6 inches of duct should show in the room beneath.

Mount the boot at the top of the duct. The boot's base should be 6 feet above the floor. If necessary, lengthen the duct with a piece from a 2-foot section, sold as a flat sheet. Cut a sheet to length at the plain end, then snap the sides together to make a round insert.

2 **Connecting the flue.** Replace the elbow and slide a trim collar onto the length of the flue that will connect the elbow and the wall opening. With the finished side of the trim collar facing you, push one end of the triple-insulated Class A flue through the wall spacer until you are able to position the other end in front of the elbow opening. Connect the flue and elbow *(right)*. Slide the trim collar toward the wall until it completely conceals the opening.

3 **Mounting the wall support.** Connect the chimney T to the plate of the wall support. Use the T as a positioning guide by inserting it into the wall and aligning it with the end of the flue pipe. It may be necessary to push the flue pipe back slightly—or to have a helper pull it back from inside—to allow the T to fit snugly, about 3 inches into the wall. Use a level to be sure the top of the T is perfectly horizontal, then have a helper mark the bolt positions through holes in the braces and bolting flanges *(right)*. Screw the support to the wall with the diagonal braces above the plate, as here, or below it.

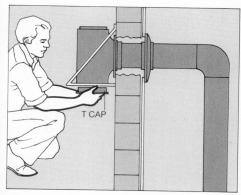

4 **Connecting the flue to the T.** Have a helper hold the T firmly outside the house while you push against the flue from inside until the end of the flue locks tightly about an inch inside the T. If they do not lock, uncouple the flue pipe from the elbow, apply a thin coat of lubricating oil around the outer edge of the rim, and work it into the T before reconnecting it to the elbow.

When the flue has been firmly locked into the T, push in the T cap—used for inspection and cleaning—from beneath the support plate *(above)*. Caulk around the T at the wall spacer.

5 **Running the chimney up the wall.** Place the first length of insulated chimney pipe into the opening at the top of the T and twist it until it locks firmly. Place a level across the top of the pipe to be sure it is straight. Repeat the procedure, locking the bottom of each successive length of pipe to the top of the one below, until the chimney extends from the T to a point just below the roof overhang.

To anchor the chimney to the wall while retaining the required 2-inch clearance, wall bands should be attached at 8-foot intervals. Slide the wall band down the pipe to the proper position and tighten the screw clamp to fasten it to the pipe. Then nail the wall band to the side of the house *(left)*.

6 **A passage to the roof.** If the center of the chimney pipe will be 4 inches or less from the edge of the roof overhang—check with a plumb line—use a pair of 15° elbows to carry the chimney around the overhang. Otherwise, mark the center line on the underside, or soffit, of the overhang and cut a hole in the same way as in an interior wall *(page 332)*. If, despite earlier planning to route the chimney between rafters, the hole uncovers a lookout support, use an elbow to reroute the pipe. Use the plumb line inside the opening to mark the center for the second opening. Drill a guide hole upward through the roof. Cut the second hole from above, through shingles and wood. Nail a fire-stop spacer, similar to a wall spacer *(page 332)*, to the soffit opening to provide for pipe clearance.

7 **Covering the roof hole.** Prepare to work safely on the roof *(page 340)*. Extend the chimney pipe through the holes in the soffit and roof until it reaches at least 2 feet above the roof peak. Spread roofing cement around the opening before sliding the flashing, which can be adjusted to the pitch of most roofs, down the pipe *(below)* until it lies flat against the roof and cement. Nail the flashing to the roof without removing shingles.

8 **Protecting the chimney.** Slip a storm collar over the chimney and slide it down to cover the opening where the chimney passes through the flashing. Tighten the collar's screw clamp. Then push a chimney cap onto the top of the chimney to keep rain, snow and birds out. Spread roofing cement around the top edge of the storm collar and the edges of the flashing. If required locally, install spark-arresting mesh around the chimney cap opening.

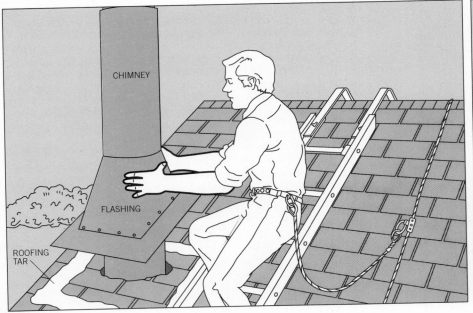

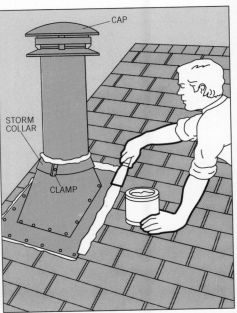

Running a Chimney through the House

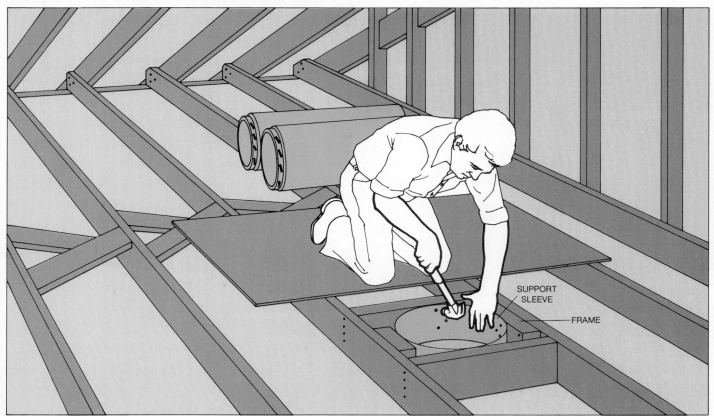

SUPPORT SLEEVE
FRAME

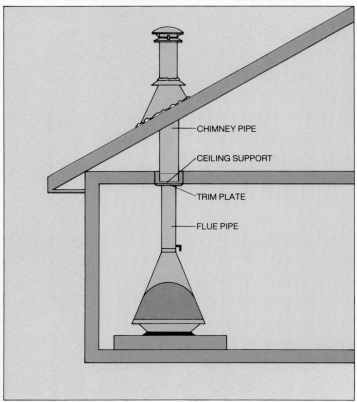

CHIMNEY PIPE

CEILING SUPPORT

TRIM PLATE

FLUE PIPE

1 **Installing the ceiling support.** Attach a length of decorative flue to the fireplace. Use a plumb line to align the center of the flue opening with a predetermined point on the ceiling midway between joists. If necessary, move the fireplace slightly to get the opening centered between joists. Cut a hole wide enough for the support sleeve in the ceiling as you would in a wall *(page 332)*. From above, cut away flooring necessary to frame the opening with wood the same size as the joists. The frame should touch the circular opening on all four sides. From below, slide the support into the opening and nail the trim plate through the ceiling into the frame. From above, nail the sleeve to the frame *(above)*.

2 **Running pipe up.** Insert a length of triple-insulated chimney pipe into the sleeve from above. Connect it below to the fireplace with flue pipe. Follow the steps used in an outside chimney run to open the roof and add chimney pipe to complete the job.

Where an inside chimney must pass through more than one ceiling, as for a fireplace located in a lower level of a multilevel home, only a spacer is needed in the second opening. But you should plan ahead to minimize the problem of running pipe through second-floor space. Route it through a closet, or run it through a corner where it can be boxed in like a duct *(page 324)*.

5 EXTERIOR IMPROVEMENTS

The Structure of Roofs and Walls

Before you can cover a house with roofing or siding, you must know the skeleton that lies beneath the exterior—what builders call the framing. The type of framing depends on whether you have a masonry house or a wood-frame house.

A wood frame *(opposite)* consists entirely of lengths of wood, named for their location and function. Normally, vertical studs frame the walls, horizontal joists support the ceilings and floors and diagonal rafters hold up the roof. These framing members are generally installed with a narrow edge facing outward or upward, and this edge provides a nailing surface for the layers of the house's skin.

Generally, the innermost layer is a sheath of plywood or fiberboard panels. A moisture-permeable covering is stapled to the sheath as a barrier against air entry, and the siding *(pages 346-347)* is nailed through the sheath and into the studs.

The spacing of the studs determines the nailing pattern of sheathing and siding. In most frame houses studs are either 16 or 24 inches apart, but the spacing may vary between a full stud and the shorter cripple and jack studs that are used to frame

doors and windows, or between a stud and a corner post.

The spacing problem takes a different form in a masonry house *(below)*. Here, the skeleton consists of solid brick, stone or concrete blocks covered with brick veneer, stucco or ordinary siding. If siding is used, it hangs on vertical wood supports called furring strips, spaced 16 or 24 inches apart on the outside walls.

In most modern dwellings the roofs are built with joists and rafters *(below and opposite)* and decked, or sheathed, with boards or plywood panels. Depending on the roofing material, boards may be butted together, tongue and grooved or spaced up to 4 inches apart. The boards or panels are nailed to the rafters and covered with asphalt felt paper; flashing is then installed at chimneys, vents, dormers, skylights and valleys.

The final roof covering *(pages 370-371)* is as variable as the siding on the walls. On a pitched roof, the covering may be asphalt shingles, tiles, slates, wood shakes or shingles; a roof that is flat or has negligible pitch must be covered with built-up or cemented roll roofing.

A masonry house. In this example of masonry construction, a hip roof covered with tiles rests on concrete-block walls finished with stucco. To anchor the roof framing to the walls, a wood sill plate is bolted to the top row, or course, of concrete blocks. Hip rafters extend from the sill plate to the horizontal ridge board; these rafters are supported by hip jack rafters fastened to the sill. The main part of the roof is also supported by common rafters, which are fastened to the ridge board and the sill plate. Ceiling joists span the width of the house, resting on the sill plate and nailed to either jack or common rafters. Horizontal braces called collar beams tie opposite rafters to give the roof added strength.

The roof sheathing is 4-by-8-foot plywood sheets nailed to the rafters and covered with roofing felt and tiles. On the walls, two coats of mortar create the stucco exterior: a thick base coat, applied directly to the blocks; and a finish coat, spread over the base. (Stucco can also be applied to a wood-frame house in three coats.)

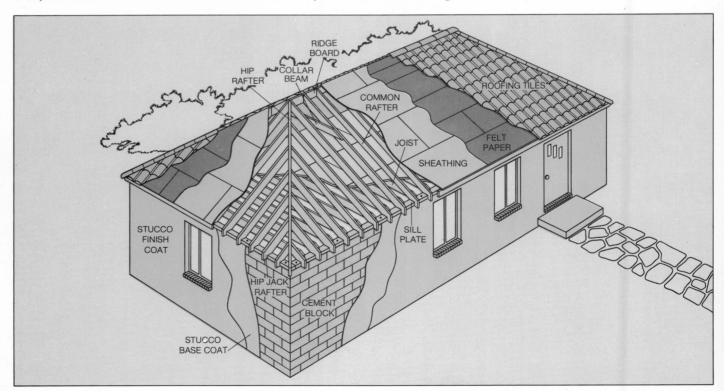

A wood-frame house. Beneath the clapboard siding and asphalt shingles of this typical frame house, vertical wall studs and sloping rafters make up the main structural members. The studs rest on a horizontal 2-by-4 called a sole plate, and a horizontal top plate consisting of doubled 2-by-4s runs across the top of the wall studs. The lower ends of the rafters rest on the top plate; the upper ends are attached to a horizontal ridge board. Horizontal ceiling joists, nailed to the rafters, rest on the top plate, and collar beams add rigidity to the structure.

Special framing is needed wherever walls are interrupted by windows or doors and wherever roof slopes or walls intersect. In the roof, the valley is framed with a valley rafter, which runs from the ridge boards to the top plate and is supported on each side by shorter valley jack rafters. In the walls, windows and doors are framed horizontally with headers and plates, vertically with jack and cripple studs. Corner posts consist of three studs nailed together, and each gable wall is framed with end studs installed between the top plate and the end rafters.

To create a solid surface for the final coverings, both roofs and walls are sheathed with plywood sheets; building paper shields the sheathing against water. The valley and other critical joints are protected with metal flashing and the roofing and siding are nailed over the roof sheathing.

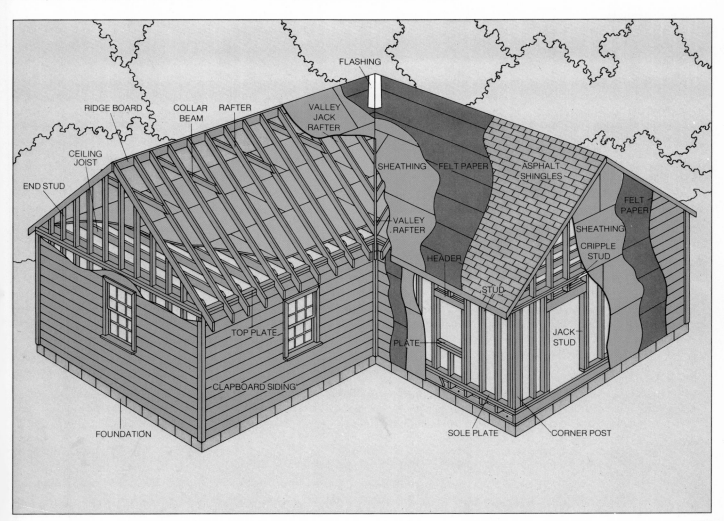

Extreme caution is required at all times when working at heights on a ladder or scaffolding, or on the roof. Avoid injuries by reading this section carefully and following the instructions for safe working practices. Never use a ladder or scaffolding or work on the roof in wet, cold or windy weather; wait for optimal weather conditions. Do not set up a ladder or scaffolding near utility lines, or otherwise work near power cables. Wear footgear with a well-defined heel and a non-slip sole. Stop working when you feel tired and avoid undertaking a repair during the hottest part of the day. Have a helper on hand while you are working, but keep others away from the work area.

Caution: If working near an antenna, unplug any radio or television connected to it. In addition, everyone below the top worker should wear a hard hat, in case something falls; for maximum safety, the top worker should wear one as well.

A typical stepladder, extension ladder and scaffolding are shown opposite. To work safely and comfortably on the siding and stand up to 10 feet from the ground, set up a stepladder *(page 342)*; allow for about 5 to 10 minutes of set-up time. To work safely and comfortably on the siding and stand more than 10 feet from the ground, or to work on the roof, set up an extension ladder *(page 343)*; add about 20 to 30 minutes for setting it up to the estimated time needed for your repair. To work safely and comfortably, extensively along the siding at a height you cannot reach from the ground, or along the roofing at an eave, set up scaffolding *(page 344-345)*; allow about 15 to 20 minutes to assemble each single level.

Before climbing onto your roof, determine its pitch *(page 342)*. If the pitch of your roof is more than 6 in 12, call for a professional evaluation rather than undertake a repair on it yourself. If the pitch of your roof is 4 to 6 in 12, take an added precaution: Wear a safety harness or belt *(right)* while working on the roof. Roofing of tile or slate breaks easily under pressure and should not be walked on; if you cannot perform a roof repair safely and comfortably from the eave, call for a professional evaluation.

If you need to use a ladder, choose an appropriate type for the job; verify its duty rating, which is the total weight that it is designed to support. There are three grades of ladders: Household, Commercial and Industrial; a Type I or I A Industrial ladder with non-slip rubber shoes is recommended. To work from an extension ladder on the siding, use standoff stabilizers for added lateral stability or to bridge a window; foam or fabric covers are available for the end caps to avoid marring the siding. Store your extension ladder horizontally on hooks. Keep a wooden ladder in a dry area, out of direct sunlight. Never paint a wooden ladder, which could hide defects; apply a clear wood preservative, if necessary.

When ordering scaffolding units, request prefabricated decks; they hook onto the end frames and are stronger and safer than wooden planks. Order extra decks to leave on each intermediate scaffolding level. Make sure you obtain guardrails and toeboards for the working platform, as well as enough frame couplers to secure each level and standoffs to stabilize the scaffolding against the house.

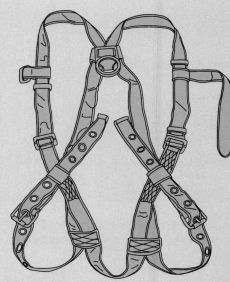

SAFETY HARNESS
A fully adjustable body harness, usually made of nylon. A metal ring on the back attaches to the fall-arrest system: the lanyard, the rope grab and the fall-arrest rope.

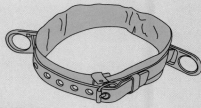

SAFETY BELT
A substitute for the safety harness, usually made of nylon. Worn around the waist with a metal ring over the hip attached to the fall-arrest system: the lanyard, the rope grab and the fall-arrest rope.

LANYARD
A thick rope about 2 feet long with a locking hook on each end; clips onto the safety harness or belt and the rope grab.

ROPE GRAB
Attached to the lanyard and connected to the fall-arrest rope. Designed to allow controlled movement up and down on the rope, but to lock if jerked suddenly. Usually made of stainless steel with an arrow to indicate the direction of orientation for the rope.

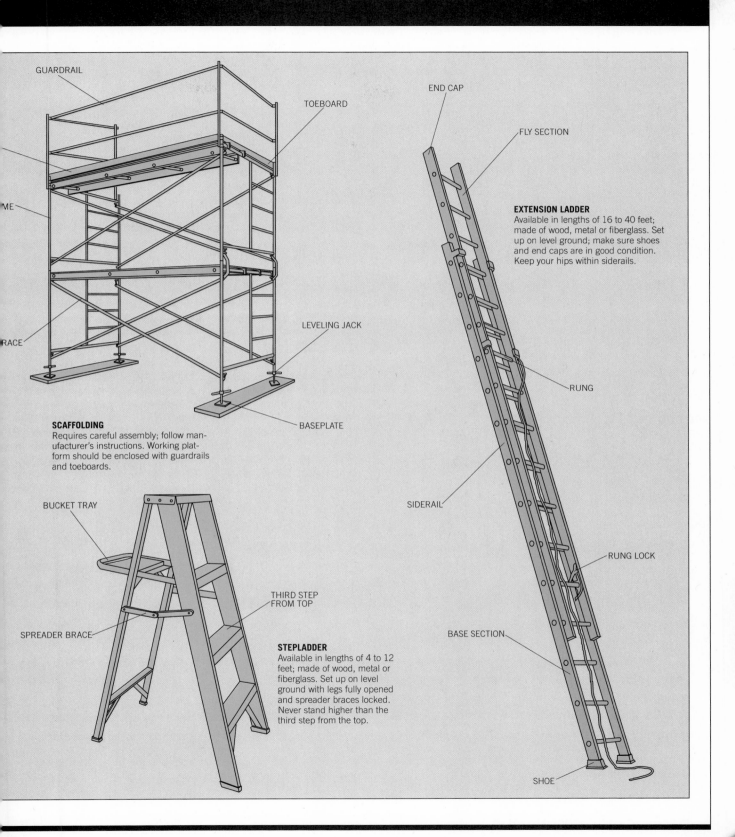

GUARDRAIL

TOEBOARD

END CAP

FLY SECTION

EXTENSION LADDER
Available in lengths of 16 to 40 feet;
made of wood, metal or fiberglass. Set
up on level ground; make sure shoes
and end caps are in good condition.
Keep your hips within siderails.

ME

RACE

LEVELING JACK

RUNG

SCAFFOLDING
Requires careful assembly; follow manufacturer's instructions. Working platform should be enclosed with guardrails
and toeboards.

BASEPLATE

SIDERAIL

BUCKET TRAY

RUNG LOCK

THIRD STEP
FROM TOP

BASE SECTION

SPREADER BRACE

STEPLADDER
Available in lengths of 4 to 12
feet; made of wood, metal or
fiberglass. Set up on level
ground with legs fully opened
and spreader braces locked.
Never stand higher than the
third step from the top.

SHOE

Setting up and Using a Stepladder

SPREADER BRACE

Setting up a stepladder. To work safely and comfortably on the siding and stand up to 10 feet from the ground, set up a stepladder; as a rule, use a stepladder at least 2 feet longer than the height at which you need to stand. Inspect the stepladder before using it; do not use it if, for example, a foot is worn, a step is loose or a spreader brace does not open fully. Read the safety instruction label, usually located on a siderail.

Set up the stepladder on firm, level ground, opening its legs completely and locking its spreader braces. If the ground is soft or uneven, place boards under the front and back feet of the stepladder, as shown; dig up the soil with a spade to level them, if necessary. Never use an unanchored object such as a stone to prop the feet up. Pull down on the bucket tray to open it and place tools and materials on it before climbing the stepladder; or carry tools in a tool belt.

Wearing footgear with a well-defined heel, face the stepladder to climb up or down it, using both hands to grasp the steps rather than the siderails. While working from the stepladder, lean into it and keep your hips between the siderails *(left)*; do not stand higher than the third step from the top. Never overreach or straddle the space between the stepladder and the siding; instead, climb down from the stepladder and reposition it.

Measuring Roof Slope to Determine the Pitch

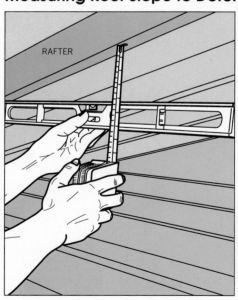

RAFTER

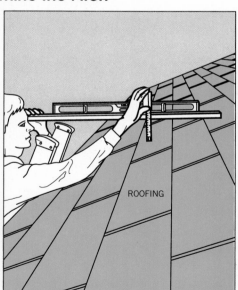

ROOFING

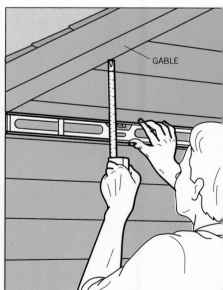

GABLE

Determining roof pitch. A roof's slope, or pitch, is the measurement of its vertical rise in inches every 12 horizontal inches and is expressed as a number in 12. If your roof rises vertically by more than 6 inches every 12 inches horizontally, a pitch greater than 6 in 12, call for a professional evaluation rather than undertake a repair on it yourself. To determine the pitch of

your roof, climb to your attic or set up an extension ladder *(opposite)* to reach an eave or a rake (the sloping edge of the roof framing gable). On a carpenter's level or a board, mark a reference line 12 inches from one end. Hold the level or the board with a level on it horizontal, the end of it against a reference structure and the reference line on it facing the roof;

then, measure the vertical distance between the reference structure and the reference line. For the reference structure in the attic, use a rafter *(above, left)*; at the eave, use the roofing *(above, center)*; at the rake, use the top of the gable *(above, right)*. The pitch of your roof is the vertical distance, measured in inches, in 12.

Setting up an Extension Ladder

FLY SECTION

SIDERAIL

FLY SECTION

STABILIZER

RUNG LOCK

1 Positioning and raising the ladder. To work safely and comfortably on the siding standing more than 10 feet from the ground or on the roof, set up an extension ladder; to work on the roof, determine its pitch *(opposite)* and do not climb onto it if the pitch is more than 6 in 12. To calculate the length of ladder you need, estimate height by multiplying the number of stories you need to reach by the interior ceiling height (usually 8 to 10 feet), adding about 1 foot per floor (usually the distance between it and the ceiling below it) and adding the distance from the ground to the first floor; if you are getting off the ladder onto the roof, add another 3 feet. Inspect the ladder and do not use it if, for example, a shoe is worn or missing, a rung is loose, or a rung lock or the rope and pulley system is faulty. Read the safety instruction label, usually located on a siderail. Place the unextended ladder on the ground, perpendicular to the wall where it will be positioned, with its fly section on the bottom and its feet out from the wall 1/4 of the height to which it will be raised; to work on the roof, set it up at an eave. To increase side-to-side stability or to bridge a window, attach standoff stabilizers to the ladder following the manufacturer's instructions. With the helper's feet bracing the bottom of the ladder, use both hands to raise the top of it above your head *(left)*. Walk under the ladder toward its bottom, moving your hands along the siderails, until it is upright.

2 Extending the fly section. With a helper supporting the ladder, stand slightly to one side of it, bracing the bottom with one foot; pull on the rope to disengage the rung locks and raise the fly section *(left)*. When the fly section is extended to the height desired, gently release pressure on the rope to engage the rung locks. If your ladder does not have a rope and pulley system, keep both feet on the ground against the bottom of the siderails to push the fly section up with your hands; never stand on the ladder to raise the fly section. Carefully rest the ladder against the siding or eave; if the roof is covered with tiles or slates, be careful not to break them. Check that the bottom of the ladder is out from the wall by 1/4 the height of the ladder. If you installed standoff stabilizers on the ladder, make sure they rest properly against the siding *(inset)*, following the manufacturer's instructions. If you plan to get onto the roof, make sure the ladder extends at least 3 feet, or rungs, above the eave. If necessary, work with your helper to raise the fly section higher. If the ladder does not stand steady on firm, level ground, place a board under the feet. Then drive a stake into the ground between the ladder and the house; tie each siderail to the stake. If you are working on an eave or plan to get off the ladder, stabilize the top of the ladder: Install an eye screw into the fascia near each siderail and tie each siderail to it.

Setting up Scaffolding

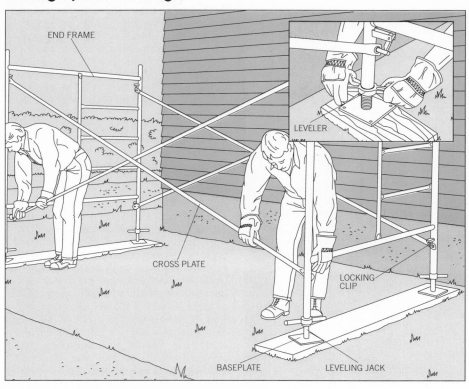

1 Assembling the base level. Rent scaffolding at a tool rental agency. Estimate the height at which you will be working and order the appropriate number of units. (Each unit includes end frames, cross braces, frame couplers, baseplates, leveling jacks, prefabricated decks or wooden planks, and guardrails.) Inspect the scaffolding and do not use it if an end frame is rusted, a baseplate is bent, a deck or plank is cracked or warped, or it is otherwise damaged. If the ground is soft, use 2-by-6s or -10s under the end frames to support them. Position the baseplates and leveling jacks. Working with a helper, wear work gloves and slide each end frame onto its leveling jacks. Install cross braces on the locking clips of the end frames *(left)*. Use a carpenter's level to ensure the end frames are vertical and horizontal; if necessary, adjust a leveler *(inset)*. Adding another end frame for each extra length of scaffolding you need. To work at the height of the scaffolding, set up a full working platform of decks or planks on top of the end frames; if using planks, make sure they overhang each end frame by at least 1 foot and no more than 2 feet. Then, install guardrails *(Step 4)*. Otherwise, set up one deck or two planks alongside the climbing bars and assemble additional scaffolding levels *(Step 2)*.

2 Assembling additional levels. Kneeling on the working platform, have your helper pass up each end frame for the next level *(left)*, then slide it onto one of the end frames for the level below it; align its climbing bars with those on the end frame below it, as shown. Install cross braces as you did for the base level *(Step 1)*. Then, install a frame coupler at the bottom of each foot on the end frames to anchor it to the top of the end frame below it; depending on your scaffolding model, the frame coupler is a type of locking arm or pin *(inset)*. To work at the height of the scaffolding, set up a full working platform of decks or planks on top of the end frames; if using planks, make sure they overhang each end frame by at least 1 foot and no more than 2 feet. Then, install guardrails *(Step 4)*. Otherwise, set up one deck or two planks alongside the climbing bars and assemble an additional scaffolding level. If necessary, pull up each component from the ground using a 3/8-inch diameter nylon rope; tie the rope using a non-slip knot. After assembling an additional scaffolding level above each story of the house, secure it to the wall *(Step 3)*.

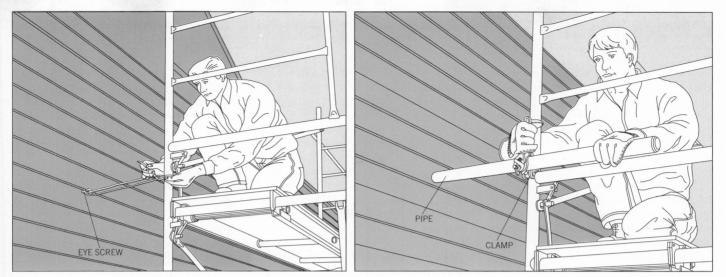

EYE SCREW

PIPE

CLAMP

3 **Securing the scaffolding to the wall.** Secure every second end frame of the scaffolding to the wall at each story above the first story of the house; reposition a deck or two planks as close to the wall as possible, if necessary, for a working platform. To prevent the scaffolding from falling away from the house, install an eye screw in the wall and tie the end frame to it *(above, left)*; locate a wall stud for the eye screw or, if the wall is masonry, first install a lead anchor. To prevent the scaffolding from falling against the house, install a stand-off following the manufacturer's instructions; the type shown consists of a metal pipe and adjustable swivel clamp. Fit the clamp onto the end frame and slide the pipe through the clamp until its end is 1 inch away from the wall. Using an adjustable wrench, tighten the bolts on the clamp to secure the pipe *(above, right)*.

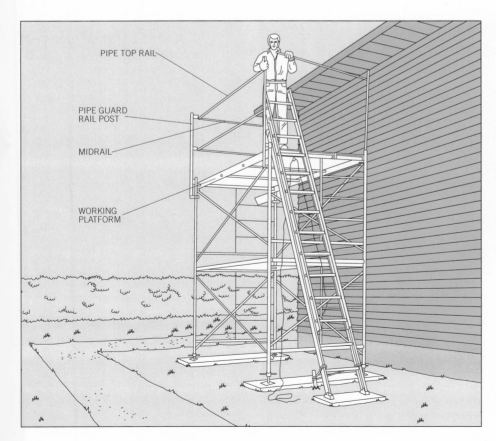

PIPE TOP RAIL

PIPE GUARD RAIL POST

MIDRAIL

WORKING PLATFORM

4 **Installing guardrails.** After assembling the number of scaffolding levels you need. set up an extension ladder *(page 343)* at one end of the scaffolding, if necessary, for easy access to the working platform; tie the top of it to the end frame as you would at the eave. Then, enclose the working platform with a guardrail along each open side of it and a toeboard along each side at the bottom of it. Have your helper on the ground pass up each component or pull it up from the ground using rope tied using a non-slip knot. Slide a guardrail post onto the top of each end of the end frames and secure it with a locking pin. Attach the toprails and midrails onto the locking pins on the posts; on the end with the ladder, install only a toprail *(left)*, omitting a midrail, and be careful getting on and off the ladder. Attach each toeboard to the guardposts following the manufacturer's instructions.

Choosing the Right Siding, Preparing the Walls

Beyond the obvious considerations of cost and appearance, your choice of a new siding should take into account the problems of installing a specific siding material, the kind of regular maintenance it will need, and its special physical characteristics, which may make it more or less suitable for your purposes.

The drawings and chart on these pages enable you to compare eight widely available materials. In the drawings, you can compare their surface appearances and judge their suitability to the architecture of your home.

The appearances may be deceiving. Clapboard, stucco and wood shingles and shakes are traditional materials that have set the familiar styles in exterior wall coverings for centuries. The other sidings, developed more recently, are usually shaped and finished to resemble the traditional ones. At their best, these imitations are not wholly successful: The newer types of siding lack the elegance of the old materials. But what they lack in appearance they may make up in economy or convenience. Vinyl, for example, has become a favored material for new siding on both new and old houses because it is relatively inexpensive, easy to install and all but maintenance free. It is factors like these that are compared in the chart at right. Detailed descriptions of all the sidings appear in the remainder of this chapter.

One element of a siding job that does not show up in the drawings or the chart is the exterior wall beneath the siding. Depending on its condition and on the siding you choose, this wall may need some measure of repair or preparation, by methods described on pages 348-354.

Eight Styles of Siding

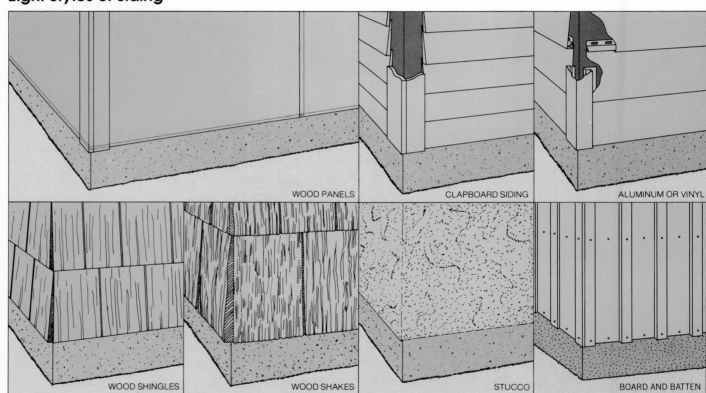

WOOD PANELS

CLAPBOARD SIDING

ALUMINUM OR VINYL

WOOD SHINGLES

WOOD SHAKES

STUCCO

BOARD AND BATTEN

A range of materials. The types of siding shown above are varied. Some look alike, but each has distinctive qualities. Large, rectangular panels of plywood or hardboard are available unfinished for painting or staining, or in finishes that resemble any of the other materials. Long planks nailed horizontally to walls can be installed in a variety of patterns. Clapboard, the most common, consists of lapped boards tapered toward one edge; in tongue-and-groove siding the board edges are fitted together; in shiplap they are rabbeted and overlapped; board and batten is rough-sawn for a less finished look. In each case the boards can be painted. Vinyl and aluminum are generally designed to resemble clapboard when installed, but come from the factory precolored in several shades.

Wood shingles and shakes are similar in size and identical in material—redwood or cedar—but shingles are milled to an exact and uniform size while shakes are thicker and irregularly shaped. Both can be stained or painted, or in the case of cedar, simply left unfinished for an attractive, weathered look. Masonry siding, represented here by stucco, is made from a wet cement that is spread over a wall in layers. Stucco may be left uncolored; more often, it is either precolored or painted after installation. Its surface may be smooth or textured, lined and grouted, or embedded with light-colored stones.

A Guide to Siding Materials

Siding type	Cost	Maintenance	Advantages	Limitations
wood panels	inexpensive (unfinished plywood) to moderate (finished hardboard)	periodic painting or staining	quick installation; goes over most existing sidings; available in a wide variety of styles	poor fire resistance; installation always requires two workers, and can be especially difficult at the borders of windows, doors and rake
clapboard	moderate	periodic painting or staining	goes over most existing sidings	poor fire resistance; installation requires two workers; some types are subject to rot
board and batten	inexpensive	periodic painting or staining	quick installation; goes over most existing sidings	poor fire resistance; coverage not as tight as clapboard
vinyl	inexpensive to moderate	none	easy installation; goes over most existing sidings	may melt near intense heat; brittle in very cold weather; narrow range of colors, subject to fading; cannot be painted
aluminum	inexpensive to moderate	none	easy installation; goes over most existing sidings; fire resistant, available in wide variety of styles; can be repainted	scratches and dents easily; may clatter in wind and hail if not insulated; needs electrical grounding
wood shingles	expensive	regular replacement of missing or damaged pieces; regular painting or staining for some woods	goes over most existing sidings; single pieces easily replaced; can be left unfinished for rustic look	flammable unless treated; slow installation
wood shakes	expensive	regular replacement of missing or damaged pieces	goes over most existing sidings; single pieces exceptionally durable and easily replaced; can be left unfinished for rustic look	flammable unless treated; slow installation, often difficult around windows and doors
stucco	moderate	periodic painting	fire resistant; surface can be molded or decorated	requires wire-mesh backing over wall or existing siding; long and difficult installation, requiring special skills, cracks must be done in good weather; or crumbles if incorrectly applied

Comparing siding materials. In the chart above, "Cost" refers to the relative cost of each material as compared with all the others; it does not reflect the labor involved in a professional installation. In general, labor costs are considerably higher for the traditional materials—clapboard, wood shingles and shakes and stucco— than for the newer types of siding, most of which are relatively easy to install. With stucco, the materials alone are only moderately expensive, but if professionally installed, it is the most expensive of all sidings. For some materials a range of costs is given. Aluminum, for example, can be bought in two thicknesses, each with or without an insulation backing. Thin aluminum without backing is inexpensive; thick aluminum with backing is moderately expensive.

With reasonable care, all the materials listed will last as long as the houses they cover. The column headed "Maintenance" indicates what must be done to keep a siding structurally sound and weatherproof. It does not take into account the gradual deterioration of materials like aluminum and vinyl, which, though sound, may look weathered after a number of years.

The last two columns summarize the general advantages and limitations of each material. Under these headings the most important considerations for the amateur are ease of installation and the ability to cover existing siding.

A Solid Base for New Siding

The principal requirement for any type of siding is a flat, sound nailing surface and there are three ways of obtaining it. The old wood siding will do if it is in good condition. If not, the usual solution is to mount furring strips over the old siding—shimming the strips on uneven surfaces—and nail the siding to the strips. The third and most time-consuming way to guarantee a good nailing surface is to remove the old siding and begin as you would with new construction. This often must be done when the old siding is asbestos shingles, crumbling stucco or aluminum—all difficult to nail through to a firm wood backing.

Whichever technique you choose, always begin by removing accessories that could interfere with the re-siding—downspouts, light fixtures, shutters, decorative trim. You will need professional help if you must temporarily remove a utility meter. It may be necessary to shut down all power; in that case be prepared to mount the necessary pieces of siding quickly so power can be restored.

Preparing the walls for re-siding offers an excellent opportunity to add to wall insulation. If you plan to keep the old siding in place, you can drill holes through it to have loose-fill insulation blown into the stud cavities, or you can mount plastic foam insulation boards between old and new siding. If old siding is removed, install batts or blankets between the studs. If removing cement/asbestos siding, do not saw it or create dust; wear a dust mask or respirator *(page 76)* rated to protect against asbestos fibers.

Removing asbestos shingles. Because brittle asbestos shingles provide a poor nailing surface for new siding, strip them from the walls with a pry bar. Break the shingles near the nailheads and pull off the pieces and backer strips; then pound the nails into the sheathing. Use 15-pound asphalt felt to patch any old felt torn in the process, making sure the new paper overlaps the old by about an inch all around.

Stripping the Walls

Removing trim. To save molding and other trim for reuse, pry it off gently with a utility bar. Begin at one end, inserting the flat end of the bar under the molding and tapping the curved end with a hammer. Remove the frieze—the board at the top of the siding under the soffit—only if you plan to replace it with siding. Otherwise, build out the old frieze with an identically sized strip of lumber to meet the projection of the new siding.

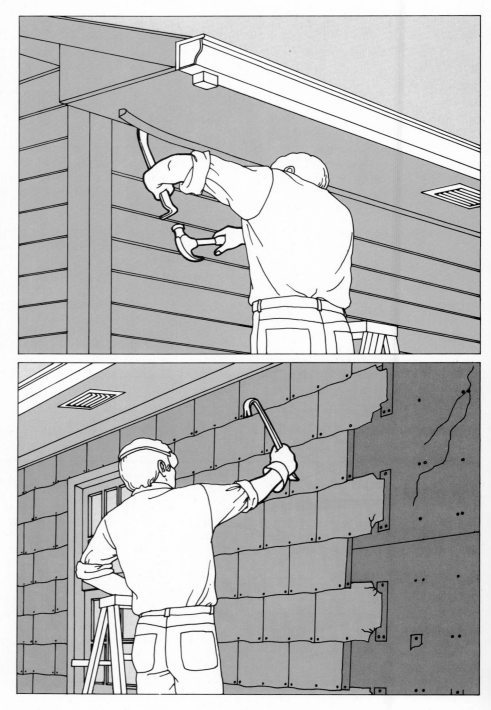

Resealing the Walls

Sheathing a stud wall. If studs are exposed after removing old siding, add any necessary insulation—with the vapor barrier inside—before sheathing the wall with APA-rated plywood or oriented strand board sheathing rated for the stud spacing of your wall. Mount 4-by-8-foot sheets horizontally for greater rigidity, leaving about 1/4 inch at panel edges and 1/8 inch at panel ends for expansion. Space nails 6 to 12 inches apart on the studs at edges and 12 inches apart along the panel. Do not overlap the board ends at corners, but caulk the seam. Overlap the house foundation by at least an inch, and be sure to nail into the exposed sill.

Sheath behind window casings and door frames by inserting sheathing into space from which old siding has been removed, or by prying off the trim and renailing it over the sheathing.

Nailing sheathing paper. For additional moisture protection, especially when siding with stucco, staple or nail a layer of the building paper required by your local building code to the sheathing. Attach the paper in long horizontal rows from the bottom, lapping each row about 4 inches over the row below. Be sure to mount strips of sheathing paper recommended by your local code, at least 8 inches wide, around windows and doors—even if none is used elsewhere—to reduce drafts.

New Insulation over the Old Siding

Attaching plastic foam insulation boards. If the interior wall has no vapor barrier—to keep warm inside air from condensing in the wall—drill half-inch vent holes through the old siding and sheathing *(left)* at the top and bottom of each stud cavity. Nail 2-by-8-foot panels horizontally on the siding. Leave about 1/16-inch space at corners so that trapped vapor can escape. Caution: Use an electric drill only under dry conditions; plug it into a GFCI-protected outlet or use a cordless drill.

Furring for Panels and Horizontal Siding

1 Locating studs. Find and mark the tops of studs by examining the nailing pattern in your present siding or by using a density sensor *(page 46)*. This will establish the stud pattern at 16-inch or 24-inch intervals. Hang a plumb bob and mark the stud bottoms below the siding.

2 Checking for straightness. Hold a straight-edge such as a 2-by-4 against the wall vertically, horizontally and diagonally to locate bulges. If possible, pound and nail them into alignment.

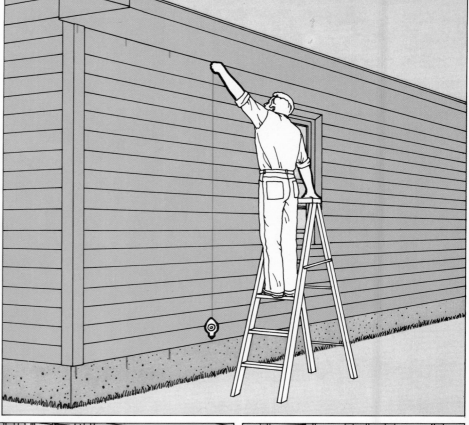

3 Nailing the furring strips. Attach 1-by-3-inch furring strips to each stud, using 2 1/2 inch nails at 16-inch intervals to penetrate siding and sheathing. Drive the nails into the high spots of beveled siding. Where the wall bows, shim as necessary to keep the strips straight, checking frequently as in Step 2. Fur completely around windows and doors as well; if necessary, saw off projecting sill ends. If you do not plan to use corner boards with the new siding, nail furring strips at corners that do not have existing corner boards or adjacent to existing corner boards. If you plan to use corner boards, see Step 4. If you are re-siding with 4-by-8-foot plywood or hardboard panels, nail horizontal furring strips at the bottom and top of the wall, and at any intermediate point where rows of panels will join.

4 Installing corner boards. For outside corners, attach corner boards as thick as the furring strips plus the new siding, overlapping them at the corner. If corner boards already exist, nail the new ones directly over them. For inside corners *(inset)*, nail a 2-by-2 strip, 1 1/2 inches square, over the old post and the adjacent furring strips. Plane one edge of the new post, if necessary, to ensure a close fit.

Furring for Shingles and Vertical Siding

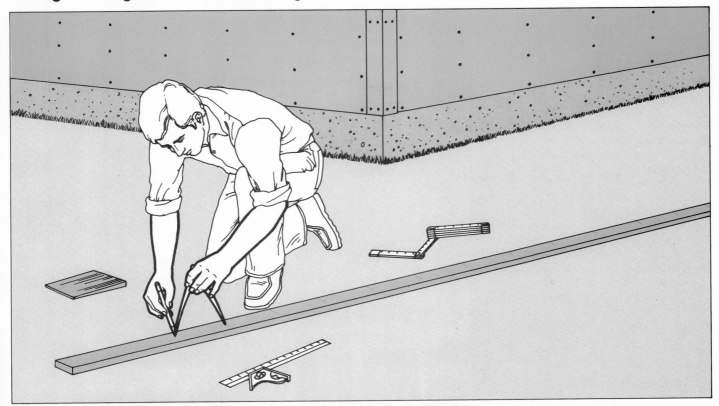

Laying out a story pole. To align horizontal furring, mark the intervals on a story pole—a straight piece of 1-by-2-inch wood long enough to cover the distance from the soffit to 2 inches below the existing siding. Set a pair of dividers at the height of a single piece of siding and mark the wide side of the pole evenly from top to bottom, squaring the lines with a combination square. Nail the pole tightly to the corners of the house and transfer the markings to the corner boards or furring strips. Snap chalk lines around the house to serve as nailing guides in mounting furring strips.

Furring out masonry. Using a story pole and chalk lines to establish the horizontal lines, nail 1-by-4-inch strips to masonry if you are siding with shingles. For vertical board siding, use 1-by-3-inch strips spaced 24 inches apart. Before choosing a type of fastener, consult a knowledgeable representative at your lumberyard or home supply center: Some will recommend that you drill holes for masonry anchors at 16-inch intervals, fit the anchors through the strips and into the masonry, then drive nails or screws into the anchors. Others will suggest toggle bolts or lead shield anchors.

Retrimming Doors and Windows

The joints where new siding meets windows and doors can pose problems. If the old siding is so thick that the door or window casing protrudes only slightly or not at all, you must protect the edges of the new siding by altering the casing.

Strips of molding nailed to the outer edges of the casing may bring the casing out as much as needed. If adding molding will not suffice, you can remove the casing, build out the jamb and install new casing *(opposite)*. For windows and doors recessed into masonry walls, make a liner to cover the masonry *(page 354)*.

Both extending jambs and lining masonry windows require ripsawing to exact widths. Use the method shown below.

A Jig for Accurate Ripping

The best way to make a dead-straight rip cut with a circular saw is to slide the edge of the saw's base plate along a true straightedge, which you can make by cutting a strip about 6 inches wide from the long side of a piece of plywood. Using nails, sandwich a 1-by-2 between the strip and a wider piece of plywood, so that the factory-milled edge of the strip overhangs the wide platform. Nail the platform to the top of a workbench. Slide the lumber under the overhanging straightedge; the distance between the rip line and the straightedge should equal that between the saw blade and the base-plate edge. Then tack two nails through the overhang to immobilize the lumber, and rip it with a saw set to cut slightly into the platform.

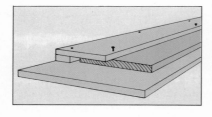

Building Out the Casing

Applying a molding. Bend the bottom edge of the existing drip cap out to the horizontal and nail the molding to the casing. If you use cove molding, as shown here, fasten it flush to the outer edge of the casing with weather-resistant nails driven through the narrow face at a slight inward angle. Nail backband molding *(inset)* from the side through the backband. Bevel the bottom ends of the side moldings to the slope of the sill. Miter the corners, set the nails and fill the nail holes.

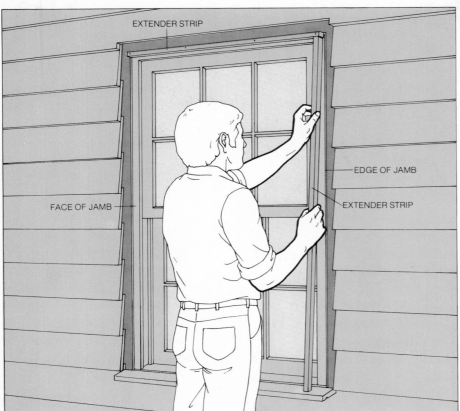

EXTENDER STRIP

FACE OF JAMB

EDGE OF JAMB

EXTENDER STRIP

Building Out the Jamb

1 **Extending the jambs.** After gently prying off the old casing, nail 3/4-inch extender strips flush with the outside edge of the jamb. The strips must be wide enough to project exactly the distance from the face of the jamb to the plane of the old siding. Butt side strips to the top one and saw the lower ends to the angle of the sill.

2 **Nailing on the casing.** Miter the top strip so that its bottom edge measures 1/4 inch longer than the inside width of the new jamb. Use weather-resistant casing nails to fasten it to the extender strip with the bottom edge 1/8 inch above the inner edge of the top strip. Bevel the bottom ends of the side strips to the slope of the sill, miter the top ends to fit and nail them to the jambs 1/8 inch offset from the inner corner. Then set the nails and fill the nail holes.

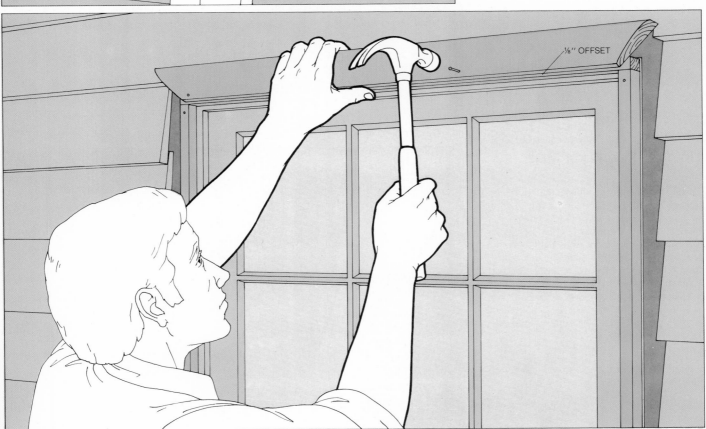

⅛″ OFFSET

3 Extending the sill. Using a plane at least 10 inches long, plane the front edge of the sill flat and square. Then build the sill out 1 1/2 inches with a strip of wood or of round-nose molding as thick as the sill.

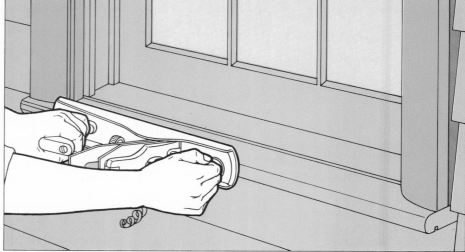

4 Installing drip caps. Shape a strip of flashing metal to overlap the front of the top casing strip by 1/2 inch, to cover the top of it and to run 3 inches up the existing wall. Nail it at its top edge only. Apply clear silicone rubber sealant along the top edge of the drip cap with a caulking gun.

Lining a Recess in Masonry

Cutting the liner boards. Measure from the casing out to the front of the furring strips that will support the new siding. To this measurement add the thickness of the new siding plus 1/2 inch to bring the liner out slightly beyond the siding. Rip 3/4-inch boards to this width. Saw to length so that the side boards will butt against the top board and fit the angle of the sill. Glue the boards in place with exterior panel adhesive applied generously. Caulk the joints where the liner meets the casing and the sill.

Precut Panel Siding that Covers a Wall Fast

For covering a wall both quickly and durably, panels of textured plywood or hardboard are hard to equal. Such panels can be nailed directly over sound clapboard or shingles, and because they are stiff they will flatten small irregularities in these surfaces. Most are designed to be installed vertically and are made 4 feet wide and long enough to extend from the foundation to the eaves of one-story houses. The standard thicknesses—19/32 inch (APA 303 plywood siding) for plywood, 7/16 inch for hardboard—are best.

In one common style, 3/8-inch vertical grooves spaced 8 inches apart give the appearance of boards backed by battens. Another has a rough surface resembling wood fresh from the saw, and another a high-relief grain made by wire brushing. Hardboard is also molded into simulations of stucco, shakes or shingles. Even plain hardboard can be patterned with vertical battens.

Panels should overlap the foundation by 2 inches; allow an expansion gap of 1/8 inch along panel edges and ends and where panels meet the soffits, rake boards and door and window casings. When the height of a wall exceeds the length of the panels, as in a gable wall or a two-story house, install a second course above the first. Locate the plate—the stud that lies along the tops of the studs—and cut panels so that the horizontal seam lies over the center line of the plate. Nail the panels into the plate.

BACK-LAP EDGE

1 Positioning the first panel. Set a panel, cut to length, to overlap the corner of a wall, with the top snugged up to the soffit and the back-lap edge 1/4 inch short of the center line of a stud; mark the corner edge in line with the thickest parts of the clapboards or shingles of the adjoining wall.

Cut the panel at the mark and start a nail midway on each long edge at the stud positions.

Set the panel back in place with a 1/8-inch spacer stick—a yardstick will do—between it and the soffit; then, while a helper secures the panel by lean-ing into it hard, drive the nails home. Drive additional nails every 6 inches around the top, bottom and corner edges and every 12 inches along the intermediate studs, but not into the back-lap edge; drive each nailhead just to the surface of the panel. Remove the spacer stick.

2 Joining panels. Install each succeeding panel with its front lap over the back lap of the preceding panel; align the seam between two panels at top and bottom, and fasten the new panel in place. At joints do not nail through laps; instead drive nails through the body of the new panel *(inset)*, leaving the adjoining panel free to expand and contract.

SPACER

SHEATHING — STUD
OLD SIDING — BACK LAP
PANEL BODY — FRONT LAP

3 Fitting around windows and doors. Cut the siding to fit around door- and window casings with a 3/16-inch gap on all sides for caulking. To retain lapped outer edges, cut lengths from full-width panels rather than remnants.

Use a circular saw to make the inside cut shown below. Work in dry conditions and use a GFCI-protected circuit *(page 171)*. Pull the guard out of the way, line the blade up over the cut mark with the forward edge of the base plate resting on the panel and the blade slightly above the panel. Start the saw and, using the base-plate edge like a hinge, slowly lower the blade into the panel. Saw to the marked corners and cut out the small remaining arc of material with a handsaw.

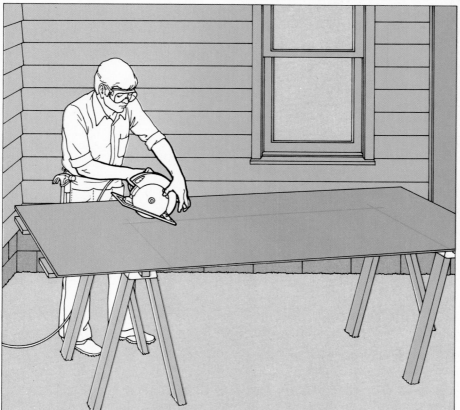

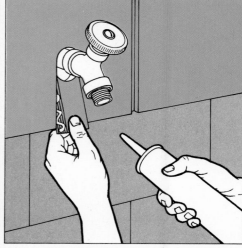

4 Slotting the panel for a pipe. Where a pipe or utility cable must pass through the siding and cannot be disconnected and later passed through a hole, mark the point by measuring the vertical distance from the bottom edge-line of the panel and the horizontal distance from the edge of the adjacent panel. Drill a hole slightly larger than the pipe and bevel-cut toward it so that the slot cut is slightly wider at the front than at the back. With a plane, bevel the sides of a strip of panel material so that you can push it in just flush to the surface. Apply panel adhesive to the sides of the filler strip and press it into place.

5 **Installing a course in a gable wall.** Use a plumb bob to mark points on the rake board or soffit that are directly above the joints. Measure from the joints to the marked points to find the edge dimensions of angle-topped panels to be fastened to the gable wall.

To waterproof the joint between the upper and lower panels, double-bend strips of flashing metal 3 inches wide so that the cross section roughly resembles a Z. Tack the strips in place so that one bent edge extends down in front of the top of the lower panels and the other will lie behind the bottom of the upper panels *(inset)*. End-lap the strips 3 inches. Nail on the panels.

1 × 3 — 1 × 4

6 **Capping outside corners.** Make corner boards by nailing a 1-by-3 on one side of the corner, then overlap with a 1-by-4 on the other; the direction of the overlap should duplicate that of the panels. Fasten each strip to the panels with staggered nails; do not nail the strips to each other. Lay a heavy bead of caulking on the end grain of any board with an exposed top, shaping the caulking to drain water.

7 **Capping inside corners.** Install inside cove molding *(inset)* to protect the joint where the panels meet. Fasten through both edges of the molding, using galvanized siding nails and butting the top of the molding to the soffit.

COVE MOLDING

8 **Installing a frieze board.** Seal the joint where the top edge of the siding meets the soffit with a new frieze board. Cut 1-by-6s into lengths so the joints will lie over the studs. Use bevel joints where the boards meet, and butt joints against the corner boards and inside cove moldings.

9 **Protecting the top edge.** If the rake board does not cover the upper edge of the siding and the gable has no overhang, double the board with a strip of lumber about 1 1/2 inches wide and thick enough to cover the exposed edge. Seal the strip with caulking between the strip, the rake board and the siding edge, and caulk any butt joints along the length of the strip. If the overhang is deep enough, run the siding up to it and nail on a new rake board in the same way that you fastened the frieze boards.

The Versatile Siding Board

A few rotting clapboards can turn a handsome house into an eyesore. In many cases, the offensive boards can be cut out and replaced *(page 360)*. But if you decide to apply an entirely new skin of wood siding, you have a wide choice.

Clapboards may be either plain or beveled. Other styles of wood siding boards have interlocking edges, and still others make a flat surface. Many types can be applied either horizontally or vertically, while some are suitable only for one or the other. Siding ranges up to 1 inch in thickness, 12 inches in width and 20 feet in length. Though cedar is the most common siding wood, boards are also available in redwood and in the man-made wood composition called hardboard.

Aside from the type of siding to use and whether to apply it vertically or horizontally, the only major consideration before starting work is how to finish corners. With horizontal siding, one option is to use corner boards *(page 363)*. You can substitute metal corners for outside corner boards; these corners simulate the effect obtained by mitering the ends of siding boards, a procedure too demanding for all but a seasoned carpenter. Vertical siding is applied much like horizontal siding except for a few details *(page 363)*.

Siding must be fastened to a sound surface. Existing siding that is badly damaged must be removed. Peeling paint may be a sign of moisture problems to be corrected. Window frames, doorframes and trim boards usually have to be built up to accommodate new siding *(pages 352-353)*. Downspouts and other wall fixtures must be removed. Furring strips are a necessity when re-siding over masonry or applying new horizontal siding over old clapboards. Horizontal siding on top of a flat wood surface, such as tongue-and-groove siding or vertically applied siding, requires no furring strips unless the surface of the wall is uneven.

Nails should be aluminum or stainless-steel siding nails with spiral or annular ring shanks for the tightest grip. Follow the nailing patterns below and overleaf, and when fastening the end of a board, especially a thin beveled one, drill a small pilot hole for the nail to prevent splitting.

Before nailing the first board, determine whether the old siding is level. If it consists of straight boards or panels, lay a level against the bottom edge of the siding on each side of the house. If the old siding is level, use it as a guide for the new. If the courses are canted or if the siding has an irregular edge, measure the house to be sure that the old siding will not show below the new *(page 361)*.

How to Nail the Joints

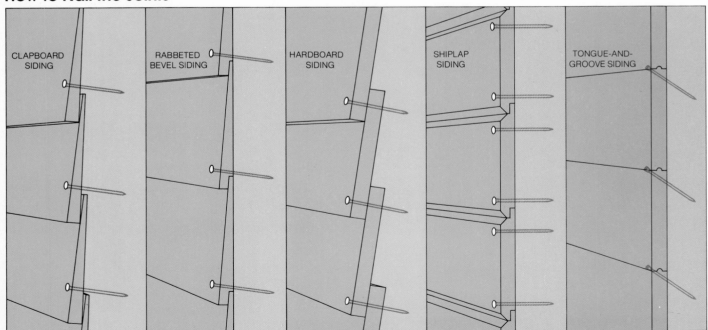

CLAPBOARD SIDING

RABBETED BEVEL SIDING

HARDBOARD SIDING

SHIPLAP SIDING

TONGUE-AND-GROOVE SIDING

Horizontal siding. Clapboard and rabbeted bevel siding closely resemble each other and are both nailed to studs or furring strips so that the nail misses the board below. Use one eightpenny nail in each stud or furring strip for 3/4-inch-thick siding, one sixpenny nail for thinner boards.

Hardboard siding, less likely to split, is nailed through the piece below. Shiplap sidings wider than 6 inches are face nailed with two eightpenny nails hammered one quarter of the board width from the end of the board. With narrower shiplap the upper nail is unnecessary. Tongue-

and-groove siding 6 inches wide or less is blind nailed—fastened at the base of the tongue with a 45° nail so that the head is hidden by the board above—with a single eightpenny finishing nail. Countersink the nail with a nail set. Wider boards are face nailed like shiplap siding.

Vertical siding. In the board-and-batten style, strips called battens cover joints between the wider boards. Fasten the boards first. Space them 1/2 inch apart and hammer eightpenny nails through the center of each board at 24-inch intervals. Cover the gaps between the boards with battens at least 1 1/2 inches wide, nailed through the center every 24 inches with a tenpenny nail.

Board-on-board siding, similar to board-and-batten, has underboards spaced to allow a 1 1/2-inch overlap by the top boards at both edges and nailed through the center with eightpenny nails. Top boards are attached with tenpenny nails driven next to the underboards.

Channel siding is a variety of shiplap used only vertically. Face-nail it with two eightpenny nails spaced to miss the rabbets in the board edges by 1/2 inch.

In addition to these styles, shiplap and tongue-and-groove sidings can also be applied vertically with the nailing patterns shown on page 359.

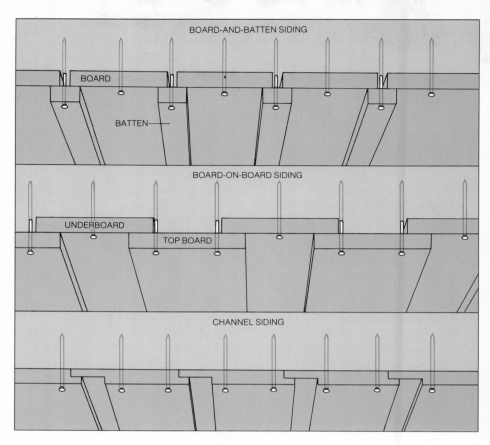

BOARD-AND-BATTEN SIDING

BOARD

BATTEN

BOARD-ON-BOARD SIDING

UNDERBOARD

TOP BOARD

CHANNEL SIDING

Working with Board and Batten

Installing new board and batten. To install boards on vertical board-and-batten siding, place the board properly spaced from the previously installed board and nail it, working from the top to bottom. Use the nailing pattern rec-

ommended for that type of siding *(above, center)*. Then position a batten centered over the joint between boards and nail it in the same way *(far right)*. Use the same procedure on board-on-board and channel siding. In any

case, it is good practice to apply wood preservative or wood primer to boards and battens, ensuring that the end grain, in particular, is adequately coated. When using wood preservative, follow all manufacturer's instructions for safety.

Installing Horizontal Boards

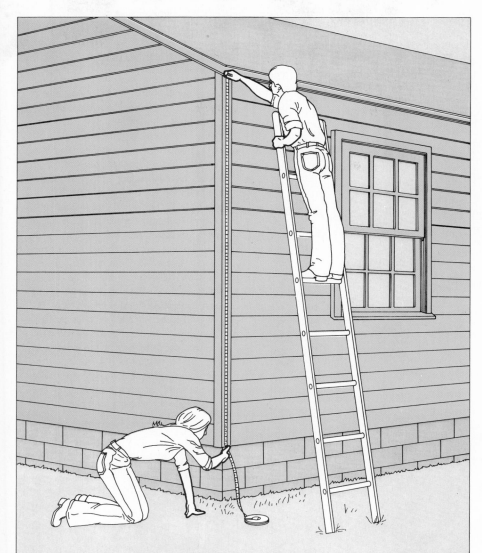

1 Measuring for a level first course. If the old siding is not level—check with a level along the bottom—record the height of the siding at each corner of the house; measure from the soffit to the bottom edge of the existing siding. Transfer the longest measurement to each corner, then snap a horizontal chalk line between the marks around the house.

Between the chalk lines, nail vertical furring strips to the old siding and add new corner boards *(page 350)*, unless you plan to install metal corners. Extend window and door casings *(pages 352-353)* and gable-ends *(page 357)*, if necessary, to accommodate the new siding.

2 Nailing the starter strip. For clapboards, nail a starter strip over the furring strips , flush with their bottom edges. Use a board about 1 1/2 inches wide and as thick as the top edge of the siding, and fasten it to each furring strip with a sixpenny nail.

Rabbeted-bevel, shiplap and tongue-and-groove sidings require no starter strips.

3 **Applying the siding.** For the first course, start a nail near the end of the board so the nails will enter furring strips or studs. With a helper, hold the board so that it overlaps the bottom edge of the starter strip by 1/8 inch or, where no starter strip is used, overlap the joint between sheathing and foundation by 1 inch. If you use corner boards, be sure to make tight joints between them and the siding. Butt lengths of siding at furring strips or studs, staggering the joints for weathertightness.

Subsequent courses of rabbeted-bevel, shiplap and tongue-and-groove siding space themselves. For clapboard siding, make a story pole with divisions the width of the exposure. Use the pole to mark corner boards, then snap a chalk line for each course.

A Story Pole for Horizontal Siding

To determine the ideal starting point for each course of shingles or shakes, use a story pole. Make one from a 1-by-2 the height of the major wall of your house—measured from the soffit to 1 inch below the existing siding or sheathing. In a two-story house, you will have to splice pieces to make a long story pole. Draw marks on the wood at evenly spaced intervals equal to the desired exposure for each course. Then hold the story pole alongside a window casing with the top of the pole jammed against the soffit. Adjust the spacing marks if necessary so courses above and below the casing will be at least 4 inches deep. Transfer the markings to both sides of each inside and outside corner, and to all window and door casings. Then drive a hardened masonry nail partway into each corner of the foundation at the bottom marker of the major wall of your house. Stretch a string between the nails to indicate the butt line for the starter courser of shingles or shakes.

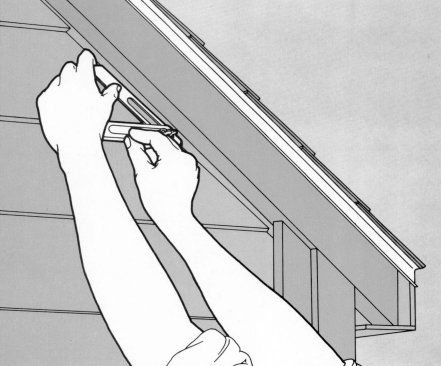

STORY POLE COURSE MARKINGS

4 **Fitting at obstacles.** At gables, measure the rake angle with a T bevel and cut the ends of the siding to match. Trim the width of the topmost course if necessary. Caulk all joints between the ends of siding boards and the house. To fit siding around corners of windows and doors, saw away part of the board to leave a tongue that fits snugly into the space above or below the opening. Do not drive nails into tongues narrower than 2 inches.

Installing Vertical Boards

1 Installing the first board. If you find that the corners of the house are not plumb, plane or rip an edge of the first board so that when nailed in place, one edge will be flush with the corner or corner board and so that the other edge will be vertical (exaggerated for clarity below). Align the bottoms of boards with a chalk line around the house *(page 361)* and nail them in place, using the nailing patterns shown on page 360.

2 Butting vertical boards. To help keep water from seeping into a joint, bevel the ends of adjoining boards before nailing either to the wall. Stagger joints for a pleasing appearance.

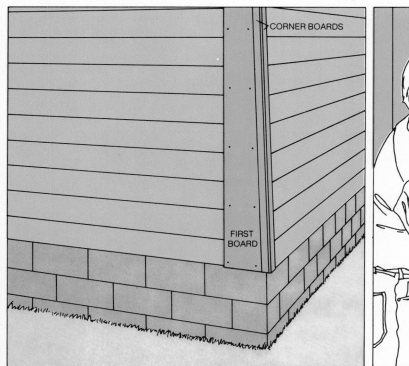

CORNER BOARDS

FIRST BOARD

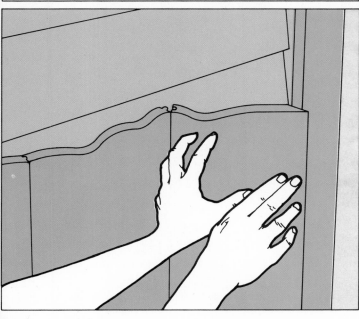

3 Beveling for a tight fit. When fitting a shiplap or tongue-and-groove board along a window or doorframe, rip the board to fit the space, then bevel the edge with a plane to the shape shown at left. Insert the tongue into the groove of the preceding board, then push the beveled edge against the wall. Nail the board in place.

If the board is cut out to fit around the frame, use a chisel to complete any part of the bevel in a corner that the plane cannot reach.

Metal and Plastic—Boards without Wood

Low cost and ease of installation make lightweight vinyl and aluminum siding the most popular materials for re-siding jobs, and increasingly, for the outer covering of new walls. Both are available with insulation backing if desired.

Choosing between the two, which are remarkably similar in panel sizes and shapes, mounting techniques and durabililily, is mostly a matter of taste and availability. Vinyl is a bit easier to work, does not dent or show scratches and resists heat and cold better than aluminum. But it can crack when struck in cold weather and cannot be repainted.

Aluminum is usually less costly than vinyl, and comes in a brighter palette of factory-baked enamel finishes. But it is easily dented and scratched, and some codes require electrical grounding.

Whichever material you use, the key to professional-looking work is in the installation of the accessories—F channel, J channel, corner posts, starter strips and trim. When these are mounted level or plumb in their correct locations, the rest of the siding job is mostly routine sawing and hammering. Aluminum requires no special tools, but you will need a snap-lock punch, available at hardware stores and siding dealers, to indent the edges of some vinyl panels *(page 366)*. When replacing vinyl panels, you will also need a handy zipper tool *(right)*.

Both vinyl and aluminum siding expand and contract more than wood does, and allowances must be made for this movement. Always provide a 1/4- to 1/8-inch space at joints and panel ends. Never pull vinyl panels taut before nailing, since this may cause dimpling or rippling as they expand. With either material, drive nails straight into the wall or sheathing behind it through the centers of the oval nailing slots, leaving a gap of about 1/32 of an inch between the nailheads and the material—the thickness of a matchbook cover.

While it is possible to apply vinyl or aluminum siding without installing a new soffit—or vice versa—it is usually advisable to do both. If you already have a soffit, you may simply want to cover it with new material. If you do not have one—or choose to rip out the old one—use at least one perforated panel every 10 feet for ventilation.

Like wood, vinyl and aluminum siding can be installed horizontally, vertically or—by special arrangements of mounting appliances—in both directions on the same wall. To make the lines of overlapping joints virtually invisible, begin siding at a point farthest from the usual viewing locations—front sidewalk, front entrance, driveway—and work toward those locations, lapping the previous panel. The finished wall will appear to be an unbroken expanse of siding when viewed from the "favored" side.

Punching and Zipping to Replace Vinyl Panels

Installing vinyl siding panel. A snap-lock punch and a zipper tool are used to install vinyl siding panels. Installing panels is easy: Mark the last panel at the top to size and cut it with tin snips, smoothing the cut edges with a utility knife. If necessary, measure and fit the panel around obstructions; then, using the snap-lock punch, dimple the panel every 16 inches along the edge to be fitted into the undersill trim channel *(inset)*. Working with a helper, slide the panel into place. First, fit into place the edge of the panel overlapped by an adjacent panel, J channel or corner post and snap the dimpled edge into the trim channel; if necessary, pry out the trim channel slightly, using an old flat-tipped screwdriver *(below)*.

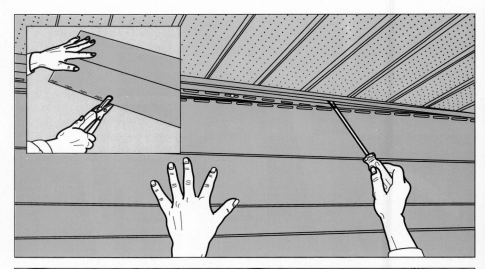

Locking the panel into place. To lock the panel onto the panel it overlaps, use the zipper tool. Starting at one end of the panel, slip the tip of the zipper tool behind it, hooking onto its lip, and pull firmly, snapping it onto the panel it overlaps *(above)*, zipping it in place.

A Horizontal Layout

1 **Installing a soffit track.** If you plan to include a new soffit with the siding, begin by mounting a track of F channel to receive the soffit panels at the top edge of the siding. Use a level to mark points on the wall that line up with the bottom of the fascia board, then strike chalk lines between those points. If using vinyl, nail facing strips of F channel both to the bottom of the fascia and to the wall; with aluminum, only the wall channel is needed. If you are not adding a soffit, simply nail strips of undersill or general-purpose trim *(page 366)* along the upper edge of the existing siding.

2 **Nailing in corner posts.** To provide vertical support for horizontal panels, attach grooved corner posts the height of the siding, setting them 1/4 inch below the top trim. To make sure they are vertical, pin each with a couple of nails at the center and check for plumb *(below)* before nailing. Drive nails at 12-inch intervals along the nailing flanges *(inset)* on both sides.

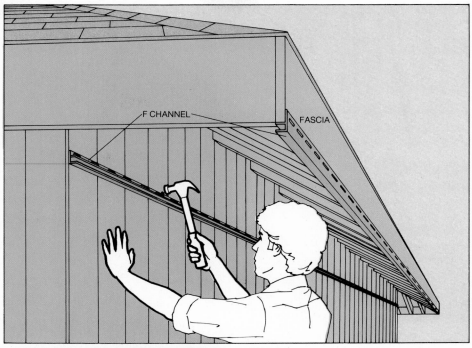

F CHANNEL

FASCIA

NAILING FLANGE

CORNER POST

J CHANNEL

3 **Mounting window and door trim.** Nail strips of J channel, mitered at the corners, to the tops and sides of all large wall openings—windows, doors, louvers, air-conditioner recesses. To allow for mitering, cut the top piece longer than the top by two channel widths, and the side pieces longer than the sides by one channel width. Nail the top piece first, then carefully fit and nail the side pieces *(left)*.

4 **Installing the panels.** Lock the first panel into the lip of a starter strip, nailed along the bottom of the old siding, before sliding it into the corner post *(below)* and nailing at 16-inch intervals. After the starter course, lock each panel into the one below it. Where a panel meets a corner, allow 1/4 inch for expansion.

STARTER STRIP

5 **End-to-end joints.** To join panels on the same course, lap the factory-notched end of one panel by about an inch with the unnotched end of the next, leaving a gap between nailing strips. If you use aluminum, slip a small metal backer plate behind each joint for support, and nail it to the wall before nailing the panel. Stagger joints in adjoining courses by at least 4 feet.

6 **Cutting around wall openings.** When there is less than a panel width between the top of a course and the bottom of a window or other opening, notch a panel to fit snugly underneath. Hold the panel against the opening to mark the cutout dimensions, adding 1/4 inch in each direction for expansion. Make vertical cuts with metal shears *(below)*; score the hori-

zontal cut with a utility knife and snap out the section. If you are using insulation-backed panels, cut the insulation before scoring. To secure the cutout section under a window, nail a strip of undersill or general-purpose trim beneath the sill. If necessary, add furring to maintain the pitch of the siding when the panel is locked to the trim *(inset)*.

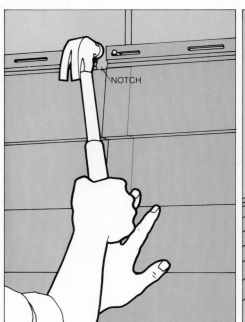

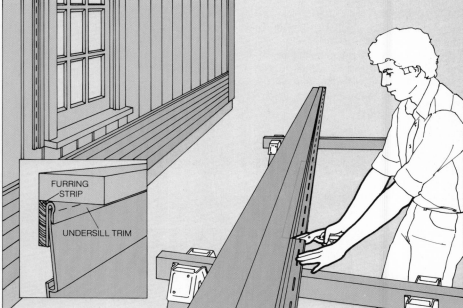

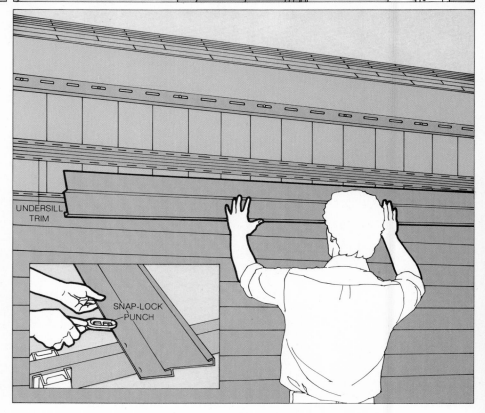

7 **Installing the top panel.** The top course is not nailed, but is tucked into a strip of undersill trim. After the trim has been nailed just beneath the soffit track, or along the top of the existing siding, measure the gap between the last course and the trim. Cut the final panels to fit, and use a snap-lock punch to indent the upper edge of each panel every 6 inches *(inset)*. Then push the panel into the trim while locking its bottom edge into the lip of the panel below. The indentations will lock the top into the trim.

366

A Vertical Layout

1 **Mounting the starter strip.** If you are using vertical vinyl panels, start from the center of the wall. After you have nailed in corner posts, mount strips of drip cap along the bottom of the wall, and J channel along the top. Then drop a plumb line from the center of the wall to mark the location of the double-channeled starter strip. Nail the strip precisely on the plumb marks, allowing 3/8 inch at the top for expansion.

If you are using aluminum instead of vinyl, install J channel at both top and bottom; omit the corner posts and starter strip.

2 **Mounting the panels.** After cutting panels to fit between trim strips, allowing 3/8 inch for expansion, install each one by inserting it into the top strip *(below)* and then lowering it onto the bottom strip before locking it to the adjoining panel. With vinyl, work from the center until you are a panel width or less from the corners.

With aluminum, begin about a foot from the end of the wall. Cut off the simulated batten at the outer edge of the starter panel and plumb carefully before nailing on both sides. Then proceed across the wall.

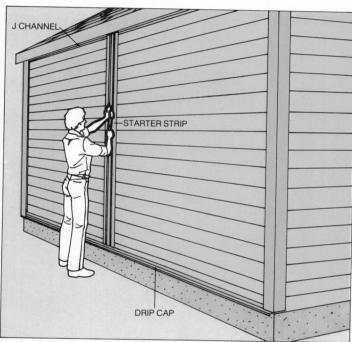

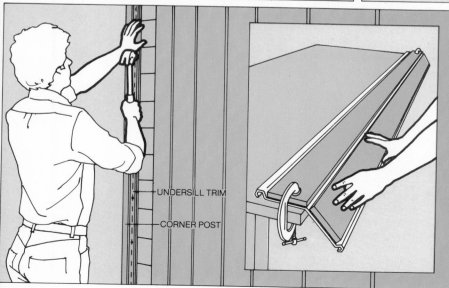

3 **Finishing the corners.** If you are using vinyl, nail a piece of undersill trim inside the corner post *(left)* and add furring if necessary to keep it straight. Do not nail the trim through a post nailing flange. Cut the last panel to fit, allowing about 1/4 inch for expansion; indent its edge with a snap-lock punch so it will lock into the corner trim.

With aluminum, fit the last panel on each wall so that it extends past the corner and mark points 1/8 inch beyond the corner at top and bottom. Remove the panel, clamp it between boards and use another board to bend it to a 90° angle at the marks *(inset)*. Remount the bent panel and nail it around the corner. When you reach the last corner and return to the starting point, mount a strip of general-purpose trim over the nailheads along the outer edge of the starter panel to receive the last corner panel.

Mounting a Soffit

1 **Installing soffit panels**. Soffits are made of specially constructed panels, their sides locked into one another and their ends fitted into tracks. For vinyl *(below, left)*, cut the panels to fit between the channels of the soffit track *(page 365)*, allowing 1/4 inch for expansion. If the span is greater than 18 inches, hang nailing strips,

2-by-2 inches, from the rafters to the soffit mid-point. Bend the panels slightly to slip them into the ends of the track and lock them together while you push them toward the center of the soffit run. If you have a nailing strip, use a pair of aluminum trim nails to fasten each panel to it. For aluminum *(below, right)*, where only one

mounting channel is used, cut the panels to cover three fourths of the fascia bottom, leaving space for the fascia cover *(Step 3)*. Set one end of each panel into the channel, allowing 1/8 inch for expansion. Make sure it is square and locked into the preceding panel, then nail the other end to the fascia with aluminum nails.

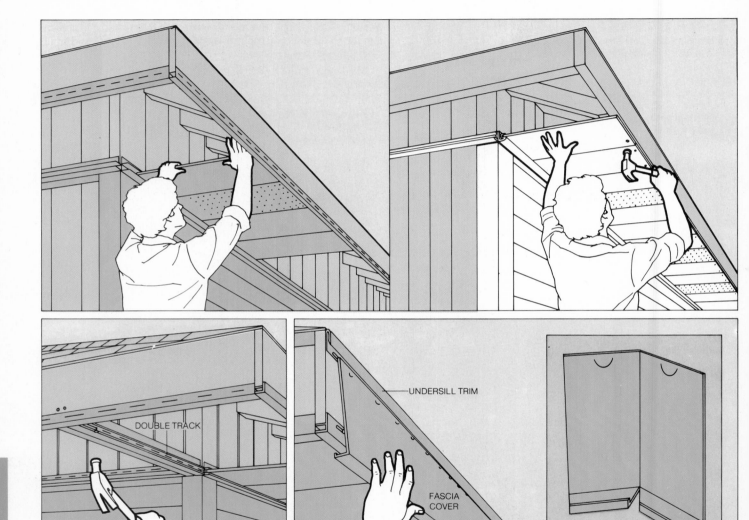

DOUBLE TRACK

UNDERSILL TRIM

FASCIA COVER

2 **Finishing a soffit corner**. When two runs of soffit panels meet at a corner, a simple channel extension permits one run to fill the corner gap. Nail a double track to the bottom of a 2-by-2 strip nailed between the wall and fascia, parallel to one row of soffit panels and perpendicular to the other. Install panels to fill the two runs, trimming and bending the last panels to fit securely.

3 **Covering the fascia**. Finish the soffit installation by covering the fascia board with special J-shaped panels. If you are using vinyl, nail a strip of undersill trim along the top of the fascia, cut fascia covers to the correct width and indent the top edges with a snap-lock punch *(page 366)*. Install the covers by hooking them over the soffit channel and locking them into the

trim *(above)*. Make a corner cap *(inset)* by cutting off a 5 1/2-inch piece of fascia cover, marking and lightly scoring a vertical center line on the back, and cutting out a 90° section of the flange. When indented and bent, the cap will fit snugly. If you use aluminum, nail the covering to the fascia top, where the nailheads will be concealed by gutters or an L-shaped trim.

368

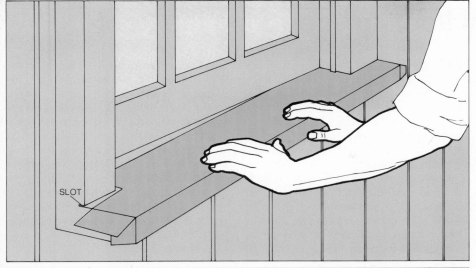

A Vinyl Cover for Window Frames

1 **Covering the sill.** Although sills and casings are usually left uncovered, some manufacturers provide optional vinyl coverings that can be installed before mounting window trim *(page 43)*. Before covering the sill, trim the ends flush with the outside edges of the casings and saw a slot about 1/16 inch wide—the width of a keyhole-saw blade—and 1/8 inch deep at the bottom of both casings. Cut the cover big enough to overlap the sill 2 inches at each end, and apply vinyl cement on the back and the sill. Press the cover onto the sill, slipping it into the slots before folding the ends. Seal the folds with single nails, and nail every 6 inches beneath the sill.

2 **Covering the casings.** The L-shaped coverings for the casings are fitted first onto the sides and then to the top. Cut the side casings to extend all the way from the sill to the upper edge of the top casing, notching the inside edge to pass over the top casing. Fit the covering onto the casing; nail the inner edge every 6 inches. Measure and cut the top casing long enough to extend across both side casings. Then cut out a 45° angle at each end, so that the angles lap the top of the side casings *(left)*. Nail the covering along the inner edge.

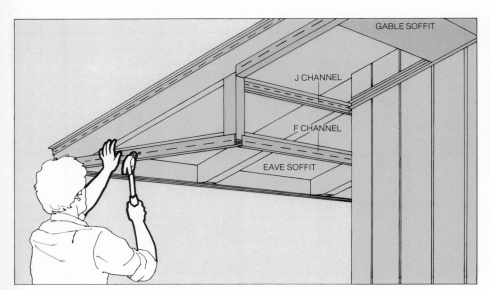

Corner Framing for Uneven Soffits

Boxing in gable ends. On some gabled houses two runs of soffit meet unevenly at the corners, and you may have to build a frame of 2-by-2s nailed into the fascia and corner studs. Nail strips of F channel to provide an extension for the eave soffit and J channel to hold the pieces of fascia cover that box in the frame.

Choosing the Right Roofing, Preparing the Roof

The choice of a roofing material, like the choice of a siding, involves such factors as appearance, cost, durability and ease of installation. But in roofing, an added factor—the slope of the roof you plan to cover—limits the choice of materials.

The more nearly level the slope, the slower the runoff of water from the roof, and a slow runoff calls for an especially waterproof covering. A completely flat roof, for example, must be covered by soldered metal or by built-up roofing—and because these materials need special installation skills and tools, a flat roof should be laid by a professional. But a roof with a gentle slope can be covered by a homeowner, using roll roofing *(pages 82-83)*.

On steeper slopes, the range of practical materials increases. Asphalt shingles, for example, are widely used on roofs with moderate to steep slopes because they are inexpensive, easy to install and available in a wide variety of colors. To enhance the value of your house, you may prefer to reroof with such traditional materials as slate, ceramic tile, or wood shingles or shakes. All are attractive and durable—but they are also expensive, hard to install and may need special roof preparations: Slate and tile are particu-larly heavy and require sturdy roof supports, while wood shingles must be laid over open planks for ventilation.

The chart on the next page compares the factors of cost and convenience in widely available roofing materials. The drawings on this page show how to measure the slope and area of a roof—information you need in order to choose a roofing material and to estimate the amount to buy. Most materials are sold in units called squares, each capable of covering 100 square feet; the only exception is roll roofing, which comes in rolls of varying lengths and weights.

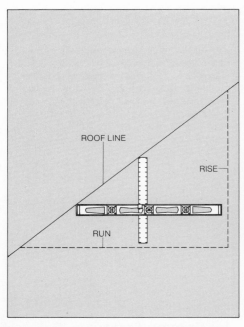

Measuring the slope of a roof. A roof's slope is the rate at which it rises, expressed as inches of vertical rise for each foot of horizontal run; for example, a roof that rises 3 inches vertically while covering 12 inches of the house beneath it is said to have a slope of 3 in 12. To measure slope from outside a house, mark off 12 inches on a level and set the end of the level at the rake of the roof. With the level itself aligned horizontally under the rake, use a ruler to measure the vertical distance between the 12-inch mark and the rake (in the example above, a 10-inch reading on the ruler would indicate a slope of 10 in 12). To measure a slope from inside a house, follow the same method but measure along a rafter rather than the rake.

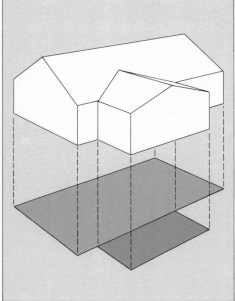

Measuring area of a roof. Make a plan of the ground space covered by each surface of a roof, including overhangs at gables and eaves. Break the ground spaces down into rectangles and calculate the area of each rectangle. In the example above, the house occupies two rectangles, covered by roofs of two different slopes.

To convert flat ground areas into slanted-roof areas, use the table above, right. Find the figure in the right-hand column that corresponds to the slope of the roof, and multiply this figure by the ground area under the roof to get the area of the roof. To estimate the amount of material you need to cover roofs of different slopes, take the total of the roof areas, add 10 percent to

Slope	Conversion factor
1 to 3 in 12	1.054
4 in 12	1.083
5 in 12	1.09
6 in 12	1.12
7 in 12	1.16
8 in 12	1.20
9 in 12	1.25
10 in 12	1.30
11 in 12	1.36
12 in 12	1.414

this total to allow for double layers of covering along ridges, eaves and hips, and round the new total to the next higher square—that is, the next 100 square feet—of material.

In the house shown here, one of the rectangles measures 1,600 square feet, covered by a roof with a slope of 10 in 12; the other measures 400 square feet, covered by a roof with a slope of 5 in 12. The area of the first roof is 1,600 by 1.30, or 2,080 square feet; that of the second is 400 by 1.09, or 436 square feet; and the total roof area is 2,516 square feet. An additional 10 percent allowance makes the total 2,768 square feet, which should be rounded to 2,800 square feet, or 28 squares.

A Guide to Roofing Materials

Type	Cost	Durability (years)	Minimum slope	Advantages	Limitations
asphalt shingles	inexpensive	12-25	2 in 12	easy installation; available in a variety of weights and colors; requires little maintenance, easy to repair	lower fire resistance
roll roofing	inexpensive	10-15	1 in 12	easy installation and maintenance	poor fire resistance; drab appearance
built-up roofing	moderate	10-20	0 in 12	most waterproof of all roofing	lower fire resistance; must be installed professionally; leaks difficult to locate
wood shingles and shakes	moderate to expensive	15-30 (shingles) 25-75 (shakes)	3 in 12 (steeper in humid climates)	easy installation; attractive rustic appearance; natural insulator	highly flammable unless specially treated; shingles must be laid over open planks
slate	expensive	50-100	4 in 12	attractive traditional appearance, fire resistant	heavy, brittle; requires sturdy roof support; long and delicate installation may require special tools; needs regular replacement of damaged pieces; difficult to repair
ceramic tiles	expensive	50-100	4 in 12	attractive traditional appearance, fire resistant	heavy, brittle; requires sturdy roof support; time-consuming installation requires special tools; availability of replacement pieces unreliable; difficult to repair
metal panels	inexpensive to moderate	25-50	2 in 12	easy installation and patching; can be painted any color; fire resistant	subject to damage from wind, trees, any contact; may decrease value of house

Comparing roofing materials. In this chart, "Cost" refers to the relative cost of materials alone; it does not include the cost of labor. In most cases, the cost of professional installation is higher for the traditional roofing materials—slate, tile and wood shingles and shakes—than for the newer materials, which are designed to be installed more quickly. The minimum slope is the slope at which a specific material begins to provide adequate protection against water. All the materials listed can be applied to surfaces steeper than the minimum, but as slopes increase, such considerations as appearance and durability become more important. Roll roofing, for example, provides adequate covering for steep as well as gentle slopes, but its plainness and poor durability make it an unlikely choice for any but the most gradual slopes.

"Durability" is a rough measure of how long a roof will last with proper maintenance; the figures given apply to temperate climates. The columns listing advantages and limitations for each material concentrate on installation and maintenance.

Materials for Roofs

Roofs are covered in a variety of materials, many of them illustrated here. For everyday purposes, a house roof can be described by naming the materials that cover it, for example, an asphalt shingle roof.

Over its lifetime a roof is drenched by more than 3,500 tons of water, baked by 50,000 hours of direct sunlight, squeezed by temperature changes totaling half a million degrees and swept by two million miles of passing wind. Only then—after 20 years—is an asphalt-shingle roof ready for replacement. Roofs of slate and tile do even better, shrugging off the ravages of nature for a century or more.

The shape of a roof affects somewhat the roofing material that may be used on it. Most roof shapes are variations on two types: the gable roof and the hip roof. The gable roof slopes on two sides and has eaves and rakes, while the hip roof slopes on four sides and has only eaves. Different styles may be combined on one house. Any substantial interruption in a roof—the joints around projections or where a roof meets a wall—must be waterproofed with metal flashing.

The job of reroofing a house has been made simpler by standardized roofing materials designed for easy installation.

Asphalt shingles, in a wide assortment of styles, colors and weights, are appropriate to an increasing variety of roofing situations.

The shingles are easily applied and come with dabs of adhesive that automatically seal them against lifting in a high wind.

Classic shakes, thin slabs split from a section of a cedar log, were formerly made by hand. Now they are machine made. These modern shakes go onto a roof more easily and tightly, but retain their hand-split ancestors' rustic look.

Slates for roofing come in standard sizes with prepunched nail holes. Clay tiles and concrete tiles (which look almost exactly like clay tiles) are manufactured in classic patterns that fit together like building blocks.

Often a new roof can be laid directly over the old one, with no more preparation than the removal of material at the ridge and hips and the installation of new flashing. But if there is already more than a single layer of roofing in place—as is likely on any house more than 20 years old—you must pry off the old material down to the wood sheathing covering the rafters. And sometimes the sheathing or rafters may also need repair.

All roofing except wood shingles and shakes requires solid sheathing, preferably of plywood. Shingles and shakes are generally laid over an open roof deck made of 1-inch-thick boards spaced 2 to 4 inches apart. If you have an open deck you can reroof with wood using the existing boards, provided you keep the same distance between courses. If the spacing will change, move the existing boards or replace them. If you are reroofing with any other material, provide a solid deck by replacing the spaced boards with plywood or by nailing plywood over the boards. Caution: Remove and replace sheathing one side at a time only; removing all of the sheathing at once may allow the roof to shift or even collapse.

Once the deck is prepared, protect its perimeter with drip edge, metal or plastic preformed to direct runoff away from fascia boards at eaves and rakes.

Underlayment—which is generally a heavy asphalt-impregnated paper called roofing felt—is used under the roofing except for wood or roll roofing. It adds protection to the roof and shields it from rain while the new roof is installed.

In any climate, low-sloped roofs—those with pitches of less than 4 inches per foot—call for a double layer of underlayment. For steeper pitches in climates generally free of ice, apply one layer of felt. If there is occasional icing, add a layer of roll roofing at the eaves. Where icing is severe, you will need a double layer of felt over the entire deck. Use 15-pound felt underlayment—it weighs 15 pounds per 100 square feet—for most roofs; 30-pound felt is recommended for slate roofs, and 45-pound felt for tile roofs.

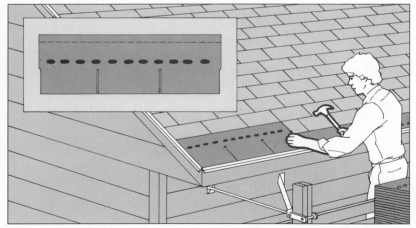

Asphalt shingle roofs. Asphalt shingles generally are made as 3-foot-long, 1-foot-wide strips of wood-fiber, rag-fiber or fiberglass felt impregnated with asphalt and coated with fine gravel or ceramic granules. A pair of 5-inch-deep slots called cutouts divides each strip into three 1-by-1-foot sections called tabs. Most contain dabs of adhesive across each strip just above the cutout tabs. When the adhesive is softened by the heat of the sun, it seals down the tabs over the overlapping shingles against wind and heat-caused curling. Shingles are laid in courses starting at the eaves. The first course overlaps a starter course of shingles with their tabs cut off along the eaves. A variety of weights is available, the heavier weights being longer lasting, except fiberglass felt, which is both lightweight and long lasting. Shingle roofs are subject to fire started by falling embers, and shingles are rated according to their resistance to fire. Those with a Class A fire rating are most fire-resistant; those with a Class C fire rating less resistant.

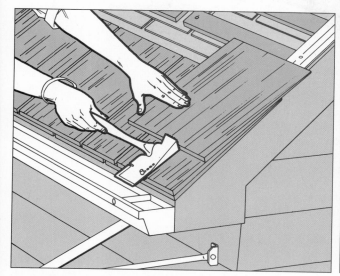

Wood shingle roofs. Wood shingles come as hand-split or smooth-surfaced and are installed over wood strips. Wood shingles are laid in courses, beginning at the eaves, with those installed on lesser-sloped roofs laid with less exposure (greater overlap) to shed water more readily. This makes the roof more waterproof, but requires more shingles. A shingler's hatchet contains an adjustable peg to gauge exposures, for uniformity from bottom to top (above). On a 3-in-12 to 4-in-12 pitch roof, exposure is usually 3 3/4 inches for 16-inch shingles, 4 1/4 inches for 18-inch shingles and 5 3/4 inches for 24-inch shingles, more for steeper roofs. Wood shingles are subject to fire and may not be permitted in areas of high fire risk. Those that have been treated with fire retardant have improved resistance to fire.

Wood shake roofs. Wood shakes have a rougher surface than wood shingles making them naturally ventilated beneath so they can be laid directly over underlayment. A doubled starter course of underlayment at the eaves gets the job going, then a course of underlayment overlaps the starter course. Subsequent courses of shakes are installed and overlapped with a course of underlayment. A piece of tape placed on the handle of the shingler's hatchet is used to gauge the desired exposure: usually 7 1/2 inches with 18-inch shakes and 10 inches with 24-inch shakes. Wood shake roofs have a low resistance to fire and may not be permitted in high-fire-danger areas. The fire resistance of some shakes is improved by special treatment.

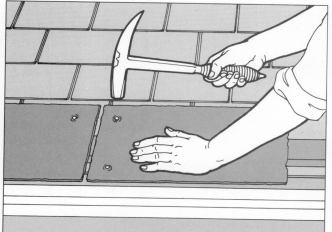

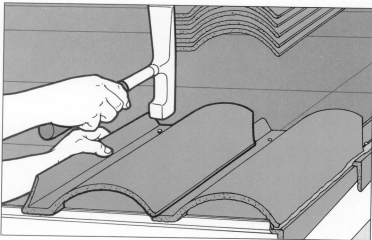

Slate tile roofs. Slate tiles may be applied over old asphalt shingles (above) as well as over a freshly felted roof, provided the roof structure is made for the load. (A professional engineer should check.) Standard roofing slate is 3/16 inch thick and 18 to 24 inches long, and generally is sold in random widths that vary from about 8 to 14 inches. Most roofs are covered with assorted widths of uniform length. Slates come with nailing holes and irregularly sloped or beveled edges. When installing them, be sure the exposed bevel faces upward. A slater's hammer is used to shape and nail the slates. Slate tile roofs are highly resistant to fire from falling embers, since the slates themselves will not burn.

Clay and concrete tile roofs. Formed tiles of clay and concrete come in myriad sizes, shapes and colors, but the most familiar is the single-barrel style shown above. Most clay and concrete tiles contain prepunched nail holes at the upper corner, and a single nail driven with a mason's hammer is used to hold each tile. Single-barrel tile is 13 1/4 inches long, 9 3/4 inches wide and 3/8 inch thick. Because a tile roof is quite heavy and requires a roof structure that will support it, consult a professional engineer before you order any tiles. Tiles start with one or two courses at the eaves, overlapping horizontally as well as vertically, so you must measure the width of your roof as well as its height to plot regular courses in both directions. Since you will need an assortment of specially shaped accessory tiles to finish the eaves, rakes, ridge and hips, enlist the help of your roofing supplier to determine the exact exposure. Like slate, clay and concrete tile roofs are highly resistant to fire.

Roll Roofing for Economy

Superficially, a scrap of roll roofing resembles asphalt shingle: Like the shingle, the roll material consists of asphalt-impregnated felt—wood and rag fibers—covered with mineral granules. There the resemblance ends. The roofing comes in rolls that weigh between 50 and 90 pounds and unroll into strips 36 feet long and 3 feet wide. What is more, roll roofing has only half the life of shingles and lacks their esthetic appeal. But it is the fastest, easiest and least expensive roofing to install.

Roll roofing is especially suitable for low-slope roofs. It can be applied to roofs with pitches as little as one inch per foot—half the minimum pitch for shingles—and because the surface of low-slope roofs is not normally visible, the plain appearance of the roll material usually does not matter.

The double coverage, concealed-nail application method shown on these pages gives the neatest appearance, the greatest protection and the longest life. To follow it, use roofing with a 19-inch selvage—the material that is hidden when the roofing is installed.

For the best job, remove the old roof covering, repair the deck if necessary and install drip edges along the eaves and rakes. However, you can reroof under roll or shingle roofing if you nail down loose or torn material and repair blisters. Unroll the roofing and cut it into pieces slightly longer than the roof. For a roof longer than 20 feet, it may be more convenient to cut shorter lengths and combine the pieces on the roof with lap joints. In either case, pile the strips near the top of the roof—on a day when the temperature is over 45°—and let them flatten out for a day or so. During the job, move each strip down for installation; when you near the top of the roof, move the pile down.

1 Laying the starter course. Cut a starter strip 19 inches wide from the selvage portion of a roll, and fasten it to the sheathing with roofing nails spaced a foot apart in three horizontal rows. Locate these nails 1 1/2, 8 and 14 1/2 inches up from the lower edge of the strip, and start them an inch in from the rake. The lower edge of the starter strip should overhand the eaves by 1/2 inch; trim the rake edges for a 1/2-inch overhang.

2 Laying the first course. Cover the starter course with a full-width, 36-inch sheet of roofing, which is trimmed after nailing to overhang rakes and eave 1/2 inch. Space nails a foot apart, in two horizontal rows, 4 1/2 and 13 inches below the upper edge of the sheet.

3 Cementing laps. Fold the first course back to expose the starter strip and brush on asphalt cement *(below)*. Unfold the first course and press it firmly into the cement with a stiff broom. Nail and cement additional courses until you reach the ridge.

4 Making vertical joints. To join sheets of roofing that are shorter than the roof, make vertical lap joints *(below)*. Nail and cement a sheet in place, then drive a vertical row of nails an inch in from the end of the sheet with the nails spaced 4 inches apart. Install a second sheet, aligned to overlap the first by 6 inches, but do not nail through the overlap; instead, hold the second sheet back to expose the overlap, apply cement to the last 5 1/2 inches of the first sheet, and press the end of the second sheet down into the cement. Drive a vertical row of nails into the selvage of the second sheet; locate the row 1 inch in from the lapped end and the nails 4 inches apart.

5 Finishing hips and ridges. Cut strips 12 inches wide and 36 inches long from a roll of roofing to make pieces to be nailed and cemented over hips and ridges *(left)*. Use the 17-inch selvage of one of these pieces as a starter at the bottom of a hip or the end of a ridge. Snap a chalk line 5 1/2 inches to one side of the hip or ridge; using the chalk line as a guide, fasten the starter in place with rows of nails 4 inches apart and an inch from the edges. Coat the starter with asphalt cement. Lap the granule-covered end of a second piece over the starter, nail the selvage as you did the starter, and press the piece into the cement. Apply cement to the selvage of this piece and repeat the procedure for all subsequent pieces. Trim the selvage of the last complete piece to fit the end of the hip or ridge, then apply a granule-covered piece cut to fit the selvage. Lap the ridge over hips.

The Basics of Building with Bricks: A Brick Wall

Not everyone can match the expertise of Winston Churchill, an amateur mason who could lay a brick a minute (the average beginner's rate is about 75 to 100 bricks a day) and was invited to join the brick-layers' union. But anyone who wants to can lay bricks well, in structures that are both useful and good-looking. The work is not difficult—bricks are light and easy to handle, and their uniform size makes planning and patterning surprisingly simple. The finished structure can range from a freestanding wall made of brick alone to a complex affair—a flight of stairs or a backyard barbecue, for instance—consisting of an inexpensive cinder-block core with a handsome brick veneer covering. The freestanding wall, lending charm to the smallest yard or enclosing spaces such as flower beds and play areas, is probably the most common and the most popular. You can build your own—a wall standing on a concrete footing and rising up to 4 feet high—by using the techniques that are shown in the illustrations on the following pages.

The planning of a brick-construction job begins when you choose a location, well before the first brick is laid. For the brick wall, start by consulting local ordinances, building codes, your neighbors and (if you do not own the property) your landlord, to be sure

that are no legal obstacles to your proposed wall. Next, check your soil for drainage; the best-built wall may buckle or sink if it rests on marshy or spongy ground. Study the exact site of the wall with special care: A hill or slope presents special difficulties; avoid large trees with thick and widespread roots; and make sure that the concrete footing of the wall, which will extend about 2 inches to the front and rear, will not overlap an adjacent property line or sidewalk.

Now plan the wall itself in detail. To avoid the complexities of reinforcement, you should keep the wall under 4 feet high, but you can make it as long as you like and shape it with square corners. You can choose among a number of pattern bonds—that is, different ways of interlocking the bricks—but you are probably best off with the simplest pattern, called running bond, in which the bricks overlap one another so that vertical joints are staggered from course to course. (The basic wall shown in these pages is laid in running bond.)

When you have decided upon the size and shape of the wall, estimate the amount of materials you will need and bring them to the site all at once. An 8-by-12-inch concrete footing contains 6.66 cubic feet of concrete for each 10 feet of its length. To de-

termine the number of standard-size bricks, multiply the length of the wall by its height, double this figure (because the finished wall will be two bricks thick), and multiply by 7.5. Plan on about 1 cubic foot of mortar for each 5 square feet of wall surface.

When you place your order at a building supply dealer, select bricks that are roughly twice as long as they are wide, so that the topmost course, when placed across the parallel rows of bricks below it, will cover them completely. Be sure that the dealer has more of the same bricks on hand—bricks are often delivered broken or chipped, and you may spoil more bricks than you expect when you have to split them so that they will fit the running-bond pattern. In freezing climates, be sure to order bricks made for such temperatures.

When you have completed the footing, let the concrete cure a day or so before going on to bricklaying. As you work, set separate piles of bricks at convenient points to save time and keep them dampened. Keep a bucket of clean water or a hose nearby to clean your trowel and your level. Wet down the completed wall, and keep it moist for several days as the mortar cures. After two weeks or so, clean off all mortar stains and any areas of efflorescence that may have developed.

A Story Pole for Brick

To control the heights of courses in any brick structure, use a homemade measuring stick called a story pole. For a brick wall, cut a piece of scrap lumber to the total planned height of the wall. With a felt-tip marker or a similar indelible marker, draw a line near one end of the pole to indicate the top of the bricks in the first course. This first mark on the story pole should be equal to the combined height of a 1/2-inch mortar bed plus the exact height of a single brick (usually 2 1/4 inches). Then mark the brick height and mortar bed of each successive course all the way up the pole. As you build the wall, set the pole against newly laid bricks to make sure that the courses of brick rise evenly at every point.

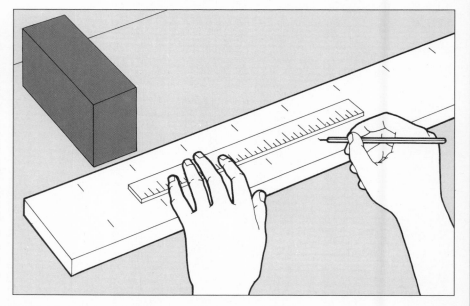

The anatomy of a brick wall. A freestanding brick wall, shown here in cross section, is actually a combination of simple structures. Like all walls, it rests on a footing—in this case, a 6-inch deep bed of gravel, topped by a cast-in-place reinforced concrete footing slab 8 inches deep and 12 inches wide. Reinforce the footing with two 1/2-inch reinforcing bars to prevent cracks from opening in the footing. The top of the footing is about 3/4 inch below ground level. Some walls consist of a single row of bricks; for added strength and better proportions, this one has two parallel rows, separated by a narrow air space and bound together at regular intervals by metal strips called wall ties. Both rows are formed by stretcher courses—bricks placed end to end, with 1/2-inch-thick vertical and horizontal mortar joints. At the top, the rows are locked together by a rowlock course—bricks set on their long narrow sides and extending from the front of the wall to the

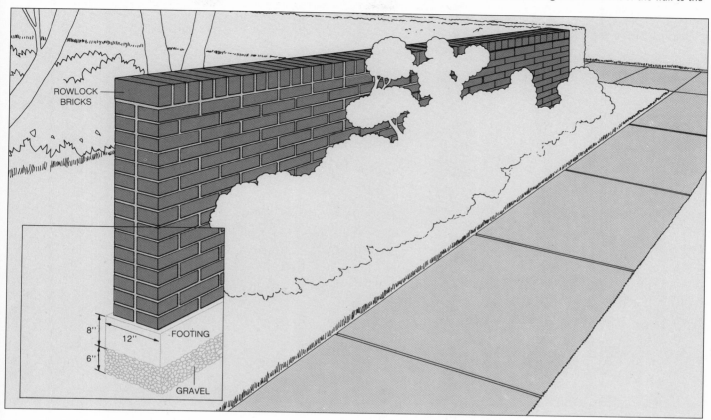

The Plan

A dry run for the first courses. From a fixed horizontal reference line, such as the side of your house, driveway or property line, measure out to the baseline you have chosen for the face, or front, of the wall. Drive stakes at the ends of this line and stretch a string between them. Then lay out the first face course of bricks on the ground between the stakes, following the string as a guide and using your forefinger to make 1/2-inch gaps between bricks. If the end bricks do not quite reach the stakes or fall slightly beyond them, move the stakes to fit the bricks.

Begin the rear, or backup, course of bricks about 1/2 inch behind the face course starting with a half brick and continuing with full-length stretchers. When you have placed several bricks, set a rowlock brick across the parallel rows; if it does not fit exactly across the bricks, adjust the width of the space between front and back courses. Lay out the remaining backup bricks, using a second half brick for the far end.

The Footing

Building and marking the footing. Outline the slab by driving pairs of stakes on both sides of the proposed footing at the beginning and end of the site. Tie strings to the stakes, then mark the string line on the ground by taking a handful of sand and letting it trickle out over the strings to make a sand outline. Remove the stakes, and use the sand outline as a guide for a trench about 14 3/4 inches deep. The trench must be long and wide enough to extend 2 inches beyond the ends of the baseline and about 12 inches wide, overlapping the baseline 2 inches in front and 10 behind. Fill the bottom with a layer of gravel 6 inches deep, then assemble forms, mix concrete and place the footing to 3/4 inch below ground level. In the final smoothing, taper the edges of the concrete downward very slightly—no more than 1/8 inch—to provide a runoff for excess moisture. Finally, mark the baseline again, 2 inches from the front of the footing, with a chalk line (*drawing*).

CHALK LINE

The Lead

1 Laying the first bricks. Hose down about 25 bricks or immerse them in water for a few minutes, then let the surface moisture evaporate. (Follow this procedure each time you use more bricks.) Mix a cubic foot of ready-packaged mortar. Moisten about 3 feet of the surface at one end of the foundation with a hose set to a fine spray and let this surface moisture evaporate. Throw a mortar line just behind the chalk line and lay up three bricks on the mortar bed. These first bricks will begin to form the lead, or end of the wall.

To make sure the bricks exactly follow the chalk line, align a level from the bricks to the chalk line beyond them. Adjust the bricks, if necessary to make them perfectly straight and flush to the chalk line. Set a story pole beside the bricks at various points to be sure that the bed joint measures 1/2 inch; the top of the brick should align with the first mark on the pole. (Repeat these story-pole checks as each course of brick is laid.)

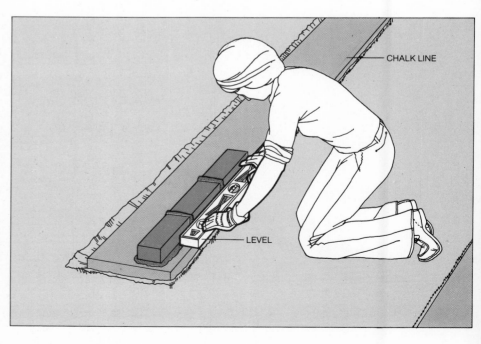

CHALK LINE

LEVEL

2 **Starting the backup course.** Throw a mortar line parallel to the three bricks you have laid for the face course and about 1/2 inch behind them. Place a half brick at the end of the mortar line, 1/2 inch behind the first face brick—or at a similar spacing determined in your dry run—then continue the backup course with two stretcher bricks. (As the wall rises, half bricks will alternate between the ends of the face and backup courses.) Use a level to align the backup bricks, and set the level across both courses at several points to be sure that the front and back bricks are level with each other.

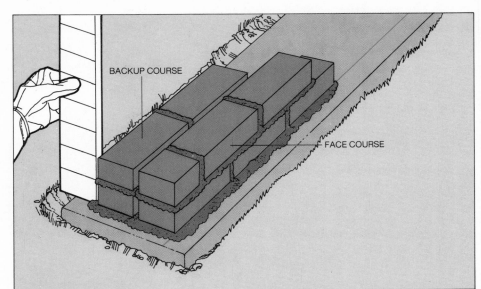

BACKUP COURSE

FACE COURSE

3 **Placing the first ties.** Metal wall ties *(inset)* are placed along the wall atop the second course and all other even-numbered courses. Throw a mortar line on the second face course and embed ties in the mortar about 12 inches apart, with the free ends of the ties lying over the backup course *(drawing)*. Then lay two whole stretcher bricks of the third face course over the embedded ties.

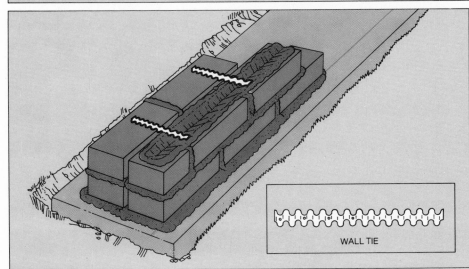

WALL TIE

4 **Mortaring the ties.** When the mortar below the third face course has begun to set, bend the wall ties up from the tops of the backup bricks. Caution: This phase of the job calls for special care to avoid disturbing the bricks that are already in place. Throw a mortar line on the backup bricks, then bend the ties down into the fresh mortar bed. Lay the backup course—one half brick followed by a whole one.

5 **Completing the first lead.** Lay five courses of the face and backup, with wall ties between the fourth and fifth courses; the lead should now be stepped up to a single brick at the end of the face and a half brick at the end of the backup. Use the level to check alignment. If you find a protruding brick, tap the level gently with your trowel handle to push the brick back into line. If a brick recedes, tap it from behind to bring it flush to the level. Do not worry about minute irregularities; correct only those that are obtrusive.

6 **Building the opposite lead.** At the opposite end of the footing, repeat Steps 1 through 5 to form a five-course lead. Checks with the story pole and the level are especially important at this stage of the job. The two leads must match exactly; if they do not, the completed wall will be unstable, with no way to correct the problem short of tearing down the leads and starting afresh.

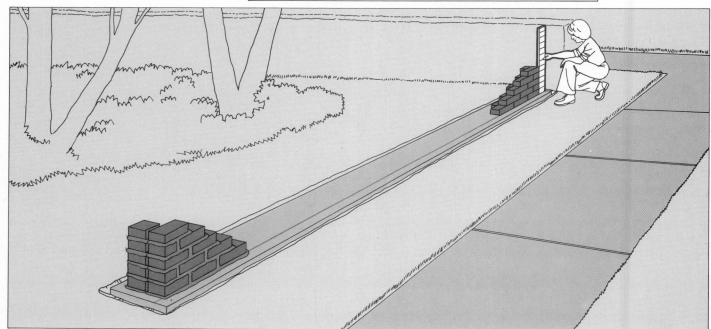

The Corners

1 **Preparing a mason's line.** As a guideline from lead to lead, use a mason's line—a string, slightly longer than the wall, stretched between wood or plastic blocks. Tie one end around a block, then fit it into the lengthwise groove. Hook the block around the end brick in the first course at either end of the wall, aligning the string precisely to the top edge of the brick. Extend the line to the other end of the wall, fasten the string to the second block, and hook this block around the corresponding brick in the first course; just as before, the string should be flush with the top edge of the brick.

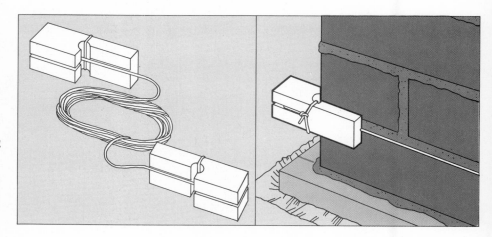

2 **Laying bricks between the leads.** Working from the ends of the wall toward the middle, lay the first face course between the leads, using the mason's line as a guide; the line should be 1/16 inch in front of the bricks and flush with the top edges. At the center of the course, place a closure brick, buttering both ends. Then lay the first backup course, using the line at the back of the wall.

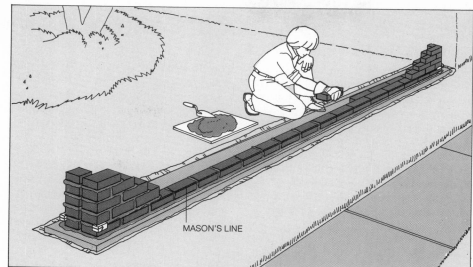

MASON'S LINE

3 **Building up to the top of the leads.** Always working from the ends toward the middle of the wall, lay the next four face and backup courses. Move the mason's line up one course at a time as you proceed, and insert wall ties about every 12 inches atop the second and fourth courses. When you have inserted closure bricks in the last course, the wall will be approximately 14 inches high. If you wish to complete it at this point, lay a cap course of rowlock bricks and fill the joints between end bricks of the two parallel rows with an inch of mortar.

4 **Extending the wall upward.** If you want a higher wall, built new leads at the ends and fill in the courses between the leads, always working from the ends toward the middle. As before, use a story pole as a guideline for the leads and a mason's line for the bricks between them. Five additional courses will give a wall 28 inches high; a third set of five courses makes it about 3 1/2 feet high. Two more courses of brick—making 17—raise the wall to maximum practical height.

Brick Patterns to Set in Sand or Cement

Brick has been used for centuries to surface plazas, roads and walks throughout much of the world. The qualities that make it suitable for these uses make brick a good choice for a patio surface that is at once elegant and practical. A brick surface is enduring, weather-resistant and low-glare, and it is composed of small standard units that are simple to install and easy to maintain.

Durable enough to use on driveways, brick makes an attractive low-cost veneer for a concrete-slab patio. Alternatively, for a patio, it can be laid without mortar, over sand, an underlayment that has certain advantages. A sand base allows rain water to seep down to nearby tree or shrub roots, and it lets bricks move independently as the earth below settles or shifts with freezing and thawing. In addition, loose bricks allow you flexibility: They can be removed in order to accommodate a broadening tree trunk or an additional flower bed.

Many bricklike blocks used today are not the traditional clay brick baked in the sun or fired in an oven, but are made of molded concrete. For this reason, the popular reddish-brown rectangular brick is only one of a wide array of colors and shapes. A variety of surface textures is also available. The best paving materials are relatively smooth, because a rough or grooved surface collects rain water; if the water freezes, the bricks may crack. But avoid bricks that are glazed or so smooth that they become slippery when wet. In a climate where the ground freezes, use bricks that are rated SW, which means they are capable of withstanding severe weather conditions.

The dimensions of paving materials also vary widely: They can be as thin as 1/2 inch (if laid in mortar on a concrete slab) or as thick as 3 1/8 inches, and they range in length from 7 1/2 to 11 1/2 inches and in width from 3 1/2 to 5 1/2 inches. This range of sizes allows you to plan a patio with or without gaps between the bricks. For a pattern laid tight on sand—desirable for preventing weed growth—you will need

special paving bricks, exactly half as wide as they are long.

Common building or face bricks are sized to accommodate a 1/2-inch gap for mortar—a gap that not only accentuates the pattern but serves to channel off rain water, down the long side of the brick. (To take advantage of this function, you should orient the pattern to carry water down the slope of the patio, away from the house.) For patterns set in mortar, you will also need fewer bricks—4 1/2 bricks per square foot as against 5 bricks for patterns set tight in sand.

A sand bed should start far enough from the base of a tree for the bricks to lie level. The composition of a sand bed depends on how well the underlying soil drains. Usually a 2-inch sand base on well-tamped earth is sufficient, but you may need a 4-inch layer of washed gravel under the sand if you live in an area where rainfall is heavy or where the soil is hard-packed clay. To prevent the sand from sifting down into the gravel, cover the gravel with overlapping strips of 15-pound roofing felt or polyethylene sheeting that has been punctured with drainage holes at 4- or 6-inch intervals. If drainage is a particular problem, slope the bed about 1 inch every 4 to 6 feet. You can also lay perforated draintile or plastic piping in the gravel layer to drain water away from wet spots.

Sand-laid bricks must be contained by a permanent edging, to check horizontal shifts. The edging is usually set at soil level, or 2 inches above the soil at the edge of a flower bed.

You can further limit shifting by filling the joints between bricks with a mixture of sand and cement, brushed in dry and then misted with water. Use a mixture of one part cement to three parts sand, and keep the patio damp for three days. To avoid staining the brick, remove all traces of cement from the surface before misting. A thin coat of silicone brick sealer, applied to the dried-out brick with a paint roller before you sweep in the cement mixture, will help prevent staining.

Weeds may grow in the sand bed if the

bricks are not laid tight. A vapor barrier of perforated roofing felt or plastic sheeting directly below the bricks will control most weeds, but herbicides or weeding may be needed to rid cracks of all unwanted plants. Be careful not to use weed killers close to trees and other desirable plants.

The moss that sometimes grows between bricks in shady areas can be attractive, but on the patio surface it can be a slippery hazard; if necessary, you can remove it with ammonium sulfamate, sold at garden-supply stores. In damp areas, bricks sometimes are discolored by mildew; you can remove it by scrubbing the bricks with household bleach.

If weeds are a problem—or if a stronger, more permanent patio is wanted—bricks can be set in mortar on a concrete slab. To ensure a good bond between brick and concrete, prepare the slab yourself, if you have appropriate experience; otherwise have a professional do it. The best mortar for outdoor use—type M—is available in ready-packaged form from masonry and building suppliers. Using a hoe, mix the mortar in a wheelbarrow according to the package instructions; add more water if necessary as you work, to keep the mortar just soft enough to slide easily off the hoe. Dampen the bricks thoroughly before applying mortar; use leather-palmed gloves to protect your hands from irritants.

You will not need an edging for mortared brick, but you may want to add one to protect and hide the edges of the concrete slab. Set such a border before surfacing the slab, so that the border will serve as a reference level for the surface bricks. If the slab has contraction joints, matching joints are required in the brick veneer. Fill the expansion joint between bricks with polyethylene rope, then cover the rope with self-leveling polysulfide or silicone-rubber caulk. To avoid the need for contraction joints, build the slab of reinforced concrete using 6-by-6 No. 6/6 wire mesh sheets placed in the slab halfway between the bottom and top. Overlap sheets by at least 8 inches on all sides.

Brick used for paving. Of the thousands of sizes, shapes and shades available in bricks and brick-like blocks, those used for paving fall into three categories: common or building brick, face brick and interlocking concrete pavers. Common or building brick *(top)* is ordinary clay brick, whose color varies with the natural color of clay in an area. Dimensions are about 2 1/4 by 3 5/8 inches—to accommodate mortar joints. Face brick, more durable and expensive than common brick, includes bricks called pavers *(middle)*, with widths exactly half their lengths, to fit mortarless patterns. Interlocking pavers *(bottom)*, long used in Europe and usually made of concrete, are defined by their shape. When pavers are combined in a pattern, each one locks its neighbor into place, preventing shifting.

Primary paving patterns. These four patterns can be used as shown, or in combination to give varied surface designs. Bricks laid in rows for a jack-on-jack pattern *(top)* are difficult to align over a large area, but a double row of jack-on-jack pattern is often used to frame another pattern. In a variation, running bond *(below)*, the bricks are staggered. It is an easy all-purpose pattern, laid with or without mortar. Two locking patterns, herringbone *(middle)* and basket-weave *(bottom)*, increase the durability of a mortarless patio; each brick is held in place by a brick perpendicular to it. Herringbone can be laid diagonally, to direct a viewer's eye in a certain direction. To vary basket-weave, shown here with brick faces exposed, set the bricks on their sides, three to a square, for a tighter pattern.

Two designs for added drama. A circular patio *(top)* around a tree, statue or fountain emphasizes the object you wish to feature. Beginning with two circles of half bricks, the pattern radiates outward to fill an area of any shape.

The scalloped pattern *(bottom)*, often used on European boulevards, adds a graceful touch to a patio. Rows of bricked arcs enclose scalloped spaces loosely filled with whole and half bricks.

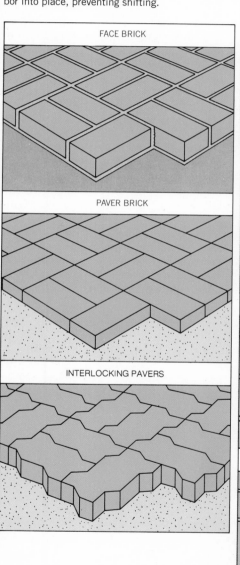

FACE BRICK

PAVER BRICK

INTERLOCKING PAVERS

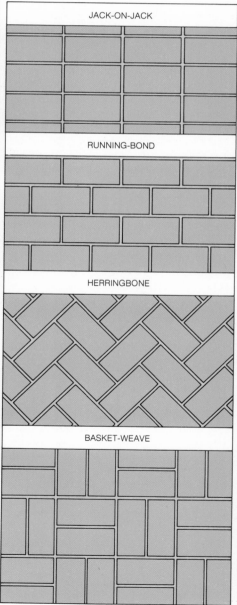

JACK-ON-JACK

RUNNING-BOND

HERRINGBONE

BASKET-WEAVE

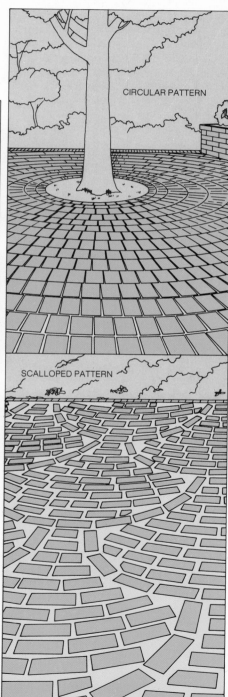

CIRCULAR PATTERN

SCALLOPED PATTERN

Setting Fence Posts Straight and Secure

The key to a good-looking, long-lasting fence is a series of sturdy fence posts, securely anchored and properly aligned and spaced. The posts are the working members of a fence, bearing and bracing the gates and railings. But the posts are also an important element in the design of a fence, creating evenly spaced visual breaks in long runs of railings or panels.

Generally, the function and size of the fence determines the characteristics of its posts. Heavy fences and any fence more than 4 feet high should be supported by posts no smaller than 4-by-4-inch lumber. Low picket fences can be anchored with 2-by-4 intermediate, or line, posts, but even on a lightweight fence the end, corner and gateposts should be at least 4-by-4s. Use pressure-treated Ground-Contact (LP-22) lumber, impregnated with wood preservative under pressure so that the entire post is highly resistant to rot and fungus. Pressure-treated posts last up to 50 years, while untreated posts may have to be replaced after five.

The depth of the posthole and what filling to use within it are the next considerations. As a general rule, one third of the post should be belowground; a 6-foot fence, for example, requires 9-foot posts sunk 3 feet into the earth. In relatively stable soil, tamped earth or gravel will hold the post securely. Concrete makes a more secure setting and is advisable in loose or sandy soils. The gateposts and the end and corner posts, which are subjected to greater stress, should be set in concrete wherever possible; if you prefer not to go to the trouble and expense of using concrete, use longer lengths of lumber for these key posts and sink them deeper into the ground.

Though concrete settings provide the most solid base, they are subject to frost damage in colder climates. As freezing water expands under and around the setting, a phenomenon known as frost heaving tends to force the post up out of the ground. If the frost depth in your area is quite shallow, you can set the concrete below the frost line, but it is generally impractical to sink posts deeper than 3 to 3 1/2 feet. To minimize frost heaving in shallower postholes, widen the hole at the base into a bell shape so that the surrounding earth holds the concrete in place. If wet posts in your locality sometimes freeze and expand, and crack concrete footings, drive wood shims between the post and the concrete while the concrete is still wet. Then remove the shims and fill the gaps with roofing cement after the concrete has set.

The exposed end grain at each end of the post requires additional protection. To prevent the bottom from resting in ground water, shovel several inches of gravel into each hole to act as a drain. To help protect the top from rain, cut the post at a 30° to 45° angle, or cover it with a metal post cap, available at hardware stores to fit standard post sizes.

Post spacings are determined by standardized widths of fence sections and railings; if you build your own fence, it is simpler to use standard lumber sizes to reduce cutting and fitting on site. In general, posts should not be spaced more than 8 feet apart; at this spacing, a standard 16-foot length of lumber spans three posts. After measuring the length of the fence and allowing for gates, you may find that you must use tighter spacing and shorter lengths of lumber to avoid ending a fence with a narrow section.

Measuring and marking post locations is relatively simple on flat ground; on sloping or uneven ground the type of fence determines the measuring method. For fences that slope, measurements should be made along the surface. For fences of panels with level tops, measure spacings along a level line above the ground. On hillsides, the panels are often stepped down in level sections, with posts evenly spaced along a level line.

Where to Place Postholes

Locating posts on flat ground. Drive stakes at the locations of the end posts, stretch a string between the stakes, just high enough to clear the ground, and measure the length of the string to determine the standard lengths of lumber or fencing that will make up the fence with a minimum of cutting. Make a gauge pole—a piece of straight 1-by-2 lumber cut to the length of the fence sections and marked off in 1-foot increments—and set it repeatedly on the ground against the string to set the locations of the intermediate posts. Use the markings on the pole to adjust locations for gateposts and to avoid ending the fence with a very short section.

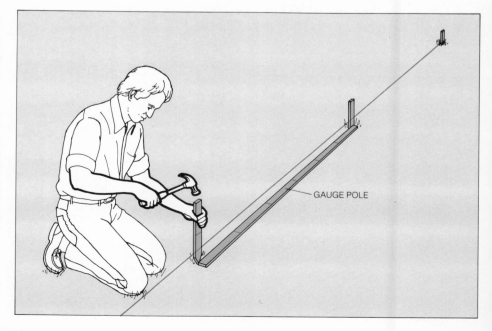

GAUGE POLE

Staking posts on uneven ground. For a fence with rigid rectangular panels, or one with a level top, such as a picket fence *(page 391)*, stretch a line between two end stakes, level it with a line level and, working with a helper if necessary, measure along it with a gauge pole. Drop a plumb bob from the line to pinpoint each post location on the ground *(below, top)*

and drive marker stakes at all the post locations. For a fence such as a post-and-rail, with a top that follows the natural contours of the ground, drive stakes at the fence ends and at each high and low point in between. Join all the stakes with string and use a gauge pole to space the remaining posts evenly between the post locations already marked *(below, bottom)*.

Using a posthole digger. After removing the marker stake, use a manual posthole digger or hand auger to dig a posthole. For a post set in concrete, make the hole at least three times the post width and angle the digger to widen the bottom. For posts set in tamped earth, dig a hole that is twice the post width. Make the hole about 6 inches deeper than the depth of the post belowground. Fill the bottom with 4 to 6 inches of gravel, topped with a flat rock.

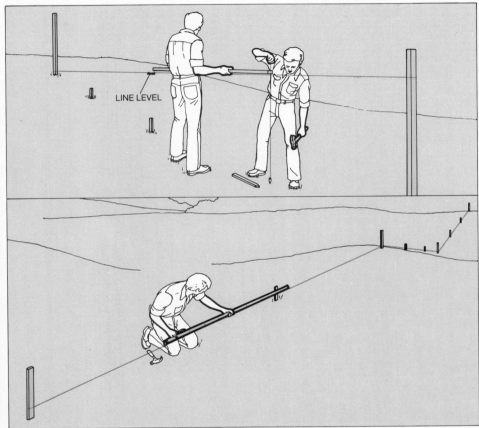

LINE LEVEL

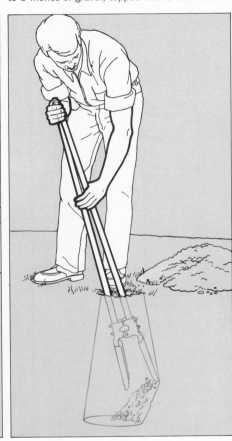

A Timesaving Tool for Digging Holes

A gasoline-powered auger, available from tool-rental shops, saves both time and effort, especially if you are setting 10 or more fence posts, unless you are working in very rocky soil.

Power augers weigh between 35 and 40 pounds and come with a removable spiral-shaped boring bit that can excavate holes up to 4 feet deep. Some models can be operated by one person, but the two-man auger at right is safer to use, because the bit is braced by handles on two sides

and is less likely to kick out of the hole when it hits a rock or other obstruction.

To use a power auger, mark the depth of the posthole on the bit with tape and see it over the marked position. Turn on the motor, adjust the speed with the handle-mounted clutch and exert an even downward pressure from both sides. After digging a few inches, slowly raise the bit to clear the dirt from the hole. If you hit a rock, stop the motor and use a digging bar or pick and shovel to pry it loose.

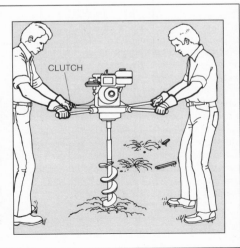

CLUTCH

Getting Your Posts in Line

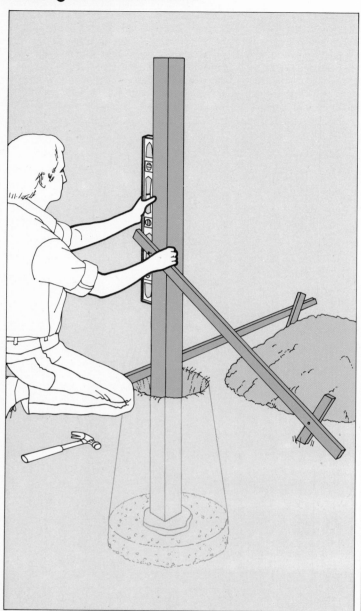

Bracing an end post plumb. Drive two stakes on adjacent sides of the posthole and fasten a 1-by-2-inch bracing board to each stake with a single nail. Set an end post in the hole, centered over the flat stone at the bottom, and use a carpenter's level to plumb a side of the post adjacent to a bracing board. When that side is plumb, nail the upper end of the bracing board to the post. Then plumb the side adjacent to the other board and nail that board to the post. Brace the other end post in the same way. Recheck the level in both directions.

Aligning intermediate posts. Stretch two strings between the sides of the end posts, one near the top and the other close to ground level. While a helper aligns one side of an intermediate post with the two strings and plumbs an adjacent side with a level, sight along the top string to check both the post height and the alignment. To make minor adjustments in height, add or remove gravel; to alter alignment, move the rock on which the post is centered.

If the posts are anchored in tamped earth, fill the holes with soil or gravel and tamp *(opposite)* as you set each post; if you are setting the posts in concrete, brace all the posts as shown until the concrete has hardened *(above, left)*.

Two Ways to a Secure Support

In tamped earth. While a helper holds the posts plumb, fill the hole with earth, in 6-inch layers; as each layer is put in, tamp the soil with the flat end of a digging bar *(above)* or a 2-by-4. Overfill the hole and shape a cone of earth around the post to channel away runoff.

In concrete. Check the braced post for alignment and plumb, then fill the hole with concrete mix—one part cement, two and one quarter parts sand and three parts gravel. Overfill the hole slightly and use a trowel to bevel the concrete down from the post for runoff. Within 20 minutes, recheck the post for plumb and make small adjustments, adding additional concrete as necessary. Allow the concrete to cure for at least 24 hours before removing the braces or attaching fencing. If the concrete leaves a slight gap around the posts as it dries, caulk the space or fill it with roofing cement.

To save both concrete and the effort of mixing it, some professionals simply empty half a bag of dry ready-packaged concrete into the hole on top of the gravel and fill the rest of the hole with earth. Though this is not as strong as a full concrete setting, natural seepage of ground water will eventually solidify the concrete base while the tamped earth holds the post up.

Wooden Fences: Variations on a Basic Theme

Almost every wooden fence is built on a framework of upright posts and connecting rails or stringers. This simple skeleton can carry a range of fences that will meet practically any need.

Whatever fence style you choose, your first concern is the quality of the building materials. Use pressure-treated lumber (*right*) or naturally decay- and insect-resistant woods, such as cedar or heart redwood. All are more expensive than construction-grade lumber, but they will last longer.

The basic post-and-board fence on these pages is made of 1-inch lumber, face-nailed to 4-by-4 posts. The posts—36 to 42 inches high for a three-rail fence, 48 to 54 inches for a four-rail one—can be topped with metal

post caps or with an angled cap rail (*opposite*) to protect the ends, which rot easily, from moisture. Space the posts to use standard lengths of board lumber as much as possible.

Post-and-rail fences, with tapered rail ends that fit into mortised posts, are sturdier than post-and-board fences and almost as easy to install. Prefabricated mortised posts and tapered stringers are sold by lumber suppliers in a variety of styles. All are assembled like the split-rail fence illustrated on page 390.

Picket fences can also be built in a wide range of styles, though prefabricated pickets are becoming difficult to find in some areas. A picket fence can be any desired height but is usually 3 to 4 feet, with pickets projecting about 6 inches above the top stringer.

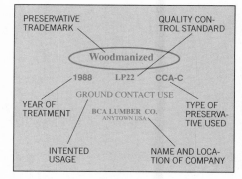

Shopping carefully. All pressure-treated wood should carry a quality control stamp (*above*). Only certain woods, notably pine, can be pressure-treated effectively. Pressure-treated wood is guaranteed against damage caused by decay or insects. Request a consumer information sheet from the manufacturer or merchant. It outlines health precautions to take with pressure-treated wood, and the conditions of the guarantee. If you fail to treat cut end grain, for example, the guarantee may be voided.

The Simplest Fence of All

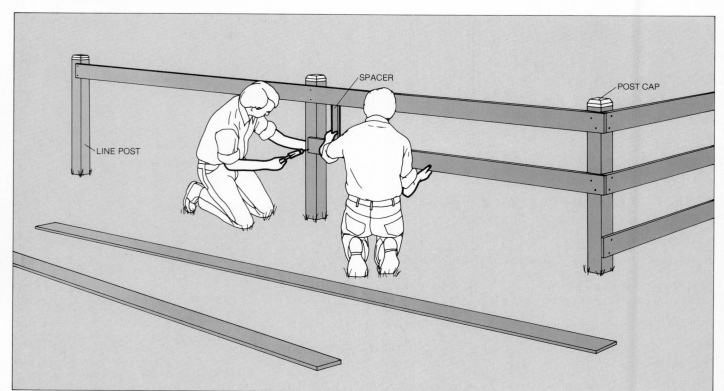

Building a post-and-board fence. To start from an end or corner, trim 1-by-4 or 1-by-6 boards to extend from a corner or end post to the center of the second line post, and stagger these long boards with others extending only to the center of the first line post. Nail on these boards. Use a piece of scrap wood as a spacer to position the lower rails. Continue to add boards cut to the longer length until you need short pieces for ends. Nail metal caps onto the posts.

Desirable Extras: A Cap Rail and Battens

1 **Beveling the posts.** To prepare the posts for the cap, saw a 30° angle at their ends—you can start the cut with a power saw set to the angle, but it will not cut all the way through and you must finish with a handsaw.

To prepare a corner post, make a second cut at a 30° angle across an adjacent side *(below, right)*.

Set all posts, placing the corner ones so that their bevels slant to support mitered cap rails.

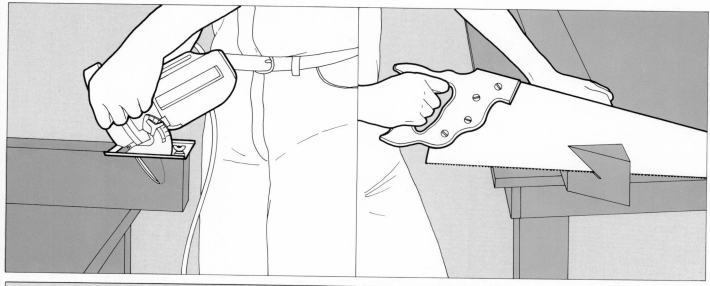

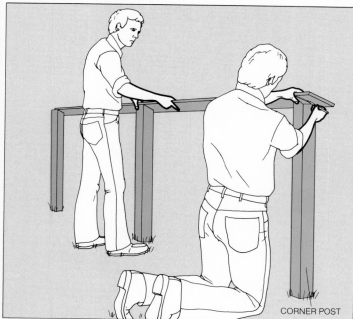

CORNER POST

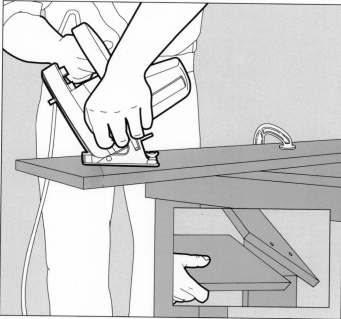

2 **Marking the cap rail.** With a helper, hold a 1-by-6 in position on top of a corner post and a line post. Have the helper set one end of the board at the center of the line post while you mark the underside of the board along the angle of the corner-post top. Then mark a second 1-by-6 cap-rail board to fit across the other angled face of the corner post. Use a carpenter's square to transfer the marks to the other side of each board to facilitate sawing.

3 **Cutting the cap rail.** With a circular saw, cut the rails along the corner-post marks at 30°, beveling the ends of the boards so that they can be mitered flush.

Nail the cap-rail sections to the corner and line posts, aligning the tops of the rails with the top edges of the beveled posts *(inset)*.

4 **Installing the battens.** When all the rails are fastened, cut 1-inch-thick batten boards to reach from the underside of the cap rail to an inch or two off the ground and nail them to the posts.

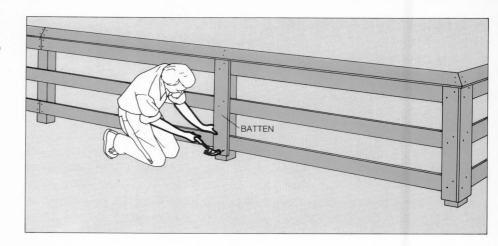

BATTEN

Fitting Together a Rail Fence

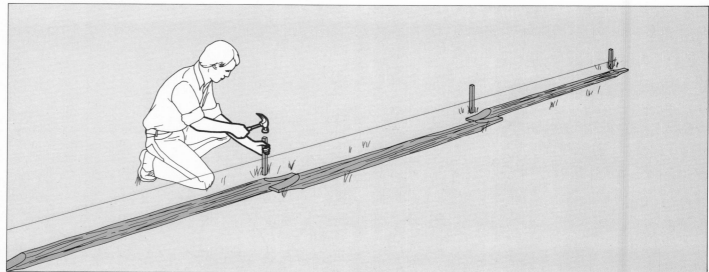

1 **A dry run of rails.** Drive stakes for the end posts and string a line between them *(page 384)*. Lay precut rails on the ground along the fence line, overlapped as they will be in the mortises of the posts—if the rails do not fit evenly, move the end stakes if possible or cut short rails for one or two sections of the fence. Drive additional stakes at the centers of the overlaps. Dig holes for the posts at the stake locations.

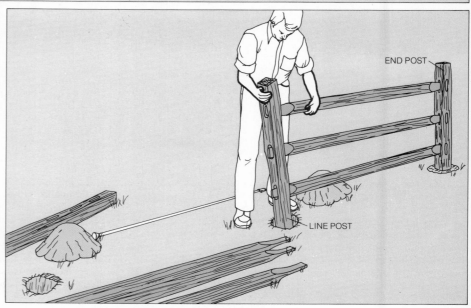

END POST

LINE POST

2 **Fitting the rails in place.** Set an end post in tamped earth *(page 387)* and lower the first line post into its hole; then insert the ends of the rails into the slots of the end post and, as you lift the line post upright, fit the other ends of the rails into the line-post mortises. Plumb the line post, secure it with tamped earth and set succeeding sections the same way.

Putting Up a Picket Fence

1 Installing the stringers. For the bottom stringers, trim 2-by-4s to fit between each pair of posts and nail galvanized 4-inch angle irons or other rail supports to their ends. Attach the stringers to the posts about 8 inches above the ground, nailing through the angle irons and then toenailing.

Use long 2-by-4s for top stringers to span as many posts as possible. Nail the stringers on top of the posts, cutting them to meet in the centers of line and corner posts. At line posts, bevel the stringer ends at an angle of 45° so that they overlap; at corner posts, miter the stringer ends.

2 Attaching the pickets. Using a piece of scrap the length of a picket, make a spacer as wide as the distance between pickets. Nail a block of wood about 6 inches from one end of the spacer as a cleat; hang the spacer on the fence by hooking the cleat over a top stringer. Set the first picket at the edge of an old post, align its point with the top of the spacer, plumb it with a level and nail it in place. Proceed along the fence, using the spacer to locate each picket. Check with a level every few pickets to be sure they are not drifting out of plumb. Stop a few feet from the end of the fence and check the fit of the remaining pickets; adjust the spacing if necessary, so that the last picket will be flush with the outside edge of the end post.

ANGLE IRON

SPACER

CLEAT

Pickets in Patterns

1 Building a panel. Build rectangular frames of 2-by-3s to fit between each pair of posts. Cut picket slats to the length of the longest picket in your pattern and, starting from the ends, nail several of them to the frame laid out on the ground. Align the pickets evenly along the bottom of the frame, using a spacer with a cleat that holds the spacer's end about 4 inches below the frame bottom. In the center of the panel, lay the pickets on the frame without nailing, adjust their spacing, mark their positions on the stringers and nail them in place.

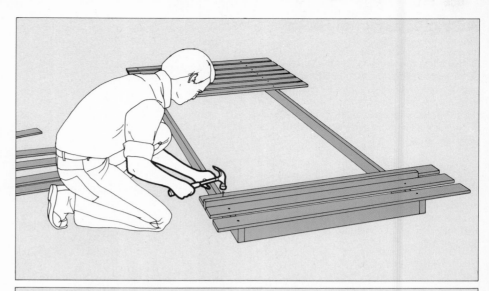

2 Marking a curved pattern. Measure down from the top center of the panel of pickets the full depth of the curve and drive a central nail. Drive two end nails at the top of the picket panel, each a distance from the central nail equal to half the panel length. Tie a cord to one end nail, pull it around the central nail and fasten it to the other end nail. Now remove the central nail, substituting for it the point of a pencil. Keeping the cord taut, use the pencil to draw a curve on the picket panel. Then mark each panel in the same manner and cut along the curves.

3 Installing the panels. Have a helper hold each panel in position against the posts so that the post tops fit into the picket pattern. The bottom stringer should be about 8 inches above the ground. Nail the panels to the posts through the uprights and, for additional support, toenail through the bottom stringer from the side.

A Rack of Dowels

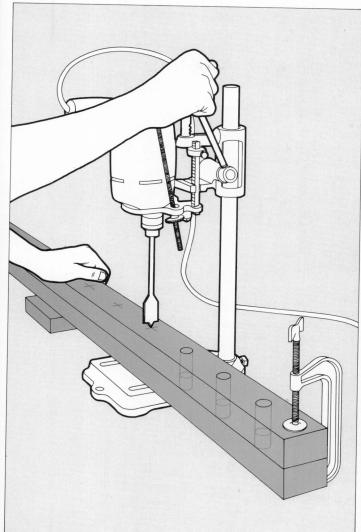

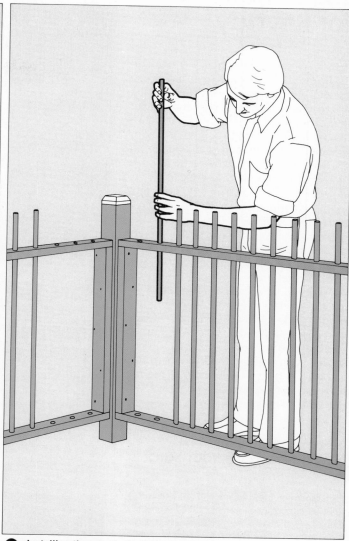

1 **Preparing the stringers.** Cut 2-by-3 stringers to fit between posts, clamp each pair together and mark the positions for the dowels. Bore 3/4-inch holes through the top stringer and a third of the way into the bottom one at each marked point. The holes must be straight; use a drill-press stand or a jig made for guiding dowel holes.

2 **Installing the panels.** Build frames for a picket panel from the stringer pairs. In all but the last three or four holes at the ends of each panel, insert 3/4-inch dowels through the top stringer, resting them in the depressions in the bottom stringer, and glue the dowels to the bottom stringer with exterior-grade carpenter's glue. Finally, nail the fence panels to the posts, and insert and glue the remaining dowels.

Tall Fences for Privacy

Although they are higher and heavier, most privacy fences are built much like the picket fences on page 391. Common lumber nailed to simple post-and-stringer frames will produce a variety of attractive fences; prefabricated panels—in styles ranging from patterned plywood to latticework—can be nailed directly to posts or framed inside posts and stringers.

Some fences, however, require more sophisticated carpentry. A tall louvered fence, for example, is heavier and more prone to warp than some of the simpler designs and should be made with sturdier joints. To build a louvered fence, you will need a router *(page 454)* to cut grooves in the posts and the stringers. The key to using the router safely and effectively is a solidly made jig to guide the bit. Always clamp or nail the jig to whatever you are cutting and make sure the lumber is steady. Wear goggles and keep the router at chest height or below. To make the high cuts in the posts, stand on a stepladder steadied by a helper.

Five Screens for Your Yard

High fences on basic frames. All of the fences at right are supported on frames of 4-by-4 posts and 2-by-4 stringers. The posts are 6 to 8 feet high, set 6 to 8 feet apart. The simplest privacy fence is made of vertical boards or tall narrow slats, like redwood grape stakes, nailed directly to the top and bottom stringers (and to a middle stringer if the fence is taller than 6 feet). Almost as simple is a fence of horizontal boards face-nailed to the posts and to 2-by-4 studs that are toenailed to the top and bottom stringers 24 to 36 inches apart. The same framework will also support solid plywood panels.

A board-and-board fence admits breezes and looks equally well from either side. Vertical boards are nailed to both sides of the frame, separated by less than their own widths. The boards on one side are positioned opposite the spaces on the other. Ready-made panels in elaborate styles like latticework are mounted against 1-by-2s nailed in advance to the posts and stringers. Ready-made panels or precut boards and vertically grooved posts *(right)* are available for basket-weave fences.

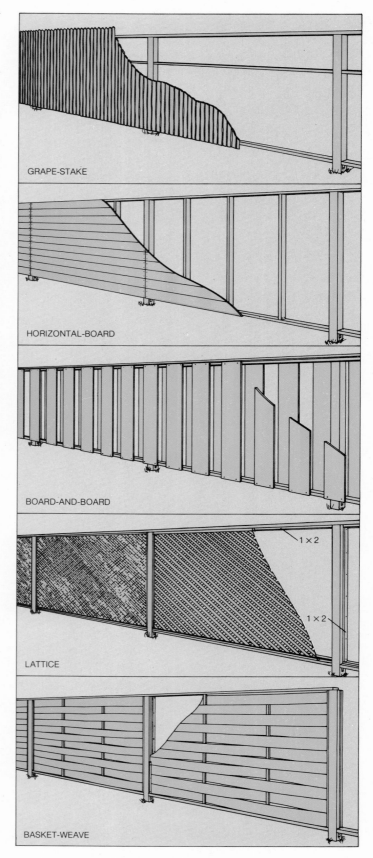

GRAPE-STAKE

HORIZONTAL-BOARD

BOARD-AND-BOARD

1 × 2

1 × 2

LATTICE

BASKET-WEAVE

Building and Repairing Gates

A wooden fence gate is often an ornery object—indeed, the faulty ones sometimes seem to outnumber the good ones. They sag, they bind, they refuse to latch. But by following three simple precepts, you can have a gate as trouble-free as anyone can reasonably expect.

The first requirement is a pair of strong, plumb gateposts, set in concrete *(page 387)* to a depth equal to one half the height of the part aboveground. Space the posts to accommodate the gate width plus a 1/2-inch clearance for the latch as well as enough clearance for the kind of hinge you plan to install.

The second critical element is a frame that is braced by a diagonal board between the top rail at the latch side and the bottom rail at the hinge side. But no brace can sufficiently stiffen a gate wider than 5 feet; for a larger opening, install two gates. One gate is held closed with a cane bolt, a 1/2-inch sliding rod that

drops through brackets on the edge of the gate into a hole in the pavement or in a block of concrete; the second gate latches to the first. To provide bottom clearance, hang all gates at least 1 inch above the highest point of ground within the arc of the opening gate.

The third crucial requirement is strong hardware, particularly the hinges *(below)*; weak hinges are the most frequent cause of gate problems. To prevent rusting, use cadmium-coated or galvanized hardware. Among latches, the simplest and most trouble-free are the thumb-and-string types; sliding bolts are not recommended because even a slight sag in the gate throws them out of alignment.

Even a carefully built gate may eventually sag and bind as its weight pulls hinge screws loose or causes the supporting post to lean. Problems of this nature are relatively easy to correct—leaning posts can be pulled up-

right with turnbuckles; loose hinge screws can be either tightened or replaced.

To tighten screws, first take the gate off the post and, using a twist drill, enlarge the width of the old screw holes to 1/2 inch and drill the holes to a depth that is three fourths of the thickness of the post. Cut 1/2-inch dowels to the depth of the holes, coat them with waterproof glue and tap them into the holes with a mallet. Then drill pilot holes in the dowels, three fourths the root diameter of the screws, and rehang the gate. For an inexpensive improvement on this method, replace loose screws with bolts that go completely through the post and are secured by nuts on the other side. But it is best not to attempt repairs of basic damage, such as rot that severely weakens the wooden parts. It is easier to build a new gate instead.

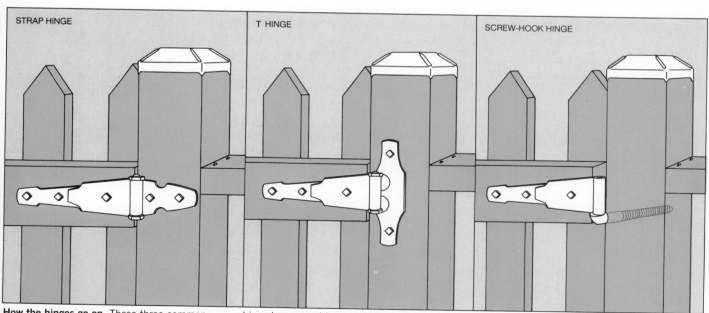

How the hinges go on. These three common styles of hinge have one element in common: All attach to the gate with a strap, which should be at least 7 inches long. But the method of attachment to the post varies. The strap hinge has a post strap—preferably one that runs the full width of the post. The T

hinge has a roughly rectangular pad, resembling the crossbar on a T; for 3 1/2-by-3 1/2-foot gate the pad should be at least 7 inches high and 2 inches wide. The screw-hook hinge has an L-shaped screw hook driven into the post; the hook should be at least 1/2 inch thick and the screw 4 inches long. The screw-hook

hinge *(page 397, Step 3)* has special advantages. It permits easy removal of the gate for minor repairs, and it is the simplest to attach to a masonry wall—either insert a flat-shank hook into a mortar joint while the wall is being built or drive a screw hook into a lead anchor.

Making and Hanging a Gate

1 **Assembling the frame.** Cut rot-resistant 2-by-4s the width of the gate for stringers and, using a steel square to guarantee right angles, nail pickets or 2-by-4s to the stringer ends. Position the pickets or rails so the stringers of the gate will align with those of the main fence. For a fence 6 feet tall or more, add a third rail or stringer at the middle of the frame. Before you proceed to the next step, nail both of the end pickets to the stringers, then turn the frame over.

2 **Bracing the frame.** Mark and cut a 2-by-4 brace with angled ends to fit diagonally between the gate's top corner at the latch side and the bottom corner at the hinge side. Secure it with 4-inch wood screws started about 2 inches in from each end and angled into the stringers.

Nail the remaining pickets to the stringers and the brace. Fasten the hinge straps to the ends of the stringers with lag screws.

3 **Hanging the gate.** Set the gate on wood scraps to align it with the fence and, holding the back of the frame flush with the back of the post, mark the post at the bottom of the top hinge. Drive a screw hook diagonally into the post at the mark *(right inset)* and slip the hinge strap over the hook. Install the bottom screw hook in the same way and hang the gate.

To make a gatestop, nail a strip of 1-by-1/2 flush with the front of the latch post. Install a latch bar on the gate and a latch on the post *(left inset)*. A string latch is shown here; most gate latches are installed in the same way.

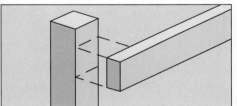
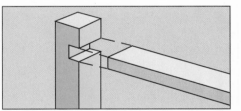
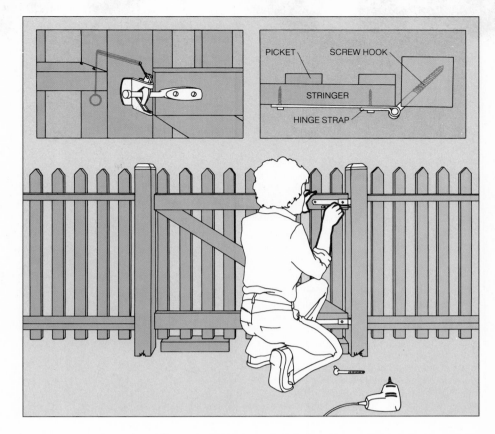

Making Wood Joints

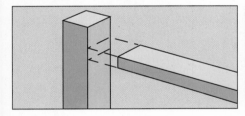

Butt joint. End of first piece fits against side *(shown)* or end of second piece, concealing end grain. To measure and mark angle at end of first piece, use a try square, a carpenter's square or a sliding bevel. Cut with a crosscut saw or a circular saw. Nail or screw pieces; reinforce with hardware.

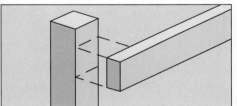

Overlap joint. First piece fits against second piece; end grain of first piece exposed *(shown)* or end of first piece butted against end or side of third piece. To measure and mark angle at piece ends, use a try square, a carpenter's square or a sliding bevel. Cut with a crosscut saw or a circular saw. Nail or screw pieces.

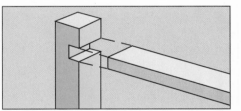

Dado joint. End of first piece fits into dado in second piece, concealing end grain. To measure and mark dado, trace first piece, or use a try square or a carpenter's square. Cut dado using a backsaw or a circular saw and a wood chisel, or use a router. Nail or screw pieces.

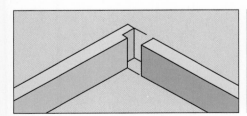

Rabbet joint. End of first piece fits into half lap of the same width and depth on second piece, concealing its end grain. To measure and mark, trace first piece or use a try square or a carpenter's square. Cut with a crosscut saw, a backsaw or a circular saw. Nail or screw pieces.

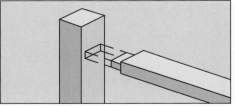

Mortise-and-tenon joint. Tenon on first piece, usually one third its width and thickness and 2 inches long, fits matching mortise in second piece. To mark tenon, use a try square or a carpenter's square; to cut, use a backsaw and a wood chisel. To make mortise, trace tenon and chisel. Nail pieces.

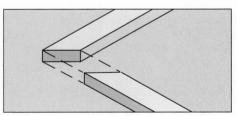

Miter joint. Ends of two pieces fit together at an angle, usually of 45°, concealing end grain. To measure and mark, use a try square or a carpenter's square. Make miter cuts on small pieces with a backsaw and miter box; on large pieces with a crosscut saw or a circular saw. Nail or screw pieces.

Outdoor Lighting Around the Yard

Low-voltage outdoor lighting, with thin cables and inexpensive fixtures, makes it easy to have exactly the yard lighting you want. The fixtures connect to the cables with outdoor pin connectors or weatherproof splice caps. They can be clipped to tree branches or staked into the ground; properly rated waterproof models can be set underwater, in a pool or fountain. And, because the connecting cables need not be deeply buried (they are generally hidden along hedge, fences and walks, sta-pled to tree trunks or tucked into a shallow slip cut with a lawn edger) the lights can be pulled up and moved at will.

Most outdoor lights come in a kit containing a 12-volt transformer sealed in a weatherproof box, a length of cable and six to 12 fixtures, although you may prefer to assemble the elements separately with a variety of fixtures.

The transformer can be mounted on a wall near an outdoor receptacle. If this location requires more than 100 feet of cable to supply the fixtures, you must allow for voltage drop—a slight consumption of electrical pressure by wires that can dim distant lights. Heavier cable solves the problem but it is harder to hide and less flexible than the standard sizes. Many installers prefer to mount the transformer on a post well away from the house and run a properly buried 120-volt line to it. In a very large yard, it may be best to mount two transformers at widely spaced locations for separate groups of fixtures.

Installing the transformer. Mount the wall bracket supplied with the transformer at least 12 inches above the ground on a wall or post, and within 6 feet of a receptacle; then push the transformer onto the bracket.

Place the fixtures and string the low-voltage cable from the transformer, leaving enough slack to follow walkways and flower beds. Leave 12 inches of additional slack at each fixture.

Clipping a fixture to a cable. If your fixtures have pin connectors, make sure the transformer is unplugged, then make a 3-inch cut in the cable sheathing to separate the conductors, but do not strip any insulation from the conductors; lay the wires into the slots at the base of the fixture, then press them firmly onto the contact pins and screw the protective cap into place.

Using splice caps. For a fixture with wire leads, make sure the transformer is unplugged, then cut the cable at the locations you have chosen. Strip 3/8 inch of insulation from each cable and fixture wire, and twist each fixture wire to conductors from each end of the cut cable; crimp a splice cap over each three-wire connection with a multipurpose tool *(right)*.

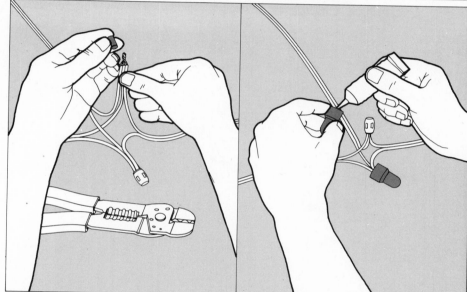

Hiding low-voltage cable underground. Push an edging tool into the ground with one foot, rocking it back and forth to exert a downward and sideward pressure. Overlapping strokes will cut a narrow slip; tuck the low-voltage cable into the slit and step along the top to press the turf back together.

6 MAJOR ADDITIONS

The Art of Making an Addition Look Right

An ugly addition is a bad bargain. It ruins the architecture of a house, antagonizes neighbors and may reduce the value of your property; worse still, it often proves difficult to live in. But properly designed, an addition enhances a house, as the drawings on the opposite page show.

Achieving the proper design for an addition requires the talents of a good architect. If you possess them, you may want to create your own design. But most people rely on a professional. You can hire an architect—either for a prearranged sum (generally about 11 percent of a contractor's estimated cost for the addition) or an hourly rate. The architect will usually supervise the job for an additional 4 percent of the estimated cost, but most do-it-yourself builders dispense with this service. If you need advice later, you can pay an hourly fee for it.

An architect or building designer will provide the drawings needed to obtain building permits. If you prepare the design yourself, you can still hire a draftsman to prepare working drawings or make the drawings yourself; most building departments accept fairly rough sketches.

Regardless of who designs the addition, the first step is to prepare what architects call a program, listing the use and approximate dimensions of each new room. Rectangular rooms, approximately half again as long as they are wide, are generally most comfortable. For the best light and ventilation, locate windows on two walls; try to place doors near corners to provide more unbroken wall space for chairs and tables. Also consider how each room should relate to surrounding ones, with an eye toward problems with noise, access and light: A noisy family room should not be next to a bedroom, for example. Where possible, illustrate your program with photographs, magazine clippings and sketches.

Site conditions, zoning ordinances and your space requirements together will determine which of three options you will pursue: building out horizontally from the house, building up above it or building a major addition—a two-story wing, perhaps, or a full second story. A particular type of addition—a bay window, for example—can be adapted to fit houses of several architectural styles. The techniques apply to any type of addition and any additions can be adapted to other architectural styles.

Theoretically, any style of addition can be made to look attractive on any style of house. All-glass modern wings have been grafted onto fussy Victorian structures with success—by architectural geniuses. But most designers play safe by following two simple rules. First, the architecture of the addition should echo that of the original house wherever possible. Ideally, the addition should mimic the house so well that you cannot tell where one stops and the other begins. The second rule applies when the addition must depart from the style of the house: The departure should be clear and intentional, in subdued contrast to the original. An inexact imitation may seem a mistake. These rules apply to all structural elements of the addition.

Three elements are particularly important: roof, windows and siding. The roof of an addition is seldom as high as an existing roof—the difference adds pleasing variety. The addition roof need not even be the same style as the house roof. Most houses have straight gable or hip roofs; a shed-roofed addition to either is a traditional style. However, adding a hip-roofed addition to a gable-roofed house or vice versa calls for discretion; either combination can look awkward unless carefully integrated.

The aspects of the roof that are crucial to appearance are details: slope, overhang and covering. The best-looking additions generally have roofs that match those of their existing houses in all three details. The principal exception to this rule is the addition with a shed roof. If the addition is not very deep, limiting the size of the roof, a very shallow slope often is used to contrast with the steep slope of the house roof.

In most cases, it is fairly simple to match roof slopes and—with some carpentry tricks *(page 431)*—overhangs. This is not true of the roof covering. While you usually can find roofing materials of the same size and shape as the ones you have, they almost never will match perfectly. Generally you can settle for an approximate match, but if the roof is a dominant feature, you may want to re-roof the entire house.

Similar considerations must be taken into account for windows. If windows on an addition match those on the house in style—casements with casements, multi-paned double-hung types with their exact counterparts—the addition will be least obtrusive, although deliberate contrasts can be attractive.

More important than window style is position. Horizontal spacing often varies, although for the most pleasing appearance it should not seem random. The crucial aspect of window position is vertical alignment. If the tops of the windows do not line up, a distracting jagged line is introduced.

Siding generally is the simplest detail of an addition to match to the house. Many old-fashioned patterns still can be found in stock in lumberyards and, if necessary, you can order pieces specially milled to match at a fairly reasonable cost. In some cases you may not want to match the existing siding—combinations of shingles, clapboard, brick or vertical planking are traditional, although they can create a fussy effect on a small house or when several variations are used.

All these details combine to create the new look your addition gives to your home. In planning for this result, consider the effect inside on room layout and outside on what architects call the focus of the house—the point that naturally draws and holds your eye, such as the front door or a large window. Ideally, each side of the house has its own focus—with its own striking shape, perhaps, or with a major feature like a sliding glass door. Partly for this reason, most additions are built at the rear, leaving facades unchanged.

All these rules are overruled, of course, by gifted designers—the most strikingly beautiful additions achieve their impact because their builders dared to disregard convention. Individual taste must be the final authority. It is your house, and its addition must please you.

A new room. A modest addition outward—front, side or back—is the most common. To prevent the addition from looking like a bump on the house, it generally is given a roof that echoes the original. (Here the original lines of a house are indicated in gray.) On a split-level house *(top)*, for example, an addition often duplicates the shape of the one-story portion. The two roofs have the same height and pitch and so meet naturally in valleys. The same approach works at the back or front of a ranch house *(center)*. On a massive, boxy house, however, it is better to extend the original shape. For example, the walls and roof on one side of a colonial house *(bottom)* can be extended to create a classic salt-box shape, with a half-story of storage space opposite the second floor of the house. A clash of styles between old and new windows is averted by the distance between them and by the clear contrast of the large-scale simplicity of the new windows.

Planning the Job to Run Smoothly

Deciding what you want to build is just the first step in planning an addition. Another might be finding the labor to build it, either doing all the work yourself as an owner-builder or supplementing your labor with hired and volunteered help.

Still another step is getting a plan of the addition onto paper. Homeowner-drawn sketches are generally acceptable to building departments, lenders and subcontractors. The most workable scale for plans is 1/4 inch equals 1 foot. This way, the entire plan should fit on one sheet of typing paper. Details can be drawn separately in a larger scale, perhaps 1 inch equals 1 foot. For making the drawings you will need some sharp, hard pencils, a 45° plastic triangle and an architect's scale containing 1/4- and 1-inch scales along with others.

If an architect is involved, he or she will probably supply working drawings; otherwise you must develop your own. If you do not feel able to draw the plans yourself, the services of a building designer or drafter may prove useful. The plans not only serve as a guide to construction, they also can be used to make a list of materials, estimate costs, secure financing and obtain building permits. The lumber dealer where you buy your materials will often do what is called a takeoff from your plans, listing all the materials required for your addition.

By providing your own labor, you can save some 50 percent of what a contractor would charge. And you can build in custom touches that you might otherwise have to forgo. However, building an addition is a great deal of work, requiring hours and hours of labor. It is best not to attempt it unless you are willing to make it a major part of your life until finished. As a rough rule of thumb, it takes about three hours per square foot of addition to finish the job, slightly more if you are unfamiliar with some of the tasks involved. For this reason, you may prefer to act as a general contractor, selecting the jobs you want to do and hiring subcontractors to do the rest, the jobs needing specialized skills or costly equipment. These include deep excavations, extensive grading, large concrete slabs and plastering. Do small or complicated jobs yourself; leave large open surfaces that can be covered quickly to a subcontractor. If you plan to hire any subcontractors, you will need to get bids on labor and materials from them.

Simple Drawings for Official Approval

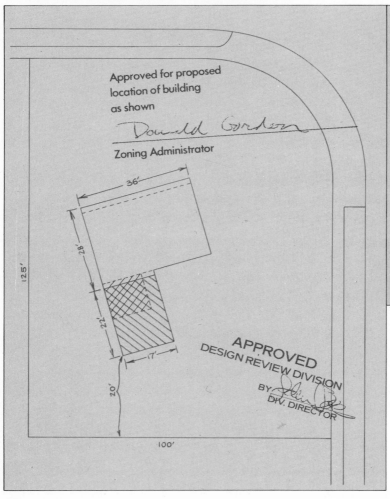

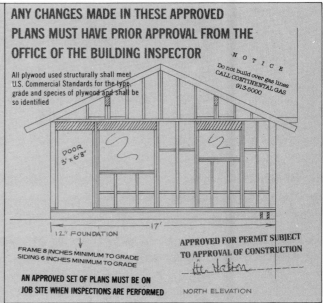

Two simple plans. Boldly stamped with building-department dos and dont's, the plot plan *(left)* and elevation view *(above)* shown here were part of a set of drawings that one homeowner used to estimate his materials costs, and later submitted with his application for a building permit. The shaded area of the plot plan shows the proposed location of his addition, at the back of the house over an old patio site, and gives its distance from the nearest property line. The elevation drawing shows an interior view of the addition's north wall as seen from the main house; similar drawings were submitted for the other walls.

Many home-improvement firms use their own contract forms when bidding. You can modify these forms so they spell out your expectations about workmanship, materials and approximate schedules.

Schedules will be firmed up later, but the specifications covering workmanship and materials should be unmistakably clear from the start. Wall-finishing materials, for instance, should be described by type, thickness and method of finishing; windows, doors, faucets, lighting fixtures and other equipment should be listed by manufacturer and model numbers, to be sure of getting what you wish.

A good contract leaves you with bargaining power if any work or materials do not meet your requirements, and gives you at least a year's guarantee on workmanship and materials. Specify that you will pay no more than 25 percent of the total cost as a down payment, and that you will hold back at least 10 percent until you have inspected the finished work and received the waivers of lien and receipts stating that the contractor has paid all suppliers and subcontractors. Your lending agency may be able to give you a contract form that covers the necessary points.

Before you sign a contract or buy materials, make a chronological checklist of all the jobs that must be done. The possibilities include excavating, laying a foundation, framing, masonry, plumbing and electrical work, heating and air-conditioning installations, insulation, putting up wallboard, painting and finish-flooring. Add such steps as buying material for each job, applying for permits, scheduling subcontractors and calling—and waiting—for inspections. Allow at least two days per month for bad weather or unforeseen interruptions. And do not underestimate the drudgery of the digging that must be done at various stages. Then you can set firm schedules and get under way. Computer software is available to help you in organizing the scheduling.

Ask your building inspector what is the right time for each inspection (*chart, page 406*). In most areas an addition must pass several inspections before it can receive the necessary certificate of occupancy. The inspections listed in the chart are in the sequence in which they normally occur; while not all of them will be required in every area, a building permit generally requires at least four inspections. These are an inspection of the foundation work, one of the framing, one after insulation is in, and a final inspection when all work is complete. The separate permits for electrical, plumbing or heating and air conditioning work commit you to inspections of the rough installation and the finished work. Sometimes these inspections can be combined with others.

The formal language of blueprints. Use these symbols, representing elements commonly included in an addition, when you render plans that will be used by others. All are readily recognized by building tradesmen and many, such as those for lavatories or doors, are obvious at first glance. More abstract symbols, standing for such elements as switches or thermostats, are easy to decipher in the context of the floor plans, elevations and section views.

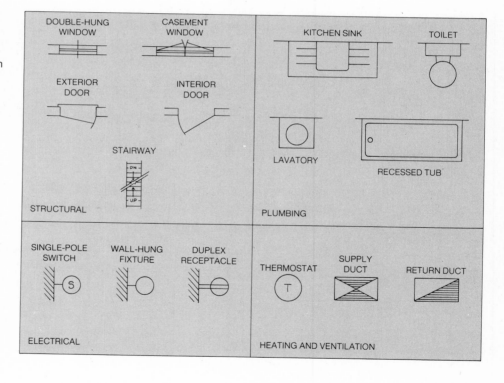

Scheduling Permits and Inspections

Inspection	When to call an inspector	Major checkpoints
Footing	After preparing the trenches, but before placing concrete	Excavation, soil conditions, reinforcement
Backfill	After consctructing the foundation walls and floor, but before backfilling	Walls, backfill material
Slab	After forms, gravel, vapor barriers, wire mesh or steel are in place, but before placing concrete	Forms, soil condition, reinforcement
Rough plumbing	Underground plumbing: after installing pipes, but before filling trenches or placing concrete Above-ground plumbing: after installing pipes, stacks, and vents in framing, but before walls are finished and fixtures installed	Stacks, vents, pipes
Rough electrical	After running cable and grounding boxes, but before walls are finished or electrical devices installed	Circuits, grounding
Framing	After plumbing and electrical rough-in work is approved, but before insulation or wall finish materials are installed	Sizes, spacing, holes, notches
Mechanical	After ductwork and insulation are installed, but before walls are finished and equipment installed	Ductwork and insulation surrounding it
Close-in	After installing all insulation materials, but before installing wall or ceiling finish materials	Insulation
Final plumbing, electrical, mechanical and building	After walls are finished and all plumbing, electrical and mechanical equipment and fixtures are installed and working, but before occupancy	Plumbing: fixtures and pipes watertight; electrical: outlets, switches and other devices operational; mechanical: ductwork unobstructed; building: structure weathertight, doors and windows in operation, grading completed

Tips for Choosing a Contractor

There is no easy way of judging the skill and reliability of a home-improvement contractor or subcontractor, but you can check his past business dealings before you invest any money in his work.

Ask the local building department or licensing bureau whether the contractor or subcontractor has a trade license. States, Canadian provinces and some local jurisdictions license plumbers, electricians, air-conditioning and heating contractors and home-improvement or remodeling specialists. A licensed contractor or tradesperson has passed a test proving competence in a particular specialty, and in some areas must post a bond as insurance against noncompletion of the work.

Look through the building permits on file at the building department. Find jobs similar to yours, call the owners of the houses and ask about the contractor's work; for a more thorough check, ask for permission to inspect the jobs. If you already have a contractor in mind, check the permits for that contractor's jobs and call the owners for references and permission to see the work. Call the local Better Business Bureau or consumer protection agency to see if there have been complaints about the contractor. If there is a history of complaints, be wary.

Finally, ask the contractor several questions: Does he or she carry workmen's compensation and liability insurance? Will the contractor give you lien waivers from suppliers and subcontractors, stating that they have been paid? Will a down payment of 25 percent be adequate on large jobs? If the answer to any of these questions is no, keep shopping.

Transforming a Porch into a Year-Round Room

Enclosing a porch is easier than building an addition from scratch—and produces a room almost as snug. If the structure is sound, walling in the porch will create new living space you can heat in winter, cool in summer and enjoy all year.

Before you start, check local building regulations and acquire a permit, if you need one. Then strip the porch down to basics: roof, support posts and floor. Take out the ceiling so you can insulate between the joists when you finish the room. If you want the section of house wall that will be inside the new room to match other interior walls, remove any wood or aluminum siding or rough stucco. If the siding is smooth stucco or other masonry, however, you can leave it as is, and put furring strips over it to hold wallboard when you finish the interior.

Enclosing the stripped-down porch be-

gins with laying an insulated subfloor. If the existing floor is level wood, you can insulate the underside and cover the top with plywood *(page 412)*. But most porch floors slope to drain off rain so you need to install a framing to compensate for the slope, then insulate between the joists before you put down plywood *(page 408)*.

Building new exterior walls over the subfloor calls for the same framing techniques used for interior partitions. An exterior door is framed like an interior one; windows are framed similarly, but with sills and cripple studs under the openings. Exterior walls, however, need 2-by-4 fire stops, inserted between the studs midway from floor to ceiling. The stops retard fires that otherwise would use the stud spaces as chimney stacks.

Finishing the exterior requires adding both sheathing and siding to the walls. Alu-

minum and vinyl siding *(pages 409-411)* is lightweight enough so you can sheathe the walls inexpensively with asphalt-impregnated board—pressed paper coated with tar that functions as a vapor barrier. With heavier wood siding, you need plywood sheathing covered outside with building paper. Aluminum siding is available plain or insulated with fiberboard or plastic foam. Various building codes require that metal siding be electrically grounded to the same ground as the house electrical service.

Once the exterior is complete, most of the steps involved in finishing the interior are familiar ones: wiring, insulating the ceiling and new walls, applying wallboard and covering the subfloor. The only unusual part may be walling over a window opening *(page 412),* and even that job is only simple carpentry.

Preparing the porch. Using a utility bar, tear down the ceiling and its trim. Remove the frieze boards, if any, but leave the soffit and fascia. Take off any shutters, screens, screen supports, partial walls or railings. Then use a handsaw to cut through the sill of the door from the house, sawing down to the subflooring along the inner edges of the side jambs. Pull the sill out. If you plan to retrim the door, pry off the top and side exterior casings. If you plan to wall over any window, remove the window.

For wood or aluminum siding, use a circular saw and utility bar to expose the sheathing inside the porch area; be careful not to cut into the sheathing. For a rough-textured stucco-finished house, use a hammer and hacksaw to remove the stucco and the metal lath under it.

Laying a Level Subfloor on a Sloping Slab

1 Attaching the header. To make the new floor flush with the interior floor, measure from the top of the interior subflooring to the slab and deduct 1/2 inch. Using 2-inch lumber of this width, or ripped to this dimension, cut a header the width of the porch area. (If you do not want the floors to be flush, use at least a 2-by-2 for the header.) Set the header on the slab and attach it to the house wall with 16-penny nails (use lead shield anchors and leg screws for masonry).

2 Putting up front boards. With metal shears, cut strips of 6-inch aluminum flashing to fit between the header and corner post on each side and between each pair of posts opposite the header. (If the corner posts are inset on the slab, use flashing at least 4 inches wider than the inset.) Lay the strips along the edges of the slab with one side projecting 2 inches, then bend down the projecting flashing. To level the floor, extend a carpenter's line from the top of the header to a corner post and hang a level on the

line. Mark the post where the line crosses it. Measure from the outside mark to the slab and use 2-inch lumber ripped to this width for the front boards; cut a front board to fit between each pair of posts. All lumber in contact with concrete should be Ground-Contact (LP-22) pressure treated. Stand the boards on the flashing, keeping their outer edges flush with outside edges of the posts, and toenail the front boards to the posts. Bend the inner edge of the front flashing up flat against the front board.

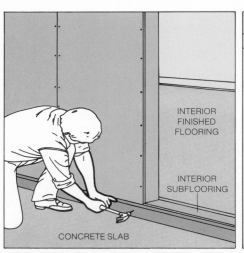

INTERIOR FINISHED FLOORING

INTERIOR SUBFLOORING

CONCRETE SLAB

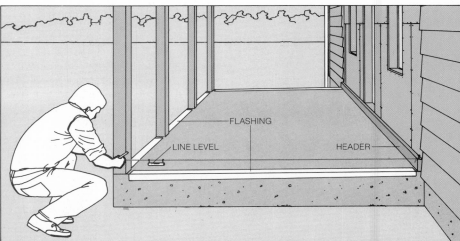

FLASHING

LINE LEVEL

HEADER

FRONT BOARD

SIDE JOIST

HEADER

PLYWOOD

FLASHING

3 Laying sleeper joists. For the sleeper joists at the sides of the slab, measure from the header to the corner posts; for intermediate joists, measure to the front boards. Using 2-inch pressure-treated lumber at least as wide as the front boards, cut two side joists and enough intermediate joists to allow for spacing them 16 inches on center. Rip each joist to match the height of the header at one end, the front board or inner post marking at the other end. Toenail the joists to the header and posts,

butt-nail them to the front board. Check the top and bottom level of each joist and, if needed, shim underneath so it fits flush against the slab; plane off high spots. Where joists are less than 2 1/2 inches high, secure them to the slab with lead shield anchors and lag screws. Elsewhere, set 2-by-4 bridges between them and nail the bridges to the joists, then anchor to the slab. Bend the inner edges of the side flashing up flat against the side joists.

4 Finishing the subflooring. Lay foil-backed insulation batts at least 3 inches thick between the joists. Then cover the subfloor framing with APA-rated sheathing plywood that is rated for use with floor framing on 16-inch centers. Finally, to make the bottoms of the posts watertight, fit a strip of aluminum flashing 10 inches long against each post, letting the bottom of the strip extend 2 inches below the framing and the ends overlap the front boards and side joists. Secure the top of the flashing to the posts with galvanized nails.

An Aluminum-Clad Exterior

1 Putting up new walls. Build wall frames *(page 77-80)* to fit from the ceiling joists to the subflooring on both sides and the front of the porch. Frame rough openings for the door and windows and add fire stops to the walls by nailing 2-by-4s between each pair of studs about 4 feet above the sole plate. Anchor the frames in place with 16-penny nails.

To sheathe the walls, cut asphalt-impregnated board to fit from the top of each wall frame to about an inch below the bottom of the floor frame. Butt the boards against the door and window openings. Stagger the joints between boards to avoid four adjoining corners. Attach the sheathing to the wall frames with roofing nails, then install the exterior doors and windows *(Chapter 3, page 176)*.

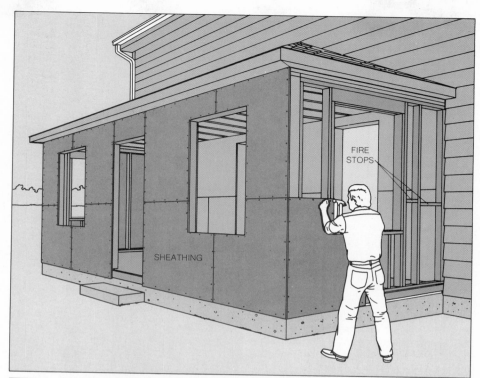

2 Covering an outside corner. With metal shears, cut an aluminum outside corner post strip, as shown in the inset, to fit from the top to the bottom of the sheathing. Working at a convenient height, secure the strip to the corner by driving 1 1/2-inch aluminum siding nails into both sides—through the nailing groove or the prepunched holes. Plumb the strip, then continue inserting nails on both sides at 12-inch intervals.

Caution: Aluminum expands and contracts with heat and cold; therefore the corner posts as well as the other trim and the siding panels should "hang" from the nails that secure them. Drive in the nails only to within 1/32 inch of the aluminum. If the nails are too tight, they will make the finished siding ripple like a washboard.

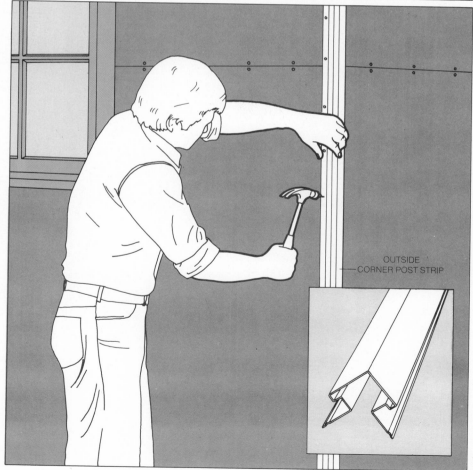

OUTSIDE CORNER POST STRIP

3 **Covering an inside corner.** Cut a strip of aluminum J channel the height of the sheathed wall. Keeping the nailing flange flush with the sheathing, butt the channel as close as possible to the existing aluminum, wood or masonry wall. Straighten the strip with a level, then drive aluminum nails through the flange into the sheathing and stud behind it at 12-inch intervals. Seal the joint between the channel and the wall with silicone rubber sealant or butyl rubber caulk.

4 **Completing the aluminum trim.** Cut continuous strips of J channel to fit around the top and both sides of each exterior door and window. Center each strip above the top casing and bend it down against the sides, notching the nailing flange with metal shears so the channel fits snug around the corners. Secure the channel with aluminum nails. To seal the bottom or a window, cut a strip of general-purpose trim the length of the sill and nail it underneath the sill.

Cut strips of general-purpose trim to fit between the corner post strips at the top of each new wall. With a helper, butt the curved side of the trim against the soffit, level the trim and nail the flange to the sheathing. To piece the trim, leave about 1/4 inch between the strips.

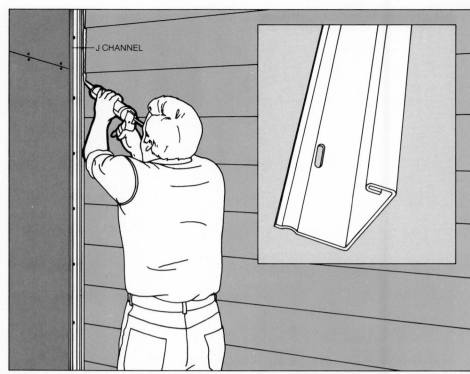

J CHANNEL

J CHANNEL

GENERAL-PURPOSE TRIM

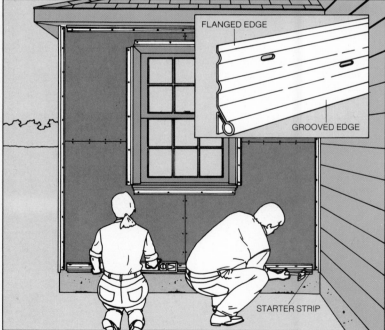

FLANGED EDGE

GROOVED EDGE

STARTER STRIP

5 **Applying the starter strips.** Snap chalk lines about 1 1/2 inches above the bottom of each section of sheathing. Check at the corners to make sure the lines are at the same level around the entire perimeter. Cut a starter strip to the length of each line. Then, with a helper, position the flanged top edge of the starter strip on the chalk line, letting the grooved bottom edge extend below the sheathing. Secure the strip with nails, driven at 8-inch intervals.

6 **Attaching siding panels.** Cut siding panels 1/2 inch longer than the distance between the projecting edges of the corner strips, or between a corner strip and the J channel around a door or window. To join two panels end to end, allow at least 1/2 inch for overlap and plan the cutting so you can stagger the joints; notch out 1/2 inch of the nailing flange on the cut end of one panel so it will slide under the other panel.

Fit the ends of the first panel under the projecting edges of the corner strips of J channel, then lift the panel up until the lower inside lip hooks into the groove in the starter strip. Secure the panel with nails driven into the flange at 16-inch intervals. If the panel is not insulated, insert a backer plate *(inset)* at each end before nailing it. Seat each successive panel similarly, hooking the lip into the groove of the preceding panel.

7 **Shaping the panels.** At windows and above doors, notch the panels before nailing them. Cut through the lip or groove side to the desired depth, then score the panel lengthwise between the cuts. Set a heavy ruler inside the score line and bend the panel over the ruler to break off the unwanted portion. At the soffit, score and break off the top edge of the panel so it will lie under the projecting edge of the attached trim. In most cases the trim will hold the panel edge securely; if not, insert nails near the top of the trim at 18-inch intervals.

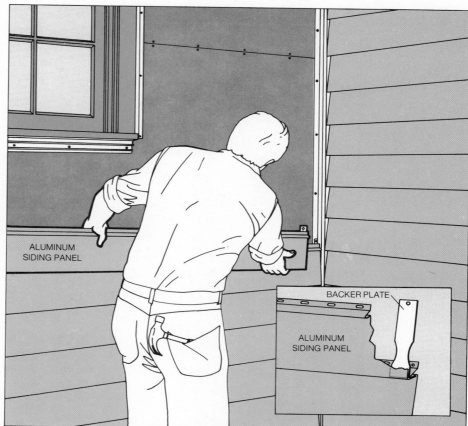

ALUMINUM SIDING PANEL

BACKER PLATE

ALUMINUM SIDING PANEL

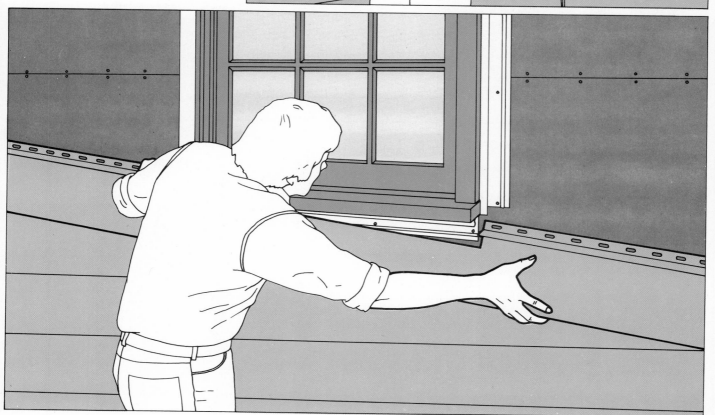

Finishing the Interior

A sheathed existing wall. Wire and insulate the new room, then cover the ceiling and walls with wallboard *(pages 80-86)*. To close up a window, butt-nail 2-by-4s inside all four sides of the jamb. Then extend the cripple studs above and below it by toenailing a 2-by-4 between the header and rough sill of the opening. Cover the opening with sheathing and insulate before installing wallboard inside the house; fill the openings with wallboard patches *(page 81)*. To retrim the door, extend the top and side jamb flush with the sheathing by attaching 3/4-inch-wide wood strips ripped to the required thickness. To replace the door, rip out the jamb and install a prehung unit *(page 196)*, or have a professional hang a new door in the old jamb.

A masonry existing wall. Wire and insulate the new room, then cover the ceiling and new walls with wallboard. To put wallboard over all or part of the masonry wall, first install 1-by-3 furring strips spaced 16 inches on center. Attach the strips with adhesive anchors, hammering the strips over the anchor nails. To hide a window recess, butt-nail 2-by-4 sleepers to the side walls of the opening, keeping the outside edges level with the masonry surface. Toenail two or more 2-by-4s between the sleepers to provide nailing surfaces for the furring strips. Inside the house, extend the cripple studs above and below the window with 2-by-4s and insulate before putting wallboard over the opening. At the door, you can fasten furring strips inside the recess to install wallboard over the masonry, then retrim the door in the new room with quarter round. To replace the door, rip out the jamb and install a prehung unit *(page 196)* or have a professional hang a new door in the old jamb.

Working with a Wood-Floored Porch

Prepare the porch *(page 408)*, then saw off the edges of the floor flush with the support frame. If the floor joists are less than 2-by-8, butt-nail a reinforcing joist to each of them—or have a masonry foundation installed after sealing the floor.

Where the floor is level and at the desired height, nail heavy 1/2-inch underlayment-grade plywood on top. Then insulate under the porch by pushing 6-inch batts between the joists, vapor-barrier side up, and securing the batts with braces cut from wire hangers to a length a bit longer than the space between joists *(right)*. Cover the ground beneath the porch with strips of 6-mil polyethylene, overlapped by about 6 inches and weighted down with bricks or stones. (If you cannot crawl under the porch, pry up the floor planks, lay the polyethylene through the joists onto the ground, staple the insulation between the joists, then replace the planks and install the plywood.)

Where the floor slopes, or is lower than the height desired, you do not need to insulate under the porch. Instead install an insulated wood frame on top of the porch floor and cover it with plywood, following the techniques for installing a subfloor over concrete *(page 408, Steps 1-4)*, but using 16-penny nails for the joists. Pressure-treated lumber need not be used. Frame, sheathe and finish the exterior walls *(pages 409-411)*.

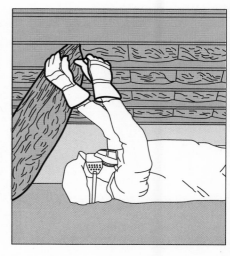

Foundations to Support an Added Room

An addition that looks like a part of the original house plan rather than an afterthought begins with a foundation that is not only structurally sound but allows you to match the floor level in the house and to make a seamless extension of a house wall, if you wish.

The problem of matching the floor levels is generally attacked by building the foundation of the addition flush with the top of the house foundation. You can compensate for slight differences in lumber dimensions or errors in building the foundation by shimming or notching floor framing members—or sleepers, in the case of a slab—to make the addition subflooring flush with that of the house.

If the addition will extend an interior wall of the house, you must place the foundation so that you can tie the addition wall to the end framing of the house wall. And where you are extending the façade of your house, the addition foundation generally should line up with the house foundation.

In a frame house finished with shingles, clapboards or metal siding, you can find the subfloor level, the top or side of the foundation, and the end framing of walls simply by removing a strip of siding and sheathing from the bottom of the wall as shown below, a step also necessary to install joists for the addition floor. You may also have to chip away some of the waterproofing mortar on many block foundations to place the addition building line flush with the house foundation.

Brick-veneer, solid-brick or block construction complicates the task of positioning the foundation. To mark the floor level or the end of an interior wall, for example, you must measure carefully inside the house from a door, a window or a pilot hole, then transfer the distances outside. The top of the new foundation is found by measuring down from floor level a distance equal to the total height of new-floor framing members. To find the foundation side of a brick-veneer house, you may have to dig below the brick.

What kind of foundation to build for the addition depends on the house foundation; consult a building designer or architect to design and draw the plans. If your house has a basement or crawl space, for example, build a crawl-space foundation for your addition as detailed on these and the following pages. If joists of your addition will span more than 15 feet, add piers for a girder. If your house rests on a slab, choose between two concrete-slab foundations (page 418). If the house slab rises no more than 12 inches above ground and if the footings of the new slab need to descend no deeper than 2 feet below grade to reach below the frost line, a turned-down slab is adequate. But if the slab must be built higher than 12 inches, or if unstable soil makes it difficult to dig the narrow trenches necessary to form the turned-down edge of the slab, build a combination slab-on-block foundation.

If the ground drops more than 24 inches from the house to the outer wall of the proposed addition, a crawl-space foundation will be the most economical choice, regardless of your house foundation. But if the land drops as much as 36 inches, you may need a stepped foundation, a complicated structure that requires considerable expertise to build.

After excavating a foundation that conforms to the local code, have the trenches checked by the building inspector. If your soil is wet or poorly compacted, more digging may be necessary to reach firm soil.

A Three-Sided Foundation

1 Attaching the marker boards. After removing a strip of siding and sheathing about 15 inches high—or extending to at least 1 inch above the sole plate—between the corners of the addition, nail two 8-foot 1-by-4 marker boards that are shimmed to make up for missing siding, flush with the top of the house foundation. The boards should extend 3 1/2 feet inside the corners marked at the house. Center a nail in the top edge of each marker board at the corners.

If the addition will extend an interior house wall, position the nail 4 inches—8 inches if you are going to finish the addition with brick veneer—outside the inner edge of the tie-in stud. If you are extending an exterior wall, align the corner nail with the house foundation.

TIE-IN STUD

MARKER BOARD

2 **Making the addition square.** Lay out building lines using the 3-4-5 triangle method. To do this, drive a nail at the center of the marker-board edge, 3 feet from a corner nail. Have two helpers cross measuring tapes hooked to the two nails so that the 4-foot mark on the corner-nail tape meets the 5-foot mark on the other tape. Drive a 3-foot stake at this point, then drive a nail into the top of the stake. Position a similar stake opposite the other marker board.

Use a string to extend the line between the corner nails in the marker boards and the nails in the stakes. Drive stakes to mark the ends of the addition side walls. Measure the diagonals of the resulting rectangle; if they are not equal, move the end stakes to make them so.

3 **Building and marking batter boards.** With a water level, mark the height of the house foundation on 2-by-4s driven to form right angles at the end stakes, 5 feet beyond the building lines. Then nail 1-by-6 batter boards, aligning the top edges with the marks. Stretch strings from the marker boards to extend the building lines to the batter boards. Drive nails in the boards to mark the lines. Drive nails into the batter boards and marker boards for the foundation wall and the footing trench and main trench, using the dimensions shown in the inset. (For brick veneer, drive the foundation-wall nails 11 5/8 inches inside the building lines.) Remove the end stakes and dig the trenches so that the bottom of the footing trench is below the frost line and the top lies a multiple of 8 inches below the top of the house foundation.

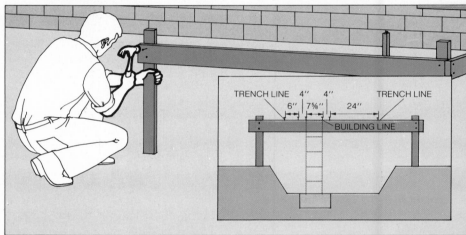

4 **Leveling the trench.** In a level site, the new footings will be the same depth as the old ones. After driving 1-by-2 stakes at the corners of the footing trench—and every 3 feet along it in a zigzag pattern, 3 inches from the sides—mark the top of the footing trench on one stake and transfer the mark to the other stakes with a water level. Deepen the footing trench where marks are less than 8 inches from the bottom; do not fill in the trench where it is deeper than 8 inches.

Drive two 16-inch lengths of 1/2-inch reinforcing bar, called grade pegs, on each side of the trench adjacent to each corner stake, and level with the mark. Remove the corner stakes and tamp the dirt around each grade peg.

5 **Placing the footing.** Place two lengths of No. 4 (1/2-inch) reinforcing bar on bricks in the footing trench and wire the bars to the grade pegs. Where two pieces of bar meet, overlap them 12 inches and wire them together with a tight double wrap of No. 16 mechanic's wire at each end of the splice. Cast the footing so that the concrete comes to the tops of the grade pegs, roughen the top surface, and let the concrete cure under sheets of polyethylene for 24 hours.

Run taut strings between the building-line nails on the batter boards and marker boards; then transfer the lines to the footing with a plumb bob and chalk line. Now you can remove the strings, batter boards and marker boards.

6 **Beginning the foundation wall.** Lay a dry run for the first course of the foundation, then lay stepped sets of 8-by-8-by-16-inch blocks three courses high as leads at the corners and ends of the foundation. Lay the block walls using a mason's line as a guide. Place wire-mesh block reinforcement into the mortar bed of every third course of blocks.

On opposite sides of the addition, install two ventilators in place of foundation blocks in the middle of the wall. Pack mortar around the edges, sloping the bottom for drainage. In the next course, lay solid blocks over each vent.

If you intend to finish the addition with brick veneer, build the wall with 12-by-8-by-16-inch blocks to a point immediately below ground level, and complete the wall with 8-inch blocks laid flush with the inside of the foundation wall.

7 **Setting anchor bolts.** Lay mesh block reinforcement under the top course of the
foundation, fill all the cores with mortar and,
before the mortar sets, install anchor bolts for
the sill place 1 foot from each corner and doorway and every 4 feet in between. Use 1/2-inch
anchor bolts 8 inches long and position each
with a piece of 2-by-6 that has a 5/8-inch hole
drilled in the center. Insert the bolt in the hole,
fit a washer and nut, then set the 2-by-6 back
1/2 inch from the outside of the foundation
wall or, if you are extending an exterior wall,
match the setback of the house sill plate. Tap
the anchor bolt into the mortar as far as it will
go. After 24 hours, remove the nuts and washers and lift the 2-by-6 jogs from the bolts.

8 **Installing the sill plate.** Place atop the
wall a pressure-treated 2-by-6 that is 1/2
inch shorter than a foundation side wall (measured from the house sill plate), and use a
combination square to mark it with the anchor-
bolt locations. Drill 3/4-inch holes centered at
the marks.

Install a layer of sill sealer, available in rolls 6
inches wide, and bolt the sill plate on. Install
the remaining sill plates in the same fashion,
shim them level and check them for squareness, then toenail the ends together.

Tying the New Floor to the Old

1 Installing header and stringer joists. Cut a header joist equal to the distance between the outside edges of the side-wall sill plates and fasten it to the exposed joist on the house, using 1/2-inch lag bolts 4 inches long and 16 inches apart in a zigzag pattern, starting 2 inches from one end of the joist. Do not bolt a joist to brick veneer; toenail it to the sill plates at each end.

Toenail two stringer joists 3 inches shorter than the side-wall sill plates to the header joist. Butt-nail another header joist to the stringer joists and toenail all three to the sill plates.

2 Securing floor joists and subfloor. Install joists the same size as those on the house every 16 inches, butt-nailing them to the sill joists where possible or using joist hangers or anchors. Face-nail and toenail blocking between joists every 4 feet.

After filling the trenches inside the walls, cover the earth within a crawl space with 6-mil polyethylene sheeting weighted down with rocks as a vapor barrier. Staple insulation between the joists, vapor barrier side up, then install subflooring, leaving an area in the center of the floor temporarily uninsulated and uncovered for access to the crawl space for the utility work. Waterproof the outside of the foundation with a 1/2-inch layer of mortar up to grade level—or higher, to match your house.

Precision Fitting for a Concrete Slab

A slab foundation. Some slabs rest on a block wall and footings identical to those built for a crawl-space foundation *(Steps 1-6, pages 413-415)*, except that air vents are omitted and the final course of the wall is laid with L-shaped header blocks to form a shelf. The area between the foundation walls is filled with compacted gravel to the level of the slab shelf, the gravel is covered with 6-mil polyethylene, and expansion-joint material is placed along the house.

The other three sides of the slab, and part of the bottom, are insulated with rigid styrofoam insulation. Wire mesh reinforces the slab. Sole plates are attached with anchor bolts set into mortar-filled cores of the blocks. In warm cli-

mates the block foundation shown here can be omitted. Instead, use simple forms and footing trenches to shape the concrete placed for the slab into turned-down edges that will serve as both footing and foundation. Reinforcing bars strengthen the edge of the foundation, mesh strengthens the slab itself. Anchor bolts for sole plates are set into the wet concrete.

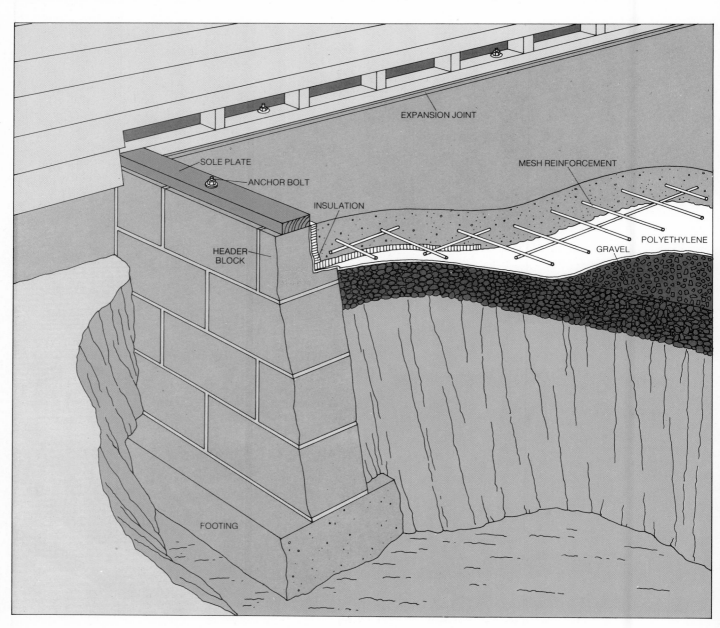

418

Grafting New Walls to the Side of a House

Erecting the walls, the most impressive stage in the construction of an addition, is also the simplest. In a single day, stud walls—made from vertical 2-by-4s and horizontal top and sole plates—can be assembled, tilted upright, tied to the house, braced, and covered with sheathing. The process differs from standard wall construction only at the joint between the house and the addition wall.

To tie the addition to a house that has wooden siding or stucco, you have to cut through the siding and sheathing and nail the addition wall to a corner post or to extra studs that you insert into the house wall. If the existing wall surface is masonry, you anchor-bolt the new walls on.

When buying materials, be sure you get perfectly straight 2-by-4s for wall plates and corner and window studs. You can straighten a crooked stud after the walls are upright by making a shallow horizontal saw cut across the inner edge of the stud, pushing the stud straight and nailing a short strip of plywood to each side of it, over the saw cut.

The wall studs for the addition must be the same length as those in the house if the ceilings are to match. To determine the correct length, make a small hole through the ceiling covering of the existing room next to the addition and measure vertically from a ceiling joist to the finish floor; subtract the distance between the finish floor and the bottom of the studs *(measured in Step 1, page 417)* and then subtract 3 inches for the double top plate of the new walls.

Make the addition walls plumb, regardless of tilt in the existing walls—to compensate for tilt, angle end studs and adjust the lengths of top plates.

Making the Incisions

1 **Making the siding.** If an addition wall will meet the middle of an existing wall, snap a vertical chalk line on the siding 5/8 inch outside the edge of the platform side, then snap another vertical line over the platform, about 12 inches from the first. If the new wall will meet a corner of the existing house, snap a single vertical line about 10 inches in from the corner.

Cut the siding along each chalk line, then pry away the wall covering between the cuts.

2 **Removing the cornice.** Prepare to work safely at heights *(page 340)*. If the roof overhang extends below the planned height of the addition walls, remove the section of roofing material over the addition platform to expose the roof sheathing. With a framing square, extend the outer two lines you marked in Step 1 onto the frieze board, the soffit, the fascia board and the roof sheathing. At the service panel, turn off all branch electrical circuits to and through the wall *(page 11)*. Make sure that there are no electric cables or water pipes in the wall, then cut the frieze board along both lines with a rented demolition saw—a powerful reciprocating saw with a long straight wood- and nail-cutting blade—and pry away the section between the cuts. Cut the soffit and the fascia board along the lines and pry them away. If lookouts supported the soffit *(page 427, bottom),* pry them off.

FASCIA BOARD

FRIEZE BOARD

SOFFIT

3 **Cutting off the overhang.** Drill a pilot hole through the roof sheathing from underneath, directly above each point where the outer face of an addition wall will meet the outer edge of the house-wall top plate. Snap a chalk line between the holes, perpendicular to the two lines you extended across the roof sheathing in Step 2. Cut the roof sheathing along the lines with a circular saw and pry it away from the rafters. With a level, mark a vertical line across each exposed rafter, flush with the outer edge of the top plate; cut the rafters off with a demolition saw.

Building Braces into the Cuts

Extra studs for a platform-frame wall. If a new wall will meet the middle of a platform-frame wall, slide a straight stud into the house wall through the slot in the siding and toenail it to top and sole plates flush with the siding. Outside, nail the siding to the stud every 6 inches. Toenail a second straight stud alongside the first but with its face set flush with the outside edge of the house plates. Slide a third stud alongside the second but perpendicular to it, toenail it to the house plates and then face-nail it to the second stud. If a stud in the house wall blocks the new studs, do not attempt to move it—simply nail the new studs alongside the old one.

Support in a balloon-frame wall. If an addition wall will meet the middle of a balloon-frame wall, remove the interior wall covering opposite the addition wall and nail 2-by-4s horizontally between studs every 2 feet, 1 1/2 inches from the outside edge of the studs. Nail a 2-by-8 vertically where the addition wall will meet the house wall and nail the siding to the 2-by-8.

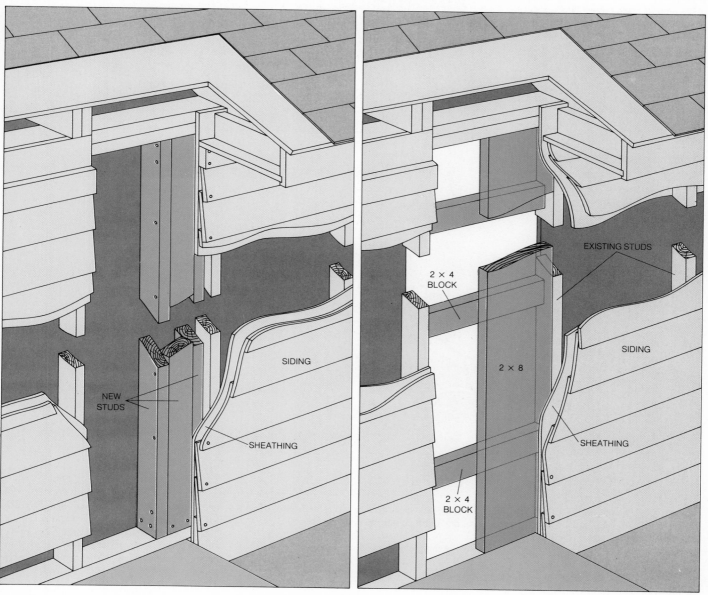

421

Tying walls to a masonry house. Lay a 2-by-4 flat on the platform as a spacer, hold a pressure-treated stud vertically on the block and flat against the masonry wall, and mark the height of every sixth mortar joint on the edge of the stud. Drill staggered 1/4-inch holes through the face of the stud at the marks. Hold the stud against the masonry in exactly the position the new wall will occupy, flush with the outer edge of the platform and on top of the spacer block; plumb the stud with a carpenter's level *(page 424, Step 4)* and fasten it temporarily with masonry nails. Use the stud as a template to drill matching pilot holes in the mortar joints, then remove it. Insert a masonry anchor in each hole. Prepare a stud for the other edge of the platform in the same way.

When you put the addition walls together *(page 423, Step 2)*, install the drilled studs at the house end of each side wall; when the walls have been erected, fasten the studs to the house with bolts and washers *(page 424, Step 4)*.

SPACER

Assembling the Walls

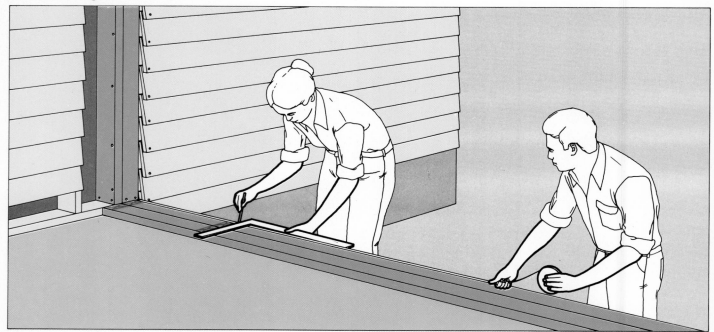

1 Laying out the plates. If your addition has wooden floor joists, measure from the sole plate of the house *(exposed on page 418, Step 1)* to the edge of the platform end and cut straight 2-by-4 top and sole plates to this length for each side wall; if your addition has a concrete slab foundation, unbolt the sole plates you installed when the slab was placed *(page 418)* and cut top plates to match.

Set the top and sole plates side by side along their respective walls and, measuring from the ends next to the house, mark locations for studs, windows and doors. Determine the width of door and window rough openings from manufacturers' specifications, and mark for jack and king studs beside each. Make end-wall plates 7 inches shorter than the end of the platform; mark them for studs and openings, including an extra nailer stud flush with the ends of the plates if a stud would not fall there normally.

2 **Nailing walls together.** Butt-nail studs to the top and bottom plates at layout marks, omitting the studs for each door or window. For each wall corner, make a post from straight studs and 2-by-4 blocks *(inset)* and nail it to the outer ends of the plates at the corners of the addition.

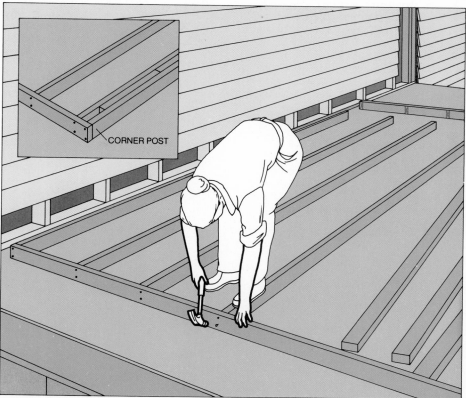

CORNER POST

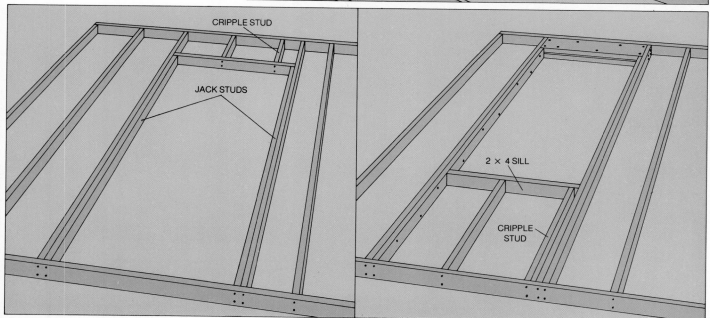

CRIPPLE STUD

JACK STUDS

2 × 4 SILL

CRIPPLE STUD

3 **Framing the rough openings.** Cut jack studs long enough to reach the top of each door rough opening *(shown above, left for a nonbearing wall)* and nail each to a straight, wall-height stud—called a king stud in this situation—then nail these double studs to the plates to frame each door and window opening. In a bearing wall, make a header for the opening *(see chart, page 73 for estimated dimen-*sions) and nail it horizontally between the king studs. Nail cripple studs, if needed, snugly between the header and the top plate at 16-inch intervals. For a window frame *(above, right)*, nail a 2-by-4 sill across the opening and nail cripple studs beneath the sill.

Tilt the wall upright and, if you are building on a slab foundation, slide the predrilled holes in the sole plate over the anchor bolts, then nail 2-by-4 braces to studs and to the platform every 8 feet along the wall. Drive the end of the sole plate tight against the sole plate of the house wall and flush with the edge of the platform. For a block foundation, nail the sole plate to the stringer or header joist with staggered 16-penny nails at 8-inch intervals; on a slab foundation, bolt the plates down.

4 **Tying the wall to the house.** While a helper holds a 4-foot level against the side of the end stud of the addition wall, push the stud in or out until it is plumb. If you are working in a house made of wood, drive staggered 16-penny nails through the top of the stud into the stud behind it—either the stud you inserted or an existing corner stud of the house; in a masonry house, fasten the stud to masonry anchors, using bolts and washers. In a platform-frame house, toenail the top and sole plates of the addition wall to those of the house wall.

Repeat Steps 1 through 3 to build the other side wall of the addition, then the end wall. Plumb and brace the corner posts of the two side walls first, then the end studs of the end wall.

5 **Straightening the walls.** To eliminate bows in the top plate, stretch a string taut across the surfaces of 2-by-4 blocks at each end of one of the addition walls. Have a helper free the bottom of each brace along the wall; hold a 2-by-4 block between the string and the top plate and push or pull the wall until the string barely touches the 2-by-4, then have your helper renail the brace. Adjust the other walls similarly.

When all of the walls are straight, nail the studs at each end of the end wall to the corner posts of the side walls. Lap a second top plate for the end wall, 7 inches longer than the first one, over the original top plates of the side walls and nail it to the original plates; then nail a second top plate to each of the side walls.

2 × 4 BLOCK

HEADER

2 × 4 BLOCK

6 **Sheathing the walls.** Have a helper hold a sheet of APA-rated plywood or oriented strand board sheathing rated for the stud spacing of your wall horizontally against the studs. The bottom of the plywood should be flush with the bottom of the sill plate and one end should be tight against the house-wall sole plate. Fasten the plywood to the sill plate, the header or stringer joist and the studs with sixpenny nails every 6 inches around the edges and every 12 inches in the center of the sheet. Leave 1/4-inch gaps at panel edges and 1/8 inch at panel ends. Continue the sheathing horizontally around the addition; when you come to a window or doorway, nail the sheathing in place, snap chalk lines along the edges of the opening and cut the sheathing with a circular saw.

Start the second course with a piece of plywood 4 feet square, so that the joints between the sheets are staggered with those in the first course. For the third course, cut the sheets to the width required before you nail them up.

A Glassed-In Sunroom

In this energy-conscious age, builders rarely include a glassed-in sunroom in new houses—even in sunny climates. They could be making a mistake, for a sunroom can be surprisingly energy-efficient. In cool weather, sunlight can warm a glassed-in room to summer temperatures during the day; at night, insulation and a snugly fitting door in the house wall will keep heat from leaking away from the house. In summer, ventilation through sunroom windows often can substitute for air conditioning—and when air conditioning is necessary, the addition can be closed off.

A sunroom—for relaxation or for use as a greenhouse-like plant room—is an addition easy to build but it requires professional assistance in design. Because the walls contain so many windows, they are relatively weak; the size of headers and the size and spacing of studs should be specified by an architect or building designer.

A sunroom generally is fitted with a concrete-slab floor *(page 418))*, awning and jalousie windows and a shed roof *(pages 428-429)*. The walls of the typical sun-

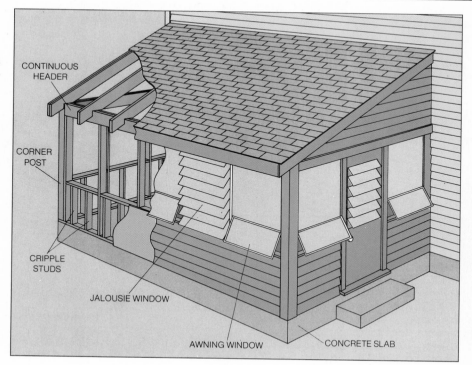

room, shown above, resemble the stud walls shown on the preceding pages, with one important difference: A continuous header runs the length of each sunroom wall, combining the functions of separate rough-framing headers and conventional 2-by-4 top plates. The header ends are supported by jack studs nailed to heavy posts.

How to Splice the New Roof onto the Old

The roof for a small one-story addition generally is built in one of two common forms: a shed roof, with a single sloping surface; or a gable roof, with two sloping surfaces that meet at a peak, or ridge. An architect or building designer can help you choose a roof for your addition, and will recommend a specific slope—that is, the inches of vertical rise per foot of horizontal run.

The slope is critical not only for practical reasons but also because it can make the difference between an ugly addition and an attractive one. For a shed roof, a professional is likely to recommend a gentle slope of 4 inches or less per foot of horizontal span; for a gable roof, a slope that matches that of the existing roof. (An easy method for measuring this slope is shown opposite, top.) These general rules must be adapted to special circumstances. In a gable roof fitted to a house wall, for example, clearing second-floor windows may require a shallow slope.

The type of roofing material you select may also affect the slope of your roof. Tile and slate cannot be used on a roof that slopes less than 4 inches in 12. Wood shingles and shakes need a minimum slope of 3 inches in 12, asphalt shingles

and metal panels 2 inches in 12, while roll roofing requires only 1 inch in 12.

A shed roof is relatively easy to build. Rafters secured to the side of the house support the sheathing and roofing, and light joists support the new ceiling. If you like a high sloping ceiling or if you build a nearly flat roof, you can omit the joists.

A gable roof built against the side of a house is little more difficult than the shed type. In one respect, in fact, it is easier: because the span of each rafter is half the rafter span in a shed roof of the same size, you can use lighter lumber. But a gable roof always must have ceiling joists to keep the rafters from spreading apart at the bottom, and for a roof with a slope of less than 4 inches in 12, you may need additional braces called collar beams between pairs of rafters.

Joining a gable roof to the side of an existing roof presents special problems. The rafters between the old roof and the new ridge beam must be made progressively shorter up to the point where the two roofs meet. At their bases these short rafters or jack rafters, must be set back from the joint between the old and the new roofs, and must be cut at a specified angle to match the roof slope *(chart be-*

low). In addition, the eaves of the new roof must both meet and blend with those of the existing structure.

Blending eaves is primarily a matter of duplicating the detail work of the cornice—that is, the trim of the eaves—in the existing house (two common types are shown opposite). Making eaves meet at the same level, so that the roofs of both the addition and the main house appear to have a single continuous eave, is trickier if the rafters of the addition are narrower than those of the main roof.

In such a roof with an overhang of at least 12 inches, the discrepancy can be corrected by making a shorter overhang on the addition *(page 431, Step 7)*. For roofs with little or no overhang, professional carpenters use a variety of methods to raise the addition rafters to the level of the main rafters at the eaves. Some alter the angle cuts, called bird's-mouths, of the addition rafters to match the heel—the vertical distance above the eave wall—of addition and main rafters. Others raise addition rafters by installing extra top plates or thin shims between rafters and wall. For amateurs the best method is to avoid the problem entirely by making the addition rafters of the same size lumber as the main rafters.

Fitting the Rafters to the Roof

Roof Slope	Height of vertical end cuts in common lumber sizes					Jack rafters	
	2 x 4	2 x 6	2 x 8	2 x 10	2 x 12	Setback	Foot angle
1"	3½"	5½"	7¼"	9¼"	10¼"	4¼"	5°
2"	3½"	5½"	7⅜"	9⅜"	11⅜"	2⅛"	10°
3"	3⅝"	5⅝"	7½"	9½"	11⅝"	1⅜"	15°
4"	3¾"	5¾"	7⅝"	9¾"	11⅞"	1"	19°
5"	3¾"	6"	7⅝"	10"	12¼"	⅞"	23°
6"	3⅞"	6⅛"	8⅛"	10⅜"	12⅝"	¾"	27°
7"	4"	6⅜"	8⅜"	10¾"	13"	⅝"	31°
8"	4¼"	6⅝"	8¾"	11⅛"	13½"	½"	34°
9"	4⅜"	6⅞"	9"	11½"	14"	½"	37°
10"	4½"	7⅛"	9⅜"	12"	14⅝"	½"	40°
11"	4¾"	7⅜"	9¾"	12½"	15¼"	⅜"	43°
12"	5"	7¾"	10¼"	13"	15⅞"	⅜"	45°

Data for making addition rafters. This table provides specifications essential to the pages that follow, organized according to rafter slopes, which are given as inches of rise per foot of span. It lists heights of the angles end cuts of five sizes of rafters so that, by using the figure for the size and slope of your rafters, you can determine where to place a rafter plate *(page 428, Step 1)* or a ridge beam *(page 429, Step 1)*.

The last two columns apply to jack rafters, short rafters that support an addition roof wherever it overlaps the main roof. One column indicates setback, the placement relative to a chalk line of these rafters and the plate that supports them *(page 430, Step 3)*; the other indicates the angle at which to set the blade of a circular saw to fit the foot of a jack rafter to the roof beneath it *(page 431, Step 5)*.

Measuring a roof slope. Mark the top of a level 12 inches from one end, set that end against the underside of a rafter inside the attic or a rake board outside the house and, with the level horizontal, set a ruler or carpenter's square vertically at the mark. The distance in inches between the top of the level and the underside of the rafter or rake board is the rise of the roof in a 12-inch unit of run; in this example, the reading indicates a slope of 6 inches in 12.

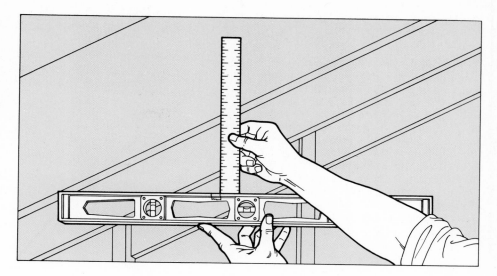

Two Basic Cornice Styles

A closed cornice. This relatively simple assembly creates a roof without an overhanging eave. After the roof sheathing has been installed, a plywood filler strip is nailed to the vertical ends—called the heels—of the rafters. A frieze board is nailed to the filler strip, and metal drip-edge flashing is fastened over the frieze. The gable edges are finished with a spacer board nailed to the edge of the roof, and a rake board, the same width as the frieze, nailed to the spacer.

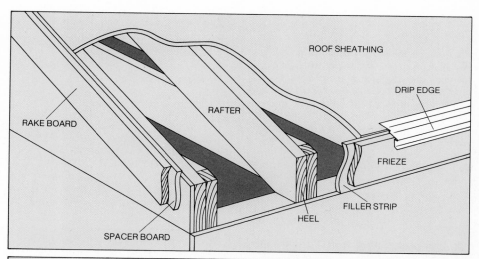

A box cornice. In this style the rafters project to frame an overhang at the eaves. A notch called a bird's mouth near the end of each rafter fits the rafter to the top and outer edge of the top plate; the end of the rafter is cut vertically, the lower corner horizontally. A fascia and a drip edge cover the ends of the rafters, a plywood soffit protects the undersides, and a frieze board covers sheathing beneath the soffit. The rakes are treated as in the closed cornice described above, except that the lower end of the rake board has specially cut pieces (including a final piece called a pork chop) over the cornice end.

In a wide box cornice (inset) horizontal members called lookouts are set between rafter ends and sheathing to frame and support the soffit.

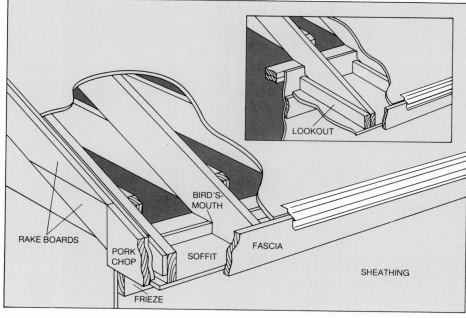

Building a Shed Roof

1 Mounting the plates. Attach plates for ceiling joists and rafters to the house, cutting both plates to the distance between the outer edges of the top plates on the addition side walls. Make the joist plate of lumber the same size as the joists, and set it on the side-wall top plates. Make the rafter plate as wide as the vertical end cut for the size and slope of your rafters *(chart, page 426)*. To set the height of the top of this plate above the side-wall top plates, subtract 5 1/2 inches from the length of a side wall, divide by 12 and multiply by the roof slope (for example, if the slope is 4 in 12, multiply by 4); then add the figure for the vertical end cut.

2 Hanging the joists. Fasten metal joist hangers to the face of the joist plate at 2-foot intervals with framing anchor nails, beginning 1 1/2 inches from one end and setting the bottom strap of each hanger flush with the bottom of the plate. Position the last hanger 1 1/2 inches from the other end of the plate. Fasten metal joist anchors atop the outer wall of the addition in corresponding positions, then cut and install the ceiling joists.

3 Hanging the rafters. Nail a length of rafter stock temporarily to the side of the addition and the end of the rafter plate, setting its position by the following method. Trim the upper end of the rafter at an angle roughly estimated to make it rest against both the house wall and the end of the rafter plate. Align the rafter with the upper edge of the upper end flush with the top of the rafter plate, and the lower edge of the other end aligned with the inner edge of the end-wall top plate *(inset)*. On the temporarily nailed rafter, trace around the end wall for the bird's-mouth cut; trace the rafter plate at the other end for an accurate angle cut. Mark the outer edge of the rafter for the cornice style you have chosen. Cut the rafter at the marks and use it as a template for the other rafters.

Set the first rafter alongside the first joist, flush with the side wall; nail the rafter to the joist, and use metal plates and framing anchor nails to fasten it to the top and rafter plates. Install the remaining rafters 2 feet apart except for the last one, which—like the first—should be flush with the side wall.

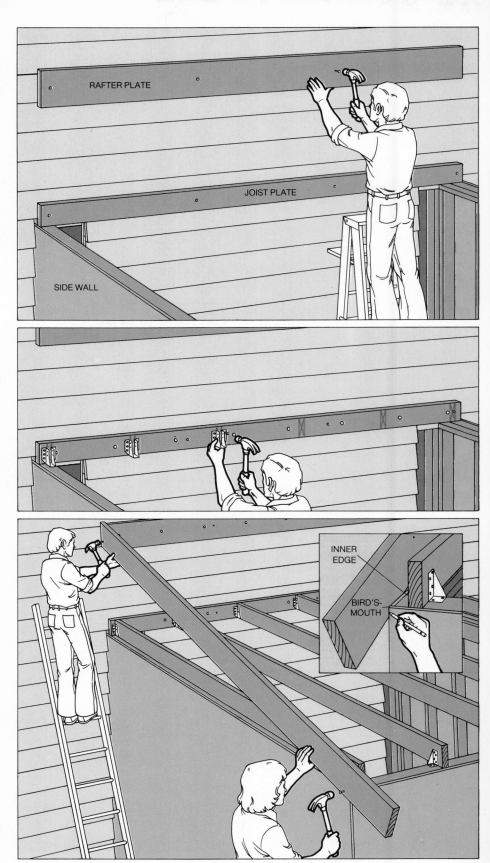

4 **Installing cripple studs.** Cut 2-by-4 studs to fit at 16-inch intervals between the outermost rafters and the side-wall top plates with the wide sides of the studs facing outward, and toenail the studs to the rafters and the top plates. At the house wall, turn the studs so that the wide sides are resting flat against the wall, and nail the studs to the wall between the rafter and joist plates.

At the addition end wall, saw off the corners of the joists so they are flush with the upper edges of the rafters.

Building a Gable Roof

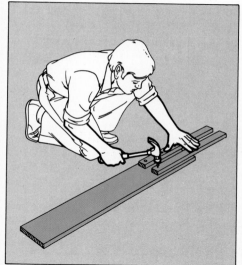

1 **Braces for a ridge beam.** Make two temporary supports for the ridge beam by nailing pairs of 1-by-2s 1 1/2 inches apart to the ends of 2-by-6s cut to the height of the ridge beam above the addition walls. To calculate this height, subtract 9 1/2 inches from the width of the addition and divide by 24. Multiply the result by the roof slope, then add the figure for the end cut of your rafters (*chart, page 426*). Finally, subtract the width of the ridge beam.

Install ceiling joists between the side walls of the addition, using metal anchors at 2-foot intervals and setting the outermost joists 1 1/2 inches from the ends of the plates (*Step 2, opposite*). Nail and brace a ridge-beam support to the center of each outermost joist, placing the bottom of the support flush with the bottom of the joist. Cut a set of rafters (*Step 3, opposite*).

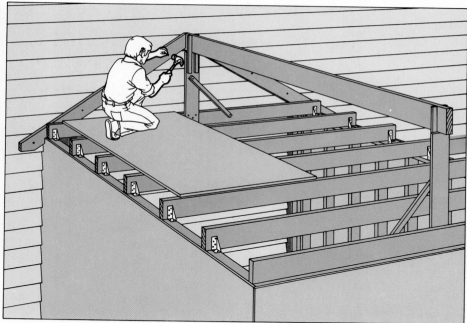

2 **Mounting the rafters.** Set the ridge beam in place; then, at the house wall, nail a pair of rafters in place atop the plates and against the ridge beam, and secure the rafters to the wall with bolts. Mount the remaining pairs at 2-foot intervals, using nails at the joists and metal angle plates at the top plates and the ridge beam. Saw off the outer corners of the joists flush with the upper edges of the rafters; install cripple studs, cut to fit between the end-wall top plate and the end rafters, at the gable end of the addition roof (*Step 4, above*).

Intricate Angles
of Intersecting Roofs

1 Cutting the ridge beam. Set a length of ridge-beam stock in temporary braces *(page 429, Step 1)*. At the point where it touches the roof of the house, drive a marker nail down into the attic; then hold a board on the roof against the beam, and trace the roof slope onto the beam. Cut the beam to fit and mark it for rafters at 2-foot intervals; then set it back in place. If the point of the marker nail protrudes inside the attic between two rafters, install a bracing board of rafter stock between those rafters. On the roof, nail the end of the new ridge beam through the roof into a bracing board or a rafter.

2 Installing rafters. Cut pairs of rafters *(page 428, Step 3)*, but for the main part of the roof, leave the rafter ends uncut and long enough to extend below the edge of the existing roof; for the position just outside the edge of the existing roof make the rafters 2 feet longer. If a rafter position falls inside the existing roof, trim the ends of this pair *(inset)* for a closed cornice as described on page 427, center. Install all but one pair of the rafters, starting at the gable end of the addition. Use a reserved rafter as a template for the end cuts of the jack rafters *(Steps 5 and 6, opposite)*. Install cripple studs at the gable end of the addition *(page 429, Step 4)*.

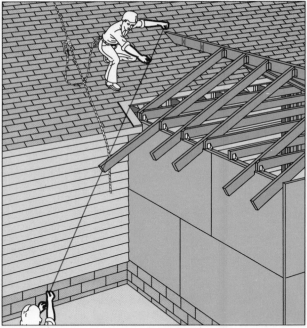

3 Positioning roof plates. With a helper, extend a chalk line from the point where the top of the ridge beam meets the main roof down over the tops of the long rafters on each side of the addition; the line should graze both the roof and the rafters. Snap this line on each side of the addition roof. Then snap a second line inside the first on each side; to find how far inside—the "setback" distance between the first and second lines—use the chart on page 426.

430

4 **Installing the roof plates.** Nail roof plates of 1/2-inch plywood, 12 inches wide, between the ridge beam and the cut edge of the main roof, aligning the outer edges of each plate with the second of the chalk lines made in Step 3. To mark the roof plates for the lower ends of the jack rafters, drop a plumb line from the rafter positions you marked along the ridge beam and, at the points where the plumb bob touches the existing roof, run horizontal lines on the roof to the roof plates.

5 **A compound cut for a jack rafter.** Using a template rafter reserved in Step 1, trace the horizontal cut of its bird's-mouth at the middle of a piece of rafter stock that is close to twice as long as the template *(right, top)*. Extend the line across the stock. Set a circular saw to the angle required for your roof slope *(chart, page 426)* and cut along the marks *(right, bottom)*, creating left- and right-hand pieces. Cut other jack rafters in the same way, estimating lengths approximately.

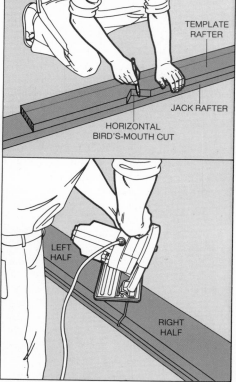

TEMPLATE RAFTER

JACK RAFTER

HORIZONTAL BIRD'S-MOUTH CUT

LEFT HALF

RIGHT HALF

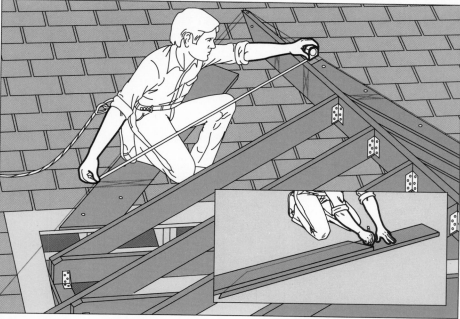

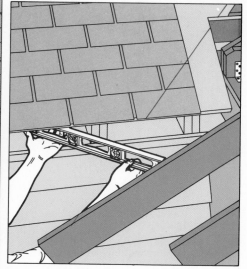

6 **Completing jack rafters.** With a tape, measure from the top of the ridge beam to the outer edge of the roof plate at each jack-rafter location. Mark this distance on each left-hand jack rafter cut in Step 5, measuring along the upper edge. Set the ridge end of a template rafter at this mark, aligning its longest edge with that of the jack rafter, trace the ridge cut of the template *(inset)*, and saw the jack rafter there. Use the left-hand rafters as templates to mark ridge cuts on right-hand ones. Toenail the jack rafters to the roof plate and fasten them to the ridge beam with metal angle plates. Add any other fasteners required by your local code. Install the template rafters last.

7 **Trimming the rafters.** At each side of the addition, remove a short section of the fascia from the main roof of the house and set a level under the edge of the main-roof sheathing, then swing the level until its end touches the top of the nearest addition rafter. Mark that rafter at this point, cut it at the mark to match the ends of the main-roof rafters; cut the other addition rafters to match the first. To complete the framing, match the cornice trim of the addition to that of the main roof.

431

The Special Problems of an Extended Roof

A gabled addition at the gable end of a house has a unique roof design. Instead of running the addition roof into the side or roof of the main house, as on pages 429-431, the builder generally must extend the main roof to cover the addition. When the addition is as high and wide as the house, the entire roof is extended. When the addition has a front or back wall as high as that of the house, but is not as wide, an extension of the main roof is generally built at the front or back of the house; for the other half of the addition, a new roof is run into the side of the house *(right)*.

If the original main roof has an overhang at its gables, the addition will generally look best with a similar or identical overhang on the roof extension. Other problems arise when the addition is almost, but not quite, as wide as the main house. If you find that the new roof meets the rake trim of the old, remove the trim; flash the completed addition roof in the usual way *(pages 434-435)*, and reinstall the trim over the flashing. If the new roof meets the old just under the rake trim, so that you do not have enough room to install roofing and flashing, extend the existing rake trim down onto the new roof and flash to it.

Two roof treatments. Because this addition has been built flush with the front of the main house but is set back at the rear, its roof is matched to the house in two different ways. At the front of the house, the main roof is extended to cover the addition; at the rear, the addition roof runs beneath the main roof and meets the house at the gable wall. If the addition were not set back at the rear of the house, the entire main roof would be extended to cover it.

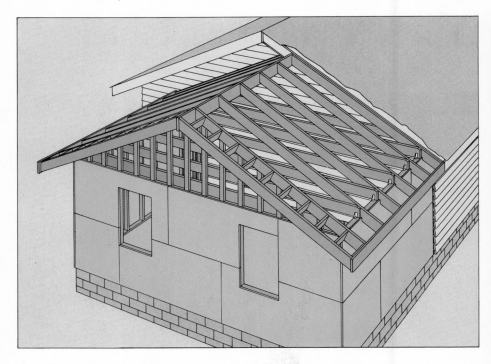

Setting the Ridge Beam, End Rafter and Overhang

Putting up the ridge beam. Lay down sheets of plywood atop the joists to provide a working surface. Remove the rake trim from the main roof—on one side for an extension of part of the roof; on both sides for a complete extension—and install joists and a ridge beam on the addition in the usual way *(page 429, Steps 1 and 2)*. For the partial extension shown here, align the upper edge of the ridge with the upper edge of the end rafter. If you are extending both roof slopes, butt the new ridge beam to the end of the old one *(inset)*. Fasten the new ridge beam to the end rafters of the main house with angle plates and nails.

Putting up the rafters. Install rafters on the addition *(page 428-431)*, starting at the gable end and, in this partial extension, fastening the innermost rafters to an end rafter and to the gable wall of the main house. If you are extending both slopes of the main roof, fasten the innermost addition rafters to the end rafters of the house. To set the slope of the rafter next to a gable wall, have a helper hold a perfectly straight board against the undersides of the installed rafters, and align the rafter with this board and with the top plate of the addition. Cut the upper end of this rafter to fit beneath the soffit board in the overhang trim of the main roof.

Although the addition roof will be sheathed and flashed in the usual way *(pages 434-435)*, you must notch the sheathing to fit the overhang of the main roof. You need not fasten the sheathing to the soffit of the overhang, but you must install flashing along the joint between the old rake and the new roof. Cover this rake flashing with new rake trim, installed between the peaks of the old and new roofs.

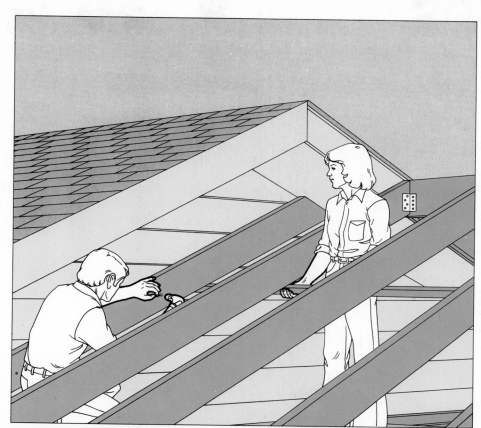

Building an overhang at the rake. Match the cornice trim of the addition to that of the main roof *(page 427)*, but extend the fascia beyond the outermost rafter to the outer edge of the planned rake overhang. At this edge, install a rafter between the fascia and the ridge beam, then nail bracing blocks the same size as the rafters between the rake rafter and the outermost main rafter at 16-inch intervals.

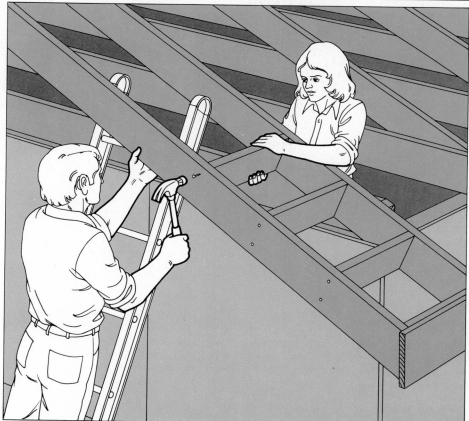

Finishing an Addition Roof

Roofing for an addition generally duplicates that on the existing house. In most cases it will consist of sheathing of plywood; felt underlayment; flashing at edges and valleys, best made of aluminum; and the same shingles used for the house. However, if the roofing is shakes, you need sheathing of 1-by-3 slats; if the slope of the addition roof is less than 2 inches per foot, use roll roofing instead of shingles or shakes. Because all addition roofs must be flashed at newly created joints, most drawings on these pages concern flashing.

Matching new roofing material to old can be tricky. Old roofing changes color as it weathers. Also, you may encounter an odd installation pattern in asphalt shingles or in the depths of the courses in wooden shingles and shakes. If you cannot make a good match, it is best to reroof the main house.

On a small addition roof, gutters are not generally necessary. The exception is an intersecting gable roof, where there is a heavy flow of water from the valleys between the main and addition roofs. In this case, either extend the main-roof gutters around the addition (*opposite, bottom*) or install gutters on both roofs.

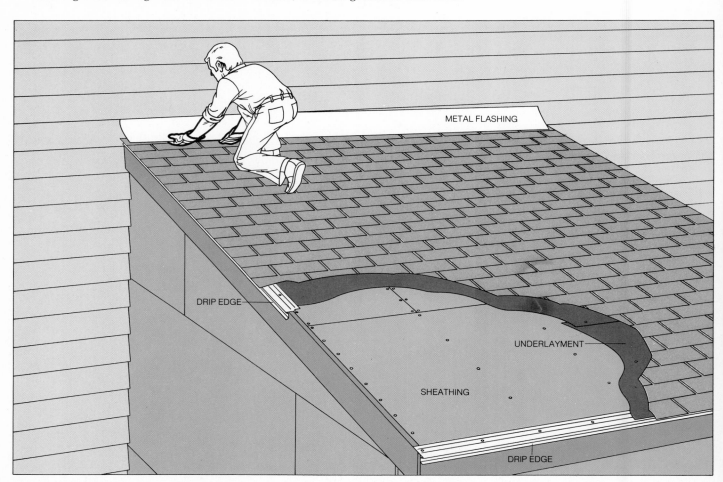

Flashing a shed roof. Sheathe the roof and add drip edges, underlayment and roofing. For clapboard siding, slip a strip of aluminum flashing up underneath the siding board just above the addition roof and bend the bottom of the strip to lap over the roof. Nail through the siding board and flashing at 12-inch intervals. For plywood or vertical board siding, cut a 1-inch slot above the roof, install the flashing in the same way, and caulk the joint between the upper edge of the slot and the flashing.

In brick siding, use a circular saw with a masonry blade to cut a groove 1/2 inch deep into a horizontal mortar joint about 6 inches above the top of the roof. Install one strip of bent flashing flat to the wall and the roof, nailing it with masonry nails driven into mortar joints. Install a second strip—called counterflashing—into the groove, then bend it down over the first strip. Nail and caulk the counterflashing at the groove.

Flashing a gable roof at a wall. To seal the joints at the edge of this roof, small individually cut rectangles of flashing are installed alternately with courses of roofing. Start the job by installing sheathing, drip edges and underlayment, with the underlayment lapped 3 inches up the adjoining wall. As you lay each course of roofing, cover at least 2 inches of its upper half with a rectangle of flashing cut to fit; bend the piece and set its upper edge under a clapboard, in a diagonal slot cut into plywood or vertical wooden siding, or under a piece of counter-flashing on brick siding. In clapboard, caulk the vertical gaps between the flashing strips.

The flashing at the roof peak consists of two precut pieces: one folded over the ridge and extending up the wall on each side, the other piece extending down the wall over the first and notched to fit the roof peak.

Flashing an intersecting roof. A special type of valley flashing, shaped like a W in cross section and fitted with nailing cleats, protects the valleys between old and new roofs. Carefully remove the existing roofing back 3 inches from the center of each valley and remove any nails within 7 inches of the centers; remove shingles directly above the peak of the addition roof to clear about 2 square feet of sheathing. Working from the addition side of each valley, slip the edges of the valley flashing underneath the edges of the existing roofing and nail the flashing to the roof through its cleats. Trim the flashing 1 foot above the peak of the valleys, hammer it flat to the roof, and replace the shingles you removed.

Running a Gutter Around a Corner

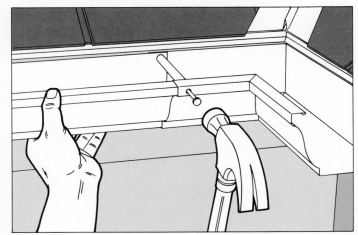

Adding the gutters. To reinstall the existing gutters, add a corner piece to each end that was cut away for the addition and extend the gutter along the new fascia to a downspout at the end of the wall. If water overflows the gutter at a valley, install an extra downspout there.

Inside the House: An Opening in the Common Wall

In most cases, the opening between an addition and the house—installed after the addition is roofed and weathertight—is easy to provide. It raises special problems in only one instance—an addition to the first floor of a two-story house that must be a seamless extension of an existing room, leaving walls and ceilings uninterrupted. Even then, the problem is solved simply in nonbearing walls; only a seamless opening that breaches a bearing wall (the front and back walls in most houses) requires the additional construction indicated in the drawing below.

Most additions, however, are not extensions but separate rooms. Entry can be provided by making use of an existing door, or if there is none, by converting an existing window or making an entirely new door or framed opening as described on page 423. Many extensions can be handled similarly—a wide framed opening serves well if the extension is meant to create space for a distinct purpose—to be a dining area, for example.

When the addition is used to expand a cramped room, an entire wall must be shifted. The shift may be slight—but a few feet added to the width of a long, narrow living room will improve its proportions, and 5 or 6 extra feet can convert a single bedroom into a comfortable double. In cases like these, a framed opening with its header beam visible just below ceiling level is objectionable. Such a construction can be avoided except when the opening is in a one-story house; in such a house there is no easy way to support the existing roof rafters except with a header that hangs beneath the existing ceiling.

To provide a seamless opening in a nonbearing wall of a two-story house, cut away part of the ceiling adjacent to it, revealing the ceiling joists, which run parallel to a nonbearing wall. Reinforce the stringer joist—the joist above the wall—by nailing to it a piece of 1/2-inch plywood and a board the same size as the joist. Then the wall can be removed.

How you provide a seamless opening in a bearing wall of a two-story house depends on the width of the opening. If the opening is more than 12 feet wide, a steel I-beam supported by steel pipe columns and reinforced foundation footings will be needed; such a job requires considerable experience in heavy construction, as well as the advice of a structural engineer or other professional.

For an opening less than 12 feet wide, however, you can reinforce the header joist to make it a substitute for the bearing wall. The existing header joist sits atop the existing bearing wall, and the ceiling joists, revealed when the adjacent ceiling sections are removed, run perpendicular to it. The reinforcement is made by bolting a 3/8-inch steel plate and another joist alongside the original one, as described on these pages.

Before you order the steel plate, make a diagram showing where each ceiling joist meets the header joist. Use this diagram to prepare a guide for the steel supplier to follow in drilling the boltholes. They should fall between joists in the pattern required by the local building code—holes every 8 inches, staggered 2 inches from the top and bottom, are usually sufficient.

Because the ceiling joists meet the inside face of the existing header joist, the reinforcement must be bolted to the outside face. If you are using a shed roof—usual for a room extension—install the roof rafters in the normal way (page 428, Steps 1-3), but do not add ceiling joists to the addition until you have finished the opening. You then can fasten both the original ceiling joists and the ceiling joists of the addition to the reinforced header joist, using steel brackets.

Supports for a seamless opening. In a two-story house, the weight of the second floor—formerly supported by a bearing wall—is carried by a header joist reinforced with a steel plate and a 2-inch board. The ends of the joists, which had rested on the top plate of the old bearing wall, are supported by steel joist hangers. The ends of the reinforced header are supported by posts made from 2-by-4s.

This method cannot be used to replace a bearing wall more than 12 feet wide. Nor does it serve in a one-story house; there the supporting header must be below ceiling level.

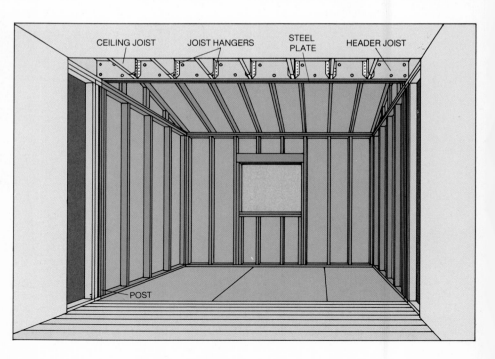

CEILING JOIST   JOIST HANGERS   STEEL PLATE   HEADER JOIST

POST

A Hidden Header for a Seamless Ceiling

1 **Removing the wallboard.** Support the second floor with temporary shoring *(page 109, Step 1)*, remove the studs and sole plate of the existing wall, then saw horizontally along the side-wall covering on each side of the opening, cutting through the wall covering until you hit a stud. Next, saw vertically along the stud, cutting from floor to ceiling, and remove the section of side-wall covering next to the opening. Snap a chalk line across the ceiling, in line with the studs that you have revealed; saw along the line and remove the covering of the ceiling.

2 **Prying out the last studs.** If a corner stud remaining from the old wall protrudes at each side of the opening, pry it away from the side-wall studs behind it, starting at the bottom and working up. Cut off the piece of sole plate that is left beneath the stud, using a handsaw, and pry it up from the floor. (For clarity, the temporary shoring shown in Step 1 has been omitted here.)

437

3 **Removing the top plates.** Cut the double top plates of the old wall flush with the side walls, using the side-wall studs as a guide; be careful not to saw into the header joist. Wedge a pry bar between the upper top plate and the bottom of each joist; pry the plates away and knock them free with a sledgehammer.

Reinforce the connection between the addition wall and the existing side wall by driving staggered 16-penny nails through the end studs of the addition wall every 6 inches.

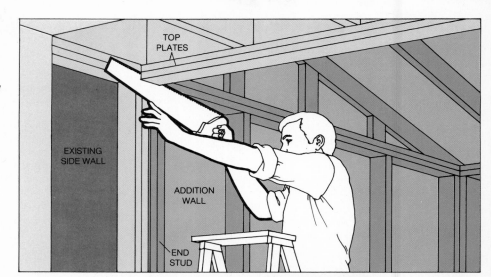

4 **Supporting the header joist.** Cut a stud 1/8 inch longer than the studs in the addition walls and hammer it tight against the end stud. Nail the new stud to the end stud with staggered 16-penny nails every 6 inches and toenail it to the top and sole plates. Build a post at the other edge of the opening in the same way.

5 **Reinforcing the header joist.** Align the
pre-drilled steel plate on top of a 2-inch
board that is as wide as the header joist and
long enough to span the top plates of the addition walls. Using the steel plate as a template,
drill matching holes through the board.

With a helper, set the steel plate on the top
plates, alongside the header joist, and use it as
a template to drill matching holes in this joist.

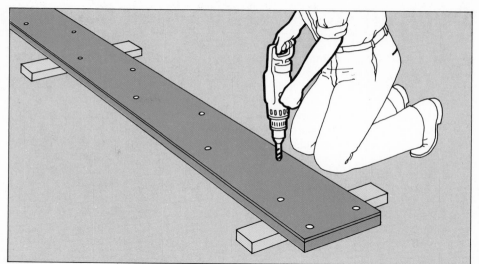

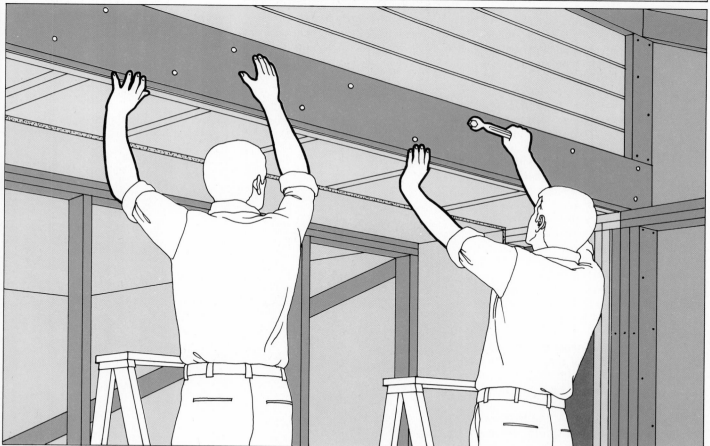

6 **Bolting the header together.** Set the drilled
board beside the plate. Bolt the drilled board,
the plate and the header joist together with machine bolts, large washers and nuts. Toenail each
end of the drilled board to the top plate. Nail metal
hangers to the existing ceiling joists and to the
header joist. Install the ceiling joists of the addition
(page 428, Step 2) and fasten them to the header
joist with joist hangers.

Decks That Blend into Their Surroundings

A deck is a crossbreed, combining some of the best features of both porches and patios. Like the old-fashioned porch, it is made of wood and sits aboveground. But it also has the open, airy feeling of a patio, serving as an architectural transition zone between indoors and out.

There are almost as many ways to build a deck as to build a house. The method shown on these page exploits a deck's most desirable qualities. Because the number of support posts is kept to a minimum, the structure seems to float in space and to be part of both the house and the landscape.

Built in this way, a deck can hug the ground or ride high above it. And the basic design can be modified or embellished for a variety of situations. Differing railing and decking treatments can be used. Multiple levels can be achieved with separate structures, linked by stairways to allow passage from one level to another. Sliding glass doors *(pages 205-207)*, installed just before the railings, provide easy access from the house to a second-story deck.

Deck building has been simplified by the availability of lumber that has been pressure-treated with wood preservative to resist rot. But pressure-treated wood often has a green tinge that takes up to a year to bleach to gray. Alternatively, you can use heart redwood or cedar for the decking and railing. Both are rot-resistant and have pleasant color and texture. Unfinished redwood and cedar will also eventually turn gray—redwood, dark gray.

Plan your deck on paper first by making a scale drawing of the side of the house to which it will be attached. Establish positions for the basic structural elements: the ledger board to be attached to the house wall, the two end joists that run perpendicular to the house at the ends of the ledger, and the ribbon board, which defines the outer edge of the deck. Then decide where you want the supporting posts and add a beam, paralleling the ledger, right over the posts. Use a deck plan approved in your area or get a building designer or architect to design your deck. This will cover the wood species, sizes, spacing, span, location and fastening of all members. Also apply for a building permit.

In plotting the post locations, beware of buried telephone cables and underground lines for gas, water and electricity; utility companies can tell you where they are. Keep in mind, too, that the beam should fall somewhere in the last quarter of the distance between the ledger and the ribbon board.

The span between the beam and the ledger—as designed by a professional—dictates joist size and spacing.

When you have the basic structure designed, add to your deck plan any other features you wish to incorporate. Then make a list of materials needed. When you buy the lumber, get an extra board or two in each size and, if possible, get decking boards in lengths just slightly longer than you need. Also look for straight decking boards, to eliminate the tricky carpentry needed to correct warped boards.

In assembling the deck you will need lag bolts for joining the ledger to the house wall, 1/2-inch carriage bolts for attaching the railings and posts, and 12-penny (3 1/4-inch) spiral-shanked electroplated nails to attach the decking and railings. The joists are suspended from joist hangers and metal angle reinforcements. Supporting posts and beams are joined with metal post-and-beam ties and joists are fastened to the beam with metal brackets called tie-downs. Allow four 60-pound bags of ready-packaged concrete for the footing of each post.

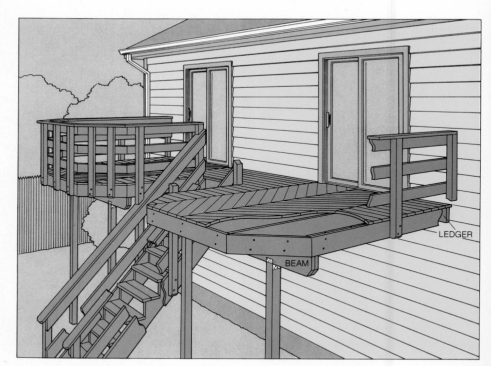

A subdivided deck. This deck in two parts, serving two rooms of a house, consists of a pair of platforms with a stairway between them. The platforms are anchored to the house by a single ledger and are supported at the other end by two beams, each resting on two 4-by-4 posts. The platform joists rest on the beams and extend beyond them, just as the outside ends of the beams project beyond the posts. The posts are anchored 6 inches above the ground in concrete footings. Railings, omitted from the front platform here for clarity, are made of 4-by-4 posts with 2-by-6 rails and handrail. The 2-by-6 decking is laid in both straight and herringbone patterns.

Building the Basic Deck

1 Starting the platform. Put up a ledger 3 inches shorter than the planned width of the platform. Mark joist positions on it, following the designer's plan. Then triple-nail a side joist, 1 1/2 inches shorter than the planned depth of the deck, to one end of the ledger while a helper holds up the far end of the joist and keeps it level. Nail a temporary support to the far end of the joist, toenailing this support to a scrap of wood at ground level. Attach a second side joist to the opposite end of the ledger in the same way. Choose sound, straight boards for these two joists.

If the ledger is attached to lapped clapboard siding and does not rest on the crowns of two strips of clapboard, trim the ends of the side joists, and all intermediate joists, so that they will fit the siding angle snugly.

2 Adding a ribbon board. Cut a ribbon board to the planned width of the deck, and mark joist positions on it corresponding to those on the ledger. Triple-nail the ribbon board to the ends of the joists, to complete the basic frame of the platform. Shift the position of the frame slightly, if necessary, to square its corners. Cut two more joists to fit between the ledger and the ribbon board and attach them using an L-shaped, all-purpose metal hanger.

If you are building a deck close to the ground, so that using a posthole digger beneath the frame would be difficult, locate and dig the postholes *(Steps 6 and 7)* before constructing the frame.

RIBBON BOARD

3 **Stabilizing the frame**. While a helper holds a steel square against an outside corner of the frame, check the position of the ribbon board again, shifting it sideways until the corner of the frame nests exactly into the square. Then nail a long diagonal brace across the tops of the ribbon board, one or both intermediate joists and a side joist. Give the corner a final check to be sure the frame is absolutely square. Then hang the remaining joists with joist hangers nailed to the ledger and ribbon boards. Add metal framing anchors or joist hangers, as required by the plan, to the inside corners where the joists meet the ledger and the ribbon board.

4 **Marking the beam position.** Measure out from the ledger along each side joist to the point where the plan indicates that the inside face of the support beam is to fall. Mark these points, then snap a chalk line across the underside of the joists between the marks. Nail metal tie-down anchors to the joists along the chalk line, using framing anchor nails.

5 **Hanging the beam.** Cut two beam boards the width of the deck, and have a helper hold the first beam board in place while you are driving framing anchor nails through the tie-downs into the board. Nail the second beam board against the outside face of the first one. If the beam is at head height or if you want to improve its appearance, cut off the lower corners of the beams at a 45° angle before installing them. If the deck is too long for the available lumber, use two boards for each section, but offset the joints so that the boards meet at different points on the two sections.

6 **Locating the footings.** Mark the post positions along the beam. Use a plumb bob to find the corresponding points on the ground, and mark these points with stakes. If you are building a low deck, mark the post positions by squaring up the frame as in Step 3, marking the beam position on the side joists as in Step 4, and stretching a string between the marks. Locate the post positions on this string, and drop a plumb bob to find the corresponding positions on the ground.

7 **Digging the footing holes.** With a posthole digger, open a footing hole at each stake; make the holes at least 24 inches deep and 8 inches below the local frost line. Make the bottom diameter of the holes for the outer posts at least 12 inches across, those for the intermediate posts 16 inches across. The upper portion of each hole can be narrower than the bottom.

8 **Hanging the supporting posts.** Use post-and-beam ties to hang the 4-by-4 posts from the beam at the marks used in Step 6. Cut each post to reach from the beam to a point in the footing hole at or just above the frost line. Nail the post-and-beam ties to the posts with framing anchor nails, then hold the posts up against the beam. For a tight fit, shim the back flange at each post with a 1/2-inch spacer. The posts should hang plumb but, if necessary, add braces at ground level to hold them in position.

POST-AND-BEAM TIE

9 **Anchoring the posts.** Mix concrete and place it into each footing hole, using enough to fill beneath the post and at least 6 inches up the sides. Tamp the wet concrete well to remove air pockets. Let the concrete set for 24 to 48 hours, then remove the temporary supports. Fill the rest of the hole with soil, remove the diagonal brace from the top of the deck and reinstall it underneath.

Simple Decking

1 **Nailing down the first board.** Put silicone rubber caulking compound in the joint between the ledger and the house siding, then lay a 2-by-6 plank trimmed to the exact width of the deck next to the house wall. Space it slightly away from the wall if the siding is wood; fasten this first board to each joist with two nails. If the deck is too wide for a single board to span, use two lengths, joining them at the midpoint of a joist. Position subsequent boards to overhang the edge of the deck; they can all be trimmed at once later. Leave 1/8 inch between boards; the blade of a brickset makes a convenient spacer. Alternate joints when more than one length of board is needed, but always center the joint over a joist.

2 **Straightening a bowed board.** Position the convex edge of a bowed board against the straight edge of a previously installed board. Nail one end of a joist in the usual way; then insert a brickset at the center of the bow, and note the distance between the two decking boards at the other end. This is the amount they are out of alignment. Hold the free end of the board above the joist by the amount of misalignment, and toenail at a 45° angle through its outer edge into the joist. (The nail should enter the joist at a point closer to the house than where it would if the board were being nailed flat.) Continue hammering the nail, drawing the bowed board toward the straight board, so that by the time the nail is completely driven the gap between the two board ends has narrowed to the desired 1/8 inch. Then nail down the once-bowed board in the usual fashion. Remove the brickset.

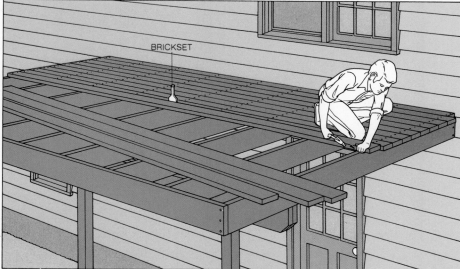

BRICKSET

3 **Trimming the excess.** Snap a chalk line above the edges of the deck onto the tops of the deck boards. Cut along the chalk line with a circular saw. Set the saw blade just deep enough to cut through the boards, watching the blade as it moves along the edge of the deck frame, to make sure it does not cut into the frame.

If you wish, and especially for cedar or redwood decking, add 3/4-inch-thick fascia boards to hide the ribbon board, the end joists and the cut edges of the decking. Set the upper edge of the fascia flush with the decking.

Decking Alternatives

A diagonal pattern. Lay the first board of a diagonal decking pattern *(inset)* so that it crosses the ribbon board and one end joist equidistant from a corner of the frame; mark the frame first to indicate this distance. Nail the decking board to each joist with two nails; leave the ends of the board free, to be trimmed later as on page 445, Step 3, when all boards are in place. Space the boards 1/8 inch apart, as in Step 1, page 445.

When a board butts against the side of the house, cut off its end at a 45° angle before laying it. If the board also crosses the end joist at the house wall, cut a second 45° angle, perpendicular to the first. When more than one decking board is needed to span the frame, join the two boards at a joist, trimming their ends at a 45° angle to meet at the midpoint of the joist.

A herringbone pattern. To form a herringbone pattern, lay two diagonal patterns at a right angle *(inset)*. Select a joist to serve as a central spine for the herringbone, adding an extra joist if none exists at the desired location. Lay the first side of the herringbone as shown above, allowing the boards to overhang the central joist until all are laid. Then snap a chalk line down the floorboards, directly over the midpoint of the central joist, and trim the boards with a circular saw set to the exact depth of the boards.

Lay the second side of the herringbone as you did the first, but trim the board ends along the central joist at a 45° angle before installing them. When a board also meets the house wall, and must be precut at both ends, cut and position the end against the house wall first. Then mark the board where it meets the end of its companion board on the other side of the herringbone spine, and make the second diagonal cut.

A Standard Railing

1 Cutting the rail posts. With the deck's access installed, cut 4-by-4 posts for the railing, 43 1/2 inches tall (or otherwise according to local building code), allowing for a span of 5 feet or less between posts and positioning posts within 2 feet of each corner. Cut the tops off at an 85° angle, so the hand rail will drain rainwater. For style and safety, bevel the outer edge of the bottom of each post. To mark the bevel, draw a line 1 inch above the bottom of the post. Then cut along the line with a circular saw set at 45°, being careful to avoid kickback.

2 Attaching the rail posts. Drill a 1/2-inch hole through the post, 1 inch above the bevel and slightly to the left of the center line of the post. Drill a second hole 5 inches above the bevel, slightly to the right of the center line. Drive a carriage bolt into the lower hole, and place the post against the edge of the deck in the desired location, positioning the bottom of the post 8 3/4 inches below the top of the deck. Strike the head of the bolt with a hammer, to mark the deck frame; drill through the frame at the mark. At the post position nearest the middle of each end joist, nail a wooden brace between the end joist and the next joist in, using lumber of the same dimensions as the joists. Bolt each post to the frame with a washer and a nut, but plumb the post before you tighten the nut. Drill through the second hole in each post, into the deck frame. Add a nut, a bolt and a washer at each hole.

BRACE

3 **Installing the railings.** Nail three 2-by-6 railings to the posts; set one railing so that its top is flush with the top of the posts, the other two with their tops 23 inches and 11 1/2 inches above the deck surface, or as required by local code. To simplify this job, drive nails into the end posts, 5 1/2 inches below each railing position; rest the railing there while you attach it. Join sections at the center of a post. At each corner, rest one section of railing in place, then butt the second section against the first and trim the end of the first board flush with the outer face of the second. You may also use four 2-by-4 railings evenly spaced. Where codes permit more than 6 inches between railings, you may use fewer boards.

4 **Adding the handrail.** Nail a 2-by-6 handrail to the top of the posts, letting it overhang the inner face of the top rail by 1/2 inch; use three nails at each post. To mark boards that will meet at a corner, rest the boards on the posts, ends overlapping, and level the upper board by sliding a 2-by-6 spacer under it at each post. Mark the points where the inside and outside edges of the boards intersect. Join these marks with a diagonal line across the face of each board, then make compound miters in the boards along the lines. Reposition the boards atop the posts, angled ends butted together, and nail the boards to each post with three nails; drive an extra nail through the handrail into the top rail every 12 inches.

A Picket Railing

Nailing the pickets into place. To make a picket-pattern railing, substitute two 2-by-4 boards for the three 2-by-6 boards in the railing shown above. Nail one board flush with the top of the posts, and position the top of the other board 5 1/2 inches above the deck. Cut 2-by-2 pickets 32 1/2 inches long, or as required by local code, and nail them to the railings on 7 1/2-inch centers. Add a 2-by-8 top railing, allowing it to overhang the inside face of the pickets by 3/4 inch.

A Slanted Railing

1 **Making post openings in the deck.** Cut openings in the decking for the posts of a slanted railing. Space the posts evenly and no more than 5 feet apart, beginning within 2 feet of each corner. Outline the openings by drawing a rectangle 3 3/4 inches wide and 3 7/8 inches long, with one short side 1 1/4 inches away from the deck edge. Along the ribbon board, position each rectangle so that one long side is beside a joist. To start the cut, drill holes at a 15° angle at the corners of the rectangle, tilting the top of the drill toward the edge of the deck. Saw the long sides of the rectangle vertically with a saber saw. Then, for the shorter sides, tilt the saw to produce a 15° angled cut *(inset)*. Along the end joists, install a brace underneath the deck *(Step 2, page 447)* beside one edge of each of the openings.

2 **Attaching the posts.** Bolt a 4-foot-high post to the joist or the brace nearest one corner of the deck, using the method described in Step 2, page 447. To position the post, have a helper hold a carpenter's protractor, set at 15°, against the deck and the edge of the post. On the underside of the deck, align an inner corner of the post with the bottom of the joist or the brace. Install a second post at the other end of the deck in the same manner. Measure along the inner face of each post 35 3/4 inches up from the top of the deck, and stretch a chalk line between the marks. Then install the remaining posts along that side, aligning their inner faces with the chalk line. Cut the posts off in a 5° slope to drain water at the height of the chalk line. Repeat this procedure to attach posts to the remaining sides of the deck.

15°

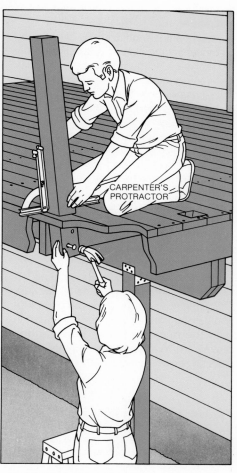

CARPENTER'S PROTRACTOR

3 **Adding the railings.** Drive support nails 5 7/8, 17 5/8 and 29 3/8 inches from the top of the posts, or as required by local code, to position 2-by-6 railings. At each level, butt the first railing board against the side of the house, its far end extending beyond the corner of the deck. Butt the adjoining railing board against it, and mark the first board where the second board touches its lower inner edge. Mark the lower edge of the second board 3 inches from the end. Remove the boards, and extend cutting lines upward from the marks, using a carpenter's protractor set to 14 1/2° and angled to make the upper edge of each board longer. Then cut the board with a circular saw set to 44°, so that the outer face of each board is longer than the inner one. Nail the first board against the posts, and repeat the fitting procedure for subsequent corners. After all the railing boards are attached to posts, nail the boards together at the corners, driving nails into their ends from both directions. Install a handrail in the same way as for an upright railing *(Step 4, opposite)*.

Add-on Options

Simple modifications and additions to the basic structure of a deck permit you to adapt it to almost any situation or whim. Stairs connect a second-story deck to the yard. A ledger board extending past the corner of the house allows the deck to open up another view and provides a point of attachment for a wraparound deck. A ledger board fastened to the studs of a house wall instead of to a joist allows the deck to project from the house at any level you choose. And by shortening some joists and joining them with angled ribbon boards, you can shape a deck edge just as you please.

Incorporating modifications calls for extra thought at the planning stage, especially for stairways. If there is to be a stairway landing—as most codes required for stairs that descend more than 8 feet—the height of the landing must be based on a multiple of 7 1/4 inches, the height of a riser. Begin the measurement from the top of the frame, not the decking. And the distance of the landing from the deck will be governed by the number of risers, multiplied by 10 3/4 inches—the width of an average tread—with 15 inches subtracted from the result so that half the bottom tread extends over the landing. If these calculations put the landing at an awkward place, you may elect to modify the deck plans.

It is best to build stairs and landing before adding railings to the deck, because the railing posts for the deck can often support the stair railings as well. Sometimes, in fact, the deck posts can be extended downward to support the railings of the stairs, as shown on page 440.

2 **Adding an angled corner board.** Set a circular saw to cut a 45° angle, and cut the corner board at the marks so that the outer face of the board will be longer than the inner one. Position the board against the cut ends of the end joist and ribbon board, and nail the board in place.

By cutting the frame elsewhere along the deck edge, you can create different shapes. Shortening a joist near the midpoint of an edge and adding angled ribbon boards creates a notch. Cutting the joists progressively shorter from two corners of the deck out to the midpoint of one edge approximates a curve (inset).

Shaping Cutaway Corners

1 **Cutting the frame** To shape the corners or edges of a deck, construct the frame in the usual fashion *(pages 441-444)*, then cut away portions according to the shape you want. For an angled corner, make a cutting mark on the end joist between the outside corner and the supporting beam, then make a mark on the ribbon board at the same distance from the corner. Cut the two boards at the marks you have just made, removing the corner of the frame. Measure the distance between the outside edges of the cut frame members *(inset)*, and transfer this measurement to a corner board that is the same lumber size as the frame members.

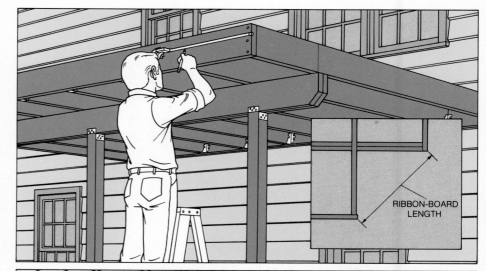

RIBBON-BOARD LENGTH

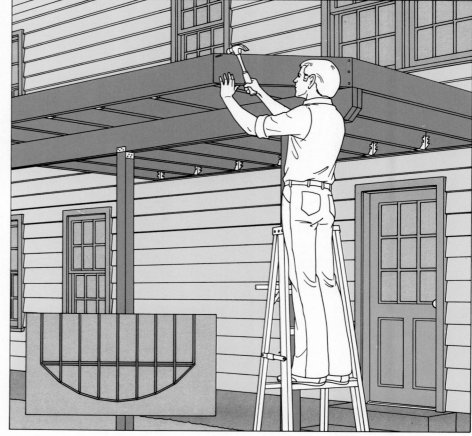

3 **Fitting an angled railing.** After the decking is installed, add 4-by-4 railing posts around the edge of the deck as in Steps 1 and 2, using at least two posts for each section of deck, no matter how short the section. Drive nails to support railings along each section, as in Step 3, page 448, then mark the railing boards for corner joints. Rest a board on its supporting nails, outer end extending beyond the deck. Hold the board for the other railing underneath it, resting the second board against its two posts. Mark where the two boards intersect along both their inner and their outer faces, and draw guidelines across the edges of the boards, connecting the two points. Extend a squared line down the inner face of each board, and cut along it with a circular saw set to match the angled guidelines. Replace the first board, and nail it on. Butt the cut end of the second board against the first, and mark the cutting lines for the next corner joint. Add a handrail as on page 447.

Adding a Stairway

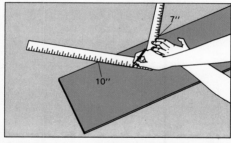

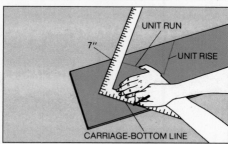

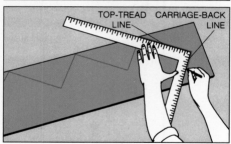

1 **Marking and cutting the carriage.** Set a framing square near one end of a 2-by-12 that has been cut 1 foot longer than the diagonal distance from the top of the band beam to the front edge of the concrete footing. Locate the unit-run number on one arm of the square, the unit-rise number on the other, and place the square on the 2-by-12 in such a way that both of the numbers (10 and 7, in the example here, but you may choose to use the standard 10 3/4 and 7 1/4 measurements) are touching the upper edge of the board. Then mark the outline of the framing square's outer edges *(left, top)*.

Turn the framing square clockwise until the unit-rise number—7, in this example—touches the end of the previously drawn unit-run line. Again mark the outline of the square's outer edges, extending the carriage-bottom line all the way to the edge of the stock *(center)*. Continue marking off pairs of perpendicular lines, one pair for each step—in this example, four pairs. Trace the last unit-run line—the line for the top tread—and continue around the framing square to the edge of the stock, to scribe the line for the back of the carriage. Cut along the unit-rise and unit-run lines and along the lines for the carriage back and carriage bottom. Then use this first carriage as a template to cut as many carriages as required.

2 **Building the steps.** Cut the stair carriages as in Step 1. Extend the depth of the next-to-last tread to allow for the thickness of the frame; if your framing lumber is larger than a 2-by-8, notch the back of the next-to-last tread to fit around it. Extend the last tread to the end of the carriage. Use a carriage as a template for marking the ends of two facing boards. Nail up the carriages, butting the last riser against the back of the frame; then nail the facing boards to the carriages and the frame. Add treads made of pairs of 2-by-6 boards, nailing through the facing board into the treads.

3 **Trimming the post tops.** Bolt 4-by-4 railing posts, 4 feet long, to the carriage assemblies as in Step 2, page 447. Position the top posts no more than 5 feet apart, with the bottom post near the bottom of the carriage. Set the bottom of each post so that the corner nearest the deck is aligned with the bottom of the carriage. Mark the tops of the posts to match the angle of the stairway; to do this, slide the 16-inch arm of a steel square along the top of the facing board while holding a pencil at the end of the 24-inch arm. Saw along the lines with a circular saw, a handsaw or, if necessary, both.

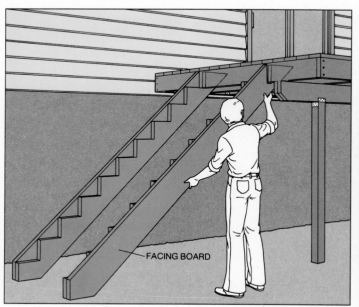

FACING BOARD

4 **Cutting the railings.** Drive supporting nails for the railing boards as in Step 3, page 448, and temporarily tack a top railing board into position. Mark the back of the board where it meets the upper edge of the top post and the lower edge of the bottom post. Remove the board, cut the ends, then nail the board in place. Repeat for all the rest of the railing boards.

5 **Fitting the handrail.** Rest a 2-by-6 handrail board on the upper railing, allowing it to project about 4 inches beyond the post at the bottom of the stairs. Mark the side of the board where it meets the upper and lower edges of the top post, and draw lines at these marks across the top of the board. Then shift the board onto the top of the lower posts, outer edge of the board flush with the outer edge of the posts. Butt the board against the top post, and draw a line down the face of the board even with the inner face of the post. Cut a notch at the marked lines *(inset)*.

Mark and notch the opposite handrail board in the same way. Trim off the bottom corners of the handrails, if desired, and nail the handrails to the posts and top railings.

Dig around and under the ends of the stair carriage 4 inches deep. Prop the ends up on small stones so that the stair treads are level, then place a concrete footing *(page 444)*, or have a professional place it.

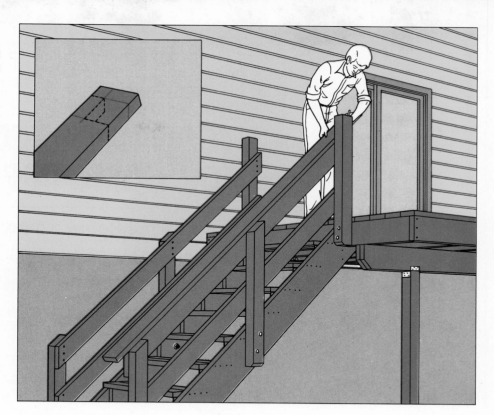

Enlarging the Deck Area

Extending a ledger board. A deck that extends beyond the corner of a house needs a ledger board that extends similarly. The ledger must be plumb, which means that on a clapboard house you will have to rest it upright. In addition, the ledger extension will require structural support. If the extension is part of a wraparound deck, the beam of the adjacent deck section will provide this support. If the deck extension stands alone and does not project beyond the house more than 4 feet, you can just double the entire ledger board, in effect creating a cantilevered beam. If the deck does extend beyond the house more than 4 feet, the ledger will need supporting posts within 2 feet of its outer end and at 8-foot intervals in between. When posts support the extension, only the projecting section of the ledger needs to be doubled.

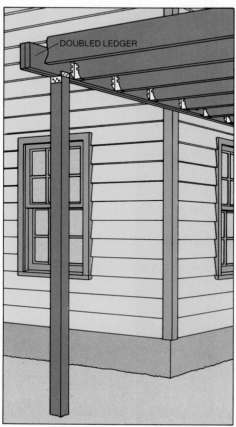

DOUBLED LEDGER

TOOLS AND TECHNIQUES FOR HOME IMPROVEMENT

Planning the Home Workshop

In selecting tools for any home workshop, first consider the kinds of projects to be done. The main consideration, and the key to selecting hand tools, is quality. When you are equipping a workshop, look for reputable brand names and for tools that have earned medium-to-high ratings in consumer tests. Such tools may be more costly than their lower-quality counterparts, but well-made tools provide decades of service; some last for a lifetime.

It is sometimes possible to find bargains, however. To cut costs, watch for sales, but be sure that the sale price includes a normal guarantee. Screw-drivers, chisels and wrenches are generally less expensive when purchased in sets. Stores that cater to professionals with top-of-the-line tools at less-than-retail prices are often interested in selling to nonprofessionals as well. Finally, garage sales and country auctions may offer rock-bottom prices, but be sure to examine the merchandise with care.

In equipping your workshop, you will not buy everything at once, of course. Begin with the essentials—listed below, then add other tools as you can afford them. It helps to make a purchase plan in advance; this helps avoid impulse purchases and the acquisition of gimmick tools that may be in fashion at the moment, but of limited value to you in the long run.

On pages 456-457, various types of tools are grouped according to function. The chart on pages 458-459 is intended as a guide to selecting tools for specific kinds to work, enabling you to decide which tools match your requirements and which will be used infrequently. The list is not all-inclusive: Many highly-specialized tools have been omitted. Nor does it include "found" tools—cotton swabs, toothbrushes, tweezers and the like—which are endlessly useful for all sorts of remodeling chores.

Building a Basic Tool Kit

Chisels. Four wood chisels with blades ranging in widths from 1/4 to 1 inch suffice for most basic jobs. For metalwork, the standard tool is a cold chisel with a flat 1/2-inch blade. For masonry work, a brick set is used to split bricks.

Clamps. Clamps come in various shapes, sizes and materials for a variety of jobs. C clamps are the most useful. Pipe clamps may be bought in two parts that fit over a 3/4-inch galvanized pipe to span long distances.

Cutting tools. At least five saws form the complement of a home workshop: crosscut, ripsaw, backsaw used in a miter box, coping saw and keyhole saw, both used for cutting curves.

Drilling tools. Eggbeater-type hand drill and push drill with ratchet mechanism bores small holes.

Files and rasps. Basic files are the 10-inch half-round double-cut, adaptable for either metal or wood, and the 10-inch half-round rasp, for wood only. All files should be fitted with handles.

Hammers. Hammers are more specialized than is thought. Curved-claw and straight-claw hammers are for driving nails only. Tempered-head ball-peen hammers are meant to striking cold chisels and other metal tools, while a two-headed mallet, with replaceable rubber and plastic faces, is used on chisels and for shaping sheet metal.

Measurers and markers. Tools for accurate measuring and marking come in various shapes, sizes and materials. Of prime importance are rulers, especially flexible steel tape. A 6-foot folding extension ruler made of hard wood is also useful.

Planes. The block plane for trimming end grain, and the jack plane for shaving along the grain are the two most essential planing tools.

Pliers. Often thought of as multipurpose tools, pliers actually have specialized purposes and should be used only on jobs for which they were designed. A pair of 8-inch slip-joint pliers is for bending and gripping. Diagonal-cutting pliers cut wire and small nails. A pair of locking-grip pliers can be adjusted to clamp onto an object, acting as a wrench. Long-nose pliers are able to reach into recessed areas and are especially handy for making terminal loops of electric wires.

Screwdrivers. Every tool collection needs at least four common sizes of flat-tipped screwdrivers for single-slot screws and two sizes of Phillips screwdrivers for cross-slot screws. In Canada, and increasingly elsewhere, you will also need square-tipped Robertson screwdrivers. In addition, a spiral ratchet screwdriver can speed jobs requiring the setting of a great many screws.

Wrenches. The most useful wrench is the 10-inch adjustable open-end wrench with smooth jaws that accept nuts and bolt heads up to 1 inch wide. Other types are open-end wrenches with fixed jaw widths, and box-end wrenches that fit over, chiefly, hexagonal nuts and bolts. Combination wrenches put together the two types. Socket wrenches, driven by handles with ratchet mechanisms, speed the task of tightening bolts and of working in tight spots. A good basic model has a 3/8-inch-wide drive post and sockets with six interior corners.

Miscellaneous. Tools to round out a collection can be of many different types, from basic to highly specialized. Buy miscellaneous items, such as putty knives and nail sets, with the same care used in selecting other tools.

Portable power tools. Small portable power tools have become practically indispensable in the home workshop. An electric hand drill can bore, sand, polish, grind; some, called driver/drills, can even drive screws. Circular saws, routers and pad sanders far out pace their hand tool counterparts.

Guidelines for Tools and Safety

The following pages cover basic tools and techniques that are often used in home renovation, such as measuring, hammering, sawing, the safe use of power tools, and guidelines for setting up a workshop. The chart on page 461 gives guidelines for selecting the proper nail; see also the fastener chart on the inside back cover of the book.

Always wear the proper clothing and safety gear for the job: gloves when handling sharp, rough, dirty or hazardous materials; safety goggles for work that creates dust or flying debris or when there is a risk of chemical splash; and a dust mask or respirator when using dust-creating drilling or sanding tools or chemicals that emit hazardous vapors. Wear hearing protection when working with noisy power tools. Special features throughout the book—such as those shown on pages 63, 76, 272 and 340-345, for example—give valuable information about safe working practices and equipment. Follow common-sense rules when you are working with power tools. Never use a faulty

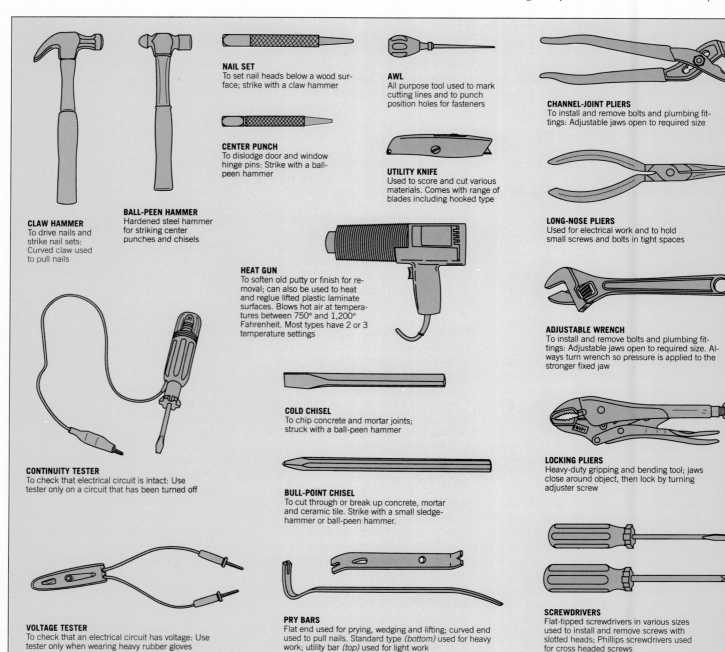

NAIL SET
To set nail heads below a wood surface; strike with a claw hammer

CENTER PUNCH
To dislodge door and window hinge pins: Strike with a ball-peen hammer

CLAW HAMMER
To drive nails and strike nail sets: Curved claw used to pull nails

BALL-PEEN HAMMER
Hardened steel hammer for striking center punches and chisels

HEAT GUN
To soften old putty or finish for removal; can also be used to heat and reglue lifted plastic laminate surfaces. Blows hot air at temperatures between 750° and 1,200° Fahrenheit. Most types have 2 or 3 temperature settings

CONTINUITY TESTER
To check that electrical circuit is intact: Use tester only on a circuit that has been turned off

VOLTAGE TESTER
To check that an electrical circuit has voltage: Use tester only when wearing heavy rubber gloves

AWL
All purpose tool used to mark cutting lines and to punch position holes for fasteners

UTILITY KNIFE
Used to score and cut various materials. Comes with range of blades including hooked type

COLD CHISEL
To chip concrete and mortar joints; struck with a ball-peen hammer

BULL-POINT CHISEL
To cut through or break up concrete, mortar and ceramic tile. Strike with a small sledgehammer or ball-peen hammer.

PRY BARS
Flat end used for prying, wedging and lifting; curved end used to pull nails. Standard type *(bottom)* used for heavy work; utility bar *(top)* used for light work

CHANNEL-JOINT PLIERS
To install and remove bolts and plumbing fittings: Adjustable jaws open to required size

LONG-NOSE PLIERS
Used for electrical work and to hold small screws and bolts in tight spaces

ADJUSTABLE WRENCH
To install and remove bolts and plumbing fittings: Adjustable jaws open to required size. Always turn wrench so pressure is applied to the stronger fixed jaw

LOCKING PLIERS
Heavy-duty gripping and bending tool; jaws close around object, then lock by turning adjuster screw

SCREWDRIVERS
Flat-tipped screwdrivers in various sizes used to install and remove screws with slotted heads; Phillips screwdrivers used for cross headed screws

power tool and never operate a power tool in wet conditions. Always use grounded or double-insulated power tools; plug them into a grounded outlet or a portable ground-fault circuit interrupter *(page 466)*.

Take the time to care for your tools properly. Avoid laying tools down unprotected where they can be damaged or cause injury.

Clean, sharpen and lubricate tools according to the manufacturer's instructions. Store tools on a shelf safely away from children, in a locked metal or plastic tool box, or hand them well out of their reach. As your tool collection grows with your home improvement expertise, the addition of a workbench in the garage or basement may prove useful.

Consult the information on page 472 for ideas about setting up a well-planned workspace with adequate lighting and space for the projects you will work on. Remember, the experience of do-it-yourselfers varies widely; if you are ever in doubt about your ability to complete a project, do not hesitate to consult a professional.

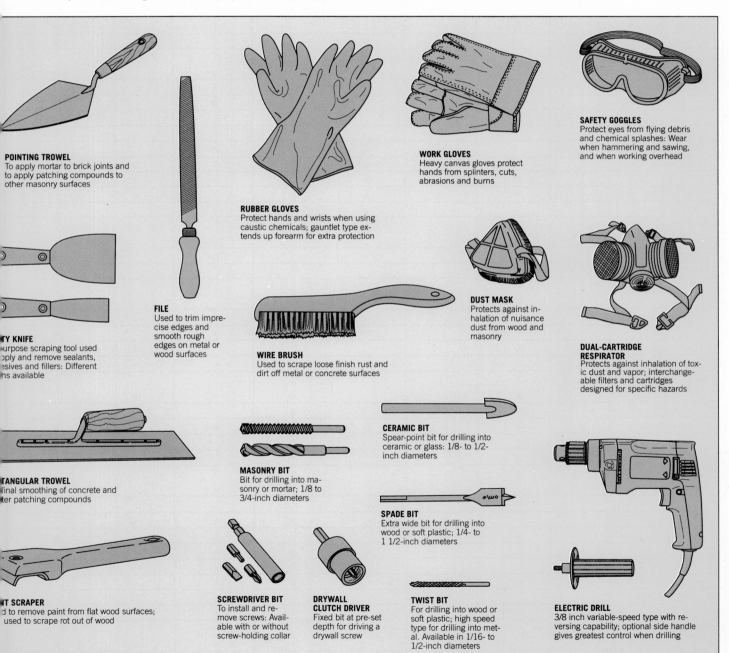

POINTING TROWEL
To apply mortar to brick joints and to apply patching compounds to other masonry surfaces

FILE
Used to trim imprecise edges and smooth rough edges on metal or wood surfaces

RUBBER GLOVES
Protect hands and wrists when using caustic chemicals; gauntlet type extends up forearm for extra protection

WORK GLOVES
Heavy canvas gloves protect hands from splinters, cuts, abrasions and burns

SAFETY GOGGLES
Protect eyes from flying debris and chemical splashes: Wear when hammering and sawing, and when working overhead

WIRE BRUSH
Used to scrape loose finish rust and dirt off metal or concrete surfaces

DUST MASK
Protects against inhalation of nuisance dust from wood and masonry

DUAL-CARTRIDGE RESPIRATOR
Protects against inhalation of toxic dust and vapor; interchangeable filters and cartridges designed for specific hazards

...TY KNIFE
...urpose scraping tool used ...pply and remove sealants, ...esives and fillers: Different ...ns available

...ANGULAR TROWEL
...final smoothing of concrete and ...er patching compounds

MASONRY BIT
Bit for drilling into masonry or mortar; 1/8 to 3/4-inch diameters

CERAMIC BIT
Spear-point bit for drilling into ceramic or glass: 1/8- to 1/2-inch diameters

SPADE BIT
Extra wide bit for drilling into wood or soft plastic; 1/4- to 1 1/2-inch diameters

...T SCRAPER
...d to remove paint from flat wood surfaces; ...used to scrape rot out of wood

SCREWDRIVER BIT
To install and remove screws: Available with or without screw-holding collar

DRYWALL CLUTCH DRIVER
Fixed bit at pre-set depth for driving a drywall screw

TWIST BIT
For drilling into wood or soft plastic; high speed type for drilling into metal. Available in 1/16- to 1/2-inch diameters

ELECTRIC DRILL
3/8 inch variable-speed type with reversing capability; optional side handle gives greatest control when drilling

The Right Tool to Make the Task Easier

Tools	Basic Household Maintenance	Plumbing	Electrical Repair	Masonry	Carpentry	Metalworking	Woodworking
CHISELS							
Brickset chisel				★			
Cold chisel	☆	☆		★		★	
Paring chisels							★
Wood chisels	☆		☆		★		★
CLAMPS							
Bar clamp					★		★
C clamp	★				★		★
Screw clamp							★
Web clamp	☆						★
CUTTING TOOLS							
Backsaw and miter box		☆			★		★
Coping saw	☆				★		★
Crosscut saw and ripsaw	★				★		★
Dovetail saw					☆		★
Hacksaw	★	★			☆	★	
Keyhole saw		★	★		☆		
Pipe cutter		★	★				
Tin snips	☆		☆			★	
Utility knife	★		★		☆		
Wire stripper			★				
DRILLING TOOLS (MANUAL)							
Brace and bit					☆		☆
Hand drill	☆				☆		★
Push drill	☆						★
FILES							
Flat file	☆					★	
Forming tools					☆		☆
Rasp					★		★
Round and half-round files	★					★	☆
Triangular file					★	★	
HAMMERS							
Ball-peen hammer	★	☆		★		★	
Bricklayer's hammer		★		★			
Claw hammer	★	★	☆	★	★		★
Soft-faced mallet				☆		★	★
Tack hammer	☆						
MEASURING AND MARKING TOOLS							
Awl					★		★
Center punch						☆	
Chalk line				★	★		
Combination square	★				★		★
Flexible tape	★	★	★	★	★		★
Folding rule	☆				★		★
Level	★	★		★	★		☆
Marking gauge					☆		☆
Steel square	☆			★	★		★
MISCELLANEOUS							
Bench vise		★			★	★	★

★–Essential ☆–Desirable

Tools	Basic Household Maintenance	Plumbing	Electrical Repair	Masonry	Carpentry	Metalworking	Woodworking
File card						★	☆
Nail set	☆				★		★
Plunger	★	★					
Pointing trowel				★			
Propane torch		★				★	
Pry bar	★			☆	★		
Putty knife	★				☆	★	
Staple gun	★		☆		☆		
Star drill				★			
Voltage tester			★				
Whetstone	☆				★		★
PLANES							
Block plane	★				★		★
Jack plane	☆				★		☆
Jointer plane							☆
Rabbet plane							☆
Spokeshave							☆
PLIERS							
Channel-joint pliers		★					
Diagonal-cutting pliers	☆		★				
Electrician's pliers			★				
Locking-grip pliers	★	★			★	★	
Long-nosed pliers	☆	★	★				
Slip-joint pliers	★	★			★	☆	☆
PORTABLE POWER TOOLS							
Belt sander					☆		☆
Circular saw	☆				★		☆
Electric drill	★	★	★	★	★	★	★
Orbital sander	☆				☆		★
Router					☆		★
Saber saw	☆		☆		★	☆	☆
SCREWDRIVERS							
Flat-tipped screwdriver	★	★			★		★
Offset screwdriver			☆				☆
Phillips-head screwdriver	★	★	★				☆
Spiral ratchet screwdriver	☆				★		☆
WRENCHES							
Adjustable wrench	★	★			★		☆
Basin wrench		★					
Box and open wrenches	☆				☆		
Pipe wrench		★					
Socket wrench	☆	★				★	
Spud wrench		★					

Determining your tool needs. In the left-hand column of this chart, tools are listed in groups according to their functions. Each of the next seven columns is headed by a work category. To find out which tools are required for a given type of work, read down any one of these seven columns. To determine how useful a particular tool can be, locate it under its function category in the first column, then read across the chart. The tools that are essential to a specific type of work are marked by a solid star; tools that are helpful in advanced, special or infrequent tasks are indicated by an open star. Of course, these designations are not rigid; for example, the spiral ratchet screwdriver that is indispensable to a person who works with piano hinges may be considered a specialty tool by someone who makes a hobby of model building.

Using a Claw or Ball-Peen Hammer

Choosing and inspecting a claw or ball-peen hammer. Choose the right hammer for the job: a claw hammer for driving most nails and striking a nail set; a ball-peen hammer for driving hardened nails and striking a center punch or a cold chisel. If you are using a claw hammer, ensure that it is the correct weight for the nailing to be done: 16 ounces for general purposes; 12 ounces for driving small nails in fine woodwork; 20 ounces for driving nails when sheathing and framing; and 28 ounces for driving spikes 4 inches or more in length.

Inspect the hammer before using it *(right)*. If the handle is bent, cracked or dented, the head is loose, or the poll, neck, face or cheek is cracked, chipped, scored or otherwise damaged, do not use the hammer; replace it. Check also that the hammer is clean. If the handle is dirty or greasy, wipe it using a soft cloth damp-ened with a solution of mild household detergent and water; dry it thoroughly with a clean cloth. To clean gum, pitch or glue off the face, wear rubber gloves and use a soft cloth dampened with min-eral spirits *(inset)*. To remove rust from the head, wear work gloves and use steel wool. When the hammer is in good condition, make sure you know how to use it properly *(below)*.

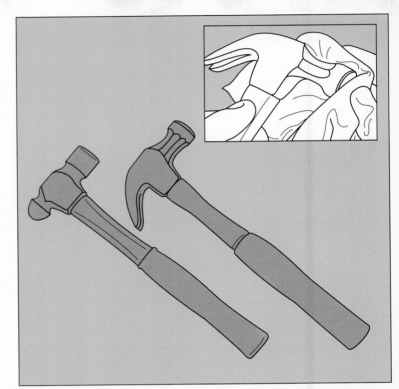

Hammering with a half swing. To start a nail, drive or set a small nail or nail in a tight space, hammer with a half swing. Wearing safety goggles *(page 130)*, grip the hammer firmly in your hand at the center of the han-dle, extending your thumb to help steady it. To start a nail, set the ham-mer face squarely on the nail head, then pull the hammer straight back to a point in front of you, bending your arm at the elbow and cocking your wrist slightly. Then, swing the hammer forward in a smooth arc, striking the nail head lightly with its face. Repeat the procedure, as shown above, until the nail is started. To drive or set a small nail or nail in a tight space, retract your thumb around the handle and continue hammering the same way. Otherwise, hammer with a full swing *(right)*.

Hammering with a full swing. To drive a large nail, hammer with a full swing after hammering with a half swing to start it *(left)*. Wearing safety goggles *(page 130)*, grip the hammer firmly in your hand near the base of the handle, retracting your thumb around it. Stepping back slightly from your initial position to start the nail, set the hammer face squarely on the nail head, then pull the hammer straight back to a point behind your ear, rolling your shoulder and bending your arm at the elbow *(above)*; avoid cocking your wrist. Then, swing the hammer forward in a smooth arc, striking the nail head sharply with its face. Repeat the procedure until the nail is driven, gradually increasing your momentum as well as the striking force applied by the hammer face.

Choosing a Nail

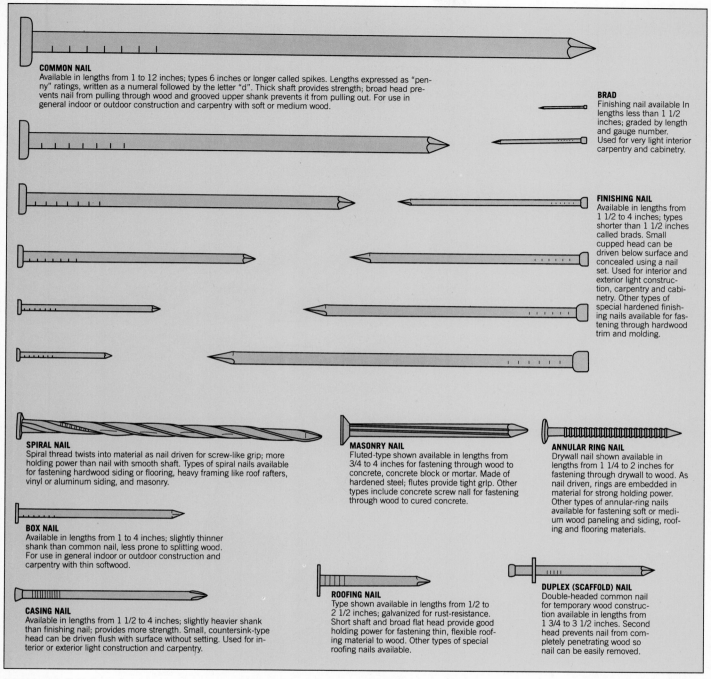

COMMON NAIL
Available in lengths from 1 to 12 inches; types 6 inches or longer called spikes. Lengths expressed as "penny" ratings, written as a numeral followed by the letter "d". Thick shaft provides strength; broad head prevents nail from pulling through wood and grooved upper shank prevents it from pulling out. For use in general indoor or outdoor construction and carpentry with soft or medium wood.

BRAD
Finishing nail available in lengths less than 1 1/2 inches; graded by length and gauge number. Used for very light interior carpentry and cabinetry.

FINISHING NAIL
Available in lengths from 1 1/2 to 4 inches; types shorter than 1 1/2 inches called brads. Small cupped head can be driven below surface and concealed using a nail set. Used for interior and exterior light construction, carpentry and cabinetry. Other types of special hardened finishing nails available for fastening through hardwood trim and molding.

SPIRAL NAIL
Spiral thread twists into material as nail driven for screw-like grip; more holding power than nail with smooth shaft. Types of spiral nails available for fastening hardwood siding or flooring, heavy framing like roof rafters, vinyl or aluminum siding, and masonry.

MASONRY NAIL
Fluted-type shown available in lengths from 3/4 to 4 inches for fastening through wood to concrete, concrete block or mortar. Made of hardened steel; flutes provide tight grip. Other types include concrete screw nail for fastening through wood to cured concrete.

ANNULAR RING NAIL
Drywall nail shown available in lengths from 1 1/4 to 2 inches for fastening through drywall to wood. As nail driven, rings are embedded in material for strong holding power. Other types of annular-ring nails available for fastening soft or medium wood paneling and siding, roofing and flooring materials.

BOX NAIL
Available in lengths from 1 to 4 inches; slightly thinner shank than common nail, less prone to splitting wood. For use in general indoor or outdoor construction and carpentry with thin softwood.

ROOFING NAIL
Type shown available in lengths from 1/2 to 2 1/2 inches; galvanized for rust-resistance. Short shaft and broad flat head provide good holding power for fastening thin, flexible roofing material to wood. Other types of special roofing nails available.

DUPLEX (SCAFFOLD) NAIL
Double-headed common nail for temporary wood construction available in lengths from 1 3/4 to 3 1/2 inches. Second head prevents nail from completely penetrating wood so nail can be easily removed.

CASING NAIL
Available in lengths from 1 1/2 to 4 inches; slightly heavier shank than finishing nail; provides more strength. Small, countersink-type head can be driven flush with surface without setting. Used for interior or exterior light construction and carpentry.

Selecting a nail. Refer to the chart above; shown are typical nails for fastening through and to wood or other materials around the home. For other types of fasteners, refer to the inside back cover. For fastening through most materials to wood, a common nail, a box nail, a finishing nail or a casing nail can do the job. For fastening through or to material such as masonry, metal or drywall and fastening through flooring, siding, paneling or roofing material, there are many special types of nails available. Consult your local hardware store or building-supply center for specific recommendations.

After choosing a suitable type of nail for the materials through and to which you are fastening, determine if any special features are needed. If the nail is to be installed in a wet or damp location, for example, use a rust-resistant variety: hot-dipped galvanized-steel or aluminum for outdoors. If you

are fastening through or to metal, ensure that the nail is of the same metal to prevent a corrosive reaction.

Use a nail of suitable length for the dimensions of the materials through and to which you are fastening. For fastening through wood, plastic or metal to wood, choose a nail of a length about three times the thickness of the material through which you are fastening; ensure that it is also at least 1/4 inch shorter than the combined thickness of the materials through and to which you are fastening. If you are fastening through plywood or composition board to wood, choose a nail suitable to its thickness: for 1/4-inch panels, a 1-inch nail; for 3/8-inch panels, a 1 1/2-inch nail. For fastening through drywall to wood or through wood to masonry, use a nail 3/4 to 1 inch longer than the drywall or wood thickness.

Using a Try Square

Using a try square. Mark a line at 90° to an edge with a try square. If necessary, use a tape measure to mark any end point for the line, then press the handle flush against the edge with the blade flat on the surface, its outer edge aligned with any marked end point. Holding a sharp pencil firmly against the outer edge, draw lightly along it *(below)*.

Marking a line parallel to an edge. A combination square may be used in place of a try square. In addition, it can be used to mark a line parallel to an edge. If necessary, use a tape measure to mark any end point for the line, then press the 90° face of the handle against the edge and loosen the lock nut; adjust the blade position, aligning its end with any marked end point or to the set distance from the edge, then tighten the lock nut. Holding a sharp pencil firmly against or in the notch at the end of the blade, slide the handle along the edge *(below)*.

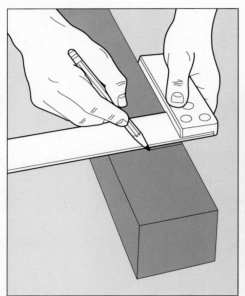

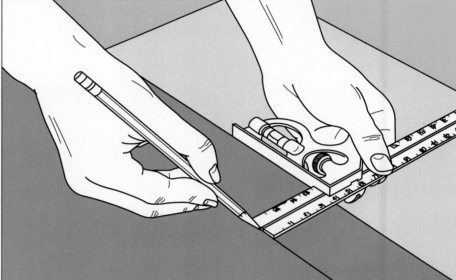

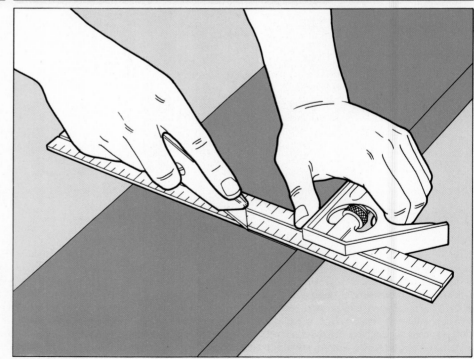

Marking for greatest precision. For the neatest job and greatest accuracy in marking for most 90° crosscuts, hold the handle of the square against the edge of the board and mark along the blade with a utility knife or scratch awl instead of a pencil. By scoring the work several times with a utility knife, the scored line will help prevent splintering of the wood as it is sawed.

Using a T Bevel

Transferring an angle. When making odd-angle miters, extend the blade of a T bevel and adjust the wing nut on the handle so that the blade moves easily but does not swing free. Fit the T bevel to the angle you plan to transfer *(below, left)* with the blade corresponding to the line you are going to cut, and tighten the wing nut. Hold the handle of the T bevel against the edge and the blade across the face of the board to be cut, then mark the cutting line along the blade *(below, right)*.

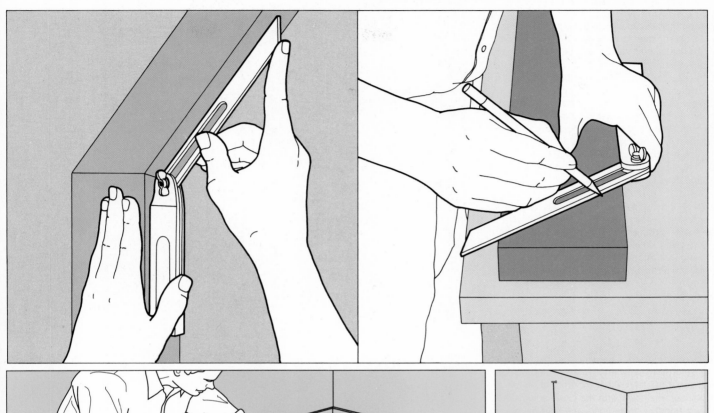

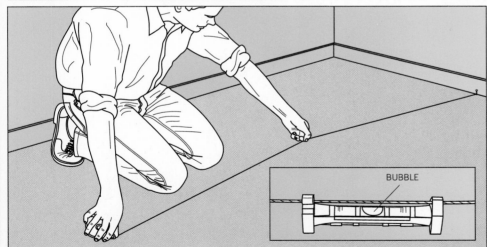

BUBBLE

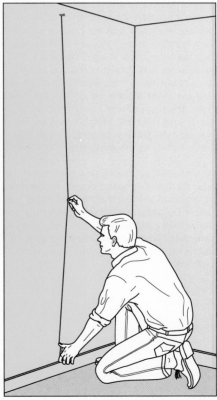

Marking a straight line. Use a chalk line to mark a straight line longer than a few feet. If necessary, use a tape measure to mark any end point for the line. To check that marked end points on a vertical surface are perfectly horizontal, use a line level *(inset)*; to check that marked end points on a vertical surface are perfectly vertical, hang the chalk line as you would a plumb bob. Drive a nail partway into the surface at one end point; on a vertical surface, at the top. Hook the chalk line over the nail and unreel it to the other point, keeping it off the surface. Pull the string taut and press it against the end point with the thumb of one hand. If the line is less than 12 feet in length, use the other hand to lift the string near the center and snap it once only against the horizontal *(above)* or vertical *(right)* surface. If the line is 12 feet or more in length, have a helper press the string at the center, then snap it twice the same way, once only on each side of the center. Unhook the chalk line and reel it in.

Crosscutting Using Hand or Power Tools

Crosscutting with a hand saw. Lay the board across sawhorses, steady it with the knee and grip the saw so that your index finger extends along the blade to help keep the course true. Set the heel, or handle, end of the blade on the board edge at an angle of about 20° with the saw teeth resting on the waste side of the cutting mark. Holding the thumb of your free hand against the blade as a guide, draw the saw halfway back toward you, pressing lightly to start the cut. Lift the blade and repeat a few times until the saw kerf is as deep as the teeth. Then lengthen and deepen the kerf with short, smooth back-and-forth strokes that cut in both directions.

When the cut is about an inch long, gradually increase the angle to 45° and lengthen your strokes, cutting mainly on the forward stroke and using moderate pressure. Before the waste piece falls and splinters the wood, reach over the top of the saw and support it as you finish the cut.

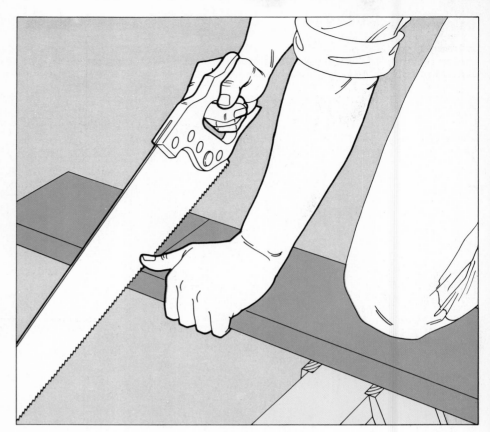

Crosscutting with a circular saw. Wearing safety goggles, lay the board across sawhorses and clamp it in place. Place the front of the base plate on the board with the blade at least 1/2 inch from the board edge, and hold the saw so that the entire plate is level; then use the guide mark in the plate, or the blade itself, to align the blade with the waste side of the cutting line. Start the saw, let it reach full speed, then, applying pressure forward but not downward, push the blade smoothly into the board, watching the guide or blade to be sure that the blade cuts along the waste side of the line.

Near the end of the cut, slow the forward motion, then quickly push through the remainder of the board in a single stroke to finish the cut before the piece can fall and splinter the wood. Immediately release the switch and move the saw away from the board, checking to be certain the blade guard has returned to its closed position.

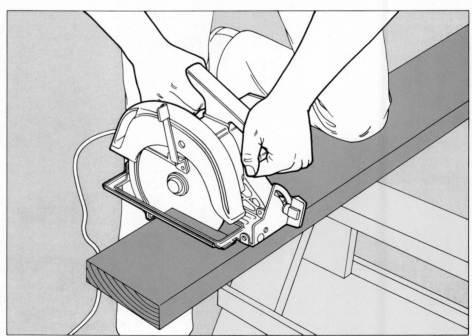

Rip Cutting by Hand and Power

Ripping with a ripsaw. Set a small board on a sawhorse as you would for a crosscut; support a large one across two sawhorses. Start the cut as you would a crosscut *(opposite)*; then, when the cut is about an inch long, raise the angle of the saw to about 60° and apply most of the force on the push stroke. If the blade buckles or skips through the cut, lower the angle of the saw slightly; if the board pinches the blade, tap wooden wedges into the kerf *(inset)*.

When using one sawhorse, edge the board forward little by little; halfway through the cut, turn the board around and saw from the other end. When using two sawhorses, cut to within a few inches of a horse, then slide the board back and resume cutting on the other side of the horse.

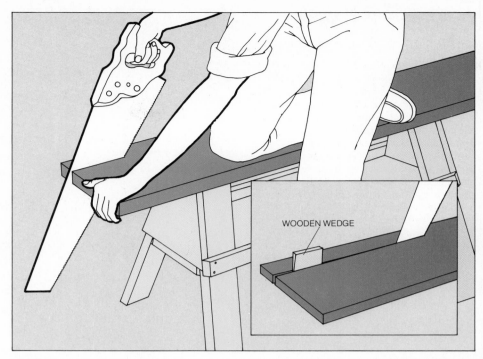

WOODEN WEDGE

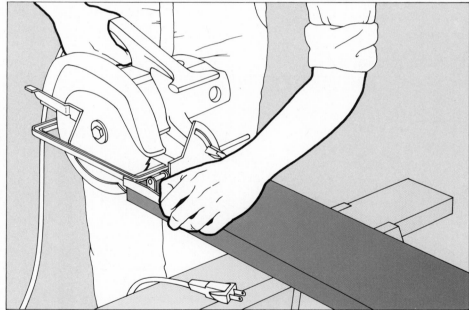

Ripping with a circular saw and a rip guide. Wearing safety goggles and with the saw unplugged, set the nose of the base plate flat on the board and align the blade with the marked line. Slide the arm of the guide through its base-plate holder until the guide shoe fits against the edge of the board, then tighten the guide arm in position. Plug in the saw, and when you make the cut, maintain a gentle sideways pressure on the saw to keep the guide shoe tight against the edge of the board.

A Miter Box for Precision

Using a miter box. A miter box ensures accuracy of angled cuts. Set the angle of the cut desired on an adjustable miter box or choose the proper pair of saw kerfs in a preset miter box, lower the saw and position the board so that the waste side of the cutting line is directly beneath the blade. With a thumb and miter box clamp, steady the board against the frame. Begin the kerf with several backward strokes of the backsaw, as for any crosscut, but hold the saw level to cut the entire upper surface of the wood along the cutting line. Then, cutting on both forward and backward strokes, cut the rest of the way through the board. Use long, smooth strokes that fall just short of pulling the blade from the rear guide or running the blade into the front guide.

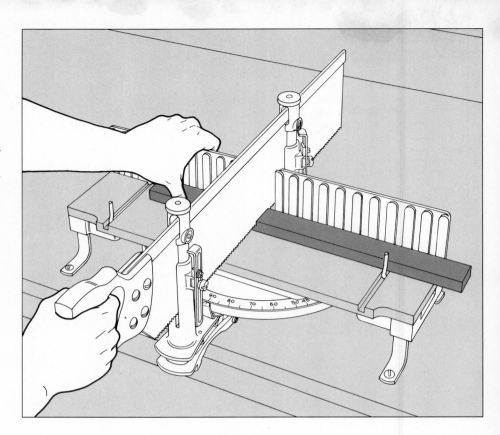

Plugging in Safely

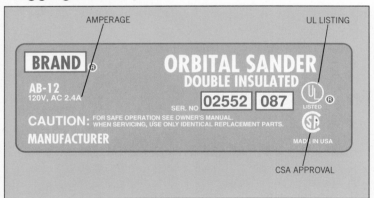

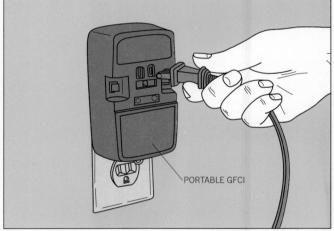

PORTABLE GFCI

Checking grounding and load requirements. Ensure that a power tool is rated electrically safe, checking its nameplate *(above)*; it should be UL (Underwriters Laboratories) listed or CSA (Canadian Standards Association) approved. Also ensure the power tool is grounded or double-insulated. A grounded tool has a three-prong plug and may be marked "grounding required"; a double-insulated tool is marked "double insulated" and may bear the symbol shown. For a power tool or extension cord with a three-prong plug, use only a similar outlet; but bend or remove the third, or grounding, prong of a plug. Ensure that the outlet, usually on a 15- or 20-ampere electrical circuit, can provide sufficient current for the power tool. Check the amperage rating of the power tool on its nameplate; if it is rated at 10 or more amperes, turn off any high-current-drawing appliances operating on the electrical circuit. After ensuring that the electrical circuit is GFCI-protected *(right)*, plug in the power tool or extension cord.

Using a portable ground-fault circuit interrupter (GFCI). A GFCI provides protection against electrical shock by monitoring the flow of current in an electrical circuit; the moment an irregularity in the current is detected, the GFCI automatically shuts off the electrical circuit. A home built or wired before 1975 is unlikely to have GFCIs permanently installed. If you do not have GFCIs permanently installed, use a portable GFCI as a safety precaution at any outlet outdoors or in a workshop, basement, utility room, kitchen, bathroom or garage. Plug the GFCI into the outlet following the manufacturer's instructions; after checking the grounding and load requirements of the power tool *(left)*, then plug the power tool or extension cord into the GFCI *(above)*.

Using a Saber Saw

Working with a saber saw. Set up the workpiece with its finished side facing down, and clamp it in position and set the saw for the work according to owner's manual instructions. For a straight cut parallel to and less than 6 inches from a straight edge, fit a ripping guide to the saw. Wearing safety goggles and respiratory protection, plug in the saw and, standing to one side of the cutting line, hold the saw by the handle and the front of the housing. Butt the blade against the cutting line just to the waste side and rest the base plate on the surface. Then, pull the saw back slightly so the blade is not touching the workpiece *(below, left)*; keep the front edge of the base plate flat on the surface. If you are using a ripping guide, first slide it against the workpiece *(below, right)* and tighten its setscrew, then plug the saw in and position it. Before sawing, ensure that the power cord is clear of the blade.

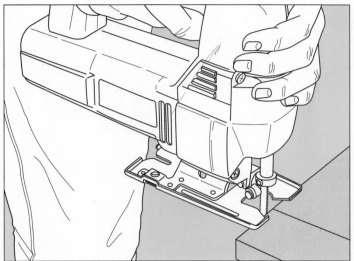

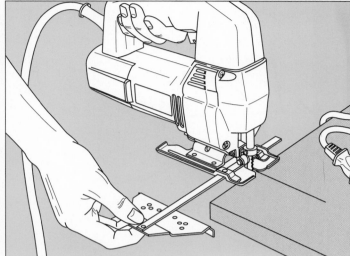

Using a Reciprocating Saw

Using a reciprocating saw for a plunge cut. Set up the workpiece, then measure and mark cutting lines on it; if you are working on a wall, ensure that there are no electric wires or plumbing pipes behind it. Set the saw for the job according to the owner's manual instructions. Wear safety goggles and respiratory protection. Plug in the saw and, for most materials, make a plunge entry. Holding the saw at one end of a cutting line with the teeth of the blade facing away from you, rest the edge of the shoe on the surface and align the blade with the cutting line just to the waste side. Then, pivot the saw on the edge of the shoe, raising the blade off the surface *(inset)*; ensure that the power cord is clear of the blade. Gripping the saw firmly, depress and hold the trigger switch. When the blade is moving at full speed, carefully lower it straight into the workpiece at the cutting line *(right)*. If you cannot make a plunge entry, use a drill to make a starting hold for the blade slightly larger than it and to the waste side of the cutting line.

When the shoe rests flat on the surface, guide the saw along the cutting line, letting the blade cut at its own speed and watching its position. If the blade veers from the cutting line, gently guide the saw ahead of it; avoid twisting the blade. When the blade reaches the end of the cutting line, release the trigger switch and let the blade stop, then lift the saw. Use the same procedure along each cutting line.

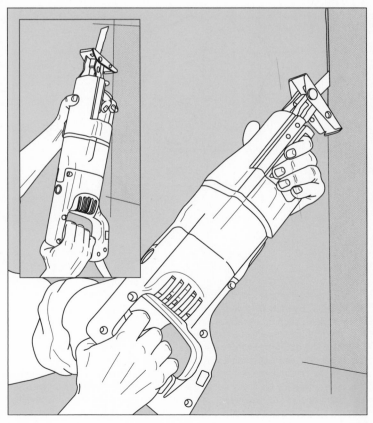

Using a Power Drill

Cradling for a small bit. To start a twist or a brad-point bit, push an awl into the wood at the center mark for the hole. Grip the drill handle with one hand, cradle the underside of the drill with the other and set the point of the bit in the awl hole. Gently press the drill into the wood and squeeze the trigger slowly until the bit starts to turn. When the bit has made a hole that is approximately 1/8 inch deep, increase the speed of the drill to its maximum and bear down firmly. When the bit has drilled almost to the full depth of the board, reduce the pressure but maintain the speed of the drill as the bit bores through the last fraction of an inch. If the hole must be perfectly perpendicular to the surface of the wood, set a combination square against the board and sight the bit against it *(inset)* or use a jig for precision work.

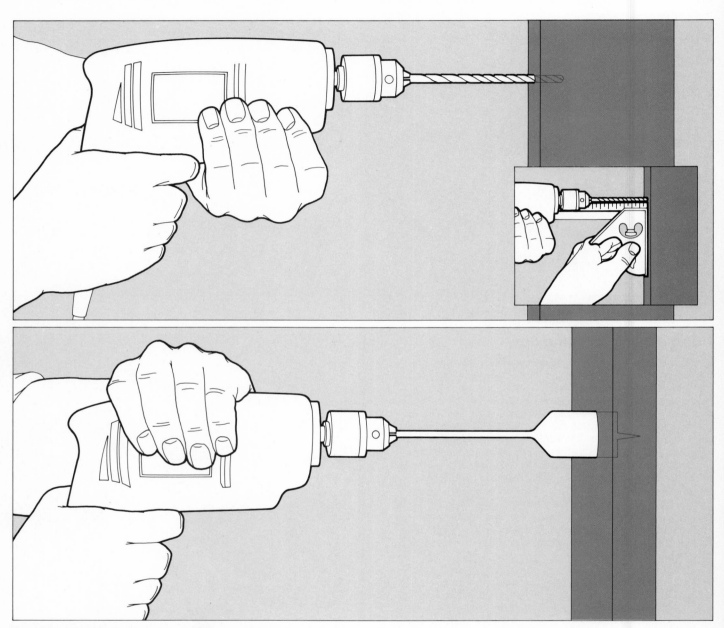

Steadying a large bit. To drive a bit with large cutting edges, such as a spade or Forstner bit, hold the drill handle with one hand and grasp the top of the drill firmly with the other, a grip that resists the twisting tendency of the drill better than the cradling grip illustrated at the top of this page. Press the bit firmly into the awl hole and begin the hole at a fairly high speed.

If the bit binds momentarily, maintain speed, but pull the drill back a fraction of an inch, then bear down again (slowing the speed will increase the tendency to bind). When the bit nears the other side of the board, reduce pressure and brace yourself; the drill may jerk and bind as it breaks through. Turn off the drill as soon as the bit is cleanly through the board.

With an auger bit, work at a somewhat slower speed: If the motor begins to labor, press the trigger to maintain speed. Reduce the drilling speed as you come close to the end of the hole; when the feed screw breaks through the other side, the bit no longer will pull itself into the wood and you must bear down on the bit with additional force to finish boring the hole.

Chisels and Their Care

Making a mortise. Chisels are useful for mortising door hardware and hinges. Press the hardware—in this example, the faceplate of a door catch—against the wood and score along its edges with a utility knife, using repeated light strokes to cut the wood fiber so that the chisel will be less likely to splinter the surface. If the mortise will be open on one side, as for a door hinge, mark the mortise depth on the open side.

Chiseling the edges. Set a heavy-duty butt chisel to the wood, with its bevel facing the outlined area and its cutting edge on the score line. Holding the blade vertical, tap the chisel with a hammer. Cut slightly deeper than the thickness of the hardware—you can gauge the depth of the cut directly on the chisel blade by holding a thumbnail at the junction of the blade and the wood, then pulling the chisel out of the cut. Repeat the cuts along all the score lines.

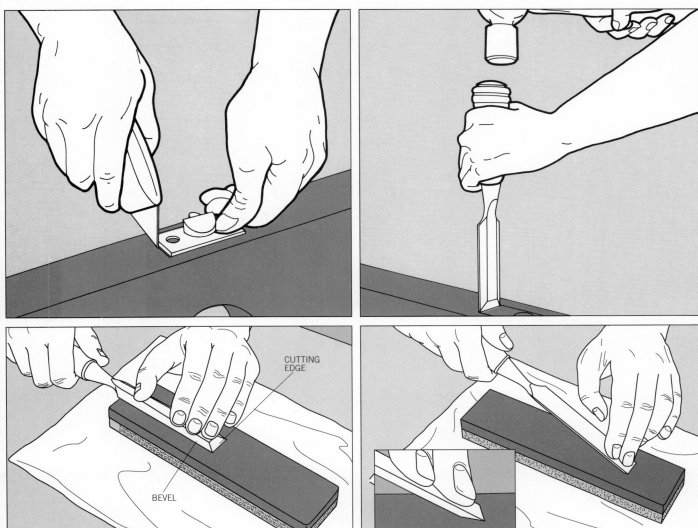

CUTTING EDGE

BEVEL

Grinding and honing the chisel. To grind or hone a chisel, use a combination waterstone such as a 250-1000 grit model. Soak the waterstone in water for 5 minutes, then set it down on a rubber mat on a work surface; keep the coarse 250-grit surface face up for grinding, the fine 1000-grit surface face up for honing. Before grinding or honing the chisel, set the back of the blade on the waterstone to lap it. Gripping the handle with one hand and pressing the blade flat with your other hand, pull the chisel across the waterstone *(above, left)*, stopping before the cutting edge reaches the edge of it. Lift the chisel and lap the back of the blade again several times, then turn it over. To grind the chisel, grip the handle with one hand and press the bevel flat against the 250-grit surface of the waterstone *(inset)*; or, support the chisel using a grinding and honing guide, following the manufacturer's instructions to install the chisel at the correct angle to it. Then, draw the chisel across the waterstone *(above, right)*, stopping before the cutting edge reaches the edge of it. Lift the chisel and grind it again, continuing until any nick is removed and a thin line of metal is raised along the cutting edge. Stop periodically to splash water onto the waterstone; rinse it to remove accumulated grit. To remove the thin line of raised metal, turn over the chisel and lap the back again. To hone the chisel, follow the same procedure used to grind it, working with the 1000-grit face of the waterstone. Continue honing the chisel until the angle between the bevel and the back of the blade is uniform and barely visible. Stop periodically to examine the cutting edge under a bright light and to test it for sharpness: Draw the top of a fingernail very lightly along it; your fingernail should slide along easily rather than catching. If honing does not sharpen the cutting edge, take the chisel for professional regrinding.

Using a Hacksaw and Mini-Hacksaw

Cutting with a hacksaw. Set up the workpiece and mark the cutting lines on it. Holding the hacksaw steady, align the blade with the cutting line just to the waste side. With a metal-cutting blade fine enough to place more than one tooth in the stock, position at least three teeth on the workpiece, then push the saw away from you several times to notch it; lift the saw slightly to pull it back. Start the cut with short, smooth strokes, then gradually lengthen them; push away firmly *(below)* and pull back lightly. Angle the frame to follow the cutting line; do not twist the blade. If necessary, smooth the cut edge with a file.

Cutting with a mini-hacksaw. Gripping the handle of the mini-hacksaw, butt the blade against the workpiece along any cutting line just to the waste side. For example, fit the blade in a narrow opening *(below)* or set it flush with another surface, pressing the handle to bend it slightly. Make the cut using short, smooth strokes, pushing the saw away firmly and pulling it back lightly. If necessary, smooth the cut edge with a file.

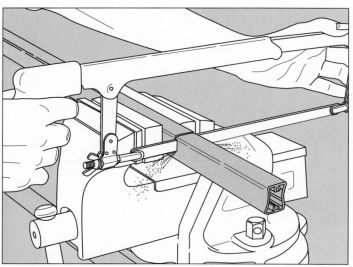

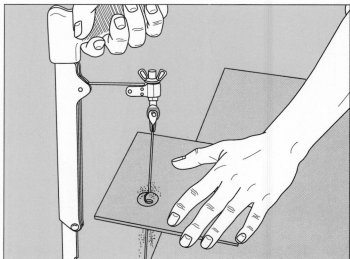

Leveling and Plumbing a Surface

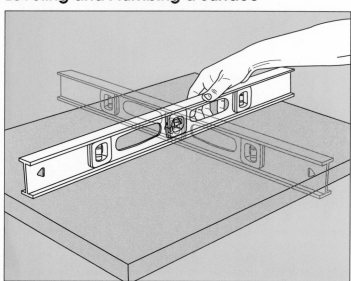

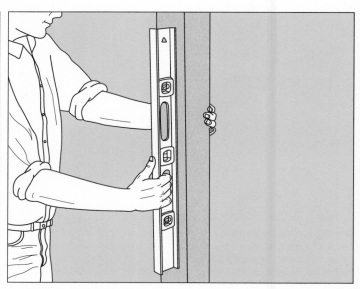

Checking for a level surface. A carpenter's level is used to level and plumb surfaces. To check that a flat surface is level, stand along one long edge across the center of the surface and examine the bubble in the horizontally-oriented vial. Turn the level 90° and stand it on the same edge across the same spot *(above)*; examine the bubble in the horizontally-oriented vial again. If the bubble is exactly centered for both readings, the surface is level.

Checking for a plumb surface. To check that a flat surface is plumb, hold one long edge of the level against the surface and examine the bubble in the horizontally-oriented vial. If the bubble is exactly centered, the surface is plumb. To check that a vertical object is plumb, check two adjacent surfaces the same way *(above)*; if each surface is plumb, the object is plumb.

Using Clamps

Installing a C clamp. For pressure or holding power over a span of up to 12 inches, using C clamps. C clamps are available in different sizes with reaches from 1 to 12 inches; a 6-inch type is usually sufficient. For clamping well back, away from the edges of materials, use deep-throated C clamps. Plan to install a C clamp across the materials you are joining every 6 to 8 inches along the joint.

To install a C clamp, turn the T handle of the screw enough to position the jaws loosely across the materials you are joining. If one material is less than 1 inch thick, use a flat block of hardwood equal in length to the joint to distribute the pressure of the C clamp evenly along it. Otherwise, use a thin, flat block of wood as a shim to keep the shoe or the foot of the C clamp from marking the materials. For example, set one shim under the foot and hold the C clamp in position. Setting another shim under the shoe, turn the T handle of the screw by hand to tighten the shoe against it *(below, left)*; do not use a tool to apply the turning force. If necessary, use a wedge-shaped wood block to provide parallel clamping surfaces for the foot of the shoe *(inset)*. Install a C clamp across the materials every 6 to 8 inches along the joint in the same way, tightening each shoe in turn a little at a time *(below, right)*.

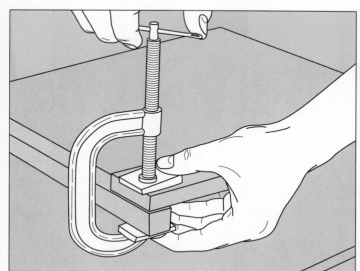
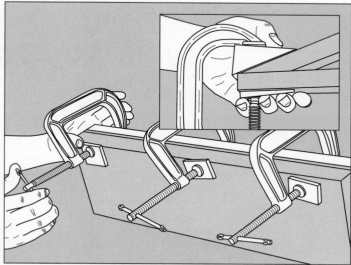

Installing a pipe clamp. For pressure or holding power over a span of more than 12 inches, use pipe clamps. To install a pipe clamp, position it loosely across the materials you are joining. If one material is less than 1 inch thick, use a thick, flat block of hardwood equal in length to the joint to distribute the pressure of the pipe clamp evenly along it. Otherwise, use a thin, flat block of wood as a shim to keep the shoe or foot of the pipe clamp from marking the materials.

For example, set one block along the joint under the foot of the fixed jaw, then hold the pipe clamp in position. Setting another block along the joint under the shoe of the movable jaw, turn the wing handle of the screw by hand to tighten the shoe against it *(right, top)*; do not use a tool to apply turning force.

Install a pipe clamp across the materials every 6 to 8 inches along the joint the same way, tightening each shoe in turn a little at a time. If you are using more than two pipe clamps, raise the materials onto wood blocks, then install a pipe clamp alternately across the top and bottom of them to help keep them from bowing and warping *(right, bottom)*.

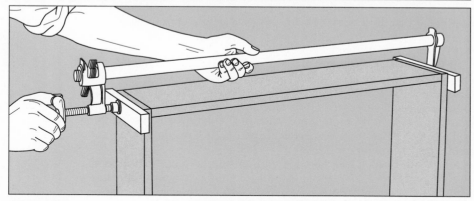
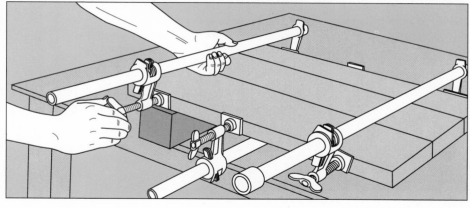

Setting Up to Work

The professional-caliber workshop, filled with stationary power tools and fine woodworking benches, is a dream for many do-it-yourselfers. However, most home-repair tasks can be undertaken safely and effectively with a selection of good hand and portable power tools in a modest basement or garage workshop. The basic workshop at right illustrates the main features of any good shop: adequate lighting and ventilation, a safe, dependable supply of electrical power, sturdy and versatile work surfaces, well-organized storage units and essential safety devices. More important than the size or layout of your workshop is your ability to marshal its many resources when you set up for a renovation project; you will need to choose not only the best tools, but the best work surface, lighting and ventilation. A safe, well-organized job setup is the key to good work; it ensures that you can handle your tools and materials comfortably and properly, and work with care and precision.

The first requirement for any job is to choose a work surface. A stationary worktable, a utility vise, a portable workbench, a pair of sawhorses and an assortment of C clamps provide a good range of options for holding most workpieces. Choose the surface or combination of surfaces large and sturdy enough to hold your workpiece securely—that also permits you to work comfortably and safely. Ensure that the work area is well lit. There should be bright overhead light; for precision tasks, also use direct, focused light on your workpiece and tools. To use a power tool far from an outlet, choose an extension cord that is properly rated for the job. Before plugging in a power tool or extension cord, check that the outlet can provide sufficient power and has ground-fault protection *(page 171)*. Ensure that the workshop is adequately ventilated—for both your comfort and safety. If you are using a material or substance that is flammable or emits hazardous vapors, work outdoors, if possible. If you must work indoors, ensure a supply of fresh air by opening windows and doors to the outdoors and setting up a sturdy fan to direct vapors out of the workshop.

Always wear the appropriate safety gear for the job. To handle sharp, rough, dirty or hazardous materials, wear gloves. For work that creates dust or flying debris or when there is a risk of a chemical splash, wear safety goggles; if necessary, also a face shield. For work with noisy power tools, use hearing protection. With dust-creating cutting, grinding, drilling or sanding tools or chemicals that emit hazardous vapors, use respiratory protection.

After completing a job, take the time to store all your tools and supplies properly, accessible and in good condition for the next job. Storage options are practically limitless; cabinets, shelves, boxes, bins and containers of every size, shape and description are sold at most hardware stores and building-supply centers, and can be used in imaginative combinations to organize your materials. Clean the workshop thoroughly, properly disposing of hazardous refuse. Keep the workshop locked when it is not in use.

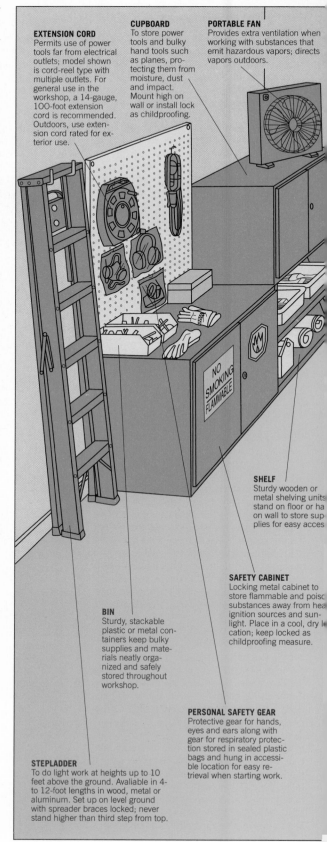

EXTENSION CORD
Permits use of power tools far from electrical outlets; model shown is cord-reel type with multiple outlets. For general use in the workshop, a 14-gauge, 100-foot extension cord is recommended. Outdoors, use extension cord rated for exterior use.

CUPBOARD
To store power tools and bulky hand tools such as planes, protecting them from moisture, dust and impact. Mount high on wall or install lock as childproofing.

PORTABLE FAN
Provides extra ventilation when working with substances that emit hazardous vapors; directs vapors outdoors.

SHELF
Sturdy wooden or metal shelving units stand on floor or ha on wall to store sup plies for easy acces

SAFETY CABINET
Locking metal cabinet to store flammable and poiso substances away from hea ignition sources and sunlight. Place in a cool, dry l cation; keep locked as childproofing measure.

PERSONAL SAFETY GEAR
Protective gear for hands, eyes and ears along with gear for respiratory protection stored in sealed plastic bags and hung in accessible location for easy retrieval when starting work.

BIN, Sturdy, stackable plastic or metal containers keep bulky supplies and materials neatly organized and safely stored throughout workshop.

STEPLADDER
To do light work at heights up to 10 feet above the ground. Available in 4- to 12-foot lengths in wood, metal or aluminum. Set up on level ground with spreader braces locked; never stand higher than third step from top.

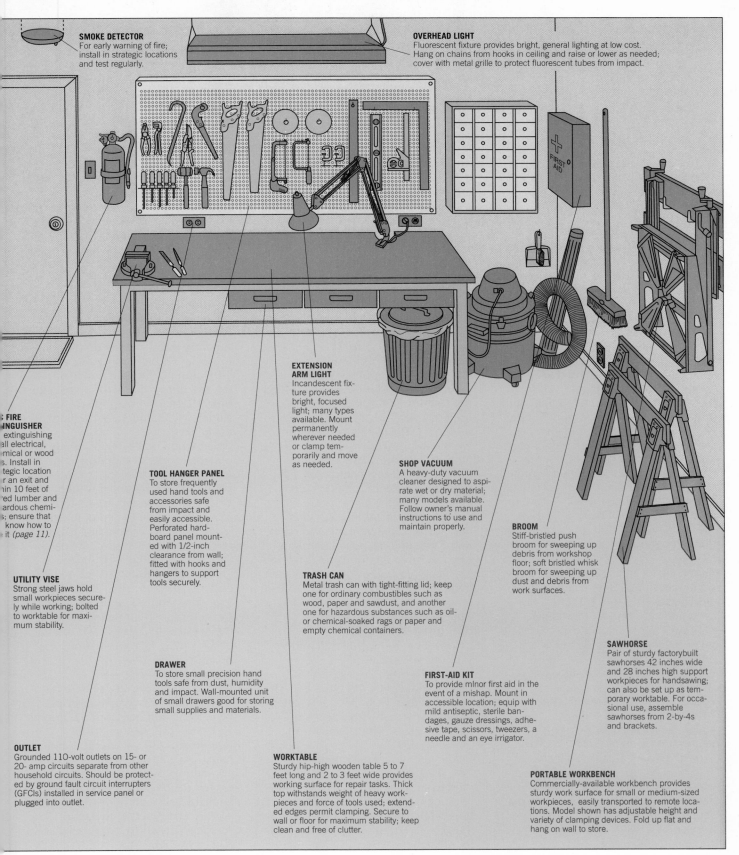

SMOKE DETECTOR
For early warning of fire;
install in strategic locations
and test regularly.

OVERHEAD LIGHT
Fluorescent fixture provides bright, general lighting at low cost.
Hang on chains from hooks in ceiling and raise or lower as needed;
cover with metal grille to protect fluorescent tubes from impact.

**FIRE
EXTINGUISHER**
extinguishing
all electrical,
mical or wood
. Install in
tegic location
r an exit and
in 10 feet of
ed lumber and
ardous chemi-
; ensure that
know how to
it *(page 11).*

UTILITY VISE
Strong steel jaws hold
small workpieces secure-
ly while working; bolted
to worktable for maxi-
mum stability.

TOOL HANGER PANEL
To store frequently
used hand tools and
accessories safe
from impact and
easily accessible.
Perforated hard-
board panel mount-
ed with 1/2-inch
clearance from wall;
fitted with hooks and
hangers to support
tools securely.

**EXTENSION
ARM LIGHT**
Incandescent fix-
ture provides
bright, focused
light; many types
available. Mount
permanently
wherever needed
or clamp tem-
porarily and move
as needed.

SHOP VACUUM
A heavy-duty vacuum
cleaner designed to aspi-
rate wet or dry material;
many models available.
Follow owner's manual
instructions to use and
maintain properly.

BROOM
Stiff-bristled push
broom for sweeping up
debris from workshop
floor; soft bristled whisk
broom for sweeping up
dust and debris from
work surfaces.

TRASH CAN
Metal trash can with tight-fitting lid; keep
one for ordinary combustibles such as
wood, paper and sawdust, and another
one for hazardous substances such as oil-
or chemical-soaked rags or paper and
empty chemical containers.

DRAWER
To store small precision hand
tools safe from dust, humidity
and impact. Wall-mounted unit
of small drawers good for storing
small supplies and materials.

FIRST-AID KIT
To provide minor first aid in the
event of a mishap. Mount in
accessible location; equip with
mild antiseptic, sterile ban-
dages, gauze dressings, adhesive tape, scissors, tweezers, a
needle and an eye irrigator.

SAWHORSE
Pair of sturdy factory-
built
sawhorses 42 inches wide
and 28 inches high support
workpieces for handsawing;
can also be set up as temporary worktable. For occasional use, assemble
sawhorses from 2-by-4s
and brackets.

OUTLET
Grounded 110-volt outlets on 15- or
20- amp circuits separate from other
household circuits. Should be protected by ground fault circuit interrupters
(GFCIs) installed in service panel or
plugged into outlet.

WORKTABLE
Sturdy hip-high wooden table 5 to 7
feet long and 2 to 3 feet wide provides
working surface for repair tasks. Thick
top withstands weight of heavy workpieces and force of tools used; extended edges permit clamping. Secure to
wall or floor for maximum stability; keep
clean and free of clutter.

PORTABLE WORKBENCH
Commercially-available workbench provides
sturdy work surface for small or medium-sized
workpieces, easily transported to remote locations. Model shown has adjustable height and
variety of clamping devices. Fold up flat and
hang on wall to store.

INDEX

Page references in *italics* indicate an illustration of the subject mentioned.

Frames, installing, 184-185, *186-191*, 205
Furring: for ceilings, 91, *95-96*; and gridiron pattern of strips, *37*; installing, *38-40*; and insulation, *64, 66-68*; for paneling, 41, *42, 50, 53, 56, 58, 61*; and re-siding, 348, *350-351*, 359

G

Gable roofs, building, 426, *429, 432-433*, 434-435
Garbage disposals, installing, *267-268*
Gates, building and repairing, *395-397*
Glass: double-pane, 232, *236*; for picture windows, 232; and sliding doors, *188, 205-207, 440*; as walls, 236
Glossary, of electrical terms, 270-271; of home renovation terms, *inside front cover*
Gloves, safety, *272, 456, 457, 472*
Glue. *See* Adhesives
Goggles: and breaking openings in masonry, 192; with ceramic tiles, 152; with drills, *287*; with joint compound, 80, *86*; with laminates, 161; with propane torch, 246, 247; and removing walls, *71*; with routers, *394*; and sanding, *167*; using, *130*; in the workshop, 456, *457, 460*, 472
Ground-Contact retention rating, 78
Ground-fault circuit interrupter (GFCI): installing, *170-171*; in kitchens, 135; portable, *466*; with power tools, *457*; in the workshop, *472-473*
Grout: applying and sealing, *156-157*; silicone, *157*; for tiles, *32*, 152
Gutters, reinstalling, *434-435*
Gypsum board. *See* Wallboard

H

Hacksaws, *chart* 458; using, *470*
Halls, installing wood flooring at, *23*
Hammers, *chart* 458; using, 455, *456*, 460
Hangers, *inside back cover*
Hardware, *inside back cover*
Hardwoods: for floors, 20; for solid-wood paneling, 48; for spiral stairs, 112
Headers, 185, *charts* 73; base for, 74; for basement stairs, *119*; butting, to walls, *76*; and removing walls, *73-75*; steel-core, 185; wide, *189-190*; wood-core, 185
Heat guns, using, *456*

Heating: by baseboard units, *326-327*; forced-air system for, *316-319*; hot-water system for, *327-331*; and prefabricated fireplaces, *332-335*. See also Ducts; Registers
Helmets: and renovating walls, *86*; and removing walls, *73*; and sanding, *167*; using, *76*
Hinges: for doors, 211, *217*; for gates, *395*
Hot-water heating systems: adding convectors to, *328-331*; modernizing, *327*
Household maintenance tools, *chart* 458-459

I

Inlaid sheet vinyl: cutting, 147-148; as rolled flooring, 144
Inspections, *chart* 406; for code work, 130, 402-405
Insulation: on concrete subfloor, 141; double-pane glass for, 232, *236*; for enclosed porches, 407, 412; for noise reduction, 261, 263; and re-siding, 348, *349*. See also Superinsulation

J

Joint compound: applying, 81, *85-86*; for wallboard, 77, 80
Joints: butt joints vs. mitered, 163; concealing, *85-86*; in copper pipes, 242-243, 244, *245-247*; in plastic pipes, *248-249*; sealers for pipes, *250*; shiplap, *49*; in steel and brass pipes, *250-251*; in subfloor sheets, *142*; tongue-and-groove, *49, 52*; types of, *397*; wood, *397*
Joists: attaching, *111*; and bathtubs, 136; and bearing and nonbearing walls, 70; and ceilings, 91; and disappearing and spiral stairs, 112; false, *95*; and fans, 312-313; and framing, 66, 186, 189; locating, *38, 46*; and masonry house, *338-339*; and openings for additions, *436-439*; passages for pipes in, 254, *260*; reinforcing, 140, *141*; and removing walls, 73, *74-76*; repairing holes at, *307*; for stairways, *108-111*; and subfloors, 18; swelling of, 142; ventilation fans between, 175; and wet walls, 256-257; and wiring outlet boxes, 278, 281, *287-297*; and wood floors, *21*

K

Keyhole brackets, installing, *101*
Kitchen island: as activity center, 132; light fixtures over, 135; and rolled flooring, 144; ventilation for, 172, 173
Kitchens, 130, *diagrams* 134-135; activity centers in, 132, *133-135*; cabinets in, *167-169*; carpeting in, 149; covering seams in, *151*; electrical problems in, 170-171; installing fixtures for, *267-268*; laying tile in, 152, *153-157*; molding for, 150; plumbing for, 254-255; rolled flooring in, *144-149*; subfloor and underlayment for, *142-143*; ventilation for, *172-175*; water-resistant wallboard for, 168
Knee brackets, fastening, *229*
Knives, *chart* 458-459; using, *456, 457*

L

Ladders, *diagram* 341; built-in, 102, *103*; safety on, *340-343, 345*; setting up, *63*; using, 340, *341-343, 345*; for the workshop, *472-473*
Laminates, mounting and maintaining, *160-162*, 163
Lavatory. *See* Sinks, bathroom
Leveling, method for, *470*
Light fixtures: adjusting, *96*; fluorescent, 91, *93-94*; recessing, 91; and safety in kitchens, 135
Lighting, outdoor, installing, *398-399*
Linoleum: as base for laminates, 160; invention of, 26; in rolled sheets, 144
Lintels, *chart* 192; supporting masonry with, *193-194*
Locksets: fitting, 196, 204, 211, *218*; parts of, *204*
Loop-pile carpeting, *33, 34*

M

Marble: and covering floor seams, *151*; as tile for floors, 30
Masonry: attaching furring strips to, 37; basement stairs near, *111*; breaking openings in, 185, *192-195*; and fitting panels, *54*; hangers and fasteners for, *inside back cover*; lining a recess in, 352, *354*; and partitions, 77; preparing for siding, *351*; ventilation in, 314, *315*
Mastic: for bonding wood, *19*, 26, 29; and furring anchors, 37

ACKNOWLEDGMENTS

For help given in the preparation of this book, the editors wish to thank the following:

Marc Cassini; Genova Products; Donald Harman; Shirley Sylvain; Jim Walker, American Floor Covering Institute

Hangers and Fasteners

Four bare walls never stay that way for long—a plain wall seems to beg for adornment. Hung with bookshelves or towel bars, fine lithographs or exotic plants, walls and ceilings can provide practical storage as well as good looks.

A wall's ability to carry a load depends in part on its condition. Before hanging anything on a wall or ceiling, check that it is sound; perform repairs if necessary. Learn what the wall is made of so that you can choose the right hanger or fastener for the job.

Hanging hardware must be suited both to the construction of the wall and to the weight placed upon it. The chart below lists common hangers and the types of walls and ceilings to which they are best suited. The load-carrying ratings are listed for comparison purposes only. Follow the weight guidelines listed on the hardware package or ask a hardware professional for assistance.

Several types of hangers are available, and each type supports a load in a different way. Metal expansion anchors and toggle bolts, designed for hollow walls, have wings or leaves that pop open behind the wall when they are screwed in, gripping the wall from behind. Anchors and screw shields made of metal, plastic or fiber come in many styles for use in hollow, solid or masonry

	Hollow wall expansion anchor (with sleeve)	Hollow wall expansion anchor (sleeveless)	Hollow wall expansion anchor (hammered type; no drilling required)	Toggle bolt (shank can be headless)	Plastic anchor (also called wall plug)
Hollow Wall (includes gypsum drywall and plywood panels over furring or studs)	very good for medium loads; choose sleeve length that matches wall thickness	good for light loads in drywall	good for light loads in drywall	very good for medium to heavy loads; avoid studs or furring	good for light to medium loads
Plaster on lath	good if sleeve length matches wall thickness including lath and plaster keys	good for light loads	not recommended	good for medium to heavy loads; bolt length must clear lath and plaster keys	good for light to medium loads
Ceramic tile	good for tile over hollow wall; sleeve length must match wall thickness; file off prongs on sleeve	not recommended	not recommended	fair for tile over hollow wall; do not overtighten; bolt may crack tile	good for light loads; do not force too large a screw into anchor; it may crack tile
Masonry (includes concrete, concrete block, brick, and plaster over masonry)	good for hollow concrete block; sleeve length must match block thickness; not recommended for solid masonry	not recommended	not recommended	very good for hollow concrete block; not recommended for solid masonry	fair for light loads; do not use in crumbly masonry
Ceilings	very good for hollow ceiling; sleeve length must match ceiling thickness	fair for very light loads only	fair for very light loads in drywall ceilings only	very good for hollow ceiling; bolts available with head or headless	fair for very light loads only